Kaleidoscope

Topic	Author	Abbreviated Title	Kaleido-scope (pages)	Those Who Can, Teach (chapters)	Foundations of Education (chapters)
Emotional intelligence	O'Neil	*On Emotional Intelligence*	91–95	4, 13	9, 12, 13
Ethics of teaching	Jesness	*Why Johnny Can't Fail*	40–43	1, 2, 12	1, 2, 16
	Strike	*The Ethics of Teaching*	307–311	12	2
Finance	LoVette	*You Ask, "Why Have School Costs Increased So Greatly?"*	324–329	9	7
Gender issues	Bailey	*Shortchanging Girls and Boys*	477–481	5	9
	Shakeshaft et al.	*Boys Call Me Cow*	67–72	5, 12	8, 9
Harassment	Shakeshaft et al.	*Boys Call Me Cow*	67–72	5, 12	8, 9
Home schooling	Lines	*Home Schooling Comes of Age*	140–144	12, 13	8, 16
Inclusion	Giangreco	*What Do I Do Now?*	460–464	4	11
	Shanker	*Where We Stand on the Rush to Inclusion*	454–459	4	11
International education	Sato & McLaughlin	*Context Matters: Teaching in Japan and in the United States*	267–275	2, 8, 15	15
Law and the teacher	McDaniel	*The Teacher's Ten Commandments*	312–323	12	8
	Shakeshaft et al.	*Boys Call Me Cow*	67–72	5, 12	8, 9
Learning styles	Guild	*The Culture/Learning Style Connection*	447–453	4	9, 10, 11
Multicultural education	Banks	*Multicultural Education in the New Century*	439–442	4, 13	5, 11, 16
	Guild	*The Culture/Learning Style Connection*	447–453	4	9, 10, 11
	Minicucci et al.	*School Reform and Student Diversity*	465–470	4, 13	11, 16
	Ravitch	*Multiculturalism*	432–438	4, 11	9, 10, 11
	Stotsky	*Multicultural Illiteracy*	443–446	4, 11, 13	9, 10, 11
Multiple intelligences (MI) theory	Gardner	*A Multiplicity of Intelligences*	230–236	4, 8	11, 14
Parental involvement	Comer	*Parent Participation*	132–139	2, 4, 9	6, 16
	Finders & Lewis	*Why Some Parents Don't Come to School*	126–131	2, 4, 9	6, 9

Kaleidoscope
Readings in Education

Ninth Edition

Kevin Ryan
Boston University

James M. Cooper
University of Virginia

Houghton Mifflin Company ▪ Boston ▪ New York

Senior Sponsoring Editor: Loretta Wolozin
Development Editor: Lisa Mafrici
Project Editor: Rebecca Bennett
Production/Design Coordinator: Jodi O'Rourke
Senior Manufacturing Coordinator: Marie Barnes
Marketing Manager: Jean Zielinski DeMayo
Senior Cover Design Coordinator: Deborah Azerrad Savona

Cover Design and Image: Diana Coe/ko Design Studio

Printed in the U.S.A.

Library of Congress Catalog Card Number: 00-103023

ISBN: 0-618-04280-6

1 2 3 4 5 6 7 8 9–CRS–04 03 02 01 00

OCLC 44886535
Aug. 2001

Contents

Part Three
Schools

Part Four
Curriculum

Part Five
Instruction

Part Nine
Diversity

Preface

When we were children, one of our favorite toys was the kaleidoscope, the cylindrical instrument containing loose bits of colored glass between two flat plates and two mirrors so placed that shaking or rotating the cylinder causes the bits of glass to be reflected in an endless variety of patterns. We chose *Kaleidoscope* as the name of this book because it seems that education can be viewed from multiple perspectives, each showing a different pattern or set of structures.

Audience and Purpose

This is the ninth edition of *Kaleidoscope: Readings in Education*. It is intended for use either as a supplemental book of readings to accompany any "Introduction to Education," "Foundations of Education," or "Issues in Education" textbook, or as a core textbook itself.

Today is a time of unprecedented educational debate and reform in the United States. It is our hope that this collection of seventy-five high-interest selections will help readers participate in these national discussions in a more informed way.

The book's wide range of sources and writers—from the classic John Dewey and Carl Rogers to the contemporary Ted Sizer, Diane Ravitch, Linda Darling-Hammond, and James Comer—makes it highly flexible and responsive to a broad variety of course needs.

The material we have selected for *Kaleidoscope* is not technical and can be understood, we believe, by people without extensive professional backgrounds in education. The articles are relatively brief and come from classroom teachers, educational researchers, journalists, union leaders, and educational reformers. Some selections are summaries of research. Some are classic writings by noted educators. Some are descriptions of educational problems and proposed solutions. And, we hasten to add, we agree with some articles and do not agree with others. Our aim is to present a wide variety of philosophical and psychological positions to reflect the varied voices heard in education today.

Coverage

Kaleidoscope is divided into nine parts. Part One concentrates on teachers, with articles ranging from personal reports by teachers to an article about what constitutes great teaching. Part Two contains selections about students, dealing with topics from the changing nature of childhood in the United States to child abuse. Part Three looks at schools and describes some of their current problems as well as a number of recent recommendations for developing more effective schools. Part Four examines curriculum issues and deals with the classic question: What is most worth knowing? Part Five focuses on instruction and includes selections on cooperative learning, multiple intelligences, constructivist learning, and research on effective teaching. Part Six contains articles on the foundations of education that discuss the historical, philosophical, and psychological roots of contemporary education. Part Seven contains articles on contemporary educational reform efforts in the United States. Part Eight examines various aspects of how educational technology is affecting or is likely to affect teaching and learning. New to this edition, Part Nine focuses on various elements of how diversity is affecting education in the United States today. Selections in Part Nine address ethnic and linguistic diversity as well as gender issues and special education inclusion efforts.

Features of the Revision

Given that over 25 percent of the selections are new to this edition, *Kaleidoscope* covers current topics such as student multicultural education, standards-based education, professional development, teacher reflection, technology, emotional intelligence, brain research, inclusion, school reform, and curriculum reform.

New Diversity Section   In previous editions, we have often included several articles on diversity. It is apparent to us, however, that the many forms of diversity in our society and schools warrant additional coverage and a separate section devoted to the topic. The selection of articles in the new Part Nine examine such topics as multiculturalism, inclusion, learning styles, and bilingual education.

Beginning Teachers' Web Site   This brand-new web site accompanies *Kaleidoscope* and *Those Who Can, Teach,* ninth edition, and will offer several articles from

Kaleidoscope—annotated and enhanced with links and critical thinking questions. Also included on this site are interactive activities and self-tests to supplement learning.

Special Features of the Book

To facilitate understanding of the selections in this book, the ninth edition of *Kaleidoscope* includes a number of especially helpful features.

■ Each of the nine major sections is introduced by a section-opening overview to help put the readings into a broader context.

■ At the end of each reading are our Postnote and several Discussion Questions. The Postnote comments on the issues raised by the article, and the Discussion Questions prompt readers to do some additional thinking about the major points made in the reading.

■ A glossary of key terms—especially useful to those students taking their first course in education or those using this book as a primary text—and a detailed subject index appear at the end of the book.

■ The Article Review Form, found at the end of the book, will help you analyze and discuss the articles in the text.

■ The Student Response Form, also at the end of the book, gives you the opportunity to comment on each of the readings and to suggest new readings or topics for the next edition. We sincerely hope that you will take the time to complete this form and mail it back to us. Your comments will be invaluable to future students and us as you help us select the best readings.

■ The Correlating Table, arranged alphabetically by topic, relates each *Kaleidoscope* selection to specific chapters in both *Those Who Can, Teach*, ninth edition, by Kevin Ryan and James M. Cooper, and *Foundations of Education*, seventh edition, by Allan Ornstein and Daniel Levine. We hope this chart will serve as a handy cross-reference for users of these books. This chart is printed on the inside covers of the text for easy reference.

Acknowledgments

We are especially grateful to a number of reviewers for their excellent recommendations and suggestions, most notably

Wanda Alderman-Swain *Seton Hall University*
Robert Barkman *Springfield College*
Glenda Boone *Emmanuel College*
Anne Claytor *Fairleigh Dickinson University*
Judy Leach *St. Louis Community College*
Cathleen Kinsella Stutz *Assumption College*
Patricia J. Schindler *Xavier University of Louisiana*
Dawn M. VanGunten *Eastern Illinois University*
Elizabeth A. Wilkins-Canter *Eastern Illinois University*

In addition, we would like to offer a special note of thanks to the many users of this book who have been kind enough to share with us their impressions of it and their suggestions on how we might improve it in subsequent editions. We hope this tradition will continue as you complete and return the Student Response Form or send us your comments via the Houghton Mifflin web site (http://www.college.hmco.com).

Kevin Ryan
James M. Cooper

Kaleidoscope

Part One

Teachers

Being a teacher today has special drawbacks. It is difficult to be a teacher in an age that mocks idealism. It is difficult to be a teacher without the traditional authority and respect that came with the title in the past. To be a teacher in the midst of a permissive time in childrearing, when many students are filled with antiauthoritarian attitudes, causes special strains. It is punishing to work at an occupation that is not keeping up economically. It is painful to be part of a profession that is continually being asked to solve deep social problems and to do the essential job of educating children and then regularly criticized for its failings. A good case can be made for discouragement, even for self-pity.

This negativism, or at least acknowledgment of the negative, obscures the fact that teaching is one of the great professions. These passing conditions ignore the greatness that resides in the teacher's public trust. Many adults struggle with the question: Am I engaged in significant work? Teachers always know that they are engaged in crucial, life-shaping work.

1 The Influence of Teachers

Mihaly Csikszentmihalyi and Jane McCormack

The ordered pattern of human energy that we call a social system can run into trouble in many different ways. It can, for instance, be broken up by the invasion of more numerous and desperate people, as happened to innumerable civilizations from the Sumerians to the Romans. Its economy can be made obsolete by the discovery of new trade routes, as happened to the Venetian Republic when the Atlantic became the main avenue for commerce; or by the development of a new technology, as when plastics undercut the production of leather, on which the affluence of Uruguay depended. Powerful nations have been destroyed by natural catastrophes, by changes in the ecology, or by epidemics that decimated the population and sapped its will to live.

In addition to such external dangers, every society faces an internal threat to its continuity. Appearances to the contrary, such seemingly powerful and enduring entities as "state," "nation," and "culture" are in reality quite vulnerable. If just one generation of young people were to grow up rejecting the language of their parents, the values of their community, or the political commitments of their elders, the nation to which they belong would be changed in irreversible ways. A social system can survive only as long as people are willing to support it.

If there is such a thing as "America," with its peculiar dreams, its unique political and economic patterns, its values and habits of lifestyle, it is because generation after generation of fathers and mothers have passed on to their sons and daughters some distinctive information that makes these offspring think and behave differently from youngsters growing up elsewhere. If this information were no longer transmitted successfully, "America" as we know it would no longer exist. Neither words carved in stone nor constitutions and laws written on paper can preserve a way of life, unless the consciousness of people supports their meaning.

At first glance, it might seem that such a "danger" is too far-fetched to worry about. After all, how likely is it that a majority of young Americans in a given generation will turn their backs permanently on the example of their elders? Moreover, a certain rebelliousness in adolescents is normal, even desirable. We expect teenagers to reject the ways their parents dress and talk, to despise the music their parents enjoy, and to ridicule the values their parents hold. But this is only a passing phase. By the time these youngsters move into young adulthood, they retain—in the guise of new lifestyle fashions—only the most superficial traces of their former rebelliousness. In all important respects, children end up repeating the pattern of their parents' lives.

All of this is true. But there are also times when, instead of disappearing in the course of maturation, the customary rebelliousness of adolescence leads to permanent changes in the ways young people see the world. The outcome is often an irreversible transformation of the society. The young people of most "underdeveloped" nations are obvious examples; fascinated by the miracles of western technology, they are no longer interested in learning the traditions of their cultures—which, as a result, will eventually become extinct.

At the time this article was written, Mihaly Csikszentmihalyi was a professor in the Department of Psychology at the University of Chicago, and Jane McCormack was a clinical psychologist in private practice in Chicago. "The Influence of Teachers," by Mihaly Csikszentmihalyi and Jane McCormack, *Phi Delta Kappan,* February 1986, pp. 415–419. © February 1986 by Phi Delta Kappa, Inc. Reprinted by permission of authors and publisher.

Many western sociologists and psychologists consider this a positive trend. The spread of "modernization" through education is, they believe, a welcome advance over the superstitious nonsense on which preliterate traditions were based. To a certain extent, they are right—for, without constant experimentation and change in ways of living, human society would become rigid and closed to the possibility of further evolution.

On the other hand, it is also clear that not all change leads to improvement. Sometimes a population gets used to an easy way of life and forgets the technological or moral skills that allowed it to survive in the past. If conditions then take a turn for the worse again, that population may no longer be able to cope with the challenge. Some scholars claim, for example, that the Appalachian settlers once had a vigorous and complex material culture. They were masters of many crafts and technologies that were state of the art in the 17th and 18th centuries. But by now the memory of those skills has decayed, and the way of life in Appalachian communities today is more primitive than it was a few centuries ago—not only in relation to the rest of the world, but in absolute terms as well. Why did this regression take place? We could list many reasons, but one factor was clearly essential: over time, young men and women no longer felt that it was worthwhile to learn what their parents had known.

Indeed, if we were to look at history from this point of view, we might discover that many of the great changes that have befallen the human race had as their source an erosion of belief, or will, or interest that undermined the younger generation's inclination to follow in the footsteps of its elders. Sometimes this reluctance to follow the elders yields positive outcomes; liberating new ideas can arise out of a stagnating culture. But probably more often, when youths reject the messages passed on to them by their elders, important information that has proved its value in helping the society to survive is lost as well.

A timely example is the so-called "sexual revolution" of the last 30 years. During this period messages concerning the physical dangers of sexual promiscuity were quickly discredited. It is true that the "wisdom" of the elders on this score was quite garbled and often hypocritical. Yet their moralistic warnings were based on thousands of years of experience with disease and psychic disintegration. They may not have had a scientific understanding of the situation, but they had a pretty clear idea of what eventually happens to individuals who indiscriminately satisfy their sexual needs.

Yet entire cohorts of young people dismissed the warnings as "repressive victorian morality." With the hubris of a generation that believed itself to be emancipated from the weakness of the past, that felt in control of its destiny because it was privy to the magic of science, the sexually liberated stepped boldly into a new world of ultimate self-indulgence—only to discover there some of the ugly realities that had forced their ancestors to counsel self-discipline. It was not ignorance that made the Victorians praise sexual restraint after all, but knowledge of the dangers of venereal diseases and of the dislocations prompted by illegitimate births. As it turned out, our liberated contemporaries were the ignorant ones—ignorant of the painfully accumulated experiences of previous centuries.

It is bad enough when a culture fails to communicate to its youngster those facts (such as the need for sexual restraint) that bear on its chances for physical survival. But a more subtle and dangerous loss of information occurs when the elders cannot pass on to the young convincing goals that make living worthwhile. When this occurs, the younger generation is left in an emotional morass. Without meaningful goals, the behavior of young people can easily become self-destructive.

This lack of meaningful goals most likely accounts for the unprecedented surge of social pathology in the U.S. over the past 30 years. The worst explosion in teenage suicide (a 300% increase in barely a generation) has occurred among white, middle-class boys—the privileged heirs to the richest society the world has ever known. Vandalism, crime, drug use, and venereal diseases all show similar gains. Clearly, the material affluence of suburbia is not enough to make young people happy. It is not even enough to make many of them want to go on living. What youngsters need, more than anything else, is purpose: meaningful goals toward which to channel their energies.

But how does one learn about meaningful goals? The simple answer is, "from other people." Certainly, books that enshrine past wisdom help. And personal experiences might move us to confirm our purpose. But the most pervasive and effective information about what makes life worth living comes from older people with whom children and adolescents interact—assuming, of course, that the elders have some useful information to impart. In any given instance, they may not. By and large, however, it is safe to assume that the older generation—simply by virtue of the fact that it has weathered the hazards of existence—can help those who have less experience to set worthwhile goals.

If this is the case, the hitch in transmitting information between generations these days becomes readily apparent. Typical American adolescents spend only five minutes a day alone with their fathers, and half of this time is spent watching television. Moreover, typical American adolescents spend only about 40 minutes a day alone with their mothers, an hour a day with both parents, and about 15 minutes a day with other adults—for a total of about two hours a day in the company of mature individuals. But almost all this time is spent unwinding from the tensions of school or work and in such repetitive maintenance activities as eating, shopping, or cleaning. Very little information of any moment is passed on in these routine interactions.

By contrast, the same teenagers spend more than four hours each day with their friends. This is time spent outside of school and beyond the influence of elders, and it is during this time that most of the information vital to teenagers' lives is exchanged. But values and goals that develop in peer groups—exciting and novel though they may be—have not passed the test of time and thus are of unknown survival value. To round out the picture, most teenagers spend from four to five hours each day alone, left to their own devices—and

perhaps two additional hours with the media, which essentially means "in front of the television set." Although scholars have argued that television is a conservative socializing influence, we have not found a single youngster in the course of our research who claims to have derived a meaningful goal from watching television.

Of course, in describing the network of relationships that define adolescence, we left out a crucial element: the roughly three hours each day that teenagers spend with their teachers. This is the single most important opportunity for them to learn from adults in our culture—a culture that has essentially delegated the upbringing of its young to educational institutions.

Unfortunately, the transmission of adult goals in classrooms takes place under far from ideal circumstances. In the first place, teachers, tend to be out-numbered, by a ratio of at least 20:1. Second, regardless of how much real or theoretical authority teachers have, they are isolated and cannot participate in the kinds of spontaneous interactions that generate internally binding norms and values. Thus the values of the peer group become real to the students, because those are the values that they help to develop and are able to experience directly.

Moreover, because school attendance is compulsory, the school cannot count on the loyalty of students. Our research shows that, of all the places teenagers hang out, the school is the one place they least wish to be. Moreover, when they are in school, the classroom is the one place they most strongly wish to avoid. They far prefer the cafeteria, the library, or the hallways.

Since the audience is a captive one, the teacher's task of passing on the central goals of the culture (and thus a sense that life has meaning and worth) becomes exceedingly difficult. In fact, when they are listening to teachers' lectures, students' levels of alertness and motivation are about as low—and their levels of passivity are about as high—as they get all day.

Yet, despite these obstacles, teachers do manage (almost miraculously) to make a positive difference in the lives of many students. When we asked teenagers to tell us who or what influenced them to become the kinds of people they are, 58% mentioned one teacher or more. However, 90% mentioned their parents, and 88% mentioned peers.

At first glance, these figures do not seem to give teachers a great deal of weight. That 30% more teenagers should mention peers than teachers as having shaped their lives is a thought-provoking commentary on the relative influence of the two groups. Moveover, these students saw only about 9% of all the teachers whom they had encountered in the course of their school careers as having made a difference in their lives. In other words, at least 91% of the teachers left no memorable mark. But, considering the difficult circumstances under which teachers usually struggle, even these meager figures inspire some hope.

What distinguishes those teachers who, despite all the obstacles, are able to touch students' lives, giving them shape and purpose? Or, to phrase the question in more general terms, What makes an adult an effective carrier of cultural information?

Psychological theories of modeling, which describe how young people imitate and internalize the behavior of their elders, suggest that, for a teacher to have an impact on the behavior of students, the teacher must be perceived as having control over resources that the students desire. According to social learning theory, an influential teacher is one who can reward and punish or who has outstanding command of a particular field of knowledge. Because adolescents wish to identify with adults who have status and power, they will choose as models those teachers who are strong, powerful, or extremely skilled.

Our interviews with adolescents, however, suggest that this picture of what motivates a teenager to let a teacher influence his or her life is much too simple. Clearly, an adult who attracts the attention of a young person strongly enough to make a difference must possess a "resource" that is attractive to the young. But this resource is not what psychologists have assumed it to be. The obvious traits—power and control, status and expertise—do not move most teenagers. When adolescents try to explain why particular teachers have helped to shape who and what they are, this is the kind of thing they say:

> Mr. R. has really interesting classes because he's so full of pep and energy when he's teaching. It's not like the boring lectures you get in other classes when you listen to some guy drag on. He really gets into it, he's interesting, and it's fun to learn that way. It's easy to learn, because you are not bored.

Most often, the teenagers described influential teachers in terms of their ability to generate enthusiasm for learning through personal involvement with the subject matter and skill in teaching it. Such responses far outnumbered mentions of power, status, or intelligence. Adolescents respond to teachers who communicate a sense of excitement, a contagious intellectual thrill. When excitement is present, learning becomes a pleasure instead of a chore. Thus teachers' involvement with subject matter translates into effective learning for students.

But involvement with subject matter does not come at the expense of involvement with the students. On the contrary, teenagers see influential teachers as exceptionally approachable—"easy to talk to" and ready to listen when students have difficulty understanding the material.

> Mrs. A. was the best teacher I ever had. . . . When you had problems, you could always go to her. Other teachers just yell at you when you don't understand something; they tell you to bring a note home to your parents.

> Mr. M. has the ability to create an atmosphere where you don't feel scared to ask a question. Even if you *feel* dumb, he doesn't make you look dumb by asking the question in class or by saying, "I really don't understand."

> Mr. N. was a teacher you could really talk to. He *listened* to you, and he helped you to learn because he didn't shoot you down when you asked a question.

The most obvious consequence of teachers' nurturant attitudes is that students gain the self-confidence necessary for perseverance in learning: "Mr. J. was always kind and helpful. . . . He'd go over things as many times as you needed, which really helped you learn."

But many more teenagers saw nurturance as important because, in one teenager's words, "It shows you that the teacher really cares, and just seeing that makes *you* want to learn." The teacher's investment of psychic energy proves to students that learning is worth *their* time and effort. The teacher's enthusiasm and dedication are the main vehicle for socializing the young into meaningful academic experiences. To paraphrase Marshall McLuhan, the medium of education is the message; the attitude of the instructor toward teaching is what is being conveyed to the students.

In addition to caring about students and about the subjects they teach, influential teachers are remembered for taking the trouble to express their messages in unusual, memorable ways.

Mr. C. is such a fantastic teacher because he has a special way of thinking that catches your attention. He makes brains *go,* he makes brains *think,* and he says things in a way that you just can't forget them.

Mr. J. was influential because he gave us a lot of unusual assignments to do—it was never just "read Chapter 2 and answer the questions at the back of the book." When we were studying about Africa, he came up with the idea of having us do some research on what it would be like to take a trip there. We had to go to a travel agency and find out all kinds of things because he wanted us to come in and tell him where we'd go and what we'd *see* there. We even had to tell him what it would cost to travel around Africa in a boat, a plane, a car, and on a bicycle. . . . He *really* opened your eyes, and his class wasn't like any class I've ever had before.

This ability to engage the attention of students by presenting material in an original way is often seen as an expression of a teacher's creativity. But to label such behavior as "creative" could be misleading, because that term implies that only exceptionally gifted teachers have the capability. It seems more probable that a teacher who presents material in an original manner is not necessarily highly creative but simply more willing to spend time thinking about how best to convey information to a specific audience. In other words, creativity—like nurturance and involvement—is probably a reflection of a teacher's enthusiasm for teaching.

Perhaps the most important accomplishment of influential teachers is that they are able to transform the usual drudgery of the classroom into an enjoyable experience. Teenagers typically say about the classes of such teachers, "You learn a lot because it doesn't seem like work; it's something you really *want* to do." One adolescent expressed this idea in a particularly pointed way:

What made Mrs. R. influential was that she made it *fun* to learn. . . . When something is fun, it's not like learning. I mean, I learned *a lot* in her class, but things would stick in my head. In other classes, things don't stay in my head; they just fly out!

Another student made a statement that highlights an important outcome of effective teaching:

Mrs. A. was influential because her [English] class was a lot of fun. . . . After all these years, I found out for the first time that I really *liked* English—it was really fun—and I've kept up my interest even though I'm not doing as well as other kids.

When teaching is effective, students not only enjoy the class but also learn to enjoy the subject matter. Only after a student has learned to love learning does education truly begin. Having caught a teacher's enthusiasm for the ordered pattern of information that constitutes "English," or "mathematics," or "chemistry," the student is ready to pursue the subject for its own sake, without threats or bribes from adults.

Past studies of teacher effectiveness have often noted that good teachers are "warm," "accessible," and "enthusiastic." But such traits are almost always lumped with the *expressive* dimensions of teaching. They are seen as characteristics that a teacher ought to possess to be popular with students, not as task-relevant traits. Indeed, they are seen as hindrances to the serious purpose of teaching. A recent article on research related to course evaluations reflects this widespread misunderstanding of the teaching process. This research suggests that jokes and theatrics, along with well-chosen materials and well-delivered lectures, are often of major importance to achieving high course ratings. In order to obtain higher ratings, an instructor should make his or her course one that students enjoy attending.

Most scholars in the field assume that enthusiasm, a sense of humor, and the ability to make learning enjoyable are dubious gimmicks to be used only by those teachers who wish to cater to their students' foibles. But this attitude is built on a mistaken view of what young people need most from their teachers. They don't need just information; they need *meaningful* information. They don't need just knowledge; they need knowledge that makes sense and inspires belief. They need knowledge that helps them understand why learning and living are worthwhile.

But how can young people believe that the information they are receiving is worth having, when their teachers seem bored, detached, or indifferent? Why would teenagers trust knowledge that brings no joy? Indeed, teenagers are following a perfectly sound survival strategy when they ignore information that has no relevance to the central business of life, which is enthusiastic involvement with enjoyable activities. To the extent that teachers cannot become joyfully involved in the task of teaching, their efforts will be largely in vain. Their message will be eliminated from the stream of cultural evolution as well, because the younger generation will have no interest in retaining it.

This obvious connection between enjoyment and education has been missed in the past because we have viewed the learning process in terms of the stimulus-response model developed by the behavioral psychologists. Most educational psychologists have tried to look at what

happens in schools according to rules developed to describe the behaviors of dogs, pigeons, or rats in laboratories. The educational process has been broken into tiny learning steps, and we have spent our time analyzing the "laws" of learning related to relationships among these microscopic units. Teacher trainers and developers of educational software for computers have all been guided by the assumption that, if the structural units of, say, mathematics are correctly sequenced and rewards are provided at appropriate points in the sequence, students will "learn mathematics."

We believe that it is more useful to see the learning of a complex system of information—be it trigonometry, music, or chemistry—as an outcome of a conscious commitment to the particular domain of knowledge. Of course, the steps of learning proceed piecemeal, according to the laws of effect specified by behaviorist theories. But to understand why mastering a new skill in computation will reward one person but not another requires knowledge of the motivational systems involved.

All complex learning that requires concentrated effort over time depends on intrinsic motivation. If an individual doesn't *like* to do math, he or she will never become a real mathematician. Extrinsic motives—the ones manipulated through the so-called operant rewards and punishments that are administered by outsiders to increase the desired behaviors—can cause students to cram for tests, pass them, and meet professional standards of knowledge. But extrinsic motives alone are not enough to cause students to identify with a body of knowledge and internalize it. And unless young people come to "love" mathematics (or music, physics, poetry, psychology, or any other discipline)—unless they try to make the body of knowledge their own—it is premature to speak of genuine learning. Knowledge that is not the outcome of intrinsic motivation is very fragile. It needs external inputs of energy, in the form of rewards and punishments, if it is to be maintained. Such knowledge remains static, because it lacks intrinsic incentives to grow. Only a student who wants to know something for its own sake can be said to be really learning.

The same is true of the much more complex process of learning to become an adult member of society. To grow up to be an "American" means to accept with enthusiasm the values, habits, and patterns of behavior that set this culture apart from others, that give it a particular historical identity and evolutionary significance. If young people fail to encounter adults who are enthusiastically involved with the culture, they cannot be expected to replicate the patterns of that culture in their own lives. If the adults who represent mainstream values to the young are bored, listless, and disinterested, their way of life will be rejected by the coming generations. And this would be a catastrophe comparable to those visited on past generations by wars or by the bubonic plague. ∎

POST NOTE

When this article first appeared, in February of 1986, the United States was facing forecasts of a deep shortage of teachers. Reports and commentaries predicted classrooms without teachers. But the authors of this article discuss a much more serious and dangerous possibility: youth without meaningful contact with adults. When this happens, society begins to crumble. Its sustaining values no longer make sense to the young. The social glue no longer sticks.

Because of the decline in the power of the family, teachers are increasingly being called upon to act as transmitters of values. They must not only teach content but do it in a way that inspires the young to "buy into" the values of the culture. For this reason, the authors believe that the affective elements of teaching are of enormous importance.

DISCUSSION QUESTIONS

1. What are the forces that currently diminish the power of parents and teachers to affect the values of the young?

2. In the view of these authors, what are the skills or qualities of "the effective teacher"?

3. Are these authors suggesting that the main job of teachers is to socialize children into society's core values? Why? Why not?

2 Letter from a Teacher

John C. Crowley

Dear Bill:

Well, your baptism by fire is about over. You have passed through that vague state appropriately mislabelled as "Student Teacher." Soon you will return to the more familiar and secure world of the college campus.

I hope your teaching experience was of some value. Throughout the time we worked together I made repeated plans to sit down with you and have a long talk—a "tell it like it is" type session. Unfortunately, except for between-class chats and noontime gab sessions, our talks never did get down to the nitty-gritty. So, with due apologies for a letter instead of a talk, this will have to do.

If you leave here feeling to some degree satisfied and rewarded, accept these feelings. You have worked diligently and consistently. For your part you have a right to feel rewarded. Teaching offers many intangible bonuses; feeling satisfied when a class goes well is one of them. The day teaching no longer offers to you the feelings of satisfaction and reward is the day you should seriously consider another profession.

Mingled with these feelings is also one of discouragement. Accept this too. Accept it, learn to

John C. Crowley was a high school teacher in Massachusetts. He died shortly after the publication of this letter. "Letter from a Teacher" by John C. Crowley. From the *Massachusetts Teacher* (Sept.–Oct. 1970), pp. 2, 34, 38. Copyright 1970 by the Massachusetts Teachers Association. Reprinted by permission.

live with it, and be grateful for it. Of course certain classes flopped; some lesson plans were horror shows; and some kids never seemed to get involved or turned on. This is not a phenomenon experienced only by student teachers. We all encounter this. The good teacher profits from it— he investigates the reasons for the failure and seeks to correct himself, his approach, or his students. And in so doing, the good teacher further improves and gets better.

Bad teachers develop mental calluses, blame it on the kids, and sweep the failures under the rug. Always be discouraged and unsatisfied; it's the trademark of a good, professional teacher.

I don't know if you plan to make teaching your career—perhaps, at this point, you don't know yourself—but if you do, I'm sure you will do well; you have the potential. In the event you do elect a teaching career, I would offer these suggestions:

1. Develop a philosophy for yourself and your job. Why do you teach? What do you expect of yourself and your students? Do not chisel this philosophy on stone. Etch it lightly in pencil on your mind, inspect it frequently. Do not be surprised that it changes—that can be a good sign. Be more concerned with the reasons for a change rather than the change itself. Unless you base your teaching on a foundation of goals and ideals, you are wasting time. If you as the teacher-model cannot show a solid basis of beliefs, how can you expect your student-imitators to develop any definite beliefs?

2. Do not be just "a teacher," be a professional teacher. Teaching is the most rewarding, demanding, and important job in the world. We deal with the minds of men and the future of the world. It is not a task to be taken lightly. Demand professionalism of yourself and your associates. Do not shut yourself up in a classroom, isolated from and ignorant of the real world. Be prepared to teach at any time, in any place, to anyone. Ferret out ignorance with the zeal of a crusader and the compassion of a saint. Teach as if the fate of mankind rested squarely upon your shoulders and you'll know, in part, what I mean.

3. Always be a learner. Never assume you know all the answers or enough material to teach your class. Read constantly. Do not become an encapsulated specialist. Vary the material. Talk to others. Most of all, learn to listen to your students . . . not to what they say but to what they mean.

A good teacher learns as much from his students as he teaches to them. Do not discourage dialogue. Do not be so dogmatic as to accept only your own views. Do not use the textbook as a mental crutch.

Any fool can break a book up into 180 reading assignments and still manage to keep one section ahead of the students, but such a fool should not assume the title of teacher. At best, he would be a grossly overpaid reading instructor.

4. Develop the feeling of empathy. Try to feel how the student feels. Do not lapse into the warm complacency of a seating chart, names without faces. Do not accept the cold facts of a rank book, marks without personality.

See the girl in the second row, homework undone because her parents fought all night. She couldn't even sleep, let alone concentrate on homework. Does that deserve an "F"?

Or the boy in the back of the room. Bad teeth, poor complexion, shabby clothes. No known father, a promiscuous mother, and a cold-water flat in a bad part of town. Of course he acts up and appears rebellious; wouldn't you? How have we alleviated his problems by assigning detention time and writing a bad progress report? How does it feel to sit in a class day after day hungry, ill, knowing that when the last bell rings it will be back to the sewer?

Is it any wonder that Jacksonian Democracy, the English morality plays, or Boyle's Law leaves these kids cold? But if they are to even...ally move into society we must reach them, and the first step comes when we, as teachers, understand them.

I am not advocating that you become a "softy." Do not rationalize every failure with some outside cause. But be prepared to evaluate a student on the basis of your understanding of him and his problems. A grade is something more than a mathematical total and an average.

Before assigning a grade, look closely at the particular student and ask yourself, "Why?"

5. Finally, alluding to the misadventures of Don Quixote, I would counsel—"Do not be afraid of windmills!" As a conscientious, professional teacher you will find your path constantly bestraddled with windmills of one type or another.

These may come in the form of other teachers, guidance departments, administrators, department heads, school committees, parents, or heaven knows what. They will obstruct, criticize, belittle, and attack you for a variety of reasons and motives. If you think you are right, do not back down! Always be willing to go as far as necessary to defend your convictions and beliefs. Do not avoid experimentation for fear of mistakes or criticism!

If we accept the status quo and maintain a conservative view toward change, we will not progress. In fact, we'll probably regress. We have an obligation, as educators, to constantly seek better ways of doing things. If that means putting our own heads on the chopping block, so be it. Either we stand for something or we stand for nothing. If we stand for something it should be so important that any sacrifice to preserve and further it is worthwhile. And, as educators, we are under a moral and ethical responsibility to stand for something.

Well, I hope these words of advice have proved helpful. Repeating an earlier statement, you have a great deal of potential and I personally hope you put it to use as a teacher.

I know of no other job that compares with teaching. We need every promising candidate who comes along. It goes without saying of course that should you need a letter of recommendation I will be only too glad to supply it. Having participated in your student teaching experience I also feel morally obliged to assist you should you, at some future date, require and want such assistance. It's there for the asking.

With confidence in the nature of man, I remain

Very truly yours,
Jack Crowley ■

POST OTE

"With confidence in the nature of man, I remain . . ." This letter, one of the last Jack Crowley wrote before he died, is overflowing with one of life's rarest commodities—wisdom. His closing, though, speaks to a value that stands behind the huge edifice of education. "Confidence in the nature of man" captures the hope and conviction that must undergird the teacher's work. Without this confidence, teachers may find their goodwill eroding. The phrase also reminds us that as teachers, we must be dedicated to more than the status quo. We must try to bring human nature to a higher level.

DISCUSSION QUESTIONS

1. What are your reactions to the suggestions Jack Crowley makes to Bill, the student teacher?

2. How would you feel if you received such a letter from your supervising teacher? Why?

3. What attitudes toward teaching and toward students does Jack Crowley reveal in this letter?

3 Room to Learn

Greg Michie

"Okay, who can tell me what a bills is?"

According to the clock above the door, sixth period had already been under way for five minutes, but my class of eighth-graders was still milling about, looking for materials, finishing up hallway conversations. I stood between them and a chalkboard on which I had written, "How a bill becomes a law."

"Ervin, how about it? What's a bill?"

Ervin turned around in his chair. "A what?"

"A bill."

"A bill?"

"Yeah, a bill."

"Like a phone bill?" Ervin offered jokingly.

"Not exactly," I said, willing to play along. "A different kind of bill."

"A cable bill?" asked LaRhonda with a knowing smile.

"Come on, you know what I mean. Another whole use of the word *bill*."

"It's a name," said Tasha. "A white name. You know how white boys have them real short names? Bill, Frank, Tom—"

"Jim," Raynard called out.

Greg Michie teaches seventh- and eighth-graders at Seward Elementary School in Chicago. Some of the names in the article have been changed. Reprinted by permission of the publisher from Michie, G., *Holler If You Hear Me* (New York: Teachers College Press, © 1999 by Teachers College, Columbia University. All rights reserved.), "Room to Learn."

"Jack," said someone else.

"Bob!"

"George Bush."

"Yeah!" Tasha said. "They got them boring names!"

"Okay, okay. I get the point," I said. "I have one myself. But what I want to know is how the word *bill* relates to how laws are made. Remember what we started talking about yesterday?"

"Oooh, Mr. Michie! Mr. Michie!" Tobias' hand shot up like a flare. An excitable kid who was at times hot-tempered, Tobias loved to distract me from my planned activities. He'd wait just long enough for me to pick up steam on a topic and then quickly figure out how he could best derail the train.

"Tobias?"

"You know what Ms. Tucker did today?" Tobias asked me.

"Oooh, yeah," Tasha hissed. "That lady make me sick."

"She bugged out," added Raynard.

"Wait," I said. "Does this have anything to do with what we're talking about?"

"Yeah, she got a husband named Bill," a voice from the back of the class piped in.

"Nah, it don't really have nothin' to do wit' it," admitted Tobias, "but look at what she done—"

"You know how we can't eat or drink or chew gum or nothin' in class, right?" Tasha inserted.

"Well, today she was eating a big cream doughnut right in front of us," said Tobias, continuing the story. "And drinking a 16-ounce pop—a diet Dr. Pepper—right there in the class! Now, that ain't right, Mr. Michie. You know that ain't right."

Yeah, I knew it. It wasn't right. But it was beside the point, at least at the moment. "Look," I said. "I'm trying to help you guys get ready to take this Constitution test. And I don't think there're gonna be any questions on there about Ms. Tucker, diet Dr. Pepper, or cream doughnuts."

"But y'all ain't fair," added LaRhonda. "Y'all can drink whenever y'all want to and we gotta be up in here all sweatin' and hot."

"Y'all?" I shot back. "What do you mean, '*y'all*'?"

"I mean y'all," LaRhonda said. "Y'all teachers. You know—you all?"

"And how many times have you seen me drinking anything in class?" I asked, trying to separate myself from the ranks of the enemy.

"But you eat them teacher lunches, don't you?"

Busted. I looked over to my right. Vincent's pudgy body was hanging halfway out the window. "Vincent!" I yelled out. He pulled his shoulders and head back in and looked at me as if he had no idea why I'd called his name. "What are you doing?" I asked.

"Nah, I thought I heard somebody outside sayin' my name," Vincent answered.

"It was probably Bill," said another voice.

"Could you sit back down, please?" I asked. Vincent hesitated. "Vincent, sit down! C'mon, I'm not playing! Let's go!" I was raising my voice again. Which meant I feared I was losing control again. It was nothing new. Sometimes it seemed like that's all my first year in the classroom had been—one long fight for control.

I grew up in a middle-class family in Charlotte, North Carolina, the oldest of three children. As a kid, I collected baseball cards and memorized lyrics to Partridge Family records. At school I was fascinated with dinosaurs and was co-captain of the crossing guards. I spent summer nights in the backyard playing neighborhood games of Kick-the-Can, and, when I was lucky, got to stay up late to watch Johnny Carson. My Childhood, in many ways, was typical, white-bread Americana.

But there were differences. Charlotte in the early '70s was a place of court-ordered desegregation but also a place of tentative reconciliation between blacks and white. I spent my elementary school years in a neighborhood that, due to a sudden outbreak of white flight, became integrated almost overnight. I walked to school and played ball with as many blacks as whites, had plenty of friends of both races, and sang gospel music in a biracial Presbyterian church from the age of five. Because of these early experiences, I considered myself somewhat well-informed on issues of race and class—more so at least than the average white person. Then I came to Chicago.

What I found, at least on first impression, was more separation and racial mistrust than I remembered even experiencing in the "backward" South. Although Chicago was certainly one of the nation's most diverse cities, it was also arguably the most segregated. In many sections of the city, ethnic and color lines clearly marked one neighborhood from the next. Poverty seemed both more severe and more widespread than anything I'd seem before. So it was not surprising that many of the city's public grammar schools were essentially single-race institutions, with almost all of their students coming from poor or working-class families.

I began subbing in the fall of 1990 at Ralph Ellison Educational and Vocational Guidance Center—a euphemistic mouthful that really meant *School for Seventh and Eighth-Graders Who'd Been Booted Out Someplace Else*. My first day there I was assigned to a rowdy but jovial group of eighth-graders who, for the first hour or so, didn't even seem to notice there was an adult in the room. They calmed down only when I off-handedly mentioned that I'd gone to college with Michael Jordan. It didn't matter to them that I hadn't actually known him. They wanted to know the details of every occasion we had even crossed paths. After class, I heard some of them in the hall telling friends, "Hey, that man know Michael Jordan." In subsequent years I would use the MJ connection often as a last-ditch means of regaining control of a classroom. It never failed and even took on a life of its own. Once a kid at the park tapped me on the shoulder and asked, "Hey, did you really used to play on the same team with Michael Jordan?"

I didn't think I had turned in a particularly Jordanlike performance that first day at Ellison, but apparently getting subs to come there wasn't easy. When the principal saw that I wasn't making a mad dash for the exit at the end of the day, she asked if I'd like to return to sub again the following morning. I said I would. The same thing happened the next day and the next, until soon I became a familiar face at the school.

In early November, Ellison's reading lab teacher abruptly resigned. A matronly, kind-hearted Polish woman of about fifty, she had taught for years at a local Catholic school before deciding the previous summer that she needed a fresh challenge. The challenge she chose was the Chicago Public Schools, and she regretted it almost immediately. The kids at Ellison ran her over like a steamroller on wet asphalt. It was the first time I'd seen someone's will totally broken by experiences with children. It wouldn't be the last.

That afternoon, the principal asked if I'd be interested in taking over the reading lab. She felt I'd begun to develop a rapport with the kids and that my stepping in would be an easier transition than bringing in someone unfamiliar. I wondered aloud if there was a set curriculum for the class—all I'd seen the kids bringing out of there were spelling lists. She explained that the intent of the course was to prove extra practice in reading and to build comprehension skills. Since many of Ellison's students were below grade-level in reading—whatever that meant—the lab was intended to serve as a place for remediation.

I didn't know the first thing about teaching reading. Thinking back on my own early experiences with books, I couldn't even begin to piece together how the process worked. I remembered my parents and grandmother reading to me, I remembered loving certain books, and then— poof!—I remembered reading on my own. It seemed more like magic than anything else. Yet as I mulled over the thought of having my own classroom, I knew I didn't have any tricks up my sleeve. Because I had done no education coursework, I would still be paid as a day-to-day substitute. I'd have all the responsibilities of a fully certified teacher for $54 a day. But there were also obvious advantages—I'd have steady work, I'd have my own space, and I'd get more of a feel for what it was really like to be a teacher. The thought of it was scary, but I'd been saying I wanted to teach, and here was a chance to do it staring me right in the face. I decided to give it a shot.

The principal allowed me one day to prepare. I arrived early that Monday to rummage through the lab's available resources. Opening the doors of a large metal supply cabinet, I peered inside, hoping, I suppose, to stumble upon some kind of lesson-plan jackpot. Instead, it looked and smelled more like a musty attic, stuffed with outdated equipment, aging materials, and other assorted junk. One shelf was full of the clunky tape recorders and headache-inducing plastic headphones I remembered from the language labs of my youth. On a higher shelf were—literally— hundreds of purple ditto masters and worksheets. The copyright date at the bottom of the pages I examined read "1972." Above those was a boxed set of the Mastery Learning series, a reading program I'd heard rode a brief wave of popularity in the mid-seventies before dying out just as quickly. Other odds and ends lay about randomly: an old sweater, a broken trophy, a whistle, a rolled-up American flag. Disappointed, I closed the cabinet's doors and decided to go to Plan B: I would plunge in and rely on instinct, trusting it to carry me through until I came up with something better.

The next day I had the students in my lab classes complete a questionnaire that covered a wide range of home, community, and school-related topics. Many wrote that they disliked, even hated, to read. To the question, "What kinds of things do you most enjoy reading?" many replied: "Nothing." I decided that my initial goal would be to try to spark the kids' interest in reading. I knew this would be nearly impossible to accomplish with moldy dittos or workbook pages, so I brought in as many outside sources as I could. We read excerpts from Malcolm X's autobiography and Claude Brown's *Manchild in the Promised Land*. We read up on African Americans of note, from Marcus Garvey to Mary McLeod Bethune to Charles Drew. We explicated poems of Gwendolyn Brooks and Langston Hughes alongside rap songs by Boogie Down Productions and A Tribe Called Quest. We studied the censorship controversy then surrounding the rap group 2 Live Crew and used that as a starting point for examining the Bill of Rights and how it affected the kids' lives. Of course, those were the good days. Good days occurred maybe once a week.

The rest of the time, I was fighting for survival. Of the five classes that came to me each day, none was easy, but one eighth-grade group had become a particular problem. I found the students to be bright and energetic; they seemed to genuinely like me. But I often found it impossible to maintain control of the classroom. While most of their other teachers ran extremely tight ships, I wanted my classes to be relaxed, open forums. But it usually only took about ten minutes for relaxed and open to turn into wild and loose. The sudden freedom I dumped at the kids' feet proved too much to handle. They didn't know what to do with it, and I failed to give them much guidance. On several occasions, things had gone so completely awry that I just sat down at my desk, frustrated and angry, and waited for the storm to pass. Sometimes it did.

I never broke down and cried in front of those students, thought there was a time or two when I came close. I fought back the tears because I knew crying would only make my job harder—it would make me appear weaker in their eyes, and that was the last thing I needed. Some of the kids already considered me a poor excuse for a man. One day I had come to school with a bandage on my hand. When I began writing on the board, a student noticed.

"What happened to your hand, Mr. Mitchell?" Several of the kids had settled on the more familiar "Mitchell" as the preferred pronunciation of my name.

I stopped writing and showed the bandage to the group. "Oh, I broke a glass last night washing dishes. Just cut it a little bit."

"Washing dishes?" one of the male students asked incredulously. "Why you washing dishes? Ain't you got a woman to do that?" This led to a period-long discussion of gender roles and relationships, but despite my attempts at feminist rhetoric, few of the guys budged in their positions. As they were leaving, one kid just looked at me and shook his head. "Washing dishes," he kept repeating with disgust. "Washing dishes."

The class wanted me to take a stronger hold, to become more authoritarian. That was the style of discipline many of them were used to, and they respected it. It felt safe. Raynard, a tall and witty kid who was one of the group's natural leaders, often lingered after class to serve as my mentor. He could tell I was floundering and had a sincere desire to help. "You gotta be meaner, Mr. Michie," he would say. Then, as if he was no longer one of them, he would add, "That's what these kids understand." I knew what Raynard meant, and sometimes I'd act on his advice. I'd get so fed up with the class's behavior that I'd blow up on them and then make them do busywork for a couple of days. They'd sit silently, mindlessly copying down words from the dictionary, and I'd play overseer at my desk, my power restored. But inside I was hating it, and I knew there had to be some middle ground, a better way.

So there I stood, trying to get through my introductory remarks on "How a bill becomes a law." It was the third week of May. An oscillating fan buzzed beside me, ineffective in the stifling air. As Vincent finally made his way from the window back to his seat, Tammy stood up and turned to face Carlton, who was sitting behind her. "Boy, you better give me back my pen!" Tammy said with a snake-like roll of her neck.

"Tammy—"

"I want my pen back!"

"Carlton, could you give her the pen back?"

"I ain't take no pen! She musta lost it."

"All right," I said. "Tammy, how about if you sit down, and we'll figure out what happened to your pen after class?"

Amazingly, Tammy obeyed. "But I better have my pen back 'fore we leave up outta here or I'mo pop that boy in his lip!" Tammy had once threatened to pop me in the lip also, so I knew how Carlton was feeling.

"Okay—" I was momentarily at a complete loss as to what I'd been talking about. "Where were we?"

Tobias again raised his hand.

"Does this have to do with how a bill becomes a law?"

"Kinda," Tobias answered.

"What do you mean, 'kinda'?" I was irritated; we were getting off track. I could tell I was about to lose the kids, if I hadn't already.

"Look, Mr. Michie, I think this is what we oughta do," Tobias explained. "The teachers around here, they not being fair, right?" They telling us we can't bring food in the school, but yet and still they eating and drinking in class, right? Well, this is what I think we oughta do. We oughta put this school on trial. The students versus Ellison. We oughta hold a trial right here and charge them with unfair rules."

It was as if the idea has an electric current running through it. The entire room was spontaneously energized. Students who seconds earlier were lifelessly slumped over their desks were now out of their seats and animated. Within minutes the class had agreed on the proposal, decided on a case to try, and begun to assign roles. I folded up my notes and marveled as they excitedly worked out the details. The plan was to put the school administration and teachers on trial for what the students considered unfair double standards: Despite a school rule forbidding food or drinks in class, several teachers apparently thought they were above the law. In addition, the kids noted that teachers were served different, higher-quality lunches than the students. They wanted the rules changed to allow students to bring food, candy, and pop into the building.

I loved the idea. Throughout the year I'd talked with the kids about the importance of speaking up intelligently about matters that concerned them. Of course, I'd had in mind some of the larger problems that affected them— discrimination, police brutality, erratic city services. Equal access to pop and cream doughnuts didn't seem quite as noble a cause, but to the kids, the bottom-line issue was essentially the same: unfair treatment.

After spending a few days discussing courtroom roles and procedure, preparing arguments, and arranging testimony, we were ready for our day in court. Seven judges—all students—and a small gallery looked on somberly as Marvin, the first witness, was sworn in by placing his right hand on a dictionary. Nathan, a playful and gangly teen who was to serve as the students' lawyer, got the proceedings started.

NATHAN: I heard that some teachers be eating and drinking in the classroom. Is that true?

MARVIN: Yep.

NATHAN: Well what do you feel about that?

MARVIN: I think they should let the kids bring it, too.

NATHAN: Thank you, sir.

It was a brief interrogation, but then again we were just getting started. It took most kids a few minutes to warm up. But it didn't take Tobias any time. Though he had originally wanted play the role of the prosecutor and had lobbied for the part, he lost out in a class vote to the more popular Nathan. Now, as the defense attorney for "the other side"—the administration—Tobias vaulted from his chair and hit the ground running.

TOBIAS: Isn't it true that every day in the lunchroom, you eat the school food?

MARVIN: Yeah.

TOBIAS: Then why should the students be allowed to bring candy and stuff when you eat the food?

MARVIN: 'Cause. . . . well, not food but we should be able to bring pop.

TOBIAS: Don't they serve you milk?

MARVIN: Yeah. So?

TOBIAS: What's the matter with the milk?

MARVIN: It's spoilt.

TOBIAS: So you're saying every day when you go downstairs to eat lunch the milk be spoiled—every time?

MARVIN: Not every time. Sometimes.

TOBIAS: And when the milk is spoiled, have you ever tried to make an effort to go back and get another one?

MARVIN: No.

TOBIAS: No more questions, your honor.

As Tobias walked back to his seat, I sensed a shared thought running through the mind of every kid in the room: This thing was serious! Tobias had destroyed the students' first witness, and the determined look in his eyes said it was no fluke. The students looked to Nathan, hoping he was up to the challenge. Nathan called the next witness. It was Carlton, a slightly built, rambunctious child who wore a patch over his right eye.

NATHAN: Carlton, do teachers drink in the classroom?

CARLTON: Yes.

NATHAN: What do you think about that?

CARLTON: That's wrong. Students should have the right to eat and drink just like the teachers.

Mindful of Tobias's previous attack, Nathan decided to proceed by confronting head-on the issue of students willfully eating the school's food.

NATHAN: Do you eat the food in the lunchroom?

CARLTON: The only thing I eat is the nuggets and the pizza.

NATHAN: Ain't it nasty?

CARLTON: Not the nuggets and pizza, but the rest of the stuff taste like dog food.

NATHAN: Don't the teachers have better lunches than you all?

CARLTON: Yes, they have roast beef sandwiches and other stuff.

NATHAN: Well, I think we should be able to bring food if we want. What do you think—

TOBIAS: Objection! The lawyer is not on the stand here.

Tobias recognized that Nathan was making arguments and leading his witness. The objection sustained, Tobias took over the questioning a few minutes later, walking in slow circles around the witness chair.

TOBIAS: Is it true that you've brought chips and candy in the school?

CARLTON: Yes, we can bring chips and candy in some classes.

TOBIAS: So that's true that you can bring chips and candy in the school?

CARLTON: Yes, in some classes. But you can't bring pops.

TOBIAS: Have you ever brought pops in the school?

CARLTON: Yes.

TOBIAS: Even though you were not supposed to, but you did?

CARLTON: Yes.

TOBIAS: No further questions, your honor.

Tobias was ripping apart witnesses like they were flimsy paper dolls. The next in line to testify for the students was Tianna Johnson, an outspoken and expressive girl whose comments were always eagerly anticipated by the others. I wondered if she could save the day.

NATHAN: Ain't it right that everybody should be treated equal in the school?

TIANNA: Yes, it is. Teachers be drinkin' pops, and I don't think it's right, because if we can't drink pop, why should the teachers?

NATHAN: Yeah, true. And don't it be hot in those classrooms?

TIANNA: Yes. It be so hot Ms. Sanders make me stand in the corner, 'cause I fall asleep.

NATHAN: So don't you think we should have some pops in there?

TIANNA: Yes, 'cause it be too hot in those classrooms.

Tobias knew Tianna would be a tough witness. He approached her cautiously and waited a few seconds before addressing her.

TOBIAS: Miss Johnson, you said teachers were allowed to bring pops in the school. Wouldn't you think they were a little more responsible than the students were?

TIANNA: No I do not. 'Cause, see, we know how to drink our pops just like they do.

TOBIAS: All right. Miss Johnson, you say you were sleeping in the classroom?

TIANNA: No, I had my head down on the desk, but this don't have nothin' to do with the pops—

TOBIAS: No, no. You said Ms. Sanders made you stand up in the classroom because you were asleep.

TIANNA: But this don't have nothin' to do with the pops. I'm up here—

TOBIAS: Answer the question, Miss Johnson. You said she made you stand up because you were sleeping in the classroom. Is that true?

TIANNA: I said it didn't have nothin' to do with it.

TOBIAS: Your honor, would you make her answer the question?

STUDENT JUDGE: Answer the question.

TOBIAS: Were you sleeping in the classroom?

TIANNA: Yes.

TOBIAS: Well, how can you be responsible when you come in the classroom and you go to sleep?

TIANNA: I don't be asleep, I had my head down!

TOBIAS: No further questions, your honor.

TIANNA: Wait! Wait a minute!

STUDENT JUDGE: Order! Order in the court!

I then testified as a witness for the administration. I was fully on the kids' side, but I tried to play my part with conviction. Keeping a straight face wasn't easy. "We strive to make our food meet two standards," I said. "Delicious and nutritious!" The students groaned. Most of the food kids brought in, I alleged, was junk. Nathan objected: "The kids say the cafeteria food is rotten! It's no good!" The highlight of the final witness, Shaundra's testimony was when she claimed she had never brought food into the school. Nathan broke out laughing. "Ooooh-eeeeee," he said, "you tellin' a story." Tobias objected, saying Nathan was putting words in the witness's mouth. Cedric, who was serving as chief judge, knew he had to rule on the objection but couldn't remember the correct terminology. "Enclosed!" he shouted. The entire class burst into laughter. Cedric searched his brain some more. "Exclosed!" Kids were falling out of the seats, rolling on the floor. The judge next to Cedric whispered something to him. "Overruled, I mean!" Cedric bellowed, smacking the desk with a makeshift gavel. "Overruled!"

When all the testimony had been completed, the seven judges were granted time to make their decisions. We had agreed that, as with the Supreme Court, majority would rule. Though I had hoped the students' side would emerge victorious, after witnessing the proceedings, there was no question in my mind who had won. But I wondered if the kids saw it the same way. And even if they did, would they vote with their consciences or their stomachs? A short while later, the judges informed us that their opinions were ready to be delivered. Everyone took a seat. One at a time, the judges stood and read their opinions. The final tally was 6-1 in favor of the administration. Tobias's skill at discrediting witnesses and laying bare lame arguments had stolen the show. Still, some in the class weren't pleased.

"See, man," yelled Carlton. "This here fixin' to help us in the future for havin' pops and stuff and y'all mess it up!"

Lonnie, a judge who had just read his opinion, responded tersely: "Hey, y'all didn't have y'all's stuff together!" They might not have admitted it at the time, but I think everyone in the class knew Lonnie was right.

That summer, thinking back on what I had accomplished over the course of my first year in the classroom, I held the trial up as the highlight of my teaching, a shining moment among dozens of dark days. It was the one experience I could point to with some sense of certainty and say, "There. That's how I think school should be." Yet it was clear that my involvement in the trial's conception, planning, and execution was only peripheral. Not that my presence wasn't important. I was there to facilitate, to guide, to keep things on track—but the kids were the real decision makers, from the genesis of the idea all the way through to its completion. It was a powerful realization for me.

From the beginning, I had hoped to create an "open" classroom where kids' ideas were sought out and valued. But questions of discipline soon demanded the bulk of my energy and attention. Other teachers at Ellison, sensing my struggle, repeatedly told me that I was too soft, that I gave the kids too much freedom, that I should clamp down, get tough. After all, they would say, that's the way we handle things, and the same kids who raise holy hell in your class don't say a word in ours. Gradually their words began to take hold and, before I knew it, the quest for control became my primary focus. I began classifying days as good or bad solely in relation to how quiet and obedient the class had been. Other concerns, such as whether the kids had learned anything of value, lessened in importance. On the worst days, they didn't matter at all.

It was an easy trap to fall into. I became so obsessed with establishing control in the classroom that once I did—fragile as that control seemed— I was afraid to let go. I began to feel that I always had to be the center of attention, the imparter of knowledge, the setter of agendas and bounds. But the positive energy that sparked the trial reminded me that it doesn't have to be that way. Letting go doesn't have to mean a loss of control.

It is possible—even desirable—to step aside and let the kids take control.

Stepping aside can be a difficult thing for a teacher. A few years back I was attempting to teach something at the blackboard of a tiny closet-sized classroom, and the kids weren't getting it. I thought I was explaining things clearly, but they weren't following me. I couldn't understand why. Then Santiago, a kid who always sat in the seat furthest from me, said, "If you'd get outta the way so we could see what you're doing, it might help." I hadn't realized it, but my body was partially blocking their view of the board. I moved over and things cleared up quite a bit. Sometimes that's what being a teacher is. Knowing when to crumple up your plans, get out of the way, and give the kids room to learn. ■

P O S T N O T E

In this essay, Greg Michie gives a peek at what many new teachers experience, but few openly talk about: the fight for personal survival. He, like many rookie teachers, has come to teach and what he finds instead is a subtle undercurrent of warfare. And, sometimes, not so subtle. As he struggles to engage students in some Big Idea, they are testing, testing, testing. Most occupations have break-in periods for beginners, which are often deeply frustrating and discouraging. But expecting it is not enough. The struggle should be accepted as a problem to be solved, a problem with a solution, but one that may take months to solve. As Greg's essay indicates, the solution takes courage and creativity. The good news is that the overwhelming majority of teachers come out the other side of the struggle for survival a good deal more secure and savvy.

D I S C U S S I O N Q U E S T I O N S

1. When you were in grade school and high school, can you recall situations similar to Greg's, where the students were "breaking in" a new teacher?

2. What do you believe were the mistakes that Greg was making with this class? What would you do differently, and why?

3. What are the sources of support available to new teachers, and what are the pluses and minuses of each?

4 Calling in the Cosmos

Margaret Metzger

Dear Christine Greenhow,

You have asked one of the hardest questions about teaching or perhaps about any profession. You have asked how a teacher moves from competence to excellence. I could postpone an answer by saying that your question is premature; you have been a student teacher for only a few weeks, and your task now is to learn the basic skills of teaching. But I admire your thinking about the larger questions. You are not getting mired in the panic of inexperience. So let me try to answer as best as I can.

How does a teacher move from competence to excellence? Partially it's just experience. If you expect excellence immediately, you degrade the craft of teaching. You would not expect to do brain surgery during your first month in medical school.

My advice is to be gentle with yourself. Teaching is an art form. All art, done with integrity, is excruciatingly difficult. You are just learning. As my mother, a gifted math teacher, bluntly told me during my first year of teaching, "For the first three years of teaching, new teachers should pay the schools for the privilege of practicing on the children. If you struggle enough, you'll get better."

At the time this article was written, Margaret Metzger had been a teacher of English at Brookline High School in suburban Boston for over twenty-five years. Metzger, Margaret, "Calling in the Cosmos," Part I of "Maintaining a Life," *Phi Delta Kappan*, January 1996. Copyright © 1996 by Phi Delta Kappa. Reprinted by permission of publisher and author, a teacher at Brookline High School, Brookline, MA.

You are struggling to improve. I watch you searching for the perfect assignment, the perfect classroom activity, the perfect lesson plan. Perhaps you are looking for answers in the wrong places. Instead of seeking just the right tidbit of knowledge or pedagogy, I suggest that you look at the larger picture. Think about what it means to be educated.

It seems to me that the missing ingredient in the lessons you teach is the subtle and explicit message that education is important. Students must be dedicated to their own growth, enthusiastic about academic work, and willing to take intellectual risks.

You must convince adolescents that being educated will enhance their lives. Students need to know, believe, and accept the idea that what they are doing is important. They are becoming educated adults; they are not just playing school. Christine, I know that you value your own education. You enjoy your intellectual life. You are in this profession because you believe that education matters. Now you must convey those values to the students.

My colleague Liz Kean teases me about how I convey the importance of education to my students. "Kids think your class is the most important event since the discovery of ice cream," she says. "You insist that what they are doing is important, that it matters in the great scheme of the universe. Even during routine work, you 'call in the cosmos.'"

I have never seen the concept of "calling in the cosmos" addressed in the research literature on teaching. Perhaps the ideal is too lofty or too unquantifiable to be included in teaching theory. Still, all the outstanding teachers I have known at Brookline High School, at Harvard, and at Brown University regularly "call in the cosmos," even if they would never use this silly term.

Strong teachers convey to their students a passion for a particular discipline, theory, or idea. But these teachers go beyond their own enthusiasm for the subject; they convince their students that learning has intrinsic value. When you are in their classes, you believe that the material matters.

Let me give you a concrete example of calling in the cosmos. Please remember that I developed this lesson after a decade of teaching. I want you to think about calling in the cosmos as an ideal, not as a requirement for a new teacher. When you first begin to teach, you can barely think about yourself, the students, and the material simultaneously, much less the cosmos. This sample is meant only to clarify the concept, not to intimidate you.

On the first day of some literature classes, I hand out a copy of Plato's "Parable of the Cave" (sometimes called "The Allegory of the Cave"). We read it, diagram it on the board so that everyone understands where the characters are standing in relation to one another, and then act it out (complete with bicycle chains and a candle on a desk to represent the fire). This makes for a dramatic beginning, but the most important part of the lesson is my introduction.

I say to the class, "I am giving you this reading as an intellectual gift, in honor of the work that we will do together this year. I first read Plato when I was your age, more than 35 years ago. As a high school sophomore, I wrote a paper on 'The Parable,'—and received, to my delight, an A. So when my college professor passed out 'The Parable,' I smugly assumed that I understood it. Yet when I reread Plato's work, I realized that I had changed my mind in three years and now understood it in a new way. I wrote another paper and again did well.

"I have been reading 'The Parable' every year of my life, and I keep changing my mind about its meaning. It has become a benchmark of my own intellectual growth. At different times, I identify with different characters in the story. More important, I understand that the tale contains a great truth about the world. Things happen in my life, and I say to myself, 'Ah, here it is again—a Parable-of-the-Cave experience.' I hope that you will think about this reading for years and years and that it will help you understand the world. We will also look for Parable-of-the-Cave experiences in the literature we read this semester. I teach you this work by Plato not as I now understand it, but as an introduction—a first exposure. I hope you receive this reading as a gift."

Sometimes I follow Plato's "Parable" with Maurice Sendak's *Where the Wild Things Are*. Particularly when I am dealing with stuffy advanced classes, we sit on the floor and I hold the book up as kindergarten teachers do. Then we talk about archetypes and language and imagination. I tell them to watch for Sendak's and Plato's ideas in Homer, Twain, Dante, and Shakespeare.

That first-day introduction contains many elements that I use to "call in the cosmos." Authentic material in any discipline moves beyond schoolwork to a larger context. I show my students that other authors and ordinary people like me think about literature. I include students in the society of educated people throughout history. Finally, I try for an almost liturgical tone because I believe that education is a sacred act.

High school teaching requires energy and drama. But flash without substance is mere gimmickry. Therefore, teach what is important. Don't claim that something is important if it isn't. Be truthful with students about whether you are required to teach particular material or whether that material will lead to more interesting ideas.

You can always call in the cosmos simply by telling students the "big reasons" for learning. Why do we learn to write? To gain personal and academic power. We need to be able to write a college essay, to complete an insurance form, to compose a love letter. Why do we read literature? To enlarge our puny vistas. Literature shows us other people, other cultures, other times and ideas. Why should we educate ourselves? Tell your students about Seneca, who believed that education should produce a free people who are responsible for their own thinking and can examine their own world critically.

Emphasize *how* to learn, rather than *what* to learn. Students may never need to know a particular fact, but they will always need to know how to learn. Teach students how to read with genuine comprehension, how to shape an idea, how to master difficult material, how to use writing to clarify their thinking. A former student, Anastasia Koniaris, wrote to me: "Your class was like a hardware store. All the tools were there. Years later I'm still using that hardware store that's up there in my head. At Harvard they just tell us to learn stuff; they never stop and explain how to learn anything." Empower your students to learn.

Empowering students is not just a faddish notion. Include students in the process of teaching and learning. Every day ask such basic questions as: What did you think of this homework? Did it help you learn the material? Was the assignment too long or too short? How can we make the next assignment more interesting? What should the criteria for assessment be? Remember that you want students to take ownership of their learning.

For every assignment, explain the larger purpose. Students are entitled to know why they should do the work, even when it comes to something as insignificant as studying a spelling list. "You must know how to spell correctly because people who can spell make judgments about those who can't. Spellers think correct spelling is an indication of intelligence and character. I don't want anyone else to assume you aren't intelligent just because you can't spell. So, let's learn these blasted words. Not all learning is fun or even interesting; sometimes we just have to memorize."

Explain common knowledge. High school students need guidance regarding academic and cultural conventions. For example, they need to know that it is not appropriate to call Thoreau "Henry," that educated people recognize the name Hamlet, that footnotes are done in a certain fashion, that in the U.S. it is a sign of respect to look the teacher in the eye.

Although the curriculum is important, students are most fascinated with one another. Instead of deploring peer pressure, try to establish a community of learners. Despite the high school's emphasis on individual learning, much success in adulthood depends on the ability to work with others. Students must respect one another's intellectual and cultural differences. Students must learn to work collaboratively, to accept editing from peers, to discuss various ways of solving a problem, to share both their knowledge and their

confusion. Adolescents, like all of us, hunger for exciting work within a community.

You, too, are a member of the community of learners. Do your own assignments. Talk to students about the things you've been reading. Show students drafts of your writing. Promise not to bore your students by giving them busywork or by wasting class time; in return, expect students to teach you by writing interesting papers and giving you new insights into life and literature.

Students want to be part of a classroom community, but they also want to be part of the larger community. Much of high school seems disconnected from real life and thus irrelevant to them. Whenever possible—and I hope you're able to do this far more frequently than I have ever managed—connect classroom learning to the outside world.

During my first semester of teaching, a particularly recalcitrant student refused to learn any grammar or mechanics, and his writing was unreadable. At the end of the course, I asked my students to write to their elementary school principals to arrange visits to their former schools. The boy demanded that I proofread and fix his letter. "Why?" I asked. "You've never cared about correctness."

"I know," he replied, "but if it's full of mistakes my old principal will think that I'm dumb, and maybe he won't let me visit."

"Okay," I said. "Now you're ready to learn mechanics." He did.

Despite all your best intentions and hardest work, Christine, in the end the students must decide whether they are ready to give up ignorance and take the scary step into knowledge. Like parenting, teaching makes us humble. There is only so much a teacher can do. A teacher can present learning experiences, but each student must ultimately take responsibility for becoming educated.

A former student, Chris Hummel, told me that when he read Martin Luther King's *Letter from a Birmingham Jail*, he decided to become educated. Chris described his thinking in this way: "So this is what it means to be well-educated. King sat in a jail, and all those references and quotes were right at his fingertips. He could see his predicament in larger terms because he had read all those authors. I want to have a mind like that."

Keep providing opportunities to think and good role models. Challenge students to think carefully about their assumptions by giving them interesting materials, questions, and alternatives. Don't just call in the cosmos, but question it.

Useful research has been conducted lately on learning styles and frames of intelligence. Read that research. The basic axiom to keep in mind is that students should think for themselves. Your job is to teach them how to think and to give them the necessary tools. Your students will be endlessly amazed at how intelligent they are; you do not need to show them how intelligent you are.

Calling in the cosmos means asking the big questions. Be careful, though, not to stereotype students' lives. Adolescents are prickly about condescension. Do not ask them questions that you would not ask an adult: What was your most embarrassing moment? How do you deal with family problems? Instead, ask students about issues that arise out of literature: When is it necessary to surrender? What is the use of solitude? How does language reveal character? What is the difference between forgiving and forgetting?

Even your least academic students want to discuss big ideas; you just need to explain the ideas more simply. Do not water down material for less academic students. They need more rigorous teaching, not less, because they are behind.

Every day, make thorough and precise lesson plans. But remember that you can always abandon your plans to take advantage of the teachable moment. Once my class was reading *King Lear,* and a thunderstorm crashed down just as we encountered the lines: "Blow, winds, and crack your cheeks. Rage, blow." I took the students outside, and we screamed Lear's lines into the storm. I love moments like that!

For the final calling in of the cosmos, I help students envision their own futures. During the last week in all my classes, my students write letters to themselves that I mail to them 10 years later. They can write about whatever they wish: predictions for the future, accounts of daily life, a list of friends. I suggest that they write down the most important knowledge that they possess. "What do you know that, if you didn't know it, would make you someone else?" Then I read a few letters that former students have written to me after they have received their 10-year-old letters.

This assignment affirms that students have important things to say at this stage of their lives—things that they will want to know 10 years from now. I am affirming the importance of the examined life.

Christine, as a beginning teacher you cannot reach all these goals right away. Even my most benign suggestions are fraught with dangers. For example, it sounds easy enough to explain to students why they ought to do something. But brand-new teachers often have no idea why they are doing something—beyond the fact that they have 180 days to fill. It takes a long time for teachers to develop the philosophical underpinnings for everything they do in the classroom.

Teaching thinking, creating communities, and engaging students in their own education are standards I have set for myself. But as I teach, I keep raising my standards. Joseph MacDonald, a professor at Brown University, helped me to clarify my thinking about that metaphor. Instead of my thinking of standards as ultimate goals, he suggested that I think of them as the banners held by the standard bearers at the head of an army. You never quite reach them, but they tell you where you are going, and they lead you forward.

You are not going into battle (though on some days teaching seems so). You are going into joy. For when you teach well, when classes sing, you will feel great jubilation. Treat your students as adults, walk beside them as they educate themselves, and they will respond with respect—even joy. They will lead you. I wish you a good journey.

Sincerely,
Margaret Metzger ■

Survival in the classroom is usually very much on the mind of new teachers. For many, their first experiences as teachers truly test their mettle. But, overwhelmingly, teachers survive. They learn to cope and get past whatever blocks they encounter in their first experiences. That is the good news. The bad news is that too many of us settle in just a little further up the scale than survival—at "adequacy" or "competency." This author is interested in something more. She wants "excellence," and in this selection (the first part of a four-part article) she lays out some goals and strategies for teachers.

Our junior and senior high schools, which have been repeatedly identified as the soft underbelly of our educational system, are the places where many of our students, too, settle for adequacy. Many settle for even less, doing only what they are driven to do. As a twenty-five-year veteran of life in a demanding high school, Margaret Metzger tells us that we must be "standard bearers" for these children who have quit on themselves as students. There are few greater missions in education today.

D I S C U S S I O N Q U E S T I O N S

1. What is your personal response to the author's call to move from competence to excellence?

2. Have you yourself been taught by teachers who could rally students mired in low expectations?

3. What teaching tips or perspectives in this article do you believe are of most value to you?

5 Reflection Is at the Heart of Practice

*Simon Hole and
Grace Hall McEntee*

The life force of teaching practice is thinking and wondering. We carry home those moments of the day that touch us, and we question decisions made. During these times of reflection, we realize when something needs to change.

A protocol, or guide, enables teachers to refine the process of reflection, alone or with colleagues. The Guided Reflection Protocol is useful for teachers who choose to reflect alone. The Critical Incidents Protocol, which we developed through our work with the Annenberg Institute for School Reform at Brown University, is used for shared reflection. The steps for each protocol are similar; both include writing.

Guided Reflection Protocol

The first step in guided reflection is to collect possible episodes for reflection. In his book *Critical Incidents in Teaching: Developing Professional Judgement* (1993), David Tripp encourages us to think

Simon Hole is a fourth grade teacher at Narragansett Elementary School in Narragansett, Rhode Island. He may be reached at 36 White Oak Dr., Wyoming, RI 02898 (e-mail: ropajavi@aol.com). Grace Hall McEntee is cofounder of Educators Writing for Change. She may be reached at Box 301, Prudence Island, RI 02872 (e-mail: Gmcente@aol.com). Hole, Simon and Grace McEntee, "Reflection Is at the Heart of Practice." *Educational Leadership*, May 1999, pp. 34–37. Reprinted by permission from ASCD. All rights reserved.

about ordinary events, which often have much to tell us about the underlying trends, motives, and structures of our practice. Simon's story, "The Geese and the Blinds," exemplifies this use of an ordinary event.

Step One: What Happened?

Wednesday, September 24, 9:30 A.M. I stand to one side of the classroom, taking the morning attendance. One student glances out the window and sees a dozen Canada geese grazing on the playground. Hopping from his seat, he calls out as he heads to the window for a better view. Within moments, six students cluster around the window. Others start from their seats to join them. I call for attention and ask them to return to their desks. When none of the students respond, I walk to the window and lower the blinds.

Answering the question What happened? is more difficult than it sounds. We all have a tendency to jump into an interpretive or a judgmental mode, but it is important to begin by simply telling the story. Writing down what happened—without analysis or judgment—aids in creating a brief narrative. Only then are we ready to move to the second step.

Step Two: Why Did It Happen?

Attempting to understand why an event happened the way it did is the beginning of reflection. We mush search the context within which the event occurred for explanations. Simon reflects:

It's not hard to imagine why the students reacted to the geese as they did. As 9-year-olds, they are incredibly curious about their world. Explaining my reaction is more difficult. Even as I was lowering the blinds, I was kicking myself. Here was a natural opportunity to explore the students' interests. Had I stood at the window with them for five minutes, asking questions to see what they knew about geese, or even just listening to them, I'd be telling a story about seizing the moment or taking advantage of a learning opportunity. I knew that even as I lowered the blinds. So, why?

Searching deeper, we may find that a specific event serves as an example of a more general category of events. We need to consider the underlying structures within the school that may be a part of the event and examine deeply held values. As we search, we often find more questions than answers.

Two key things stand out concerning that morning. First, the schedule. On Wednesdays, students leave the room at 10:00 A.M. and do not return until 15 minutes before lunch. I would be out of the classroom all afternoon attending a meeting, and so this half hour was all the time I would have with my students.

Second, this is the most challenging class I've had in 22 years of teaching. The first three weeks of school had been a constant struggle as I tried strategy after strategy to hold their attention long enough to have a discussion, give directions, or conduct a lesson. The hectic schedule and the need to prepare the class for a substitute added to the difficulty I've had "controlling" the class, so I closed the blinds.

There's something satisfying about answering the question Why did it happen? Reflection often stops here. If the goal is to become a reflective practitioner, however, we need to look more deeply. The search for meaning is step three.

Step Three: What Might It Mean?
Assigning meaning to the ordinary episodes that make up our days can feel like overkill. Is there really meaning behind all those events? Wouldn't it be more productive to wait for something extraordinary to happen, an event marked with a sign: "Pay attention! Something important is happening." Guided reflection is a way to find the meaning within the mundane. Split-second decision making is a crucial aspect of teaching. Given the daily madness of life in a classroom, considering all the options and consequences is difficult. Often, it is only through reflection that we even recognize that we had a choice, that we could have done something differently.

Like a football quarterback, I often make bad decisions because of pressure. Unlike a quarter-back, I don't have an offensive line to blame for letting the pressure get to me. While it would be nice to believe that I could somehow make the pressure go away, the fact is that it will always be with me. Being a teacher means learning to live within that pressure, learning from the decisions I make and learning to make better decisions.

Our growing awareness of how all events carry some meaning is not a new concept. In *Experience and Education* (1938), John Dewey wrote about experience and its relationship to learning and teaching: "Every experience affects for better or worse the attitudes which help decide the quality of further experience" (p. 37). He believed that teachers must be aware of the "possibilities inherent in ordinary experience" (p. 89), that the "business of the educator [is] to see in what direction an experience is heading" (p. 38). Rediscovering this concept through the examination of ordinary events creates a fresh awareness of its meaning.

The search for meaning is an integral part of being human. But understanding by itself doesn't create changes in classroom practice. The last phase of guided reflection is more action oriented and involves holding our practice to the light of those new understandings.

Step Four: What Are the Implications for My Practice?
Simon continues:

My reaction to the pressure this year has been to resort to methods of control. I seem to be forever pulling down the blinds. I'm thinking about how I might better deal with the pressure.

But there is something else that needs attention. Where is the pressure coming from? I'm sensing from administration and parents that they feel I should be doing things differently. I've gotten subtle and overt messages that I need to pay more attention to "covering" the curriculum, that I should be finding a more equal balance between process and product.

Maybe they're right. What I've been doing hasn't exactly been a spectacular success. But I think that what is causing the lowering of the blinds stems from my not trusting enough in the process. Controlling the class in a fairly traditional sense isn't going to work in the long run. Establishing a process that allows the class to control itself will help keep the blinds up.

Cultivating deep reflection through the use of a guiding protocol is an entry into rethinking and changing practice. Alone, each of us can proceed step-by-step through the examination of a particular event. Through the process, we gain new insights into the implications of ordinary events, as Simon did when he analyzed "The Geese and the Blinds."

Whereas Guided Reflection is for use by individuals, the Critical Incidents Protocol is used with colleagues. The goal is the same: to get to the heart of our practice, the place that pumps the lifeblood into our teaching, where we reflect, gain insight, and change what we do with our students. In addition, the Critical Incidents Protocol encourages the establishment of collegial relationships.

Critical Incidents Protocol

Schools are social places. Although too often educators think and act alone, in most schools colleagues do share daily events. Stories told in teachers' lounges are a potential source of rich insight into issues of teaching and learning and can open doors to professional dialogue.

Telling stories has the potential for changing individual practice and the culture of our schools. The Critical Incidents Protocol allows practitioners to share stories in a way that is useful to their own thinking and to that of the group.

Three to five colleagues meet for the purpose of exploring a "critical incident." For 10 minutes, all write a brief account of an incident. Participants should know that the sharing of their writing will be for the purpose of getting feedback on what happened rather than on the quality of the writing itself.

Next, the group decides which story to use with the protocol. The presenter for the session then reads the story while the group listens carefully to understand the incident and the context. Colleagues ask clarifying questions about what happened or why the incident occurred, then they discuss what the incident might mean in terms of the presenter's practice. During this time, the presenter listens and takes notes. The presenter then responds, and the participants discuss the implications for their own practice. To conclude, one member leads a conversation about what happened during the session, how well the process worked, and how the group might change the process.

The sharing of individual stories raises issues in the fresh air of collegial support. If open dialogue is not already part of a school's culture, however, colleagues may feel insecure about beginning. To gain confidence, they may choose to run through the protocol first with a story that is not theirs. For this purpose, Grace offers a story about an incident in the writing lab from her practice as a high school English teacher.

Guided Reflection
Protocol (For Individual
Reflection)

1. *Collect stories.* Some educators find that keeping a set of index cards or a steno book close at hand provides a way to jot down stories as they occur. Others prefer to wait until the end of the day and write in a journal.

2. *What happened?* Choose a story that strikes you as particularly interesting. Write it succinctly.

3. *Why did it happen?* Fill in enough of the context to give the story meaning. Answer the question in a way that makes sense to you.

4. *What might it mean?* Recognizing that there is no one answer is an important step. Explore possible meanings rather than determine the meaning.

5. *What are the implications for practice?* Consider how your practice might change given any new understandings that have emerged from the earlier steps.

Step One: What Happened?

We went into the computer lab to work on essay drafts. TJ, Neptune, Ronny, and Mick sat as a foursome. Their sitting together had not worked last time. On their single printer an obscene message had appeared. All four had denied writing it.

The next day Ronny, Neptune, and Mick had already sat together. Just as TJ was about to take his seat, I asked him if he would mind sitting over at the next bay of computers. He exploded. "You think I'm the cause of the problem, don't you?"

Actually I did think he might be, but I wasn't at all certain. "No," I said, "but I do want you to sit over here for today." He got red in the face, plunked down in the chair near the three other boys, and refused to move.

I motioned for him to come with me. Out in the hall, I said to him quietly, "The bottom line is that all of you need to get your work done." Out of control, body shaking, TJ angrily spewed out, "You always pick on me. Those guys. . . . You. . . ." I could hardly hear his words, so fascinated was I with his intense emotion and his whole-body animation.

Contrary to my ordinary response to students who yell, I felt perfectly calm. I knew I needed to wait. Out of the corner of my eye, I saw two male teachers rise out of their chairs in the hallway about 25 feet away. They obviously thought that I, a woman of small stature, needed protection. But I did not look at them. I looked at TJ and waited.

When he had expended his wrathful energy, I said softly, "You know, TJ, you are a natural-born leader." I waited. Breathed in and out. "You did not choose to be a leader; it was thrust upon you. But there you are. People follow you. So you have a tremendous responsibility, to lead in a positive and productive way. Do you understand what I am saying?"

Like an exhalation after a long in-breath, his body visibly relaxed. He looked down at me and nodded his head. Then he held out his hand to me and said, "I'm sorry."

Back in the room, he picked up his stuff and, without a word, moved to the next bay of computers.

Step Two: Using the Critical Incidents Protocol

At first you'll think that you need more information than this, but we think that you have enough here. One member of the group will take the role of Grace. Your "Grace" can answer clarifying questions about what happened or why it happened in whatever way he or she sees fit. Work through the protocol to figure out what the incident might mean in terms of "Grace's" practice. Finally, discuss what implications the incident in the writing lab might have for her practice and

Critical Incidents Protocol
(For Shared Reflection)

---

1. *Write stories.* Each group member writes briefly in response to the question: What happened? (10 minutes)

2. *Choose a story.* The group decides which story to use. (5 minutes)

3. *What happened?* The presenter reads the written account of what happened and sets it within the context of professional goals. (10 minutes)

4. *Why did it happen?* Colleagues ask clarifying questions. (5 minutes)

5. *What might it mean?* The group raises questions about the incident in the context of the presenter's work. They discuss it as professional, caring colleagues while the presenter listens. (15 minutes)

6. *What are the implications for practice?* The presenter responds, then the group engages in conversation about the implications for the presenter's practice and for the participants' own practice. A useful question at this stage might be, What new insights occurred? (15 minutes)

7. *Debrief the process.* The group talks about what just happened. How did the process work? (10 minutes)

for your own as reflective educators. Then, try an event of your own.

We think that you will find that whether the group uses your story on someone else's, building reflective practice together is a sure way to get to the heart of teaching and learning. ■

References

Dewey, J. (1938). *Experience and education.* New York: Macmillan.

Tripp, D. (1993). *Critical incidents in teaching: Developing professional judgement.* New York: Routledge.

POST NOTE

A common complaint of teachers is that they don't have enough time to do all the things that they either need or want to do. There just doesn't seem like the day has enough hours to do everything that needs doing. When time is precious, making the time to reflect on one's teaching seems extravagant. After all, there are so many more pressing items. On the other hand, if teachers are asked if they want to improve their teaching, it's hard to imagine one saying, "No." The authors of this article make the case that teacher reflection is the key component for improving our teaching. And, if you think about it, improving your teaching without seriously reflecting on it is virtually impossible.

Reflective teaching involves a process of examination and evaluation in which you develop the habits of inquiry and reflection. By describing two structured ways of reflecting, one individually and one with colleagues, the authors give us useful protocols for conducting a reflective process. The use of journal writing, observation instruments, simulations, and videotaping can also help you examine teaching, learning, and the contexts in which they occur. Comparing your perspectives with those of fellow students, professors, and school personnel will broaden your interpretations and give you new insights. As you reflect on your experiences you will come to distrust simple answers and explanations. Nuances and subtleties will start to become clear, and situations that once seemed simple will reveal their complexities. Moral and ethical issues are likely to be encountered and thought about. By practicing reflective teaching, you will grow and develop the attitudes and skills to become lifelong students of teaching—you will become an effective, professional teacher.

DISCUSSION QUESTIONS

1. What do you see as the primary benefits of reflecting on your teaching? What concerns do you have about it?

2. What case do the authors make for reflecting on ordinary, as opposed to special, events? Do you agree?

3. Are you more likely to use an individual or cooperative form of reflection? Why?

6 The Heart of the Matter

Robert Fried

When you get right down to it, every teacher faces one existential question: "What am I here for—to journey with young people into the great world of knowledge and ideas or to shepherd a bunch of mostly unwilling students through the everyday rituals of instruction and assessment?" Who among us has not sought the former and suffered through the latter time and again in our teaching?

Just maybe it's time to face this issue head-on and resolve to no longer accept an answer that defines a teacher as a "classroom manager," or "deliverer of instruction," or "assertive disciplinarian," or "keeper of the grade book."

The alternative to such roles is to assert that one is a passionate teacher: someone truly enamored of a field of knowledge, or deeply stirred by issues and ideas that challenge our world, or drawn to the crises and creativity of the young people who come into class each day—or all of these. To be a passionate teacher is to stop being isolated within a classroom, to refuse to submit to a culture of apathy or cynicism, to look beyond getting through the day.

Only when teachers bring their passions about learning and life into their daily work can they dispel the fog of passive compliance or surly disinterest that surrounds so many kids in

Robert Fried is the author of *The Passionate Teacher—A Practical Guide,* published by Beacon Press. Reprinted with permission from *Teacher Magazine,* Vol. 7, Issue No. 2, October 1995. By permission of Robert Fried, author of *The Passionate Teacher: A Practical Guide* (Boston: Beacon Press, 1995).

school. I believe that we all have it within us to be passionate teachers and that nothing else will quite do the trick.

In too many classrooms, we see the sound and smoke of note-taking, answer-giving, homework-checking, test-taking, and the forgetting that so quickly follows. And in the end, there is creativity for a few, compliance for most, rebellion for some, but not much fiery engagement of the mind and spirit.

What counts is students' willing engagement. They have to want to see where their ideas and energies might take them, to follow their curiosity and intuition to useful places. They have to get unshy about being smart—to stop using their brains to put each other down or to get around doing the work we assign them. Today's students need help from teachers who are more than well-prepared or genial or fair. They need teachers who have passions.

Passion itself isn't the goal of education. It's a bridge that connects us to the intensity of young people's thoughts and life experiences—things that they too rarely see as part of school. Once that connection has been made, we can help transfer passions about ideas into habits of hard work and discipline that will remain with students even when peers cajole them to "take it easy." It's not the whole story, of course, but passion is at the heart of what teaching should be if we want to be mentors for young people who sorely need (but rarely seek) heroes of the mind to balance the heroes of brute strength and exotic fashion that surround them in the media.

Yet as I look into hundreds of classrooms, watch all kinds of teachers working with a bewildering variety of students, when I ask myself what makes the greatest difference in the quality and depth of student learning—it is a teacher's passion that leaps out. More than knowledge of subject matter. More than variety of teaching techniques. More than being well-organized, or friendly, or funny, or fair.

Passionate people are the ones who make a difference in our lives. By the intensity of their beliefs and actions, they connect us with a sense of value that is within—and beyond—ourselves.

Sometimes that passion burns with a quiet, refined intensity. Sometimes it bellows forth with thunder and eloquence. But in whatever style a teacher's passion emerges, students know they are in the presence of someone whose devotion to learning is exceptional. It's what makes a teacher unforgettable—this caring about ideas and values, this fascination with the potential for growth within people, this fervor about doing things well and striving for excellence.

Passion may just be the difference between being remembered as a "pretty good teacher" who made chemistry or algebra "sort of interesting"—or being the person who opened up a world of the mind to some students who had no one else to make them feel that they were capable of doing great things with test tubes, trumpets, trigonometry, or T. S. Eliot.

How, then, is a teacher "passionate"?

You can be passionate about your field of knowledge: in love with the poetry of Emily Dickinson or the prose of Marcus Garvey; dazzled by the spiral of DNA or the swirl of Van Gogh's cypresses; intrigued by the origins of the Milky Way or the demise of the Soviet empire; delighted by the sound of Mozart or the sonority of French vowels.

You can be passionate about issues facing our world: active in the struggle for social justice or for the survival of the global environment; dedicated to the celebration of cultural diversity or to the search for a cure for AIDS.

You can be passionate about children: about the shocking rate of violence experienced by young black males; about including children with disabilities in regular school activities; about raising the low rate of high school completion by Latino children; about the insidious effects of sexism, racism, and social class prejudice on the spirits of all children; about the neglect of "average" kids in schools where those at the "top" and "bottom" seem to get all of the attention.

To be avowedly passionate about at least some of these things puts one apart from those who approach each day in a fog of fatigue, or who come to work wrapped in a self-protective cocoon. The passion that accompanies our atten-

tion to knowledge, values, and children is not just something we offer our students. It is a gift we grant ourselves, a way of honoring our life's work, our profession. It says: "I know why I am devoting this life to children."

Let's distinguish passionate teaching from mere idiosyncrasies. Lots of teachers have pet peeves or fixations: points of grammar, disciplinary practices, eccentricities of diction. These may, indeed, make them memorable to their students (for better or worse). But the passions I am speaking about convey much more.

What impresses me about truly passionate teachers is that there is no particular style of teaching, much less a common personality type, that epitomizes them. What unites them are the ways they approach the mission of teaching. They organize their curricula and their daily work with students in practical ways that play to their own strengths.

But how do we make passionate teaching happen? How do we shove aside all the stuff we're supposed to do and make room in our lesson plans for things we feel strongly about?

We may want to ask our students to study in depth the Cuban Missile Crisis, rather than surveying the entire Cold War history. Or study the ecology of one small nearby pond instead of covering all the chapters in the biology text. Or learn a lot about Emily Dickinson and leave other 19th-century poets to be discovered later in students' lives. Language arts teachers in an urban middle school may decide that learning to write good, clear, convincing prose is so vital to students' future success that they enlist colleagues in science and social studies and math to teach writing across the curriculum.

A high school history teacher in a rural New Hampshire town brought her intense interest in archaeology into the classroom by taking her students out into the woods in search of a long-forgotten graveyard. After watching her begin to carefully restore the site, they pitched in to clean and prop up the headstones. A week later, the class traveled to the local historical society to search for the records of the people whose graves they had tended. Each student became a 200-year-old former resident of the town and shared his or her life story in a presentation for the townspeople.

As passionate teachers, we share our commitment to active learning by showing, not just telling. We are readers, writers, researchers, explorers of new knowledge, new ideas, new techniques and technologies, new ways of looking at old facts and theories Our very excitement about these things helps young people reach beyond their social preoccupations and self-centeredness. When we are no longer learning, we no longer teach because we have lost the power to exemplify for young people what it means to be intellectually active. Even though we may still be able to present them with information, we have become simple purveyors of subject matter, "deliverers of educational services," in the jargon of the field.

Students need us, not because we have all the answers but because we can help them discover the right questions. It's not that we always know what's good for them but that we want to protect them from having to face life's dilemmas in ignorance or in despair. Those adults to whom young people look for advice on serious life issues know how important they are to kids' futures. For all teachers, the recovery of passion can mean a recovery of our dynamic and positive influence in the lives of children.

This, I argue, is what education *is*. There simply is no education without a commitment to developing the mind and the character of learners. And in our time and culture, perhaps as never before, that commitment must be a passionate one if we want young people to heed that calling. ■

POST NOTE

The passion a teacher has for the subject that he or she teaches is often not discussed in teacher education programs. Hollywood, however, frequently employs passionate teachers as the protagonists in films: Robin William's character in *Dead Poets Society*, Maggie Smith's in *The Prime of Miss Jean Brodie*, and Richard Dreyfus's in *Mr. Holland's Opus* display fire and passion in their teaching.

Some of our most memorable teachers are probably the ones who cared deeply and passionately about what they taught. Equally or perhaps more important are caring and passion for one's students. Teachers who care about their students—and let those students know it in various ways—are often the ones who affect their students the most.

DISCUSSION QUESTIONS

1. Think of two or three of the best teachers you've ever had. What was it that made them so good? How were they alike or different?

2. Have you ever had a really good teacher who didn't have passion for his or her subject?

3. Can passion for the subject be learned, or is it something one just has or doesn't have? Why do you think so?

The Great Teacher Question: Beyond Competencies

Edward R. Ducharme

I begin this essay by defining a great teacher as one who influences others in positive ways so that their lives are forever altered, and then asking a question I have asked groups many times. How many teachers fitting that description have you had in your lifetime? It is rare for anyone to claim more than five in a lifetime; the usual answer is one or two.

I ask this question of groups whose members have at least master's degrees, often doctorates. They have experienced anywhere from eighty to one hundred or more teachers in their lifetimes and usually describe no more than 2% of them as great. Those voting are among the ones who stayed in school considerably longer than most people do; one wonders how many great teachers those dropping out in the 9th or 10th grade experience in their lifetimes. My little experiment, repeated many times over the years, suggests that the number of great teachers is very limited. They should be cherished and treasured because they are so rare; we should do all that we can to develop more of them.

Edward R. Ducharme is a writer and consultant, living in Brewster, Massachusetts. From "The Great Teacher Question: Beyond Competencies" by Edward R. Ducharme in *Journal of Human Behavior and Learning*, Vol. 7, No. 2. Copyright © 1991. Used with permission.

This paper is purely speculative; no data corrupt it; no references or citations burden it. It began as I sat with a colleague at a meeting in 1987 in Washington; we were listening to a speaker drone on about the competencies teachers need. I asked my friend: "How would you like to write a paper about qualities great teachers have that do not lend themselves to competency measurements?" The proposed shared writing exercise did not get much beyond our talking about it the next couple of times we saw each other, but I have continued to speculate on these qualities as I have read, taught, studied, talked with others, and relived my own learning experiences.

The remarks result from years of being with teachers, students, and schools; of three decades of being a teacher; of five decades of being a learner. There is no science in the remarks, no cool, objective look at teaching. These are personal reflections and observations to provoke, to get some of us thinking beyond numbers, test scores, attendance rates, and demographics, to reflect on the notion of the Great Teacher.

I am weary of competencies even though I recognize the need for specific indicators that teachers possess certain skills and knowledge. I believe, however, that good teacher preparation programs do more than a reasonable job on these and are doing better and better. Three conditions lead me to believe that most future graduates of teacher education programs will be competent. First, the overall quality of teacher candidates is improving; second, there is a great deal more known about helping to develop people to the point where they are competent; third, the level of the education professoriate has improved dramatically. Thus, I think that *most* preparation programs will be graduating competent teachers. We should begin to worry about what lies beyond competency.

My interests extend beyond competencies to qualities that I see from time to time as I visit classrooms. Few teachers possess even several of the qualities I will describe—no great teacher lacks all of them. In the remainder of this paper,

I will name and describe the qualities and show what these qualities might look like in prospective teachers.

1. Penchant for and Skill in Relating One Thing with Another with Another and with Another

John Donne, the 17th century English poet and cleric, once wrote "The new science calls all into doubt." He was referring to the Copernican contention that the earth is not the center of the universe, that humankind may not be the cynosure of divine interest, countering beliefs that the old Ptolemaic system of earthcenteredness had fostered.

Donne saw relationships among things not readily apparent to many others. He recognized a new truth cancelled another belief, one that had affected attitudes and actions among his fellow Christians for a long time, and would have a dramatic effect. He knew that if something held eternally true were suddenly shown to be false, conclusively false, then other things would be questioned; nothing would be steadfast.

Many of us do not see the implications and relationships among seemingly unrelated events, people, places, works of art, scientific principles. Some great teachers have the ability to see these relationships and, equally important, help others see them. Donne saw them. His collected sermons evidence the intellectual force of great teachers.

I once took a course in which John Steinbeck's *The Sea of Cortez* and *The Grapes of Wrath* were among the readings. *The Sea of Cortez* is Steinbeck's ruminations on the vast complexity and interrelatedness of life under the water; *The Grapes of Wrath*, his ruminations on the complexities of life on land, on what happens when a natural disaster combines with human ineptness and lack of concern, one for the other. The professor used a word not much in vogue in those ancient days: ecology. He defined it as the "interrelatedness of all living things." He raised

questions about the relationships of these issues to the problems of New York City and its schools, as we sat in class in Memorial Lounge at Teachers College, Columbia.

E. D. Hirsch, in *Cultural Literacy: What Every American Needs to Know,* has a series of provocative listings under each letter of the alphabet. His point is that in order to grasp the meanings of works on pages, readers must know things not part of the page. Hirsch's book contains pages of items. Under the letter C, he lists caste, cool one's heels, *Crime and Punishment,* coral reef, and czar. One would "know" such things by studying sociology, language, literature, biology, and history or, perhaps equally often, simply by living for a period of time and reading newspapers, watching movies, and so forth. Hirsch's point is that when one hears a sentence like "He runs his business as though he were the czar," one would think of autocratic, harsh rule, tyranny, Russia, lack of human rights. Some might think of how the word is sometimes spelled tsar and wonder why. Others might think of the song about the czar/tsar from *Fiddler on the Roof,* while a few would think the person incapable of pronouncing the word tsar. Hirsch has in mind one kind of "relating one field to another": that which occurs when one sees a known reference and makes the associative leap.

Edna St. Vincent Millay, in her poem on Euclid's geometry, also drew associations from seemingly unrelated things. She saw the design and texture in poetry related to the design and texture of a geometric theorem. The quality described here is the same quality that Donne and Steinbeck manifested: seeing the interrelatedness of things.

What does that quality look like in prospective teachers? Sometimes it is the person who sees the connections between sociological and educational themes; sometimes, the person who wants to introduce students to the variety of language by teaching them about snowflakes and the vast number of words Eskimos have for them; sometimes, the person who understands mathematics through music, in fact, it may be the person who says mathematics is a kind of music or that music is a kind of mathematics.

2. Lack of Fondness for Closure or, Put Another Way, Fondness for Questions over Answers

Many of us are constantly on the lookout for answers to questions. For example, we might give a great deal to know the answer to the two-part question: What makes a great teacher and how do we produce one? Of course, the answer to the first part of the question depends on who is answering it. For someone in need of specific guidance at some point in life, the great teacher may be the one pointing the way to a different kind of existence, the one making the individual feel strong. To another person, confident about life, the great teacher may be the one raising questions, challenging, making the person wonder about certitudes once held dearly.

I teach Leadership and the Creative Imagination, a course designed as a humanities experience for doctoral students in educational administration. In the course, students read twelve novels and plays, discuss them effectively, and write about them in ways related to the leadership theory literature, their own experience, and the works themselves. In the fall semester of 1987, I had what has become a redundant experience. A student in the course stopped me in the hall after class one night in November. She said that she had taken the course because her advisor had said it would be a good experience for her. And, said she, she had truly enjoyed the early readings and the discussions. But now she found the readings troubling; they were causing her to question things she does, ways she relates to people, habits of thinking. She said that she was losing a sense of assuredness of what life was all about. The books, she said, just kept raising questions. "When do we get answers?" she asked.

We talked for awhile, and I reminded her of a point I had made repeatedly during the first couple of classes: there are two kinds of books, answer books and question books. Writers of answer books raise provocative questions and then provide comfortable, assuring answers. Then there are the writers who raise the provocative issues— "Thou know'st 'tis common,—all that lives must die, passing through nature into eternity," (if you get the source of that, Hirsch will like you)—and then frustrate the reader looking for facile answers by showing that the realization in the statement prompts questions: Why must all that lives die? What does it mean to pass through nature into eternity? What or when is eternity? Are we supposed to know that all that lives must die?

The predisposition to raise questions is present in all of us to varying degrees. In young, prospective teachers, the predisposition takes on various shades and hues. They ask questions like: Why do some children learn more slowly than others? Tell me, why is that, whatever that may be, a better way to do it? But how do I know they learned it? In more mature prospective teachers coming back for a fifth year and certification, it might look different: Why is this more meaningful than that? Why should we teach this instead of that? Why does my experience teach me that this is wrong? What happens next? How do I know if this is right or wrong?

Persons with fondness for questions over answers recognize that most "answers" to complex questions are but tentative, that today's answers provoke tomorrow's uneasiness. As prospective teachers, they show a disrespect for finite answers to questions about human development, the limits of knowledge, the ways of knowing, the ways of doing. They itch to know even though they have begun to believe that they can never really know, that there is always another word to be said on every subject of consequence. Often, to answer-oriented teacher educators, these students are seen as hindrances instead of prospective great teachers. In truth, they stand the chance of provoking in their future students the quest to explore, to question, to imagine, to be comfortable with the discomfort of never "really knowing," of lifelong pursuit of knowledge.

3. Growing Knowledge, Understanding, and Commitment to Some Aspect of Human Endeavor; for example, Science, Literature, Mathematics, or Blizzards

In the last several years, the point that teachers must know something before they can teach it has been made ad nauseum. We have admonitions from the Carnegie Forum to the Holmes Group to Secretary Bennett to the person on the street to all the teachers in the field who prepared with BS degrees in education all belaboring the obvious need for knowledge, albeit with a slightly different twist than the argument had the first twenty times around: teachers must have a bachelor's degree in an academic major before being admitted to a teacher preparation program.

But we all know that to know is not enough. Merely holding a bachelor of arts does not answer the question of the relationship between teacher and knowledge. What answers the question?

Teachers are rightfully and powerfully connected with knowledge when, even early in their learning careers, they begin to make metaphors to explain their existence, their issues and dilemmas, their joys and sorrows, from the knowledge they are acquiring. I speak not of that jaded notion of students being excited by what they are learning. I get excited watching a baseball game, but it doesn't have much meaning for me the next day. I mean something including and transcending excitement. Great teachers are driven by the power, beauty, force, logic, illogic, color, vitality, relatedness, uniqueness of what they know and love. They make metaphors from it to explain the world; they are forever trying to understand the thing itself, always falling a bit short yet still urging others on. They are the teachers who make learners think what is being taught has value and meaning and may actually touch individual lives.

This quality shows itself in a variety of ways in prospective teachers. Often, it is hidden because that which captures the imagination and interest of a student may not be part of the course, may have no way of being known. I have never forgotten a young woman in a class I taught fifteen years ago. She was a freshman in one of those horrible introduction to education courses. For the last assignment, each student in the class had to teach something to the class. This young woman, who had spoken, but rarely and only when challenged during the semester, asked if the class might go to the student lounge when her turn came. I agreed; we went as a group. There was a piano in the room and she proceeded to play a piece by Chopin and explain to the class why it was an important piece of music. I suspected—and subsequent discussions with her bore out my thought—that this young woman saw the world through music, that she could explain almost anything better if she could use music as the metaphor, the carrier of her thoughts.

Most of us do not have students in our classes capable of playing a piece by Chopin, but we all have students who understand the world through a medium different from what the rest of the group may be using. Experience has taught many young people to hide this quality because it is not honored in classrooms.

4. A Sense of the Aesthetic

The development of the aesthetic domain in young people is critical to their growth and development; it is a fundamental right. The ability to grasp the beautiful makes us human; to deny that to young people is to deny their humanity. Great teachers often have an acutely developed sense of the aesthetic; they are unafraid to show their fondness for beauty in front of young people; they do so in such a manner as to make the young people themselves value beauty and their own perceptions of it.

For many young people, the world is a harsh and barren place, devoid of beauty. But in every generation, there are those who emerge spiritually changed from their schooling experiences, eager to face what is at times a hostile world. The changes are sometimes the result of a teacher with a sense of the aesthetic, one able to see beyond the everydayness and blandness of institutional life.

In a world stultified by the commercial definitions of beauty, individuals preparing to teach with this embryonic sense of the aesthetic are rare. Our own jadedness and mass-produced tastes make it difficult for us to recognize this quality in students. What does it look like? In its evolutionary phases, it might be an impulse to make the secondary methods classroom more attractive; it might be a choice of book covers; it might be in the selection of course materials for young people; it might be in the habits of an individual. I'm uncertain as to its many forms, but I am quite certain that when we see it we should treasure its existence and support its development.

5. Willingness to Assume Risks

There are teachers who say the right things, prescribe the right books, associate with the right people, but never take risks on behalf of others, beliefs, and ideas, never do more than verbalize. They are hollow shams.

The quality of risk-taking of great teachers is subtle, not necessarily that which puts people on picket lines, at the barricades, although it might be. The quality is critical to teacher modeling, for great teachers go beyond the statement of principles and ideas, beyond the endorsement of the importance of friendships, as they move students from the consideration of abstract principles to the actualization of deeds.

The 1960s and 1970s were filled with risk-taking teachers. While neither praising nor disparaging these obvious examples, I urge other instances for consideration inasmuch as the "opportunity" for collective risk-taking is a rare occurrence in the lives of most of us. While it was not easy to be a risk-taker then, it wasn't very lonely either. Other instances, some more prosaic,

abound: teachers in certain parts of the country who persist in teaching evolution despite pressure to desist, teachers who assign controversial books despite adverse criticism, teachers who teach the Civil War and the Vietnam War without partisanship or chauvinism. These quiet acts of risk-taking occur daily in schools and universities; they instruct students of the importance of ideas joined with actions.

I recall my high school art teacher who took abuse from the principal because she demanded the right for her students to use the gymnasium to prepare for a dance. He rebuked and embarrassed her in front of the students for "daring to question [my] authority." His act prompted some of us to go to the superintendent to complain about him; we got the gym. But we also each had a private interview with the principal in which he shared his scorn and derision for us for having "gone over [my] head to the superintendent." We learned that acting on principles is sometimes risky, that we had to support a teacher who took risks for us, that actions have consequences, that a "good" act like defending a brave teacher can lead to punishment. But her risk-taking led us to risk-taking on behalf of another person and the resolution of a mild injustice.

Detecting this quality in the young is difficult. The young often appear cause-driven and it is hard to distinguish when students are merely following a popular, low-risk cause and when they are standing for something involving personal decisions and risk. We might see it in its evolutionary form in some quite simple instances. Many teacher educators suffer the indignity of seeing their ideas and principles distorted by the wisdom of the workplace, of having their students grow disenchanted with what they have been taught as they encounter the world of the school: "We'll knock that Ivory Tower stuff out of you here. This is the *real* world." Of course, we all know some of it should be knocked out, but much of it should remain. It is a rare student who during practical, internship, and early years of teaching remains steadfast to such principles as: all student answers, honestly given, merit serious consideration; or worksheets are rarely good instructional materials. It is risky for young pre-professionals and beginning professionals to dispute the wisdom of the workplace and maintain fidelity to earlier acquired principles. Perhaps in these seemingly small matters lies the quality to be writ large during the full career.

6. At-Homeness in the World

Great teachers live effectively in what often seems a perverse world. Acutely aware of life's unevenness, the disparities in the distribution of the world's goods, talents, and resources, they cry out for justice in their own special ways while continuing to live with a sense of equanimity and contribute to the world. They demonstrate that life is to be lived as fully as one can despite problems and issues. They show that one can be a sensitive human being caring about and doing things about the problems and issues, and, at the same time, live a life of personal fulfillment. They are not overwhelmed by the insolubility of things on the grand scale, for they are able to make sense of things on the personal level.

I once had a professor for a course in Victorian poetry. In addition to his academic accomplishments, the professor was a fine gardener, each year producing a beautifully crafted flower garden, filled with design and beauty.

We were reading "In Memoriam," the part in which Tennyson refers to nature, red in tooth and claw. All of a sudden, the professor talked about how, that morning, while eating his breakfast, he had watched his cat stalk a robin, catch it, and devour part of it. He related the incident, of course to the poem. (Clearly he had the quality alluded to earlier, the sense on interrelatedness of things.) I am uncertain what I learned about "In Memoriam" that morning, but I know I learned that this man who earlier in the semester had pointed out the delicate beauty of some of Tennyson's lyrics had integrated death into his life while remaining sensitive to beauty, to love. It was partly through him that I began to see that the parts of life I did not like were not to be ignored nor to be paralyzed about. All this in the death of a bird? No, all this in a powerful teacher's reaction to the death of a bird in the midst of life.

And what does at-homeness in the world look like in prospective teachers? I am quite uncertain, very tentative about this one. Perhaps it shows itself in a combination of things like joy in life one day and despair over life the next as the young slowly come to grips with the enigmas of life, its vicissitudes and sorrows. The young are often studies in extremes as they make order of life, of their lives. As a consequence, one sees a few students with vast energy both to live life and to anguish over its difficulties. But one cannot arrive at the point of my professor with his lovely garden and dead robin simultaneously entertained in his head without a sense of the joyful and the tragic in life, without a constant attempt to deal with the wholeness that is life, without a sense of being at home in the world.

All prospective teachers have touches of each of these qualities which should be supported and nurtured so that their presence is ever more manifest in classrooms. But a few students have some of these qualities writ large. Buttressed by programs that guarantee competency in instructional skills, these individuals have the potential to become great teachers themselves, to be the teachers who take the students beyond knowledge acquisition and skill development to questioning, to wondering, to striving. We must, first, find these prospective teachers, help them grow and develop, treasure them, and give them to the young people of America, each one of whom deserves several great teachers during thirteen years of public schooling.

And what has all this to do with the preparation of teachers? Surely, preparing teachers to be competent in providing basic instruction to as many students as possible is enough of a major task. Clearly, the raising of reading scores, of math achievement levels, of writing skills, of thinking processes are significant accomplishments. Of course, all these things must be accomplished, and teacher preparation programs around the country are getting better and better at these matters.

But we must have more; we must have an increase in the presence of greatness in the schools, in the universities. Love for a teacher's kindness, gratitude for skills acquired, fondness for teachers—these are critically important. But equally important is the possibility that students will encounter greatness, greatness that transcends the everydayness of anyplace, that invites, cajoles, pushes, drags, drives, brings students into the possibilities that questions mean more than answers; that knowledge is interrelated; that there is joy to be had from beauty; that knowledge can affect people to the cores of their being; that ideas find their worth in actions; that life is full of potential in a sometimes perverse world. ■

POST NOTE

Ducharme's article is provocative in its challenge to go beyond competence to reach for greatness in our teaching. The characteristics that he suggests embody greatness in teaching are difficult to challenge because they ring true. They also are formidable if we dare to want to become teachers who possess these characteristics.

In an effort to ensure that prospective teachers will be "safe to practice," many teacher educators focus their instruction on the knowledge and skills (competencies) new teachers will need to function effectively in classrooms. It may be a rare instance where the focus of teacher education is on what it will take to become a *great* teacher, not merely a *competent* one.

DISCUSSION QUESTIONS

1. Is a particular kind of teacher preparation needed to produce great, rather than just competent, teachers? Or does a prospective teacher need to earn competence before greatness can be achieved? Explain your answers.

2. Think of the great teachers you have had. Did they possess the characteristics Ducharme describes? Briefly discuss what made these teachers great.

3. Can you think of any other characteristics that great teachers possess that were not identified by Ducharme? If so, what are they?

8
Why Johnny Can't Fail

Jerry Jesness

I confess. I am a grade-inflating teacher guilty of "social promotion." I have given passing grades to students who failed all of their tests, to students who refused to read their assignments, to students who were absent as often as not, to students who were not even functionally literate. I have turned a blind eye to cheating and outright plagiarism, and have given As and Bs to students whose performances were at best mediocre. Like others of my ilk, I have sent students to higher grades, to higher education, and to the workplace unprepared for the demands that would be made of them.

I am, in short, a servant of the force that thwarts nearly every effort to reform American education. I am a servant of the floating standard.

I was introduced to the floating standard in 1979, while teaching for the Bureau of Indian Affairs on a reservation in western South Dakota. My predecessor, considered a capable if imprudent instructor by his former students and peers, had been forced to resign after failing nearly half of his students. In his absence, the failing grades were changed and his students were promoted to the next grade.

Even though I knew my predecessor's fate, I gave some failing grades the first term. After a few warnings, however, I fell into line. There was no point in doing otherwise. The students already knew that failing grades would mysteriously self-correct over the summer. I opted for self-preservation.

A few years later I moved to Texas's lower Rio Grande Valley. Since I now was more experienced, I was confident that I would be able to grade fairly. Besides, my future principal spoke movingly at my interview about the need to push our students to their limits. In the first grading period, I boldly flunked a number of students, including the daughter of an administrator of a local elementary school and a star fullback who was also the nephew of a school-board member.

Shortly thereafter I was called in to meet with my principal and the aggrieved parents. Such was my naïveté that I actually bothered to bring evidence. I showed the administrator her daughter's plagiarized book report and the book from which it had been copied, and I showed the fullback's father homework bearing his son's name but written in another person's handwriting. The parents offered weak apologies but maintained that I had not treated their children fairly.

My principal suddenly discovered a number of problems with my teaching. For the next few weeks he was in my class almost daily. Every spitball, every chattering student, every bit of graffiti, was noted. When there were discipline problems, my superiors sided with the offending students. Teaching became impossible.

So again I learned to turn a blind eye to cheating and plagiarism, and to give students especially athletes, extra credit for everything from reading orally in class to remembering to bring their pencils. Along the way, I gained the cooperation of my students and the respect and support of my superiors.

But not until my fifth year of teaching did I finally accept that my only choices were to embrace the floating standard or to abandon public education. That year my assignment was to teach English as a second language and lower-level language arts. My principal was particularly adamant about having all the students pass.

In language arts, no test was to be graded below 50, even one that was turned in blank. Daily assignments were to be graded according to the number of questions answered, even if all of the answers were wrong. If eight of ten questions were answered, the grade was to be 80, regardless of the quality of the answers. Those who still were failing at the end of the grading period were to be offered the opportunity to do reports or projects for extra credit. My neighbor, another lower-group teacher who was held up to me as a mentor, boasted that he left the week's spelling words on the blackboard during spelling tests and recommended that I do the same. I pulled in my horns too late to save myself that year. The principal recommended that my contract not be renewed.

That job and its $17,000 annual salary were hardly worth fighting for, so I left quietly. After a year as a salesperson and graduate student, however, I began to miss the classroom and decided to give teaching one more try. I returned to the district where I had flunked the star fullback. My superiors correctly assumed that I had learned my lesson and welcomed the return of the prodigal teacher. Just as Orwell's Winston Smith was finally able to achieve victory over himself and love Big Brother, I was ready to embrace the floating standard.

In the ensuing seven years, only two of my students failed. My evaluations were "above expectations" twice and "clearly outstanding" five times. By my fifth year I had climbed to the top of the Texas teachers' career ladder and earned an annual bonus of $3,300.

The funny thing is that I really did become a better teacher after my reincarnation, if only because my students and superiors were now cooperative. My classes were better behaved once I stopped trying to force students to learn more than they cared to. I no longer met with hostility when I sent students to the principal's office. I tried to be as honest as possible with my charges. All of my student and any parents who bothered to visit my classroom or return my phone calls

understood that grades above 80 honestly reflected performance, while those in the 70 range were fluffed up with extra credit. I explained to the parents of my immigrant students that here in America passing grades may be given for attendance and minimal effort and do not necessarily reflect mastery of the course material. Students who needed to be pushed lost out, but that was the price of harmony.

It does not matter what changes we make in curricula. The floating standard guarantees the reign of mediocrity. If standards are set high but students lack the skills or motivation to meet them, the standards will inevitably change. If a number of students in a given class take part-time jobs, homework will be reduced. If drugs sweep through a school, lower expectations will compensate for weakened ability. Americans want quality education, but when lower grades and higher failure rates reach their own children's classes, they rebel and schools relent. Americans hate public education because standards are low but love their local schools because their children perform so well there.

Schools have their own reasons to play along. Flexible standards mean fewer complaints. When parents are happy, there are fewer lawsuits; when students are happy, there are fewer discipline problems. What's more, schools that fail students assume the expensive and unpopular obligation of retaining them.

In the short term, floating standards make everybody a winner. Students build self-esteem, parents gain peace of mind, and schools save money. By giving high grades and class credit to anyone willing to occupy space in a classroom, schools create the illusion that their students are learning. Only after leaving school and facing work or college do the students discover that they are ignorant and ill prepared.

Imagine that you are required to teach *Hamlet* to a group of students who are either unwilling or unable to read such a work. If you demand that your charges read and understand the play, most will fail and you will be blamed. If you drop *Hamlet* and convert the class into a remedial reading course, you will be out of compliance with the curriculum. If you complain that your students are not up to the mandated task, you will be labeled insensitive and uncaring.

Fear not: The floating standard will save you. If the students will not or cannot read the play, read it to them. If they will not sit still long enough to hear the whole play, consider an abridged or comic-book version, or let them watch the movie. If they cannot pass a multiple-choice test, try a true-or-false or a fill-in-the-blank test that mirrors the previous day's study sheet. If they still have not passed, allow them to do an art project. They could make a model of the Globe Theatre with Popsicle sticks or draw a picture of a Danish prince, or Prince Charles, or even the Artist Formerly Known As Prince. Those not artistically inclined could make copies of Shakespearean sonnets with macaroni letters on construction paper. If all else fails, try groups projects. That way you can give passing grades to all the students, even if only one in five produces anything.

Keep dropping the standard, and sooner or later everyone will meet it. If anyone asks, you taught *Hamlet* in a nonconventional way, one that took into account your students' individual differences and needs.

For three decades, dismayed Americans have watched their children's test scores slip relative to those of children in other industrialized nations. Our leaders have responded with hollow excuses. Too many American children live in poverty, they say. But so do many Koreans. Many American children are raised in single-parent homes. But so are many Swedes. The United States is an ethnically diverse country. But so is Singapore. The biggest lie is that we are the only nation in the world that seeks to educate children of all socioeconomic classes. That has not been true for decades. The reality is simpler than that. Those other nations have fixed standards.

American schools offer fixed standards for their best and worst students, but not for the largest group, those in the middle. Advanced

Placement tests are the same throughout the country. The International Baccalaureate program offers uniform curricula and standards to top-notch students in the United States and in English-language schools throughout the world. Ever-increasing numbers of states have mandated that their students pass a basic skills test before graduating. In Texas, the Texas Assessment of Academic Skills (TAAS) is the standard. In order to prevent schools from ignoring any class of students, Texas wisely chose to track test scores by racial and economic group. The state has demanded basic skills for all students, and the schools are delivering.

For those who seek to learn more than basics, however, the result has been negative. Like other state-mandated minimum skills tests, the TAAS is helping to solve one problem while creating another: basic skills are now so strongly stressed that real academics suffer. In should be obvious that a student who has read and analyzed the works of Charles Dickens or Mark Twain would be better able to determine the sequence of events or identify the main idea of a paragraph than would a student who spent his academic year reading sample test passages, yet teachers who once taught from novels now assign reams of single-page reading passages followed by multiple-choice questions.

Perhaps there is another way. Those who take Advanced Placement or International Baccalaureate tests submit to a voluntary outside standard. There is no reason that we cannot extend this option to other students as well. Textbook publishers, educators, and others could produce competing tests, to be given at the end of certain courses. Schools could submit the works of literature read and historical eras studied to private testing companies and receive tests based on that material. These tests would free teachers from the pressure to adjust the content of their courses and would assure students and their parents that the standard for each course is fixed, not floating. If *Hamlet* is tested, then *Hamlet*, not Popsicle-stick or macaroni art, will be taught. ■

All of us are called to be people of character, people who are honest and fair with one another, people who stand by principles. This painfully candid account of a teacher lowering his standards and "going along to get along" is not only about a weakness in character, but a cancer on the character of education. Everyone is getting an easy ride and everyone seems to be happy about it. But, in fact, everyone is being cheated. Grade inflation is a form of dishonesty. So is lowering the standards for what ought to be learned about a particular school subject. Much of the current reform effort in education is about refocusing schools on academic excellence and mastery. Said another way, it is about returning honesty to schools.

D I S C U S S I O N Q U E S T I O N S

1. Was "grade inflation" an issue in your high school experience? Is it discussed in your current situation?

2. In what ways are students cheated by the dishonesty described in this essay? In what ways is the community cheated?

3. What specific steps would you suggest to teachers in a school where grade inflation has gotten out of hand?

9

Selecting "Star" Teachers for Children and Youth in Urban Poverty

Martin Haberman

No school can be better than its teachers. And the surest and best way to improve the schooling of the approximately 12 million children and youth in poverty is to get better teachers for them. The strategy for doing this is not mysterious and has been evolving for more than 35 years.

The premise of the strategy is simple: selection is more important than training. My calculated hunch is that selection is 80% of the matter. The reason is that the functions performed by effective urban teachers of students in poverty are undergirded by a very clear ideology. Such teachers not only perform functions that quitters and burnouts do not perform, but they also know why they do what they do. They have a coherent vision. Moreover, it is a humane, respectful, caring, and nonviolent form of "gentle teaching" that I have described elsewhere.[1] My point here is that teachers' behaviors and the ideology that undergirds their behaviors cannot be unwrapped. They are of a piece.

At the time this article was written, Martin Haberman was a Distinguished Professor in the School of Education, University of Wisconsin, Milwaukee. Martin Haberman, "Selecting 'Star' Teachers for Children and Youth in Urban Poverty," *Phi Delta Kappan*, June 1995. Copyright © 1995 by Phi Delta Kappa. Reprinted by permission of author and publisher.

Nor can this ideology be readily or easily taught in traditional programs of teacher preparation. Writing a term paper on Piaget's concept of conservation or sharing with other student teachers such problems as why Ray won't sit down will not provide neophytes with the ideological vision of "star teachers." This ideology, while it is open to development, must be selected for. What can be taught are the functional teaching behaviors that are built on the foundation of this belief system. And like the ideology, the teaching behaviors are not typically learned in traditional programs of teacher education but on the job, with the benefit of a teacher/coach, a support network, and some specific workshops.

There are four dimensions of excellence that programs claiming to prepare teachers for children of poverty can and should be held accountable for: 1) the individuals trained should be adults; 2) they should have demonstrated ability to establish rapport with low-income children of diverse ethnic backgrounds; 3) they should be admitted as candidates based on valid interviews that reliably predict their success with children in poverty; and 4) practicing urban teachers who are recognized as effective should be involved in selecting candidates.

My colleagues and I have identified three related truths that grow out of the recognition that selection is the heart of the matter where teachers for the urban poor are concerned: 1) the odds of selecting effective urban teachers for children and youth in poverty are approximately 10 times better if the candidates are over 30 rather than under 25 years of age; 2) there is no problem whatsoever in selecting more teachers of color, or more males, or more Hispanics, or more of any other "minority" constituency if training begins at the postbaccalaureate level; and 3) the selection and training of successful urban teachers is best accomplished in the worst schools and under the poorest conditions of practice.

This last truth requires some comment. States routinely give out teaching licenses that are deemed valid for any school in the state. The most reasonable basis for awarding such licenses would be to prepare teachers in the poorest schools and assume they will be able to deal with the "problems" presented by smaller classes, more and better materials and equipment, and safer neighborhoods if they should ever be "forced" to teach in more advantaged schools. Traditional teacher education makes almost the reverse assumption: create professional development centers (the equivalent of teaching hospitals) and then assume that beginners will be able to function in the poverty schools to which city school districts typically assign them. "Best practice" should not be thought of as ideal teaching under ideal conditions but as effective practice under the worst conditions.

Functions of "Star" Urban Teachers

By comparing the behaviors and undergirding ideologies of "star" urban teachers with those of quitters and failures, my colleagues and I have identified 14 functions of successful teachers of the urban poor that are neither discrete behaviors nor personality attributes. Instead, these functions are "midrange" in the sense that they represent chunks of teaching behavior that encompass a number of interrelated actions and simultaneously represent beliefs or commitments that predispose these teachers to act. "Stars" are those teachers who are identified by principals, supervisors, other teachers, parents, and themselves as outstanding. They also have students who learn a great deal as measured by test scores and work samples. Between 5% and 8% of the staff members who now teach in urban poverty schools are such "star" teachers. The quitters and failures with whom their functioning is compared constitute a much larger group: 30% to 50%, depending on the particular district. In a continuing series of interviews with a population of star urban teachers every year since 1959, we have found that the 14 functions have remained stable. What has changed in some cases are the questions needed to elicit interviewees' responses related to these functions.

The structured interview we use has been developed to select beginning teachers who can be prepared successfully on the job. This means that they can function at satisfactory levels while they are learning to teach. The highest success rate for selecting such exceptional neophytes has been achieved by combining both the interview and the opportunity to observe the candidates interacting with and teaching children in the summer prior to their assuming the role of beginning teacher. When the interview is combined with such observation, there is less than a 5% error rate. Use of the interview alone raises the error rate to between 8% and 10%.

Compare these figures with the fact that approximately 50% of newcomers to urban schools who were prepared in traditional programs quit or fail in five years or less. And these "trained" beginners are only the very small, self-selected group who choose to try teaching in an urban school and not a representative sample of those currently being prepared to teach. It boggles the mind to imagine what the failure rate would be if a truly representative sample of those now graduating from traditional programs of teacher education were hired as first-year teachers in the largest urban school districts.

In the rest of this article, I will briefly outline the seven functions that the star teacher interview assesses (and the additional seven for which we have never been able to develop interview questions). In order for a candidate to pass the interview, he or she need not respond at the level of a star teacher. The interview predicts applicants' potential functioning from "average," through "high," to "star." A zero answer on any of the functions constitutes a failure response to the total interview. The interview is couched in behavioral terms; that is, it attempts to determine what the applicant would do in his or her class and why. (Readers should note that merely reading about these functions does not constitute preparation to conduct an interview.)

The Dimensions of Effective Teaching

1. *Persistence.* Many urban teachers honestly believe that most of their students (all in some cases) should not be in their classrooms because

they need special help; are not achieving at grade level; are "abnormal" in their interests, attentiveness, or behavior; are emotionally unsuited to school; or are in need of alternative schools, special classes, or teachers trained to work with exceptional individuals. In some urban districts and in individual urban schools many teachers perceive 90% of their students to be not "normal."[2]

Effective urban teachers, on the other hand, believe it is their responsibility to find ways of engaging all their students in learning activities. The continuous generation and maintenance of student interest and involvement is how star teachers explain their jobs to themselves and to others. They manifest this persistence in several ways. They accept responsibility for making the classroom an interesting, engaging place and for involving the children in all forms of learning. They persist in trying to meet the individual needs of the problem student, the talented, the handicapped, and the frequently neglected student who falls in the gray area. Their persistence is reflected in an endless search for what works best with each student. Indeed, they define their jobs as asking themselves constantly, "How might this activity have been better—for the class or for a particular individual?"

The persistence of star teachers demonstrates several aspects of their ideology: teaching can never be "good enough," since everyone could always have learned more in any activity; teaching inevitably involves dealing with problems and problem students, and such students will be in every class, every day; and better materials and strategies can always be found. The basic stance of these teachers is never to give up trying to find better ways of doing things. The quip attributed to Thomas Edison, "The difference between carbon and diamonds is that diamonds stayed on the job longer," might describe these teachers as well.

2. *Protecting learners and learning.* Star teachers are typically involved in some life activity that provides them with a sense of well-being and from which they continually learn. It might be philately, Russian opera, a Save the Wolves Club,

composing music with computers, travel, or some other avocation from which they derive meaning as well as pleasure. Inevitably, they bring these activities and interests into their classrooms and use them as ways of involving their students in learning. It is quite common to find teachers' special interests used as foci that generate great enthusiasm for learning among the students. The grandiose explanation for this phenomenon is that people who continually experience learning themselves have the prerequisites to generate the desire to learn in others. A more practical explanation would be that we teach best what we care most about.

In any event, star teachers frequently involve their students in learning that transcends curriculum, textbooks, and achievement tests. Their commitment to turning students on to learning frequently brings them into noncompliance with the extremely thick bureaucracies of urban schools. Stars do not view themselves as change agents, per se, but they do seek ways to give themselves and their students greater latitude within the traditional curriculum.

Consider the following episode. The teacher has succeeded in truly involving the class in a learning activity. It might be an environmental issue (What happens to our garbage?); a biological study (How does a lie detector work?); or the production of a class play dealing with violence in the neighborhood. Imagine further that the intense student interest has generated some noise, the use of unusual equipment, or a need for extra cleaning of the classroom. The principal learns of the activity and requests that it be discontinued. The principal also instructs the teacher to stick with the approved texts and to follow the regular curriculum. At this point the lines are clearly drawn: continuing a genuine learning activity in which the students are thriving versus complying with the directive of a superior and following a school policy.

The way star teachers seek to work through such a problem is in direct opposition to the reaction of quitters and failures. Star teachers see protecting and enhancing students' involvement in learning activities as their highest priority;

quitters cannot conceive of the possibility that they would diverge from the standard curriculum or that they would question a school administrator or a school policy.

To the uninitiated, such struggles over red tape may seem atypical. Experienced star teachers, however, find themselves involved in a continuous, day-to-day struggle to redefine and broaden the boundaries within which they work. One reason they so often find themselves at odds with the bureaucracy of urban schools is that they persist in searching for ways to engage their students actively in learning. Indeed, their view that this is their primary function stands in stark contrast to the views of teachers who see their primary function as covering the curriculum.

Star teachers try to resolve their struggles with bureaucracy patiently, courteously, and professionally. They seek to negotiate with authority. Quitters and failures perceive the most professional response to be unquestioning compliance.

3. *Application of generalizations.* Some teachers have 30 years of experience, while others have one year of experience 30 times over. One basis for professional growth is the ability to generate practical, specific applications of the theories and philosophies. Conversely, successful teachers can also reflect on their many discrete classroom activities and see what they add up to. If you ask stars to give examples of some principle they believe in (e.g., "What would an observer see in your classroom that would lead him/her to believe that you believe all children can learn?"), they are able to cite clear, observable examples. Conversely, if a star is asked to offer a principle or make a generalization that accounts for a series of behaviors in which he or she engages, the star is equally able to move from the specific to the general.

The importance of this dimension is that teachers must be able to improve and develop. In order for this to happen, they must be able to take principles and concepts from a variety of sources (i.e., courses, workshops, books, and research) and translate them into practice. At the same time, stars can explain what their day-to-day work adds up to; they have a grasp not only of the learning principles that undergird their work but also of the long-range knowledge goals that they are helping their students achieve.

At the other extreme are teachers who are "concretized." They do not comprehend the difference between information and knowledge; neither do they see any connection between their daily lessons and the reasons why children and youth are compelled to go to school for 13 years. Indeed, quitters and failures frequently respond to the question, "Would you give an example of a principle in which you believe that guides your teaching?" with, "I don't like to generalize" or "It's wrong to make generalizations."

The ability to derive meaning from one's teaching is also a function of this ability to move between the general and the specific. Without this ability to see the relationship between important ideas and day-to-day practice, teaching degenerates into merely "keeping school."

4. *Approach to "at-risk" students.* Of all the factors that separate stars from quitters and failures this one is the most powerful in predicting their future effectiveness with urban children of poverty. When asked to account for the large numbers of at-risk students or to suggest what might be done about cutting down on the number of at-risk students, most teachers are well-versed in the popular litany of causes. The most common causes cited are poverty, violence, handicapping conditions, racism, unemployment, poor housing, lack of health care, gangs, drugs, and dysfunctional families. But while the quitters and failures stop with these, the stars also cite irrelevant school curricula, poor teaching, and overly bureaucratic school systems as additional causes.

Since quitters and failures essentially blame the victims, the families, and the neighborhoods, they do not come up with any measures that schools and teachers can or should take to improve the situation. Indeed, they say such things as "You can't expect schools to be all things to all people" or "Teachers can't be social workers, nurses, and policemen." Stars also see all the societal conditions that contribute to students' problems with school. But they are able to suggest that more relevant curricula and more effective teaching strategies are things that schools and teachers could try and should be held accountable for. Star teachers believe that, regardless of the life conditions their students face, they as teachers bear a primary responsibility for sparking their students' desire to learn.

5. *Professional versus personal orientation to students.* Stars expect to find some youngsters in their classrooms that they may not necessarily love; they also expect to be able to teach them. Stars expect that some of their students will not necessarily love them, but they expect these students to be able to learn from them. They use such terms as caring, respect, and concern, and they enjoy the love and affection of students when it occurs naturally. But they do not regard it as a prerequisite for learning.

Quitters and failures, on the other hand, cannot and do not discriminate between the love of parents for their children and the love of teachers for their students. They regard such love as a prerequisite for any learning to occur. They also believe that the children should feel a similar sort of love for their teachers. Consequently, it is not uncommon for quitters and failures to become disillusioned about their work in poverty schools. Once they realize that the children do not love them or that they cannot love "these" children, they find themselves unable to function in the role of teacher. For many quitters and failures, this love between students and teachers was a major reason for seeking to become teachers.

Star teachers have extremely strong, positive feelings toward their students, which in many cases might be deemed a form of love. But these feelings are not the primary reasons that stars are teachers, nor are these feelings the basis of their relationships with their students. Indeed, when their students misbehave, star teachers do not take it as a personal attack. Neither do they maintain class order or inspire effort by seeking to instill guilt. Genuine respect is the best way to describe the feelings star teachers have for their students.

6. *Burnout: its causes and cures.* Star teachers in large urban school systems are well aware that they work in mindless bureaucracies. They recognize that even good teachers will eventually burn out if they are subjected to constant stress, so they learn how to protect themselves from an interfering bureaucracy. As they gain experience, they learn the minimum things they must do to function in these systems without having the system punish them. Ultimately, they learn how to gain the widest discretion for themselves and their students without incurring the wrath of the system. Finally, they set up networks of a few like-minded teachers, or they teach in teams, or they simply find kindred spirits. They use these support systems as sources of emotional sustenance.

Without such organizational skills—and lacking the awareness that they even need such skills—failures and quitters are literally beaten down by the system. The paperwork, the conflicting rules and policies, the number of meetings, the interruptions, the inadequate materials, the lack of time, large classes, and an obsessive concern with test scores are just some of the demands that drive the quitters out of the profession. Moreover, quitters and failures are insensitive to many of the conflicting demands that every large, impersonal organization makes. And worst of all, they don't believe a good teacher "should" ever burn out. They believe that a really good person who really wants to be a teacher should *never* be ground down by any bureaucracy. This set of perceptions leads them to experience feelings of inadequacy and guilt when they do burn out. And unlike stars, who use their support networks to offset the expected pressures, quitters and failures respond to the pressures by feeling that they probably should never have become teachers.

7. *Fallibility.* Children and young people cannot learn in a classroom where mistakes are not allowed. One effective way to ensure that we find

teachers who can accept the mistakes of students is to select those who can accept their own mistakes. When teachers are asked, "Do you ever make mistakes?" they answer, "Of course, I'm only human!" or "Everyone makes mistakes." The difference between stars and quitters is in the nature of the mistakes that they recognize and own up to. Stars acknowledge serious problems and ones having to do with human relations; quitters and failures confess to spelling and arithmetic errors.

Functions Beyond the Interview

Thus far I have outlined seven teaching functions for which we have been able to create and validate interview questions. While the actual questions we use in the interview cannot be shared, I have described above the goals of the questions. It is noteworthy that there are seven additional functions for which we have never been able to develop interview questions but which are equally powerful in discriminating between stars and quitters. These functions and brief explanations follow.

- *Organizational ability:* the predisposition and ability to engage in planning and gathering of materials.
- *Physical/emotional stamina:* the ability to persist in situations characterized by violence, death, and other crises.
- *Teaching style:* the predisposition to engage in coaching rather than directive teaching.
- *Explanations of success:* the predisposition to emphasize students' effort rather than ability.
- *Basis of rapport:* the approach to student involvement. Whose classroom is it? Whose work is to be protected?
- *Readiness:* the approach to prerequisite knowledge. Who should be in this classroom?

For children in poverty, schooling is a matter of life and death. They have no other realistic options for "making it" in American society. They lack the family resources, networks, and out-of-school experiences that could compensated for what they are not offered in schools. Without school success, they are doomed to lives of continued poverty and consigned to conditions that characterize a desperate existence: violence, inadequate health care, a lack of life options, and hopelessness. The typical high school graduate has had approximately 54 teachers. When I ask successful graduates from inner-city schools, "How many of your teachers have led you to believe that you were particularly good at anything?" the modal response is none. If graduates report this perception, I wonder what those who have dropped out would say?

I recognize that getting better teachers is not a reconstructive change strategy. Indeed, I may well deserve the criticism that I am offering a Band-Aid solution by finding great people who are merely helping to shore up and preserve bad systems.

As I listened to the great change experts of the 1950s, I bet myself that they would not succeed, and I set myself the modest task of doing whatever I could to save young people in schools as they are currently constituted by getting them a few better teachers. After 35 years the movers and shakers seem further behind than ever. School systems serving poor children have become more rigid, less financially stable, more violent, and further behind their advantaged counterparts.

During the same period the school districts using my selection and training methods have become a national network. We now know how to recruit and select teachers who can succeed with children in poverty. The number of such teachers in every urban school system will continue to grow. So, too, will the impact these star teachers are making on the lives of their students.

Mark Twain once quipped, "To do good things is noble. To advise others to do good things is even nobler—and a lot easier." I fail to understand why *talking* about the reconstruction of urban schools in America is noble work, while what star teachers and their students *actually accomplish* in these schools is merely a palliative. In my own admittedly naive view, it seems that the inadequate nostrums of policy analysts and change agents are being given more attention than the effective behaviors of people who are busy making schools work better. A society that values ineffectual physicists over effective plumbers will find itself hip-deep in insoluble problems. ■

Notes

1. Martin Haberman, "Gentle Teaching in a Violent Society," *Educational Horizons,* Spring 1994, pp. 131–36.

2. Charles M. Payne, *Getting What We Ask For: The Ambiguity of Success and Failure in Urban Education* (Westport, Conn.: Greenwood, 1984).

P O S T N O T E

It is no secret that the teachers in our schools—and in preparation programs in our colleges and universities—are disporportionately white and middle class. Many of our urban schools, in contrast, have high proportions of minority students who live in poverty. Together, these two facts mean that now and in the immediate future our urban schools will be staffed by teachers who, at least initially, are sociological strangers to the worlds of their students. While many white, middle-class teachers perform well in urban schools, the need for the type of "star" urban teachers suggested by Martin Haberman is clear. In this article Haberman, a long-time commentator on urban education, focuses on the process of selecting teachers who can provide the best education for urban students.

Some educators have argued that we have an ideal opportunity to open the doors of our urban schools to such potential "star" teachers. We are in the process of reducing our armed forces, and thousands of minority noncommissioned officers come up for retirement each year. These men and women, most of whom have had extensive experience as both teachers and leaders in the military, could be a tremendous resource to our schools. Many of them have gone through urban schools themselves. Like Haberman's star teachers, they typically are over thirty, mature, organized, and disciplined. They could be the role models that are so often missing in the lives of children of poverty. Yet, as far as we know, no program has been established to recruit these people as teachers.

D I S C U S S I O N Q U E S T I O N S

1. Which of Haberman's seven "dimensions of effective teaching" do you believe is most important? Why?

2. Which of these seven dimensions is least important in middle-class schools? Why?

3. Does reading this article make you more or less eager to teach in urban schools? Why?

10 Developing an Effective Teaching Portfolio

Kenneth Wolf

Educators have used student portfolios to assess student performance for many years. Recently, they have turned their attention to portfolios for teachers.[1]

Why the interest in teaching portfolios? Although portfolios can be time-consuming to construct and cumbersome to review, they also can capture the complexities of professional practice in ways that no other approach can. Not only are they an effective way to assess teaching quality, but they also provide teachers with opportunities for self-reflection and collegial interactions based on documented episodes of their own teaching.

Essentially, a teaching portfolio is a collection of information about a teacher's practice. It can include a variety of information, such as lesson plans, student assignments, teachers' written descriptions and videotapes of their instruction, and formal evaluations by supervisors. If not carefully thought out, however, a portfolio can easily take the form of a scrapbook or steamer trunk. The "scrapbook" portfolio is a collection of eye-catching and heart warming mementos that has strong personal meaning for the portfolio owner. The "steamer trunk" portfolio is a larger container filled to the brim with assorted papers and projects.

Unfortunately, these kinds of portfolios do not allow for serious self-reflection, and others cannot examine them in an informed way. They do not illustrate an underlying philosophy of teaching, and they provide no information about instructional goals or teaching context. They do not explain the contents of the portfolio or connect them to intended instructional outcomes. Perhaps most important, such portfolios contain no written reflections by the creators on their teaching experiences.

A teaching portfolio should be more than a miscellaneous collection of artifacts or an extended list of professional activities. It should carefully and thoughtfully document a set of accomplishments attained over an extended period. And, it should be an ongoing process conducted in the company of mentors and colleagues.

Why Develop a Portfolio?

Teachers create portfolios for a variety of reasons. In teacher education programs, students develop portfolios to demonstrate their achievement. Later, they may present these portfolios at job interviews. Experienced teachers construct portfolios to become eligible for bonuses and advanced certification. And, some administrators have invited teachers to become architects of their own professional development by having them create portfolios based on individual growth plans.

In Colorado, for example, teachers are preparing portfolios in many different settings. In the Douglas County School District south of Denver, teachers submit portfolios to demonstrate their teaching excellence. Those who meet district standards receive annual performance bonuses. Some teachers also are striving to earn national recognition by preparing portfolios for the National Board for Professional Teaching Standards. And

At the time this article was written, Kenneth Wolf was an assistant professor at the University of Colorado at Denver. Wolf, Kenneth, "Developing an Effective Teaching Portfolio." *Educational Leadership*, March 1996, pp. 34–37. Reprinted by permission from ASCD. All rights reserved.

soon, Colorado will require all educators, including administrators, to develop portfolios in order to renew their professional licenses.

Selecting the Contents

A portfolio might include items such as lesson plans, anecdotal records, student projects, class newsletters, videotapes, annual evaluations, letters of recommendation, and the like. It is important, however, to carefully select the contents of the finished portfolio so that it is manageable, both for the person who constructs it and for those who will review it.

While the specific form and content of a portfolio can vary depending upon its purpose, most portfolios contain some combination of teaching artifacts and written reflections. These are the heart of the portfolio. The introductory section, in which the teacher broadly describes his or her teaching philosophy and goals, and the concluding section, which contains evidence of ongoing professional development and formal evaluations, provide a frame for these artifacts and reflections. (Figure 1 provides a suggested outline for organizing a teaching portfolio.)

Here's (in part) how Susan Howard, a pre-service elementary school teacher at the University of Colorado at Denver, described her philosophy of teaching:

Visitors to my classroom would see a supportive, risk-free environment in which the students have an active voice in their learning and in classroom decision making. Students would be engaged in a variety of individual and collaborative work designed to accommodate their diverse learning styles. Curriculum would combine basic skills, authentic learning, and critical thinking. Finally, visitors also would see parental involvement demonstrated in a variety of ways. . . .

Students should help establish class rules, have a vote in the topics for the year, and have a voice in as much of their learning as possible. I believe it is important to use a variety of presentation styles and provide a range of learning experiences to support students' diverse learning styles. . . .

In my classroom, language arts would pair phonics with literature enrichment. Math would combine basic skills and application. Science and social studies would emphasize application and

Figure 1 How to Organize a Teaching Portfolio

TABLE OF CONTENTS

I. Background Information
  ■ Résumé
  ■ Background Information on Teacher and Teaching Context
  ■ Educational Philosophy and Teaching Goals

II. Teaching Artifacts and Reflections
  Documentation of an Extended Teaching Activity
  ■ Overview of Unit Goals and Instructional Plan

  ■ List of Resources Used in Unit
  ■ Two Consecutive Lesson Plans
  ■ Videotape of Teaching
  ■ Student Work Samples
  ■ Evaluation of Student Work
  ■ Reflective Commentary by the Teacher
  ■ Additional Units/Lessons/ Student Work as Appropriate

III. Professional Information
  ■ List of Professional Activities
  ■ Letters of Recommendation
  ■ Formal Evaluations

problem-solving exercises while targeting basic area knowledge.

I would invite parents to share information about hobbies, skills, jobs, and cultures. I would communicate with them frequently, and would encourage them to become involved in their child's learning in as many ways as possible.

Artifacts (unit plans, student work samples) are essential ingredients in a teaching portfolio, but they must be framed with explanations. For example, Linda Lovino, a high school English teacher from the Douglas County School District, included surveys of students, parents, and colleagues in the portfolio she submitted for the Outstanding Teacher Program. She commented in her portfolio on what she learned from these surveys:

> I felt validated when the client surveys indicated that my students and their parents feel I use a variety of teaching strategies and methods, and that I am knowledgeable in my subject area. Although I received high ratings from over 80 percent of parents and students on the statements, "The teacher effectively communicates information regarding growth and progress of my child," and "The teacher effectively motivates the student," the remaining 20 percent of the respondents gave me a "neutral" rating.

I feel these areas are essential to being an outstanding teacher. Therefore, I am currently researching and developing methods that might help me better motivate students and assess their progress.

Each artifact also should be accompanied by a brief statement, or caption, which identifies it and describes the context in which it was created. This often can be done in one or two sentences. Figure 2 shows the kinds of captions Colorado educators include in their license renewal portfolios.

Reflective commentaries are another important part of the portfolio. These commentaries do more than describe the portfolio contents; they examine the teaching documented in the portfolio and reflect on what teacher and students learned.

Valerie Wheeler, a middle school teacher from Boulder included an account of a unit she taught on communicable diseases in the portfolio she submitted to the National Board for Professional Teaching Standards:

> The primary goal for teaching about communicable diseases is to educate students about their own role in leading a safe and healthy life. . . . When young people are informed, chances are they will act in ways that protect their own and others' health.

Figure 2 Sample Portfolio Caption

Title: Weekly Classroom Newsletter

Date: March 15, 1996

Name: John Stanford

Description of context: Students write, edit, and punish this weekly newsletter in writer's workshop.

Interpretation: This newsletter is one way that I keep parents informed about classroom events. It is also an example of how I engage students in meaningful learning activities.

Additional Comments: Parents have told me how they use the newsletter to talk with their children about what is happening in school. I also learn more about what my students find important or newsworthy in class each week!

This is an example of the kind of captions Colorado teachers use in License Renewal Portfolios.

The day I introduced this topic to my students, we used the entire period to discuss the meaning of the term "communicable disease." Together, we brainstormed questions about disease—its history, status, and future.

As in most class discussions, students eventually began to share relevant personal or family experiences. The energy and participation level was high, and by the end of class, two themes had emerged: Students wanted to know more about the most common communicable diseases, and they wanted to know more about AIDS.

Because student understanding is enhanced by prior experiences, I assigned each student to write a brief history of his or her own health.

In addition to the written account, Valerie included a videotape of her teaching along with samples of her teaching materials and her students' work. These included a newspaper article about the rights of tuberculosis patients, which her students had read and annotated; a letter they wrote to the mayor about the confinement of TB patients; thank you letters to guest speakers from the local AIDS center; and photographs of a quilt the class made after reading about the AIDS quilt.

Developing Your Profile

There are many approaches to developing a teaching portfolio. The following one involves articulating an educational philosophy and identifying goals, building and refining the portfolio, and framing the contents for presentation to others.

■ Explain your educational philosophy and teaching goals. Describe in broad strokes the key principles that underlie your practice. These principles will help you select goals for your portfolio.

■ Choose specific features of your instructional program to document. Collect a wide range of artifacts, and date and annotate them so you will remember important details when assembling the final portfolio. Consider keeping a journal for written reflections on your teaching.

■ Collaborate with a mentor and other colleagues. This is an essential, but often overlooked,

part of the process. Ideally, your mentor will have experience both in teaching and in portfolio construction. And consider meeting at regular intervals to discuss your teaching and your portfolio with a group of colleagues.

■ Assemble your portfolio in a form that others can readily examine. While any number of containers will work, the easiest to organize and handle seems to be a loose-leaf notebook. (Electronic portfolios may soon replace notebooks.)

■ Assess the portfolio. Assessment can range from an information self-assessment to formal scoring by the National Board for Professional Teaching Standards. Such assessments are tied to specific performance standards. (The Douglas County School District in Colorado has identified three categories, each of which contains specific criteria, for assessing outstanding teachers: assessment and instruction, content and pedagogy, and collaboration and partnership.)

A Means to an End

Portfolios have much to offer the teaching profession. When teachers carefully examines their own practices, those practices are likely to improve. The examples of accomplished practice that portfolios provide also can be studied and adapted for use in other classrooms.

Too often, good teaching vanishes without a trace because we have no structure or tradition for preserving the best of what teachers do. Portfolios allow teachers to retain examples of good teaching so they can examine them, talk about them, adapt them, and adopt them.

Finally, it is important to remember that the objective is not to create outstanding portfolios, but rather to cultivate outstanding teaching and learning. ■

Note

1. L. S. Shulman, (1988), "A Union of Insufficiencies: Strategies for Teacher Assessment in a Period of Reform," *Educational Leadership* 46, 3: 36–41.

POST NOTE

Portfolios are likely to play an increasingly larger role in the assessment of both beginning and experienced teachers. Already, the National Board for Professional Teaching Standards requires experienced teachers to prepare a teaching portfolio as part of the assessment for national board certification. Both state licensing and accreditation processes are moving away from a focus on courses and experiences; instead, they are putting more stress on what teacher education graduates actually know and are able to do. As this trend continues, teaching portfolios should become more and more important.

DISCUSSION QUESTIONS

1. How does the notion of developing a teaching portfolio as part of your teacher education program strike you? What would be the advantages? Disadvantages or limitations? What works or evidence would you want to put into such a portfolio?

2. How structured or open-ended should the requirements for a teaching portfolio be? That is, should everyone have to submit evidence that certain proficiencies have been met, or should the contents of the portfolio be left to the discretion of the teacher education student?

3. Portfolios are being urged by educators to play a major role in assessment and evaluation. Do you see a drawback, or downside, to the new emphasis?

Part Two
Students

Education is one of life's most complex activities. So much is involved. There are the knowledge, attitudes, values, and skills to be learned; there is the process of instruction; there is evaluation; there is the management of the learning environment. To teach well, to be an effective educator, demands so much of our attention that an essential element in the teaching-learning process may be lost: the student.

The entire purpose of teaching is to make some positive change in students. They are the main event, but sometimes we teachers lose focus. We become so involved in the knowledge to be conveyed or in the process of instruction that we lose sight of our students. We need to remind ourselves continually that the entire enterprise of education fails if the student is ill served. And we need to constantly remind ourselves that each student has a different set of needs, preferences, and goals.

One thing that should help us stay attuned to the student is the fact that modern life regularly requires us all to become students. No longer is the term *student* reserved for a relatively few young people receiving formal education. With the explosion of education in the last quarter century, people continually move in and out of student status. A knowledge- and information-oriented society such as ours requires continuous education. Whether it is acquiring computer literacy or learning how to run cooperative learning groups, we all return to being students from time to time. Having to struggle with new information or trying to master a new skill may be the best thing we can do to improve our teaching.

11 Who Is This Child?

Robert D. Barr

During my spring vacation, I visited my grandson Sam's first-grade classroom in Eugene, Oregon—home of author Ken Kesey, the University of Oregon's Fighting Ducks, and a T-shirt that proudly proclaims, "Me Tarzan, Eugene." Eager to start the day, Sam and I traded a couple of high-fives and sallied forth. He carried his books and an authentic Mighty Morphin Power Ranger lunch box; I carried a note pad and wore a sappy grin. This was the essence of grandparenting: a bright spring day in Oregon and off to school, hand-in-hand with Sam.

On arrival, Sam threw down his things and yelled over his shoulder, "Watch my stuff," as he ran off to join his friends in a soccer game. Almost immediately, I felt a small arm slide around my waist. Surprised, I looked down into the face of a little girl. "Who is this child?" I wondered. She flashed me a ragged smile that was missing half a dozen teeth. "I am from Chicago," she said and buried her head in my side. Suddenly uneasy, I looked around for some other adult. Having served on teacher licensure boards in two states and having sat through a dozen or so hearings to revoke the certification of child molesters, I was well aware of the taboos governing interactions between old guys like me and this small child.

As I tried to disentangle myself, she looked up at me with huge, longing eyes. "We don't have a

father in our family," she said in her small voice. Then, as if repeating from a script, she whispered, "My father is a deadbeat dad. He ran away because he couldn't pay his bills." She blew her bangs up out of her eyes and sighed. "They found him, though. He is somewhere, I forgot . . . maybe in Portland, but I don't know where that is." She stared up at me with moist eyes. "But it's all right. My mom says we don't need him." Once again she burrowed into my side.

The longing and need of this small child caught me off guard. Her yearning for affection was almost palpable. And suddenly I knew this child—not her name or her address, but her identity. In her ragged dress, with her dirty fingernails, she carried the staggering weight of research predictability, of statistical probability. I had pored over the data far too long; I knew where she came from, where she was bound, and where her sad journey would end. I knew that a deep yearning for denied love can soon wither into anger—perhaps even hate—and that one generation will impose its tragic story on the next.

Was there even a chance that this small child would one day graduate from the University of Oregon School of Law and walk crisply into the world, clad in a Brooks Brothers pin-striped jacket and miniskirt, swinging an Armani briefcase? More likely, she was a teenage parent in the making. I could envision a burned-out, unemployed 28-year-old, recovering from a messy second divorce and pregnant with her third child. Yes, I thought, I knew this child.

Just then a bell rang, setting off a wild rush to classes. My little friend gave me a final squeeze, waved goodbye, and skipped away. Sam ran up laughing—and, after he had gathered his things, we walked hand-in-hand into the school.

Still troubled by my encounter with the little girl, I watched her up ahead as she turned into a classroom. When I came abreast of that particular classroom door, I paused and looked in. What I saw was a teacher kneeling to hug the little girl and to say, "Melody, it's so good to see you! I'm so glad you made it to school today!" The teacher held the little girl at arm's length and gave her a thousand-watt smile that lit up the entire class-

Robert D. Barr is Professor of Secondary Education, Boise State University, Boise, Idaho, and the co-author, with William H. Parrett, of *Hope at Last for At-Risk Youth* (Allyn and Bacon, 1995). Barr, Robert D., "Who Is This Child?" *Phi Delta Kappan*, January 1996. Copyright © 1996 by Phi Delta Kappa. Reprinted by permission of author and publisher.

room. Then she took the little girl's hand and walked her to a desk. "Won't we have a great time today?" the teacher asked. "We'll paint today and sing—and of course we'll read some books." Bathed in the warmth of the teacher's care, the little girl seemed almost to glow.

Watching this touching tableau reminded me that researchers often jump to hasty conclusions, overgeneralizing from far too little data. I knew all the grim predictions that could be derived from the research literature, but I also knew the power of a good school and of caring and demanding teachers. I knew that schools could make a difference, could transform the lives of children, could overcome the deficiencies of the home and the dysfunctions of the family. I knew about resilient children and about the power of education, done well, to transform.

With a sigh of relief, I turned back to Sam, who was impatiently tugging at my hand. "Come on, Bob," he said. "We're gonna be late for class." With a final wave at the little girl, this 55-year-old researcher—now filled with hope—headed once again into a first-grade classroom. ∎

POST NOTE

This brief, poignant article reminds us of the potential power of education to make a difference in the lives of children. While statistical norms and stereotypical images tempt us to form expectations that can lead to self-fulfilling prophecies, this article helps us to see that each child is an individual with potential to overcome the circumstances that place him or her at risk of not succeeding in life. For many of these children, education is their best chance to beat the odds and improve their lot in the world, but only if educators take it upon themselves to provide the extra care and love these children need.

DISCUSSION QUESTIONS

1. The author uses the term *resilient children*. What do you think he means by it? What research can you find on the topic?

2. What are some of the factors that put children at risk for failure? What role can/should schools play in addressing these risk factors?

3. What did you learn from the way the teacher greeted Melody?

12

Problem Students: The Sociocultural Roots

D. Stanley Eitzen

Although many of today's students are a joy to work with in the classroom, some are not. Some children are angry, alienated, and apathetic. A few are uncooperative, rude, abrasive, threatening, and even violent. Some abuse drugs. Some are sexually promiscuous. Some belong to gangs. Some are sociopaths. Why are some children such problems to themselves, to their parents, to their teachers, and to the community? Is the cause biological—a result of flawed genes? Is the source psychological—a manifestation of personalities warped by harmful experiences? My strong conviction is that children are *not* born with sociopathic tendencies; problem children are socially created.

Now you might say, "Here we go again; another bleeding-heart liberal professor is going to argue that these problem children are not to blame—the system is." Well, you are partly right. I am politically liberal, and as a social scientist I embrace a theoretical perspective that focuses on the system as the source of social problems. However, I do recognize that, while human actors are subject to powerful social forces, they make choices for which they must be held accountable.

D. Stanley Eitzen is a sociologist and an emeritus professor at Colorado State University, Fort Collins. Eitzen, Stanley, "Problem Students: The Sociocultural Roots" from *Phi Delta Kappan,* April 1992. Copyright © 1992 by Phi Delta Kappa. Reprinted by permission of author and publisher.

But I also believe that it is imperative that we understand the social factors that influence behavior and impel a disproportionate number of children in certain social categories to act in socially deviant ways.

Children of this generation manifest more serious behavioral problems than children of a generation ago. I believe that four social forces account for the differences between today's young people and those of 15 years ago: the changing economy, the changing racial and ethnic landscape, changing government policies, and changing families. Moreover, these structural changes have taken place within a cultural milieu, and they combine with one another and with that culture to create the problem students that we face today. We must understand this sociocultural context of social problems in order to understand problem students and what we might do to help them.

The Changing Economy

I begin with the assumption that families and individuals within them are shaped fundamentally by their economic situation, which, of course, is tied directly to work. I want to consider two related features of the changing economy: 1) the structural transformation of the economy and 2) the new forms of poverty.

Transformation of the Economy   We are in the midst of one of the most profound transformations in history, similar in magnitude and consequence to the Industrial Revolution. Several powerful forces are converging to transform the U.S. economy by redesigning and redistributing jobs, exacerbating inequalities, reorganizing cities and regions, and profoundly affecting families and individuals. These forces are technological breakthroughs in microelectronics, the globalization of the economy, capital flight, and the shift from an economy based on the manufacture of goods to one based on information and services. I want to focus here on the significance of the last two factors.

The term *capital flight* refers to investment choices to maximize profit that involve the movement of corporate funds from one investment to another. This activity takes several forms: investment overseas, plant relocation within the U.S., and mergers and buyouts. These investment choices, which are directly related to the shift from manufacturing to services, have had dramatic and negative impacts on communities, families, and individuals.

Across the country such capital flight has meant the loss of millions of well-paid industrial jobs as plants have shut down and the jobs have migrated to other localities or the companies have shifted to other types of work. Similarly, there has been a dramatic downward tug on organized labor and wages. . . . Although many new jobs have been created by the shift to a service economy, . . . the large majority of these jobs are "bad" jobs—with much lower pay and fewer benefits than the manufacturing jobs that were lost. . . .

This is the first generation in American history to have more downward social mobility than upward. Downward mobility is devastating in American society, not only because of the loss of economic resources, but also because self-worth is so closely connected to occupational status and income. Individual self-esteem and family honor are bruised by downward mobility. Those affected feel the sting of embarrassment and guilt. Moreover, such a change in family circumstances impairs the chances of the children—both as young people and later as adults—to enjoy economic security and a comfortable lifestyle.

Some families find successful copying strategies to deal with their adverse situations. Others facing downward mobility experience stress, marital separation and divorce, depression, high levels of alcohol consumption, and spouse and child abuse. Children, so dependent on peer approval, often find the increasing gap in material differences between themselves and their peers intolerable. This may explain why some try to become "somebody" by acting tough, joining a gang, rejecting authority, experimenting with drugs and sex, or running away from home.

Poverty   One especially unfortunate consequence of capitalism is that a significant proportion of people —13.5% in 1990 and rising[1]—are officially poor. (Of course, many additional millions are just above the official government poverty line but poor nonetheless.) Poverty in the 1980s declined for some categories of the population (whites and the elderly) and *increased* for others: racial minorities, fully employed workers (the working poor), households headed by women, and children.

There is an important historical distinction that we must draw regarding the poor. Before 1973 the poor could hope to break out of poverty because jobs were generally available to those who were willing to work, even if the prospective workers were immigrants or school dropouts. The "new poor," on the other hand, are much more trapped in poverty because of the economic transformation. Hard physical labor is rarely needed in a high-tech society. Moreover, those few available unskilled jobs now offer low wages and few, if any, benefits or hopes of advancement. This situation diminishes the life chances of the working class, especially blacks, Hispanics, and other racial minorities who face the added burden of institutional racism.

Consequently, poverty has become more permanent, and we now have a relatively permanent category of the poor—the underclass. These people have little hope of making it economically in legitimate ways. This lack of opportunity explains, in part, their overrepresentation in the drug trade and in other criminal activities. Moreover, their hopelessness and alienation help us to understand their abuse of alcohol and other drugs. All of these conditions stem from the absence of stable, well-paid jobs. A further consequence of this state of affairs is that it undermines the stability of families.

Poverty is especially damaging to children. Poor children are more likely to weigh less at birth, to receive little or no health care, to live in substandard housing, to be malnourished, and to

[1]The proportion of Americans living in poverty reached 14.5% by 1995.—Eds.

Problem Students: The Sociocultural Roots

be exposed to the health dangers of pollution. Let me provide one example of this last point. Poor children are much more likely than others to be exposed to lead from old paint and old plumbing fixtures and from the lead in household dust. Sixteen percent of white children and 55% of black children have high levels of lead in their blood, a condition that leads to irreversible learning disabilities and other problems. Children suffering from exposure to lead have an average I.Q. four to eight points lower than unexposed children, and they run four times the risk of having an I.Q. below 80.

The Changing Racial Landscape

American society is becoming more racially and ethnically diverse. Recent immigration (both legal and illegal), especially by Latinos and Asians, accounts for most of this change. If current trends continue, Latinos will surpass African-Americans as the largest racial minority by the year 2020. In some areas of the country, most notably in California, the new immigration has created a patchwork of barrios, Koreatowns, Little Taipeis, and Little Saigons. These changes have also created competition and conflict over scarce resources and have led to battles over disputed turf among rival gangs and intense rivalries between members of the white working class and people of color. Moreover, communities, corporations, and schools have had difficulty providing the newcomers with the services they require because of the language and cultural barriers.

We are currently experiencing a resurgence of racial antipathy in the U.S. This is clear in various forms of racial oppression and overt acts of racial hostility in communities, in schools and universities, and in the workplace. We can expect these hateful episodes to escalate further if the economy continues to worsen.

Racial and ethnic minorities—especially African-Americans, Native Americans, and Latinos—are also the objects of institutional racism, which keeps them disadvantaged. They do not fare as well in schools as white children, their performance on so-called objective tests is lower, the jobs they obtain and their chances for advancement are less good, and so on. They are negatively stereotyped and stigmatized. Their opportunities in this "land of opportunity" are drastically limited. They are blamed for their failures, even when the causes are structural. Is it any wonder that a disproportionate number of them are "problem" people?

The Changing Government Policy

One of the reasons that the disadvantaged are faring less well now than a generation ago is that government policies today are less helpful to them. At the very time that good jobs in manufacturing began disappearing, the government was reducing various forms of aid to those negatively affected by the changing economy. During the administrations of the last three presidents—Reagan, Bush, and Clinton—the funds for government programs designed for the economically disadvantaged have diminished by more than 25 percent. In 1996, for example, Congress passed legislation that: 1) ended the 61-year-old federal guarantee of cash assistance to people whose need makes them eligible; 2) reduced federal spending on food stamps by $23 billion over six years; 3) made legal immigrants ineligible for most federal benefits for their first five years in the U.S.; and 4) demanded that each of the states require at least half of all single mothers on welfare be working by 2002 or lose some federal funds. The Urban Institute estimates that among the negative consequences of these policies, the number of children in poverty will increase by more than 10 percent, adding 1.1 million to the officially impoverished and worsening the conditions for millions already below the poverty line. The bitter irony is that these disadvantaged young people will end up, disproportionately, as society's losers, and most Americans will blame them for their failure.[2]

[2]This paragraph was updated by Professor Eitzen in January 1997.—Eds.

The Changing Family

A number of recent trends regarding the family suggest a lessening of family influence on children. Let me note just a few. First, more and more families include two primary wage earners. This means, in effect, that more and more women are working outside the home. Over 50% of mothers with children under age 6 work outside the home, and about 70% of mothers with children between the ages of 6 and 17 are in the workplace. As a result, more and more children are being raised in families in which the parents have less and less time for them. This also means that more and more preschoolers are being cared for by adults who are not their parents—a situation that is not necessarily bad, though it can be.

Second, although the divorce rate has declined slightly since 1981, it remains at a historically high level. More than one million children each year experience the divorce of their parents, up from about 300,000 a year in 1950.

Third, it is estimated that 60% of today's 5-year-olds will live in a single-parent family before they reach the age of 18; 90% of them will live with their mothers, which usually means that they will exist on a decidedly lower income than in a two-parent family. Research has shown that children from one-parent families differ significantly from the children of two-parent families with regard to school behaviors. Children from single-parent families are less likely to be high achievers; they are consistently more likely to be late, truant, and subject to disciplinary action; and they are more than twice as likely to drop out of school.

Fourth, about three million children between the ages of 5 and 13 have no adult supervision after school. One study has found that these latchkey children are twice as likely to use drugs as those who come home from school to find an adult waiting.

These trends indicate widespread family instability in American society—and that instability has increased dramatically in a single generation. Many of the children facing such unstable situations cope successfully. Others do not.

Rejection from one or both parents may lead some children to act out in especially hostile ways. Low self-esteem can lead to sexual promiscuity or to alcohol or drug abuse. Whatever the negative response of the children, I believe that we can conclude that the victims of family instability are not completely to blame for their misbehaviors.

The Cultural Milieu

The structural changes that I have noted occur within a cultural milieu. I will address only two aspects of that culture here: American values and the messages sent by the media. Let's begin with values. The highly valued individual in American society is the self-made person—that is, one who has achieved money, position, and privilege through his or her own efforts in a highly competitive system. Economic success, as evidenced by material possessions, is the most common indicator of who is and who is not successful. Moreover, economic success has come to be the common measure of self-worth.

Competition is pervasive in American society, and we glorify the winners. That is never truer than in economic competition. What about the losers in that competition? How do they respond to failure? How do we respond to them? How do they respond to ridicule? How do they react to the shame of being poor? How do the children of the poor respond to having less than their peers? How do they respond to social ostracism for "living on the other side of the tracks"? They may respond by working harder to succeed, which is the great American myth. Alternatively, they may become apathetic, drop out, tune out with drugs, join others who are also "failures" in a fight against the system that has rejected them, or engage in various forms of social deviance to obtain the material manifestations of success.

The other aspect of culture that has special relevance here is the influence of the media, particularly the messages purveyed by television, by the movies, and by advertising. These media outlets glamorize—among other things—materialism, violence, drug and alcohol use, hedonistic life-styles, and easy sex. The messages children receive are consistent. They are bombarded with materialism and consumerism, with what it takes to be a success, with the legitimacy of violence, and with what it takes to be "cool."

Consider the following illustrations of the power of the media. Three-year-olds watch about 30 hours of television a week, and by the time an American child graduates from high school she or he will have spent more time in front of the television set than in class. Between the ages of 2 and 18 the average American child sees 100,000 beer commercials on television, and young people see on average some 12,000 acts of televised violence a year.

A study by the University of Pennsylvania's Annenberg School of Communications revealed that children watching Saturday morning cartoons in 1988 saw an average of 26.4 violent acts each hour, up from 18.6 per hour in 1980. Two of the conclusions by the authors of this study were that: 1) in these cartoons children see a mean and dangerous world in which people are not to be trusted and disputes are legitimately settled by violence, and 2) children who see so much violence become desensitized to it. The powerful and consistent messages from television are reinforced in the movies children watch and in the toys that are spun off from them.

Given these strong cultural messages that pervade society, is it any wonder that violence is widespread among the youth of this generation? Nor should we be surprised at children using alcohol, tobacco, and other drugs and experimenting with sex as ways to act "adult." Moreover, we should not be puzzled by those young people who decide to drop out of school to work so that they can buy the clothing and the cars that will bring them immediate status.

The current generation of young people is clearly different from earlier ones. Its members manifest problems that are structural in origin. Obviously, these social problems cannot be solved by the schools alone, although the community often blames the schools when these problems surface.

Since the problems of today's young people are largely structural, solving them requires structural changes. The government must create jobs and supply job training. There must be an adequate system for delivering health care, rather than our current system that rations care according to ability to pay. There must be massive expenditures on education to equalize opportunities from state to state and from community to community. There must be equity in pay scales for women. And finally, there must be an unwavering commitment to eradicating institutional sexism and racism. Among other benefits, such a strategy will strengthen families and give children both resources and hope.

The government must also exert more control over the private sector. In particular, corporations must pay decent wages and provide adequate benefits to their employees. In addition, corporations contemplating a plant shutdown or a dramatic layoff must go beyond the present 60-day notification, so that communities and families can plan appropriate coping strategies.

These proposals seem laughable in the current political climate, where politicians are timid and citizens seem interested only in reducing their tax burden. The political agenda for meeting our social problems requires political leadership that is innovative and capable of convincing the public that sacrifices to help the disadvantaged today will pay long-term benefits to all. Such leadership will emerge from a base of educated citizens who are willing to work to challenge others to meet societal goals.

At the community level, we must reorder our priorities so that human and humane considerations are paramount. This means that community leaders must make the difficult decisions required to help the disadvantaged secure decent jobs, job training, health care, housing, and education. Schools must be committed to the education of all children. This requires a special commitment to invest extra resources in the disadvantaged, by assigning the most creative and effective teachers to them and by providing a solid preschool foundation to children through such programs as Head Start. Most important, though, all children must be shown that the school and the community want them to succeed. Then the self-fulfilling prophecy we create will be a positive one.

In 1990 Roger Wilkins presented a visual essay on the Public Broadcasting Service series "Frontline," titled "Throw-away People." This essay examined the structural reasons for the emergence in this past generation of a black underclass in Washington, D.C. His conclusion is appropriate for this discussion.

> If [the children of the underclass] are to survive, America must come back to them with imagination and generosity. These are imperiled children who need sustained services to repair the injuries that were inflicted on them before they were born. Adults need jobs, jobs that pay more than the minimum wage, that keep families together, that make connections with the outside world, and [they need] the strength to grow. We can face the humanity of these people and begin to attack their problems, or we can continue to watch the downward rush of this generation, in the middle of our civilization, eroding the core of our conscience and destroying our claim to be an honorable people.

Every day teachers are confronted by the unacceptable behaviors of students. Obviously, they must be handled. I hope that this discussion will help teachers and administrators understand the complex sources of these objectionable and seemingly irrational behaviors. We must begin with an understanding of these problem children. From my point of view, such an understanding begins with underlying social factors.

Most important, we must realize that social and economic factors have battered down certain children and increased the likelihood that they will fail and that they will behave in ways that we deplore.

Everyone needs a dream. Without a dream, we become apathetic. Without a dream, we become fatalistic. Without a dream and the hope of attaining it, society becomes our enemy. We educators must realize that some young people act in antisocial ways because they have lost their dreams. And we must realize that we as a society are partly responsible for that loss. Teaching is a noble profession whose goal is to increase the success rate for *all* children. We must do everything we can to achieve this goal. If not, we—society, schools, teachers, and students—will all fail. ■

Sources and Recommended Readings

Eitzen, D. Stanley, and Maxine Baca Zinn, eds. *The Reshaping of America: Social Consequences of the Changing Economy.* Englewood Cliffs, N.J.: Prentice-Hall, 1989.

Ellwood, David T. *Poor Support: Poverty in the American Family.* New York: BasicBooks, 1988.

Levy, Frank. *Dollars and Dreams: The Changing American Income Distribution.* New York: Russell Sage Foundation, 1987.

MacLeod, Jay. *Ain't No Makin' It: Leveled Aspirations in a Low-Income Neighborhood.* Boulder, Colo.: Westview Press, 1987.

Mattera, Philip. *Prosperity Lost: How a Decade of Greed Has Eroded Our Standard of Living and Endangered Our Children's Future.* Reading, Mass.: Addison-Wesley, 1991.

Schorr, Lisbeth B., with Daniel Schorr. *Within Our Reach: Breaking the Cycle of Disadvantage.* New York: Doubleday, 1988.

POST NOTE

A century and a half ago, Alexis de Tocqueville (1805–1859), one of the most perceptive commentators on American politics and culture, wrote, "America is great because it is good. When it is no longer good, it will cease to be great."

The article you just read suggests two issues: First, adult Americans have turned away from their responsibilities as parents; and second, American children are growing up with values and behaviors that not only threaten their happiness but threaten the republic, as well. All segments of society—homes, schools, churches, and communities—must devote more time and energy to our children. The stakes could not be higher.

DISCUSSION QUESTIONS

1. Of the problems of youth identified by Eitzen, which is most serious? Why?

2. What strong and positive actions can schools take to help solve problems of youth?

3. In what ways are schools limited in their efforts to help the young? What boundaries define schools' roles?

13

Boys Call Me Cow

Charol Shakeshaft, Laurie Mandel,
Yolanda M. Johnson, Janice Sawyer,
Mary Ann Hergenrother, and
Ellen Barber

If you were something the other kids will laugh at or if you sit in something or get caught, you know, having your period, then the whole class will see and make fun of you. It's nerve-wracking. Someone is always saying something. Someone is always watching. You have to be careful.

—A middle school girl

We hear a lot today about student-to-student harassment in newspapers, on TV, and even from our own children. In an effort to understand how students treat one another—even in ordinary adolescent banter—we (a professor and five doctoral students in educational administration) developed a research team to study peer harassment and understand how it occurs and how we can learn to stop it.

Charol Shakeshaft is Professor and Chairperson of Administration, Policy Studies, and Literacy at Hofstra University. Laurie Mandel and Janice Sawyer are Adjunct Assistant Professors at the university. Yolanda M. Johnson is a doctoral student working on her dissertation. Mary Ann Hergenrother is Program Administrator at Cooperative Educational Services in Trumbull, Connecticut. Ellen Barber is an Assistant Professor at North Adams State College in North Adams, Massachusetts. Copyright © 1997 by Charol Shakeshaft. "Boys Call Me Cow" by Charol Shakeshaft et al. appeared in *Educational Leadership*, October 1997, pp. 22–25. Reprinted by permission from Charol Shakeshaft.

During the 1992–95 academic years, we interviewed more than 1,000 Long Island, New York, students in eight middle, junior, and high schools. They represented a suburban mix of middle-class, wealthy, and low-income families. We also observed students in classes and hallways and in social settings, before and after school. Finally, we interviewed and observed school personnel at each site to understand the response of educators to peer harassment.

Patterns of Harassment

Most of the peer harassment we observed and heard about focused on verbal assaults. The pervasive nature of peer harassment—particularly sexual harassment—surprised us the most. Because peer sexual abuse was so widespread, no one appeared safe.

Everywhere we went, kids made fun of other kids—this was more usual than unusual. Although bullies and sexually aggressive students instigated some harassment, most of the persecution—especially in middle school—was random and illogical. Harassment occurred at school events, was unplanned, and, initially, was not thought out. The students we interviewed saw harassment as a way of life for themselves. "People make fun of you," said one student. "They make fun of your hair and the way you dress. They're just cruel."

A boy described what most boys told us is normal male behavior when he said, "We're always making fun of each other the whole time we are together." Another student added:

> Unless they're close friends, people talk about each other with no respect. If they don't like you, they pick on you. You can just be sittin' at the table and they start dissin' on you and stuff or talkin' about you.

We saw and heard about more harassment by boys than by girls, but both sexes harassed their peers. Girls believed that boys only picked on girls, whereas boys described their male peers as harassers. In general, boys targeted both boys and girls in a direct style that one student described as "in your face." Girls make fun of other girls indirectly or behind their backs. When a girl harassed a boy, it was almost always a response to his attack on her.

Name-calling was the most common form of harassment. In fact, practically everyone had a story to tell about their classmates' names and labels. "This one boy calls me Miss Piggy." "Boys call me cow." "Boys say things like joker to a girl with big lips and they call this other girl greasy." "Boys call one girl popcorn because she has zits." "Boys say you're stacked."

While all students were vulnerable to general harassment, some students were targeted more than others. In general, most girls were harassed by peers at some time during their school experience—more likely by boys than by girls. Not only did females experience more kinds of abuse more often, but it upset them more than it did males.

The Main Targets

Girls were teased because of how they looked and boys for how they acted.

Unattractive or Unstylish Girls   Males harassed females in this category more frequently, although sometimes females made fun of other females. Girls perceived as physically unattractive were often called fat or cows. When they entered a classroom, the boys made loud mooing sounds. One student described a repeated attack on her friend by a group of boys: "The girl isn't fat, but they call her cow, and they moo at her." Comments about a girl's weight were common, although a larger than average boys was seldom harassed.

Physically Mature Girls   Girls who developed breasts earlier than their classmates were at higher risk for name-calling. Other students accused them of sexual activity and circulated rumors about their so-called exploits. In addition, boys quizzed

more physically developed girls with questions such as, "What did you do last night?" and "How much did he pay you?" In one incident, boys teased an 8th grade girl because of her physical appearance. "They call her slut," remarked a student. "They say how far they've gotten. A lot of boys will talk about her. They'll say she's easy. Everybody talks."

Boys often confronted these girls directly, making sexual demands and comments. It was not uncommon for a boy to target a girl for sexual confrontation before, after, or during a class, as a middle school girl explained:

> In English class, right in front of the teacher, Joey will say, "I think I'm getting hard" when his girlfriend walks in or when he wants to embarrass some girl. The teacher only says, "Joey, calm down." Joey will say to girls, "I want you now." He does this to the unpopular girls to embarrass them and make them feel uncomfortable. Everyone laughs at the girl. She blushes or walks away.

Surprisingly, the double standard for girls remained strong. Fears of damage to their reputations by rumors were pervasive. Despite increased sexual activity by *all* adolescents, girls still suffered the most if they were considered sexually active. One girl described what we heard from many:

> Girls get called whores. If it gets around, even if you are not, it ruins your reputation. I had a friend who the boys called a whore. She wasn't, but she go the name. It ruined her reputation.

Boys Who Don't Fit the Stereotypic Male Mold   Harassment of boys often took the form of homophobic insult, in which boys were called queer, old lady, girl, sissy, or any name that linked them to a female or feminine behavior. Fear of being labeled a homosexual was much more common than fear of actually being one. Boys didn't want others to believe they were homosexual and worked hard to make sure that their behavior fit an imagined norm. Such insults were hurled at boys for any perceived weakness. Many boys told us that the most common verbal assault among their male peers was to equate the boy with femininity. "You'd call a person a pussy if they were afraid to do something," said one middle school boy. "Like if we were drinking and they were afraid to drink."

This description of treatment by 7th and 8th grade boys was typical of the homophobic club wielded against boys who didn't conform to a macho image:

If they were quiet, if they acted different in the way they walked or acted in the hall—like hyper or something—or if they were into karate, or acted in any way different from the rest, they'd get laughed about. Kids make up nicknames like gay and faggot.

A 7th grade boy told us that if a boy didn't talk about having sex with girls, then his peers assumed he was a homosexual.

If he's not interested in girls, they might call him gay. When we're talking about girls there is this one kid who is silent, and we wonder why he is not talking about having sex with girls. We say, "What's wrong with him?"

Boys who didn't excel in athletics became targets. A 9th grader told us,

If someone isn't good at sports, they'll call him a faggot. One time a kid missed the ball or he did something stupid, and they called him a fucking fag.

Our study showed that fear of being labeled a homosexual was central to male adolescent life and was a strong influence on male behavior.

How Do Students Respond?

Female and male responses to name-calling were the same: They felt bad about themselves. One girl told us that she felt "sad and worthless." A middle school boy said, "They make fun of me—it's depressing. I would change schools if I could." Another girl reported, "It makes you feel

powerless. They guys think it is a joke." One girl described the constant verbal abuse as wearing.

It's tiresome. It worries me. I know that I'm affected by it, but I have a tendency to pretend I'm not. We get used to it.

Five responses by the students to verbal harassment included ignoring it, rationalizing it, fighting it, changing behavior, or becoming part of a group to shield themselves from it. They often used more than one of these strategies to stop attacks. No matter which defense they took, however, students reported that verbal abuse hurt.

How Do Adults Respond?

Typical adult responses to allegations of harassment in schools almost always discouraged students from further reports, seldom curbed harassment, and left kids feeling as though they had no place to turn for help. Very often, when students reported harassment, they felt uncomfortable and responsible for the harassment. In many cases, staff and other students penalized them for going public by reporting a crime. In these cases, students were violated twice—first by the harassment and then by the treatment of adults and other students.

The majority of students didn't report harassment in schools. Only about 6 percent of students told an adult in authority when they were harassed. The rest either didn't tell anyone or only told a fried. Because adults seldom heard harassment complaints, they mistakenly believed that the climate was not troublesome to adolescents. When students did report peer harassment, they were often told: "You're overreacting," "That's the way life is," or "What do you expect when you wear clothes like that?" Thus, students didn't feel particularly supported by staff when they reported abuses, and most students in our study believed that teachers and administrators didn't care or that it wasn't their job to stop them.

Students said that teachers and administrators rarely intervened when harassment occurred. Some students believed that teachers saw the harassment, but didn't want to get involved. This incident is typical:

> In science class, the boys snap our bras. The [male] teacher doesn't really care. He doesn't say anything. The teacher has to keep teaching. The boys just laugh.

Other students believed that teachers didn't stop peer harassment because they didn't care about students. A few thought the teachers had too much to do, and that stopping abuse was not part of their job description. "Teachers don't really have time—they have 200 people to think about. I don't expect them to care."

Either way, students didn't view talking to school personnel as a possible recourse. One girl spoke for most when she said, "No way I'd report harassment to the principal or anyone else. I'd be the laughingstock of the school."

In cases of peer abuse, teachers—particularly male teachers—often sided with student athletes accused of harassment, especially sexual. They defended the athletes, often describing a female target as setting a trap or encouraging the athletes. These same teachers often isolated the student accuser or failed to act on allegations of sexual abuse by male athletes. These teachers gave male students this message: "Watch out or you will be falsely accused." Rarely did we find evidence that teachers talked with males, particularly athletes, about sexual harassment. Instead, most male students got the message to be careful *not* to get caught.

In cases of verbal harassment, most students and teachers alike reported that teachers only intervened minimally. One girl said:

> For name-calling, they'll [teachers] just say, "I don't want to hear that," and then that's it. They really don't do anything else. . . . I wish teachers would stop it right away; even if they hear only one thing.

Another student described ineffectual teacher response this way:

> They [teachers] don't take as much control as they should. They say, "Don't do it next time." And when they [the harassers] do it the next time, they [the teachers] keep on saying the same thing. They don't take control.

Supporters of victims tended to be quiet, often not even telling the other student they believed the story. Many students thought that anyone who was harassed brought it on themselves. For example, one student said, "If girls are flirting or flaunting, then both guys and girls would call them names, like 'ho'." Another student reported that any student who "wears short shorts is a slut." Although this student and her friends wore short shorts, she stressed that "we're definitely not sluts. There are a lot of other girls in our grade who are."

Putting an End to It

Stopping peer harassment requires changing the adolescent culture of the school. Because students don't report harassment and because the peer culture requires that they act as though it doesn't affect them, adults must take the lead in behavioral change.

Help the School Community Become Conscious of Harassing Behavior. This takes some time and involves students, teachers, other staff, and parents. Students initially downplay the effects of harassment. Therefore, we need to use reflective activities to raise consciousness and raise students' awareness of their own feelings. Teachers can plan these activities through academic projects and assignments in all areas. In literature classes, focus on the issues of acceptable community behavior when discussing fiction. In science and math classes, ask students to conduct surveys about teasing and harassment and analyze the results. In art courses, encourage students to portray in paintings and other representations how they feel about verbal attacks.

Westbury Friends School in Westbury puts a priority on conflict resolution.[1] This school is an institution that honors its Quaker roots by its peaceful settlement of everyday conflict. Teachers try to spot potential conflicts between students and defuse them by talking to students before conflicts get out of hand.

Define Appropriate Behavior.   Once aware of the extent of harassment and the harm it does, students and faculty can move toward defining the behavior they would like to see replace harassment. These definitions must include detailed explanations of what students and teachers believe is acceptable behavior. In small-group activities, community participants can share their definitions of respectful and caring behavior. For example, students can explain how and when they feel it is appropriate to be touched by others. Teachers might share a list of words they prefer that students do not use. During this phase, allow students and faculty to freely speak about the kind of language that makes them feel uncomfortable. Remember that teachers and other staff members are part of the community. Expecting students to conform to the comfort level of the adults is not only a reasonable expectation but it is also a responsible one. The purpose is to end up with guidelines for behavior in a caring, inclusive environment.

Monitor and Change the Behavior.   If teachers give these problems at least a year of close attention, three things can happen: students and faculty will learn about expectations; teachers will monitor student behavior; and students will realize the harmful consequences of unchanged behavior.

The main point is to stay attentive to behavior. Teachers can use staff meetings, student meetings, assemblies, staff inservices, special projects, plays, school newspaper articles, PTA meetings, and other community activities to discuss harassment issues. Teachers must also monitor their own behavior because sarcasm and ridicule by teachers is no more acceptable than peer harassment.

Changing adolescent culture isn't easy. It is necessary, however, if we are to ensure a safe environment for learning and growing. ∎

Note

1. J. Hildebrand (March 11, 1996), "Taking the Fight Out of Students in School" (*Newsday,* p. A23).

POST NOTE

Anyone who claims never to have encountered people being cruel to one another must have skipped high school. This article pinpoints the real-life, everyday problems faced by many students: harassment, putdowns, intimidation, and cruel ridicule. The authors suggest that the solution "requires changing the adolescent culture of the school." Actually, most high schools have several adolescent cultures and it is the tensions and competition among them that lead to much of the mean-spiritedness described. Groups of students, such as the jocks, the cybernerds, the artsy crowd, the intellectuals, the druggies, and others, create their own cultures. Each of these cultures has its own heroes, its own rules, and often its own language system. These, in turn, are imported from the "outer world," the world of popular culture. However, another way to look at this situation is that the culture (the customs, mores, and approved ways to doing things), for which teachers and administrators have the responsibility, is a weak culture. It doesn't "engage" the students, and, therefore, the students create their own. In contrast, a good school is a school with a strong, positive culture that supports both learning and human decency.

DISCUSSION QUESTIONS

1. How do you explain the cruel behavior described in this article?

2. In your own school experience, was this type of behavior evident and what was the response of the school's teachers and administrators?

3. What are your opinions about the suggestions the authors provide to alter the adolescent culture of the schools? What suggestions can you offer to bring about more civility and kindness?

14

How to Create Discipline Problems

M. Mark Wasicsko and
Steven M. Ross

Creating classroom discipline problems is easy. By following the ten simple rules listed you should be able to substantially improve your skill at this popular teacher pastime.

1. *Expect the worst from kids.* This will keep you on guard at all times.

2. *Never tell students what is expected of them.* Kids need to learn to figure things out for themselves.

3. *Punish and criticize kids often.* This better prepares them for real life.

4. *Punish the whole class when one student misbehaves.* All the other students were probably doing the same thing or at least thinking about doing it.

5. *Never give students privileges.* It makes students soft and they will just abuse privileges anyway.

6. *Punish every misbehavior you see.* If you don't, the students will take over.

7. *Threaten and warn kids often.* "If you aren't good, I'll keep you after school for the rest of your life."

8. *Use the same punishment for every student.* If it works for one it will work for all.

At the time this article was written, M. Mark Wasicsko was provost at Aurora University in Aurora, IL, and Steven M. Ross was professor of education at Memphis State University. *The Clearing House,* May/June 1994, pp. 248–251. Reprinted with permission of the Helen Dwight Reid Educational Foundation. Published by Heldref Publications, 1319 Eighteenth Street, NW, Washington, DC, 20036-1802. Copyright © 1994.

9. *Use school work as punishment.* "Okay, smarty, answer all the questions in the book for homework!"

10. *Maintain personal distance from students.* Familiarity breeds contempt, you know.

We doubt that teachers would deliberately follow any of these rules, but punishments are frequently dealt out without much thought about their effects. In this article we suggest that many discipline problems are caused and sustained by teachers who inadvertently use self-defeating discipline strategies. There are, we believe, several simple, concrete methods to reduce classroom discipline problems.

Expect the Best from Kids

That teachers' expectations play an important role in determining student behavior has long been known. One author remembers two teachers who, at first glance, appeared similar. Both were very strict, gave mountains of homework, and kept students busy from the first moment they entered the classroom. However, they differed in their expectations for students. One seemed to say, "I know I am hard on you, but it is because I know you can do the work." She was effective and was loved by students. The other conveyed her negative expectations, "If I don't keep these kids busy they will stab me in the back." Students did everything they could to live up to each teacher's expectations. Thus, by conveying negative attitudes toward students, many teachers create their own discipline problems.

A first step in reducing discipline problems is to demonstrate positive expectations toward students. This is relatively easy to do for "good" students but probably more necessary for the others. If you were lucky, you probably had a teacher or two who believed you were able and worthy, and expected you to be capable even when you presented evidence to the contrary. You probably looked up to these teachers and did whatever you could to please them (and possibly even became a teacher yourself as a result). Now is the time to return the favor. Expect the best from *each* of your students. Assume that *every* child, if given the chance, will act properly. And, most important, if students don't meet your expectations, *don't give up!* Some students will require much attention before they will begin to respond.

Make the Implicit Explicit

Many teachers increase the likelihood of discipline problems by not making their expectations about proper behavior clear and explicit. For example, how many times have you heard yourself saying, "Now class, BEHAVE!"? You assume everyone knows what you mean by "behave." This assumption may not be reasonable. On the playground, for example, proper behavior means running, jumping, throwing things (preferably balls, not rocks), and cooperating with other students. Classroom teachers have different notions about proper behavior, but in few cases do teachers spell out their expectations carefully. Sad to say, most students must learn the meaning of "behave" by the process of elimination: "Don't look out the window. . . . Don't put hands on fellow students. . . . Don't put feet on the desk . . . don't . . . don't . . . don't. . . ."

A preferred approach would be to present rules for *proper* conduct on the front end (and try to phrase them positively: "Students should . . ."). The teacher (or the class) could prepare a poster on which rules are listed. In that way, rules are clear, explicit, and ever present in the classroom. If you want to increase the likelihood that rules will be followed, have students help make the rules. Research shows that when students feel responsible for rules, they make greater efforts to live by them.

Rewards, Yes! Punishments, No!

A major factor in creating classroom discipline problems is the overuse of punishments as an answer to misbehavior. While most teachers would agree with this statement, recent research indicates that punishments outweigh rewards by at least 10 to 1 in the typical classroom. The types of punish-

ments identified include such old favorites as The Trip to the Office and "Write a million times, 'I will not. . . .'" But punishments also include the almost unconscious (but frequent) responses made for minor infractions: the "evil eye" stare of disapproval and the countless pleas to "Face front," "Stop talking," "Sit down!" and so on.

Punishments (both major and minor) have at least four consequences that frequently lead to increased classroom disruption: 1) Punishment brings attention to those who misbehave. We all know the adage, "The squeaky wheel gets greased." Good behavior frequently leaves a student nameless and unnoticed, but bad behavior can bring the undivided attention of the teacher before an audience of classmates! 2) Punishment has negative side effects such as aggression, depression, anxiety, or embarrassment. At the least, when a child is punished he feels worse about himself, about you and your class, or about school in general. He may even try to reduce the negative side effects by taking it out on another child or on school equipment. 3) Punishment only temporarily suppresses bad behavior. The teacher who rules with an iron ruler can have students who never misbehave in her presence, but who misbehave the moment she leaves the room or turns her back. 4) Punishment disrupts the continuity of your lessons and reduces the time spent on productive learning. These facts, and because punishments are usually not premeditated (and frequently do not address the real problems of misbehavior such as boredom, frustration, or physical discomfort), usually work to increase classroom discipline problems rather than to reduce them.

In view of these factors, the preferred approach is to use rewards. Rewards bring attention to *good* behaviors: "Thank you for being prepared." Rewards provide an appropriate model for other students, and make students feel positive about themselves, about you, and about your class. Also, reinforcing positive behaviors reduces the inclination toward misbehavior and enhances the flow of your lesson. You stay on task, get more student participation, and accentuate the correct responses.

Let the Punishment Fit the Crime

When rewards are inappropriate, many teachers create discipline problems by using short-sighted or ineffective punishments. The classic example is the "whole class punishment." "Okay, I said if anyone talked there would be no recess, so we stay in today!" This approach frustrates students (especially the ones who were behaving properly) and causes more misbehavior.

Research indicates that punishments are most effective when they are the natural consequences of the behavior. For example, if a child breaks a window, it makes sense to punish him with clean-up responsibilities and by making him pay for damage. Having him write 1,000 times, "I will not break the window," or having him do extra math problems (!) does little to help him see the relationship between actions and consequences.

In reality, this is one of the hardest suggestions to follow. In many cases, the "natural consequences" are obscure ("Okay, Steve, you hurt Carlton's feelings by calling him fat. For your punishment, you will make him feel better"). So, finding an appropriate punishment is often difficult. We suggest that after racking your brain, you consult with the offenders. They may be able to come up with a consequence that at least appears to them to be a fit punishment. In any case, nothing is lost for trying.

If You Must Punish, Remove Privileges

In the event that there are no natural consequences that can serve as punishments, the next best approach is to withdraw privileges. This type of punishment fits in well with the actual conditions in our society. In "real life" (located somewhere outside the school walls) privileges and responsibilities go hand in hand. People who do not act responsibly quickly lose freedoms and privileges. Classrooms provide a great opportunity to teach this lesson, but there is one catch: *There must be privileges to withdraw!* Many privileges already exist in classrooms and many more should be created. For example, students who

finish their work neatly and on time can play an educational game, do an extra credit math sheet, work on homework, or earn points toward fun activities and free time. The possibilities are limitless. The important point, however, is that those who break the rules lose out on the privileges.

"Ignor"ance Is Bliss

One of the most effective ways to create troubles is to reward the very behaviors you want to eliminate. Many teachers do this inadvertently by giving attention to misbehaviors. For example, while one author was observing a kindergarten class, a child uttered an expletive after dropping a box of toys. The teachers quickly surrounded him and excitedly exclaimed, "That's nasty! Shame! Shame! Don't ever say that nasty word again!" All the while the other kids looked on with studied interest. So by lunch time, many of the other students were chanting, ". . . (expletive deleted) . . ." and the teachers were in a frenzy! Teachers create similar problems by bringing attention to note passing, gum chewing, and countless other minor transgressions. Such problems can usually be avoided by ignoring minor misbehaviors and, at a later time, talking to the student individually. Some minor misbehavior is probably being committed by at least one student during every second you teach! Your choice is to spend your time trying to correct (and bring attention to) each one *or* to go about the business of teaching.

Consistency Is the Best Policy

Another good way to create discipline problems is to be inconsistent with rules, assignments, and punishments. For example, one author's daughter was given 750 math problems to complete over the Christmas holidays. She spent many hours (which she would rather have spent playing with friends) completing the task. As it turned out, no one else completed the assignment, so the teacher extended the deadline by another week. In this case, the teacher was teaching students that it is all right to skip assignments. When events like this recur, the teacher loses credibility and students are taught to procrastinate, which they may continue to do throughout their lives.

Inconsistent punishment has a similar effect. By warning and rewarning students, teachers actually cultivate misbehavior. "The next time you do that, you're going to the office!" Five minutes pass and then, "I'm warning you, one more time and you are gone!" And later, "This is your last warning!" And finally, "Okay, I have had it with you, go stand in the hall!" In this instance, a student has learned that a punishment buys him/her a number of chances to misbehave (she/he might as well use them all), and that the actual punishment will be less severe than the promised one (not a bad deal).

To avoid the pitfalls of inconsistency, mean what you say, and, when you say it, follow through.

Know Each Student Well

Discipline problems can frequently be caused by punishing students we intended to reward and vice versa. When a student is told to clean up the classroom after school, is that a reward or punishment? It's hard to tell. As we all know, "One person's pleasure is another's poison."

One author remembers the difficulty he had with reading in the fourth grade. It made him so anxious that he would become sick just before reading period in the hope that he would be sent to the clinic, home, or anywhere other than to "the circle." One day, after helping the teacher straighten out the room before school, the teacher thanked him with, "Mark, you've been so helpful, you can be the first to read today." The author made sure he was never "helpful" enough to be so severely punished again.

The opposite happens just as often. For example, there are many class clowns who delight in such "punishments" as standing in the corner, leaving the room, or being called to the blackboard. The same author recalls having to stand in the school courtyard for punishment. He missed math, social studies, and English, and by the end

of the day had entertained many classmates with tales of his escapades.

The key to reducing discipline problems is to know your students well; know what is rewarding and what is punishing for each.

Use School Work as Rewards

One of the worst sins a teacher can commit is to use school work as punishments. There is something sadly humorous about the language arts teacher who punishes students with, "Write 1,000 times, I will not. . . ." or the math teacher who assigns 100 problems as punishment. In cases like these we are actually punishing students with that which we want them to use and enjoy! Teachers can actually reduce discipline problems (and increase learning) by using their subjects as rewards. This is done in subtle and sometimes indirect ways, through making lessons meaningful, practical, and fun. If you are teaching about fractions, bring in pies and cakes and see how fast those kids can learn the difference between ½, ¼, and ⅛. Reading teachers should allow free reading as a reward for good behavior. Math teachers can give extra credit math sheets (points to be added to the next test) when regular assignments are completed. The possibilities are endless and the results will be less misbehavior and a greater appreciation for both teacher and subject.

Treat Students with Love and Respect

The final suggestion for reducing discipline problems is to treat students kindly. It is no secret that people tend to respond with the same kind of treatment that they are given. If students are treated in a cold or impersonal manner, they are less likely to care if they cause you grief. If they are treated with warmth and respect they will want to treat you well in return. One of the best ways to show you care (and thus reduce discipline problems) is to surprise kids. After they have worked particularly hard, give them a treat. "You kids have worked so hard you may have 30 minutes extra recess." Or have a party one day for no good reason at all. Kids will come to think, "This school stuff isn't so bad after all!" Be careful to keep the surprises unexpected. If kids come to expect them, surprises lose their effectiveness. Recently, one author heard a student pay a teacher the highest tribute. He said, "She is more than just a teacher; she is our friend." Not surprisingly, this teacher is known for having few major discipline problems.

Final Thoughts

When talking about reducing discipline problems, we need to be careful not to suggest that they can or should be totally eliminated. When children are enthusiastic about learning, involved in what they are doing, and allowed to express themselves creatively, "discipline problems" are apt to occur. Albert Einstein is one of numerous examples of highly successful people who were labeled discipline problems in school. It was said of Einstein that he was "the boy who knew not merely which monkey wrench to throw in the works, but also how best to throw it." This led to his expulsion from school because his "presence in the class is disruptive and affects the other students." For dictators and tyrants, robot-like obedience is a major goal. For teachers, however, a much more critical objective is to help a classroom full of students reach their maximum potential as individuals.

The theme of this article has been that many teachers create their own discipline problems. Just as we teach the way we were taught, we tend to discipline with the same ineffectual methods that were used on us. By becoming aware of this and by following the simple suggestions presented above, learning and teaching can become more rewarding for all involved. ■

POST NOTE

A friend of ours, Ernie Lundquist, claims that as a student he actually saw a sign on his principal's door that read, "The beatings will continue until the morale improves." While over the years Ernie has not proved to be a particularly reliable source in these matters, his reported sign-sighting underlines the point that student misbehavior often brings out the very worst in educators. In dealing with disruptive, misbehaving students, we who are supposed to stand for the use of intelligence, compassion, and imagination all too often demonstrate stupidity, insensitivity, and a complete lack of imagination.

The authors of this essay take the problem and turn it inside out, suggesting how we can create discipline problems for ourselves. But the real answer they offer us, and one the teacher frequently forgets in the heat of dealing with a discipline problem, is to *be creative*! We expect creativity from our students. Why not show a little in dealing with our discipline problems?

DISCUSSION QUESTIONS

1. Which of the authors' "ten simple rules" have you seen demonstrated most frequently in our schools?

2. What do you believe is the central message of this article?

3. What, in your judgment, are the three most practical suggestions offered by the authors? Why?

15

At Risk for Abuse: A Teacher's Guide for Recognizing and Reporting Child Neglect and Abuse

Dennis L. Cates,
Marc A. Markell,
and Sherrie Bettenhausen

In 1992, 2.9 million children were reported as suspected victims of abuse or neglect, an increase of 8% from 1991 (Children, Youth, & Families Department [CYFD], 1993). The exact number of children who are abused is, of course, difficult to determine because many cases of abuse go unreported and the definition of abuse varies from state to state (Winters Communication [WCI], 1988). Not only does the definition of abuse differ among states, but professionals also define abuse in different ways (Pagelow, 1984). Additional reasons for the difficulty in determin-

At the time this article was written, Dennis L. Cates was an assistant professor in Programs in Special Education at the University of South Carolina in Columbia, Marc A. Markell was an associate professor in the Department of Special Education at St. Cloud State University in St. Cloud, Minnesota, and Sherrie Bettenhausen was an assistant professor in the College of Education and Technology at Eastern New Mexico University in Portales. Dennis L. Cates, Marc A. Markell and Sherri Bettenhausen, "At Risk for Abuse: A Teacher's Guide for Recognizing and Reporting Child Neglect and Abuse," from *Preventing School Failure*, Vol. 39, No. 2, Winter 1995. Reprinted by permission of the authors.

ing an accurate rate is that there may be a failure to recognize and report child abuse among professionals. Giovannoni (1989) stated that the failure to uncover child abuse and neglect is generally a result of three factors: a) failure to detect injury caused by abuse, particularly when parents use different medical treatment facilities each time or do not seek medical treatment; b) failure to recognize the indicators of abuse and neglect, especially for middle- and upper-income families; and c) failure to report the case to the appropriate agency when injury is detected and recognized as abuse or neglect.

Although exact numbers for children who are abused are not available, it is known that an alarming number of children are abused each year. These children are in our classrooms throughout the United States.

Child abuse can lead to the development of a full range of problems in children, from poor academic performance and socialization to a variety of physical and cognitive disabilities. Because children are required to attend school, teachers and other educators are faced with the responsibility of maintaining a protective and vigilant posture in relation to their students' well-being.

Studies have shown that children with disabilities are at greater risk for abuse and neglect than are nondisabled children (Ammerman, Lubetsky, Hersen, & Van Hasselt, 1988). Meier and Sloan (1984) suggested that "most certifiably abused children have been identified as suffering from various developmental handicaps" (p. 247). They further stated that "it is seldom clear whether or not the handicapping conditions are a result of inflicted trauma or, because of a misreading of the child's abilities by parents, such disappointing delays precipitate further abuse" (pp. 247–248). Blacher (1984) suggested that children with disabilities are more likely to supply the "trigger mechanism" for abuse or neglect. It has further been indicated that parents who abuse often describe their children as being backward, hyperactive, continually crying, or difficult to control.

The premise that a disability, developmental delay, or problem adjusting to the school environment may be directly linked to an abusive home environment requires that educators must be especially vigilant in dealing with those children who are at risk for the development of educational disabilities or poor school performance. Because many children will not report abuse directly, teachers need to be aware of specific behavioral and physical indicators that may indicate that abuse has occurred (Parent Advocacy for Educational Rights [PACER], 1989). The purpose of this article is to provide teachers with potential indicators of abuse, guidelines in dealing with child abuse in at-risk children, and information related to their legal responsibilities in reporting suspected child abuse.

Definitions and Extent of the Problem

The Child Abuse Prevention and Treatment Act of 1974 defines child abuse and neglect as follows:

> the physical or mental injury, sexual abuse or exploitation, negligent treatment, or maltreatment of a child under the age of eighteen, or the age specified by the child protection law of the state in question, by a person who is responsible for the child's welfare under the circumstances which indicate that the child's health or welfare is harmed or threatened thereby (42 U.S.C. § 5102).

Maltreatment of a child can be further described in terms of neglect and physical, verbal, emotional, and sexual abuse.

Neglect typically involves a failure on the part of a parent, guardian, or other responsible party to provide for the child's basic needs, such as food, shelter, medical care, educational opportunities, or protection and supervision. Further, neglect is associated with abandonment and inadequate supervision (Campbell, 1992).

Verbal abuse may involve excessive acts of derision, taunting, teasing, and mocking. Verbal abuse also involves the frequent humiliation of the child as well as a heavy reliance on yelling to convey feelings. Physical abuse can involve shaking, beating, or burning.

Emotional abuse is a pattern of behavior that takes place over an extended period of time,

characterized by intimidating, belittling, and otherwise damaging interactions that affect a child's emotional development (PACER, 1989). It may be related to an intent to withhold attention or a failure to provide adequate supervision, or relatively normal living experiences. Sensory deprivation and long periods of confinement are also related to emotional abuse. Emotional abuse is very difficult to define or categorize.

Sexual abuse of children is also referred to as child sexual abuse and child molesting. It is typically defined in terms of the criminal laws of a state and involves intent to commit sexual acts with minors or to sexually exploit children for personal gratification (Campbell, 1992). Sexual intercourse need not take place and, in fact, is rare in prepubertal children. Sexual abuse involves coercion, deceit, and manipulation to achieve power over the child (PACER, 1989).

In Table 1, we provide possible physical and behavioral indicators of neglect and physical, emotional, and sexual abuse. A child who persistently shows several of these characteristics *may* be experiencing the symptoms of abuse or neglect.

It is important to note that the physical and behavioral indicators of neglect and emotional, sexual, and physical abuse *suggest* or *indicate* that abuse *may* have taken place. They *do not prove* that abuse has occurred and may be indicators of other situations happening in the child's life. Additionally, educators need to be cognizant of the fact that children who are motorically delayed or impaired may be prone to accidents and as a result have bruises, scrapes, cuts, or other minor injuries. This may also be true of children with severely limited vision. Children with diagnosed medical conditions may develop symptoms that result in a change of demeanor or physical appearance. It is important that teachers who serve these children become familiar with the child's condition and be well acquainted with the child's family, Frequent meetings, by telephone and in person, will assist the teacher in keeping up to date with changing medical conditions and aid in monitoring changes in family life patterns.

A teacher who is equipped with knowledge of the symptoms of child abuse and neglect and the characteristics of the child and the family will be able to better determine whether an at-risk learner or child with a disability is a victim of abuse.

Legal Obligations

Children who are at risk for developmental delays are at greater risk for child abuse than children who are not. Teachers who work with these students should, therefore, be aware of their responsibilities relative to child abuse and neglect.

Child abuse cannot be legally ignored by school officials. Teachers and administrators are required by law in all 50 states to report suspected child abuse (Fossey, 1993; Trudell & Whatley, 1988). In most jurisdictions, it is a criminal offense for a person to fail to report abuse when he or she

Table 1 Physical and Behavioral Indicators of Possible Neglect and Abuse

PHYSICAL INDICATORS	BEHAVIORAL INDICATORS
Emotional Abuse and Neglect	
■ Height and weight significantly below age level ■ Inappropriate clothing for weather, scaly skin ■ Poor hygiene, lice, body odor ■ Child left unsupervised or abandoned ■ Lack of a safe and sanitary shelter ■ Unattended medical or dental needs ■ Developmental lags ■ Habit disorders	■ Begging or stealing food ■ Constant fatigue ■ Poor school attendance ■ Chronic hunger ■ Dull, apathetic appearance ■ Running away from home ■ Child reports that no one cares for/looks after him/her ■ Sudden onset of behavioral extremes (conduct problems, depression)
Physical Abuse	
■ Frequent injuries such as cuts, bruises, or burns ■ Wearing long sleeves in warm weather ■ Pain despite lack of evident injury ■ Inability to perform fine motor skills because of injured hands ■ Difficulty walking or sitting	■ Poor school attendance ■ Refusing to change clothes for physical education ■ Finding reasons to stay at school and not go home ■ Frequent complaints of harsh treatments by parents ■ Fear of adults
Sexual Abuse	
■ Bedwetting or soiling ■ Stained or bloody underclothing ■ Venereal disease ■ Blood or purulent discharge from genital or anal area ■ Difficulty walking or sitting	■ Excessive fears, clinging ■ Unusual, sophisticated sexual behavior/knowledge ■ Sudden onset of behavioral extremes ■ Poor school attendance ■ Finding reasons to stay at school and not go home

is required by law to do so (Fossey, 1993). Therefore, failure to act may result in the filing of criminal charges or civil suits. The courts have also ruled against teachers for delaying their actions (McCarthy & Cambron-McCabe, 1992). The possibility of criminal or civil proceedings may give many teachers pause and result in undue anxiety or overreaction to the problem. Educators must, therefore, become aware of their legal and administrative responsibilities.

The state laws governing the reporting of child abuse generally require teachers, doctors, school counselors, nurses, dentists, and police, to name a few, to report suspected child abuse to those human services agencies responsible for child welfare. Generally, teachers are required only to have a reasonable suspicion that child abuse has occurred before they are required to report it. Reasonable suspicion suggests that one is relieved of the responsibility of researching a case or of having specific facts related to the incidence of abuse. Given teachers' training in child behavior and their daily contact with children, they are in a position to recognize unusual circumstances. Exercising prudence in reporting suspected abuse will generally protect the teacher from criminal or civil action. Persons who report abuse and neglect *in good faith* to the appropriate state agency are immune from civil liability (Fossey, 1993). Laws vary from state to state in this regard, however.

Reporting laws in all states give final authority to investigate abuse charges to agencies other than the schools (Fossey, 1993). The advantage of reporting suspected abuse to agencies other than the school lies in the fact that the burden of gathering facts does not rest with the school. These agencies can research each case objectively and determine the need for action. Teachers may report child abuse to law enforcement officials; however, most states require them to report to local service agencies such as children's protective services, child abuse hotlines, local welfare departments, local social service agencies, public health authorities, school social workers, nurses, or counselors. In extreme cases, teachers may be required to report cases to hospital emergency rooms. Questions often arise, however, about the procedures for reporting abuse.

Should teachers report suspected abuse directly to the appropriate human service agency or to their building principal or immediate supervisor? These questions may be difficult to answer if specific policies and procedures have not been outlined. If no policy exists, and a teacher reports suspected abuse to the principal, and the principal fails or refuses to report the case to the proper authorities, both teacher and principal may be subject to legal action. In such a case, a teacher may be held responsible depending upon specific circumstances involved.

A specific policy or procedure for reporting abuse should protect the teacher from legal liability if those procedures are followed. A policy requiring a teacher to report to the principal or school counselor relieves the teacher of the need to second-guess the system. Teachers are encouraged to familiarize themselves with existing law as well as district policies related to child abuse. If policies do not exist or are not clear, teachers should work through their professional organizations to help promote institutionalization of such policies.

McCarthy and Cambron-McCabe (1992) suggest that low levels of reporting by teachers may be related to the lack of clearly defined administrative policy. Additionally, they recommend the development of in-service programs to acquaint teachers with their legal responsibilities as well as the signs of abuse.

Even though specific laws may require the person suspecting abuse to report specific information, the following suggestions from PACER (1989), CYFD (1992), and WCI (1988) should answer many questions a teacher may have concerning the reporting of suspected abuse.

1. *To whom should I report suspected child abuse?* If the teacher suspects that a child has been abused, she or he must report the suspected abuse to the local social service agency, the local police, or the local county sheriff's department. Reporting the suspected abuse to another teacher or the school principal may not be enough to fulfill the requirements of mandatory reporting.

2. *Should I tell the parents or alleged abuser of my suspicion of child abuse?* The teacher should not disclose the suspicion of abuse or neglect of a child to either the parents, the caregiver, or the alleged perpetrators. The teacher should report the suspected abuse to the local social service agency, the local police, or the county sheriff's department.

3. *What should I report?* The teacher should report the following information (if known):

- identifying information about the child (name, age, grade, address, and names of parents)
  - name of the person responsible for the abuse
  - where the alleged abuse took place
- description of the child, any relevant statements made by the child, and any observations made
- how long ago the incident described took place
- the reporter's name, address, and phone number
- if the child has a disability, any information that may be helpful to the officials (i.e., if the child has difficulty with communication, uses a hearing aid, has mental retardation, emotional, or behavioral difficulties, or has a learning disability that indicates special needs)

Summary

To ensure that accurate information is reported to the appropriate human service agency, teachers who serve children at risk for the development of educational problems must be prudent in their efforts to know their children and their families well. Parents who abuse or neglect their children often exhibit characteristics that may be heightened or triggered during family crises. This is of critical importance to teachers of children at risk for developing educational problems because of the additional stress that often results from the child's presence. Parents who abuse or neglect their child may exhibit low self-esteem or appear to be isolated from the community. They typically fail to appear for parent–teacher conferences and are often defensive when questioned about their child. Their child's injuries are often blamed on

others or unsatisfactorily explained. The child may relate stories of abuse or unusual behavior by his or her parents. Limited parenting skills may be a result of lack of education, experience, or maturity. Parents may lack patience and be overly demanding of a child who, because of developmental difficulties, is unable to meet their demands in a timely manner. Often, parents who abuse their children were abused themselves.

In determining whether a child is subject to abuse or neglect, the teacher should make note of consistent behaviors or physical evidence, being aware that one incident may not be evidence of child abuse. An isolated incident should be recorded for future reference but should not necessarily be reported immediately. This will depend, of course, on the severity of the injury or the effect on the child's behavior. Knowing the parents well will certainly aid in making a decision relative to reporting of abuse and neglect.

Recognizing abuse and reporting it to the appropriate agency is expected of all teachers and administrators. The experienced teacher makes the extra effort to gather information about the family, to become well acquainted with the parents, and to monitor all of his or her students' physical and behavioral conditions. Teachers must know their students if they intend to effectively deal with child abuse and neglect.

In addition to understanding the procedures for reporting abuse and neglect, teachers may also contribute to improved parent–student relations by participating in the development of parenting education programs or in setting up a more flexible schedule for parent conferences. Efforts should be made to help parents see the advances and improvements made by their children. As parents develop a more realistic view of their child's abilities and potential, they may become more patient and understanding of their child's actions. Teachers should preface a note home with a friendly telephone call or an informal letter discussing the child's overall performance in school. Given a situation in which abuse is present, a teacher's first note home detailing a disciplinary action may precipitate undue punishment. One key to reduced child abuse is improved parent–teacher communication. Teachers cannot afford to wait for the parent to initiate contact. Open lines of communication must be established and supported by the school's administration.

Children at risk for the development of educational problems are at greater risk for abuse and neglect than those children who develop normally. Teachers who serve these children must be aware of this and be able to recognize the warning signs. They must also have a complete understanding of the legal and administrative procedures for reporting abuse. Most important, they must know their students and work to establish effective parent–teacher communication. To stem the tide of abuse and neglect among disabled and at-risk children, teachers must be vigilant, understanding, observant, prudent, and effective record keepers.

Acknowledgment

We wish to thank Dr. J. David Smith and Dr. Mitchell L. Yell for their editorial assistance in the preparation of this manuscript. ■

References

Ammerman, R., Lubetsky, M., Hersen, M., & Van Hasselt, V. (1988). Maltreatment of children and adolescents with multiple handicaps: Five case examples. *Journal of the Multihandicapped Person, 1,* 129–139.

Blacher, J. (1984). A dynamic perspective on the impact of a severely handicapped child on the family. In J. Blacher (Ed.), *Severely handicapped young children and their families: Research in review* (pp. 3–50). New York: Academic Press.

Campbell, R. (1992). Child abuse and neglect. In L. Bullock (Ed.), *Exceptionalities in children and youth* (pp. 470–475). Boston: Allyn and Bacon.

Child Abuse Prevention and Treatment Act of 1974, 42 U.S.C. § 5101 et. seq.

Children, Youth, and Families Department (CYFD). (1993). *Stop child abuse/neglect: Prevention and reporting kit.* Available from Children, Youth and Families Department, Social Services Division, Child Abuse Prevention Unit, 300 San Mateo NE, Suite 802, Albuquerque, New Mexico 87108-1516.

Fossey, R. (1993). Child abuse investigations in the public school: A practical guide for school administrators. *Education Law Reporter* . St. Paul, MN: West.

Giovannoni, J. (1989). Definitional issues in child maltreatment. In D. Cicchitti & V. Carlson (Eds.), *Child maltreatment: Theory and research on the causes and consequences of child abuse and neglect* (pp. 48–50). New York: Cambridge University Press.

McCarthy, M., & Cambron-McCabe, N. (1992). *Public school law: Teachers' and students' rights.* Boston: Allyn and Bacon.

Meier, J., & Sloan, M. (1984). The severely handicapped and child abuse. In J. Blacher (Ed.), *Severely handicapped young children and their families: Research in review* (pp. 247–272). New York: Academic Press.

Pagelow, M. D. (1984). *Family violence.* New York: Praeger Publishing.

Parent Advocacy for Educational Rights (PACER). (1989). *Let's prevent abuse: An informational guide for educators.* Available from PACER Center, Inc., 4826 Chicago Avenue South, Minneapolis, Minnesota 55407-1055.

Trudell, B., & Whatley, M. H. (1988). School sexual abuse prevention: Unintended consequences and dilemmas. *Child Abuse and Neglect, 12,* 103–113.

Winters Communication Inc. (WCI). (1988). *Child abuse and its prevention.* Available from Winter's Communications, Inc., 1007 Samy Drive, Tampa, Florida 33613.

P O S T N O T E

The abuse (or, more accurately stated, the torture) of a helpless child by an adult is one of those crimes that truly cries out for attention. The effects of abuse usually spill over into a child's school life and can make him or her impervious to the best schooling. Recently, greater attention has been given to child abuse in the hope of alerting teachers and other youth workers to the problem and sensitizing adults to its long-term harm.

The National Clearinghouse on Child Abuse and Neglect Information (in the U.S. Department of Health and Human Services) distributes materials, collects data, and conducts research into this problem area. If you wish to obtain more information, one especially useful report from the Center is titled, "The Role of Educators in the Prevention and Treatment of Child Abuse and Neglect," which can be found at http://www.calib.com/nccanch/.

DISCUSSION UESTIONS

1. Describe a case of child abuse you know of personally or through media accounts. What was the outcome of the case for all parties involved?

2. What legal responsibilities do teachers have in your state for reporting child abuse? Do they have any legal protection (such as anonymity) once they have reported a case?

3. What services are available in your area for children who have been abused? Consider child protection or welfare services as well as law enforcement agencies at the state, county, and city levels.

16

What Do Students Want (and What Really Motivates Them)?

*Richard Strong,
Harvey F. Silver, and
Amy Robinson*

Ten years ago, we began a research project by asking both teachers and students two simple questions: What kind of work do you find totally engaging? and What kind of work do you hate to do? Almost immediately, we noticed distinct patterns in their responses.

Engaging work, respondents said, was work that stimulated their curiosity, permitted them to express their creativity, and fostered positive relationships with others. It was also work at which they were *good*. As for activities they hated, both teachers and students cited work that was repetitive, that required little or no thought, and that was forced on them by others.

How, then, would we define engagement? Perhaps the best definition comes from the work of Phil Schlecty (1994), who says students who are engaged exhibit three characteristics: (1) they are attracted to their work, (2) they persist in their

work despite challenges and obstacles, and (3) they take visible delight in accomplishing their work.

Most teachers have seen these signs of engagement during a project, presentation, or lively class discussion. They have caught glimpses of the inspired inner world of a child, and hoped to sustain this wonder, enthusiasm, and perseverance every day. At the same time, they may have felt stymied by traditions of reward and punishment. Our challenge is to transcend these very real difficulties and provide a practical model for understanding what our students want and need.

Goals and Needs: The SCORE

As the responses to our questions showed, people who are engaged in their work are driven by four essential goals, each of which satisfies a particular human need:

- *Success* (the need for mastery),
- *Curiosity* (the need for understanding),
- *Originality* (the need for self-expression),
- *Relationships* (the need for involvement with others).

These four goals form the acronym for our model of student engagement—*SCORE*. Under the right classroom conditions and at the right level for each student, they can build the motivation and *Energy* (to complete our acronym) that is essential for a complete and productive life. These goals can provide students with the energy to deal constructively with the complexity, confusion, repetition, and ambiguities of life (the drive toward *completion*).

Rethinking Motivation

The concept of "score" is a metaphor about performance, but one that also suggests a work or art, as in a musical score. By aiming to combine achievement and artistry, the SCORE model can reach beyond strict dichotomies of right/wrong and pass/fail, and even bypass the controversy about intrinsic and extrinsic motivation, on which theories of educational motivation have long been based.

Robert Strong is vice president and director of curriculm development, Harvey F. Silver is vice president and director of program development, and Amy Robinson is director of Research and Publishing for Silver Strong and Associates of 34 Washington Rd., Princeton, NJ 08550. Strong, Richard, Harvey F. Silver, and Amy Robinson, "What Do Students Want (and What Really Motivates Them)?" *Educational Leadership*, September 1995, pp. 8–12. Reprinted by permission from ASCD. All rights reserved.

Extrinsic motivation—a motivator that is external to the student or the task at hand—has long been perceived as the bad boy of motivational theory. In *Punished by Rewards,* Alfie Kohn (1995) lays out the prevailing arguments against extrinsic rewards, such as grades and gold stars. He maintains that reliance on factors external to the task and to the individual consistently fails to produce any deep and long-lasting commitment to learning.

Intrinsic motivation, on the other hand, comes from within, and is generally considered more durable and self-enhancing (Kohn 1993). Still, although intrinsic motivation gets much better press, it, too, has its weaknesses. As Kohn argues, because intrinsic motivation "is a concept that exists only in the context of the individual," the prescriptions its proponents offer teachers are often too radically individualized, or too bland and abstract, to be applied in classroom settings. . . .

Perhaps it is the tradition of separating extrinsic and intrinsic motivation that is flawed. Robert Sternberg and Todd Lubart recently addressed this possibility in *Defying the Crowd* (1995). They assert that any in-depth examination of the work of highly creative people reveals a blend of both types of motivation.

Knowing the SCORE

After taking into consideration the needs and drives we've mentioned, our model poses four important questions that teachers must ask themselves in order to score the level of engagement in their classrooms.

1. Under what conditions are students most likely to feel that they can be successful?

2. When are students most likely to become curious?

3. How can we help students satisfy their natural drive toward self-expression?

4. How can we motivate students to learn by using their natural desire to create and foster good peer relationships?

Much of what we will discuss is already taking place in classrooms across the country. The point of our SCORE model of engagement is first to help teachers discover what they are already doing right and then to encourage the cultivation of everyday classroom conditions that foster student motivation and success.

Convincing Kids They Can *Succeed*

Students want and need work that enables them to demonstrate and improve their sense of themselves as competent and successful human beings. This is the drive toward mastery. But success, while highly valued in our society, can be more or less motivational. People who are highly creative, for example, actually experience failure far more often than success.

Before we can use success to motivate our students to produce high-quality work, we must meet three conditions:

1. We must clearly articulate the criteria for success and provide clear, immediate, and constructive feedback.

2. We must show students that the skills they need to be successful are within their grasp by clearly and systematically modeling these skills.

3. We must help them see success as a valuable aspect of their personalities.

All this seems obvious enough, but it is remarkable how often we fail to meet these conditions for our students. Take skills. Can you remember any crucial skills that you felt you did not successfully master because they were not clearly taught? Was it finding themes in literature? Reading and interpreting primary texts? Thinking through nonroutine math problems? Typically, skills like these are routinely assigned or assumed, rather than systematically modeled or practiced by teachers.

So how can we help students master such skills? When teaching your students to find themes, for example, deliberately model interpretation. Ask your students to give you a poem you have never seen, and then interpret it both for and with them. If they are reading primary texts, use what we call the "main idea" strategy. Teach them how to find the topic (usually a noun or noun phrase), the main idea (a sentence that states the text's position on the topic), and reasons or evidence to support the main idea. If students are concerned about writer's block, remember that perhaps the most difficult task of a teacher is to teach how to think creatively. Model the process of brainstorming, demonstrating that no idea is unworthy of consideration.

These are not revolutionary ideas. They simply illustrate how easily classroom practices can be improved, thus increasing the chance that your students will succeed.

But what of the *criteria* for success? Teachers define success in many ways. We must not only broaden our definition, but also make sure the definition is clear to everyone. In this way, students will *know* when they have done a good job, and they will *know* how to improve their work.

To achieve this clarity, we can present examples of work that illustrate high, average, and low levels of achievement. Such exemplars can significantly motivate students, as well as increase their understanding of their own ability to achieve.

Arousing *Curiosity*

Students want and need work that stimulates their curiosity and awakens their desire for deep understanding. People are naturally curious about a variety of things. Einstein wondered his whole life about the relationships among gravity, space, and electromagnetic radiation. Deborah Tannen, the prominent linguistic psychologist, has spent years pondering the obstacles that prevent men and women from conversing meaningfully.

How can we ensure that our curriculum arouses intense curiosity? By making sure it features two defining characteristics: the information about a topic is fragmentary or contradictory, and the topic relates to students' personal lives.

It is precisely the *lack* of organization of a body of information that compels us to understand it further. This may explain why textbooks, which are highly organized, rarely arouse student interest. We have stimulated students' curiosity by using a strategy called "mystery." We confront the class with a problem—for example, "What killed off the dinosaurs?"—and with the actual clues that scientists or historians have used to try to answer that question and others. Clues might include:

- Mammals survived the changes that killed the dinosaurs.
- Chickens under stress lay eggs with thinner shells than do chickens not under stress.
- While flowering plants evolved, dinosaurs increased in population and in number of species.
- Some flowering plants contain alkaloids.

Students then work together in groups, retracing the steps scientists took in weighing the available evidence to arrive at an explanation. We have seen students work diligently for several days dealing with false hypotheses and red herrings, taking great delight when the solutions begin to emerge.

As for topics that relate to students' lives, the connection here cannot be superficial; it must involve an issue or idea that is both manageable and unresolved. We must ask, With what issues are adolescents wrestling? How can we connect them to our curriculum? Figure 1 illustrates some possibilities for adolescents.

Encouraging *Originality*

Students want and need work that permits them to express their autonomy and originality, enabling them to discover who they are and who they want to be. Unfortunately, the ways schools traditionally focus on creativity actually thwart the drive toward self-expression. There are several reasons for this.

First, schools frequently design whole programs (art, for example) around projects that teach technique rather than self-expression.

Figure 1   The Curiosity Connection: Relating Content to Students' Lives

ADOLESCENT ISSUE	TOPIC	CONNECTION
Independence: How can I separate myself from parents and other adults?	American Revolution	When is rebellion justified?
The search for identity: Who do I want to be? What do I want to become?	Percentages	To determine your likes and dislikes, compute the percentage of your life spent in various activities.
Relationships and stature: How important are my opinions of my peers, my family?	Jane Austen's *Emma*	Discuss how stature and reputation affect Emma's decisions and your own.
Responsibility: For what do I want to take responsibility? What is expected of me?	Ecology	Investigate social organizations working to improve the environment.

Adapted from Beane, J. A., and R. P. Lipka. (1986). *Self-Concept, Self-Esteem, and the Curriculum.* New York: Teachers College Press.

Second, very often only students who display the most talent have access to audiences, thus cutting off all other students from feedback and a sense of purpose. Finally, and perhaps most destructive, schools frequently view creativity as a form of play, and thus fail to maintain the high standards and sense of seriousness that make creative work meaningful.

How, then, should self-expression be encouraged? There are several ways.

■ *Connect creative projects to students' personal ideas and concerns.* One of our favorite teachers begins her study of ceramics by having students examine objects found in the homes of a variety of ancient civilizations. She then asks the class to design a ceramic object that expresses their feeling about their home.

■ *Expand what counts as an audience.* One of the most successful creative projects we have seen involved an audience of one. Each student in a middle school class was linked to an older member of the community and asked to write that person's "autobiography."

■ *Consider giving students more choice.* The medium of expression, for example, is often as important to an artist as the expression itself. What would have happened to the great tradition of American blues if the early musicians were forced to adhere to traditions of European music? This is one more argument for instructional methods that emphasize learning styles, multiple intelligences, and cultural diversity.

■ *Use the "abstracting" strategy to help students fully understand a genre and to maintain high standards* (Marzano et al. 1992). Too often, students prefer video art to a book because they perceive it as less demanding or requiring less commitment. Teaching students to abstract the essence of a genre will change their perceptions.

Begin by studying examples of high-quality work within a genre (the science-fiction story, poster art, sonnets, frontier diaries, television news programs, and so on). Examine the structure of the works and the standards by which they are judged. Then, ask students to produce their own work in that genre that expresses their own concerns, attempting to meet the high standards embodied in the original work. Finally, have the students ask themselves four questions about their work: How good is my technique?

Does my work truly express my own concerns? Does it demonstrate my understanding of the genre in which I am working? Does it successfully relate to its audience?

Some people worry that the stringency of this model might actually block self-expression, but our experience is precisely the opposite. Students' drive toward self-expression is ultimately a drive to produce work that is of value to others. Lower standards work to repress, not to enhance, the creation of high-quality work.

Fostering Peer *Relations*

Students want and need work that will enhance their relationships with people they care about. This drive toward interpersonal involvement is pervasive in all our lives. Further, most of us work hardest on those relationships that are reciprocal—what you have to offer is of value to me, and what I have to offer is of some value to you. In general, unbalanced, nonreciprocal relationships prove transient and fail to generate much energy or interest.

How does this insight apply to life in the classroom? Consider a student's perception of homework. The only relationship that can be advanced through the typical homework assignment is the one between student and teacher. And this relationship is essentially unbalanced. Students do not feel that the teacher needs their knowledge, and the teacher, with possibly 145 students a day, probably isn't seeking a deep relationship either.

But suppose student work is complementary: one student's job is to learn about tortoises, another's is to learn about snakes, and a third student is boning up on lizards. After they do their research, they jointly develop a poster comparing and contrasting these three reptile types. The students actually need one another's knowledge.

Annemarie Palincsar Brown has applied this "jigsaw" strategy to inner-city students using in-classroom computer networks (Brown et al. 1993). She found that it significantly improved their motivation, reading, and writing. Elizabeth Cohen (1994) builds reciprocal groups by asking students with different talents and abilities to work on one project that requires all of their gifts.

Orchestrating Classroom Performance

As teachers, the first thing we should try to "score" is our *own* performance. Different people value the four goals we have discussed to different degrees in different situations. Which ones are particularly important to you? How does this preference affect the way you run your classroom? By observing and understanding how classroom conditions can create or repress student engagement, we can gradually move toward a more successful, curious, creative, and reciprocal school system.

All students, to some extent, seek mastery, understanding, self-expression, and positive interpersonal relationships. But they are all different as well. Imagine what could happen if we engaged our students in a discussion of these four types of motivation. What might they tell us about themselves and their classrooms? Could we actually teach them to design their own work in ways that match their own unique potential for engagement?

Last, we can score the change process itself. What professional conditions block teachers' motivation? We can redesign staff development to promote understanding and respect among school staff members.

By seeking to break down boundaries between teacher and teacher, teacher and student, student and the learning process, we will learn what students want and need. As a result, more and more teachers may go to bed at night remembering the images of wonder, enthusiasm, and perseverance on the faces of their students. ∎

References

Brown, A., D. Ash, M. Rutherford, K. Nakagawa, A. Gordon, and J. Campione. (1993). "Distributed Expertise in the Classroom." In *Distributed Cognitions: Psychological and Educational Considerations,* edited by G. Salomon. New York: Cambridge University Press.

Cohen, E. G. (1994). *Designing Groupwork: Strategies for the Heterogeneous Classroom.* 2nd Edition. New York: Teachers College Press

Kohn, A. (1993). *Punished by Rewards: The Trouble with Gold Stars, Incentive Plans, A's, Praise, and Other Bribes.* Boston: Houghton Mifflin.

Marzano, R., D. Pickering, D. Arredondo, G. Blackburn, R. Brandt, and C. Moffett. (1992). *Dimensions of Learning.*

Alexandria, Va.: Association for Supervision and Curriculum Development.

Schlecty, P. (January 1994). "Increasing Student Engagement." Missouri Leadership Academy.

Sternberg, R. J., and T. I. Lubart. (1995). *Defying the Crowd: Cultivating Creativity in a Culture of Conformity.* New York: The Free Press.

POST NOTE

Student engagement is an important concept related to educational success. A recent book by Lawrence Steinberg, *Beyond the Classroom,* identifies the lack of student engagement in American high schools as an alarming problem in our educational system. According to Steinberg, the problem results from peer culture influence that devalues educational effort, from part-time employment that undermines students' commitment to school, and from reduced involvement by parents in school activities. No amount of school reform will succeed, Steinberg contends, unless we as a nation face and resolve this issue.

This article examines what schools can do to increase motivation among students. Selection 41 in this book addresses the same topic from the perspective of an individual teacher. Together, these articles offer plenty of good advice. But unless the underlying factors identified by Steinberg are also addressed, schools are not likely to be successful.

DISCUSSION QUESTIONS

1. What reactions did you have to the SCORE model of student engagement?

2. In your opinion, what is the appropriate role of extrinsic motivation in school? What were your reactions to Kohn's proposition that extrinsic motivation is ineffective in producing long-lasting learning?

3. What steps would you encourage to decrease student apathy and increase student engagement in school?

On Emotional Intelligence: A Conversation with Daniel Goleman

17

John O'Neil

Traditional conceptions of intelligence focus on cognitive skills and knowledge. You've investigated the idea of "emotional intelligence." What do you mean by that term? Emotional intelligence is a different way of being smart. It includes knowing what your feelings are and using your feelings to make good decisions in life. It's being able to manage distressing moods well and control impulses. It's being motivated and remaining hopeful and optimistic when you have setbacks in working toward goals. It's empathy; knowing what the people around you are feeling. And it's social skill—getting along well with other people, managing emotions in relationships, being able to persuade or lead others.

And you contend that emotional intelligence is just as important as the more familiar concept of IQ? Both types of intelligence are important, but they're important in different ways. IQ contributes, at best, about 20 percent to the factors that deter-

Daniel Goleman, author of *Emotional Intelligence: Why It Can Matter More Than IQ,* covers the behavioral and brain sciences for *The New York Times.* John O'Neil is Senior Editor of *Educational Leadership.* O'Neil, John, "On Emotional Intelligence: A Conversation with Daniel Goleman." *Educational Leadership,* September 1996, pp. 6–11. Reprinted by permission from ASCD. All rights reserved.

mine life success. That leaves 80 percent to everything else. There are many ways in which your destiny in life depends on having the skills that make up emotional intelligence.

Has research shown such a correlation? Yes. For example, boys who are very impulsive, who are always getting in trouble in 2nd grade, are six to eight times more likely than other kids to commit crimes and be violent in their teen years. Sixth grade girls who confuse feelings of anxiety and anger, boredom, and hunger are the ones most likely to develop eating disorders in adolescence. What these girls lack is an awareness of what they are feeling; they're confused about what this feeling is and what it's called. So specific deficits in these skills can get a person in trouble, particularly a child who is growing into adulthood. On the other side, having these abilities can help you immensely in life; they affect everything from whether your marriage is going to last to how well you do on the job.

There's also a relationship between these emotional skills and academic success, isn't there? Absolutely. It's not too surprising, really. We know that skills such as being able to resist impulsivity, or to delay gratification in pursuit of a long-term goal, are helpful in the academic arena.

Your book describes some fascinating findings from the "marshmallow" study at Stanford. Right. Preschool kids were brought in one by one to a room and had a marshmallow put in front of them. They were told they could eat the marshmallow now, but if they delayed eating it until the researchers came back from running an errand, they could have two marshmallows. About one-third of them grabbed the single marshmallow right away while some waited a little longer, and about one-third were able to wait 15 or 20 minutes for the researcher to return.

When the researchers tracked down the children 14 years later, they found this test was an amazing predictor of how they did in school. The kids who waited were more emotionally stable, better liked by their teachers and their peers, and still able to delay gratification in pursuit of their goals. The ones who grabbed were emotionally unstable, they fell apart under stress, they were more irritable, more likely to pick fights, not as well liked, and still not able to delay gratification. But the most powerful finding was that the one who waited scored an average of 210 points higher on the SAT.

Was that because their emotional habits were more conducive to studying, sticking with a task and thinking that it would eventually pay off? That's part of it. Obviously, a child who can stick with a task can do his homework or can finish an assignment much better than a child who is distracted and goes off and does something else.

There's another factor, too; the physiology of the brain and the relationship between the emotional brain and the brain's executive areas. The prefrontal lobes just behind the forehead are where working memory resides. Working memory is what you are paying attention to at any given point. So everything you are mulling over, making a decision about, or are learning, is at first in working memory. All learning is in working memory. And the emotional centers that control moods like anxiety or anger have very strong connections to the prefrontal areas. So if a child is chronically anxious or angry or upset in some way, he experiences that as intruding thoughts. He can't keep his mind off the thing he is worried about.

Now working memory has a limited attention capacity. So, to the extent that it is occupied by these intrusive thoughts, it shrinks what's available in working memory to think about what you are trying to learn.

Is that what's occurring when someone has "test anxiety"? Yes, test anxiety is a very good example. You can think of nothing else except the fact that you may fail. It becomes a self-fulfilling prophecy, because your working memory cannot manage both the extreme anxiety and the demands for retrieving the information that would help you pass. So I think that's why we

find that children whose emotional lives are more under control and better managed are able to learn more.

We all know people who have a lot of self-insight, or who are virtuosos in social situations. But are those kinds of personality traits something that people are born with, or can everyone be helped to develop them? The good news about emotional intelligence is that it is virtually all learned. Even though newborn children differ in terms of their temperament, for example, they are highly malleable.

The best data on this come from Jerome Kagan, who studied shy kids. He found that you can identify a tendency toward shyness within the first two weeks of life, by looking at how much an infant startles to a noise or whether they are likely to shy away from stimulating, new, novel, uncertain experiences. He followed kids from birth into childhood and teenage years and found that this is a remarkable predictor of shyness.

But he also discovered that a subgroup of children whose newborn behaviors suggested they would be shy turned out not to be. Kagan found that the parents of this group treated them differently. Instead of catering to the children's shyness and protecting them from the world, these parents pushed them a bit into challenging situations; you know, meet a new kid, let's go to this new place. Not in a way that overwhelmed them but in a way that gave them the continued experience of mastering something new. And by the time they got to kindergarten, those kids weren't shy. They weren't the most extroverted, but they weren't inordinately shy either.

What's the significance of these findings? Well, they suggest something that, in theory, we've known all along: the brain is enormously malleable during childhood. The brain's regulatory centers for emotional response are among the last parts of become anatomically mature. They continue to grow into adolescence.

This is vitally important, because we're finding that the repeated emotional lessons of a child's life literally shape the brain circuits for that response. So if a child learns to manage his anger well, or learns to calm or soothe himself, or to be empathic, that's a lifelong strength. That's why it's so critical that we help children develop the skills of emotional intelligence.

What about children who learn the wrong emotional responses from early on; who come from abusive homes, for example. Can they relearn emotional skills or do the initial strategies become "hardwired" in the brain? It's harder, but the sooner we begin to teach children appropriate emotional responses the sooner these responses can become a part of their repertoire. A child may have learned that when you get mad, you yell and you hit. Someone has to help these children learn an alternative response that becomes stronger than the initial one. So instead of yelling and hitting, the child will stop, calm down, think before she acts, and so on.

Again, the good news about childhood is that it's a wonderful palette to work with. It may look like it's been painted on, but you can keep painting and eventually children can learn healthier emotional responses. The literature on resilient children, those who have grown up in the worst circumstances and yet thrived, shows that what made the difference wasn't the terrible circumstance of their chaotic home life, but the fact that one caring adult really got involved in their lives and helped them out. And oftentimes that person is a teacher.

Before talking about what schools can do to foster emotional intelligence, what can you say about the current state of the emotional well-being of children? Childhood is harder than it used to be; we've got data on that. For example, in the last 20 years or so the rate of teen homicide has quadrupled and teen suicide tripled, and forcible rape among teens has doubled. Those are the headline-making statistics.

But there are other more subtle indicators of a growing general emotional malaise among children. Thomas Achenbach at the University of Vermont studied a random sample of American kids in the mid-70s and a comparable sample in the late '80s. He had them rated by their parents and teachers and found that, across the board, American kids on average had a growing deficit in these emotional skills. They had gone down on 40 indicators of emotional well-being, which is very alarming. This doesn't mean there aren't great kids, but on average kids were more impulsive, more disobedient, more angry, more lonely, more depressed, more anxious, and so on.

Let's face it: childhood has changed, and not necessarily in ways that anyone intended. The state of the economy now demands that parents work much harder and longer than they had to, so they have less discretionary time to spend with their kids than their own parents had with them. More families live in neighborhoods where they're scared about the kids even playing down the street, let alone going into a neighbor's house. And kids are spending more time glued to a TV or in front of a computer, away from other children or adults. And most of the emotional skills I've discussed aren't learned on your own, they're learned through your interaction with other children and adults. That's why the emphasis on computers concerns me, helpful as they can be. More time with computers and TV means less time with other people. The changes in families are another reason I think it's vital that schools begin to teach these emotional skills, to promote "emotional literacy."

You're familiar with schools that have been trying to teach emotional literacy. How are they doing this? A good example is the program developed in the New Haven schools, which goes from 1st through 12th grade and is developmentally appropriate. The program addresses all the skills I mentioned before, like empathy, how to calm yourself down when you are feeling anxious, and so on. In some grades, lessons in emotional intelligence are taught as a separated topic three times a week. In other grades it's part of courses such as health, even math or study skills. And all the teachers are familiar with the ideas and look for opportunities to teach them. So whenever a child is upset, it's an opportunity to make sure that they learn something from that experience that will help them.

In New Haven, they also use techniques that make healthy emotional responses a pervasive part of the school culture or environment. For example, a school I recently visited had a "spotlight" poster on the wall of every room. It indicates to kids that whenever you are distressed on upset or you have a problem, red light—stop, calm down, and think before you act. Yellow light—think about a number of different things you could do and what the consequences will be. Green light—pick the best one and try it out. Now that's a wonderful lesson in impulse control, in soothing yourself, and in making the distinction between having the feeling and what you do, how you act when you have the feeling. These are crucial lessons and kids are really learning them.

That's encouraging, because one of the trends that worries educators is that students seem to be more impulsive, more prone to act without thinking about the consequences. I've taken aside 7th graders in New Haven and said, "Look, I know they teach you this stuff, but does it really make any difference to you?" And they all have stories to tell about how they're using these skills in their lives.

In the culture of adolescents in New Haven, if someone "disses" you, you have to fight them; it's the code. But I talked to this kid, and he said: "You know, this guy was dissing my sneaks, and you know what I did? I told him I didn't agree with him. I like my shoes. And then I walked away." Well, that's revolutionary, and what's happening is that children are expanding their emotional repertoire in some healthy ways.

What are they finding in terms of results? Well, it works. They've found that students are better able to control their impulses, they've improved their behavior, they have better conflict-resolution skills and skills in handling interpersonal problems. That's consistent with what's happening in other programs aimed at emotional literacy.

It seems important that this emotional literacy curriculum is a schoolwide effort; it's not just isolating the kids who appear to have the worst emotional problems. Ghettoizing is the wrong approach. For one thing, the decline in emotional well-being holds true for all groups of kids, from wealthy areas and poor ones. These lessons are not just for so-called problem kids.

The public appears to be very skeptical these days about curriculums that address social issues, or that ask kids to work on their emotions instead of on their reading and math. Isn't that a major obstacle to broader application of these ideas by schools? Actually I've encountered the reverse. Parents and teachers are very interested in bringing this sort of curriculum into the schools, because they see that children need it. When they understand that you can do this without taking any time from the basics—which they've been able to do in New Haven—they're very supportive. It just makes good sense. ■

Editor's note: For information on emotional literacy programs, contact The Collaborative for the Advancement of Social and Emotional Learning (CASEL), Yale Child Study Center, P.O. Box 207900, New Haven, CT 06520-7900; (203) 785-6107.

POST NOTE

For several decades, schools have been under great pressure to focus on academic achievement. Headlines about falling SAT scores and America's poor to mediocre academic performance in international educational studies have fueled more and more interest on raising standards and testing. As a culture, we seem to be overfocused on our students' IQ, or intelligence quotient. Daniel

Goleman, here and in his best-selling book, *Emotional Intelligence: Why It Can Matter More Than IQ*, attempts to provide another view. Clearly, though, the answer is not to select one, IQ or EQ, for our attention, but to build an educational program that is committed to developing both. However, since EQ is new on our cultural and educational radar screens and more difficult to measure, it is currently having more trouble capturing the attention of educators.

D I S C U S S I O N Q U E S T I O N S

1. What do you think is the essential message of Daniel Goleman's article?

2. What is the relationship between EQ and test anxiety? Have you noticed any other areas of school performance that might be strongly related to EQ?

3. Do you believe the school has a role in promoting EQ and, if so, in what ways to you think schools should promote EQ?

18

What Do We Know from Brain Research?

Pat Wolfe and Ron Brandt

In July 1989, following a congressional resolution, President Bush officially proclaimed the 1990s the "Decade of the Brain." And indeed in the past nine years, we have seen an unprecedented explosion of information on how the human brain works. Thousands of research projects, books, magazine cover stories, and television specials regale us with new facts and figures, colorful PET scans, and at times, suspiciously simple ways to improve our memories, prevent Alzheimer's, and make our babies geniuses.

Our knowledge of brain functioning has been revolutionized. And many of the new findings have changed medical practice. We have a much better understanding of mental illnesses and the drugs that ameliorate them. Treatment for tumors, seizures, and other brain diseases and disorders has become much more successful.

But what about the educational applications of these new findings? Have we learned enough to incorporate neuroscientific findings into our schools? Is it possible that the Decade of the Brain will usher in the Decade of Education?

Pat Wolfe is an independent educational consultant. Ron Brandt is Editor Emeritus of *Educational Leadership* and an independent educational consultant. Copyright © 1998 Pat Wolfe and Ron Brandt. "What Do We Know from Brain Research?" by Ron Brandt and Pat Wolfe. From *Educational Leadership,* November 1998, pp. 8–13. Reprinted by permission from the authors.

Interpreting Brain Research for Classroom Practice

Brain science is a burgeoning new field, and we have learned more about the brain in the past 5 years than in the past 100 years. Nearly 90 percent of all the neuroscientists who have ever lived are alive today. Nearly every major university now has interdisciplinary brain research teams.

But almost all scientists are wary of offering prescriptions for using their research in schools. Joseph LeDoux from New York University and author of *The Emotional Brain* (1996) says, "There are no quick fixes. These ideas are very easy to sell to the public, but it's too easy to take them beyond their actual basis in science." Susan Fitzpatrick, a neuroscientist at the McDonnell Foundation, says scientists don't have a lot to tell educators at this point. She warns,

> Anything that people would say right now has a good chance of not being true two years from now because the understanding is so rudimentary and people are looking at things at such a simplistic level. (1995, p. 24)

Researchers especially caution educators to resist the temptation to adopt policies on the basis of a single study or to use neuroscience as a promotional tool for a pet program. Much work needs to be done before the results of scientific studies can be taken into the classroom. The reluctance of scientists to sanction a quick marriage between neuroscience and education makes sense. Brain research does not—and may never—tell us specifically what we should do in a classroom. At this point it does not "prove" that a particular strategy will increase student understanding. That is not currently the purpose of neuroscience research. Its purpose is to learn how the brain functions. Neuroscience is a field of study separate from the field of education, and it is unrealistic to expect brain research to lead directly to pedagogy. So how do we use the current findings?

We need to critically read and analyze the research in order to separate the wheat from the chaff. If educators do not develop a functional understanding of the brain and its processes, we will be vulnerable to pseudoscientific fads, inappropriate generalizations, and dubious programs.

Then, with our knowledge of educational practice, we must determine if and how brain research informs that practice. Educators have a vast background of knowledge about teaching and learning. This knowledge has been gained from educational research, cognitive science, and long experience. Given this knowledge base, educators are in the best position to know how the research does—or does not—supplement, explain, or validate current practices.

Although we must be cautious about many neuroscientific findings, a few are quite well established. Some validate what good educators have always done. Others are causing us to take a closer look at educational practice.

Finding One

The brain changes physiologically as a result of experience. The environment in which a brain operates determines to a large degree the functioning ability of that brain.

Researchers agree that at birth, humans do not yet possess a fully operational brain. The brain that eventually takes shape is the result of interaction between the individual's genetic inheritance and everything he or she experiences. Ronald Kotulak, in his book *Inside the Brain* (1996), uses the metaphor of a banquet to explain the relationship between genes and the environment.

> The brain gobbles up the external environment through its sensory system and then reassembles the digested world in the form of trillions of connections which are constantly growing or dying, becoming stronger or weaker depending on the richness of the banquet. (p. 4)

The environment affects how genes work, and genes determine how the environment is interpreted. This is a relatively new understanding. It wasn't too many years ago that scientists thought the brain was immutable or fixed at birth. Scientists had known for some time that with a few

specialized exceptions, a child's brain at birth has all the brain cells, or neurons, that it will ever have. Unlike tissue in most other organs, neurons do not regenerate, so researchers assumed that the brain you had at birth was the brain you were stuck with for life.

However, Marian Diamond and her colleagues at the University of California at Berkeley pioneered research in the mid-1960s showing that brain structures are modified by the environment (Diamond & Hopson, 1998). Her research established the concept of neural plasticity—the brain's amazing ability to constantly change its structure and function in response to external experiences. A further finding that should please us all is that dendrites, the connections between brain cells, can grow at any age. Researchers have found this to be true in humans as well as in animals. Contrary to folk wisdom, a healthy older person is not necessarily the victim of progressive nerve cell loss and diminishing memory and cognitive abilities.

So our environment, including the classroom environment, is not a neutral place. We educators are either growing dendrites or letting them wither and die. The trick is to determine what constitutes an enriched environment. A few facts about the brain's natural proclivities will assist us in making these determinations.

1. The brain has not evolved to its present condition by taking in meaningless data; an enriched environment gives students the opportunity to make sense out of what they are learning, what some call the opportunity to "make meaning."

2. The brain develops in an integrated fashion over time. Babies don't talk one week, tie their shoes the next, and then work on their emotional development. An enriched environment addresses multiple aspects of development simultaneously.

3. The brain is essentially curious, and it must be to survive. It constantly seeks connections between the new and the known. Learning is a process of active construction by the learner, and an enriched environment gives students the opportunity to relate what they are learning to what they already know. As noted educator

Phil Schlecty says, "Students must do the work of learning."

4. The brain is innately social and collaborative. Although the processing takes place in our students' individual brains, their learning is enhanced when the environment provides them with the opportunity to discuss their thinking out loud, to bounce their ideas off their peers, and to produce collaborative work.

Finding Two

IQ is not fixed at birth.

This second finding is closely linked to the first. Craig Ramey, a University of Alabama psychologist, took on the daunting task of showing that what Diamond did with rats, he could do with children. His striking research (Ramey & Ramey, 1996) proved that an intervention program for impoverished children could prevent children from having low IQs and mental retardation.

Ramey has directed studies of early educational intervention involving thousands of children at dozens of research centers. The best programs, which started with children as young as six weeks and mostly younger than four months, showed that they could raise the infants' scores on intelligence tests by 15 to 30 percent. It is important to note that although IQ tests may be useful artifacts, intelligence is probably much more multifaceted. Every brain differs, and the subtle range of organizational, physiological, and chemical variations ensures a remarkably wide spectrum of cognitive, behavioral, and emotional capabilities.

Finding Three

Some abilities are acquired more easily during certain sensitive periods, or "windows of opportunity."

At birth, a child's cerebral cortex has all the neurons that it will ever have. In fact, in utero, the brain produces an overabundance of neurons, nearly twice as many as it will need. Beginning at about 28 weeks of prenatal development, a massive pruning of neurons begins, resulting in the loss of one-third to one-half of these elements. (So we lose up to half our brain cells before we're born.) While the brain is pruning away excess neurons, a tremendous increase in dendrites adds substantially to the surface area available for synapses, the functional connections among cells. At the fastest rate, connections are built at the incredible speed of 3 billion a second. During the period from birth to age 10, the number of synaptic connections continues to rise rapidly, then begins to drop and continues to decline slowly into adult life.

Much credit for these insights into the developing brain must be given to Harry Chugani and Michael Phelps at the UCLA School of Medicine. Phelps co-invented the imaging technique called Positron Emission Tomography (PET), which visually depicts the brain's energy use. Using PET scans, Chugani has averaged the energy use of brains at various ages. His findings suggest that a child's peak learning years occur just as all those synapses are forming (1996). Chugani states that not only does the child's brain overdevelop during the early years, but that during these years, it also has a remarkable ability to adapt and recognize. It appears to develop some capacities with more ease at this time than in the years after puberty. These stages once called "critical periods" are more accurately described as "sensitive periods" or "windows of opportunity."

Probably the prime example of a window is vision. Lack of visual stimulation at birth, such as that which occurs with blindness or cataracts, causes the brain cells designed to interpret vision to atrophy or be diverted to other tasks. If sight is not restored by age 3, the child will be forever blind. . . . Similarly, the critical period for learning spoken language is totally lost by about age 10. If a child is born deaf, the 50,000 neural pathways that would normally activate the auditory cells remain silent, and the sound of the human voice, essential for learning language, can't get through. Finally, as the child grows older, the cells atrophy and the ability to learn spoken language is lost.

Not all windows close as tightly as those for vision and language development. Although learning a second language also depends on the stimulation of the neurons for the sounds of that language, and adult certainly can learn a second language and learn to speak it quite well. However, it is much more difficult to learn a foreign language after age 10 or so, and the language will probably be spoken with an accent. We might say that learning a second language is not a window that slams shut—it just becomes harder to open.

The implications of the findings regarding early visual auditory, motor, cognitive, and emotional development are enormous. Indeed, in many places work has already begun to enrich prenatal and early childhood environments. One example is the application of the research with premature infants. Premature babies who are regularly touched in their incubators gain weight at twice the rate of those who are not touched. Preemies whose parents visit them regularly vocalize twice as much in the third week as babies who are visited infrequently or not at all.

The research findings on early development are in stark contrast with the current situation in society.

- An estimated 12 percent of infants born in this country suffer significant reduction of their cognitive ability as a result of preterm birth; maternal smoking, alcohol use, or drug use in pregnancy; maternal and infant malnutrition; and postbirth lead poisoning or child abuse (Newman & Buka, 1997). Many of these factors could be eliminated with education programs for parents (or future parents). Twenty-five percent of all pregnant women receive no prenatal care.

- The early years, which are most crucial for learning, receive the least emphasis in federal, state, and local programs. We spend at least seven times more on the elderly than we do on children from birth to age 5.

- About half of all children in the United States are in full-time day care within the first year. Yet many day care centers not only are underfunded, but they are also staffed by untrained, low-paid workers and have too high an adult/child ratio. (Thirty-eight states do not require family child care providers to have *any* training prior to serving children.)

- Our present system generally waits until children fall behind in school, then places them in special education programs. With intense early intervention, we could reverse or prevent some adverse effects. It is possible that the billions of dollars spent on special education services might be better spent on early intervention.

Finding Four

Learning is strongly influenced by emotion.

The role of emotion in learning has received a good deal of press in the past few years. Daniel Goleman's *Emotional Intelligence* (1995) and Joseph LeDoux's *The Emotional Brain* (1996) have been instrumental in increasing our understanding of emotion.

Emotion plays a dual role in human learning. First, it plays a positive role in that the stronger the emotion connected with an experience, the stronger the memory of that experience. Chemicals in the brain send a message to the rest of the brain: "This information is important. Remember it." Thus, when we are able to add emotional input into learning experiences to make them more meaningful and exciting, the brain deems the information more important and retention is increased.

In contrast, LeDoux has pointed out that if the emotion is too strong (for example, the situation is perceived by the learner to be threatening), then learning is decreased. Whether you call this "downshifting" or decreasing the efficiency of the rational thinking cortex of the brain, it is a concept with many implications for teaching and learning.

Expect More Findings

On the horizon are many more studies that may have implications for the education of the human brain from birth through old age. Current research areas include these:

- The role of nutrition in brain functioning
- How brain chemicals affect mood, personality, and behavior

■ The connection between the mind/brain and the body

Rather than passively wait for research findings that might be useful, educators should help direct the search to better understand how the brain learns. James McGaugh of the University of California at Irvine has suggested that we educators need to be more proactive and tell the scientists, "Here's what we need to know. How can you help us?"

Should the Decade of the Brain lead to an enlightened Decade of Education? Eventually, yes. Along with cognitive research and the knowledge base we already have, findings from the neurosciences can provide us with important insights into how children learn. They can direct us as we seek to enrich the school experience for all children—the gifted, the creative, the learning disabled, the dyslexic, the average students, and all the children whose capabilities are not captured by IQ or other conventional measures. We can help parents and other caregivers understand the effects of maternal nutrition and prenatal drug and alcohol use and the role of early interaction and enriched environments. Brain research can also offer valuable guidance to policymakers and school administrators as they strive to focus their priorities.

Does what we are learning about the brain matter? It must, because our children matter. ■

References

Chugani, H. T. (1996). *Functional maturation of the brain.* Paper presented at the Third Annual Brain Symposium, Berkeley, California.

Diamond, M., & Hopson, J. (1998). *Magic trees of the mind: How to nurture your child's intelligence, creativity, and healthy emotions from birth through adolescence.* New York: Penguin Putnam.

Fitzpatrick, S. (1995, November). Smart brains: Neuroscientists explain the mystery of what makes us human. *American School Board Journal.*

Goleman, D. (1995). *Emotional intelligence: Why it can matter more than IQ.* New York: Bantam.

Kotulak, R. (1996). *Inside the brain: Revolutionary discoveries of how the mind works.* Kansas City, MO: Andrews & McMeely.

LeDoux, J. (1996). *The emotional brain: The mysterious underpinnings of emotional life.* New York: Simon & Schuster.

Newman, L., & Buka, S. L. (1997). *Every child a learner: Reducing risks of learning impairment during pregnancy and infancy.* Denver, CO: Education Commission of the States.

Ramey, C. T., & Ramey, S. L. (1996). *At risk does not mean doomed.* National Health/Education Consortium Occasional Paper #4. Paper presented at the meeting of the American Association of Science, February 1996.

P O S T N O T E

One of the many powerful research findings reported in this article is about the unparalleled importance of a child's earliest years. The authors point out the sobering contrast between the importance of early brain development and the lack of attention and funding we give to the development of children's brains. Although the research evidence appears to be piling up and underlining the importance of nurturing a young child's brain, American society seems to be going in the other direction. Increasingly, children are being dumped in front of television sets to passively absorb cartoons and commercials. And while there are, admittedly, many fine daycare centers, there are huge numbers of daycare facilities that are stunting children. At this critical period in their children's development, parents leave them with untrained and often uncaring personnel to languish for precious hour after hour with only minimal human attention to their basic health needs. These current child-care arrangements suggest that we are squandering our most precious natural resource, the healthy development of our young.

DISCUSSION UESTIONS

1. Which of the findings reported in this article struck you as the most important?

2. Which of the findings was the greatest surprise to you, and why?

3. If you were the American Czar of Education, and had just read this article, how would you rearrange our education spending priorities and current arrangements?

19 Leaving No Child Behind

Marian Wright Edelman

We are living at an incredible moral moment in history. Few human beings are blessed to anticipate or experience the beginning of a new century and millennium.

How will we say thanks for the life, for the earth, for the nation, and for the children God has entrusted to our care? What legacies, principles, values, and deeds will we stand for and send to the future through our children to their children and to a spiritually confused, balkanized, and violent world desperately hungering for moral leadership.

How will progress be measured over the next thousand years if we survive them? By the kill power and number of weapons of destruction we can produce and traffic at home and abroad, or by our willingness to shrink, indeed destroy, the prison of violence constructed in the name of peace and security?

By how many material things we can manufacture, advertise, sell, and consume, or by our rediscovery of more lasting non-material measure of success—a new Dow Jones for the purpose and quality of life in our families, neighborhoods, and national community? By how rapidly technology and corporate merger-mania can render human beings and human work obsolete, or by a better balance between corporate profits and corporate caring for children, families, and communities?

By how much a few at the top can get at the expense of the many at the bottom and in the middle, or by our struggle for a concept of enough for all Americans? By the glitz, style, and banality of too much of our culture, or by the substance of our struggle to rekindle an ethic of caring, community, and justice in a world driven by money, technology, and weaponry?

The answers lie in the values we stand for and decisions and actions we take today. What an opportunity for good and evil we Americans personally and collectively hold in our hands as parents, citizens, public school leaders, and as titular world leader in the post-Cold War and post-industrial era on the cusp of the third millennium . . .

A thousand years ago the United States was not even a dream. Copernicus and Galileo had not told us the earth was round or revolved around the sun. Gutenberg's Bible was not printed, Wycliffe had not translated it into English, and Martin Luther had not tacked his theses on the church door. The Magna Carta did not exist, Chaucer's and Shakespeare's tales had not been spun, and Bach's, Beethoven's, and Mozart's miraculous music had not been created to inspire, soothe, and heal our spirits. European serfs struggled in bondage while African empires flourished in independence. Native Americans peopled our land free of slavery's blight, and Hitler's Holocaust had yet to show the depths human evil can reach when good women and men remain silent or indifferent.

A thousand years from now, will civilization remain and humankind survive? Will America's dream be alive, be remembered, and be worth remembering? Will the United States be a blip or a beacon in history? Can our founding principle "that all men are created equal" and "are endowed by their Creator with certain inalienable rights" withstand the test of time, the tempests of politics, and become deed and not just creed for *every* child? Is America's dream big enough for every fifth child who is poor, every sixth child who is black, every seventh child who is Latino, and every eighth child who is mentally or physically challenged?

Marian Wright Edelman's article is excerpted from *The State of America's Children Yearbook 1996*, published by the Children's Defense Fund. Marian Wright Edelman, "Stand for Children: Leave No Child Behind." In *The State of America's Children Yearbook 1996* (Washington, DC: Children's Defense Fund, 1996): ix–xiii.

Protecting children is the moral litmus test of our humanity and the overarching moral challenge in our world and nation where millions of child lives are ravaged by the wars, neglect, abuse, and racial, ethnic, religious, and class divisions of adults. In the last decade, UNICEF reports, 2 million children have been killed, 4.5 million disabled, 12 million left homeless, more than 1 million orphaned or sundered from parents, and some 10 million have been traumatized by armed conflicts throughout the world.

In the United States since 1979, more than 50,000 children have been killed by guns in our homes, schools, and neighborhoods in a civil war on our own young. Although we are the world's leading military power, we stand by silent and indifferent as a classroomful of children are killed violently every two days from guns. About every day and a half, gun violence kills as many children as the children killed in the tragic Oklahoma City bombing.

In the richest nation in history, we appear unashamed that a child dies from poverty every 53 minutes, that children are the poorest group of Americans, and do not express outrage as political leaders of both parties propose policies to make them poorer. We talk about family values but turn our backs on real needs of families for jobs and decent wages and child care and health care. We tolerate a child welfare system that abuses and neglects children already abused and neglected by their families. While we bemoan a few child victims of abuse like Susan Smith's young sons and beautiful Elisa Izquierdo in New York City, we do not mend our cracked child welfare system that lets an abused child die every seven hours.

How much child suffering, death, and neglect will it take for you, me, religious, civic, school, and political leaders to stand up and cry out "enough" with our hearts and voices and votes to protect our young who are our sacred trust and collective American future?

A Mass Movement

When Jesus Christ invited little children to come unto him, He did not invite only rich, middle-class, white, male children without disabilities, from two-parents families, or our own children to come. He welcomed all children. There are no illegitimate children in God's sight. James Agee eloquently reminded: "In every child who is born under no matter what circumstances and of no matter what parents, the potentiality of the human race is born again, and in him, too, once more, and each of us, our terrific responsibility toward human life: toward the utmost idea of goodness, of the horror of terrorism, and of God."

Yet every day too many of us fail our terrific responsibility toward our own children and millions of other people's children who are America's and God's potentiality.

It is not just poor or minority children who are afflicted by the breakdown of moral, family, and community values today. The pollution of our airwaves, air, food, and water; growing economic insecurity among middle-class children and young families; rampant drug and alcohol abuse, teen pregnancy, and domestic violence among rich, middle-class, and poor alike; AIDS; random gun and terrorist violence; resurging racial intolerance in our places of learning work, and worship; and the crass, empty materialism of too much of our culture threaten every American child.

Every day in America, 2,660 children are born into poverty and 27 die from poverty. And every day 7,962 children of all races and classes are reported abused or neglected, and three die from abuse; 15 die from firearms and 2,833 drop out of school; 2,700 get pregnant; and 790 are born at low birthweight. We are first in the world in military and health technology but 18th in the industrialized world in infant mortality.

But it is poor children who suffer most. What kind of country permits this? A poor one? An undemocratic one? An uncaring one? A foolish one? One that ignores the biblical injunction to "defend the poor and fatherless and do justice to afflicted and needy"?

Our failure to place children first as parents, communities, corporate, civic, cultural, educational, and political leaders is our Achilles' heel and will be our future undoing. Indeed the present unraveling of our family fabric is a portent of what is to come if we do not correct course and regain our moral moorings.

The stresses and strains of making a living leave too many parents too little time with their children. Too many affluent parents are more preoccupied with material than with eternal things—with fun rather than faithfulness in providing the family rituals, continuity and consistent companionship children need to grow up healthy, caring, loving, and productive. Parenting itself is not a valued calling and people who care for children get the least support in America. Too many neighbors look out just for themselves and take little or no interest in each other's children. Too many business people seem to forget they are parents and family members and treat children as consumers to whom they can market excessively violent, sexually charged messages and products they would not want their own children to see or use. And too many faith communities fail to provide the strong moral leadership parents and communities need to meet their shared responsibilities to children.

What you stand for and do now as educational leaders—and encourage our political leaders to stand for during the final years of the century—will shape our nation's fate and our children's futures in the next century and millennium. It is time to call the moral question about whether America truly values and will stand up for children not just with words but with work; not just with promises but with leadership and investment in child health, early childhood education, after-school programs, and family economic security; not just with a speech or photo opportunity, but with sustained positive commitment to meet every child's needs. ■

POST NOTE

Marian Wright Edelman has for years been America's conscience for children's welfare. As the founder and president of the Children's Defense Fund, she has forcefully reminded Americans that, as a nation, we have turned a blind eye and a deaf ear to the worlds of many of our children, particularly our children of color. She has worked tirelessly with presidents, congressional representatives, governors, and bureaucrats to better children's lives. In this article she once again appeals to our consciences. Although the United States is the richest country in the world, it has the highest poverty rate for children among industrialized countries. Our health care system permits millions of children to fall between the cracks. About a million verified cases of child abuse occur each year. Guns kill more children in America than in all of Europe. How can this be? Who is looking out for the children?

DISCUSSION QUESTIONS

1. What reasons can you give for the sad state of so many children living in the United States?

2. What steps would you recommend to help remedy the problems experienced by children that Edelman identifies in the article?

3. Who besides Edelman can you identify as children's advocates? What actions have they taken to improve children's lives in America?

STUDENTS

Part Three
Schools

Schools and schooling in the United States have been the object of careful scrutiny and considerable criticism in recent years. Disappointing test scores, disciplinary problems, violence, and a lack of clear direction are all points of tension. In the past few years, there has been a shift in what educators, legislators, and critics say schools must do to address these and other problems. There is a sense that schools have gotten away from their most important purpose—that is, to prepare students academically and intellectually. Schools have lost sight, they say, of a sense of excellence.

Some of the selections in this section consider this emphasis, whereas others pose alternative solutions. The topics include characteristics of good schools, the size of schools, and some of the new approaches to school improvement.

Mythology and the American System of Education

David C. Berliner

W hat is wrong with the American public school system is that it runs on myths. As we all know, myths are functional. Thus the myths about the American public school system must be serving the purposes of some, though not necessarily all, citizens. But the myths about the American public schools may also be misleading the majority of the citizenry and undermining the American people's confidence in one of their most cherished institutions.

What is right about the American education system is that the myths are so far off the mark. Contrary to the prevailing opinion, the American public schools are remarkably good whenever and wherever they are provided with the human and economic resources to succeed.

Let us examine a [number] of these myths about U.S. education and see if they hold up. As we challenge the myths about what is wrong with our schools, we may learn what is right about them.

At the time this article was written, David Berliner was professor of education at Arizona State University, Tempe. Berliner, David, "Mythology and the American System of Education," *Phi Delta Kappan*, April 1993. Copyright © 1993 by Phi Delta Kappa. Reprinted by permission of the author and publisher.

Myth 1. Today's youth do not seem as smart as they used to be.

Fact: Since 1932 the mean I.Q. of white Americans aged 2 to 75 has risen about .3 points per year. Today's students actually average about 14 I.Q. points higher than their grandparents did and about seven points higher than their parents did on the well-established Wechsler or Stanford-Binet Intelligence Tests.[1] That is, as a group, today's school-age youths are, on average, scoring more than 30 percentile ranks higher than the group from which have emerged the recent leaders of government and industry. The data reveal, for example, that the number of students expected to have I.Q.s of 130 or more—a typical cutoff point for giftedness—is now about seven times greater than it was for the generation now retiring from its leadership positions throughout the nation and complaining about the poor performance of today's youth. In fact, the number of students with I.Q.s above 145 is now about 18 times greater than it was two generations ago. If the intelligence tests given throughout the U.S. are measuring the factors the general public includes in its definition of "smart," we are now smarter than we have ever been before.

Myth 2. Today's youths cannot think as well as they used to.

Fact: The increased scores on intelligence tests throughout the industrialized world have not been associated with those parts of the tests that call for general knowledge or for verbal or quantitative ability. We could assume performance in those areas to be positively affected by the increase in schooling that has occurred throughout the industrial world during the last two generations. Rather, it turns out that the major gains in performance on intelligence tests have been primarily in the areas of general problem-solving skills and the ability to handle abstract information of a decontextualized nature.[2] That is, the gains have been in the areas we generally label "thinking skills."

If we look at statistics on the Advanced Placement (AP) tests given to talented high school students every year, we find other evidence to bolster the claim that today's American youths are smarter than ever. In 1978, 90,000 high school students took the AP tests for college credit, while in 1990 that number had increased 255% to 324,000 students, who took a total of 481,000 different AP tests. Although the population taking these tests changed markedly over this time period, the mean score dropped only 11/100 of a point. Meanwhile, the percentage of Asians taking the AP tests tripled, the percentage of African-Americans taking the examinations doubled, and the percentage of Hispanics quadrupled.[3] Something that the public schools are doing is producing increasingly larger numbers of very smart students, for those tests are very difficult to pass.

Myth 3. University graduates are not as smart as they used to be and cannot think as well as they did in previous generations.

Fact: When we look at objective data, such as the scores on the Graduate Record Examination (GRE), we discover that the talented students who take this exam are smarter and think better than students who have for some time.[4] It is a myth to believe that today's college graduates are less talented than those from some previous time.

In the verbal area these students perform at about the same level as graduates did 20 years ago. But in the area of mathematical skills they far exceed the graduates of two decades ago. And in analytic skills—a measure of what we usually mean by "ability to think"—their performance has gone up during the decade that such skills have been measured.

Reliable data exist that appear to challenge the myth of poor performance by high school and college graduates. A very good data-based case can be made that the K–12 public schools and the colleges and universities are conferring many more degrees than in previous generations, and the products of all those schools are smarter than ever before.

Myth 4. The Scholastic Aptitude Test (SAT) has shown a marked decrease in mean score over the last 25 years, indicating the failure of our schools and our teachers to do their jobs.

Fact: To be sure, since 1965 the average SAT score has fallen. The *scaled* scores showed 70- or 90-point declines, a drop that frightened many government officials and the press. The scaled scores, however, are distorted records of performance. Not noted, for example, was the fact that, if we multiplied those scores by 10, the declines would have been 700 or 900 points—and we could have scared more people—while if we divided those scores by 10, the decline would have been only 7 or 9 points over a 30-year period. If we use the *raw* score to judge performance over time, as we should, the decline has actually been only 3.3% of the raw score total—about five fewer items answered correctly over a period of 30 or so years.

Far from being ashamed of this loss, educators should celebrate it. Why? Because it is explainable by the fact that much greater numbers of students in the bottom 60% of their graduating classes have been taking the SAT since the 1960s.[5] As educational opportunities and higher education became available to rural Americans and to members of traditionally underrepresented minorities, more of these students started taking the SAT. Since they were frequently from impoverished communities and from schools that offered a less rigorous academic curriculum and fewer advanced courses than wealthier schools, it is not surprising that they tended to score lower than advantaged, suburban, middle-class white students. This is why the mean number of items correct is less than it was. Most of the drop actually occurred between 1965 and 1975, not since. And the drop was primarily in the verbal, not the mathematics, measure.

Anyone rearing a child during the 1950s probably noticed an increase in television viewing. Associated with that change in the nature of childhood was a decrease in book reading and other verbal skills among the students who graduated from high school during the 1960s. Between the changes in the population taking the test and a changed pattern of child rearing because of TV, the decline we witnessed in SAT performance seems perfectly reasonable and not easily attributable to inadequate teachers or a failing school system. In fact, one might properly ask why we do not test our children on decoding information from complex audiovisual displays, or on remembering information presented in auditory and visual forms, or on comprehending extremely fast changing video arrays of information, and so forth. The media through which our children learn about the world changed dramatically in the 1950s, and so did our children's cognitive skills. Our assessment instruments, however, have not changed at all, and therefore some decrease in measured verbal ability is to be expected.

Actually, as an educator, I am filled with pride that we have played a major role in the achievement of two of America's most prized goals of the 1960s—a higher high school graduation rate, particularly for minority children, and increased access to higher education. We accomplished both goals with a loss of only a few correct answers on the SAT.

This is a remarkable achievement, I think, particularly when we look at other data. For example, from 1975 to 1990 the mean SAT scores of white, African-American, Asian-American, and Puerto Rican high school students went up.[6] Every one of the subgroups for which there are data has increased its average score on the SAT over the period during which the mean score dropped. The most likely cause of this nationwide increase in measured student achievement is an improvement in education. The decline of the average SAT score, used to bolster the myth

that the schools are failing, seems meaningless in light of this increase in the scores of *every* subgroup that attends our public schools. These data can more easily be used to make the point that our public schools must actually be improving.

Myth 5. The bottom students now score better on achievement tests, but the performance of the better students has declined. Our top students are not as good as they were.

Fact: There has been some concern that, while the performance of underachieving students in the U.S. (primarily poor, primarily those black and brown in color) has gotten better, it has been at the cost of underserving the better students (primarily the richer and whiter students). But that myth also appears not to be true. The SAT performance of all test-takers between 1975 and 1990 was unusually stable. Whatever drops there were in performance occurred prior to 1975; since then, scores have remained steady. But if we look at the performance of only those students who match the profile of those who *used to* take the SAT (students who were primarily white, suburban, middle and upper-middle class, higher in high school class rank, and so on), we see an increase between 1975 and 1990 of more than 30 SAT points—more than 10 percentile ranks.[7] Among these advantaged, primarily white youths, who were supposedly achieving less because they suffered from harmful desegregation policies (including forced busing), low standards of performance, poor teachers, no homework, too much television, low morals, and a host of other plagues, we find considerable improvement in performance on the SAT. What boosts my pride as an educator even more is that the Educational Testing Service, the developer of the test items for the SAT, has admitted that the test today is more difficult than it was in 1975.[8]

What have we learned about our students when we look at the facts about SAT scores?

Three things stand out. First, the supposedly great loss in America's intellectual capital, as measured by the average score on the SAT, is trivial, particularly since the average scores of every minority group went up for 15 years. Even the traditional college-bound students (those white middle-class students more likely to have taken the examination in 1975) are doing dramatically better today than they did in the seventies. Second, more American students are graduating from high school and thinking about college. That is why the mean SAT score did fall somewhat. Many of the students who took the SAT actually did go on to college, with the U.S. achieving one of the highest rates of college attendance in the world.[9] Third, the data we have from this well-accepted indicator of educational achievement will not support the accusation that, overall, we have a failing school system and inadequate teachers. The public and many educators bought this spurious charge in the past, and they should not do so any longer.

Myth 6. The performance of American students on standardized achievement tests reveals gross inadequacies.

Fact: This myth can be examined first by looking at the data collected by the National Assessment of Educational Progress (NAEP). The NAEP tests are given to national samples of 9-, 13-, and 17-year-olds in the subjects of mathematics, science, reading, writing, geography, and computer skills. Since the 1970s modest gains, at best, have been the rule. But what is more important is that one group of scientists reviewing the data believe unequivocally that the "national data on student performance do not indicate a decline in *any* area" (emphasis in the original). They have concluded that "students today appear to be as well educated as previously educated students."[10]

Summaries of the NAEP test results, purporting to be the nation's report card, inform us only that our students are performing the same over time. But there are other data in which we can take greater pride. When you investigate the norming procedures used with the most commonly purchased standardized tests, you find that it takes a higher score now to reach the 50th percentile rank than it did in previous decades. For example, on average, students in the 1980s scored higher on the California Achievement Tests than they did in the 1970s. Similarly, on the venerable Iowa Tests of Basic Skills, at the time of the last norming of the test, the test developer said that achievement was at an all-time high in nearly all test areas. The same trend was found in the renorming of the Stanford Achievement Test, the Metropolitan Achievement Tests, and the Comprehensive Tests of Basic Skills.[11]

In both reading and mathematics we find meaningful annual gains in percentile ranks from one representative norming sample to the next. If a school district does not gain more than one percentile rank a year in reading or mathematics, it loses out in the subsequent norming of the test because every other district is doing better than it did previously. If a district at the 60th percentile in reading and mathematics on the last set of norms kept the same program and teachers and had the same kinds of students, that district would be at about the 50th percentile on the new set of norms without any change in performance having occurred. Each renorming sets the mean higher—clear evidence of the increased productivity of the American schools.

Major standardized tests are renormed, on the average, approximately every seven years. A reasonable estimate is that, over one generation, norms have been redone around three times. Thus we can estimate that about 85% of today's public school students score higher on standardized tests of achievement than the average parent did.[12] But, as in the high jump, the bar keeps getting higher, and it takes better performance today than it did around 1965 to hit the 50th percentile.

While on the subject of standardized test performance, we should also examine the social studies survey developed by Diane Ravitch and Chester Finn and discussed in their gloomy 1987 book, *What Do Our 17-Year-Olds Know?* Their answer was that 17-year-olds know embarrassingly and shockingly little! Their conclusions were part of a barrage of similar arguments showered on the American people by E. D. Hirsch in his book *Cultural Literacy* (1987), by Allan Bloom in his book *The Closing of the American Mind* (1987), and by William Bennett in his report *To Reclaim a Legacy* (1984).[13] The popular press, of course, promoted the claim that today's children know less than they ever did and, therefore, that we are surely a nation at risk. The authors and the editorial writers throughout the land seemed to see nothing but doom for America if we didn't return to our old ways as a nation and as a people, to those mythical halcyon days.

Dale Whittington decided to check the claim that the 17-year-olds of the 1980s knew less than their parents, grandparents, and great-grandparents.[14] She examined social studies and history tests administered from 1915 onward and found 43 items on the Ravitch and Finn test that corresponded to items from other tests given at other times. Today's students were less knowledgeable than previous generations on about one-third of the items. They scored about the same on about one-third of those items. And they scored better on about one-third of the items. When compared to historical records, the data in Ravitch and Finn's study do not support the charge that today's 17-year-olds know less than any previous generation. In fact, given the less elitist composition of today's high schools, the case can be made that more 17-year-olds today know as much about social studies and historical facts as previous generations.

There may never have been any halcyon days to which to return. Every generation of adults has a tendency to find the next generation wanting. This social phenomenon has been recorded for about 2,500 years, since Socrates condemned the youths of Athens for their impertinence and ignorance. Ravitch and Finn, continuing this grand tradition, are merely disappointed that the next generation does not know what they themselves do.

What may we reasonably conclude from these studies of standardized tests? First, there is no convincing evidence of a decline in standardized test performance. This is true of intelligence tests, the SAT, the NAEP tests, and the standardized achievement tests used by local school districts. If any case for a change in these scores can be made, it is that the scores on standardized aptitude and achievement tests are going up, not down. Educators—working under almost intolerable conditions in some settings—have not failed society. It is incredibly difficult to keep academic achievement constant or to improve it with increasing numbers of poor children, unhealthy children, children from dysfunctional families, and children from dysfunctional neighborhoods.[15] Yet the public school system of the U.S. has actually done remarkably well as it receives, instructs, and nurtures children who are poor, who have no health care, and who come from families and neighborhoods that barely function. Moreover, they have done this with quite reasonable budgets.

Myth 7. Money is unrelated to the outcomes of schooling.

Fact: Current income can be predicted from the characteristics of the state school systems in which men received their education during the first half of the century. After the usual statistical controls are applied, it is found that teachers' salaries, class size, and the length of the school year are significant predictors of future earnings. States that had spent the most on their schools had produced the citizens with the highest incomes.[16]

It has also been found that higher salaries attract teaching candidates with higher academic ability and keep teachers in the profession longer.[17] Clearly, both of those benefits pay off for students.

An unusual set of data from Texas looks at the effects of teacher ability, teacher experience, class size, and professional certification on student performance in reading and mathematics. Data on millions of students from 900 districts were examined longitudinally from 1986 to 1990. Two rather simple findings emerged. First, teachers' academic proficiency explains 20% to 25% of the variation across districts in students' average scores on academic achievement tests. The smarter the teachers, the smarter their pupils appeared to be, as demonstrated by results on standardized achievement tests administered to both groups. Second, teachers with more years of experience have students with higher test scores, lower dropout rates, and higher rates of taking the SAT. Experience counts for about 10% of the variation in student test scores across the districts. The effects are such that an increase of 10% in the number of teachers within a district who have nine or more years' experience is predicted to reduce dropout rates by about 4% and to increase the percentage of students taking the SAT by 3%. Dollars appear to be more likely to purchase bright and experienced professionals, who, in turn, are more likely to provide us with higher-achieving and better-motivated students.[18]

The Texas data also show that, in grades 1 through 7, once class size exceeds 18 students, each student over that number is associated with a drop in district academic achievement. This drop is estimated to be very large—perhaps 35 percentile ranks on standardized tests—between a class size of, say, 25 and a class size of 18.

Furthermore, the percentage of teachers with master's degrees accounted for 5% of the variation in student scores across districts in grades 1 through 7. So we learn from the Texas study *and other data that support its conclusions* that academically more proficient teachers, who are more experienced, who are better educated, and who work with smaller classes, are associated with students who demonstrate significantly higher achievement.

It costs money to attract academically talented teachers, to keep them on the job, to update their professional skills, and to provide them with working conditions that enable them to perform well. Those districts that are willing and able to pay the costs attract the more talented teachers from neighboring districts, and they

eventually get the best in a region. Those districts can improve their academic performance relative to the other districts that are unable to pay the price, resulting in an education system that is inherently inequitable.

For those who point out that education costs have been rising faster than inflation, it is important to note that special education populations have been rising as well. It costs 2.3 times as much money to educate a child in special education as it does to educate a student in the regular education program.[19] Most of the real increases in educational expenditures over the last 20 years have been the result of increased costs for transportation, health care, and special education. They have not been connected with regular instruction or teachers' salaries.

Myth 8. The American public school system is a bloated bureaucracy, top-heavy in administrators and administrative costs.

Fact: The average number of employees that each administrator supervises in education is among the highest of any industry or business in America. With 14.5 employees for every one administrator, education is leaner than, for example, the transportation industry (9.3 to one), the food products industry (8.4 to one), the utilities industry (6.6 to one), the construction industry (6.3 to one), and the communications industry (4.7 to one). Central office professionals plus principals, assistant principals, and supervisors in the public schools make up a mere 4.5% of the total employee population of the schools. If all these supervisory personnel were fired and their salaries given to teachers, the salaries of teachers would rise no more than 5%. And if those supervisors' salaries were redistributed to reduce class size, the size of classes nationwide would be reduced by an average of one student![20] The administration of education is not a major cost factor. That is a myth.

Myth 9. American schools are too expensive. We spend more on education than any other country in the world, and we have little to show for it.

Fact: Former Secretaries of Education William Bennett, Lauro Cavazos, and Lamar Alexander said we spend more on education than do our rivals Germany and Japan. Former Assistant Secretary of Education Chester Finn wrote in the *New York Times* that we "spend more per pupil than any other nation." And, just before the education summit of 1989, John Sununu, once President Bush's chief of staff and close advisor, declared that "we spend twice as much [on education] as the Japanese and almost 40 percent more than all the other major industrialized countries of the world."[21] But it appears that the people who made these claims, like David Stockman before them, made up the numbers as they went along.

The U.S., according to UNESCO data, is tied with Canada and the Netherlands, and all three fall behind Sweden in the amount spent per pupil for K–12 education and higher education.[22] We look good in this comparison because we spend much more than most nations on higher education and have two to three times more people per 100,000 enrolled in higher education than most other countries. When only the expenditures for preprimary, primary, and secondary education are calculated, however, we actually spend much less than the average industrialized nation.

In 1988 dollars we rank ninth among 16 industrialized nations in per-pupil expenditures for grades K–12, spending 14% less than Germany, 30% less than Japan, and 51% less than Switzerland. We can also compare ourselves to other countries in terms of the percentage of per-capita income spent on education. When we do that comparison, we find that, out of 16 industrialized nations, 13 of them spend a greater percentage of per-capita income spent on K–12 education than we do. If we were to come up just to the *average*

percentage of per-capita income spent on education by the 15 other industrialized nations, we would have to invest an additional $20 billion per year in K–12 education![23] The most recent report by the Organisation for Economic Cooperation and Development on education in the European Community and some other industrialized nations also finds the U.S. low in its commitment to education. That report places the U.S. behind 12 other industrialized nations in the percentage of the Gross Domestic Product devoted to public and private education.[24]

Perhaps we do not teach as much in the K–12 schools as some would like. But we do not have to. A relatively large percentage of our students go on to postsecondary studies, where they can acquire the learning the nation needs them to have. Our nation has simply chosen to invest its money in higher education. Consequently, our education system ultimately provides about 25% of each year's group of high school graduates with college degrees, and it is the envy of the world. We run a costly and terrific K–16 school system, but we must acknowledge that we run an impoverished and relatively less good K–12 school system.

Moreover, in many of the countries that spend more per capita than we do, the funding is relatively even across regions and cities. But in our nation, we have, to use Jonathan Kozol's scathing formulation, "savage inequalities" in our funding of schools.[25] Even though the national *average* for per-pupil expenditures in the primary and secondary schools is relatively low, included in the calculation of that figure are the much, much lower annual per-pupil expenditures of those school districts at the bottom of the income distribution. To our shame, conditions in many of those districts resemble conditions in the nonindustrialized nations of the world.

Former President George Bush perpetuated the myth we address here when he declared at the education summit of 1989 that the U.S. "lavishes unsurpassed resources on [our children's] schooling."[26] What he should have said was that we are among the most cost-efficient nations in the world, with an amazingly high level of productivity for the comparatively low level of investment that our society makes in K–12 education.

Myth 10. Our high schools, colleges, and universities are not supplying us with enough mathematicians and scientists to maintain our competitiveness in world mark ets.

Fact: There are solid data to suggest that the supply of mathematicians and scientists is exceeding the demand for them! First of all, we now exceed or are at parity with our economic competitors in terms of the technical competence of our work force—for example, in the number of engineers and physical scientists we have per hundred workers.[27] So, if we have lost our economic edge in the world marketplace, it may well be because of poor business management and faulty government economic policies, but it is certainly not because of the lack of a technically skilled work force. But that is the present situation. Projections of the future supply in these fields do look gloomy, but that is true only as long as the economy's demand for such individuals is not examined. When demand and supply are examined together, it turns out that the economy is not now able to absorb all the scientists and engineers that we produce. With no increase in the rate of supply of scientists and engineers, we will accumulate a surplus of about one million such individuals by the year 2010. Given the probable reduction in military spending during the next few years, the glut of trained scientists is likely to be even more serious than was forecast a year or two ago. Moreover, the National Science Foundation recently apologized to Congress for supplying it with phony data a few years back. That agency now admits that its predictions of shortages in supply were grossly inflated.

In my most cynical moments, I think that the business community and the politicians are demanding that the schools produce even more engineers and scientists because the labor of these individuals is currently so expensive. An oversupply will certainly drive down the salaries of such workers.

The myth of the coming shortage of technically able workers has been debunked by many economists.[28] In fact, it has been estimated that, if the entering workers had an average of only one-fourth of a grade level more education than those now retiring from the labor force, all the needs of the future economy would be served.

How can this be? The answer is in the mix of jobs available in the future. The five most highly skilled occupational groups will make up only about 6% of the job pool by the year 2000. On the other hand, service jobs, requiring the least technical skill, will actually grow the fastest overall in the next few years, and they will constitute about 17% of the job pool by the year 2000. Apparently this nation is not in any danger of failing to meet its technological needs.

Furthermore, research has found that, during the first eight years on the job, young adults without a college education receive no rewards for the labor market for their abilities in science, mathematical reasoning, or language arts.[29] The fact that so many American high school students avoid rigorous mathematics and science courses may actually be a rational response to the lack of rewards for these skills in the labor market. . . .

Let me be clear. We have failing schools in this nation. But where they fail we see poverty, inadequate health care, dysfunctional families, and dysfunctional neighborhoods. Where our public schools succeed—in Princeton, New Jersey; in Grosse Pointe, Michigan; in Manhasset, New York—we see well-paying jobs, good health care, functional families, and functional neighborhoods. Families that can live in dignity send the schools children who have hope. Those children we can educate quite well. Families that have lost their dignity function poorly. They send us children with no hope for the future. Those children we cannot easily educate.

The agenda America should tackle if we want to improve schooling has nothing to do with national tests, higher standards, increased accountability, or better math and science achievement. Instead, we should focus our attention and our energies on jobs, health care, reduction of violence in families and neighborhoods, and increased funding for day care, bilingual education, summer programs for young people, and so forth. It is estimated that 100,000 handguns enter the schools each day. It seems to me that this is a greater problem than the nation's performance in international mathematics competitions. ■

Notes

1. J. R. Flynn, "Massive IQ Gains in 14 Nations: What IQ Tests Really Measure," *Psychological Bulletin,* vol. 101, 1987, pp. 171–91.

2. Ibid.

3. Paul E. Barton and Richard J. Coley, *Performance at the Top: From Elementary Through Graduate School* (Princeton, N.J.: Educational Testing Service, 1991).

4. Ibid.

5. C. C. Carson, R. M. Huelskamp, and T. D. Woodall, "Perspectives on Education in America," Third Draft, Sandia National Laboratories, Albuquerque, N.M., May 1991.

6. Ibid.

7. Ibid.

8. Ibid.

9. Organisation for Economic Cooperation and Development, *Education at a Glance* (Paris: Centre for Educational Research and Innovation, 1992).

10. Carson, Huelskamp, and Woodall, op. cit.

11. Robert L. Linn, M. Elizabeth Graue, and Nancy M. Sanders, "Comparing State and District Test Results to National Norms: The Validity of Claims That 'Everyone Is Above Average,'" *Educational Measurement: Issues and Practice,* Fall 1990, pp. 5–14.

12. Robert L. Linn, personal communication, February 1991.

13. Diane Ravitch and Chester E. Finn, Jr., *What Do Our 17-Year-Olds Know?* (New York: Harper & Row, 1987); E. D. Hirsch, Jr., *Cultural Literacy: What Every American Needs to Know* (Boston: Houghton Mifflin, 1987); Allan Bloom, *The Closing of the American Mind: How Higher Education Has Failed Democracy and Impoverished the Souls of Today's Students* (New York: Simon & Schuster, 1987); and William J. Bennett, *To Reclaim a Legacy: A Report on the Humanities in Higher Education* (Washington, D.C.: National Endowment for the Humanities, 1984).

14. Dale Whittington, "What Have 17-Year-Olds Known in the Past?," *American Educational Research Journal,* vol. 28, 1991, pp. 759–83.

15. National Commission on Children, *Beyond Rhetoric: A New American Agenda for Children and Families* (Washington, D.C.: U.S. Government Printing Office, 1991).

16. David Card and Alan B. Krueger, "Does School Quality Matter? Returns to Education and the Characteristics of Public Schools in the United States," Working Paper No. 3358, Bureau of Economic Research, Washington D.C., 1990.

17. Charles F. Manski, "Academic Ability, Earnings, and the Decision to Become a Teacher: Evidence for the National Longitudinal Study of the High School Class of 1972," in David A. Wise, ed., *Public Sector Payrolls* (Chicago: University of Chicago Press, 1987); and Richard J. Murnane and R. J. Olsen, "The Effects of Salaries and Opportunity Costs on Duration in Teaching: Evidence from Michigan," *Review of Economics and Statistics,* vol. 71, 1989, pp. 347–52.

18. Ronald F. Ferguson, "Paying for Public Education: New Evidence on How and Why Money Matters," *Harvard Journal on Legislation,* vol. 28, 1991, pp. 465–98.

19. Glen Robinson and David Brandon, *Perceptions About American Education: Are They Based on Facts?* (Arlington, Va.: Educational Research Service, 1992).

20. Ibid.

21. Both Finn and Sununu are quoted in M. Edith Rasell and Lawrence Mishel, *Shortchanging Education: How U.S. Spending on Grades K–12 Lags Behind Other Industrialized Nations* (Washington, D.C.; Economic Policy Institute, 1990).

22. Ibid.

23. Ibid.

24. Organisation for Economic Cooperation and Development, op. cit.

25. Jonathan Kozol, *Savage Inequalities* (New York: Crown, 1991).

26. George H. Bush, speech delivered at education summit, University of Virginia, Charlottesville, 28 September 1989.

27. Carson, Huelskamp, and Woodall, op. cit.

28. Lawrence Mishel and Ruy A. Texeira, *The Myth of the Coming Labor Shortage: Jobs, Skills, and Incomes of America's Workforce 2000* (Washington, D.C.: Economic Policy Institute, 1991).

29. John H. Bishop, "The Productivity Consequences of What Is Learned in High School," *Journal of Curriculum Studies,* vol. 22, 1990, pp. 101–26.

P O S T N O T E

David Berliner challenges many widely held beliefs about the American educational system. He asserts that schools are not nearly as bad as many critics claim and that they are, in fact, doing as good a job of educating our youth as has ever been done in U.S. history. Where problems exist, Berliner says, they are more the result of poverty, dysfunctional families and neighborhoods, and inadequate health care. Where problems don't exist, the educational system produces good results.

Some people simply don't accept Berliner's arguments, whereas others agree with him that American schools are doing as well as ever. But even many supporters believe the educational system must be restructured to achieve a much higher level of learning for a greater number of students in order for the United States to be economically competitive in a global society. This perspective is held by many business leaders who want employees to be well-educated problem solvers.

D I S C U S S I O N Q U E S T I O N S

1. Which of the myths discussed by Berliner did you believe before reading the article? Have you changed your mind after reading the article? If so, how?

2. Do you disagree with any points that Berliner made? If so, which ones and why?

3. If Berliner's points are valid, why do you think the general public has such a negative perception about the American educational system? Or do they?

21
A Tale of Two Schools

Larry Cuban

For this entire century, there has been conflict among educators, public officials, researchers, and parents over whether traditionalist or progressive ways of teaching reading, math, science, and other subjects are best. Nowhere has this unrelenting search for the one best way of teaching a subject or skill been more obvious than in the search for "good" schools. Progressives and traditionalists each have scorn for those who argue that there are many versions of "good" schools. Partisan debates have consumed policymakers, parents, practitioners, and researchers, blocking consideration of the unadorned fact that there is more than one kind of "good" school.

What follows is a verbal collage of two elementary schools I know well. School A is a quiet, orderly school where the teacher's authority is openly honored by both students and parents. The principal and faculty seek out students and parental advice when making schoolwide decisions. The professional staff sets high academic standards, establishes school rules that respect differences among students, and demands regular study habits from the culturally diverse population. Drill and practice are parts of each teacher's daily lesson. Report cards with letter grades are sent home every nine weeks. A banner in the school says: Free Monday through Friday: Knowledge—Bring Your Own Container." These snippets describe what many would call a "traditional" school.

School B prizes freedom for students and teachers to pursue their interests. Most classrooms are multiage (6- to 9-year-olds and 7- to 11-year-olds). Every teacher encourages student-initiated projects and trusts children to make the right choices. In this school, there are no spelling bees; no accelerated reading program; no letter or numerical grades. Instead, there is a year-end narrative in which a teacher describes the personal growth of each student. Students take only those standardized tests required by the state. A banner in the classroom reads: "Children need a place to run! explore! a world to discover." This brief description describes what many would call a "progressive" school.

I will argue that both schools A and B are "good" schools. What parents, teachers, and students at each school value about knowledge, teaching, learning, and freedom differs. Yet both public schools have been in existence for 25 years. Parents have chosen to send their children to the schools. Both schools have staffs that volunteered to work there. And both schools enjoy unalloyed support: Annual surveys of parent and student opinion have registered praise for each school; each school has had a waiting list of parents who wish to enroll their sons and daughters; teacher turnover at each school have been virtually nil.

Moreover, by most student-outcome measures, both schools have compiled enviable records. In academic achievement, measured by standardized tests, School A was in the top 10 schools in the entire state. School B was in the upper quartile of the state's schools.

These schools differ dramatically from one another in how teachers organize their classrooms, view learning, and teach the curriculum. Can both of them be "good"? The answer is yes.

What makes these schools "good"? They have stable staffs committed to core beliefs about what is best for students and the community, parents

Larry Cuban is a professor of education at Stanford University, Stanford, California. Reprinted with permission from *Education Week*, Vol. 17, No. 20, January 28, 1998, and from the author.

with beliefs that mirror those of the staffs, competent people working together, and time to make it all happen. Whether one was traditional or progressive was irrelevant. The century-long war of words over traditional vs. progressive schooling is a cul-de-sac, a dead end argument that needs to be retired once and for all.

What partisans of each fail to recognize is that this pendulum-like swing between traditional and progressive schooling is really a deeper political conflict over what role schools should play in society. Should schools in a democracy primarily concentrate on making citizens who fulfill their civic duties? Should schools focus on efficiently preparing students with skills credentials to get jobs and maintain a healthy economy? Honor individual excellence yet treat everyone equally? Or should schools do everything they can to develop the personal and social capabilities of each and every child? For almost two centuries of tax-supported public schooling in the United States, all of these goals have been viewed as both important and achievable.

The war of words between progressives and traditionalists has been a proxy for this political struggle over goals. Progressive vs. traditionalist battles over discipline in schools, national tests, tracking students by their performance, and school uniforms mask a more fundamental tension in this country over which goals for public schools should have priority.

The problem lies not in knowing how to make schools better. Many parents and educators already know what they want and possess the requisite knowledge and skills to get it. Schools A and B are examples of that knowledge in action. The problem is determining what goals public schools should pursue, given the many goals that are desired and inescapable limits on time, money, and people.

Determining priorities among school goals is a political process of making choices that involves policymakers, school officials, taxpayers, and parents. Deciding what is important and how much should be allocated to it is at the heart of the process. Political parties, lobbies, and citizen groups vie for voters' attention. Both bickering and deliberation arise from the process. Making a school "good" is not a technical problem that can be solved by experts or scientific investigation into traditional or progressive approaches. It is a struggle over values that are worked out in elections for public office, tax referendums, and open debate in civic meetings, newspapers, and TV talk shows. Yet these simple distinctions between the political and the technical, between goals for schools and the crucial importance of the democratic process determining which goals should be primary, seem to have been lost in squabbles over whether progressive or traditional schools are better.

And that is why I began with my descriptions of the two schools. They represent a way out of this futile struggle over which kind of schooling is better than the other. I argue that both these schools are "good."

One is clearly traditional in its concentration on passing on to children the best knowledge, skills, and values in society. The other is progressive in its focus on students' personal and social development. Each serves different goals, each honors different values. Yet—and this is the important point that I wish to drive home—these seemingly different goals are not inconsistent. They derive from a deeply embedded, but seldom noticed, common framework of what parents and taxpayers want their public schools to achieve.

What is different, on the surface, are the relative weights that each "good" school gives to these goals, how they go about putting into practice what they seek, and the words that they use to describe what they do. The common framework I refer to is the core duty of tax-supported public schools in a democracy to pass on to the next generation democratic attitudes, values, and behaviors. Too often we take for granted the linkage between the schools that we have and the kind of civic life that we want for ourselves and our children. What do I mean by democratic attitudes, values, and behaviors? A few examples may help:

■ Open-mindedness to different opinions and a willingness to listen to such opinions.

- Respect for values that differ from one's own.
- Treating individuals decently and fairly, regardless of background.
- A commitment to talk through problems, reason, deliberate, and struggle toward openly-arrived-at compromises.

I doubt whether partisans for traditional and progressive schools, such as former U.S. Secretary of Education William J. Bennett, educator Deborah Meier, and academics like Howard Gardner and E. D. Hirsch Jr., would find this list unimportant.

Tax-supported public schools in this country were not established 150 years ago to get jobs for graduates. They were not established to replace the family or church. They were established to make sure that children grew into literature adults who respected authority, could make reasoned judgments, accept differences of opinions, and fulfill their civic duties to participate in the political life of their communities. Over time, of course, as conditions changed, other responsibilities were added to the charter of public schools. But the core duty of schools, teachers, and administrators—past and present—has been to turn students into citizens who can independently reason through difficult decisions, defend what they have decided, and honor the rule of law. Our traditional and progressive schools each have been working on these paramount and essential tasks.

Consider such democratic values as individual freedom and respect for authority. In School A, students have freedom in many activities, as long as they stay within the clear boundaries established by teachers on what students can do and what content they must learn. Staff members set rules for behavior and academic performance, but students and parents are consulted; students accept the limits easily, even enjoying the bounded freedom that such rules give them. School A's teachers and parents believe that students' self-discipline grows best by setting limits on freedom and learning what knowledge pre-

vious generations counted as important. From these will evolve students' respect for the rule of law and their growth into active citizens.

In School B, more emphasis is placed on children's individual freedom to create, diverge from the group, and work at their own pace. Students work on individually designed projects over the year. They respect teachers' authority but often ask why certain things have to be done. The teacher gives reasons and, on occasion, negotiates over what will be done and how it will be done. School B's teachers and parents believe that students' self-discipline, regard for authority, and future civic responsibility evolve out of an extended, but not total, freedom.

Thus, I would argue, both of these schools prize individual freedom and respect for authority, but they define each value differently in how they organize the school, view the curriculum, and engage in teaching. Neither value is ignored. Parents, teachers, and students accept the differences in how their schools puts these values into practice. Moreover, each school, in its individual way, cultivates the deeper democratic attitudes of open-mindedness, respect for others' values, treating other decently, and making deliberate decisions.

Because no researcher could ever prove that one way of schooling is better than the other, what matters to me in judging whether schools are "good" is whether they are discharging their primary duty to help students think and act democratically. What we need to talk about openly in debates about schooling is not whether a traditional school is better or worse than a progressive one, but whether that school concentrates on instilling within children the virtues that a democratic society must have in each generation. Current talk about national goals is *not* about this core goal of schooling. It is about being first in the world in science and math achievement; it is about preparing students to use technology to get better jobs. Very little is said about the basic purpose of schooling except in occasional one-liners or a paragraph here and there in speeches by top public officials.

What are other criteria for judging goodness? I have already suggested parent, student, and teacher satisfaction as reasonable standards to use in determining how "good" a school is. I would go further and add: To what degree has a school achieved its own explicit goals? By this criterion, School A is a clear success. Parents and teachers want children to become literate, respectful of authority, and responsible. Although School B scores well on standardized tests, parents and teachers are less interested in test results. What School B wants most are students who can think on their own and work together easily with those who are different from themselves; students who, when faced with a problem, can tackle it from different vantage points and come up with solutions that are creative. Parents and teachers have plenty of stories about students' reaching these goals, but there are few existing tests or quantitative measures that capture these behaviors.

So, another standard to judge "goodness" in a school is to produce graduates who possess these democratic behaviors, values, and attitudes. This is, and always has been, the common, but often ignored, framework for our public schools. It has been lost in the battle of words and programs between public officials and educators who champion either traditional or progressive schools. A "good" school, I would argue, even in the face of the technological revolution and globalization of the U.S. economy in this century, is one that has students who display those virtues in different situations during their careers as students and afterwards as well.

My criteria, then, for determining good schools are as follows: Are parents, staff, and students satisfied with what occurs in the school? Is the school achieving the explicit goals it has set for itself? And, finally, are democratic behaviors, values, and attitudes evident in the students?

Why is it so hard to get past the idea that there is only one kind of "good" school? Varied notions of goodness have gotten mired in the endless and fruitless debate between traditionalists and progressives. The deeply buried but persistent impulse in the United States to create a "one best system," a solution for every problem, has kept progressives and traditionalists contesting which innovations are best for children, while ignoring that there are more ways than one to get "goodness" in schools.

Until Americans shed the view of a one best school for all, the squabbles over whether a traditional schooling is better than a progressive one will continue. Such a futile war of words ignores the fundamental purposes of public schooling as revitalizing democratic virtues in each generation and, most sadly, ignores the good schools that already exist. ∎

P O S T N O T E

What one defines as a good school depends on what one values, says Larry Cuban, which makes perfectly good sense. A person's educational philosophy will determine how that person views schooling, teaching, and curriculum. Thus, many different types of good schools can and do exist.

Cuban's point argues for giving parents choice about the kind of school that their children attend. By offering different kinds of schools that represent different educational philosophies and by allowing parents to select the school of their choice, school boards can better satisfy parents' educational preferences. In this way, more parents will believe that their children attend good schools.

1. Of the two schools that Cuban describes in his article, would you prefer to teach in School A or School B? Why?

2. Describe the characteristics of the kind of school that you would consider to be "good."

3. Do you agree with Cuban's assertion that the common framework of public schools should be to "pass on to the next generation democratic attitudes, values, and behaviors." Is there anything else that you would add to this common framework?

22

The Big Benefits of Smallness

Deborah W. Meier

Small schools come as close to being a panacea for America's educational ills as we're likely to get. Smallness is a prerequisite for the climate and culture that we need to develop the habits of heart and mind essential to a democracy. Such a culture emerges from authentic relationships built on face-to-face conversations by people engaged in common work and common work standards.

A good school is a work in progress: a place to tinker, fix, and sometimes even to throw out and start over. Creating such a school requires keeping in mind both visionary ideas and mundane daily details. A good school is never satisfied with itself. As a result, there's never enough time. But it turns out that everything is easier when we get the scale right. Getting the size right is the necessary, though not sufficient, first step.

Until my own school days, small schools were the rule rather than the exception. In a few places, like New York City, rapid population booms and high-priced land produced America's first truly big school buildings. They didn't work

Deborah W. Meier was founder and director of several small New York City public schools, including Central Park East Elementary School in 1974 and Central Park East Secondary School from 1985 to 1995. She is now associated with the Teaching and Learning Department at Harvard University. Meier, Deborah, "The Big Benefits of Smallness." *Educational Leadership,* September 1996, pp. 12–15. Reprinted by permission from ASCD. All rights reserved.

then any better than they do now. I have friends who swear they did. When I show them the statistics, they are startled: "But everyone I knew graduated, I'm sure of it." True, but they just never knew all those others who didn't.

Big school buildings are mistakes that are hard to undo, but fortunately, big buildings can house small schools. Of the four Central Park East schools we created in East Harlem's District 4, none ever had its own separate building. The district used every available extra space for the new small schools, while it gradually downsized the larger ones. If four teachers had a good idea, the district said "Go to it." In the end, 52 schools occupied the original 20 buildings.

Big Buildings and Small Subschools

If one looks closely, big high schools are, in fact, always made up of small schools. The kids create them for survival's sake. The trouble is, only two groups of kids—each a small minority—are able to join the subgroup where the adults are significant people to them. These are 1) the academic stars—who are in the honors and advanced placement classes, leaders of the student government or debating society, or editors of the school newspaper; and 2) the star athletes who belong to various sports teams. The faculties know these kids well; they share common values and aspirations; and the kids and teachers thrive on their mutual admiration and respect. Occasionally there are subschools for musicians or artists or actors.

But the vast majority of kids—probably 70–80 percent—belong to enclaves that include no grown-ups. A few loners belong nowhere. In the good old days, most of this latter group dropped out along the way to join real grown-up occupations. The problem is, there are no longer grown-up occupations for the dropouts to join. So they stay with us—at least officially. Half in, half out, disconnected from the culture that schools are intended to impart. In short, the schools we've invented aren't organized to assist this other 70 percent. They make do as best they can. And the specialty schools—the honors track of one sort or another—have had to organize themselves against the grain of the school's dominant peer culture. What we small school fanatics are working for is schools that do for all kids what we now do for a few. We want to make that the dominant culture of the school.

Seven Reasons

There are at least seven reasons that smallness—300–400 students—works best and offers probably the only chance of carrying out serious reforms in pedagogy and curriculum.

1. *Governance.* Ideally, a school's total faculty should be small enough to meet around one common table. Whether it's hammering out a solution to a crisis or working though a long-range problem, sustained attention over time is required of everyone. Studies in group efficacy suggest that once you have more than 20 people in a group, you've lost it. Some people will be marking papers, some writing their lesson plans, and others silently disagreeing.

I'm always puzzled when I hear that a staff of 100 went off for a one-day retreat with parents, district personnel, and sundry others, and came up with a vision, a mission, and some objectives. The power of the ideas behind these rushed jobs is not likely to go far in the tricky business of educating kids. Committees can do useful spade work, but in running a school, committees work only for relatively unimportant decisions. Unless we're all committed to the goal, what we do behind our closed doors won't be implemented just because a committee of our peers decided on it. Further, only in a small school can we try something on Monday, put it into effect on Tuesday, and change our minds on Wednesday.

We teachers went into teaching because we love working with kids, not going to meetings. We thus need a faculty small enough so that knowing one another's ideas and work is feasible within the normal constraints of a 24-hour day, and without putting kids in second place.

2. *Respect.* Students and teachers in schools of thousands cannot know one another well. And if we do not know one another, we may mishear one another. Families, teachers, staff, and students may assume disrespect where none was intended. ("She *looked* at me." "He didn't even say hello.") The more diverse our students' backgrounds, and the greater the gap between the faculty's and kids' cultures, the greater the misunderstandings will be.

We will think we have made our point when in fact we've been thoroughly misunderstood. We will sabotage one another thoughtlessly, because we didn't know better. We will be lax and permissive when we need to be tough and demanding; we will nag when that's bound to cause trouble. Toughness that comes from respect and toughness that comes from fear and scorn produce opposite results. A culture of respect rests on mutual knowledge, and even then it's hardly automatic. Small schools make such knowledge a possibility.

3. *Simplicity.* One of the first things Ted Sizer told us when we started Central Park East Secondary School in 1985 was to keep the organizational side simple. Otherwise, he said, you'll be tempted to simplify the minds and hearts of the children and subject matter you intend to teach. In most schools we've chosen just this; we've created a complex bureaucracy, and then simplified—or standardized—the kids, teaching them a one-size-fits-all curriculum so that we can more easily grade, measure, and categorize them. The larger the school, the greater the temptation to treat one another like interchangeable parts, and our subject matter as discreet and unconnected.

4. *Safety.* Anonymity breeds not only contempt and anger, but also physical danger. The data are clear that the smaller the school, the fewer the incidents of violence, as well as vandalism and just plain rudeness. Strangers are easily

spotted, and teachers can respond quickly to a student who seems on the verge of exploding. Small schools offer what metal detectors and guards cannot: the safety and security of being where you are well known by people who care for you.

5. *Parental Involvement.* Schools are intimidating places for many parents—parents feel like intruders, strangers, outsiders. And nothing seems more foolish than going to parent night and seeing a slew of adults who don't know your kid, have very little investment in him or her, and whose opinion and advice make one feel less, not more, powerful. When kids reach high school, schools usually give up on parents entirely (except to scold them). But high school students don't need their parents any less, just differently.

When the school is small enough, probably someone there knows your kid well enough, and maybe also likes him or her enough, to create a powerful alliance with you. Smallness doesn't guarantee such an alliance, but it makes it reasonable to put time into creating one.

In small high schools like those in our New York City network, each staff member is responsible for knowing well a group of fewer than 15 students over several years. The schools schedule opportunities for the student, family, and advisor to meet—often. The student's work is at the center of these meetings, and the meetings end with an understanding and a plan for what comes next. In large urban schools, by contrast, such meetings are often not useful to any of the parties. This could be why some parents don't show up; they're reserving their time for more important things.

6. *Accountability.* No one needs long computer printouts, statistical graphs, and educational mumbo jumbo to find out how a teacher, kid, or school is doing when the scale of the school is right. Parents can simply walk around the school, listen to teachers and kids, look at the young peoples' work, and raise questions. It's not hard to know how many kids graduated,

who went on to college, and how many dropped out along the way. (Try finding this out in any big urban high school!) In a small school, the principal doesn't have to rely on bureaucratic data or the grapevine. In a glance, he or she can take the temperature of the school on a given day—see how the substitute is doing, check on a particular kid, and follow up on yesterday's conversation.

How likely is it that a principal of a school with 100 teachers knows how they really teach? Only in small schools can we figure out how to hold a faculty responsible for the work of the school as a whole; to create a responsible community instead of a collection of classrooms. There's no guarantee, of course: teachers can use their greater collegiality to make one another feel good instead of encouraging good teaching (teaching is hard, and we long for a friendly word). But there is a good likelihood of peer accountability—a hallmark of a serious profession.

Finally, scandals and outrages may be no less likely in a small school, but they're a heck of a lot harder to hide. Padded payrolls, ghost students, or missing equipment won't go unnoticed. As in a small town, phony data stick out; secrets are hard to keep. At Central Park East Secondary School, there are no closed meetings. Visitors are invited in almost daily (they're a real-life check on our standards). Schools that are small can more easily take seriously their public character. In doing so, they go a long way toward being accountable.

7. *Belonging.* In small schools, the other 70 percent belong. Every kid is known, every kid belongs to a community that includes adults. Relationships are cross-disciplinary, cross-generational, and cross-everything else. Kids don't just know the adults they naturally like, or the ones who naturally like them. They may hate some grown-ups and love others, but they recognize everyone as members of the same human club. The good news is that kids like to be members of such cross-generational clubs. (Or at least most do, at least some of the time!) And, if parents are part of the process, they like to join, too—even part-time.

In small schools, we're more likely to pass on to students the habits of heart and mind that define an educated person—not only formally, in lesson plans and pedagogical gimmicks, but in hallway exchanges, arguments about important matters, and resolutions of ordinary differences. We're more likely to show kids in our daily discourse that grown-ups—models outside their homes—use reasoning and evidence to resolve issues. We can teach them what it's like to be a grown-up—bring them into our culture, but only if we're part of a world that they find compelling, credible, and accessible. And only if we're better able as adults to make sense of and appreciate the varied cultures our students and their families are committed to. If they can't join our club and we don't know theirs, we're unlikely to influence each other.

No Idle Dream

That, after all, is what school is all about: It's a way one generation consciously tries to influence another—and in turn is influenced. For that to happen, both grown-ups and kids have to see themselves as members of a common club, or at least overlapping ones. Those who try to create such shared communities where they don't exist will run into resistance aplenty—from faculty, family, and kids themselves.

But it's not an idle dream. In New York City, nearly 50,000 youngsters now go to small schools, and the number is growing every day. Recently,

New York supported the phasing out of several big comprehensive high schools and gradually replaced them with new smaller schools. In several cases, these schools mix age groups, so that a big building now houses schools for students ranging from infancy to adulthood. The Annenberg Foundation, through its Challenge Grant, proposes not only to help foster such small schools but also to tackle the systemic issues they bring to the fore.

The routes that can take us from big to small are as varied as the communities and schools are. In New York, for example, some of the new schools that share a building keep close ties with one another and share a single administrative leader. In other cases, they act like co-tenants of the World Trade Center. Some are located in a wing or a floor with an otherwise "unreformed" school.

No single formula works best, but postponing a decision until everyone in the building agrees on change—at the cost of educating kids better—is a mistake. One starts wherever one can. Young people are eager for grown-ups to be grown-up enough to stick with what matters, however uncomfortable it may be. Growing up to be smart, thoughtful, and responsible citizens is a lot easier in schools organized in favor of such principles.

If it's the right thing to do for our kids, they'll recognize it. It's adult resistance that's hardest to overcome. Once we do, we will see that small schools allow us, too, to put our effort into what matters most to us: building a true community for teaching and learning. ■

P O S T N O T E

For most of this century, American educators were in love with big schools and big school districts. In 1928, there were 150,000 individual school districts in the United States, each one deciding what to teach and how to teach it. Each district built its schools and hired its own teachers. Today, there are fewer than 15,000 school districts, and the average number of students per district has grown enormously. Similarly, our schools themselves have become bigger and bigger, so that we now have elementary schools of 600 or 700 pupils and high schools of 4,000 or 5,000.

Proponents of these changes said that larger districts and schools would increase efficiency and comprehensiveness. Instead of supporting four small high schools in four neighboring towns, it is cheaper and more efficient to have one big school, with one principal, one guidance officer, one band, and one football team. And if all the language teachers in the four schools become part of one faculty, the big high school can now offer each student a wide array of language courses. More depth! More breadth! Better education! Or so it seemed.

At the same time, Americans have become extremely mobile, moving here and there for newer and better job opportunities. For the last few decades, sociologists have written about American adults becoming part of "the lonely crowd" and feeling "disconnected." Less attention has been given to the uprooted children who have been sent off to our huge schools. Now, however, many educators, like Deborah W. Meier, are recognizing that there are major benefits in smallness. The educational motto "Less is more" is fueled by the realization that our children need to be "rooted" and "reconnected" in more nurturing and more personal schools.

DISCUSSION QUESTIONS

1. Has your educational experience been in big schools or small schools? And how did you feel being part of those school communities?

2. What do you think is the best argument in favor of smaller schools? Why?

3. How does the movement toward smaller schools relate to the current "excellence movement" in education?

23

Why Some Parents Don't Come to School

Margaret Finders
and Cynthia Lewis

I n our roles as teachers and as parents, we have been privy to the conversations of both teachers and parents. Until recently, however, we did not acknowledge that our view of parental involvement conflicts with the views of many parents. It was not until we began talking with parents in different communities that we were forced to examine our own deeply seated assumptions about parental involvement.

From talking with Latino parents and parents in two low-income Anglo neighborhoods, we have gained insights about why they feel disenfranchised from school settings. In order to include such parents in the educational conversation, we need to understand the barriers to their involvement from their vantage point, as that of outsiders. When asked, these parents had many suggestions that may help educators re-envision family involvement in the schools.

At the time this article was written Margaret Finders was an assistant professor of English education at Purdue University, West Lafayette, Indiana. Cynthia Lewis was on the faculty at Grinnell College, Grinnell, Iowa. Finders, Margaret and Cynthia Lewis, "Why Some Parents Don't Come to School." *Educational Leadership*, May 1994, pp. 50–54. Reprinted by permission from ASCD. All rights reserved.

The Institutional Perspective

The institutional perspective holds that children who do not succeed in school have parents who do not get involved in school activities or support school goals at home. Recent research emphasizes the importance of parent involvement in promoting school success (Comer 1984, Lareau 1987). At the same time, lack of participation among parents of socially and culturally diverse students is also well documented (Clark 1983, Delgado-Gaitan 1991).

The model for family involvement, despite enormous changes in the reality of family structures, is that of a two-parent, economically self-sufficient nuclear family, with a working father and homemaker mother (David 1989). As educators, we talk about "the changing family," but the language we use has changed little. The institutional view of nonparticipating parents remains based on a deficit model. "Those who *need* to come, don't come," a teacher explains, revealing an assumption that one of the main reasons for involving parents is to remediate them. It is assumed that involved parents bring a body of knowledge about the purposes of schooling to match institutional knowledge. Unless they bring such knowledge to the school, they themselves are thought to need education in becoming legitimate participants.

Administrators, too, frustrated by lack of parental involvement, express their concern in terms of a deficit model. An administrator expresses his bewilderment:

> Our parent-teacher group is the foundation of our school programs. . . . This group (gestures to the all-Anglo, all-women group seated in the library) is the most important organization in the school. You know, I just don't understand why *those other parents* won't even show up.

Discussions about family involvement often center on what families lack and how educators can best teach parents to support instructional agendas at home (Mansbach 1993). To revise this limited model for interaction between home and school, we must look outside of the institutional perspective.

The Voices of "Those Other Parents"

We asked some of "those other parents" what they think about building positive home/school relations. In what follows, parents whose voices are rarely heard at school explain how the diverse contexts of their lives create tensions that interfere with positive home/school relations. For them, school experiences, economic and time constraints, and linguistic and cultural practices have produced a body of knowledge about school settings that frequently goes unacknowledged.

Diverse school experiences among parents. Educators often don't take into account how a parent's own school experiences may influence school relationships. Listen in as one father describes his son's school progress:

> They expect me to go to school so they can tell me my kid is stupid or crazy. They've been telling me that for three years, so why should I go and hear it again? They don't do anything. They just tell me my kid is bad.
>
> See, I've been there. I know. And it scares me. They called me a boy in trouble but I was a troubled boy. Nobody helped me because they liked it when I didn't show up. If I was gone for the semester, fine with them. I dropped out nine times. They wanted me gone.

This father's experiences created mistrust and prevent him from participating more fully in his son's education. Yet, we cannot say that he doesn't care about his son. On the contrary, his message is urgent.

For many parents, their own personal school experiences create obstacles to involvement. Parents who have dropped out of school do not feel confident in school settings. Needed to help support their families or care for siblings at home, these individuals' limited schooling makes it difficult for them to help their children with homework beyond the early primary level. For some, this situation is compounded by language barriers and lack of written literacy skills. One mother who attended school through 6th grade in Mexico, and whose first language is Spanish, comments about homework that "sometimes we can't help because it's too hard." Yet the norm in most schools is to send home schoolwork with little information for parents about how it should be completed.

Diverse economic and time constraints. Time constraints are a primary obstacle for parents whose work doesn't allow them the autonomy and flexibility characteristic of professional positions. Here, a mother expresses her frustrations:

> Teachers just don't understand that I can't come to school at just any old time. I think Judy told you that we don't have a car right now. . . . Andrew catches a different bus than Dawn. He gets here a half an hour before her, and then I have to make sure Judy is home because I got three kids in three different schools. And I feel like the teachers are under pressure, and they're turning it around and putting the pressure on me cause they want me to check up on Judy and I really can't.

Often, parents work at physically demanding jobs, with mothers expected to take care of childcare responsibilities as well as school-related issues. In one mother's words:

> What most people don't understand about the Hispanic community is that you come home and you take care of your husband and your family first. Then if there's time you can go out to your meetings.

Other parents work nights, making it impossible to attend evening programs and difficult to appear at daytime meetings that interfere with family obligations and sleep.

At times, parents' financial concerns present a major obstacle to participation in their child's school activities. One mother expresses frustration that she cannot send eight dollars to school so her daughter can have a yearbook to sign like the other girls.

> I do not understand why they assume that everybody has tons of money, and every time I turn around it's more money for this and more money for that. Where do they get the idea that we've got all this money?

This mother is torn between the pressures of stretching a tight budget and wanting her daughter to belong. As is the case for others, economic constraints prevent her child from full participation in the culture of the school. This lack of a sense of belonging creates many barriers for parents.

Diverse linguistic and cultural practices. Parents who don't speak fluent English often feel inadequate in school contexts. One parent explains that "an extreme language barrier" prevented her own mother from ever going to anything at the school. Cultural mismatches can occur as often as linguistic conflicts. One Latino educator explained that asking young children to translate for their parents during conferences grates against a cultural norm. Placing children in a position of equal status with adults creates dysfunction within the family hierarchy.

One mother poignantly expresses the cultural discomfort she feels when communicating with Anglo teachers and parents:

> [In] the Hispanic culture and the Anglo culture things are done different and you really don't know—am I doing the right thing? When they call me and say, "You bring the plates" [for class parties], do they think I can't do the cookies, too? You really don't know.

Voicing a set of values that conflicts with institutional constructions of the parent's role, a mother gives this culturally-based explanation for not attending her 12-year-old's school functions:

> It's her education, not mine. I've had to teach her to take care of herself. I work nights, so she's had to get up and get herself ready for school.

I'm not going to be there all the time. She's gotta do it. She's a tough cookie. . . . She's almost an adult, and I get the impression that they want me to walk her through her work. And it's not that I don't care either. I really do. I think it's important, but I don't think it's my place.

This mother does not lack concern for her child. In her view, independence is essential for her daughter's success.

Whether it is for social, cultural, linguistic, or economic reasons, these parents' voices are rarely heard at school. Perhaps, as educators, we too readily categorize them as "those other parents" and fail to hear the concern that permeates such conversations. Because the experiences of these families vary greatly from our own, we operate on assumptions that interfere with our best intentions. What can be done to address the widening gap between parents who participate and those who don't?

Getting Involved: Suggestions from Parents

Parents have many suggestions for teachers and administrators about ways to promote active involvement. Their views, however, do not always match the role envisioned by educators. Possessing fewer economic resources and educational skills to participate in traditional ways (Lareau 1987), these parents operate at a disadvantage until they understand how schools are organized and how they can promote systemic change (Delgado-Gaitan 1991).

If we're truly interested in establishing a dialogue with the parents of all of our nation's students, however, we need to understand what parents think can be done. Here are some of their suggestions.

Clarify how parents can help. Parents need to know exactly how they can help. Some are active in church and other community groups, but lack information about how to become more involved in their children's schooling. One Latina mother explains that most of the parents she knows think that school involvement means attending school parties.

As Concha Delgado-Gaitan (1991) points out "... the difference between parents who participate and those who do not is that those who do have recognized that they are a critical part of their children's education." Many of the parents we spoke to don't see themselves in this capacity.

Encourage parents to be assertive. Parents who do see themselves as needed participants feel strongly that they must provide their children with a positive view of their history and culture not usually presented at school.

Some emphasize the importance of speaking up for their children. Several, for instance, have argued for or against special education placement or retention for their children; others have discussed with teachers what they saw as inappropriate disciplinary procedures. In one parent's words:

> Sometimes kids are taken advantage of because their parents don't fight for them. I say to parents, if you don't fight for your child, no one's going to fight for them.

Although it may sound as if these parents are advocating adversarial positions, they are simply pleading for inclusion. Having spent much time on the teacher side of these conversations, we realize that teachers might see such talk as challenging their positions as professional decision makers. Yet, it is crucial that we expand the dialogue to include parent knowledge about school settings, even when that knowledge conflicts with our own.

Develop trust. Parents affirm the importance of establishing trust. One mother attributes a particular teacher's good turnout for parent/teacher conferences to her ability to establish a "personal relationship" with parents. Another comments on her need to be reassured that the school is open, that it's OK to drop by "anytime you can."

In the opportunities we provide for involvement, we must regularly ask ourselves what messages we convey through our dress, gestures, and talk. In one study, for example, a teacher described her school's open house in a middle-class neighborhood as "a cocktail party without cocktails" (Lareau 1987). This is the sort of "party" that many parents wouldn't feel comfortable attending.

Fear was a recurrent theme among the parents we interviewed: fear of appearing foolish or being misunderstood, fear about their children's academic standing. One mother explained:

> Parents feel like the teachers are looking at you, and I know how they feel, because I feel like that here. There are certain things and places where I still feel uncomfortable, so I won't go, and I feel bad, and I think maybe it's just me.

This mother is relaying how it feels to be culturally, linguistically, and ethnically different. Her body of knowledge does not match the institutional knowledge of the school and she is therefore excluded from home/school conversations.

Build on home experiences. Our assumptions about the home environments of our students can either build or serve links between home and school. An assumption that "these kids don't live in good environments" can destroy the very network we are trying to create. Too often we tell parents what we want them to do at home with no understanding of the rich social interaction that already occurs there (Keenan et al. 1993). One mother expresses her frustrations:

> Whenever I go to school, they want to tell me what to do at home. They want to tell me how to raise my kid. They never ask me what I think. They never ask me anything.

When we asked parents general questions about their home activities and how these activities might build on what happens at school, most thought there was no connection. They claimed not to engage in much reading and writing at home, although their specific answers to questions contradicted this belief. One mother talks about her time at home with her teenage daughter:

> My husband works nights and sometimes she sleeps with me. . . . We would lay down in bed and discuss the books she reads.

Many of the parents we spoke to mentioned Bible reading as a regular family event, yet they did not see this reading in relation to school-work. In one mother's words:

> I read the Bible to the children in Spanish, but when I see they're not understanding me, I stop (laughing). Then they go and look in the English Bible to find out what I said.

Although the Bible is not a text read at public schools, we can build on the literacy practices and social interactions that surround it. For instance, we can draw upon a student's ability to compare multiple versions of a text. We also can include among the texts we read legends, folk-tales, and mythology—literature that, like the Bible, is meant to teach us about our strengths and weaknesses as we strive to make our lives meaningful.

As teachers, of course, we marvel at the way in which such home interactions do, indeed, support our goals for learning at school; but we won't know about these practices unless we begin to form relationships with parents that allow them to share such knowledge.

Use parent expertise. Moll (1992) underscores the importance of empowering parents to contribute *"intellectually* to the development of lessons." He recommends assessing the "funds of knowledge" in the community, citing a teacher who discovered that many parents in the Latino community where she taught had expertise in the field of construction. Consequently, the class developed a unit on construction, which included reading, writing, speaking, and building, all with the help of responsive community experts—the children's parents.

Parents made similar suggestions—for example, cooking ethnic foods with students, shar-

ing information about multicultural heritage, and bringing in role models from the community. Latino parents repeatedly emphasized that the presence of more teachers from their culture would benefit their children as role models and would help them in home/school interactions.

Parents also suggested extending literacy by writing pen pal letters with students or involving their older children in tutoring and letter writing with younger students. To help break down the barriers that language differences create, one parent suggested that bilingual and monolingual parents form partnerships to participate in school functions together.

An Invitation for Involvement

Too often, the social, economic, linguistic, and cultural practices of parents are represented as serious problems rather than valued knowledge. When we reexamine our assumptions about parental absence, we may find that our interpretations of parents who care may simply be parents who are like us, parents who feel comfortable in the teacher's domain.

Instead of operating on the assumption that absence translates into noncaring, we need to focus on ways to draw parents into the schools. If we make explicit the multiple ways we value the language, culture, and knowledge of the parents in our communities, parents may more readily accept our invitations. ■

References

Clark, R. M. (1983). *Family Life and School Achievement: Why Poor Black Children Succeed or Fail.* Chicago: University of Chicago Press.

Comer, J. P. (1984). "Homeschool Relationships as They Affect the Academic Success of Children." *Education and Urban Society* 16: 323–337.

David, M. E. (1989). "Schooling and the Family." In *Critical Pedagogy, the State, and Cultural Struggle,* edited by H. Giroux and P. McLaren. Albany, N.Y.: State University of New York Press.

Delgado-Gaitan, C. (1991). "Involving Parents in the Schools: A Process of Empowerment." *American Journal of Education* 100: 20–46.

Keenan, J. W., J. Willett, and J. Solsken. (1993). "Constructing an Urban Village: School/Home Collaboration in a Multicultural Classroom." *Language Arts* 70: 204–214.

Lareau, A. (1987). "Social Class Differences in Family-School Relationships: The Importance of Cultural Capital." *Sociology of Education* 60: 73–85.

Mansbach, S. C. (February/March 1993). "We Must Put Family Literacy on the National Agenda." *Reading Today*: 37.

Moll, L. (1992). "Bilingual Classroom Studies and Community Analysis: Some Recent Trends." *Educational Researcher* 21: 20–24.

POST NOTE

Much research supports the principle that children whose parents are active in their schools are more likely to succeed in school, whereas children whose parents are not involved are more apt to do poorly. Some parents are eager to work as partners with schools to be certain that their children are well prepared for the life and career choices they will make. Other parents are almost never involved with the school.

This article is useful to educators working at schools where parental involvement is less than what they hoped for. By understanding why some parents never show up at schools, educators can take steps to help overcome the parents' reluctance. Remember, teachers need parents to help them succeed.

DISCUSSION QUESTIONS

1. List some of the main reasons Finders and Lewis give for parents not coming to school. Which of these reasons do you find compelling? Do any of the reasons surprise you?

2. Can you identify any additional reasons for parents to stay away from school, besides those given by the authors?

3. What strategies for involving parents in school have you seen employed, and how successful were they?

Parent Participation: Fad or Function?

James P. Comer

I nnovations promoted with great promise have come and gone in education with regularity over the last twenty-five years. Eventually, most are remembered as passing fads, thus leading us to ask if today's increasing enthusiasm for parental participation is just another fad. Or can the practice serve a vital function and thereby survive an otherwise inevitable backlash?

Innovative practices often fail because they promise too much and are not based on sound theoretical underpinnings. Also, often the participants are not adequately trained to implement the change, and nobody is clear about what to expect. These conditions lead to confusion, disappointment, and the eventual rejection of potentially useful practices.

To avoid such an outcome, advocates of parental participation in schools need to proceed from research-based theories about the value of the practice. These theories should suggest the most effective ways parents and schools can be brought together, as well as the potential problems involved.

Our Yale Child Study Center school intervention was field initiated by a team (psychologist, social worker, special education teacher, and psy-

chiatrist, the author) in two New Haven schools in 1968. The project was designed to develop a research-based theoretical framework for understanding poorly functioning schools and then to work with parents and school people to improve school functioning and outcomes.

From the beginning, parental participation played a key role in our ability to develop such a framework. The theory, in turn, suggested a vital function for parents in schooling. By focusing on that vital function during the evolution and implementation of our program, parental participation has been sustained over more than twenty years. This experience holds implications for all school improvement approaches.

We quickly discovered an extremely high degree of distrust, anger, and alienation between home and school—the two most important institutions in the developmental life of a child—that were only vaguely apparent and routinely misunderstood. School people viewed parents' poor participation in school programs as indicative of a lack of concern about their children's education. Parents often viewed the staff as distant, rejecting, and sometimes even hostile towards them and their children. These feelings resulted in acting out and other troublesome behaviors among parents, staff, and students that made matters worse.

Our project started out over twenty years ago, intended to bridge that gap, yet, despite our intentions, parents indicated that they felt manipulated and exploited once again by powerful mainstream people and institutions beyond their control—this time the New Haven school system and Yale University.[1] It was 1968, shortly after the assassination of Dr. Martin Luther King, Jr. The reaction of the 99 percent African-American, almost all-poor communities was swift, direct, and highly assertive. Our effort to understand and respond to these feelings forced us to consider the African-American experience within the context of American economic and social history and eventually led us to a theoretical framework for understanding schooling and the critical function of parents in it. Our intervention evolved from these understandings.

James P. Comer, M.D., is the Maurice Falk Professor of Child Psychiatry at the Yale Child Study Center in New Haven, Connecticut. This article originally appeared in *Educational Horizons* quarterly journal, published by Pi Lambda Theta international honor society and professional association in education, Bloomington, IN 47407-6626. Reprinted by permission of the author.

The two elementary schools in which we began our work were ranked the lowest academically in the city with the worst attendance and behavior problems. In 1969 they ranked 32d and 33d out of 33 New Haven schools on the Metropolitan Achievement Test. The students were nineteen and eighteen months behind in language arts and mathematics by the fourth grade. (We dropped one school after five years because of policy disagreements and worked in a replacement school with a similar profile and achievement level.)

By 1980 our new model had been institutionalized and our Child Study Center team left the schools. The program was carried on by the New Haven school system with minimal involvement of our staff. By 1984, the two project schools were tied in third and fourth place for achievement in the city. Fourth-grade students were a year above grade level in one school and seven months above grade level in the other. The rate of attendance at both schools was among the top five for five of the previous six years, and there were no serious behavior problems.[2]

Listening to Parents

During the first year, we lived in the schools with a promise to be as helpful as possible but without a clear intervention plan. Given our training, we carried child development knowledge, skills, and sensitivities, some appreciation of systems theory, and an ecological perspective. We responded to the first angry confrontation with parents by changing the project-wide Steering Committee to a school-based Governance and Management Team representative of parents, teachers, administrators, and professional support staff. We eventually added nonprofessional support staff as well as middle and high school students. In this way, all people with a stake in the outcome of the school had an opportunity to have their interests and concerns represented by peers in the governance and management process.

Our notions about child development and behavior gained credibility with staff and parents as we helped the staff successfully manage prob-

lem behaviors. By working as a Mental Health Team rather than individual professionals, as is custom, we developed a more efficient and effective approach to managing behavior problems.[3] But more importantly, working as a team enabled us to help the staff understand principles of child development and behavior and apply them in working with individual children and in developing the social and academic programs of the school. A Parent Program was established that focused primarily on supporting the social program of the school, on making the school a good place for students, staff, and parents. Behavior problems declined as a result, and parents' distrust, anger, and alienation began to subside. Directly and indirectly, parents began to share experiences that helped us understand the racial struggle that formed the basis of much of their distrust and anger.

Many of the parents were intelligent but undereducated, living on the margin or outside the mainstream of society. Some parents had had poor school experiences in segregated as well as integrated school systems. With poor education, they had been closed out of better paying, more prestigious employment in a job market that increasingly had required higher levels of education and social development since 1945. These conditions had contributed to family stress, hopelessness, and ambivalence about school—hope for their children but a sense that the school would fail them and their children.

Many parents and grandparents had attended school between 1900 and 1945 or during the period when most Americans were gaining higher levels of education that would be needed to be reasonably successful in the post–World War II job market. Most, however, attended school in one of eight states in which four to eight times as much money was spent on the education of a white child as on that of an African-American child: the disparity was as great as twenty-five times in areas that were disproportionately African American.[4] Because African Americans did not gain political, economic, or social power in those same areas, the level of racism remained high throughout the country and prevented them from gaining well-paying job opportunities or protecting their rights.

Here and there, some parents had relatives who managed to get an education and enjoy better life conditions. Many sensed that society blamed them for their undereducation and problems and the undereducation of their children. They lived in a community dominated by Yale University, a daily reminder of the value of education. A school project sponsored by Yale and the New Haven school system that promised a better chance and then did not immediately deliver was a ripe and right target for the expression of deep-seated distrust and anger.

Also, many parents were from the rural south and many staff were from small towns or remembered New Haven as a collection of small towns. They remembered community—a time before television and a great deal of transportation; a time when children gained their knowledge about what was right and wrong from the important adults around them, when any adult could censure children for inappropriate behavior. They remembered a time when the school was a natural part of the community and the authority of parents was transferred directly to the school through the interaction of parents and staff in the communities where they all lived.[5]

Parents and staff longed for that kind of authority and sensed that it had something to do with the ability of children to function well in school. In 1968, distrust, anger, and alienation did not allow parents and the school to engage in a way that would enable them to work together to help children succeed. As our Governance and Management Team, Mental Health Team, and Parents Program all began to work together to reduce behavior problems, a spirit of community began to develop in both schools and a theoretical basis for understanding schooling began to emerge for us.

The Theoretical Framework

Children are born totally dependent, and, yet, by the age of eighteen or so, they are expected to carry out all adult tasks and responsibilities. They are born into families that are a part of a social network of friends, kin, and selected institutions in which they feel welcome and belonging. Their parents carry the attitudes, values, and ways of their selected social network about work, play, academic, learning, and all aspects of life. As parents interact with and care for their children, an emotional attachment and bond develops. Through imitation, identification, and internalization, they influence the attitudes, values, and ways of their children; they channel their aggressive energy into the energy of work, play, and learning as their culture dictates; and they help their children grow along developmental pathways critical to academic learning—social/interactive, psychoemotional, moral, linguistic, and intellectual/cognitive.

In incidental ways—mediating a fight, teaching appropriate manners for particular occasions, explaining the environment around them, reading to them at bedtime, and so on—parents and other adults help children grow along all these critical developmental pathways. This enables children to go to school and interact with other children and to sit still, take in information, and be spontaneous and curious when it is appropriate to do so.

In short, children are able to meet the expectations of the school, and they elicit a positive response from school people.[6] As a result, a positive attachment and bond occur between children and school people similar to the attachment and bond that occur between parents and their children. This enables school people to relate the school program to children and to support their overall development, including an appreciation of academic learning. For children from society's mainstream, there is little discontinuity between the learning expectations of home and those of school, and most are adequately developed and prepared for academic learning.

The situation is different for many children whose parents live on the margins or outside the mainstream. Often, even when parents want their children to achieve in school, they are not able to give them the experiences that will enable them to do so. These children are not able to meet the expectations of school, and they are viewed as "bad" or "not so bright." Actually, they are underdeveloped or differently developed along the critical pathways. Often they can function well in the housing project, on the playground, or in a variety of other places, but the same skills they display there will get them into trouble in school.

Most school staffs, through no fault of their own, are not prepared to respond appropriately to these behaviors.[7] Their attempt to control behavior leads to a struggle between staff and students that makes matters worse. These children eventually fail in school or achieve far below their ability level. Many who begin to achieve adequately level off by third or fourth grade, and some decline precipitously during early adolescence.

Because of difficult staff-student interactions, the attachment and bonding that should occur between the child and the school staff do not occur. Parents' fears about school are confirmed, and underlying distrust, anger, and alienation are deepened. And, yet, the self-affirmation of the child comes more from home than from school. Without parental support for school staff and programs, very few children who sense any degree of rejection or being outside the mainstream of society will pull away from the attitudes, values, and ways that could lead to sustained school and related life success.

Because the peer group and community culture in areas of high economic and social stress often support problem behaviors,[8] parents must visibly join school staff in supporting good overall development and academic learning if children from nonmainstream environments are to succeed. The vital function of parents in schooling, then, is to endorse the work of the school through their attitudes and behaviors.

The School Development Program

Our model is designed to apply the principles of child development and the behavioral and social sciences to every aspect of a school program in a way that creates a good school climate and to facilitate the emotional attachment and bonding of students with staff and staff with parents and community.

Through trial and error, we learned that we cannot mandate a change in parents' or staffs' attitudes nor can we simply teach child development, systems theory, and the like and expect parents or staff to apply these ideas in a school setting. The mechanisms we created to deal with the initial problems and opportunities we found in the schools gradually set in motion the processes that allowed all involved to change. As we better understood the needs, we created a nine-component program designed to: (1) bring parents and school staff together and create a community within the school; (2) provide the staff with the knowledge, skills, and sensitivity to apply child development and relationship principles in their work with children and parents; and (3) create the organization and management structures that would allow parents, staff and students to interact in a cooperative, collaborative way.

The nine program components are composed of three mechanisms, three operations, and three guidelines. The three mechanisms are a Governance and Management Team, a Mental Health or Social Support Team, and a Parent Program; the three operations are a Comprehensive School Plan with social and academic goals, a Staff Development Program related to those goals, and Goal Assessment and Program Adjustment; the three guidelines are a "no fault" policy, decision making by consensus, and "no paralysis" (noninterference with needed action taking) of the team leader or principal, with full attention to input from team participants. These mechanisms, operations, and guidelines restructure or change the organization and management of the school from an authoritarian, hierarchical approach to a participatory, cooperative, collaborative one.

The Governance and Management Team, representing all involved, drives the direction of the school and provides a sense of ownership for all through the Comprehensive School Plan it develops and manages. As parents and school people interact around meaningful issues, a sense of community is established and adult authority is available to aid the development and behavior of students.

The Mental Health Team helps individual students function in the school. In addition, through its liaison on the Governance and Management Team and through its work with individual teachers in addressing problem behaviors, the Mental Health Team helps the staff develop programs and practices that are sensitive to child development and relationship needs. As a result, all staff members can help children develop along critical pathways.

The Parent Program is fully integrated into the work and mission of the school. It is geared most to the social program of the school as established in the Comprehensive School Plan developed by parents serving with others on the Governance and Management Team. Parents and staff together develop social activities that generate a good climate in the school—fairs, suppers, invited guests, and the like—and together teach the children ways to manage at these occasions. This helps children grow along critical developmental pathways. Most parents are able to contribute to the school academic program planning and implementation in one way or another. The Parent Program is further structured to enable parents to learn more about how to help their children gain school skills at home.

In our experience, parents began to feel ownership in the program, feel useful to the staff and their young people, and experienced social comfort in the school. As a result, they eventually attended programs in large numbers—from fifteen to thirty participating in major activities such as the Christmas program in the first year to four hundred parents three years later, with no change in the socioeconomic makeup of the community.

In short, the change in the structure and function of the entire school made it possible for parents to engage with staff. This, in turn, enabled children to make an emotional attachment and bond to school people and the school program. Parents and staff working together aided the overall development of students and permitted and promoted adequate teaching and curriculum development and, thus, learning.

While we strongly support the practice of direct parental involvement in the work of schools, there is evidence that children from families that support adequate development and engage in activities that facilitate academic learning at home often do well in school without direct parental involvement.[9] But there is evidence that even when parents do not participate in school programs, parental interest and involvement are needed to limit social problem behaviors such as teenage pregnancy, violence and vandalism, and alcoholism and other drug abuse.[10]

Even under the best of conditions, not all parents will participate in their children's education. When those who do are widely representative of the parent community the school serves, however, most children are able to identify with the people from their community who are involved in the work of the school, even when their parents are not. In one of the elementary schools where we are working, for example, a staff member serves as a substitute parent to children whose parents are unable to attend special activities.

Implementation Insights

We made several mistakes initially regarding the Parent Program which later added to our understanding: Some parents gained skills and confidence while working in the schools. They wanted to serve on teams every year and even to continue after their children graduated. However, continuing service limited both their own development and opportunities for others. Also, as they continued service, there was the possibility that they could have become less representative of the community and their children. Therefore, we developed policies that maintained accountability and promoted continuity and change on our teams, continued development for active parents, and opportunities for others. At least two of the six to eight parents on the Governance and Management Team had to be drawn from kindergarten or first grade and no parents could serve more than two consecutive years; they could serve only as long as their children were students in these schools.

Instead of trying to remain a part of the school program, parents with growing skills and confidence moved on to advance their own education and employment. At least seven of the parents involved during the full elaboration of our program from 1977 to 1984 returned to school, finished college, and became professionals. Many who had been depressed or lacked confidence were mobilized so that they could take jobs they would not have considered applying for previously. Many remained active in the education of their children, and these young people have completed undergraduate and professional school programs.

Our earliest Parent Program efforts floundered because we did not understand that parents need help in coping with the culture of the school and, in some cases, gaining the management skills needed to carry out an effective Parent Program. We assigned a teacher, social worker, or another support staff member to serve as a liaison to the Parent Program. This person not only assisted the parents but also facilitated staff-parent interactions. Without such a person, an adversarial relationship between parents and staff can develop or the Parent Program can be carried out poorly, without a sense of mission, and thus be ineffective.

In our first effort to disseminate the School Development Program, we trained a trainer without adequately orienting other key players in the school community—central office, principals, teachers, parents, etc. When the trainer returned to her school district, she was unable to involve others and could not establish the Governance and Management Teams. She was able to establish a Parent Program, however, and very soon the parents were better organized and more action oriented than the staff. This created a very serious adversarial relationship that required intervention or orientation of the entire school community. The importance of timing, not only in parental participation, but also in all aspects of our work, became sharply apparent through this experience.

One of our most important innovations was a parent assistant program. Parents were paid minimum wage to work ten hours a week, with one parent in each classroom. These ten to twelve parents formed the core of a parent group and were a very important force for linking home and community to the school. Support for this program was lost with cuts in Title I funds and we have never been able to replace it. While we have been able to make do with volunteers over the last eight years, we believe that the Parent Program could be much stronger and the school improvement process could move much more rapidly with ten to twelve parents of children in the school, carefully selected, serving as parent assistants.

Implications

We believe that parental participation in all schools, particularly low-income schools, is extremely important in this modern age when a high level of personal development is needed if students are to achieve well in school and when family and community support is not as strong as it used to be. But parent programs must be integrated into the work of the school in a way that allows them to be meaningful and important to parents, staff, and students. Staff and parents need training and support to work cooperatively and collaboratively. Parent participation in schools probably cannot be sustained if the major ways parents can be helpful are not understood and school programs are not structured to facilitate appropriate and effective participation.

Given what schools need to carry out successful parent-school programs, there are clear implications for preservice training. Teachers, administrators, support staff, and all other school professionals need to learn how to work together and with parents. There is a need for school professionals to know more about how systems (the building program) work and how to work with parents to promote the development of students; they also need to understand how the adequate development of students facilitate teaching, curriculum development, and learning.

There also are staff development implications. Many practicing school staff have never received training that would help them work with parents to support the development of students or to understand the relationship of development to learning. Some do not feel any responsibility to participate in school governance or to work with mental health teams and participate in a parent program because they do not understand the connection between these activities and student performance in social and academic areas. Staff development must address these issues, but more importantly, coaching is needed. It is difficult to change long-established behaviors without significant help over a reasonable length of time or until the new ways of working prove valuable and are internalized and institutionalized.

If parents are involved in supporting the staff and the program of a school in a way that promotes the attachment and bonding of their children to the program, parental involvement can be sustained as a critical function rather than declining in a few years as one more unsuccessful fad in education. ■

Notes

1. Carol M. Schraft and James P. Comer, "Parent Participation and Urban Schools," *School Social Work Quarterly* 1 (Winter 1979): 309–25.

2. James P. Comer, "Educating Poor Minority Children," *Scientific American* 259 (November 1988): 47–48.

3. Ibid., 48.

4. James P. Comer, *Maggie's American Dream: The Life and Times of a Black Family* (New York: Penguin Inc., 1988), 213–14.

5. James P. Comer, *School Power: Implications of an Intervention Project* (New York: The Free Press, 1980), 8–11.

6. Robert D. Hess and Susan D. Holloway, "Family and School as Educational Institutions," in *Review of Child Development Research: The Family*, 7, eds. Ross D. Parke et al. (Chicago: University of Chicago Press, 1984), 179–222.

7. Comer, *Maggie's American Dream*, 214–17.

8. Jewelle T. Gibbs, "Black Adolescents and Youth: An Endangered Species," *American Journal of Orthopsychiatry* 54 (January 1984): 6–20.

9. Ursula Casanova, "Conflicting Views of 'At-Risk' Students" (Paper presented at the Annual Meeting of the American Educational Research Association, New Orleans, LA, April 1988).

10. Gerald R. Patterson and Magda Stouthamer-Loeber, "The Correlation of Family Management Practices and Delinquency," *Child Development* 55 (June 1984): 1299–1307; Donna L. Franklin, "Race, Class, and Adolescent Pregnancy: An Ecological Analysis," *American Journal of Orthopsychiatry* 58 (July 1988): 339–54.

POST NOTE

In this article, James Comer reminds us of the critical importance of involving parents in children's learning in schools. Comer practices what he preaches: He is a public health physician and psychiatrist who, through his work with schools, has demonstrated that if parents become involved, it is possible for low-income African-American children to achieve at high academic and social levels.

No academic learning is possible, Comer asserts, unless there is a positive environment at the school, one in which teachers, students, parents, and administrators like each other and work together for the good of all children. In such an environment, conflict between home and school is eliminated.

1. Comer initially encountered a high level of distrust, anger, and alienation between school and home. Why do you think this was the case?

2. What are some effective ways that schools can involve parents in their children's education?

3. What aspects of your teacher education program address how to foster parental involvement?

Home Schooling Comes of Age

Patricia M. Lines

T his fall, when school bells summoned school-aged children, some did not respond. These children turned, instead, to home schooling, learning primarily at home or in the nearby community. Not so long ago, the families of these children might have gone underground, hiding from public view. Now they feel that they are simply exercising a valid educational option.

Home schooling has come of age. On any given day, more than a half million children are home schooling—perhaps little more than 1 percent of all school-aged children and about 10 percent of those who are privately schooled. This rough estimate assumes modest growth since 1990–1991, when I collected data from three independent sources—state education agencies, distributors of popular curricular packages, and state and local home-school associations. Knowing that all these figures represented the tip of the iceberg, I also used surveys of home-schoolers to estimate how many remained submerged (Lines 1991).

My current estimate rests in part on evidence of growth since then together with a rough assessment of the Census Bureau's 1994 Current Population Survey. Assuming the average home-schooling experience lasts only two years, as many as 6 percent of all families with children could have some home-schooling experience.

Making It Legal

A more favorable legal climate also signals the coming of age of home schooling. Twenty years ago, many states did not allow it. Constitutional protection for parents has always been ambiguous. The U.S. Supreme Court has never explicitly ruled on home schooling, although in 1972, in *Wisconsin v. Yoder,* the Court did restrict compulsory school requirements in a limited ruling involving the right of Amish students not to attend high school. Nearly a half century earlier, in a case involving a Catholic private school (*Pierce v. Society of Sisters,* 1925), the high court upheld, in more general terms, the right of parents to direct the education of their children.

Home-schoolers have argued that these cases protect them. But public officials have often disagreed, charging parents with violating compulsory education laws. In most cases, the courts have avoided the heart of the matter and—as is traditional in the American judicial system— ruled on narrow legal grounds, For example, some courts have struck down compulsory education laws as too vague, or found that restrictive school board regulations exceeded the board's statutory authority. Yet some courts have upheld states' legal requirements and found that parents met or did not meet them. A few parents have gone to jail for the cause.

State legislatures have responded more vigorously than the courts. Where many state once forbade home schooling, all states now allow it. At the same time, all states do expect the home-schooling family to file basic information with either the state or local education agency. And some states have additional requirements, such as the submission of a curriculum plan; the testing of students; or, in a few cases, education requirements or testing for parents.

At the time this article was written Patricia M. Lines was senior research analyst with the National Institute on Governance, Policy, Finance, and Management, Washington, D.C. Lines, Patricia, "Home Schooling Comes of Age." *Educational Leadership*, October 1996, pp. 63–67. Reprinted by permission from ASCD. All rights reserved.

Bending Stereotypes

What do today's home-schoolers look like? The stereotypical view is that they are loners who do not care about the opinions of others. But in at least one survey of home-schooling parents, 95 percent of respondents said the single most important thing that they wanted was support and encouragement from family, friends, church, and community (Mayberry et al. 1995).

Certainly the image of the isolated family does not fit any home-schooling family that I have met. On the contrary, these families seem highly connected to other families and other institutions. Indeed, the most universal resource that home-schooling families draw upon are like-minded families. Wherever there is more than a handful of home-schooling families in an area, they tend to form at least one home-schooling association.

Though home-schoolers look to one another, they hardly look *like* one another. One family may start the day with prayer or a flag salute, followed by a traditional, scheduled curriculum. Another may throw out the schedule and opt for child-led learning, providing help as the child expresses interest in a topic. In either type of family, the children are likely to take increasing responsibility for choosing and carrying out projects as they mature. And either type of family is likely to collaborate with other families.

Some home-schooled children will spend part of their time—with or without parents—at a local public or private school or at a nearby college. Substantial numbers of home-schoolers have invaded the electronic world, using it heavily for educational materials and networking. Families also draw upon resources at libraries, museums, parks departments, churches, and local businesses and organizations, and take advantage of extension courses and various mentors. In addition, they use the curriculum packages, books, and other materials that many private schools offer for use in home schooling.

Courting Public Opinion

Now that all states have adopted more flexible legislation, the most important factor contributing to the growth of home schooling may be the increased receptivity of the general public. In the 1980s, few Americans gave home-schoolers much support or encouragement. In 1985, for example, only 16 percent of respondents to the annual *Phi Delta Kappan* Gallup poll thought that home schooling was a "good thing." By 1988, 28 percent thought so. That same year, Gallup asked whether parents should or should not have the legal right to home-school. Fifty-three percent said "should" and 39 percent said "should not" (Gallup and Elam 1988; Gallup 1984).

Because the *Kappan* Gallup poll has not asked these questions again, one must turn to other sources to gauge changing attitudes. Increasingly favorable media reports are one indicator. Mayberry and her colleagues have observed that media in the 1970s reported "the most divisive and extreme home education court cases and their outcomes" and tended to show home-schooling parents "as neglectful and irresponsible" (Mayberry et al. 1995). They note that recent news stories not only portray home-schoolers in a more positive light, but sometimes as folk heroes.

In a similar vein, Pat Farenga, a home-schooling leader employed by Holt publishers, told me that 10 years ago, *Good Housekeeping* and *Publisher's Weekly* would never run stories suggesting home schooling as an option for their readers, but both now do. (Based in Cambridge, Massachusetts, Holt Associates Inc. publishes *Growing Without Schooling*, a bimonthly newsletter designed to give practical advice to home-schooling parents.)

Last April, participants in a Home-School Association online discussion group (AHAonline @aol.com) reported how dramatically things have changed over the last decade. One home-schooler recalled that 10 years ago, if she told someone what she was doing, the first response would be "Is that legal?" Often this would be followed by strong disapproval. Another participant, Ann

Lahrson (author of *Home Schooling in Oregon: The Handbook*), told how some friends, neighbors, and family members "rejected us, ignored us, clucked at us." She added that "professionally, I was shunned by colleagues at the public school where I had previously taught." Today, these home-schoolers said, they mostly hear remarks like, "Oh, do you enjoy it?" or "Oh, yeah, my brother/neighbor/cousin/fellow employee does that!"

Partnering Public Schools

Professional educators, on the other hand, remain wary. In 1988, the National Educational Association adopted a resolution calling for more rigorous regulation of home schooling. In March 1993, the National Association of Elementary School Principals adopted a resolution declaring that education is "most effectively done through cohesive organizations in formal settings" and specifically criticized home schooling. Even the national Parent-Teachers Association has passed a resolution opposing home schooling.

Other public educators have decided to work with home-schoolers. Most state education agencies have a home-schooling liaison, who at minimum will help a family understand state requirements. A small but growing number of school districts are offering home-schoolers access to schools on a part-time basis and, in some cases, special programs for home-schoolers.

In fact, the most exciting development in the home-schooling world is the emergence of partnerships between public schools and home schools, an arrangement that educators in Alaska pioneered. Teachers in Juneau work with students all over the state, staying in touch by mail and telephone and through occasional visits. Although the program was designed for students in remote areas, Alaska has never denied access to it because a child was near a school. The majority of the students now live in the Anchorage area.

Similar partnerships have emerged at the district level in other states. In California, for example, a child may enroll in an independent study program in a public school and base his or her studies in the home. Washington public schools must enroll children part-time if their families request it. The Des Moines (Iowa) School District, as well as several dozen in Washington, California, and other states, offer special programs for home-schooled children. Usually a child may enroll in such programs anywhere in the state. In a preview of education in the 21st century, these fledgling programs often rely heavily on electronic communications programs and software.

A few educators actually urge collaboration with home-schoolers, in the belief that they provide good models in exploring ways to involve parents and to individualize instruction and assessment (Weston 1996). For example, Dan Endsley, one of the founders of the Home Education League of Parents (HELP) in Toledo, Ohio, observes that

> As we helped more and more families learn about the home-school option, we found that school administrators also became more tolerant of home schooling. In several cases, public school administrators even recommended that families get in touch with HELP and gave them our address and phone numbers.

Remaining Vigilant

Given the more favorable legal climate for home schooling, families are now freer to concentrate on access to public resources and scholastic and athletic competitions. Still, home-schoolers remain watchful. There are several national organizations and at least one statewide organization in every state. Some states also have a dozen or more regional associations. All these groups monitor issues that might affect home schoolers, and they can mobilize large numbers of constituents where their interests are at stake.

The Home-School Legal Defense Association, based in Paeonian Springs, Virginia, and headed by Michael P. Farris, maintains a staff of about seven lawyers specializing in home-schooling law. The organization routinely monitors developments in every state, and keeps its national membership informed of potential problems. The group is also ready to negotiate or sue where it believes a policy might threaten its members' interests. An affiliated organization, the National Center for Home Education, runs an aggressive congressional action program with a facsimile alert system (Mayberry et al. 1995). State associations provide the same services for their constituencies. So, too, do other organizations, such as Clonlara Home-Based Education, an Ann Arbor, Michigan–based group that offers support nationwide.

As a result of these interest groups, efforts to pass stricter home-schooling laws or to seek enforcement that exceeds statutory authorization are likely to face organized and informed opposition and legal challenges. Clonlara, for example, argued successfully that the Michigan Board of Education exceeded it statutory authority to regulate (*Clonlara v. State Board* 1993).

In an interview with me, an experienced staff member of the Congressional Research Service compared the activity of the home-schooling lobby to that of the lobby for the Individuals with Disabilities Education Act. He noted, though, that unlike disability law backers, home-schoolers are merely reactive, rarely taking the offensive.

Pointing the Way for Reform?

Does home schooling help children academically? There is considerable disagreement on this question. No one has undertaken research involving controls that indicates whether the *same* children would do better or worse in home schooling than in a public or private school classroom. States that require testing, however, have analyzed test scores, and home-schooling associations have a multitude of data from these states. Yet information from both these sources may reflect only a select group of home-schoolers, as not all families cooperate with state testing requirements, and

private efforts rely on voluntary information. These caveats notwithstanding, virtually all the available data show that scores of the tested home-schooled children are above average, and comparable to the higher achievement pattern of private school students (Ray and Wartes 1991).

People also disagree on whether home schooling helps or hinders children's social development. Children engaged in home schooling spend less time with their peer group and more time with people of different ages. Most spend time with other children through support and networking groups, scouting, churches, and other associations. Many spend time with adults other than their parents through activities such as community volunteer work, home-based businesses, and tutoring or mentoring. No conclusive research suggests that time spent with same-aged peers is preferable to time spent with people of varying ages.

That said, limited testing of a self-selected group of home-schooled children suggests that these children are above average in their social and psychological development (Sheirs 1992, Delahooke 1986). At the very least, anyone who has observed home-schoolers will notice a high level of sharing, networking, collaboration, and cooperative learning.

Clearly, home schooling offers the potential for a very different educational environment for children. As such, it could be an important resource for studying how children learn, and whether and when formal or informal learning environments are superior. To the extent that home-schoolers are willing to cooperate, they could provide an opportunity to study the effects of one-on-one lay tutoring, child-led learning, and distance learning.

Although the percentage of children in home schooling on any one day is small, the number of adults in the home-schooling movement is much larger. Growth in numbers, increased acceptance by the public, and opportunities for engaging in the policy arena mean that home-schoolers could be an important part of a coalition seeking education reform at the state or national level. ∎

References

Delahooke, M. M. (1986). "Home Educated Children's Social/Emotional Adjustment and Academic Achievement: A Comparison Study." Doctoral diss. Los Angeles: California School of Professional Psychology.

Gallup, A. M. (1984). "The Gallup Poll of the Public's Attitudes Toward the Public Schools." *Phi Delta Kappan* 66, 1: 23–28.

Gallup, A. M., and S. M. Elam. (September 1988). "The 20th Annual Gallup Poll of the Public's Attitudes Toward the Public Schools." *Phi Delta Kappan* 70, 1: 33–46.

Lines, P. (October 1991). "Estimating the Home-Schooled Population," U.S. Department of Education, Office of Research Working Paper.

Mayberry, M., J. G. Knowles, B. Ray, and S. Marlow. (1995). *Home Schooling: Parents as Educators.* Thousand Oaks, Calif.: Corwin Press.

Pierce v. Society of Sisters. (1925). 268 U.S. 510.

Ray, B. D., and J. Wartes. (1991). "The Academic Achievement and Affective Development of Home-Schooled Children." In *Home Schooling: Political, Historical and Pedagogical Perspectives,* edited by J. Van Galen and M. A. Pitman. Norwood, N.J.: Ablex Publishing Corporation.

Sheirs, L. E. (1992). "Comparison of Social Adjustment Between Home- and Traditionally-Schooled Students." Doctoral diss., University of Florida.

Weston, M. (April 3, 1996). "Reformers Should Take a Look at Home Schools." *Education Week:* 34.

Wisconsin v. Yoder. (1972). 406 U.S. 205.

Author's note: For an expanded version of this article, see P. Lines, (in press). "Home Schooling," In *Private Education and Educational Choice,* edited by J. G. Cibulka (Westport, Conn.: Greenwood Press).

P O S T N O T E

Widespread criticism of our schools, along with the growing realization of education's importance, has set off an educational growth phase in the United States. As a historically innovative and experimental country, the United States is responding true to form, by striking out in new directions. The home-schooling movement is one such effort, as are charter schools, voucher experiments, and educational networks like the Coalition of Essential Schools.

Educational critics used to complain that our schools were captured by the "one right way" mentality. No longer. Home schooling is a case in point. It appears to be the right way for some, but for others it can be a disaster. To home-school well takes a special set of resources, among them a parent (or two) with the willingness and ability to teach. As this article suggests, however, home schooling seems to be satisfying the educational needs of hundreds of thousands of children and parents.

D I S C U S S I O N  U E S T I O N S

1. What do you believe are the greatest potential advantages and disadvantages of home schooling?

2. Why do you suppose there has been such strong opposition to home schooling in the United States?

3. List what you think are the resources needed by someone to be a successful home-school teacher.

26

Early Lessons of the Charter School Movement

Joe Nathan

The charter public school idea has spread rapidly in the last five years. As of late summer 1996, 25 states and the District of Columbia had adopted the idea in some fashion.

The goal of the charter movement is not just to establish innovative schools, but also to help improve the public education system. Charter schools provide families with choices and give skilled, entrepreneurial educators an opportunity, with accountability, to create more effective public schools. They also allow fair competition for public school districts.

The charter approach appeals to many educators who acknowledge that there are major societal problems but believe that schools can have significant, measurable impact on young people. In addition to retaining key aspects of public education, including no tuition, a non-sectarian nature, and no admissions test—the charter approach is based on several key principles.

- Charter schools are responsible for increased student achievement. A contract, or charter, stipulates academic goals and student assessment methods that are used to determine whether the school continues after a specified time, usually from three to five years.

- In exchange for explicit accountability, most rules and regulations are waived, other than those related to building safety and the rules mentioned above.

- Schools are free to set their working conditions and governance system, including the option to be a worker-owned cooperative.

- Charter schools receive the same per-pupil funding as other public schools.

- No one is assigned to charter school. Each is a school of choice.

- More than one organization, like a state board of education or a public university, along with a local district, can sponsor a charter school.

Many educators and legislators are concluding that the charter approach is a much fairer form of school choice than vouchers. Most voucher plans include parochial schools, permit schools to charge tuition beyond what the state provides, and allow schools to use admissions tests. The charter approach does not permit any of this. A recent national study found that most legislators proposed charters as an alternative, rather than a prelude, to vouchers (Nathan and Power 1996).

Poorly designed choice programs create more problems than they solve, but carefully created ones can produce widespread benefits.

The following four schools illustrate the potential of the charter approach.

O'Farrell Community School

San Diego's O'Farrell Community School opened as an innovative public middle school in 1988, emphasizing restructuring, teacher and community empowerment, interagency collaboration, and interdisciplinary teaching. President Bill Clinton came to O'Farrell's campus to announce the first federal grants to help start charter schools.

The school serves about 1,400 inner-city students in grades 6–8. More than two-thirds of these students come from families eligible for free or

At the time this article was written, Joe Nathan, a former public school teacher and administrator, was director of the Center for School Change at the University of Minnesota's Humphrey Institute of Public Affairs, 234 Humphrey Center, 310 19th Ave. South, Minneapolis, MN 55455. Adapted from *Charter Schools: Hope and Opportunity in American Schools* by Joe Nathan. Copyright © 1996 by Jossey-Bass, Inc. Reprinted by permission of John Wiley Sons, Inc. This article also appeared in *Educational Leadership*, October 1996.

reduced lunches. Approximately 36 percent are African American, 37 percent Filipino American, 16 percent Hispanic American, 4 percent Asian American, and 8 percent white.

Students are assigned to Educational Families of approximately 150 students and 6 teachers. All students study the same enriched curriculum, with six core challenges: *Research Process, Community Service, Exhibition, Performance in Academic Skills, Presentation of the School's Philosophy to Visitors,* and *Appropriate Problem-Solving Behavior.*

O'Farrell's governing council, which meets weekly, includes teachers, students, parents, representatives of community agencies helping the school, and Chief Education Officer Bob Stein, both leader and "Keeper of the Dream." In the early 1990s, the council decided to convert to charter status. O'Farrell, like many other innovative, award-winning public schools, wanted greater responsibility for decision making and control of its budget. For example, charter status allows each educational family to hire its own full-time Family Support Service Teacher, with money formerly spent on substitute teachers.

O'Farrell Community School is having an impact beyond its own walls. The National Education Association has asked teacher Byron King to help other public school teachers establish charters. Moreover, in the last year, 27 prospective educators from San Diego State University have either assisted or student-taught at the school.[1]

Minnesota New Country School

Unlike O'Farrell, which converted to charter status, Minnesota New Country School is a new school, established by three technologically sophisticated public school teachers from tiny Henderson, Minnesota. When their school consolidated with the nearby town of LeSueur, the teachers found that many veteran LeSueur teachers had less experience and interest in using technology. After several frustrating years trying to improve this situation, the three teachers from Henderson convinced the local school board, on their second try, to grant them a charter.

The school received start-up grants from Community Learning Centers, a New American Schools project; the Southwestern Minnesota Initiative fund; the Center for School Change; and a local business that asked the school's students and teachers to train its employees on the Internet.

The foundations of this year-round school are extensive parent involvement, teacher/student accountability, community as a place to learn, technology as a tool for learning, and Ted Sizer's Essential Principles. New Country, which serves a cross section of rural students (about 90) in grades 6–12, looks different from most schools. Its three buildings are former storefronts on Main Street in LeSueur, remodeled by teachers, parents, and students the summer before the school opened. School staff meet with each student and his or her parents in August to review student and parent priorities for the year and to plan the student's program.

New Country School does not have traditional classrooms or classes. Students work on individual and group projects based on the plans they've developed with their parents and their advisors. Multiage groupings are common. Walking into the storefronts, visitors might think they were walking into a business office, except that the "employees" are teenagers.

Every other month, students report their progress at "Presentation Nights" held in a community center. For example, two students worked with the local chamber of commerce to compile a database of local businesses. Throughout the school day, faculty move from student to student, reviewing progress, asking questions, and providing advice on projects. To graduate, students must demonstrate skills in basic areas like writing, public speaking, mathematics, and art, as well as in more applied areas like developing a post–high school plan and working effectively in a team.

Students frequently participate in field trips and internships (for example, at the local radio station). Recently, on a field trip along the nearby Minnesota River, students noticed that many of the frogs they saw had two, three, or five, rather than the typical four, legs. The youngsters collected data in their notebooks and, after their nature hike, contacted the Minnesota Pollution Control Agency. They learned that mutations in frogs may be a sign of major pollution problems. To make a long story short, after students testified, the Minnesota legislature awarded the school and the Pollution Control Agency money to continue their research. The Frog Project has gathered national attention and the interest of professional scientists.

As noted, technology is a focus of the school, and students often use one of the 40 computers. By deciding not to hire a principal, the school could afford to buy computers and to pay teachers a higher salary than the local district does. (New Country School teachers work a longer day and year than other local teachers.) As at other charter schools in states with "strong" charter laws, the school, not the district, sets teachers' working conditions. Teachers are evaluated yearly.

Like O'Farrell Community School, New Country is beginning to have an impact beyond its walls. Recently, an ABC Network crew filmed computer workshops for local district teachers taught by the school's faculty as well as some students.[2]

City Academy

The nation's first charter to have its contract renewed, City Academy is located in a low-income area of St. Paul, Minnesota. To help get the school running, Northern States Power donated computers, provided start-up funds, and hired several City Academy graduates. The City of St. Paul leases space to the school in a recreation facility built for youngsters to use after school and on weekends. Before City Academy moved in, the building was virtually empty during the day.

The school enrolls about 60 racially diverse youngsters, ages 15–21, who had left other schools without graduating. Milo Cutter, who helped found the school, sees these youngsters' strengths, not just their problems. Terry Kraabel, another City Academy teacher, shares Cutter's interest in active, hands-on approaches, and in using the youngsters' energy. He helps them learn via con-

struction projects, where they see applications of the math problems he gives them.

Under the supervision of a contractor and union workers, City Academy students have helped gut and rehabilitate several buildings. Kraabel explains, "If students make mistakes, we don't get into finger-pointing. The kids know it has to be done right. They usually do it that way the first time." The students often help neighbors, including shoveling snow for elderly residents.

Cutter and Kraabel think the small size of the school is a strength. Cutter is frustrated by the millions of dollars districts are spending to hire police and purchase metal detectors. "More and more youngsters don't fit in large schools. We know it. We have to do something about it."

Violence has not been a problem at City Academy. As one student points out, "If there's a problem, we talk it out. People listen to each other. No one is afraid."

Another student says that the teachers push her to "do my best. At a large school it seemed like most of the teachers just wanted us to be there. It's way better here."

Students help develop the school's rules, but it's not an anything-goes environment. One student explained, "It's like the teachers are saying, 'We care about you, so we expect a lot, and we'll help you get there.'"

Cutter and Kraabel worked with colleges and employers to develop graduation requirements, which call for demonstration of knowledge. Beyond the three Rs, students develop a post–high school plan. Students' goals provide a focus for City Academy courses.

The National Education Association has asked Cutter, a union member, to help other teachers start charter schools, and featured her in a film about outstanding teachers. She's pleased that the NEA is now trying to help some of its members start charter schools.

City Academy is accredited by the North Central Association of Schools and Colleges. In November 1995, the St. Paul Board of Education voted 7–0 to renew the school's charter for another three years.

Academy Charter School

In September 1993, parents and teachers started the Academy Charter School in Castle Rock, Colorado, in a former grocery store, about 25 miles south of Denver. The K–8 school's 315 students include both disabled and gifted.

Walking into the school, you might see some students building a model Parthenon with Lego blocks, while other youngsters practice a play based on a Greek classic. The school combines innovative teaching with conservative curriculum ideas. The school's parents and teachers believe in using phonics, the Saxon Math program, and the Core Knowledge Curriculum, developed by E. D. Hirsch.

Educators and parents do not think of Academy Charter as a back-to-basics school. As one teacher explained, "We believe in modern technology and active learning. But we want students to master content, not just to develop skills. I'd call it pragmatic education: we will do whatever it takes."

Academy parents praise the Douglas County School District for its support. As one parent explained, "The district could have reacted defensively to our questions and concerns. But the school board, Superintendent Rick O'Connell, and Assistant Superintendent Pat Grippe allowed our group of parents to create the kind of school we thought made sense." Grippe believes in public school choice, noting that "when families select schools, they are more committed to them, and their students do better."

The district sponsors three charter schools with differing philosophies. Randy Quinn, executive director of the Colorado School Board Association, believes that the charter law opens up new opportunities for school boards to do this kind of thing. He thinks the charter idea may help districts deal with "competing philosophies about what public schools should do or not do" (1993).

Academy students' improved scores on standardized tests support the school's approach. The first year's progress report, using the Iowa Test of Basic Skills, showed a 9 percent overall increase in math, a 4 percent increase in language, and a 3 percent gain in average reading score. Progress continued, and in the spring of 1996, after a careful study, the Douglas County Board extended Academy's charter for another two years. The state department of education also named Academy Charter a Colorado School of Excellence.

Strengthening Public Education

Schools like these interest legislators, but they are not the only reason 25 states have some form of charter legislation. Several studies show that charter schools in many states have a higher percentage of students from low-income, minority, and limited or non-English-speaking backgrounds than does the overall state public school educational system. Moreover, there is some evidence that fair competition helps stimulate improvement in public education systems. For example:

■ After Massachusetts adopted its charter legislation, allowing charter proponents to apply directly to the state for sponsorship, 18 of the first 64 charter proposals came from Boston. The Boston Public Schools and Boston Teachers Union responded by approving a proposal they had been considering, but had not yet adopted: a pilot school plan allowing educators to apply directly to the district for permission to create new schools.

■ After Colorado adopted charter legislation, parents and educators in several districts who had tried for years to start or replicate successful innovative schools found that school boards were more responsive.

■ Several Minnesota school districts had previously resisted parents' requests to create Montessori public schools. Then, after charter legislation passed, they created new within-district Montessori options.

Five years of experience show that the details of state charter laws matter enormously. The five states with the "strongest" laws allow some entity other than local school boards, such as a state board of education or public universities, to sponsor charters. As of December 1995, the five states with the strongest laws had 222 charter schools, compared to only 14 schools in the five states with the weakest laws (Bierlein 1996). Strong laws also allow charter schools to create their own work rules, rather than be bound by local labor-management agreements.

With most charter schools in their first few years, it's too early for definitive conclusions. Charter schools in California, Colorado, and Minnesota, however, have had their contracts renewed or extended because of the demonstrated progress with students. For example, the Sacramento, California, School Board recently extended Bowling Green Charter School's contract for an additional two years after students showed improvements in achievement, attendance, and behavior. These are noteworthy gains from a place that five years ago was one of the three lowest achieving schools in the district.

Younger charter schools report achievement gains as measured by standardized tests, along with other measures. For example, a first-year evaluation of the New Visions Charter in Minneapolis—a K–8 school that works predominantly with inner-city students who have not succeeded in other schools—showed a 1.5-year average gain on the Slosson Oral Reading Test among its

children of color and a 1.4-year average gain on the same test among its white students.

Educators throughout the nation are accepting the challenge and opportunity that the charter movement represents. The charter concept—combining freedom, accountability, and competition—can be an important part of redesigning and strengthening public education. ■

Notes

1. For additional information about O'Farrell, check its Internet site (http://edweb.sdsu.edu/O'Farrell/O'Farrellhome.html).

2. For additional information about New Country School, check its Internet site (http://mncs.K12.mn.us/).

References

Bierlein, L. A. (February 1996). *Charter Schools: Initial Findings.* Denver: Education Commission of the States.

Nathan, J., and J. Power. (1996). *Policy-Makers' Views of the Charter School Movement.* Minneapolis: University of Minnesota Center for School Change.

Quinn, R. (August 1993). "Charter Schools: Now What?" *CASB Agenda:* 2.

P O S T N O T E

Currently, two related educational ideas are vying for the public's support: the charter school movement and voucher plans. Both are gaining popularity in response to parents' desire for more choice in selecting education for their children. Charter schools represent choice *within* the public school system. Most voucher plans, on the other hand, propose a "purer choice" in which parents can use the voucher for a wide array of educational alternatives both inside and outside the public system.

While there has always been choice in our educational system, it has been limited. If you don't like the local school, you can move to a new locale served by a different school, or you can send your children to a private or religious school—except, that is, if you cannot move or you are poor (conditions that are often linked). Increasingly, then, school choice is being seen as an issue of justice. Why shouldn't all Americans have an opportunity currently reserved for the well off?

This article makes a strong case for charter schools. Nathan, one of the most articulate advocates of educational choice, argues that charter schools can both improve the education of individual students and strengthen public education as a whole.

DISCUSSION UESTIONS

1. Which of the four schools described in the article do you find most impressive? Why?

2. In your view, what are the main advantages of charter schools for individual students?

3. What are the major advantages of charter schools for public education as a whole?

27

Charter Schools: The Smiling Face of Disinvestment

Alex Molnar

Everyone, it seems, loves charter schools. *Time* magazine has called them the "New Hope for Public Schools" (Wallis 1994). *The New Democrat*, the Democratic Leadership Council's journal, says charter school advocates are "Rebels With a Cause" (Mirga 1994). And *The New York Times* (in an unusual note of irony) calls them the "Latest 'Best Hope' in U.S. Education" (Applebome 1994).

American Federation of Teachers President Albert Shanker launched the movement when, in a 1988 National Press Club speech, he called for empowering teachers by creating "charter" schools that focused on professional development and had a clear commitment to improving student achievement (Sautter 1993). Since then, the rise of charter schools to the top of the educational reform agenda has been spectacular.

To many educators, parents, and politicians, the charter school idea represented a public education alternative to private school voucher proposals. It was an idea they could embrace enthusiastically because it seemed to protect public education as an institution and at the same time provide for fundamental reform and

At the time this article was written, Alex Molnar was a professor of education at the University of Wisconsin—Milwaukee. This essay is derived from a chapter in his book, *Giving Kids the Business: the Commercialization of American Schools*, Westview Press, 1996. Reprinted by permission from Alex Molnar, Professor of Education, University of Wisconsin-Milwaukee.

systemic "restructuring." As a bonus, charter schools had more media sex appeal than, say, site-based management.

Zealots, Entrepreneurs, Reformers

Tom Watkins (1995), the director of the Detroit Center for Charter Schools, says charter school advocates are usually one of three types:

1. *Zealots*, who believe that "private is always better than public," market systems are always superior to public systems, "unions are always the problem," and students at private and religious schools outperform their public counterparts. Neoconservative supporters, such as Hudson Institute Fellow Chester Finn and former Secretary of Education William Bennett, probably fit most comfortably in this category.

2. *Entrepreneurs*, who want to make money running schools or school programs. Edison Project charter schools operating in Boston and in Mt. Clements, Michigan, are examples of private entrepreneurs using charter school legislation as an opportunity to turn a profit.

3. *Reformers* (child-, parent-, and teacher-centered), who want to expand public school options and provide the sort of creative tension they believe will help improve all schools. It is this group—perceived as representing a kind, moderate, educational middle—that generates most of the favorable press reports about dedicated individuals struggling to make a difference in the lives of America's schoolchildren. These are the people (and Watkins places himself here) who have given the charter school movement its air of mainstream respectability.

Despite the rosy image provided by the child-centered reformers, most of the money and political influence driving the charter movement have been provided by the zealots and the profiteers.

Prairie Fire Reform

Charter school reformers aim their rhetorical firepower at those ever-popular sources of evil in American public education: overregulation and unresponsive bureaucracies. Remove the regulation and dismantle the bureaucracies, their logic goes, and—voilà—a thousand flowers cultivated by the unfettered ingenuity, energy, and commitment of parents and teachers will bloom. The idea is simple, direct, and appealingly libertarian.

In 1991, Minnesota became the first state to pass a charter school law. The Minnesota legislation enabled school districts to "charter" schools organized by teachers. These schools were freed of most state and local regulations and operated as nonprofit cooperatives that were legally autonomous. Existing nonsectarian private schools also were allowed to apply for charter status. For the most part, the Minnesota legislation met Shanker's criterion of empowering teachers.

Within four years, charter school laws had been adopted from one end of the country to the other. At the end of 1994, 11 states had some form of charter school law on the book and 134 charter schools had been approved. By late summer 1996, 25 states and the District of Columbia had passed laws. The number of charter schools approved had jumped to 246, of which 110 were up and running.

An August 1995 survey of these 110 charter schools found that about 27,500 students were enrolled. Most of these schools were small (about 250 students on the average—only 140 if California schools were excluded). The schools were most often located in leased commercial space (in Hull, Massachusetts, for example, this meant eight rooms in the Seashore Motel). Two-thirds wanted to attract a cross section of students and about half were intended to serve at-risk students. Their academic focus was primarily on "integrated interdisciplinary curriculum" or "technology" or "back to the basics" (University of Minnesota 1995).

Clearly as a result of the political struggle among charter school advocates with different agendas, the practical meaning of the term varies considerably from state to state. At a minimum, however, all states defined charter schools as public schools that operate under a special contract or charter. Depending on the state, the sponsor granting that charter could be a school district, a university, a state education board, or some other public authority. Most, but not all, states place limits on the number of charter schools allowed.

Instead of having to meet most state or district regulations, charter schools are accountable for such matters as educational programming, academic results, and fiscal affairs under the terms of their contract with their sponsoring organization (Bierlein and Mulholland 1995). The sponsor is in turn responsible for guaranteeing compliance with the contract. In almost all cases, charter schools have been designed to be nonselective, tuition-free, nonsectarian, and based on choice. Funding depends directly on the number of students enrolled.

Laws Weak and Strong

One of the most significant differences among the various charter school laws is the degree of autonomy they grant the schools. Arizona, California, Colorado, Massachusetts, Michigan, and Minnesota have what are sometimes characterized as "strong" charter school laws because they allow these schools to operate as legally independent entities with a high degree of autonomy. In contrast, the so-called "weak" charter school laws passed by Georgia, Hawaii, Kansas, New Mexico, and Wyoming grant charter schools little more autonomy than other public schools (U.S. General Accounting Office 1995).

Obviously "strong" and "weak" are in the eye of the beholder. Given the variety of reasons offered for embracing the charter school concept—to encourage innovative teaching, to create new professional opportunities for teachers, to promote community involvement, to improve student learning and performance-based accountability, among others (U.S. General Accounting Office 1995)—it is not surprising that charter school legislation has varied considerably.

Free-Market Accountability

As yet, no national evaluation of the effectiveness of charter schools has been completed. The

Pew Charitable Trusts have funded a study to be conducted by Chester Finn and Louann Bierlein at the Hudson Institute. And the U.S. Department of Education has commissioned a study that should begin to provide some data in the next two or three years.

In the meantime there are a few clues about the impact of the reform. A 1995 report issued by the Indiana Policy Center, "Charter Schools: Legislation and Results After Four Years," found little in the way of systematic evidence that charter schools increased student achievement (Indiana Policy Center 1996).

In December 1994, the Minnesota legislature released a report on charter schools in Minnesota. The authors did not try to judge the success or failure of the charter experiment; they felt it was too early for that. They did, however, highlight a number of problems that threw into question the idea the charter schools would provide a model for public school reform (Urahn and Stewart 1994).

Because Minnesota charter schools were free of all legal requirements placed on public schools, except those clearly spelled out in their charters, the charter schools didn't necessarily have to operated in open meetings or otherwise be open to public scrutiny. That made it difficult for the public to hold them accountable for proper and efficient conduct of their activities. Accountability was further complicated by a finding that some school boards granting charters were unwilling or unable to adequately evaluate charter school outcomes or student success.

One of the biggest problems Minnesota charter schools faced was financing. Thus, in order to reduce class size and afford other reforms, the schools relied on experienced teachers to accept low salaries and take on administrative and other responsibilities. The schools also had difficulty finding facilities and paying for even the most basic equipment—books and desks—without additional income from private sources that could not be relied upon for continuing, long-term support.

These problems are not unique. In a recent survey of charter schools around the country, financial support and the lack of start-up funds were the most frequently mentioned problems (University of Minnesota 1995). The authors of the Minnesota legislative report concluded that without increased support, "it is not clear that charter schools will be able to function as anything but educational reformers 'on the margin'" (Urahn and Stewart 1994).

Despite the report's perfectly reasonable conclusion, most charter school supporters would be the last ones to admit publicly that they are backing a reform that has neither a logical nor a demonstrated relationship to increased academic achievement and that will cost someone lots of money to get off the ground and keep afloat. Most would rather claim that the market will somehow provide.

For this reason, charter school advocates often prefer to frame the issue of accountability the way voucher supporters do. Real accountability, they say, is imposed by competition in the marketplace. Parents who "know what they like" and who are "empowered" to choose the school their children attend will send their kids to a charter school if they think its program is good; and if they don't, they won't. This view assumes parents know an effective school program when they see one and that they could not possibly be satisfied with an ineffective school.

Undeniably, this position has populist appeal. In practice, however, parents' decisions about where to send their children are much more complex than a simple judgment about a school's academic program. Considerations such as proximity to the school, work schedules, availability of after-school care, and extracurricular activities get thrown into the mix. Also, the ability of parents to choose the best school for their children requires more than the freedom to walk away from schools they don't like: they also must be able to get their children into schools they like better.

The chance of a market creating a multitude of options for all parents, especially those in the most impoverished urban areas, is so small as to be nonexistent. Obviously that is why no one has yet explained in practical terms how to create the surplus of educational capacity needed to give parents such an opportunity. Should a dissatisfied parent decide to switch schools, who pays to keep a vast network of partially filled schools at the ready? In the real world, financing limits parents' choices. Charter schools do nothing to change that basic fact.

Real-World Money Problems

If the popularity of charter schools demonstrates anything, it is America's enduring faith that major educational reforms can be accomplished on the cheap. Charter school reformers in Massachusetts and elsewhere have sold the idea that charter schools won't cost anyone anything—a real win-win reform. This fiscal miracle is accomplished by a budgetary sleight of hand in which the money to educate charter school students is, for the most part, taken out of state aid to the district in which the student lives. In the case of hard-pressed urban school systems such as Boston's, such financing further undermines the district's ability to serve the children attending its schools.

Raising the necessary money is one problem; keeping track of it after it has been raised is another. Few of the institutions legally empowered to grant charters are likely to have the expertise or the resources to monitor and enforce those charters. If educational performance contracting during the Nixon administration and the more recent contract problems between Education Alternatives Inc. and the Baltimore and Hartford school systems are any indication, we will soon be reading stories of mismanagement and educational short-sheeting at charter schools.

In fact, in 1994, one California charter school, Edutrain, went belly up with more than $1 million in public money unaccounted for. Apparently the school administration had been spending money to help pay the principal's rent, lease the principal a sports car, hire a bodyguard, and fund a $7,000 staff retreat in Carmel—this while teachers lacked textbooks and supplies (Schmidt 1994).

To some charter school supporters the failure of Edutrain was an example of the educational market imposing its discipline. The problem with their logic is this: An educational "market" does not punish people who set up a school the way a financial market punishes investors in stocks and bonds when share prices plummet or a bond issuer defaults. In the Edutrain fiasco, the people punished were the students who had their education disrupted and the taxpayers and students in the Los Angeles Unified School District who were out of education money and received nothing in return. In the charter school market, the financial risks are socialized, while the financial gains are privatized.

Demonizing Teachers

The lack of a common educational vision helps assure that the argument for charter schools is dominated by economic, no educational, ideas. Central to the logic of charter schools is the idea that competition will force public schools, which now have a monopoly in providing educational services, to improve or perish as parents choose to send their children to better schools. Unfortunately, *how* the competition will result in better teaching and more learning is never specified.

The assumptions are that educators have grown fat and complacent in the warm embrace of a government monopoly and that a threat to their now-secure futures will force them to figure out how to do better. In this scenario, teachers unions are considered self-interested culprits responsible for driving up the cost of education without accepting accountability for student achievement.

Neoconservative charter school zealots, such as Chester Finn and the Center for Educational Reform's Jeanne Allen, ridicule the idea that schools (particularly those in poor, urban districts) might need more money to improve. Any increase in funding would, from their perspective, be throwing good money after bad. In what has become the conventional wisdom in the charter school movement, the enemies of school improvement are rigid union contracts; bloated, unresponsive bureaucracies; and overregulation, not fiscal constraints.

Hostility toward teachers unions and the teacher certification requirements they have achieved is built into some so-called "strong" charter school laws, including those in Arizona, California, Colorado, and Massachusetts. Under those laws, virtually any adult with "qualifications" is allowed to teach in a charter school, or administer one for that matter, without the need for certification. It's an approach that is in some ways analogous to trying to solve the problem of access to health care by allowing anyone who can attract patients to practice medicine.

"Edventures" in Exploitation

The surge of interest in charter schools seems to have energized a fledgling movement that wants to increase the number of what it calls "teachers in private practice." This is billed as a movement for teachers who want to work as entrepreneurs instead of employees. The idea of teachers as entrepreneurs is couched in the language of greater professionalism and independence for teachers freed to work when and where they want, even free to set their own fees. To those who contend that good teachers are too often yoked to incompetents by union protections, the idea also is presented as a chance for good teachers to take their competence to the marketplace and receive the greater rewards their talent will command.

In practice, however, the ability of professionals to set their own fees depends on how many others are competing in the marketplace. Because the money available for public education is constrained by political decisions, cost, not competence, will often be the most decisive factor in hiring.

Changing state laws to make it easier to be a private practice teacher would most likely result in large numbers of teachers finding themselves shut out of the more highly paid positions with fringe benefits they might have had as school district employees. These teachers would be involuntary teachers in private practice, with the freedom to do the same work for lower wages and few opportunities to raise their incomes, whatever their competence.

This mirrors what has happened at public universities over the past two decades. As money to hire professors in positions leading to tenure has steadily diminished, schools have hired more adjuncts to work on year-to-year contracts at low pay with few, if any, fringe benefits (Judson 1996). They are, as the outside critics argue, free to change careers. But a system that consistently turns away talented people undermines the quality of higher education in the long run.

Certified and uncertified teachers in private and religious schools are already in this battered boat. That's why large numbers leave those mythically superior schools as quickly as they can find a decent-paying job in a public school system. Anyone who thinks about it quickly realizes that charter schools can never occupy more than a very small corner in American public education without drastic reductions in wages or huge increases in education spending.

For the zealots and profiteers, charter schools are as much a vehicle for breaking up teachers unions and lowering wages as an education reform strategy. That is why so much of their rhetoric demonizes teachers unions and paints them as self-serving enemies of reform. They attack teachers unions for backing "weak" charter laws (for example, those that keep charter schools clearly accountable within the structure of public education). As in universities, a continuing erosion of teachers' wages could drive many of the best prospective teachers into other occupations. This most likely would lower the quality of public education, inevitably harming the poorest children the most.

Storefront Education

One of the most hotly contested aspects of charter schools is who will run them. As originally proposed by Albert Shanker, the idea was to "empower" certified teachers by freeing them from regulations so they could run their program more effectively. But charter school laws in states that allow private and for-profit schools to operate without certified teachers open the door to some strange possibilities.

Many people who start charter schools will work long and hard to accomplish their goal and some will have good results. Many of these schools, however, won't last long. People burn out, they move on, their kids grow up, and for any number of reasons the effort collapses.

The quick-buck operators, on the other hand, are likely to be much more durable. Attracted by the lack of regulations, effective fiscal controls, or academic standards, and untroubled by the welfare of their students, they will be free to set up and close down over and over again, milking the system for as much as they can get. Their role models will be the scam artists who bilk postsecondary students out of their college Pell Grant money and student loans by opening up fly-by-night schools of "business" or "technology" or even "hair styling" and "nail academies."

One of the paradoxes of the charter school idea is that the farther the schools are outside the public school system, the more they rely on the idiosyncratic vision of a few people and the more exotic their methods of funding become. As a result, even if there are some individual success stories over the next few years, they may not serve as models elsewhere because their circumstances will be unique.

The Public Debate Versus the Real One

Free-market zealots are likely to continue to claim vindication or argue that their reactionary ideas need more time to work. Supporters of public education will call the experiment a costly failure and marvel at the willingness to spend large sums on unproven alternatives while cutting resources for the public system that serves most children. With an absence of uniform standards, the war of educational anecdotes and misleading statistics will remain "subject to interpretation."

All the while, the desperation of America's poorest children and their families will grow. No state's charter schools, under laws strong or weak, will make an appreciable difference for most of these children. They are failing in public schools. They are failing in Catholic schools. They are going under. That is not because they cannot succeed, but because they have been abandoned in a political and economic debate that masks selfish interests with educational rhetoric.

No amount of entrepreneurial zeal will make up for a lack of sufficient resources to provide for them. Indeed, it is the market that has destroyed their neighborhoods and the livelihoods of the adults they rely on. Unleashing the market on the public schools will only compound the harm.

Charter schools, like private school vouchers and for-profit schools, are built on the illusion that our society can be held together solely by the self-interested pursuit of our individual purposes. Considered in this light, the charter school movement represents a radical rejection not only of the possibility of the common school, but of common purposes outside the school as well. The struggle is not between market-based reforms and the educational status quo. It is about whether the democratic ideal of the common good can survive the onslaught of a market mentality that threatens to turn every human relationship into a commercial transaction. ■

References

Applebome, P. (October 12, 1994). "Latest 'Best Hope' in U.S. Education: Chartered Schools." *The New York Times.*

Bierlein, L. A., and L. A. Mulholland. (1995). "Charter School Update and Observations Regarding Initial Trends and Impact." Policy Brief, Morrison Institute for Public Policy. Tempe: Arizona State University.

Indiana Policy Center. (March 1996). "Charter Schools: Legislation and Results After Four Years." *ERS Bulletin* 23: 7.

Judson, G. (January 17, 1996). "Yale Student Strike Points to Decline in Tenured Jobs." *The New York Times.*

Mirga, T. (April–May 1994). "Rebels with a Cause." *The New Democrat* 6, 2: 17–22.

Sautter, R. C. (1993). "Charter Schools: A New Breed of Public Schools," Policy Briefs, Report 2. Oak Brook, Ill.: North Central Regional Educational Laboratory.

Schmidt, P. (December 14, 1994). "Citing Doubts, L.A. Board Revokes School's Charter." *Education Week*: 3.

University of Minnesota Humphrey Institute of Public Affairs and Education Commission of the States. (1995).

Charter Schools: What Are They Up To? A 1995 Survey. Denver: Education Commission of the States.

Urahn, S., and D. Stewart. (1994). "Minnesota Charter Schools: A Research Report." St. Paul: Minnesota House of Representatives Research Department.

U.S. General Accounting Office, Health, Education and Human Services Division. (January 1995). "Charter Schools: New Model for Public Schools Provides Opportunities and Challenges." Report to Senators Arlen Spector and Edward Kennedy. Washington, D.C.: U.S. General Accounting Office.

Wallis, C. (October 31, 1994). "A Class of Their Own." *Time*: 53–61.

Watkins, T. (September 6, 1995). "So You Want to Start a Charter School." *Education Week*: 40.

P O S T   N O T E

This article reports the rapid rise in the number of charter schools, one of the latest answers to our search for a better education for our young. But the idea of charter schools is new and not fully tested, and the educational graveyard is littered with "latest answers." Thoughtful educators should heed Molnar's cautionary note and not rush to judgment.

Molnar points out that the charter school advocates include zealots and entrepreneurs as well as reformers. Yes, but there are also parents and teachers who hunger for something different, who feel trapped in certain public schools that are failing the students. Much of the fuel for charter schools comes from parents who want something better for their children and from teachers who want to break out of the constraints of their current teaching situation.

At the end of the article, Molnar contends that "Charter schools, like private school vouchers and for-profit schools, are built on the illusion that our society can be held together solely by the self-interested pursuit of our individual purposes." This is an interesting and debatable statement. Isn't the self-interest that motivates charters and other choice plans really child-interest? Parents have a duty and probably an instinct to seek the best for their children. In that sense, seeking the best possible schools could be described as good parenting.

D I S C U S S I O N   Q U E S T I O N S

1. How do you account for the increasing interest in charter schools?

2. What do you think is the best case for them, and what is the best case against them?

3. What evidence should we look for to judge their effectiveness?

Part Four
Curriculum

The bedrock question of education is: What knowledge is most worth knowing? This question goes right to the heart of individual and social priorities. As our world has become more and more drenched with information, information pouring out at us from many different media, the question of what is worth our limited time and attention has increased in importance. It is the quintessential curriculum question.

The question begets others, though: What is the purpose of knowledge? To make a great deal of money? To become a wise person? To prepare oneself for important work? To contribute to the general good of society?

This difficult question becomes more and more complex and swiftly takes us into the realm of values. Nevertheless, it is a question communities must regularly address in our decentralized education system. In struggling with curriculum issues, a community is really making a bet on the future needs of society and of the young people who will have to live in that society. Behind the choice of a new emphasis on foreign language instruction or on computer literacy is a social gamble, and the stakes are high. Offering students an inadequate curriculum is like sending troops into battle with popguns.

28

The Saber-Tooth Curriculum

J. Abner Peddiwell

The first great educational theorist and practitioner of whom my imagination has any record (began Dr. Peddiwell in his best professional tone) was a man of Chellean times whose full name was *New-Fist-Hammer-Maker* but whom, for convenience, I shall hereafter call *New-Fist*.

New-Fist was a doer, in spite of the fact that there was little in his environment with which to do anything very complex. You have undoubtedly heard of the pear-shaped, chipped-stone tool which archaeologists call the *coup-de-poing* or fist hammer. New-Fist gained his name and a considerable local prestige by producing one of these artifacts in less rough and more useful form than any previously known to his tribe. His hunting clubs were generally superior weapons, moreover, and his fire-using techniques were patterns of simplicity and precision. He knew how to do things his community needed to have done, and he had the energy and will to go ahead and do them. By virtue of these characteristics he was an educated man.

New-Fist was also a thinker. Then, as now, there were few lengths to which men would not go to avoid the labor and pain of thought. More readily than his fellows, New-Fist pushed himself beyond those lengths to the point where

J. Abner Peddiwell is the pseudonym for Harold W. Benjamin, a professor of education who died in 1969. From *The Saber-Tooth Curriculum* by J. Abner Peddiwell. Copyright © 1959 by McGraw-Hill, Inc. Used with permission of The McGraw-Hill Companies.

cerebration was inevitable. The same quality of intelligence which led him into the socially approved activity of producing a superior artifact also led him to engage in the socially disapproved practice of thinking. When other men gorged themselves on the proceeds of a successful hunt and vegetated in dull stupor for many hours thereafter, New-Fist ate a little less heartily, slept a little less stupidly, and arose a little earlier than his comrades to sit by the fire and think. He would stare moodily at the flickering flames and wonder about various parts of his environment until he finally got to the point where he became strongly dissatisfied with the accustomed ways of his tribe. He began to catch glimpses of ways in which life might be made better for himself, his family, and his group. By virtue of this development, he became a dangerous man.

This was the background that made this doer and thinker hit upon the concept of a conscious, systematic education. The immediate stimulus which put him directly into the practice of education came from watching his children at play. He saw these children at the cave entrance before the fire engaged in activity with bones and sticks and brightly colored pebbles. He noted that they seemed to have no purpose in their play beyond immediate pleasure in the activity itself. He compared their activity with that of the grown-up members of the tribe. The children played for fun; the adults worked for security and enrichment of their lives. The children dealt with bones, sticks, and pebbles; the adults dealt with food, shelter, and clothing. The children protected themselves from boredom; the adults protected themselves from danger.

"If I could only get these children to do the things that will give more and better food, shelter, clothing, and security," thought New-Fist, "I would be helping this tribe to have a better life. When the children became grown, they would have more meat to eat, more skins to keep them warm, better caves in which to sleep, and less danger from the striped death with the curving teeth that walks these trails at night."

Having set up an educational goal, New-Fist proceeded to construct a curriculum for reaching that goal. "What things must we tribesmen know how to do in order to live with full bellies, warm backs, and minds free from fear?" he asked himself.

To answer this question, he ran various activities over in his mind. "We have to catch fish with our bare hands in the pool far up the creek beyond that big bend," he said to himself. "We have to catch fish with our bare hands in the pool right at the bend. We have to catch them in the same way in the pool just this side of the bend. And so we catch them in the next pool and the next and the next. And we catch them with our bare hands."

Thus New-Fist discovered the first subject of the first curriculum—fish-grabbing-with-the-bare-hands.

"Also we club the little woolly horses," he continued with his analysis. "We club them along the bank of the creek where they come down to drink. We club them in the thickets where they lie down to sleep. We club them in the upland meadow where they graze. Wherever we find them we club them."

So woolly-horse-clubbing was seen to be the second main subject of the curriculum.

"And finally, we drive away the saber-tooth tigers with fire," New-Fist went on in his thinking. "We drive them from the mouth of our caves with fire. We drive them from our trail with burning branches. We wave firebrands to drive them from our drinking hole. Always we have to drive them away, and always we drive them with fire."

Thus was discovered the third subject—saber-tooth-tiger-scaring-with-fire.

Having developed a curriculum, New-Fist took his children with him as he went about his activities. He gave them an opportunity to practice these three subjects. The children liked to learn. It was more fun for them to engage in these purposeful activities than to play with colored stones just for the fun of it. They learned the new activities well, and so the educational system was a success.

As New-Fist's children grew older, it was plain to see that they had an advantage in good and safe living over other children who had never been educated systematically. Some of the more intelligent members of the tribe began to do as New-Fist had done, and the teaching of fish-grabbing, horse-clubbing, and tiger-scaring came more and more to be accepted as the heart of real education.

For a long time, however, there were certain more conservative members of the tribe who resisted the new, formal educational system on religious grounds. "The Great Mystery who speaks in thunder and moves in lightning," they announced impressively, "the Great Mystery who gives men life and takes it from them as he wills—if that Great Mystery had wanted children to practice fish-grabbing, horse-clubbing, and tiger-scaring before they were grown up, he would have taught them these activities himself by implanting in their natures instincts for fish-grabbing, horse-clubbing, and tiger-scaring. New-Fist is not only impious to attempt something the Great Mystery never intended to have done; he is also a damned fool for trying to change human nature."

Whereupon approximately half of these critics took up the solemn chant, "If you oppose the will of the Great Mystery, you must die," and the remainder sang derisively in unison, "You can't change human nature."

Being an educational statesman as well as an educational administrator and theorist, New-Fist replied politely to both arguments. To the more theologically minded, he said that, as a matter of fact, the Great Mystery had ordered this new work done, that he even did the work himself by causing children to want to learn, that children could not learn by themselves without divine aid, that they could not learn at all except through the power of the Great Mystery, and that nobody could really understand the will of the Great Mystery concerning fish, horses, and saber-tooth tigers unless he had been well grounded in three fundamental subjects of the New-Fist school. To the human-nature-cannot-be-changed shouters, New-Fist pointed out the fact that paleolithic culture had attained its high level by changes in human nature and that it seemed almost unpatriotic to deny the very process which had made the community great.

"I know you, my fellow tribesmen," the pioneer educator ended his argument gravely, "I know you as the humble and devoted servants of the Great Mystery. I know that you would not for one moment consciously oppose yourselves to his will. I know you as intelligent and loyal citizens of the great cave-realm, and I know that your pure and noble patriotism will not permit you to do anything which will block the development of that most cave-realmish of all our institutions—the paleolithic educational system. Now that you understand the true nature and purpose of this institution, I am serenely confident that there are no reasonable lengths to which you will not go in its defense and its support."

By this appeal the forces of conservatism were won over to the side of the new school, and in due time everybody who was anybody in the community knew that the heart of good education lay in the three subjects of fish-grabbing, horse-clubbing, and tiger-scaring. New-Fist and his contemporaries grew older and were gathered by the Great Mystery to the Land of the Sunset far down the creek. Other men followed their educational ways more and more, until at last all the children of the tribe were practiced systematically in the three fundamentals. Thus the tribe prospered and was happy in the possession of adequate meat, skins, and security.

It is to be supposed that all would have gone well forever with this good educational system if conditions of life in that community had remained forever the same. But conditions changed, and life which had once been so safe and happy in the cave-realm valley became insecure and disturbing.

A new ice age was approaching in that part of the world. A great glacier came down from the neighboring mountain range to the north. Year after year it crept closer and closer to the headwaters of the creek which ran through the tribe's valley, until at length it reached the stream and began to melt into the water. Dirt and gravel which the glacier had collected on its long journey were dropped into the creek. The water grew muddy. What had once been a crystal-clear stream in which one could see easily to the bottom was now a milky stream into which one could not see at all.

At once the life of the community was changed in one very important respect. It was no longer possible to catch fish with the bare hands. The fish could not be seen in the muddy water. For some years, moreover, the fish in the creek had been getting more timid, agile, and intelligent. The stupid, clumsy, brave fish, of which originally there had been a great many, had been caught with the bare hands for fish generation after fish generation, until only fish of superior intelligence and agility were left. These smart fish, hiding in the muddy water under the newly deposited glacial boulders, eluded the hands of the most expertly trained fish-grabbers. Those tribesmen who had studied advanced fish-grabbing in the secondary school could do no better than their less well-educated fellows who had taken only an elementary course in the subject, and even the university graduates with majors in ichthyology were baffled by the problem. No matter how good a man's fish-grabbing education had been, he could not grab fish when he could not find fish to grab.

The melting waters of the approaching ice sheet also made the country wetter. The ground became marshy far back from the banks of the creek. The stupid woolly horses, standing only five or six hands high and running on four-toed front feet and three-toed hind feet, although admirable objects for clubbing, had one dangerous characteristic. They were ambitious. They all wanted to learn to run on their middle toes. They all had visions of becoming powerful and aggressive animals instead of little and timid ones. They dreamed of a far-distant day when some of their descendants would be sixteen hands high, weigh more than half a ton, and be able to pitch their would-be riders into the dirt. They knew they could never attain these goals in a wet, marshy country, so they all went east to the dry, open plains, far from the paleolithic hunting grounds. Their places were taken by little ante-lopes who came down with the ice sheet and were so shy and speedy and had so keen a scent for danger that no one could approach them closely enough to club them.

The best trained horse-clubbers of the tribe went out day after day and employed the most efficient techniques taught in the schools, but day after day they returned empty-handed. A horse-clubbing education of the highest type could get no results when there were no horses to club.

Finally, to complete the disruption of paleo-lithic life and education, the new dampness in the air gave the saber-tooth tigers pneumonia, a disease to which these animals were peculiarly susceptible and to which most of them suc-cumbed. A few moth-eaten specimens crept south to the desert, it is true, but they were piti-fully few and weak representatives of a once numerous and powerful race.

So there were no more tigers to scare in the paleolithic community, and the best tiger-scaring techniques became only academic exercises, good in themselves, perhaps, but not necessary for tribal security. Yet this danger to the people was lost only to be replaced by another and even greater danger, for with the advancing ice sheet came ferocious glacial bears which were not afraid of fire, which walked the trails by day as well as by night, and which could not be driven away by the most advanced methods developed in the tiger-scaring course of the schools.

The community was now in a very difficult situation. There was no fish or meat for food, no hides for clothing, and no security from the hairy death that walked the trails day and night. Ad-justment to this difficulty had to be made at once if the tribe was not to become extinct.

Fortunately for the tribe, however, there were men in it of the old New-Fist breed, men who had the ability to do and the daring to think. One of them stood by the muddy stream, his stomach contracting with hunger pains, longing for some way to get a fish to eat. Again and again he had tried the old fish-grabbing technique that day, hoping desperately that at last it might work, but now in black despair he finally rejected all that he had learned in the schools and looked about him for some new way to get fish from that stream. There were stout but slender vines hanging from trees along the bank. He pulled them down and began to fasten them together more or less aim-lessly. As he worked, the vision of what he might do to satisfy his hunger and that of his crying children back in the cave grew clearer. His black despair lightened a little. He worked more rapidly and intelligently. At last he had it—a net, a crude seine. He called a companion and explained the device. The two men took the net into the water, into pool after pool, and in one hour they caught more fish—intelligent fish in muddy water—than the whole tribe could have caught in a day under the best fish-grabbing conditions.

Another intelligent member of the tribe wan-dered hungrily through the woods where once the stupid little horses had abounded but where now only the elusive antelope could be seen. He had tried the horse-clubbing technique on the antelope until he was fully convinced of its futil-ity. He knew that one would starve who relied on school learning to get him meat in those woods. Thus it was that he too, like the fish-net inventor, was finally impelled by hunger to new ways. He bent a strong, springy young tree over an antelope trail, hung a noosed vine therefrom, and fastened the whole device in so ingenious a fashion that the passing animal would release a trigger and be snared neatly when the tree jerked upright. By setting a line of these snares, he was able in one night to secure more meat and skins than a dozen horse-clubbers in the old days had secured in a week.

A third tribesman, determined to meet the problem of the ferocious bears, also forgot what he had been taught in school and began to think in direct and radical fashion. Finally, as a result of this thinking, he dug a deep pit in a bear trail, covered it with branches in such a way that a bear would walk on it unsuspectingly, fall through to the bottom, and remain trapped until the tribes-men could come up and despatch him with sticks and stones hat their leisure. The inventor showed his friends how to dig and camouflage other pits until all the trails around the community were furnished with them. Thus the tribe had even more security than before and in addition had the great additional store of meat and skins which they secured from the captured bears.

As the knowledge of these new inventions spread, all the members of the tribe were engaged in familiarizing themselves with the new ways of living. Men worked hard at making fish nets, setting antelope snares, and digging bear pits. The tribe was busy and prosperous.

There were a few thoughtful men who asked questions as they worked. Some of them even criticized the schools.

"These new activities of net-making and operating, snare-setting, and pit-digging are indispensable to modern existence," they said. "Why can't they be taught in school?"

The safe and sober majority had a quick reply to this naive question. "School!" they snorted derisively. "You aren't in school now. You are out here in the dirt working to preserve the life and happiness of the tribe. What have these practical activities got to do with schools? You're not saying lessons now. You'd better forget your lessons and your academic ideals of fish-grabbing, horse-clubbing, and tiger-scaring if you want to eat, keep warm, and have some measure of security from sudden death."

The radicals persisted a little in their questioning. "Fishnet-making and using, antelope-snare construction and operation, and bear-catching and killing," they pointed out, "require intelligence and skills—things we claim to develop in schools. They are also activities we need to know. Why can't the schools teach them?"

But most of the tribe, and particularly the wise old men who controlled the school, smiled indulgently at this suggestion. "That wouldn't be *education*," they said gently.

"But why wouldn't it be?" asked the radicals.

"Because it would be mere training," explained the old men patiently. "With all the intricate details of fish-grabbing, horse-clubbing, and tiger-scaring—the standard cultural subjects—the school curriculum is too crowded now. We

can't add these fads and frills of net-making, antelope-snaring, and—of all things—bear-killing. Why, at the very thought, the body of the great New-Fist, founder of our paleolithic educational system, would turn over in its burial cairn. What we need to do is to give our young people a more thorough grounding in the fundamentals. Even the graduates of the secondary schools don't know the art of fish-grabbing in any complete sense nowadays, they swing their horse clubs awkwardly too, and as for the old science of tiger-scaring—well, even the teachers seem to lack the real flair for the subject which we oldsters got in our teens and never forgot."

"But, damn it," exploded one of the radicals, "how can any person with good sense be interested in such useless activities? What is the point of trying to catch fish with the bare hands when it just can't be done any more? How can a boy learn to club horses when there are no horses left to club? And why in hell should children try to scare tigers with fire when the tigers are dead and gone?"

"Don't be foolish," said the wise old men, smiling most kindly smiles. "We don't teach fish-grabbing to grab fish; we teach it to develop a generalized agility which can never be developed by mere training. We don't teach horse-clubbing to club horses; we teach it to develop a generalized strength in the learner which he can never get from so prosaic and specialized a thing as antelope-snare-setting. We don't teach tiger-scaring to scare tigers; we teach it for the purpose of giving that noble courage which carries over into all the affairs of life and which can never come from so base an activity as bear-killing."

All the radicals were silenced by this statement, all except the one who was most radical of all. He felt abashed, it is true, but he was so radical that he made one last protest.

"But—but anyway," he suggested, "you will have to admit that times have changed. Couldn't you please *try* these other, more up-to-date activities? Maybe they have *some* educational value after all?"

Even the man's fellow radicals felt that this was going a little too far.

The wise old men were indignant. Their kindly smiles faded. "If you had any education yourself," they said severely, "you would know that the essence of true education is timelessness. It is something that endures through changing conditions like a solid rock standing squarely and firmly in the middle of a raging torrent. You must know that there are some eternal verities, and the saber-tooth curriculum is one of them!" ■

P O S T N O T E

One might think that *The Saber-Tooth Curriculum* had been written by a modern-day critic of the public school curriculum instead of someone writing in 1939. It is virtually impossible to read this selection without drawing parallels to courses and curricula that we have experienced. Fish-grabbing-with-the-bare-hands has not disappeared. It still exists today in most American schools, but it is called by a different name. And the same arguments used by the elders to defend the saber-tooth curriculum are used today to defend subjects that have outlived their right to remain in the curriculum. Why do they remain?

D I S C U S S I O N Q U E S T I O N S

1. What is the main message of this excerpt from *The Saber-Tooth Curriculum*?

2 What subjects, if any, in the current school curriculum would you equate with fish-grabbing-with-the-bare-hands? Why?

3. What new subjects would you suggest adding to the school curriculum to avoid creating our own saber-tooth curriculum? Why?

29

The Paideia Proposal: Rediscovering the Essence of Education

Mortimer J. Adler

I n the first 80 years of this century, we have met the obligation imposed on us by the principle of equal educational opportunity, but only in a quantitative sense. Now, as we approach the end of the century, we must achieve equality in qualitative terms.

This means a completely one-track system of schooling. It means, at the basic level, giving all the young the same kind of schooling, whether or not they are college bound.

We are aware that children, although equal in their common humanity and fundamental human rights, are unequal as individuals, differing in their capacity to learn. In addition, the homes and environments from which they come to school are unequal—either predisposing the child for schooling or doing the opposite.

Consequently, the Paideia Proposal, faithful to the principle of equal educational opportunity, includes the suggestion that inequalities due to environmental factors must be overcome by some form of preschool preparation—at least one year for all and two or even three for some. We

At the time this article was written, Mortimer J. Adler was chairman of the board of editors of Encyclopaedia Britannica and director of the Institute of Philosophical Research in Chicago, Illinois. From "The Paideia Proposal: Rediscovering the Essence of Education" by Mortimer J. Adler. Reprinted with permission, from *The American School Board Journal*, July 1982. Copyright © 1982, the National School Boards Association. All rights reserved.

know that to make such preschool tutelage compulsory at the public expense would be tantamount to increasing the duration of compulsory schooling from 12 years to 13, 14, or 15 years. Nevertheless, we think that this preschool adjunct to the 12 years of compulsory basic schooling is so important that some way must be found to make it available for all and to see that all use it to advantage.

The Essentials of Basic Schooling

The objectives of basic schooling should be the same for the whole school population. In our current two-track or multitrack system, the learning objectives are not the same for all. And even when the objectives aimed at those on the upper track are correct, the course of study now provided does not adequately realize these correct objectives. On all tracks in our current system, we fail to cultivate proficiency in the common tasks of learning, and we especially fail to develop sufficiently the indispensable skills of learning.

The uniform objectives of basic schooling should be threefold. They should correspond to three aspects of the common future to which all the children are destined: (1) Our society provides all children ample opportunity for personal development. Given such opportunity, each individual is under a moral obligation to make the most of himself and his life. Basic schooling must facilitate this accomplishment. (2) All the children will become, when of age, full-fledged citizens with suffrage and other political responsibilities. Basic schooling must do everything it can to make them good citizens, able to perform the duties of citizenship with all the trained intelligence that each is able to achieve. (3) When they are grown, all (or certainly most) of the children will engage in some form of work to earn a living. Basic schooling must prepare them for earning a living, but not by training them for this or that specific job while they are still in school.

To achieve these three objectives, the character of basic schooling must be general and liberal. It should have a single, required, 12-year course of study for all, with no electives except one—an elective choice with regard to a second language, to be selected from such modern languages as French, German, Italian, Spanish, Russian, and Chinese. The elimination of all electives, with this one exception, excludes what *should* be excluded—all forms of specialization, including particularized job training.

In its final form, the Paideia Proposal will detail this required course of study, but I will summarize the curriculum here in its bare outline. It consists of three main columns of teaching and learning, running through the 12 years and progressing, of course, from the simple to the more complex, from the less difficult to the more difficult, as the students grow older. Understand: The three columns (see table below) represent three distinct modes of teaching and learning. They do not represent a series of courses. A specific course or a class may employ more than one mode of teaching and learning, but all three modes are essential to the overall course of study.

The first column is devoted to acquiring knowledge in three subject areas: (A) language, literature, and the fine arts; (B) mathematics and natural science; (C) history, geography, and social studies.

The second column is devoted to developing the intellectual skills of learning. These include all the language skills necessary for thought and communication—the skills of reading, writing, speaking, listening. They also include mathematical and scientific skills; the skills of observing, measuring, estimating, and calculating; and skills in

The Paideia Curriculum

	COLUMN ONE	COLUMN TWO	COLUMN THREE
Goals	Acquisition of Organized Knowledge	Development of Intellectual Skills and Skills of Learning	Improved Understanding of Ideas and Values
	by means of	by means of	by means of
Means	Didactic Instruction, Lecturing, and Textbooks	Coaching, Exercises, and Supervised Practice	Maieutic or Socratic Questioning and Active Participation
	in these three subject areas	in these operations	in these activities
Subject Areas, Operations, and Activities	Language, Literature, and Fine Arts Mathematics and Natural Science History, Geography, and Social Studies	Reading, Writing, Speaking, Listening, Calculating, Problem Solving, Observing, Measuring, Estimating, Exercising Critical Judgment	Discussion of Books (Not Textbooks) and Other Works of Art Involvement in Music, Drama, and Visual Arts

The three columns do not correspond to separate courses, nor is one kind of teaching and learning necessarily confined to any one class.

the use of the computer and of other scientific instruments. Together, these skills make it possible to think clearly and critically. They once were called the liberal arts—the intellectual skills indispensable to being competent as a learner.

The third column is devoted to enlarging the understanding of ideas and values. The materials of the third column are books (*not* textbooks), and other products of human artistry. These materials include books of every variety—historical, scientific, and philosophical as well as poems, stories, and essays—and also individual pieces of music, visual art, dramatic productions, dance productions, film or television productions. Music and works of visual art can be used in seminars in which ideas are discussed; but as with poetry and fiction, they also are to be experienced aesthetically, to be enjoyed and admired for their excellence. In this connection, exercises in the composition of poetry, music, and visual works and in the production of dramatic works should be used to develop the appreciation of excellence.

The three columns represent three different kinds of learning on the part of the student and three different kinds of instruction on the part of teachers.

In the first column, the students are engaged in acquiring information and organized knowledge about nature, man, and human society. The method of instruction here, using textbooks and manuals, is didactic. The teacher lectures, invites responses from the students, monitors the acquisition of knowledge, and tests that acquisition in various ways.

In the second column, the students are engaged in developing habits of performance, which is all that is involved in the development of an art or skill. Art, skill, or technique is nothing more than a cultivated, habitual ability to do a certain kind of thing well, whether that is swimming and dancing or reading and writing. Here, students are acquiring linguistic, mathematical, scientific, and historical *know-how* in contrast to what they acquire in the first column, which is *know-that* with respect to language, literature, and the fine arts, mathematics and science, history, geography, and social studies. Here, the method of instruction can-

not be didactic or monitorial; it cannot be dependent on textbooks. It must be coaching, the same kind used in the gym to develop bodily skills; only here it is used by a different kind of coach in the classroom to develop intellectual skills.

In the third column, students are engaged in a process of enlightenment, the process whereby they develop their understanding of the basic and controlling ideas in all fields of subject matter and come to appreciate better all the human values embodied in works of art. Here, students move progressively from understanding less to understanding more—understanding better what they already know and appreciating more what they already have experienced. Here, the method of instruction cannot be either didactic or coaching. It must be the Socratic, or maieutic, method of questioning and discussing. It should not occur in an ordinary classroom with the students sitting in rows and the teacher in front of the class, but in a seminar room, with the students sitting around a table and the teacher sitting with them as an equal, even though a little older and wiser.

Of these three main elements in the required curriculum, the third column is completely innovative. Nothing like this is done in our schools, and because it is completely absent from the ordinary curriculum of basic schooling, the students never have the experience of having their minds addressed in a challenging way or of being asked to think about important ideas, to express their thoughts, to defend their opinions in a reasonable fashion.

The only thing that is innovative about the second column is the insistence that the method of instruction here must be coaching carried on either with one student at a time or with very small groups of students. Nothing else can be effective in the development of a skill, be it bodily or intellectual. The absence of such individualized coaching in our schools explains why most of the students cannot read well, write well, speak well, listen well, or perform well any of the other basic intellectual operations.

The three columns are closely interconnected and integrated, but the middle column—the one concerned with linguistic, mathematical, and scientific skills—is central. It both supports and is supported by the other two columns. All the intellectual skills with which it is concerned must be exercised in the study of the three basic subject-matters and in acquiring knowledge about them, and these intellectual skills must be exercised in the seminars devoted to the discussion of books and other things.

In addition to the three main columns in the curriculum, ascending through the 12 years of basic schooling, there are three adjuncts: One is 12 years of physical training, accompanied by instruction in bodily care and hygiene. The second, running through something less than 12 years, is the development of basic manual skills, such as cooking, sewing, carpentry, and the operation of all kinds of machines. The third, reserved for the last year or two, is an introduction to the whole world of work—the range of occupations in which human beings earn their livings. This is not particularized job training. It is the very opposite. It aims at a broad understanding of what is involved in working for a living and of the various ways in which that can be done. If, at the end of 12 years, students wish training for specific jobs, they should get that in two-year or in technical institutes of one sort or another.

Everything that has not been specifically mentioned as occupying the time of the school day should be reserved for after-hours and have the status of extracurricular activities.

Please note: The required course of study just described is as important for what it *displaces* as for what it introduces. It displaces a multitude of elective courses, especially those offered in our secondary schools, most of which make little or no contribution to general, liberal education. It eliminates all narrowly specialized job training, which now abounds in our schools. It throws out of the curriculum and into the category of optional extracurricular activities a variety of things that have little or no educational value.

If it did not call for all these displacements, there would not be enough time in the school day or year to accomplish everything that is essential to the general, liberal learning that must be the content of basic schooling.

The Quintessential Element

So far, I have set forth the bare essentials of the Paideia Proposal with regard to basic schooling. I have not yet mentioned the quintessential element—the *sine qua non*—without which nothing else can possibly come to fruition, no matter how sound it might be in principle. The heart of the matter is the quality of learning and the quality of teaching that occupies the school day, not to mention the quality of the homework after school.

First, the learning must be active. It must use the whole mind, not just the memory. It must be learning by discovery, in which the student, never the teacher, is the primary agent. Learning by discovery, which is the only genuine learning, may be either unaided or aided. It is unaided only for geniuses. For most students, discovery must be aided.

Here is where teachers come in—as aids in the process of learning by discovery, not as knowers who attempt to put the knowledge they have into the minds of their students. The quality of the teaching, in short, depends crucially upon how the teacher conceives his role in the process of learning, and that must be as an aid to the student's process of discovery.

I am prepared for the questions that must be agitating you by now: How and where will we get the teachers who can perform as teachers should? How will we be able to staff the program with teachers so trained that they will be competent to provide the quality of instruction required for the quality of learning desired?

The first part of our answer to these questions is negative: We *cannot* get the teachers we need for the Paideia program from schools of education *as they are now constituted*. As teachers are now trained for teaching, they simply will not do. The ideal—an impracticable ideal—would be to ask for teachers who are, themselves, truly educated human beings. But truly educated human beings are too rare. Even if we could draft all who are now alive, there still would be far too few to staff our schools.

Well, then, what can we look for? Look for teachers who are actively engaged in the process of *becoming* educated human beings, who are themselves deeply motivated to develop their own minds. Assuming this is not too much to ask for the present, how should teachers be schooled and trained in the future? First, they should have the same kind of basic schooling that is recommended in the Paideia Proposal. Second, they should have additional schooling, at the college and even the university level, in which the same kind of general, liberal learning is carried on at advanced levels—more deeply, broadly, and intensively than it can be done in the first 12 years of schooling. Third, they must be given something analogous to the clinical experience in the training of physicians. They must engage in practice-teaching under supervision, which is another way of saying that they must be *coached* in the arts of teaching, not just given didactic instruction in educational psychology and in pedagogy. Finally, and most important of all, they must learn how to teach well by being exposed to the performances of those who are masters of the arts involved in teaching.

It is by watching a good teacher at work that they will be able to perceive what is involved in the process of assisting others to learn by discovery. Perceiving it, they must then try to emulate what they observe, and through this process, they slowly will become good teachers themselves.

The Paideia Proposal recognizes the need for three different kinds of institutions at the collegiate level: The two-year community or junior college should offer a wide choice of electives that give students some training in one or another specialized field, mainly those fields of study that have something to do with earning a living. The four-year college also should offer a wide variety of electives, to be chosen by students who aim at the various professional or technical occupations that require advanced study. Those elective majors chosen by students should be accompanied, for all students, by one required minor, in which the kind of general and liberal learning that was begun at the level of basic schooling is continued at a higher level in the four years of college. And we should have still a third type of collegiate institution—a four-year college in which general, liberal learning at a higher level constitutes a required course of study that is to be taken by all students. *It is this third type of college, by the way, that should be attended by all who plan to become teachers in our basic schools.*

At the university level, there should be a continuation of general, liberal learning at a still higher level to accompany intensive specialization in this or that field of science or scholarship, this or that learned profession. Our insistence on the continuation of general, liberal learning at all the higher levels of schooling stems from our concern with the worst cultural disease that is rampant in our society—*the barbarism of specialization.*

There is no question that our technologically advanced industrial society needs specialists of all sorts. There is no question that the advancement of knowledge in all fields of science and scholarship, and in all the learned professions, needs intense specialization. But for the sake of preserving and enhancing our cultural traditions, as well as for the health of science and scholarship, we need specialists who also are generalists—generally cultivated human beings, not just good plumbers. We need truly educated human beings who can perform their special tasks better precisely because they have general cultivation as well as intensely specialized training.

Changes indeed are needed in higher education, but those improvements cannot reasonably be expected unless improvement in basic schooling makes that possible.

The Future of Our Free Institutions

I already have declared as emphatically as I know how that the quality of human life in our society depends on the quality of the schooling we give our young people, both basic and advanced. But a marked elevation in the quality of human life is not the only reason improving the quality of schooling is so necessary—not the only reason we must move heaven and earth to stop the deterioration of our schools and turn them in the opposite direction. The other reason is to safeguard the future of our free institutions.

They cannot prosper, they may not even survive, unless we do something to rescue our schools from their current deplorable deterioration. Democracy, in the full sense of the term, came into existence only in this century and only in a few countries on earth, among which the United States is an outstanding example. But democracy came into existence in this century only in its initial conditions, all of which hold out promises for the future that remain to be fulfilled. Unless we do something about improving the quality of basic schooling for all and the quality of advanced schooling for some, there is little chance that those promises ever will be fulfilled. And if they are not, our free institutions are doomed to decay and wither away.

We face many insistently urgent problems. Our prosperity and even our survival depend on the solution of those problems—the threat of nuclear war, the exhaustion of essential resources and of supplies of energy, the pollution or spoil-age of the environment, the spiraling of inflation accompanied by the spread of unemployment.

To solve these problems, we need resourceful and innovative leadership. For that to arise and be effective, an educated populace is needed. Trained intelligence—not only on the part of leaders, but also on the part of followers—holds the key to the solution of the problems our society faces. Achieving peace, prosperity, and plenty could put us on the threshold of an early paradise. But a much better educational system than now exists is needed, for that alone can carry us across the threshold. Without it, a poorly schooled population will not be able to put to good use the opportunities afforded by the achievement of the general welfare. Those who are not schooled to enjoy society can only despoil its institutions and corrupt themselves. ■

POST NOTE

This article by Mortimer J. Adler is representative of a *perennialist* philosophy. Perennialists believe that truth is best revealed in the enduring classics of Western culture and that the schools' curriculum should consist of the traditional subjects—history, language, mathematics, science, and the arts. Derived from the Greek word, *paideia* signifies the general learning that should be the possession of all human beings.

By eliminating a differentiated curriculum from elementary and secondary schools and requiring all students to take a common curriculum, Adler believes, we can give all students the quality education currently available only to those on a high track. Adler and many of his supporters have established a network of individuals who are implementing these ideas in a variety of public and private schools around the country.

DISCUSSION QUESTIONS

1. What do you see as the merits of Adler's proposal? The drawbacks? Why?

2. What kinds of individuals or groups are likely to be supportive of a curriculum structured according to Adler's "three columns"? Who is apt to oppose this type of curriculum? Why?

3. Should vocational education be eliminated from K–12 schooling? Why or why not?

30 The Core Knowledge Curriculum—What's Behind Its Success?

E. D. Hirsch, Jr.

The Mohegan School, in the South Bronx, is surrounded by the evidence of urban blight: trash, abandoned cars, crack houses. The students, mostly Latino or African-American, all qualify for free lunch. This public elementary school is located in the innermost inner city.

In January 1992, CBS Evening News devoted an "Eye on America" segment to the Mohegan School. Why did CBS focus on Mohegan of several schools that had experienced dramatic improvements after adopting the Core Knowledge guidelines? I think it was in part because this school seemed an unlikely place for a low-cost, academically solid program like Core Knowledge to succeed.

Mohegan's talented principal, Jeffrey Litt, wrote to me that "the richness of the curriculum is of particular importance" to his students because their educational experience, like that of "most poverty-stricken and educationally underserved students, was limited to remedial activities." Since adopting the Core Knowledge curriculum, however, Mohegan's students are engaged in the integrated and coherent study of topics like: Ancient Egypt, Greece, and Rome; the Industrial Revolution; limericks, haiku, and poetry; Rembrandt,

Monet, and Michelangelo; Beethoven and Mozart; the Underground Railroad; the Trail of Tears; Brown v. Board of Education; the Mexican Revolution; photosynthesis; medieval African empires; the Bill of Rights; ecosystems; women's suffrage; the Harlem Renaissance—and many more.

The Philosophy Behind Core Knowledge

In addition to offering compelling subject matter, the Core Knowledge guidelines for elementary schools are far more specific than those issued by most school districts. Instead of vague outcomes such as "First graders will be introduced to map skills," the geography section of the *Core Knowledge Sequence* specifies that 1st graders will learn the meaning of "east," "west," "north," and "south" and locate on a map the equator, the Atlantic and Pacific Oceans, the seven continents, the United States, Mexico, Canada, and Central America.

Our aim in providing specific grade-by-grade guidelines—developed after several years of research, consultation, consensus-building, and field-testing—is *not* to claim that the content we recommend is better than some other well-thought-out core. No specific guidelines could plausibly claim to be the Platonic ideal. But one must make a start. To get beyond the talking stage, we created the best specific guidelines we could.

Nor is it our aim to specify *everything* that American schoolchildren should learn (the Core Knowledge guidelines are meant to constitute about 50 percent of a school's curriculum, thus leaving the other half to be tailored to a district, school, or classroom). Rather, our point is that a core of shared knowledge, grade by grade, is needed to achieve excellence and fairness in elementary education.

International studies have shown that *any* school that puts into practice a similarly challenging and specific program will provide a more effective and fair education than one that lacks such commonality of content in each grade.[1] High-performing systems such as those in France, Sweden, Japan, and West Germany

E. D. Hirsch, Jr., is a professor at the University of Virginia in Charlottesville and founder of the Core Knowledge Foundation. From "The Core Knowledge Curriculum—What's Behind Its Success?" by E. D. Hirsch, Jr., in *Educational Leadership*, May 1993, Vol. 50, No. 8. Copyright © 1993. Used with permission.

bear out this principle. It was our intent to test whether in rural, urban, and suburban settings of the United States we would find what other nations have already discovered.

Certainly the finding that a school-wide core sequence greatly enhances achievement *for all* is supported at the Mohegan School. Disciplinary problems there are down; teacher and student attendance are up, as are scores on standardized tests. Some of the teachers have even transferred their own children to the school, and some parents have taken their children out of private schools to send them to Mohegan. Similar results are being reported at some 65 schools across the nation that are taking steps to integrate the Core Knowledge guidelines into their curriculums.

In the broadcast feature about the Mohegan School, I was especially interested to hear 5th grade teacher Evelyn Hernandez say that Core Knowledge "tremendously increased the students' ability to question." In other words, based on that teacher's classroom experience, *a coherent approach to specific content enhances students' critical thinking and higher-order thinking skills.*

I emphasize this point because a standard objection to teaching specific content is that critical thinking suffers when a teacher emphasizes "mere information." Yet Core Knowledge teachers across the nation report that a coherent focus on content leads to higher-order thinking skills more securely than any other approach they know, including attempts to inculcate such skills directly. As an added benefit, children acquire knowledge that they will find useful not just in next year's classroom but for the rest of their lives.

Why Core Knowledge Works

Here are some of the research findings that explain the correlation between a coherent, specific approach to knowledge and the development of higher-order skills.

Learning can be fun, but is nonetheless cumulative and sometimes arduous. The dream of inventing methods to streamline the time-consuming activity of learning is as old as the hills. In antiquity it was already an old story. Proclus records an anecdote about an encounter between Euclid, the inventor of geometry, and King Ptolemy I of Egypt (276–196 B.C.), who was impatiently trying to follow Euclid's *Elements* step by laborious step. Exasperated, the king demanded a faster, easier way to learn geometry—to which Euclid gave the famous, and still true, reply: "There is no royal road to geometry."

Even with computer technology, it's far from easy to find short-cuts to the basic human activity of learning. The human brain sets limits on the potential for educational innovation. We can't, for instance, put a faster chip in the human brain. The frequency of its central processing unit is timed in thousandths rather than millionths of a second.[2] Nor can we change the fundamental, constructive psychology of the learning process, which dictates that we humans must acquire new knowledge much as a tree acquires new leaves. The old leaves actively help nourish the new. The more "old growth" (prior knowledge) we have, the faster new growth can occur, making learning an organic process in which knowledge builds upon knowledge.

Because modern classrooms cannot effectively deliver completely individualized instruction, effective education requires grade-by-grade shared knowledge. When an individual child "gets" what is being taught in a classroom, it is like someone understanding a joke. A click occurs. If you have the requisite background knowledge, you will get the joke, but if you don't, you will remain puzzled until somebody explains the knowledge that was taken for granted. Similarly, a classroom of 25 to 35 children can move forward as a group only when *all* the children have the knowledge that is necessary to "getting" the next step in learning.

Studies comparing elementary schools in the United States to schools in countries with core knowledge systems disclose a striking difference in the structure of classroom activities.[3] In the best-performing classrooms constant back-and-forth interaction among groups of students and between students and the teacher consumes more than 80 percent of classroom time. By contrast, in the United States, over 50 percent of student time is spent in silent isolation.[4]

Behind the undue amount of "alone time" in our schools stands a theory that goes as follows: Every child is a unique individual; hence each child should receive instruction paced and tailored to that child. The theory should inform classroom practice as far as feasible: one hopes for teachers sensitive to the individual child's needs and strengths. The theory also reveals why good classroom teaching is difficult, and why a one-on-one tutorial is the most effective form of instruction. But modern education cannot be conducted as a one-on-one tutorial. Even in a country as affluent as the United States, instruction is carried out in classes of 25 to 35 pupils. In Dade County, Florida, the average class size for the early grades is 35. When a teacher gives individual attention to one child, 34 other pupils are left to fend for themselves. This is hardly a good trade-off, even on the premise that each child deserves individual attention.

Consider the significance of these facts in accounting for the slow progress (by international standards) of American elementary schools. If an entire classroom must constantly pause while its lagging members acquire background knowledge that they should have gained in earlier grades, the progress is bound to be slow. For effective, fair classroom instruction to take place, all members of the class need to share enough common reference points to enable everyone to understand and learn—though of course at differing rates and in response to varied approaches. When this commonality of knowledge is lacking, progress in learning will be slow compared with systems that use a core curriculum.

Just as learning is cumulative, so are learning deficits. As they begin 1st grade, American students are not far behind beginners in other developed nations. But as they progress, their achievement falls farther and farther behind. This widening gap is the subject of one of the most important recent books on American education, *The Learning Gap* by Stevenson and Stigler.

This progressively widening gap closely parallels what happens *within* American elementary schools between advantaged and disadvantaged children. As the two groups progress from grades 1–6, the achievement gap grows ever larger and is almost never overcome.[5] The reasons for the parallels between the two kinds of gaps—the learning gap and the fairness gap—are similar.

In both cases, the widening gap represents the cumulative effect of learning deficits. Although a few talented and motivated children may overcome this ever-increasing handicap, most do not. The rift grows ever wider in adult life. The basic causes of this permanent deficit, apart from motivational ones, are cognitive. Learning builds upon learning in a cumulative way, and lack of learning in the early grades usually has, in comparative terms, a negatively cumulative effect.

We know from large-scale longitudinal evidence, particularly from France, that this fateful gap between haves and have-nots *can* be closed.[6] But only one way to close it has been devised: to set forth explicit, year-by-year knowledge standards in early grades, so they are known to all parties—educators, parents, and children. Such standards are requisites for home-school cooperation and for reaching a general level of excellence. But, equally, they are requisites in gaining fairness for the academic have-nots: explicit year-by-year knowledge standards enable schools in nations with strong elementary core curriculums to remedy the knowledge deficits of disadvantaged children.

High academic skill is based upon broad general knowledge. Someone once asked Boris Goldovsky how he could play the piano so brilliantly with such small hands. His memorable reply was: "Where in the world did you get the idea that we play the piano with our hands?"

It's the same with reading: we don't read just with our eyes. By 7th grade, according to the epoch-making research of Thomas Sticht, most children, even those who read badly, have already attained the purely technical proficiency they need. Their reading and their listening show the same rate and level of comprehension; thus the mechanics of reading are not the limiting factor.[7] What is mainly lacking in poor readers is a broad, ready vocabulary. But broad vocabulary means broad knowledge, because to know a lot of words you have to know a lot of things. Thus, broad general knowledge is an *essential* requisite to superior reading skill and indirectly related to the skills that accompany it.

Superior reading skill is known to be highly correlated with most other academic skills, including the ability to write well, learn rapidly, solve problems, and think critically. To concentrate on reading is therefore to focus implicitly on a whole range of educational issues.[8]

It is sometimes claimed (but not backed up with research) that knowledge changes so rapidly in our fast-changing world that we need not get bogged down with "mere information." A corollary to the argument is that because information quickly becomes obsolete, it is more important to learn "accessing" skills (how to look things up or how to use a calculator) than to learn "mere facts."

The evidence in the psychological literature on skill acquisition goes strongly against this widely stated claim.[9] Its fallacy can be summed up in a letter I received from a head reference librarian. A specialist in accessing knowledge, he was distressed because the young people now being trained as *reference specialists* had so little general knowledge that they could not effectively help the public access knowledge. His direct experience (backed up by the research literature) had caused him to reject the theory of education as the gaining of accessing skills.

In fact, the opposite inference should be drawn from our fast-changing world. The fundamentals of science change very slowly; those of elementary math hardly at all. The famous names of geography and history (the "leaves" of that knowledge tree) change faster, but not root and branch from year to year. A wide range of this stable, fundamental knowledge is the key to rapid adaptation and the learning of new skills. It is precisely *because* the needs of a modern economy are so changeable that one needs broad general knowledge in order to flourish. Only high literacy

(which implies broad general knowledge) provides the flexibility to learn new things fast. The only known route to broad general knowledge for all is for a nation's schools to provide all students with a substantial, solid core of knowledge.

Common content leads to higher school morale, as well as better teaching and learning. At every Core Knowledge school, a sense of community and common purpose have knit people together. Clear content guidelines have encouraged those who teach at the same grade level to collaborate in creating effective lesson plans and schoolwide activities. Similarly, a clear sense of purpose has encouraged cooperation among grades as well. Because the *Core Knowledge Sequence* makes no requirements about *how* the specified knowledge should be presented, individual schools and teachers have great scope for independence and creativity. Site-based governance is the order of the day at Core Knowledge schools—but with definite aims, and thus a clear sense of communal purpose.

The Myth of the Existing Curriculum

Much of the public currently assumes that each elementary school already follows a schoolwide curriculum. Yet frustrated parents continually write the Core Knowledge Foundation to complain that principals are not able to tell them with any explicitness what their child will be learning during the year. Memorably, a mother of identical twins wrote that because her children had been placed in different classrooms, they were learning completely different things.

Such curricular incoherence, typical of elementary education in the United States today, places enormous burdens on teachers. Because they must cope with such diversity of preparation at each subsequent grade level, teachers find it almost impossible to create learning communities in their classrooms. Stevenson and Stigler rightly conclude that the most significant diversity faced by our schools is *not* cultural diversity but, rather, diversity of academic preparation. To achieve excellence and fairness for all, an elementary school *must* follow a coherent sequence of solid, specific content. ■

Notes

1. International Association for the Evaluation of Education Achievement (IEA), (1988), *Science Achievement in Seventeen Countries: A Preliminary Report*, (Elmsford, N.Y.: Pergamon Press). . . . [Data] show a consistent correlation between core knowledge systems and equality of opportunity for all students. The subject is discussed at length in E. D. Hirsch, Jr., "Fairness and Core Knowledge," *Occasional Papers 2*, available from the Core Knowledge Foundation, 2012-B Morton Dr., Charlottesville, VA 22901.

2. An absolute limitation of the mind's speed of operation is 50 milliseconds per minimal item. See A. B. Kristofferson, (1967), "Attention and Psychophysical Time," *Acta Psychologica* 27:93–100.

3. The data in this paragraph come from H. Stevenson and J. Stigler, (1992), *The Learning Gap*, (New York: Summit Books).

4. Stevenson and Stigler, pp. 52–71.

5. W. Loban, (March 1964), *Language Ability: Grades Seven, Eight, and Nine*, (Project No. 1131), University of California, Berkeley; as expanded and interpreted by T. G. Sticht, L. B. Beck, R. N. Hauke, G. M. Kleiman, and J. H. James, (1974), *Auding and Reading: A Developmental Model*, (Alexandria, Va.: Human Resources Research Organization); J. S. Chall, (1982), *Families and Literacy, Final Report to the National Institute of Education*; and especially, J. S. Chall, V. A. Jacobs, and L. E. Baldwin, (1990), *The Reading Crisis: Why Poor Children Fall Behind*, (Cambridge, Mass.: Harvard University Press).

6. S. Boulot and D. Boyzon-Fradet, (1988), *Les immigrés et l'école: une course d'obstacles*, Paris, pp. 54–58; Centre for Educational Research and Innovation (CERI), (1987), *Immigrants' Children at School*, Paris, pp. 178–259.

7. T. G. Sticht and H. J. James, (1984), "Listening and Reading," in *Handbook of Reading Research*, edited by P. D. Pearson, (New York: Longman).

8. A. L. Brown, (1980), "Metacognitive Development and Reading," in *Theoretical Issues in Reading Comprehension*, edited by R. J. Spiro, B. C. Bruce, and W. F. Brewer, (Hillsdale, N.J.: L. Earlbaum Associates).

9. J. R. Anderson, ed., (1981), *Cognitive Skills and Their Acquisition*, (Hillsdale, N.J.: L. Earlbaum Associates).

P O S T N O T E

In 1987, E. D. Hirsch, Jr., published the enormously successful book *Cultural Literacy: What Every American Needs to Know*. In that book, Hirsch argues that Americans need to possess cultural literacy—that is, knowledge of the persons, events, literature, and science that forms the basis of shared knowledge in American culture.

Since the publication of *Cultural Literacy*, Hirsch has worked with educators to develop his Core Knowledge curriculum for the elementary grades; it is currently being implemented in over one thousand schools in the United States. In a series of books, Hirsch and his collaborators have set forth the cultural knowledge that they believe should be taught at each grade level. Hirsch believes that children from advantaged homes have always had access to this knowledge but that children from disadvantaged homes have not. By teaching children a common core of knowledge in school, Hirsch believes that the barriers to adult literacy (and thus to full citizenship and full acculturation into society) can be overcome.

In spite of careful attention to including cultural knowledge from many facets of American society in his Core Knowledge curriculum, some people still believe that Hirsch promotes Western European culture over other cultures represented in our society. Examine *What Every First Grader Needs to Know*, as well as other similarly titled books for grades two through six, and decide for yourself.

1. Why doesn't the United States have a common national curriculum as many other countries do?

2. Do you agree or disagree with Hirsch's contention that cultural literacy is important in sustaining a democracy? Why? What are the counterarguments?

3. Would you like to teach in a school that has implemented the Core Knowledge curriculum? Why or why not?

31

The Quality School Curriculum

William Glasser

Recently I had a chance to talk to the staff members of a high school who had been hard at work for six months trying to change their school into a Quality School. They believed that they were much less coercive than in the past, but they complained that many of their students were still not working hard and that a few continued to be disruptive. They admitted that things were better but asked me if maybe they should reinject a little coercion back into their classroom management in order to "stimulate" the students to work harder.

I assured them that the answer to their complaints was to use less, not more, coercion. At the same time, I realized that in their teaching they had not yet addressed a vital component of the Quality School, the curriculum. To complete the move from coercive boss-managing to noncoercive lead-managing,[1] they had to change the curriculum they were teaching.

This was made ever clearer to me during the break when I talked to a few teachers individually. They told me that they had already made many of the changes that I suggest below and that they were not having the problems with students that most of the staff members were having. Until almost all the teachers change their curriculum, I

William Glasser, M.D., is a board-certified psychiatrist and founder and president of the Institute for Reality Therapy, Canoga Park, California. Glasser, William, "The Quality School Curriculum," *Phi Delta Kappan,* May 1992. Copyright © 1992 by Phi Delta Kappa. Reprinted by permission of author and publisher.

strongly believe that they will be unable to rid their classrooms of the coercion that causes too many of their students to continue to be their adversaries.

In Chapter 1 of *The Quality School,* I briefly cited the research of Linda McNeil of Rice University to support my claim that boss-management is destructive to the quality of the curriculum.[2] From feedback I have been receiving, it seems that the schools that are trying to become Quality Schools have not paid enough attention to this important point. I am partly at fault. When I wrote *The Quality School,* I did not realize how vital it is for teachers to make sure that they teach quality, and I did not explain sufficiently what this means. To correct this shortcoming, I want to expand on what I wrote in the book, and I strongly encourage staff members of all the schools that seek to move to quality to spend a great deal of time discussing this matter.

We must face the fact that a majority of students, even good ones, believe that much of the present academic curriculum is not worth the effort it takes to learn it. No matter how well the teachers manage them, if students do not find quality in what they are asked to do in their classes, they will not work hard enough to learn the material. The answer is not to try to make them work harder; the answer is to increase the quality of what we ask them to learn.

Faced with students who refuse to make much effort, even teachers who are trying to become lead-managers give a lot of low grades—a practice so traditional that they fail to perceive it as coercive. Then the students deal with their low grades by rebelling and working even less than before. The teachers, in turn, resent this attitude. They believe that, because they are making the effort to be less coercive, the students should be appreciative and work harder. The teachers fail to see that the students are not rebelling against them and their efforts to become lead-managers; they are rebelling against a curriculum that lacks quality. Therefore, if we want to create Quality Schools, we must stop *all* coercion, not just some, and one way to do this is to create a quality curriculum.

Before I describe a quality curriculum, let me use a simple nonschool example to try to explain what it is about the curriculum we have now that lacks quality. Suppose you get a job in a factory making both black shoes and brown shoes. You are well-managed and do quality work. But soon you become aware that all the brown shoes you make are sold for scrap; only the black shoes are going into retail stores. How long would you continue to work hard on the brown shoes? As you slack off, however, you are told that this is not acceptable and that you will lose pay or be fired if you don't buckle down and do just as good a job on the brown as on the black. You are told that what happens to the brown shoes is none of your business. Your job is to work hard. Wouldn't it be almost impossible to do as you are told?

As silly as the preceding example may seem, students in schools, even students in colleges and graduate schools, are asked to learn well enough to remember for important tests innumerable facts that both they and their teachers know are of no use except to pass the tests. I call this throwaway information because, after they do the work to learn it, that is just what students do with it. Dates and places in history, the names of parts of organisms and organs in biology, and formulas in mathematics and science are all examples of throwaway information.

Newspapers sometimes publish accounts of widespread cheating in schools and label it a symptom of the moral disintegration of our society. But what they call "cheating" turns out to be the ways that students have devised to avoid the work of memorizing throwaway knowledge. The honest students who are penalized are not pleased, but many students and faculty members and most of the informed public do not seem unduly upset about the "cheating." They are aware that there is no value to much of what students are asked to remember. I certainly do not condone cheating, but I must stress that, as long as we have a curriculum that holds students responsible for throwaway information, there will be cheating—and few people will care.

Elsewhere I have suggested that this throwaway knowledge could also be called "nonsense."[3] While it is not nonsense to ask students to

be aware of formulas, dates, and places and to know how to use them and where to find them if they need them, it becomes nonsense when we ask students to memorize this information and when we lower their grades if they fail to do so. Whether called throwaway knowledge or nonsense, this kind of memorized information can never be a part of the curriculum of a Quality School.

This means that in a Quality School there should never be test questions that call for the mere regurgitation of bare facts, such as those written in a book or stored in the memory of a computer. Students should never be asked to commit this portion of the curriculum to memory. All available information on what is being studied should always be on hand, not only during class but during all tests. No student should ever suffer academically because he or she forgot some fact or formula. The only useful way to test students' knowledge of facts, formulas, and other information is to ask not what the information is, but where, when, why, and how it is of use in the real world.

While a complete definition of quality is elusive, it certainly would include usefulness in the real world. And useful need not be restricted to practical or utilitarian. That which is useful can be aesthetically or spiritually useful or useful in some other way that is meaningful to the student—but it can never be nonsense.

In a Quality School, when questions of where, why, when, and how are asked on a test, they are never part of what is called an "objective" test, such as a multiple-choice, true/false, or short answer test. For example, if a multiple-choice test is used to ask where, why, when, and how, the student in a Quality School should not be restricted to a list of predetermined choices. There should always be a place for a student to write out a better answer if he or she believes that the available choices are less accurate than another alternative. For example, a multiple-choice test question in history might be: "George Washington is called 'the father of his country' for the following reasons: [four reasons would then be listed]. Which do you think is the best reason?" The student could choose one of the listed answers or write in another and explain why he or she thought it better than those listed.

In a Quality School questions as narrow as the preceding example would be rare, simply because of the constant effort to relate all that is taught to the lives of the students. Therefore, if a question asking where, when, why, and how certain information could be used were asked, it would always be followed by the further question: "How can you use this information in your life, now or in the future?"

However, such a follow-up question would never come out of the blue. The real-world value of the material to be learned would have been emphasized in lectures, in class discussions, in cooperative learning groups, and even in homework assignments that ask students to discuss with parents or other adults how what they learn in school might be useful outside of school. The purpose of such follow-up questions is to stress that the curriculum in a Quality School focuses on useful skills, not on information that has no use in the lives of those who are taught it. I define a *skill* as the ability to use knowledge. If we emphasized such skills in every academic subject, there would be no rebellion on the part of students. Students could earn equal credit on a test for explaining why what was taught was or was not of use to them. This would encourage them to think, not to parrot the ideas of others.

Continuing with the George Washington question, if a student in a Quality School said that Washington's refusal to be crowned king makes him a good candidate to be considered father of this republic, a teacher could ask that student how he or she could use this information in life now or later. The student might respond that he or she prefers to live in a republic and would not like to live in a country where a king made all the laws. A student's answer could be more complicated than this brief example, but what the student would have thought over would be how Washington's decision affects his or her life today.

Without memorizing any facts, students taught in this way could learn more history in a few weeks than they now learn in years. More important, they would learn to *like* history. Too many students tell me that they hate history, and I find this to be an educational disaster. I hope that what they are really saying is that they hate the history curriculum, not history.

Another important element in the curriculum of a Quality School is that the students be able to *demonstrate* how what they have learned can be used in their lives now or later. Almost all students would have no difficulty accepting that reading, writing, and arithmetic are useful skills, but in a Quality School they would be asked to demonstrate that they can use them. For example, students would not be asked to learn the multiplication tables as if this knowledge were separate from being able to use the tables in their lives.

To demonstrate the usefulness of knowing how to multiply, students would be given problems to solve and asked to show how multiplication helped in solving them. These problems might require the use of several different mathematical processes, and students could show how each process was used. Students would learn not only how to multiply but also when, where, and why to do so. Once students have demonstrated that they know *how* to multiply, the actual multiplication could be done on a small calculator or by referring to tables.

In a Quality School, once students have mastered a mathematical process they would be encouraged to use a calculator. To do math processes involving large numbers over and over is boring and nonessential. Today, most students spend a lot of time memorizing the times tables. They learn how to multiply, but fail to demonstrate when, where, and why to multiply. I will admit that the tables and the calculators do not teach students *how* to multiply, but they are what people in the real world use to find answers—a fact finally recognized by the Educational Testing Service, which now allows the use of calculators on the Scholastic Aptitude Test.

Teachers in a Quality School would teach the "how" by asking students to demonstrate that they can do calculations without a calculator.

Students would be told that, as soon as they can demonstrate this ability by hand, they will be allowed to use a calculator. For most students, knowing that they will never be stuck working one long, boring problem after another would be more than enough incentive to get them to learn to calculate.

In a Quality School there would be a great deal of emphasis on the skill of writing and much less on the skill of reading. The reason for this is that anyone who can write well can read well, but many people who can read well can hardly write at all. From grade 1 on, students would be asked to write: first, words; then, sentences and paragraphs; and finally, articles, stories, and letters. An extremely good project is to have each middle school student write a book or keep a journal. Students who do so will leave middle school with an education—even if that is all that they have done.

To write a great deal by hand can be onerous, but using a computer makes the same process highly enjoyable. In a Quality School, all teachers would be encouraged to learn word-processing skills and to teach them to their students. Moreover, these skills should be used in all classes. Computers are more readily available in schools today than would seem to be the case, judging from their actual use. If they are not readily available, funds can be raised to buy the few that would be needed. If students were encouraged to write, we would see fewer students diagnosed as having language learning disabilities.

At Apollo High School,[4] where I consult, the seniors were asked if they would accept writing a good letter on a computer as a necessary requirement for graduation. They agreed, and almost all of them learned to do it. One way they demonstrated that their letters were good was by mailing them and receiving responses. They were thrilled by the answers, which we used as one criterion for satisfying the requirement. Clearly, demonstrating the use of what is learned in a real-life situation is one of the best ways to teach.

While demonstrating is the best way to show that something worthwhile has been learned, it is not always easy or even possible to do so. Thus there must be some tests. But, as I stated above, the tests in a Quality School would always show the acquisition of skills, never the acquisition of facts or information alone.

Let me use an example from science to explain what would be considered a good way to test in a Quality School. Science is mostly the discovery of how and why things work. But where and when they work can also be important. Too much science is taught as a simple listing of what works—e.g., these are the parts of a cell. Students all over America are busy memorizing the parts of a cell, usually by copying and then labeling a cell drawn in a textbook. The students are then tested to see if they can do this from memory—a wonderful example of throwaway information, taught by coercion. Teaching and testing in this way is worse than teaching no science at all, because many students learn to hate science as a result. Hating something as valuable as science is worse than simply not knowing it.

The students in a Quality School would be taught some basics about how a cell works, and they would be told that all living organisms are made up of cells. To show them that this is useful knowledge, the teacher might bring up the subject of cancer, explaining how a cancer cell fails to behave as normal cells do and so can kill the host in which it grows. All students know something about cancer, and all would consider this useful knowledge.

The subsequent test in a Quality School might ask students to describe the workings of a cell (or of some part of a cell) with their books open and available. They would then be asked how they could use this information in their lives and would be encouraged to describe the differences between a normal cell and a cancer cell. They would be taught that one way to use this information might be to avoid exposure to too much sunlight because excessive sunlight can turn normal skin cells into cancer cells. For most students, this information would be of use because all students have some fear of cancer.

Readers might feel some concern that what I am suggesting would not prepare students for standardized tests that mostly ask for throw-away information, such as the identification of the parts of a cell. My answer is that students would be better prepared—because, by learning to *explain* how and why something works, they are more likely to remember what they have learned. Even if less ground is covered, as is likely to be the case when we move from facts to skills, a little ground covered well is better preparation, even for nonsense tests, than a lot of ground covered poorly.

We should never forget that people, not curriculum, are the desired outcomes of schooling. What we want to develop are students who have the skills to become active contributors to society, who are enthusiastic about what they have learned, and who are aware of how learning can be of use to them in the future. The curriculum changes I have suggested above will certainly produce more students who fit this profile.

Will the students agree that these outcomes are desirable? If we accept control theory, the answer is obvious. When the outcomes the teachers want are in the quality worlds of their students, the students will accept them. In my experience skills will be accepted as quality in almost all cases; facts and information will rarely be accepted.

Assuming that skills are taught, the teacher must still explain clearly what will be asked on tests. Sample questions should be given to the students, and the use of all books, notes, and materials should be permitted. Even if a student copies the workings of a cell from a book at the time of the test, the student will still have to explain how this information can be used in life. If students can answer such questions, they can be said to know the material—whether or not they copied some of it.

Tests—especially optional retests for students who wish to improve their grades—can be taken at home and can include such items as, "Explain the workings of a cell to an adult at home, write down at least one question that was asked by that person, and explain how you answered it." All the facts would be available in the test; it is the skill to use them that would be tested. The main thing to understand here is that, after a school stops testing for facts and begins to test for skills, it will not be long before it is clear to everyone that skills are the outcomes that have value; facts and information have none.

In most schools, the teacher covers a body of material, and the students must guess what is going to appear on the test. Some teachers even test for material that they have not covered. In a Quality School this would not happen. There would be no limitation on input, and the teacher would not ask students to figure out which parts of this input will be on the test. There would be no hands raised asking the age-old question, Is this going to be on the test?

Since it is always skills that are tested for in a Quality School, it is very likely that the teacher would make the test available to the students before teaching the unit so that, as they went through the material in class, they would know that these are the skills that need to be learned. Students could also be asked to describe any other skill that they have learned from the study of the material. This is an example of the open-endedness that is always a part of testing and discussion in a Quality School. A number of questions would be implicit in all tests: What can you contribute? What is your opinion? What might I (the teacher) have missed? Can you give a better use or explanation.

Keep in mind that, in a Quality School, students and teachers would evaluate tests. Students who are dissatisfied with either their own or the teacher's evaluation could continue to work on the test and improve. Building on the thinking of W. Edwards Deming, the idea is to constantly improve usable skills. In a Quality School, this opportunity is always open.

As I look over what I have written, I see nothing that requires any teacher to change anything that he or she does. If what I suggest appeals to you, implement it at your own pace. Those of us in the Quality School movement believe in lead-management, so there is no coercion—no pressure on you to hurry. You might wish to begin by discussing any of these ideas with your students. In a Quality School students should be aware of everything that the teachers are trying to do. If it makes sense to them, as I think it will, they will help you to put it into practice. ■

Notes

1. For a definition of *boss-management* and *lead-management*, see William Glasser, "The Quality School," *Phi Delta Kappan*, February 1990, p. 428.

2. William Glasser, *The Quality School: Managing Students Without Coercion* (New York: Harper & Row, 1990), Ch. 1.

3. See *Supplementary Information Bulletin No. 5* of the Quality School Training Program. All of these bulletins are available from the Institute for Reality Therapy, 7301 Medical Center Dr., Suite 104, Canoga Park, CA 91307.

4. Apollo High School is a school for students who refuse to work in a regular high school. It enrolls about 240 students (9–12) and is part of the Simi Valley (Calif.) Unified School District.

P O S T N O T E

William Glasser's *choice theory* represents an attempt to base schooling on different principles that satisfy students' needs for friendship, freedom, fun, and power. Glasser's philosophy has been implemented by many educators for whom his humanistic approach has great appeal.

In this article, Glasser asserts that a majority of students believe that much of the present academic curriculum is not worth the effort needed to learn it. To overcome this problem, Glasser suggests that the quality of what we ask students to learn must be increased. Some guiding principles of this quality curriculum include reducing the quantity of what students are asked to memorize, emphasizing the usefulness of knowledge and the development of useful skills (including writing skills), covering less material, and assessing performance.

Many of Glasser's ideas are compatible with the curriculum reform movement occurring in such fields as mathematics, science, and history. Asking students to construct their own knowledge, rather than memorize packaged knowledge, is clearly the direction in which these curriculum efforts are headed.

D I S C U S S I O N Q U E S T I O N S

1. Do Glasser's ideas appeal to you? Why or why not? What problems, if any, do you see in implementing them?

2. What do you think about Glasser's notion of allowing open-book tests? Explain your position.

3. Glasser states that in looking over his ideas, he sees nothing that requires teachers to change what they do. Do you agree or disagree with his statement? Why?

32 Curriculum Integration and the Disciplines of Knowledge

James A. Beane

A t a conference on curriculum integration, a speaker who admitted that he had only recently been introduced to the concept said, "From a quick look at various readings, it seems that the disciplines of knowledge are the enemy of curriculum integration." Unwittingly or not, he had gone straight to the heart of perhaps the most contentious issue in current conversations about curriculum integration. Simply put, the issue is this: If we move away from the subject-centered approach to curriculum organization, will the disciplines of knowledge be abandoned or lost in the shuffle?

As an advocate for curriculum integration, I want to set the record straight. In the thoughtful pursuit of authentic curriculum integration, the disciplines of knowledge are not the enemy. Instead they are a useful and necessary ally.

At the time this article was written, James A. Beane was professor of education, National College of Education, National-Louis University, Evanston, Illinois. Beane, James A., "Curriculum Integration and the Disciplines of Knowledge," *Phi Delta Kappan*, April 1995. Copyright © 1995 by Phi Delta Kappa. Reprinted by permission of author and publisher.

What Is Curriculum Integration?

Curriculum integration is not simply an organizational device requiring cosmetic changes or realignments in lesson plans across various subject areas. Rather, it is a way of thinking about what schools are for, about the sources of curriculum, and about the uses of knowledge. Curriculum integration begins with the idea that the sources of curriculum ought to be problems, issues, and concerns posed by life itself.[1] I have argued elsewhere that such concerns fall into two spheres: 1) self- or personal concerns and 2) issues and problems posed by the larger world.[2] Taking this one step further, we might say that the central focus of curriculum integration is the search for self- and social meaning.

As teachers facilitate such a search within a framework of curriculum integration, two things happen. First, young people are encouraged to integrate learning experiences into their schemes of meaning so as to broaden and deepen their understanding of themselves and their world. Second, they are engaged in seeking, acquiring, and using knowledge in an organic—not an artificial—way. That is, knowledge is called forth in the context of problems, interests, issues, and concerns at hand. And since life itself does not know the boundaries or compartments of what we call disciplines of knowledge, such a context uses knowledge in ways that are integrated.[3]

Notice that, in order to define curriculum integration, there must be reference to knowledge. How could their not be? If we are to broaden and deepen understandings about ourselves and our world, we must come to know "stuff," and to do that we must be skilled in ways of knowing and understanding. As it turns out, the disciplines of knowledge include much (but not all) of what we know about ourselves and our world and about ways of making and communicating meaning. Thus authentic curriculum integration, involving as it does the search for self- and social meaning, must take the disciplines of knowledge seriously—although, again, more is involved than just the correlation of knowledge from various disciplines.

What Is the Problem?

Theoretically, defining the relations between curriculum integration and the disciplines of knowledge is easy. But that act does not resolve the tension over how those relations work in the practical context of curriculum integration. Part of the reason is that the problem is not with the disciplines of knowledge themselves but with their representation in the separate-subject approach to the curriculum. Put another way, the issue is not whether the disciplines of knowledge are useful, but how they might appropriately be brought into the lives of young people. And more than that, do they include all that might be of use in the search for self- and social meaning?

A discipline of knowledge is a field of inquiry about some aspect of the world—the physical world, the flow of events over time, numeric structures, and so on. A discipline of knowledge offers a lens through which to view the world—a specialized set of techniques or processes by which to interpret or explain various phenomena. Beyond that, a discipline also provides a sense of community for people with a shared special interest as they seek to stretch the limits of what is already known in that field. Those on the front edges of a discipline know that disciplinary boundaries are fluid and often connect with other disciplines to create interdisciplinary fields and projects.[4]

Though school-based subject areas, like disciplines of knowledge, partition knowledge into differentiated categories, they are not the same thing as disciplines. Some subjects, like history or mathematics, come close, but they are really institutionally based representations of disciplines, since they deal with a limited selection of what is already known within the field. That selection is based on what someone believes ought to be known (or is worth knowing) about some discipline by people who do not work within it or are unfamiliar with its progress to date. Other subjects, like biology or algebra or home economics, are subsets of disciplines and are limited in even more specialized ways. And still other subjects, like career education or foreign languages, may lay far-reaching claims of connection to some discipline, but their presence in schools really has to do with economic, social, or academic aspirations.

In this sense, a discipline of knowledge and its representative school subject area are not the same things, even though they may be concerned with similar bodies of knowledge. They serve quite different purposes, offer quite different experiences for those who encounter them, and have quite different notions about the fluidity of the boundaries that presumably set one area of inquiry off from others. These differences are substantial enough that the identification of a school subject area as, for example, "history" amounts to an appropriation of the name attached to its corresponding discipline of knowledge. Subject areas are, in the end, a more severe case of "hardening of the categories" than are the disciplines they supposedly represent.

I make this distinction not to demean the work of subject-area teachers or to relegate them to a lower status than disciplinary scholars. Rather, I wish to point out that calling for an end to the separate-subject approach to school curriculum organization is not at all a rejection or abandonment of the disciplines of knowledge. But in saying this, I want to quickly warn that such a claim does not simply open the door to a renewal of "essentialist" conversations about the "structure of disciplines" or their "teachability" that Jerome Bruner and others encouraged in the past[5] and that are now revisited in lists of national and state content standards.

It is worth noting that Bruner himself apparently recognized this risk when, 10 years after the publication of *The Process of Education*, he reconsidered the work's place in education policy. Having just spoken of poverty, racism, injustice, and dispossession, he said this:

> I believe I would be quite satisfied to declare, if not a moratorium, then something of a de-emphasis on matters that have to do with the structure of history, the structure of physics, the nature of mathematical consistency, and deal with curriculum rather in the context of the problems that face us. We might better concern

ourselves with how those problems can be solved, not just by practical action, but by putting knowledge, wherever we find it and in whatever form we find it, to work in these massive tasks. We might put vocation and intention back into the process of education, much more firmly than we had it here before.[6]

It is from just this kind of thinking that the case for curriculum integration emerges. Creating a curriculum for and with young people begins with an examination of the problems, issues, and concerns of life as it is being lived in a real world. Organizing themes are drawn from that examination. To work through such themes, to broaden and deepen our understanding of ourselves and our world, and to communicate those meanings, we must necessarily draw on the disciplines of knowledge. Again, therein lies much of what we know about ourselves and our world, ways in which we might explore them further, and possibilities for communicating meanings. Our reach for help in this kind of curriculum is a purposeful and directed activity—and we do not simply identify questions and concerns and then sit around and wait for enlightenment to come to us. Instead, we intentionally and contextually "put knowledge to work."

Inside the Subject Approach

More and more educators are coming to realize that there is a fundamental tension in schools that current restructuring proposals are simply not addressing, no matter how radical their rhetoric might otherwise be. That tension has to do with the curriculum that mediates the relationships between teachers and young people. After all, teachers and their students do not come together on a random or voluntary social basis— they do not meet casually and decide to "do school." Instead, they are brought together to do something—namely the curriculum—and if that curriculum is fraught with fundamental problems, then the relationships between teachers and students will almost certainly be strained.

Advocates of curriculum integration, myself included, locate a large measure of that tension in the continuing organization of the planned curriculum around separate subject areas. While more complete critiques of the separate-subject approach have been offered elsewhere,[7] I want to touch on the major points of contention in order to clarify the claims made earlier in this article.

First, the separate-subject approach, as a selective representation of disciplines of knowledge, has incorrectly portrayed the latter as "ends" rather than "means" of education.[8] Young people and adults have been led to believe that the purpose of education is to master or "collect"[9] facts, principles, and skills that have been selected for inclusion in one or another subject area instead of learning how those isolated elements might be used to inform larger, real-life purposes.

Second, since the Eight-Year Study of the 1930s, we have been getting signals that the separate-subject approach is an inappropriate route even for those purposes that its advocates claim for themselves.[10] As that study and others after it have indicated, young people tend to do at least as well, and often better, on traditional measures of school achievement when the curriculum moves further in the direction of integration.

Third, the separate subjects and the disciplines of knowledge they are meant to represent are territories carved out by academicians for their own interests and purposes. Imposed on schools, the subject approach thus suggests that the "good life" consists of intellectual activity within narrowly defined areas.[11] The notion that this is the only version of a "good life," or the best one, or even a widely desirable one demeans the lives of others outside the academy who have quite different views and aspirations. It is a remnant of the same "top-down" version of the curriculum that has historically served the people in schools so poorly.

The fact that those academicians who so narrowly define the "good life" happen to be mostly white, upper-middle-class, and male means that the knowledge they prize and select is of a particular kind. Such knowledge, of course, is the cultural capital of that limited group, and thus the cultures of "other" people have been marginalized in the separate-subject approach. This is why the traditional question of the curriculum field, "What knowledge is of most worth?" has been amended to "Whose knowledge is of most worth?" as Michael Apple has pointed out, the fact that subject-centered curricula dominate most schools "is at least partly the result of the place of the school in maximizing the production of high-status knowledge."[12]

Pressing this point a bit further, we can see how such knowledge works in favor of the privileged young people in whose culture it is regularly found while working harshly against those from nonprivileged homes and nondominant cultures. In this way, the separate-subject approach and its selective content plays more than a small role in the "sort and select" system that has been an unbecoming feature of our schools for so long. While curriculum integration by itself cannot resolve this issue, the use of real-life themes demands a wider range of content, while the placement of that content in thematic contexts is likely to make it more accessible for young people.[13]

For most young people, including the privileged, the separate-subject approach offers little more than a disconnected and incoherent assortment of facts and skill. There is no unity, no real sense to it all. It is as if in real life, when faced with problems or puzzling situations, we stopped to ask which part is science, which part mathematics, which part art, and so on.

We are taken aback when young people ask, "Why are we doing this?" And our responses—"Because it will be on the test" or "Because you will need it next year"—are hardly sufficient to answer that question, let alone to justify placing anything in the curriculum.

The deadening effect the separate-subject approach has on the lives of young people cannot be overestimated. In too many places, students are still taught how to diagram complex sentences as if that were the key to the writing process, still made to memorize the names and routes of European explorers, still taught the same arithmetic year after year, page after page, with no

particular connection to their lives. I believe such irrelevance has also had a deadening effect on the lives of many teachers. Had they known that this would be their routine for 30 years or more and that high tension would result, many would probably have chosen a different line of work. And who could blame them?

The separate-subject approach is a legacy of Western-style classical humanism, which views the world in divided compartments. This view was shored up in the last century by the theories of faculty psychology and mental discipline that described the mind as a compartmentalized "muscle" whose parts were to be exercised separately by particular disciplines.[14] The reasoning faculty, for example, was supposedly exercised by the "objective logic" of mathematics, and the assumption was that the heightened reasoning abilities could then be applied to any new situations, including social ones.

Though faculty psychology and mental discipline were discredited by the turn of the century, both live on in some interpretations of split-brain and multiple intelligence theories. And suspect as it has now become, classical humanism still looms large in curriculum organization as part of "official knowledge."[15] How can this be so?

The separate-subject approach to the curriculum is protected by four powerful factors. First, any call for rethinking that approach immediately comes up against a network of educational elites whose symbiotic relationships are founded upon it. I refer here to many academicians and teacher educators in universities, state- and district-level subject supervisors, test and text publishers, subject-area associations, and others whose titles and office doors often signify particular subject areas. The struggles to form, institutionalize, and defend the subject areas have not been easy ones, and neither the areas nor the job titles are going to be given up easily, no matter how persuasive the educational arguments to do so.[16]

Second, parents and other adults are reluctant to embrace versions of the curriculum that depart from what they remember from their own schooling. They want assurance that their children will "get what they need." Thus talk about ideas like curriculum integration may feel threatening to them. And their fears are compounded when they hear arguments for national tests and curriculum or are confronted with media critiques of schools, both of which lend support to the separate-subject cause.

Third, inside the schools themselves, teachers and supervisors often build their professional identities along subject-matter lines.[17] They are not just teachers, but "math teachers" or "music teachers" or "language arts teachers." Identities are always tied to status associated with subject areas—"math is more important than physical education" and so on—and that status, in turn, often determines which teachers get preferred schedule slots or their own classrooms. Anyone who has ever worked in a school knows that this is very dangerous territory to invade.

Finally, it is no secret that we are living in a very conservative era in which historically dominant political and economic groups are noisily reclaiming ground and goods they believe have been taken away from them by progressives.[18] Most of the social road signs advise, "Merge right." In the midst of this conservative restoration comes a call for "curriculum integration"—an approach, as I have defined it, that was historically rooted in the work of the social reconstruction wing of the progressive education movement. Unlike many educators who think that curriculum integration is simply about rearranging lesson plans, conservative critics have figured out that it involves something much larger, and they don't like it.

In constructing a critique of the separate-subject approach, we must remember Dewey's admonition that any nondominant idea about education—in this case curriculum integration—must not be defended solely on the ground of rejection of another idea—here the separate-subject approach.[19] Curriculum integration does not just mean doing the same things differently but doing *something different*. It has its own theories of purpose, knowledge, and learning and is able to stand on those without the necessity of standing on the corpse of the separate-subject approach.

However, the subject-centered approach is rooted in the deep structures and folklore of schooling that its critique is necessary to raise the possibility of other approaches.[20] It is almost as if it had been conceived supernaturally instead of constructed by real people with particular values and beliefs.[21]

Knowledge in an Integrated Curriculum

Having exposed the shortcomings of the separate-subject approach, we may now turn back to the happier relations between curriculum integration and the disciplines of knowledge. How does knowledge look in the context of curriculum integration? What happens to the disciplines of knowledge? How are they used?

In practice, curriculum integration begins with the identification or organizing themes or centers for learning experiences. As previously noted, the themes are drawn from real-life concerns, such as conflict; living in the future; cultures and identities; jobs, money, and careers; or the environment. In some cases the themes are identified by teachers; in the most sophisticated instances, they emerge from collaborative planning with young people.[22] Planning then proceeds directly to creating activities to address the them and related issues. There is no intermediate step in which attempts are made to identify which subject areas might contribute to the theme.

This is a very important distinction, since curriculum integration, in theory and practice, transcends subject-area and disciplinary identifications; the goal is integrative activities that use knowledge without regard for subject or discipline lines. Pretenders to this approach, such as "multidisciplinary" or "interdisciplinary" arrangements, may not follow a strict subject-centered format, but they nevertheless retain subject-area and disciplinary distinctions around some more or less unifying theme.[23] (This structure is typically demonstrated by the fact that a student's schedule still involves a daily rotation through various subjects, even though the teachers may be attempting to use a common theme.) In curriculum integration, the schedule revolves around projects and activities rather than subjects. The disciplines of knowledge come into play as resources from which to draw within the context of the theme and related issues and activities.

For example, in a unit on "living in the future," young people might survey their peers regarding their visions of the future, tabulate the results, compare them to other forecasts, and prepare research reports. Or they might look at technological, recreational, entertainment, or social trends and develop forecasts or scenarios of probable futures for one or more areas. Or they might study past forecasts made for our own times to see if the predictions actually came true. Or they might develop recommendations for the future of their local communities in areas such as population, health, recreations, transportation, and conservation. Or they might study the effects of aging on facial features to imagine how they might look when they are older.

In a unit on "the environment" they might create simulations of different biomes with real and constructed artifacts and offer guided "tours" of their work. Or they might experiment with the effects of pollutants on plant growth. Or they might set up and manage a recycling program in the classroom or school. Or they might identify the raw products in various clothing items and investigate where they come from, find out who makes them, and analyze the environmental and economic impacts of the entire process. Or they might identify environmental problems in their local community and seek ways to resolve them.

I have used the word "or" between activities, since an integrative unit may involve one or any number of them. The point is this: any careful reading of the activities should reveal that, if they are done thoughtfully, they will draw heavily on a variety of disciplines of knowledge for facts, skills, concepts, and understandings.

For example, in constructing surveys, tabulating data, and preparing reports, one would need to draw heavily from the social sciences, language arts, and mathematics. Suppose that some young people did not know how to compute percentages or make graphs. Obviously the teacher(s) would help them learn how to do the things or, if necessary, find someone else who knew how to do them. In experimenting with the effects of pollutants on plant life, some young people might not know how to carry out controlled tests. In that case, someone would teach them how to do that. Does this mean that schools would intentionally employ teachers who know "stuff" from disciplines of knowledge? Certainly! But in curriculum integration, teachers work first as generalists on integrative themes and secondarily as content specialists.

Note that, in curriculum integration, knowledge from the disciplines is repositioned into the context of the theme, questions, and activities at hand. Even when teaching and learning move into what looks like discipline-based instruction, the theme continues to provide the context and the motivation. It is here that knowledge comes to life, has meaning, and is more likely to be "learned." Particular knowledge is not abstracted or fragmented, as is the case when its identity and purpose are tied only to its place within a discipline or school subject area.

Repositioning knowledge in this way raises two issues that cannot be ignored. First, subject-area sequences that have previously defined the flow of knowledge tend to be rearranged in curriculum integration, since knowledge is called forth when it is pertinent rather than when it is convenient. While this is upsetting to some subject-loyal teachers, we should note the irony that sequences often vary from school to school and from state to state. In other words, sequences are more arbitrary than those who construct and defend them would have us believe.[24] The fact that even some subject-area associations have moved away from traditional notions of sequencing should tell us something. In the end, though, advocates of curriculum integration are more interested in the rhythms and patterns of inquiring young minds than in the scopes and sequences of subject-area specialists. The work done within the context of curriculum integration *is* a curriculum; there is not another "curriculum" waiting in the wings to be taught.

Second, it is entirely possible, even probable, that not all the information and skills now disseminated by separate-subject teaching will come to the surface in the context of curriculum integration. But let's face it: there is a good deal of trivia now being disseminated in schools that would be necessary or meaningful only if and when one actually became a specialist in one or another discipline of knowledge, and even then some of it would probably be superfluous. In some places the separate-subject curriculum looks more like preparation for doing the *New York Times* crossword puzzle than for specializing in a discipline. Besides, the very idea of knowing all that "stuff" is a pipe dream in an era when yesterday's "truths" seem to dissolve in the high tide of today's new knowledge.

Curriculum integration, on the other hand, calls forth those ideas that are most important and powerful in the disciplines of knowledge— the ones that are most significant because they emerge in life itself. And because they are placed in the context of personally and socially significant concerns, they are more likely to have real meaning in the lives of young people, the kind of meaning they do not now have.

As boundaries disappear, curriculum integration is also likely to engage knowledge that ordinarily falls between the cracks of disciplines and subject areas. This is particularly the case as knowledge is applied to problematic situations. For example, in exploring the influences of media, young people might investigate the use of the word "average" in the context of the presumed consumer interests of the "average person." What does "average" mean here? How is "average" arrived at when used in this way? How can mathematics be used to manipulate meanings?

Indeed, this kind of knowledge is being attended to by some scholars who work in disciplines of knowledge (and their work is an important resource for those who advocate curriculum integration). But can the same be said for those who live within the boundaries of school subject areas? And if discipline-based scholars have felt the need to move beyond the boundaries of their home disciplines, why is it that so many people are adamant about leaving those same boundaries intact in schools?

Critics of curriculum integration love to convey their deep concern that it will destroy the integrity of the disciplines of knowledge. I am puzzled by this. What possible integrity could there be for any kind of knowledge apart from how it connects with other forms to help us investigate and understand the problems, concerns, and issues that confront us in the real world? Furthermore, what kind of integrity do the disciplines of knowledge now have in young people's minds? Am I missing something? Is "integrity" really a code for "subject boundaries" and "dominant-culture knowledge"?

As a last attempt, some critics suggest that perhaps curriculum integration would be a good idea, but only after a thorough grounding in the separate subjects. If we were talking about house building, the foundation metaphor might work well. However, in the case of learning, it is the "whole" context that gives particular knowledge meaning and accessibility.[25] Besides, if we have to wait for the kind of foundation that such critics mean, we will probably never see any integration.

Beyond the Debate

Despite the matter-of-fact tone I have used here, it would be a mistake to believe that the understanding and practice of curriculum integration is free of confusion. The very existence of the false dichotomy that I have addressed here between curriculum integration and the disciplines of knowledge is evidence that, as advocates of curriculum integration have criticized the use of a separate-subject approach, they have left the impression that the disciplines of knowledge are to be rejected.

Worse yet, the very meaning of curriculum integration has become so confused that the term is used in association with almost any approach that moves beyond that of strictly separate subjects. For example, "curriculum integration" is often used to describe multidisciplinary arrangements in which themes are found inside the existing subjects (e.g., "colonial living" or "ancient Greece" or "metrics") and the guiding question is, What can each subject contribute to the theme? Subject-loyal teachers typically rebel over the contrived use of their areas in such cases and resent being distracted from their usual focus on content coverage. But that kind of alienation merely signifies that this is an adaptation still closely tied to the separate-subject approach and philosophy. As we have seen, curriculum integration involves a quite different philosophy that goes far beyond these concerns.

The term "integration" has also been used to describe attempts to reassemble fragmented pieces of a discipline of knowledge—such as creating social studies out of history and geography—and to label approaches that emphasize thinking, writing, and valuing across subject areas. One might well argue that the word "integration" is technically acceptable in these instances, but they clearly do not represent what has been meant historically by "curriculum integration."

However, even if the language problem were cleared up, there is still much to learn about curriculum integration as an approach. For example, are some kinds of knowledge morel likely than others to emerge in the context of life-centered themes? Are some themes more likely than others to serve well as contexts for integrating wide ranges of knowledge? How big a chunk of life should an integrative theme encompass? How can we be certain that integrated knowledge will not simply accumulate without meaning (as separate-subject knowledge usually does) but will help young people continuously expand meaning?[26]

These kinds of questions are rooted in attempts to understand more fully curriculum integration as well as the place of knowledge within it. Notice that they are not of the sort that asks how curriculum integration might find peaceful coexistence with current conceptions of a subject-centered curriculum. Again, curriculum integration is not about doing the same things differently but about doing something truly different. For this reason, questions like "How will young people do on our subject-based tests?" or

"How does this fit into our current schedule?" are not pertinent (though they are real politically). The structures to which such questions refer grew out of the separate-subject approach to the curriculum. Shifting to a different approach thus calls the structures themselves into question.

Many educators today like to speak of paradigm shifts when describing changes they have made or are trying to make. Such shifts may involve changing the school schedule, more sharply defining the outcomes of schooling, or coming up with new methods of assessment. As I understand it, a paradigm shift entails a change in viewpoint so fundamental that much of what is currently taken for granted is called into question or rendered irrelevant or wrong. If we use this definition, it is hard to consider the kinds of changes just mentioned as "paradigm shifts." These, like most of the changes usually associated with "restructuring," ask about "how" we do things and leave alone more fundamental questions about "what" we do and "why."

Curriculum integration centers on the curriculum of life itself rather than on the mastery of fragmented information within the boundaries of subject areas. It is rooted in a view of learning as the continuous integration of new knowledge and experience so as to deepen and broaden our understanding of ourselves and our world. Its focus is on life as it is lived now rather than on preparation for some later life or later level of schooling. It serves the young people for whom the curriculum is intended rather than the specialized interests of adults. It concerns the active construction of meanings rather than the passive assimilation of others' meanings.

Described in this way, curriculum integration is more of a real paradigm shift than are the changes usually touted as such. Yet it does not reject outright or abandon all that has been deemed important by other views of schooling. This accommodation is especially apparent with regard to the disciplines of knowledge, which are necessarily drawn on in responsible curriculum integration. This point is not a matter of compromise but of common sense. Advocates of curriculum integration may criticize the separate-subject approach and the purpose of schooling it implies, they may accuse subject-area loyalists of narcissism, and they may decry the deadening effects of the separate-subject curriculum. But they do not intend to walk away from knowledge—and, for that reason, the disciplines of knowledge are clearly not the enemies of curriculum integration. ■

Notes

1. L. Thomas Hopkins et al., *Integration: Its Meaning and Application* (New York: Appleton-Century, 1937); Lucille L. Lurry and Elsie J. Alberty, *Developing the High School Core Program* (New York: Macmillan, 1957); Paul L. Dressel, "The Meaning and Significance of Integration," in Nelson B. Henry, ed., *the Integration of Educational Experiences: 57th NSSE Yearbook, Part III* (Chicago: National Society for the Study of Education, University of Chicago Press, 1958); Gertrude Noar, *The Teacher and Integration* (Washington D.C.: National Education Association, 1966); James A. Beane, *Affect in the Curriculum: Toward Democracy, Dignity, and Diversity* (New York: Routledge, 1993); and Gordon F. Vars, "Integrated Curriculum in Historical Perspective," *Educational Leadership*, October 1991, pp. 14–15.

2. Beane, op. cit.; and idem, *A Middle School Curriculum: From Rhetoric to Reality*, rev. ed. (Columbus, Ohio: National Middle School Association, 1993).

3. Here and throughout the article, I am using the term "knowledge" generically to include knowing about, knowing how, and knowing why, and so on. Thus "knowledge" would include information, skills, concepts, processes, and so on.

4. Julie Thompson Klein, *Interdisciplinarity: History, Theory, and Practice* (Detroit: Wayne State University Press, 1990).

5. Jerome S. Bruner, *The Process of Education* (Cambridge, Mass.: Harvard University Press, 1960); G. W. Ford and Lawrence Pugno, *The Structure of Knowledge and Curriculum* (Chicago: Rand McNally, 1964); Arthur R. King, Jr., and John A. Brownell, *The Curriculum and the Disciplines of Knowledge* (New York: Wiley, 1966); and Morton Alpern, ed., *The Subject Curriculum: Grades K–12* (Columbus, Ohio: Charles E. Merrill, 1967).

6. Jerome S. Bruner, "The Process of Education Reconsidered," in Robert R. Leeper, ed., *Dare to Care/Dare to Act: Racism and Education* (Washington, D.C.: Association for Supervision and Curriculum Development, 1971), pp. 29–30.

7. Marion Brady, *What's Worth Teaching?* (Albany, N.Y.: State University of New York Press, 1989); Beane, *A Middle School Curriculum*; and R. W. Connell, *Schools and Social Justice* (Philadelphia: Temple University Press, 1993).

8. John Dewey, *The School and Society*, rev. ed. (Chicago: University of Chicago Press, 1915); George Henry, "Foundations of General Education in the High School," in *What Shall the High Schools Teach?: 1956 ASCD Yearbook* (Washington, D.C.: Association for Supervision and Curriculum Development, 1956); and Brady, op. cit.

9. Basil Bernstein, *Class, Codes, and Control, Vol. 3: Towards a Theory of Educational Transmissions*, 2nd ed. (London: Routledge and Kegan Paul, 1975).

10. Wilford Aikin, *The Story of the Eight Year Study* (New York: Harper & Row, 1942).

11. See, for example, Allan Bloom, *The Closing of the American Mind* (New York: Simon & Schuster, 1987); E. D. Hirsch, Jr., *Cultural Literacy* (Boston: Houghton Mifflin, 1987); and Diane Ravitch and Chester E. Finn, Jr., *What Do Our 17-Year-Olds Know?* (New York: Harper & Row, 1987).

12. Michael W. Apple, *Ideology and Curriculum* 2nd ed. (London: Routledge and Kegan Paul, 1990), p. 38.

13. Ashgar Iran-Nejad, Wilbert J. McKeachie, and David C. Berliner, "The Multisource Nature of Learning: An Introduction," *Review of Educational Research*, Winter 1990, pp. 509–15.

14. Herbert M. Kliebard, "The Decline of Humanistic Studies in the American School Curriculum," in Benjamin Ladner, ed., *The Humanities in Precollegiate Education: 83rd NSSE Yearbook, Part II* (Chicago: National Society for the Study of Education, University of Chicago Press, 1984).

15. Michael W. Apple, *Official Knowledge: Democratic Education in a Conservative Age* (New York: Routledge, 1993).

16. Ivor Goodson, ed., *Social Histories of the Secondary School Curriculum: Subjects for Study* (Philadelphia: Falmer, 1985); Herbert M. Kliebard, *The Struggle for the American Curriculum: 1893-1958* (Boston: Routledge and Kegan Paul, 1986); and Thomas S. Popkewitz, ed., *The Formation of School Subjects: The Struggle for Creating an American Institution* (New York: Falmer, 1987).

17. Bernstein, op. cit.

18. Anne C. Lewis, "The Ghost of November Past," *Phi Delta Kappan*, January 1995, pp. 348–49.

19. John Dewey, *Experience and Education* (New York: Macmillan, 1938).

20. Michael F. D. Young, "An Approach to the Study of Curricula as Socially Organized Knowledge," in idem, ed., *Knowledge and Control* (London: Collier-Macmillan, 1971).

21. Raymond Williams, *The Long Revolution* (London: Chatto and Windus, 1961).

22. Rosalind M. Zapf, *Democratic Processes in the Classroom* (Englewood Cliffs, N.J.: Prentice-Hall, 1959); Noar, op. cit.; James A. Beane, "The Middle School: Natural Home of Integrated Curriculum," *Educational Leadership*, October 1991, pp. 9–13; idem, "Turing the Floor Over: Reflections

on *A Middle School Curriculum," Middle School Journal*, January 1992, pp. 34–40; Barbara Brodhagen, Gary Weilbacher, and James A. Beane, "Living in the Future: An Experiment with an Integrative Curriculum," *Dissemination Services on the Middle Grades*, June 1992, pp. 1–7; and Barbara L. Brodhagen, "The Situation Made Us Special," in Michael W. Apple and James A. Beane, eds., *Democratic Schools* (Alexandria, Va.: Association for Supervision and Curriculum Development, 1995).

23. Charity James, *Young Lives at Stake* (New York: Agathon, 1972); Bernstein, op. cit.; and Heidi Hayes Jacobs,

ed., *Interdisciplinary Curriculum: Design and Implementation* (Alexandria, Va.: Association for Supervision and Curriculum Development, 1989).

24. It is instructive to note that alphabetical order rather than disciplinary structure created the usual biology-chemistry-physics sequence.

25. Iran-Nejad, McKeachie, and Berliner, op. cit.

26. Arno A. Bellack, "Selection and Organization of Curriculum Content," in *What Shall the High Schools Teach?*

POST NOTE

The influential report from the Carnegie Corporation, *Turning Points: Preparing American Youth for the 21st Century*, published in 1989, recommended that the middle school curriculum be organized around "integrating themes that young people find relevant to their own lives." This was not the first time that a major reform group has advocated curriculum integration instead of the tradition of teaching history, English, mathematics, and science as separate subjects. The notion of centering school curricula on concerns "posed by life itself," as Beane puts it, has great appeal as a way of developing a more holistic understanding of the world.

Nevertheless, there is scant evidence that such changes are occurring in most of our schools, especially the high schools. The separate-subject-matter curriculum is very resistant to change. The efforts during the early and mid-1990s to develop national standards in various traditional subjects (such as history, geography, and mathematics) are examples of just how entrenched the discipline organization of school curricula has become.

DISCUSSION QUESTIONS

1. Have you ever experienced an integrated curriculum, as described by the author of this article? If so, how would you compare that experience with the more traditional subject-matter organization?

2. What disadvantages, if any, are there in using an integrated curriculum approach?

3. What are the barriers to implementing an integrated curriculum approach?

33

The Relevance of Religion to the Curriculum

Warren A. Nord

For some time now, public school administrators have been on the front lines of our culture wars over religion and education—and I expect it would be music to their ears to hear that peace accords have been signed.

Unfortunately, the causes of war are deep-seated. Peace is not around the corner.

At the same time, however, it is also easy to overstate the extent of the hostilities. At least at the national level—but also in many communities across America—a large measure of common ground has been found. The leaders of most major national educational, religious and civil liberties organizations agree about the basic principles that should govern the role of religion and public schools. No doubt we don't agree about everything, but we agree about a lot.

For example, in 1988, a group of 17 major religious and educational organizations—the American Jewish Congress and the Islamic Society of North America, the National Association of Evangelicals and the National Council of Churches,

Warren Nord is director of the Program in the Humanities and Human Values and teaches the philosophy of religion at University of North Carolina. He is the author of *Religion and American Education: Rethinking a National Dilemma* and co-author with Charles Haynes of *Taking Religion Seriously Across the Curriculum*. Reprinted with permission from the January 1999 issue of *The School Administrator* magazine.

the National Education Association and American Federation of Teachers, the National School Boards Association and AASA among them—endorsed a statement of principles that describes the importance of religion in the public school curriculum.

The statement, in part, says this: "Because religion plays significant roles in history and society, study about religion is essential to understanding both the nation and the world. Omission of facts about religion can give students the false impression that the religious life of humankind is insignificant or unimportant. Failure to understand even the basic symbols, practices and concepts of the various religions makes much of history, literature, art and contemporary life unintelligible."

A Profound Problem

As a result of this (and other "common ground" statements) it is no longer controversial to assert that the study of religion has a legitimate and important place in the public school curriculum.

Where in the curriculum? In practice, the study of religion has been relegated almost entirely to history texts and courses, for it is widely assumed that religion is irrelevant to every other subject in the curriculum—that is, to understanding the world here and now.

This is a deeply controversial assumption, however. A profoundly important educational problem lingers here, one that is almost completely ignored by educators.

Let me put it this way. Several ways exist for making sense of the world here and now. Many Americans accept one or another religious interpretation of reality; others accept one or another secular interpretation. We don't agree—and the differences among us often cut deeply.

Yet public schools systematically teach students to think about the world in secular ways only. They don't even bother to inform them about religious alternatives—apart from distant history. That is, public schooling discriminates against religious ways of making sense of the world. This is no minor problem.

An Economic Argument

To get some sense of what's at issue, let's consider economics.

One can think about the economic domain of life in various ways. Scriptural texts in all religions traditions address questions of justice and morality, poverty and wealth, work and stewardship, for example. A vast body of 20th century literature in moral theology deals with economic issues. Indeed most mainline denominations and ecumenical agencies have official statements on justice and economics. What's common to all of this literature is the claim that the economic domain of life cannot be understood apart from religion.

Needless to say, this claim is not to be found in economics textbooks. Indeed, if we put end to end all the references to religion in the 10 high school economics texts I've reviewed in the past few years, they would add up to about two pages—out of 4,400 pages combined (and all of the references are to premodern times). There is but a single reference to religion—a passing mention in a section on taxation and nonprofit organizations—in the 47 pages of the new national content standards in economics. Moreover, the textbooks and the standards say virtually nothing about the problems that are the major concern of theologians—problems relating to poverty, justice, our consumer culture, the Third World, human dignity and the meaningfulness of work.

The problem isn't just that the texts ignore religion and those economic problems of most concern to theologians. A part of the problem is what the texts do teach—that is, neoclassical economic theory. According to the texts, economics is a science, people are essentially self-interested utility-maximizers, the economic realm is one of competition for scarce resources, values are personal preferences and value judgments are matters of cost-benefit analysis. Of course, no religious tradition accepts this understanding of human nature, society, economics and values.

That is, the texts and standards demoralize and secularize economics.

An Appalling Claim

To be sure, they aren't explicitly hostile to religion; rather they ignore it. But in some ways this is worse than explicit hostility, for students remain unaware of the fact that there are tensions and conflicts between their religious traditions and what they are taught about economics.

In fact, the texts and the standards give students no sense that what they are learning is controversial. Indeed, the national economics standards make it a matter of principle that students be kept in the dark about alternatives to neoclassical theory. As the editors put it in their introduction, the standards were developed to convey a single conception of economics, the "majority paradigm" or neoclassical model of economic behavior. For, they argue, to include "strongly held minority views of economic processes [would only risk] confusing and frustrating teachers and students who are then left with the responsibility of sorting the qualifications and alternatives without a sufficient foundation to do so."

This is an appalling statement. It means, in effect, that students should be indoctrinated; they should be given no critical perspective on neoclassical economic theory.

The problem with the economics texts and standards is but one aspect of the much larger problem that cuts across the curriculum, for in every course students are taught to think in secular ways that often (though certainly not always) conflict with religious alternatives. And this is always done uncritically.

Even in history courses, students learn to think about historical meaning and causation in exclusively secular ways in spite of the fact that Judaism, Christianity and Islam all hold that

God acts in history, that there is a religious meaning to history. True, they learn a few facts about religion, but they learn to think about history in secular categories.

Nurturing Secularity

Outside of history courses and literature courses that use historical literature, religion is rarely even mentioned, but even on those rare occasions when it is, the intellectual context is secular. As a result, public education nurtures a secular mentality. This marginalizes religion from our cultural and intellectual life and contributes powerfully to the secularization of our culture.

Ignoring religious ways of thinking about the world is a problem for three important reasons.

■ *It is profoundly illiberal.*

Here, of course, I'm not using the term "liberal" to refer to the left wing of the Democratic Party. A liberal education is a broad education, one that provides students with the perspective to think critically about the world and their lives. A good liberal education should introduce students—at least older students—to the major ways humankind has developed for making sense of the world and their lives. Some of those ways of thinking and living are religious and it is illiberal to leave them out of the discussion. Indeed, it may well constitute indoctrination—secular indoctrination.

We indoctrinate students when we uncritically initiate them into one way of thinking and systematically ignore the alternatives. Indeed, if students are to be able to think critically about the secular ways of understanding the world that pervade the curriculum, they must understand something about the religious alternatives.

■ *It is politically unjust.*

Public schools must take the public seriously. But religious parents are now, in effect, educationally disenfranchised. Their ways of thinking and living aren't taken seriously.

Consider an analogy. A generation ago textbooks and curricula said virtually nothing about women, blacks and members of minority subcul-tures. Hardly anyone would now say that that was fair or just. We now—most of us—realize this was a form of discrimination, of educational disenfranchisement. And so it is with religious subcultures (though, ironically, the multicultural movement has been almost entirely silent about religion).

■ *It is unconstitutional.*

It is, of course, uncontroversial that it is constitutionally permissible to teach about religion in public schools when done properly. No Supreme Court justice has ever held otherwise. But I want to make a stronger argument.

The court has been clear that public schools must be neutral in matters of religion—in two senses. Schools must be neutral among religions (they can't favor Protestants over Catholics or Christians over Jews), and they must be neutral between religion and nonreligion. Schools can't promote religion. They can't proselytize. They can't conduct religious exercises.

Of course, neutrality is a two-edged sword. Just as schools can't favor religion over nonreligion, neither can they favor nonreligion over religion. As Justice Hugo Black put it in the seminal 1947 *Everson* ruling, "State power is no more to be used so as to handicap religions than it is to favor them."

Similarly, in his majority opinion in *Abington v. Schempp* in 1963, Justice Tom Clark wrote that schools can't favor "those who believe in no religion over those who do believe." And in a concurring opinion, Justice Arthur Goldberg warned that an "untutored devotion to the concept of neutrality [can lead to a] pervasive devotion to the secular and a passive, or even active, hostility to the religious."

Of course this is just what has happened. An untutored, naïve conception of neutrality has led educators to look for a smoking gun, an explicit hostility to religion, when the hostility has been philosophically rather more subtle—though no less substantial for that.

The only way to be neutral when all ground is contested ground is to be fair to the alternative. That is, given the Supreme Court's longstanding interpretation of the Establishment Clause, public schools must require the study of religion if they require the study of disciplines that cumulatively lead to a pervasive devotion to the secular—as they do.

Classroom Practices

So how can we be fair? What would a good education look like? Here I can only skim the surface—and refer readers to *Taking Religion Seriously Across the Curriculum,* in which Charles Haynes and I chart what needs to be done in some detail.

Obviously a great deal depends on the age of students. In elementary schools students should learn something of the relatively uncontroversial aspects of different religions—their traditions, holidays, symbols and a little about religious histories, for example. As students mature, they should be initiated into the conversation about truth and goodness that constitutes a good liberal education. Here a two-prong approach is required.

First, students should learn something about religious ways of thinking about any subject that is religiously controversial in the relevant courses. So, for example, a biology text should include a chapter in which scientific ways of understanding nature are contrasted with religious alternatives. Students should learn that the relationship of religion and science is controversial, and that while they will learn what most biologists believe to be the truth about nature, not everyone agrees.

Indeed, every text and course should provide students with historical and philosophical perspective on the subject at hand, establishing connections and tensions with other disciplines and domains of the culture, including religion.

This is not a balanced-treatment or equal-time requirement. Biology courses should continue to be biology courses and economics courses should continue to be economics courses. In any case, given their competence and training, biology and economics teachers are not likely to be prepared to deal with a variety of religious ways of approaching their subject. At most, they can provide a minimal fairness.

A robust fairness is possible only if students are required to study religious as well as secular ways of making sense of the world in some depth, in courses devoted to the study of religion.

A good liberal education should require at least one year-long high school course in religious studies (with other courses, I would hope, available as electives). The primary goal of such a course should be to provide students with a sufficiently intensive exposure to religious ways of thinking and living to enable them to actually understand religion (rather than simply know a few facts about religion). It should expose students to scriptural texts, but it also should use more recent primary sources that enable students to understand how contemporary theologians and writers within different traditions think about those subjects in the curriculum—morality, sexuality, history, nature, psychology and the economic world—that they will be taught to interpret in secular categories in their other courses.

Of course, if religion courses are to be offered, there must be teachers competent to teach them. Religious studies must become a certifiable field in public education, and new courses must not be offered or required until competent teachers are available.

Indeed, all teachers must have a much clearer sense of how religion relates to the curriculum and, more particularly, to their respective subjects. Major reforms in teacher education are necessary—as is a new generation of textbooks sensitive to religion.

Some educators will find it unrealistic to expect such reforms. Of course several decades ago textbooks and curricula said little about women and minority cultures. Several decades ago, few universities had departments of religious studies. Now multicultural education is commonplace and most universities have departments of religious studies. Things change.

Stemming an Exodus

No doubt some educators will find these proposals controversial, but they will be shortsighted if they do. Leaving religion out of the curriculum is also controversial. Indeed, because public schools don't take religion seriously many religious parents have deserted them and, if the Supreme Court upholds the legality of vouchers, as they may well do, the exodus will be much greater.

In the long run, the least controversial position is the one that takes everyone seriously. If public schools are to survive our culture wars, they must be built on common ground. But there can be no common ground when religious voices are left out of the curricular conversation.

It is religious conservatives, of course, who are most critical of public schooling—and the most likely to leave. But my argument is that public schooling doesn't take any religion seriously. It marginalizes all religion—liberal as well as conservative, Catholic as well as Protestant, Jewish, Muslim and Buddhist as well as Christian. Indeed, it contributes a great deal to the secularization of American culture—and this should concern any religious person.

But, in the end, this shouldn't concern religious people only. Religion should be included in the curriculum for three very powerful secular reasons. The lack of serious study of religion in public education is illiberal, unjust and unconstitutional. ■

POST NOTE

Parents rightfully want to pass on to their children their most deeply held beliefs. Many of these beliefs about what constitutes a good life, and what is a person's true nature, are theological questions that are embedded in their religious convictions. For a variety of reasons, many of which are touched on in this article, the public schools have ignored and marginalized religion. Besides the educational implications of this policy, the impact on the public support of public schools is beginning to show. America is a religious nation, founded on religious principles ("In God we trust" and "All men are created equal"). Also, over 90 percent of Americans believe in God and close to 90 percent report membership in a particular church. It would seem, then, that the current condition of the two powerful educational influences on children, the media and the public school system, being areligious or antireligious is bound to have political consequences. Since parents can do little to punish Hollywood, the temptation to take out their resentments on the local, tax-supported schools is strong.

DISCUSSION QUESTIONS

1. Professor Nord ends his essay with the words, "The lack of serious study of religion in public education is illiberal, unjust and unconstitutional." What is your reaction to this statement?

2. Has your previous school experience strengthened, undermined, or had no effect on your religious convictions?

3. What solutions to the problem he has outlined does Nord offer? Do you agree with them? Why? Why not?

Teaching Themes of Care

Nel Noddings

Some educators today—and I include myself among them—would like to see a complete reorganization of the school curriculum. We would like to give a central to place to the questions and issues that lie at the core of human existence. One possibility would be to organize the curriculum around themes of care—caring for self, for intimate others, for strangers and global others, for the natural world and its non-human creatures, for the human-made world, and for ideas.[1]

A realistic assessment of schooling in the present political climate makes it clear that such a plan is not likely to be implemented. However, we can use the rich vocabulary of care in educational planning and introduce themes of care into regular subject-matter classes. In this article, I will first give a brief rationale for teaching themes of care; second, I will suggest ways of choosing and organizing such themes; and, finally, I'll say a bit about the structures required to support such teaching.

Why Teach Caring?

In an age when violence among schoolchildren is at an unprecedented level, when children are

Nel Noddings is a Professor of Education at Teachers College, Columbia University. Noddings, Nel, "Teaching Themes of Care," from *Phi Delta Kappan*, May 1995. Copyright © 1995 by Phi Delta Kappa. Reprinted by permission of authors and publisher.

bearing children with little knowledge of how to care for them, when the society and even the Schools often concentrate on materialistic messages, it may be unnecessary to argue that we should care more genuinely for our children and teach them to care. However, many otherwise reasonable people seem to believe that our educational problems consist largely of low scores on achievement tests. My contention is, first, that we should want more from our educational efforts than adequate academic achievement and, second, that we will not achieve even that meager success unless our children believe that they themselves are cared for and learn to care for others.

There is much to be gained, both academically and humanly, by including themes of care in our curriculum. First, such inclusion may well expand our students' cultural literacy. For example, as we discuss in math classes the attempts of great mathematicians to prove the existence of God or to reconcile a God who is all good with the reality of evil in the world, students will hear names, ideas, and words that are not part of the standard curriculum. Although such incidental learning cannot replace the systematic and sequential learning required by those who plan careers in mathematically oriented fields, it can be powerful in expanding students' cultural horizons and in inspiring further study.

Second, themes of care help us to connect the standard subjects. The use of literature in mathematics classes, of history in science classes, and of art and music in all classes can give students a feeling of the wholeness in their education. After all, why should they seriously study five different subjects if their teachers, who are educated people, only seem to know and appreciate one?

Third, themes of care connect our students and our subjects to great existential questions. What is the meaning of life? Are there gods? How should I live?

Fourth, sharing such themes can connect us person-to-person. When teachers discuss themes of care, they may become real persons to their students and so enable them to construct new knowledge. Martin Buber put it this way:

> Trust, trust in the world, because this human being exists—that is the most inward achievement of the relation in education. Because this human being exists, meaninglessness, however hard pressed you are by it, cannot be the real truth. Because this human being exists, in the darkness the light lies hidden, in fear salvation, and in the callousness of one's fellow-man the great love.[2]

Finally, I should emphasize that caring is not just a warm, fuzzy feeling that makes people kind and likable. Caring implies a continuous search for competence. When we care, we want to do our very best for the objects of our care. To have as our educational goal the production of caring, competent, loving, and lovable people is not anti-intellectual. Rather, it demonstrates respect for the full range of human talents. Not all human beings are good at or interested in mathematics, science, or British literature. But all humans can be helped to lead lives of deep concern for others, for the natural world and its creatures, and for the preservation of the human-made world. They can be led to develop the skills and knowledge necessary to make positive contributions, regardless of the occupation they may choose.

Choosing and Organizing Themes of Care

Care is conveyed in many ways. At the institutional level, schools can be organized to provide continuity and support for relationships of care and trust.[3] At the individual level, parents and teachers show their caring through characteristic forms of attention: by cooperating in children's activities, by sharing their own dreams and doubts, and by providing carefully for the steady growth to the children in their charge. Personal manifestations of care are probably more important in children's lives than any particular curriculum or pattern of pedagogy.

However, curriculum can be selected with caring in mind. That is, educators can manifest their care in the choice of curriculum, and appropriately chosen curriculum can contribute to the growth of children as carers. Within each large domain of care, many topics are suitable for thematic units: in the domain of "caring for self," for example, we might consider life stages, spiritual growth, and what it means to develop an admirable character; in exploring the topic of caring for intimate others, we might include units on love, friendship, and parenting; under the theme of caring for strangers and global others, we might study war, poverty, and tolerance; in addressing the idea of caring for the human-made world, we might encourage competence with the machines that surround us and a real appreciation for the marvels of technology. Many other examples exist. Furthermore, there are at least two different ways to approach the development of such themes: units can be constructed by interdisciplinary teams, or themes can be identified by individual teachers and addressed periodically throughout a year's or semester's work.

The interdisciplinary approach is familiar in core programs, and such programs are becoming more and more popular at the middle school level. One key to a successful interdisciplinary unit is the degree of genuinely enthusiastic support it receives from the teachers involved. Too often, arbitrary or artificial groupings are formed, and teacher are forced to make contributions that they themselves do not value highly. For example, math and science teachers are sometimes automatically lumped together, and rich humanistic possibilities may be lost. If I, as a math teacher, want to include historical, biographical, and literary topics in my math lessons, I might prefer to work with English and social studies teachers. Thus it is important to involve teachers in the initial selection of broad areas for themes, as well as in their implementation.

Such interdisciplinary arrangements also work well at the college level. I recently received a copy of the syllabus for a college course titled "The Search for Meaning," which was co-taught by an economist, a university chaplain, and a psychiatrist.[4] The course is interdisciplinary, intellectually rich, and aimed squarely at the central questions of life.

At the high school level, where students desperately need to engage in the study and practice of caring, it is harder to form interdisciplinary teams. A conflict arises as teachers acknowledge the intensity of the subject-matter preparation their students need for further education. Good teachers often wish there were time in the day to co-teach unconventional topics of great importance, and they even admit that their students are not getting what they need for full personal development. But they feel constrained by the requirements of a highly competitive world and the structures of schooling established by that world.

Is there a way out of this conflict? Imaginative, like-minded teachers might agree to emphasize a particular theme in their separate classes. Such themes as war, poverty, crime, racism, or sexism can be addressed in almost every subject area. The teachers should agree on some core ideas related to caring that will be discussed in all classes, but beyond the central commitment to address themes of care, the topics can be handled in whatever way seems suitable in a given subject.

Consider, for example, what a mathematics class might contribute to a unit on crime. Statistical information might be gathered on the location and number of crimes, on rates for various kinds of crime, on the ages of offenders, and on the cost to society; graphs and charts could be constructed. Data on changes in crime rates could be assembled. Intriguing questions could be asked: Were property crime rates lower when penalties were more severe—when, for example, even children were hanged as thieves? What does an average criminal case cost by way of lawyers' fees, police investigation, and court processing? Does it cost more to house a youth in a detention center or in an elite private school?

None of this would have to occupy a full period every day. The regular sequential work of the math class could go on at a slightly reduced rate (e.g., fewer textbook exercises as homework), and the work on crime could proceed in the form of interdisciplinary projects over a considerable period of time. Most important would be the continual reminder in all classes that the topic is part of a larger theme of caring for strangers and fellow citizens. It takes only a few minutes to talk about what it means to live in safety, to trust one's neighbors, to feel secure in greeting strangers. Students should be told that metal detectors and security guards were not part of their parents' school lives, and they should be encouraged to hope for a safer and more open future. Notice the words I've used in this paragraph: caring, trust, safety, strangers, hope. Each could be used as an organizing theme for another unit of study.

English and social studies teachers would obviously have much to contribute to a unit on crime. For example, students might read *Oliver Twist*, and they might also study and discuss the social conditions that seemed to promote crime in 19th-century England. Do similar conditions exist in our country today? The selection of materials could include both classic works and modern stories and films. Students might even be introduced to some of the mystery stories that adults read so avidly on airplanes and beaches, and teachers should be engaged in lively discussion about the comparative value of the various stories.

Science teachers might find that a unit on crime would enrich their teaching of evolution. They could bring up the topic of social Darwinism, which played such a strong role in social policy during the late 19th and early 20th centuries. To what degree are criminal tendencies inherited? Should children be tested for the genetic defects that are suspected of predisposing some people to crime? Are females less competent than males in moral reasoning? (Why did some scientists and philosophers think this was true?) Why do males commit so many more violent acts than females?

Teachers of the arts can also be involved. A unit on crime might provide a wonderful opportunity to critique "gangsta rap" and other currently popular forms of music. Students might profitably learn how the control of art contributed to national criminality during the Nazi era. These are ideas that pop into my mind. Far more various and far richer ideas will come from teachers who specialize in these subjects.

There are risks, of course, in undertaking any unit of study that focuses on matters of controversy or deep existential concern, and teachers should anticipate these risks. What if students want to compare the incomes of teachers and cocaine dealers? What if they point to contemporary personalities from politics, entertainment, business, or sports who seem to escape the law and profit from what seems to be criminal behavior? My own inclination would be to allow free discussion of these cases and to be prepared to counteract them with powerful stories of honesty, compassion, moderation, and charity.

An even more difficult problem may arise. Suppose a student discloses his or her own criminal activities? Fear of this sort of occurrence may send teachers scurrying for safer topics. But, in fact, any instructional method that uses narrative forms or encourages personal expression runs this risk. For example, students of English as a second language who write proudly about their own hard lives and new hopes may disclose that their parents are illegal immigrants. A girl may write passages that lead her teacher to suspect sexual abuse. A boy may brag about objects that he has "ripped off." Clearly, as we use these powerful methods that encourage students to initiate discussion and share their experiences, we must reflect on the ethical issues involved, consider appropriate responses to such issues, and prepare teachers to handle them responsibly.

Caring teachers must help students make wise decisions about what information they will share about themselves. On the one hand, teachers want their students to express themselves, and they want their students to trust in and consult them. On the other hand, teachers have an obligation to protect immature students from making disclosures that they might later regret. There is a deep ethical problem here. Too often educators assume that only religious fundamentalists and right-wing extremists object to the discussion of emotionally and morally charged issues. In reality, there is a real danger of intrusiveness and lack of respect in methods that fail to recognize the vulnerability of students. Therefore, as teachers plan units and lessons on moral issues, they should anticipate the tough problems that may arise. I am arguing here that it is morally irresponsible to simply ignore existential questions and themes of care; we must attend to them. But it is equally irresponsible to approach these deep concerns without caution and careful preparation.

So far I have discussed two ways of organizing interdisciplinary units on themes of care. In one, teachers actually teach together in teams; in the other, teachers agree on a theme and a central focus on care, but they do what they can, when they can, in their own classrooms. A variation on this second way—which is also open to teachers who have to work alone—is to choose several themes and weave them into regular course material over an entire semester or year. The particular themes will depend on the interests and preparation of each teacher.

For example, if I were teaching high school mathematics today, I would use religious/existential questions as a pervasive theme because the biographies of mathematicians are filled with accounts of their speculations on matters of God, other dimensions, and the infinite—and because these topics fascinate me. There are so many wonderful stories to be told: Descarte's proof of the existence of God, Pascal's famous wager, Plato's world of forms, Newton's attempt to verify Biblical chronology, Leibnitz' detailed theodicy, current attempts to describe a divine domain in terms of metasystems, and mystical speculations on the infinite.[5] Some of these stories can be told as rich "asides" in five minutes or less. Others might occupy the better part of several class periods.

Other mathematics teachers might use an interest in architecture and design, art, music, or machinery as continuing themes in the domain of "caring for the human-made world." Still others might introduce the mathematics of living things. The possibilities are endless. In choosing and pursuing these themes, teachers should be aware that they are both helping their students learn to care and demonstrating their own caring by sharing interests that go well beyond the demands of textbook pedagogy.

Still another way to introduce themes of care into regular classrooms is to be prepared to respond spontaneously to events that occur in the school or in the neighborhood. Older teachers have one advantage in this area: they probably have a greater store of experience and stories on which to draw. However, younger teachers have the advantage of being closer to their students' lives and experiences; they are more likely to be familiar with the music, films, and sports figures that interest their students.

All teachers should be prepared to respond to the needs of students who are suffering from the death of friends, conflicts between groups of students, pressure to use drugs or to engage in sex, and other troubles so rampant in the lives of today's children. Too often schools rely on experts—"grief counselors" and the like—when what children really need is the continuing compassion and presence of adults who represent constancy and care in their lives. Artificially separating the emotional, academic, and moral care of children into tasks for specially designated experts contributes to the fragmentation of life in schools.

Of course, I do not mean to imply that experts are unnecessary, nor do I mean to suggest that some matters should not be reserved for parents or psychologists. But our society has gone too far in compartmentalizing the care of its children. When we ask whose job it is to teach children how to care, an appropriate initial response is "Everyone's." Having accepted universal responsibility, we can then ask about the special contributions and limitations of various individuals and groups.

Supporting Structures

What kind of schools and teacher preparation are required, if themes of care are to be taught effectively? First, and most important, care must be taken seriously as a major purpose of our schools; that is, educators must recognize that caring for students is fundamental in teaching and that developing people with a strong capacity for care is a major objective of responsible education. Schools properly pursue many other objectives—developing artistic talent, promoting multicultural understanding, diversifying curriculum to meet the academic and vocational needs of all students, forging connections with community agencies and parents, and so on. Schools cannot be single-purpose institutions. Indeed, many of us would argue that it is logically and practically impossible to achieve that single academic purpose if other purposes are not recognized and accepted. This contention is confirmed in the success stories of several inner-city schools.[6]

Once it is recognized that school is a place in which students are cared for and learn to care, that recognition should be powerful in guiding policy. In the late 1950s, schools in the U.S., under the guidance of James Conant and others, placed the curriculum at the top of the educational priority list. Because the nation's leaders wanted schools to provide high-powered courses in mathematics and science, it was recommended that small high schools be replaced by efficient larger structures complete with sophisticated laboratories and specialist teachers. Economies of scale were anticipated, but the main argument for consolidation and regionalization centered on the curriculum. All over the country, small schools were closed, and students were herded into larger facilities with "more offerings." We did not think carefully about schools as communities and about what might be lost as we pursued a curriculum-driven ideal.

Today many educators are calling for smaller schools and more family-like groupings. These are good proposals, but teachers, parents, and students should be engaged in continuing discussion about what they are trying to achieve through the new arrangements. For example, if test scores do not immediately rise, participants should be courageous in explaining that test scores were not the main object of the changes. Most of us who argue for caring in schools are intuitively quite sure that children in such settings will in fact become more competent learners. But, if they cannot prove their academic competence in a prescribed period of time, should we give up on caring and on teaching them to care? That would be foolish. There is more to life and learning than the academic proficiency demonstrated by test scores.

In addition to steadfastness of purpose, schools must consider continuity of people and place. If we are concerned with caring and community, then we must make it possible for students and teachers to stay together for several years so that mutual trust can develop and students can feel a sense of belonging in their "school-home."[7]

More than one scheme of organization can satisfy the need for continuity. Elementary school children can stay with the same teacher for several years, or they can work with a stable team of specialist teachers for several years. In the latter arrangement, there may be program advantages; that is, children taught by subject-matter experts who get to know them well over an extended period of time may learn more about the particular subjects. At the high school level, the same specialist teaching might work with students throughout their years in high school. Or, as Theodore Sizer has suggested, one teacher might teach two subjects to a group of 30 students rather than one subject to 60 students, thereby reducing the number of different adults with whom students interact each day.[8] In all the suggested arrangements, placements should be made by mutual consent whenever possible. Teachers and students who hate or distrust one another should not be forced to stay together.

A policy of keeping students and teachers together for several years supports caring in two essential ways: it provides time for the development of caring relations, and it makes teaching themes of care more feasible. When trust has been established, teachers and students can discuss matters that would be hard for a group of strangers to approach, and classmates learn to support one another in sensitive situations.

The structural changes suggested here are not expensive. If a high school teacher must teach five classes a day, it costs no more for three of these classes to be composed of continuing students than for all five classes to comprise new students—i.e., strangers. The recommended changes come directly out of a clear-headed assessment of our major aims and purposes. We failed to suggest them earlier because we had other, too limited, goals in mind.

I have made one set of structural changes sound easy, and I do believe that they are easily made. But the curricular and pedagogical changes that are required may be more difficult. High school textbooks rarely contain the kinds of supplementary material I have described, and teachers are not formally prepared to incorporate such material. Too often, even the people we regard as strongly prepared in a liberal arts major are unprepared to discuss the history of their subject, its relation to other subjects, the biographies of its great figures, its connections to the great existential questions, and the ethical responsibilities of those who work in that discipline. To teach themes of care in an academically effective way, teachers will have to engage in projects of self-education.

At present, neither liberal arts departments nor schools of education pay much attention to connecting academic subjects with themes of care. For example, biology students may learn something of the anatomy and physiology of mammals but nothing at all about the care of living animals; they may never be asked to consider the moral issues involved in the annual euthanasia of millions of pets. Mathematics students may learn to solve quadratic equations but never study what it means to live in a mathematicized world. In enlightened history classes, students may learn something about the problems of racism and colonialism but never hear anything about the evolution of childhood, the contributions of women in both domestic and public caregiving, or the connection between the feminization of caregiving and public policy. A liberal education that neglects matters that are central to a fully human life hardly warrants the name,[9] and a professional education that confines itself to technique does nothing to close the gaps in liberal education.

The greatest structural obstacle, however, may simply be legitimizing the inclusion of themes of care in the curriculum. Teachers in the early grades have long included such themes as a regular part of their work, and middle school educators are becoming more sensitive to developmental needs involving care. But secondary schools—where violence, apathy, and alienation are most evident—do little to develop the capacity to care. Today, even elementary teachers complain that the pressure to produce high test scores inhibits the work they regard as central to their mission: the development of caring and competent people. Therefore, it would seem that the most fundamental change required is one of attitude. Teachers can be very special people in the lives of children, and it should be legitimate for them to spend time developing relations of trust, talking with students about problems that are central to their lives, and guiding them to-

ward greater sensitivity and competence across all the domains of care. ■

Notes

1. For the theoretical argument, see Nel Noddings, *The Challenge to Care in Schools* (New York: Teachers College Press, 1992); for a practical example and rich documentation, see Sharon Quint, *Schooling Homeless Children* (New York: Teachers College Press, 1994).

2. Martin Buber, *Between Man and Man* (New York: Macmillan, 1965), p. 98.

3. Noddings, chap. 12.

4. See Thomas H. Naylor, William H. Willimon, and Magdalena R. Naylor, *The Search for Meaning* (Nashville, Tenn.: Abingdon Press, 1994).

5. For many more examples, see Nel Noddings, *Educating for Intelligent Belief and Unbelief* (New York: Teachers College Press, 1993).

6. See Deborah Meier, "How Our Schools Could Be," *Phi Delta Kappan,* January 1995, pp. 369–73; and Quint, op. cit.

7. See Jane Roland Martin, *The Schoolhome: Rethinking Schools for Changing Families* (Cambridge, Mass.: Harvard University Press, 1992).

8. Theodore Sizer, *Horace's Compromise: The Dilemma of the American High School* (Boston: Houghton Mifflin, 1984).

9. See Bruce Wilshire, *The Moral Collapse of the University* (Albany: State University of New York Press, 1990).

POST NOTE

Getting over selfishness and self-preoccupation is a major task of one's young years. Schools have a responsibility to help children develop the habit of caring for others, as Nel Noddings demonstrates in this article. She makes a strong case for giving this task a more prominent place in our educational planning.

As children get older, however, they need to develop some sterner virtues to complement caring. They need to acquire self-discipline and self-control. They need to acquire the habit of persistence at hard tasks. They need, too, to learn how to strive for individual excellence and to compete against others without hostility. We could argue that both a strong individual and a strong nation need a balance of strengths. To pursue one strength, such as caring, without developing the full spectrum of human virtues, leaves both the individual and the nation vulnerable.

DISCUSSION QUESTIONS

1. Do you agree with the primacy given to caring by the author? Why or why not?

2. What are the "supporting structures" the article suggests are necessary to teach caring effectively?

3. What practical classroom suggestions to advance caring have you gleaned from this article?

35 Mining the Values in the Curriculum

Kevin Ryan

While the development of a child's character is clearly not the sole responsibility of the school, historically and legally schools have been major players in this arena. Young people spend much of their lives within school walls. There they will learn, either by chance or design, moral lessons about how people behave.

In helping students develop good character—the capacity to know the good, love the good, and do the good—schools should above all be contributing to a child's knowing what is good. But what is most worth knowing? And for what purpose? How do educators decide what to teach? Pressing concerns for ancient philosophers, these questions are even more demanding today as we struggle to make order out of our information-saturated lives. New dilemmas brought on by such developments as computers, doomsday weaponry, and lethal viruses challenge us daily.

What Is a Good Person?

Before curriculum builders can answer "What's most worth knowing?" we have to know "For what?" To be well adjusted to the world around

Kevin Ryan is founder and director emeritus of the Center for the Advancement of Ethics and Character, School of Education, Boston University, Massachusetts. Ryan, Kevin, "Mining the Values in the Curriculum." *Educational Leadership*, November 1993, pp. 16–18. Reprinted by permission from ASCD. All rights reserved.

us? To become wealthy and self-sufficient? To be an artist? With a little reflection, most of us would come to similar conclusions as our great philosophers and spiritual leaders: education should help us become wise and good people.

What constitutes a "good person" has paralyzed many sincere educators and noneducators. Because the United States is a multiracial, multiethnic nation, many educators despair of coming up with a shared vision of the good person to guide curriculum builders. Our founders and early educational pioneers saw in the very diverse, multicultural American scene of the late 18th and early 19th centuries the clear need for a school system that would teach the civic virtues necessary to maintain our novel political and social experiment. They saw the school's role not only as contributing to a person's understanding of what it is to be good, but also as teaching the enduring habits required of a democratic citizen.

Yet the school's curriculum must educate more than just the citizen. Conway Dorsett recently suggested that a good curriculum respects and balances the need "to educate the 'three people' in each individual: the worker, the citizen, and the private person" (1993). Our schools must provide opportunities for students to discover what is most worth knowing, as they prepare, not only to be citizens, but also good workers and good private individuals.

The work of C. S. Lewis may provide us with the multicultural model of a good person that we are seeking. Lewis discovered that certain ideas about how one becomes a good person recur in the writing of ancient Egyptians, Babylonians, Hebrews, Chinese, Norse, Indians, and Greeks, and in Anglo-Saxon and American writings as well. Common values included kindness; honesty; loyalty to parents, spouses, and family members; an obligation to help the poor, the sick, and the less fortunate; and the right to private property. Some evils such as treachery, torture, and murder, were considered worse than one's own death (1947).

Lewis called this universal path to becoming a good person by the Chinese name, "the Tao." Combining the wisdom of many cultures, this

Tao could be our multicultural answer for how to live our lives, the basis for what is most worth knowing.

Over the years, teachers, curriculum specialists, and school officials have used the Tao, albeit unconsciously, to guide the work of schools. Translated into curriculum, the Tao guides schools to educate children to be concerned about the weak and those in need; to help others; to work hard and complete their tasks well and promptly, even when they do not want to; to control their tempers; to work cooperatively with others and practice good manners; to respect authority and other people's rights; to help resolve conflicts; to understand honesty, responsibility, and friendship; to balance pleasures with responsibilities; and to ask themselves and decide "What is the right thing to do?"

Most educators agree that our schools should teach these attitudes both in the formal and in the hidden curriculum.

The Formal Curriculum

The formal curriculum is usually thought of as the school's planned educational experiences— the selection and organization of knowledge and skills from the universe of possible choices. Of course, not all knowledge nor every skill contributes directly to knowing the good, but much of the subject matter of English and social studies is intimately connected to the Tao. Stories, historical figures, and events are included in the formal curriculum to illuminate the human condition. From them we can learn how to be a positive force in the lives of others, and we can also see the effects of a poorly lived life.

The men and women, real or fictitious, who we learn about in school are instruments for understanding what it is to be (or not to be) a good person. One of the strengths and attractions of good literature is its complexity. As students read, they learn about themselves and the world. For example, students come face-to-face with raw courage in the exploits of Harriet Tubman and

further understand the danger of hate and racism through *The Diary of Anne Frank*. They glimpse in Edward Arlington Robinson's poem "Miniver Cheevy" the folly of storing up earthly treasures. They see in Toni Cade Bambera's "Your Blues Ain't Like Mine" the intrinsic dignity of each human being. They gain insight into the heart of a truly noble man, Atticus Finch, in *To Kill a Mockingbird*. They perceive the thorny relationships between the leader and the led by following the well-intended, but failed efforts of Brutus in Shakespeare's *Julius Caesar*.

Our formal curriculum is a vehicle to teach the Tao, to help young people to come to know the good. But simply selecting the curriculum is not enough; like a vein of precious metal, the teacher and students must mine it together. To engage students in the lessons in human character and ethics contained in our history and literature without resorting to empty preaching and crude didacticism is the great skill of teaching.

The Hidden Curriculum

In addition to the formal curriculum, students learn from a hidden curriculum—all the personal and social instruction that they acquire from their day-to-day schooling. Much of what has been written about the hidden curriculum in recent decades has stressed that these school experiences often lead to students' loss of self-esteem, unswerving obedience to silly rules, and the suppression of their individuality. While true of some students and some schools, the hidden curriculum can lead either to negative or positive education.

Many of education's most profound and positive teachings can be conveyed in the hidden curriculum. If a spirit of fairness penetrates every corner of the school, children will learn to be fair. Through the service of teachers, administrators, and older students, students learn to be of service to others. By creating an atmosphere of high standards, the hidden curriculum can teach habits of accuracy and precision. Many aspects of school life, ranging from homework assignments to sporting events, can teach self-control and self-discipline.

While unseen, the hidden curriculum must be considered with the same seriousness as the written, formal curriculum. The everyday behavior of the faculty, staff, and other students cannot fail to have an impact on a student.

One school concerned with the hidden curriculum is Roxbury Latin, a fine academic high school in Boston. In the spring of 1992, an accredited team interviewed 27 students, ranging from 7th to 12th grade, asking them the same question, "What do you think is Roxbury Latin's philosophy of education?" Every one of the students came back with the same answer: "This school is most concerned about what kind of people we are becoming." What the review team did not know was that every September, the school's headmaster, Anthony Jarvis, assembles all the new students and delivers a short message:

> We want you to excel in academics and sports and the arts while you are here. But, remember this: we care much more about your characters, what kind of people you are becoming.

End of message. End of assembly. All indications are that the message is getting through.

Policies and Practices

A school that makes a positive impact on the character of young people helps children to know the Tao and make it part of their lives. Such a school has in place the following policies and practices.

- The school has a mission statement widely known by students, teachers, administrators, parents, and the entire school community.
- The school has a comprehensive program of service activities, starting in the early grades and requiring more significant contributions of time and energy in the later years of high school.
- School life is characterized by a high level of school spirit and healthy intergroup competition.
- The school has an external charity or cause (a local home for the elderly or educational fund-raising for a Third World community) to which all members of the community contribute.
- The school has a grading and award system that does more than give lip service to character formation and ethics, but recognizes academic effort, good discipline, contributions to the life of the classroom, service to the school and the community, respect for others, and good sportsmanship.
- The school expects not only teachers but also the older students to be exemplars of high ethical standards.
- The school's classrooms and public areas display mottoes and the pictures of exemplary historical figures.
- The school has regular ceremonies and rituals that bring the community together to celebrate achievements of excellence in all realms: academic, athletic, artistic and ethical.[1]

Our students have a major task in life: to become individuals of character. Character education, then, is the central curriculum issue confronting educators. Rather than the latest fad, it is a school's oldest mission. Nothing is better for the human soul than to discuss excellence every day. The curriculum of our elementary and secondary schools should be the delivery system for this encounter with excellence. ■

Note

1. Several of these policies and procedures are elaborated in *Reclaiming Our Schools: A Handbook for Teaching Character, Academics, and Discipline,* by E. A. Wynne and K. Ryan (Columbus, Ohio: Merrill, 1992).

References

Dorsett, C. (March 1993). "Multicultural Education: Why We Need It and Why We Worry About It." *Network News and Views* 12, 3:31.

Lewis, C. S. (1947). *The Abolition of Man.* New York: MacMillan.

Author's note: I wish to acknowledge Catherine Kinsella Stutz of Boston University for her contributions to this article.

C. S. Lewis, the late English scholar and writer of children's stories (e.g., *the Tales of Narnia* and others), used to tell a modern fable about a country that decided to abandon teaching mathematics because the curriculum was too crowded and no one was exactly sure of what to teach. Dropping mathematics from the school curriculum pleased students and teachers, as well as parents who were no longer embarrassed each night, struggling over their children's homework. All went well for several years, until shopkeepers began to complain that their clerks couldn't "do sums" and kept billing customers incorrectly. Passengers on trains and buses were furious because they were continually getting shortchanged by ticket collectors. And worst of all, politicians became frenzied because people could not fill out their taxes properly. But still, no one thought to consider that mathematics was no longer in the curriculum. Lewis intended the fable as a parable about the failure to teach religion. Today, we might see parallels between the imaginary country's abandonment of mathematics and America's recent failure to teach character and ethical values.

DISCUSSION QUESTIONS

1. What is the Tao? Should it be taught in American public schools? Why or why not?

2. Review Headmaster Anthony Jarvis's message to new students. Do you agree or disagree with it as the major purpose of schooling?

3. What are the strongest cases for and against character education in U.S. schools? And where do you stand on this issue: for or against? Why?

36

Standards for American Schools: Help or Hindrance?

Elliot W. Eisner

Efforts to reform American schools are not exactly a novel enterprise. When the Soviet Union sent Sputnik circling the globe in 1957 the U.S. Congress looked to the schools to recover what we had though we had: leadership in space. The curriculum reform movement of the 1960s was intended, in part, to help us regain our technological superiority in the Cold War. In the 1970s "accountability" became the central concept around which our education reform efforts turned. If only we could identify the expected outcomes of instruction and invent means to describe their presence, school administrators and teachers could be held accountable for the quality of their work.

In April 1983 *A Nation at Risk* was published. In its memorable opening passage the impact of the schools on U.S. society was likened to foreign invasion. By the late 1980s *A Nation at Risk*, one of the most prominent reform publications of the century, seemed to have faded, and its passing set the stage for America 2000—the reform agenda of the Bush Administration, now signed on to by the Clinton Administration. America 2000 was intended to do what the curriculum reform movement of the 1960s, the accountability movement of the 1970s, and *A Nation at Risk* and the "excellence movement" of the 1980s had been unable to accomplish.

We now have in Goals 2000 (the Clinton version of America 2000) an approach to education reform that uses standards as the linchpin of its efforts. Standards are being formulated for the certification of teachers, for the content of curricula, and for the outcomes of teaching. Virtually every subject-matter field in education has formulated or is in the process of formulating or revising national standards that describe what students should know and be able to do.

If anyone detects a slight echo of the past in today's reform efforts, let me assure you that you are not alone. We seem to latch on to approaches to reform that are replays of past efforts that themselves failed to come to grips with what it is that makes school practices robust and resistant to change.

Consider, for example, the concept of standards. The term is attractive. Who among us, at first blush at least, would claim that schools—or any other institution for that matter—should be without them? Standards imply high expectations, rigor, things of substance. To be without standards is not to know what to expect or how to determine if expectations have been realized—or so it seems.

Yet once we get past the illusions that the concept invites—once we think hard about the meaning of the term—the picture becomes more complex. To begin with, the meaning of the term is not as self-evident as many seem to believe. A standard meal, for example, is a meal that I think we would agree is nothing to rave about—and the same could be said of a standard hotel room or a standard reply to a question. A standard can also be a banner, something that trumpets one's identity and commitment. A standard can represent a value that people have cared enough about to die for. Standards can also refer to units of measure. The National Bureau of Standards employs standards to measure the quality of manufactured products. Electrical appliances, for example, must achieve a certain standards to get the UL seal of approval.

At the time this article was written, Elliot W. Eisner was professor of education and art at Stanford University. Originally published in *Phi Delta Kappan*, June 1995, pp. 758–764. Reprinted with the permission of the author.

Which conception of standards do we embrace in the reform movement? Surely we do not mean by standards a typical level of performance, since that is what we already have without an iota of invention. As for standards that represent beliefs or values, we already have mission statements and position papers in abundance, but they do not have the level of specificity that reformers believe is needed for standards to be useful.

The third conception of standards—as units of measure that make it possible to quantify the performance of students, teachers, and schools—seems closer to what we have in mind. We live in a culture that admires technology and efficiency and believes in the possibility of objectivity. The idea of measurement provides us with a procedure that is closely associated with such values. Measurement makes it possible to describe quantity in ways that allow as little space as possible for subjectivity.[1] For example, the objectivity of an objective test is not a function of the way in which the test items were selected, but of the way in which the test is scored. Objective tests can be scored by machine, with no need for judgment.

Standards in education, as we now idealize them, are to have such features. They are to be objective and, whenever possible, measurable. Once a technology of assessment is invented that will objectively quantify the relationship of student performance to a measurable ideal, we will be able to determine without ambiguity the discrepancy between the former and the latter, and thus we will have a meaningful standard.

Those who have been working in education for 20 or so years or who know the history of American education will also know that the vision I have just described is a recapitulation of older ideals. I refer to the curriculum reform movement of the 1960s. It was an important event in the history of American education, but it was not the only significant movement of that period. You will also remember that it was in the 1960s that American educators became infatuated with "behavioral objectives." Everyone was to have them. The idea then, like the notion of standards today, was to define our educational goals operationally in terms that were suffi-ciently specific to determine without ambiguity whether or not the student had achieved them.

The specifics of procedures, given prominence by Robert Mager's 1962 book, *Preparing Instructional Objectives*, required that student behavior be identified, that the conditions in which it was to be displayed be described, and that a criterion be specified that made it possible to measure the student's behavior in relation to the criterion.[2] For Mager a behavioral objective might be stated as follows: "At the end of the instructional period, when asked to do so, the student will be able to write a 200-word essay with no more than two spelling errors, one error in punctuation, and no errors in grammar."

It all seemed very neat. What people discovered as they tried to implement the idea was that to have behaviorally defined instructional objectives that met the criteria that Mager specified required the construction of *hundreds* of specific objectives. Heaven knows, school districts tried. But it soon became apparent that teachers would be bogged down with such a load. And even so ardent a supporter of behavioral objectives as James Popham eventually realized that teachers would be better off with just a few such objectives.[3] The quest for certainty, which high-level specificity and precision implied, was soon recognized as counterproductive.

Those who know the history of American education will also know that the desire to specify expected outcomes and to prescribe the most efficient means for achieving them was itself the dominant strain of what has come to be called the "efficiency movement" in education.[4] The efficiency movement, which began in 1913 and lasted until the early 1930s, was designed to apply the principles of scientific management to schools. Its progenitor, Frederick Taylor, the inventor of time-and-motion study, was a management consultant hired by industrialists to make their plants more efficient and hence more profitable. By specifying in detail the desired outcomes of a worker's efforts and by eliminating "wasted motion," output would increase, profits would soar, wages would rise, and everyone would benefit.

American school administrators thought that in Taylor's approach to the management of industrial plants they had found a surefire method for producing efficient schools. Moreover, Taylor's approach was based on "science." The prescription of expected outcomes, of the manner of performance, and of the content in which competence is to be displayed is a not-too-distant cousin of the teacher performance standards and curriculum content standards that accompany today's discussions of standards for student performance.

School administrators caught up in the efficiency movement gradually learned that the basic conception and the expectations that flowed from it—namely, that one could mechanize and routinize teaching and learning—did not work. Even if it were possible to give teachers scripts for their performance, it was not possible to give students scripts. There was no "one best method," and there was no way to "teacher-proof" instruction.

My point thus far is that what we are seeing in American education today is a well-intentioned but conceptually shallow effort to improve our schools. My point thus far is to make it plain that the current effort in which we are enmeshed is no novelty; we have been here before. My point thus far is to suggest that successful efforts at school reform will entail a substantially deeper analysis of schools and their relationships to communities and teachers than has thus far been undertaken.

To try to do justice to the aspirations of the national education reform movement, I will try to make a sympathetic presentation of its arguments. I start with the acknowledgment that there is a sense of sweet reason to the arguments that the reformers have made. After all, with standards we will know where we are headed. We can return rigor to schooling; we can inform students, parents, and teachers of what we expect; we can have a common basis for appraising student performance; and we can, at last, employ a potent lever for education reform. Without standards, we are condemned to an unbroken journey into an abyss of mediocrity; we will remain a nation at risk.

In addition, the task of formulating standards is salutary for teachers and others involved in curriculum planning. By establishing national goals for each subject that schools teach, we will be able to achieve professional consensus that will give us a unified and educationally solid view of what students are expected to learn. By trying to define standards for each field, a single vision of a subject will be created, teachers will have an opportunity to profit from the goals and standards formulated by their peers, and ambiguity will be diminished because teachers will know not only the direction their efforts are to take, but also the specific destinations toward which their students are headed. Furthermore, teachers will have something of a timetable to help determine not only whether, but when, they have arrived.

As if they had just taken a cold shower, a population of sometimes lethargic and burned-out teachers will be reawakened and will become alert. Our nation will, at last, have a national educational agenda, something that it has never possessed. Ultimately, such resources and the approach to education that those resources reflect will help us regain our competitive edge in the global economy. Parents will be satisfied, students will know what is expected of them, and the business community will have the employees it needs for America to become number one by the year 2000, not only in science and math but in other fields as well. Our students and our schools will go for and get the gold at the educational Olympics in which we are competing. Our schools will become "world class."

An attractive vision? It seems so, yet a number of questions arise. You will recall that the standards about which reformers speak are national standards. The organizations—and there are dozens—that are engaged in formulating standards are doing so for the nation as a whole, not for some specific locality. Put another way, in a nation in which 45 million students in 50 states go to approximately 108,000 schools overseen by some 15,000 school boards and in which 2.5 million teachers teach, there is the presumption that it makes good educational sense for there to be uniform expectations with respect to goals, content, and levels of student achievement. I regard this assumption as questionable on at least two counts.

First, the educational uses of subjects are not singular. The social studies can be used to help students understand history, to help create a socially active citizenry, or to help students recognize the connection between culture and ideas. Biology can be used to help students learn to think like biologists, to understand the balance of nature, to appreciate the limits of science in establishing social policy, or to gain an appreciation of life. The language arts can be used to develop poetic forms of thought, to learn to appreciate great works of literary art, to acquire the mechanics of written and spoken language, to learn to appreciate forms of life that require literary rather than literal understanding. Mathematics can be taught to help students learn to compute, to understand the structure of mathematics, to solve mathematical problems, to cultivate forms of mathematical cognition, and to help students appreciate the beauty of structures in space. Where is it written that every subject has to be taught for the same reasons to 45 million students? Despite the effort to achieve professional consensus about the educational agendas of specific subjects, the virtue of uniformity is, to my mind, questionable.

Uniformity in curriculum content is a virtue *if* one's aim is to be able to compare students in one part of the country with students in others. Uniformity is a virtue when the aspiration is to compare the performance of American students with students in Korea, Japan, and Germany. But why should we wish to make such comparisons? To give up the idea that there needs to be one standard for all students in each field of study is not to give up the aspiration to seek high levels of educational quality in both pedagogical practices and educational outcomes. Together, the desire to compare and the recognition of individuality create one of the dilemmas of a social meritocracy: the richness of a culture rests not only on the prospect of cultivating a set of common commitments, but also on the prospect of cultivating those individual talents through which the culture at large is enriched.

A second problematic feature of the aspiration to adopt a common set of standards for all is a failure to recognize differences among the students with whom we work. I am well aware of the fact that deleterious self-fulfilling prophecies can be generated when the judgments educators make about individuals are based on a limited appreciation of the potentialities of the students. This is a danger that requires our constant vigilance. However, the reality of differences—in region, in aptitude, in interests, and in goals—suggests that it is reasonable that there be differences in programs.

The framers of the U.S. Constitution implicitly recognized the need for the localities they called states to develop educational programs that addressed the values and features of the populations in those states. We do not need the U.S. equivalent of a French Ministry of Education, prescribing a one-size-fits-all program. Ironically, at a time when the culture at large is recognizing the uniqueness of us all and cultivating our productive differences, the education reform movement, in its anxiety about quality, wants to rein in our diversity, to reduce local discretion, and to give everybody the same target at which to aim.

Thus, with respect to aspiration, I think there are fundamental problems with the concept of standards as applied to the nation as a whole. But there are other problems as well, and these problems relate to the concept of standards as it applies to the process of education and to what we know about normal patterns of human development.

You will remember that I referred to standards as units of measure that make possible the "objective" description of quantitative relationships. But there are qualitative standards as well. To have a *qualitative* standard you must create or select an icon, prototype, or what is sometimes called a benchmark against which the performance or products of students are matched. To have a *quantitative* standard you must specify the number or percentage of correct answers needed to pass a test or the number of allowable errors in a performance or product and to use that specification as the standard.

In each case, there is a fixed and relatively unambiguous unit of measurement. In the qualitative case, the task for both judge and performer is one of matching a performance with a model. This kind of matching is precisely what occurs in the Olympics. Olympic judges know what a particular dive should look like, and they compare a diver's performance to the model. The diver, too, knows what the model looks like and does his or her best to replicate the model.

With respect to the quantitative case, the application of a standard occurs in two different ways. The first has to do with determining the correctness of any individual response. An item response is judged correct if the appropriate bubble is filled in, or if the appropriate selection is made, or if some other indication is given that the student has hit a prespecified mark. The prespecified correct response serves as a standard for each item. Once these item responses are summed, a determination is made as to whether the total number of correct responses meets a second standard, the standard specified as a passing grade by the test-maker or by some policy-making body.

Notice that in both cases innovation in response is not called for. The diver replicates a known model. The test-maker determines whether a student's score is acceptable, not by exercising judgment, but by counting which bubbles have been filled in and comparing the number of correct responses to a fixed predetermined standard.

There are, we must acknowledge, a number of important tasks that students must learn in school in which innovation is not useful. Learning how to spell correctly means knowing how to replicate the known. The same holds true for much of what is taught in early arithmetic and in the language arts. There are many important tasks and skills that students need to learn—i.e., convention—that are necessary for doing more important work and that educational programs should help them learn. The more important work that I speak of is the work that makes it possible for students to think imaginatively about problems that matter to them, tasks that give them the opportunity to affix their own personal signature to their work, occasions to explore ideas and questions that have no correct answers, and projects in which they can reason and express their own ideas.

Learning to replicate known conventions is an important part of the *tactical outcomes* of education, but it is not adequate for achieving the *strategic aspirations* that we hold. These strategic aspirations require curricula and assessment policies that invite students to exercise judgment and to create outcomes that are not identical with those of their peers. Again, the cultivation of productive idiosyncrasy ought to be one of the aims that matter in American schools, and, to my way of thinking, we ought to build programs that make the realization of such an outcome possible, even if it means that we will not find it easy to compare students. When we seek to measure such outcomes, we will not be able to use a fixed standard for scoring the work students have produced. We will have to rely on that most exquisite of human capacities—judgment. . . .

Standards are appropriate for some kinds of tasks, but, as I argued above, those tasks are instrumental to larger and more important educational aims. We really don't need to erect a complex school system to teach the young how to read utility bills, how to do simple computation, or how to spell; they will learn those skills on their own. What we do need to teach them is how to engage in higher-order thinking, how to pose telling questions, how to solve complex problems that have more than one answer. When the concept of standards becomes salient in our discourse about educational expectations, it colors our view of what education can be and dilutes our conception of education's potential. Language matters, and the language of standards is by and large a limiting rather than a liberating language.

The qualities that define inventive work of any kind are qualities that by definition have both unique and useful features. The particular form those features take and what it is that makes them useful are not necessarily predictable, but sensitive critics—and sensitive teachers—are able to discover such properties in the work. Teachers who know the students they teach recognize the unique qualities in students' comments, in their paintings, in the essays they write, in the ways in which they relate to their peers. The challenge in teaching is to provide the conditions that will foster the growth of those personal characteristics that are socially important and, at the same time, personally satisfying to the student. The aim of education is not to train an army that marches to the same drummer, at the same pace, toward the same destination. Such an aim may be appropriate for totalitarian societies, but it is incompatible with democratic ideals.

If one used only philosophical grounds to raise questions about the appropriateness of uniform national standards for students in American schools, there would still be questions enough to give one pause. But there are developmental grounds as well. The graded American public school system was built on an organizational theory that has little to do with the developmental characteristics of growing children. In the mid-19th century we thought it made very good sense for the school to be organized into grades and for there to be a body of content assigned to each grade.[5] Each grade was to be related to a specific age. The task of the student was to master the content taught at that grade as a precondition for promotion to the next grade. At the end of an eight- or 12-year period, it was assumed that, if the school and the teacher had done their jobs, everyone would come out at roughly the same place.

If you examine the patterns of human development for children from age 5 to age 18, you will find that, as children grow older, their rate of development is increasingly variable. Thus the range of variation among children of the same age increases with time.

For example, for ordinary, nonhomogeneous classes, the average range of reading achievement is roughly equal to the grade level: at the second grade there is, on average, a two-year spread in reading achievement. Some second-graders are reading at the first-grade level, and others are reading at the third-grade level. At the fourth grade the spread is about four years, and at the sixth grade, about six years. In the seventh grade the range is about seven years: some children are reading at the fourth-grade level, and some are reading at the 10th-grade level.

What this means is that children develop at their own distinctive pace. The tidy structure that was invented in the 19th century to rationalize school organization may look wonderful on paper, but it belies what we know about the course of human development. Because we still operate with a developmentally insensitive organizational structure in our schools, the appeal of uniform standards by grade level or by outcome seems reasonable. It is not. Variability, not uniformity, is the hallmark of the human condition.

I do not want to overstate the idea. To be sure, humans are like all other humans, humans are like some other humans, and humans are like no other humans. All three claims are true. But we have become so preoccupied with remedying the perceived weaknesses of American schools that we have underestimated the diversity and hence the complexity that exists.

The varieties of unappreciated complexity are large. Let me suggest only a few. When evaluating students in the context of the classroom, the teacher—the person who has the widest variety of information about any particular student—takes into consideration much more than the specific features of a student's particular product. The age, grade, and developmental level of the student; the amount of progress the student has made; the degree of effort that the student has expended; the amount of experience a student has had in a domain are all educationally relevant considerations that professionally competent teachers take into account in making judgments about a student's progress. Experienced teachers know in their bones that the student's work constitutes only one item in an array of educational values and that these values sometimes compete. There are times when it may be more important educationally for a teacher to publicly acknowledge the quality of a student's work than to criticize it, even when the work is below the class average.

Beyond the details of the classroom, there are more general questions having to do with the bases on which educational standards are formulated. Should educational standards be derived from the average level of performance of students in a school, in a school district, in a state, in a nation, *in the world*? How much talk have we heard of *"world class"* standards?

If national policy dictates that there will be uniform national standards for student performance, will there also be uniform national standards for the resources available to school? To teachers? To administrators? Will the differences in performance between students living in well-heeled, upper-class suburbs and those living on the cusp of poverty in the nation's inner cities demonstrate the existing inequities in American education? Will they not merely confirm what we already know?

The socioeconomic level of the students and the resources available to them and their teachers in a school or school district do make a difference. If those urging standards on us believe that the use of standards will demonstrate inequities—and hence serve to alleviate them—why haven't these already painfully vivid inequities been effective in creating more equitable schools?

And, one might wonder, what would happen to standards in education if by some magic all students achieved them? Surely the standards would be considered too low. At first blush this doesn't sound like a bad thing. Shouldn't the bar always be higher than we can reach? Sounds reasonable. Yet such a view of the function of standards will ineluctably create groups of winners and losers. Can our education system flourish without losers? Is it possible for us to frame conceptions of education and society that rest on more generous assumptions? And consider the opposite. What will we do with those students who fail to meet the standards? Then what?

Perhaps one of the most important consequences of the preoccupation with national standards in education is that it distracts us from the deeper, seemingly intractable problems that beset our schools. It distracts us from paying attention to the importance of building a culture of schooling that is genuinely intellectual in charac-ter, that values questions and ideas at least as much as getting right answers. It distracts us from trying to understand how we can provide teachers the kind of professional opportunities that will afford the best among them opportunities to continue to grow through a lifetime of work. It distracts us from attending to the inevitable array of interactions between teaching, curriculum, evaluation, school organization, and the often deleterious expectations and pressures from universities.

How should these matters be addressed? Can schools and teachers and administrators afford the kind of risk-taking and exploratory activity that genuine inquiry in education requires?

Vitality within any organization is more likely when there are opportunities to pursue fresh possibilities, to exercise imagination, to try things out, and to relinquish the quest for certainty in either pedagogical method or educational outcome. Indeed, one of the important aims of education is to free the mind from the confines of certainty. Satisfaction, our children must learn, can come from the uncertainty of the journey, not just from the clarity of the destination.

I am not sure that American society is willing at this time to embrace so soft a set of values as I have described. We have become a tough-minded lot. We believe that we can solve the problems of crime by reopening the doors to the gas chamber and by building more prisons. But it's never been that simple. Nor is solving the problems of schooling as simple as having national education standards.

And so I believe that we must invite our communities to join us in a conversation that deepens our understanding of the educational process and advances our appreciation of its possibilities. Genuine education reform is not about shallow efforts that inevitably fade into oblivion. It is about vision, conversation, and action designed to create a genuine and evolving educational culture. I hope we can resist the lure of slogans and the glitter of bandwagons and begin to talk seriously about education. That is one conversation in which we must play a leading role. ■

Standards for American Schools: Help or Hindrance?

Notes

1. The presence of subjectivity in scientific work has long been regarded as a source of bias. Most measurement procedures aspire to what is called "procedural objectivity," which represents a process in which the exercise of judgment is minimized. A competent 10-year-old can do as well as a Nobel Prize winner in measuring a room. Tasks that can be accomplished without appealing to human judgment can also be done by machine. Optical scanners can score multiple test forms more quickly and more accurately than humans. Some idealizations of science aspire to a pristine quantitative descriptive state that does not depend on human judgment or interpretation at all. For an extended discussion of the concept of "procedural objectivity," see Elliot W. Eisner, *The Enlightened Eye: Qualitative Inquiry and the Enhancement of Educational Practice* (New York: Macmillan, 1991).

2. Robert Mager, *Preparing Instructional Objectives* (Palo Alto, Calif.: Fearon Publishers, 1962).

3. W. James Popham, "Must All Objectives Be Behavioral?," *Educational Leadership*, April 1972, pp. 605–608.

4. Raymond Callahan, *Education and the Cult of Efficiency* (Chicago: University of Chicago Press, 1962).

5. John I. Goodlad and Robert Anderson, *The Nongraded Elementary School*, rev. ed. (New York: Teachers College Press, 1987).

P O S T N O T E

As young graduate students, both editors of *Kaleidoscope* were privileged to have Eisner (at the time himself a young professor) as a teacher. It was at the height of interest in B. F. Skinner's behaviorism and the application of programmed instruction and behavioral objectives to American classrooms. There was a heady belief throughout the educational community that this new movement would soon transform our schools. Professor Eisner was one of the few voices at that time to raise questions and urge caution.

Today we are in the midst of a new national movement that many believe will revolutionize our schools and lead to much higher levels of achievement among our students. As he has throughout his career, Eisner is again asking the hard questions, this time about the "standards movement." His advice in the matter of standards is profoundly important. In matters of education, there are no quick fixes; there are no simple answers. Real education reform is not a flashy sprinter's dash, but a brave marathoner's run.

D I S C U S S I O N Q U E S T I O N S

1. What is the author's central contention? What is his argument?

2. Based on your reading of this article, what do the words *educational standards* mean to you?

3. What positive suggestions does the author make for improving our schools?

Realizing the Promise of Standards-Based Education

Mike Schmoker and
Robert J. Marzano

The standards movement is arguably a major force in education today, and some researchers assert that the significance of the standards campaign will be huge. Undoubtedly, historians will identify the last decade of this century as the time when a concentrated press for national education standards emerged (Glaser & Linn, 1993, p. xiii).

But will the standards movement endure? And if it does, will it contribute significantly to higher achievement? We believe it will—but only if we rein in its most excessive tendencies. Those tendencies can be seen in the nature and length of state and professional standards documents— and in their unintended consequences.

The Promise of the Standards Movement

Make no mistake: The success of any organization is contingent upon clear, commonly defined

Mike Schmoker is author of *Results: The Key to Continuous School Improvement* (ASCD, 1996). Robert J. Marzano is co-author of *A Comprehensive Guide to Designing Standards-Based Districts, Schools, and Classrooms* (ASCD/McREL, 1997) and *Content Knowledge: A Compendium of Standards and Benchmarks for K–12 Education* (McREL/ASCD, 1996). Schmoker, Mike and Robert J. Marzano, "Realizing the Promise of Standards-Based Education." *Educational Leadership*, March 1999, pp. 17–21. Reprinted by permission from ASCD. All rights reserved.

goals. A well-articulated focus unleashes individual and collective energy. And a common focus clarifies understanding, accelerates communication, and promotes persistence and collective purpose (Rosenholtz, 1991). This is the stuff of improvement.

The promise of standards can be seen in places like

■ Frederick County, Maryland, where the number of students reaching well-defined and commonly assessed standards rose dramatically, lifting them from the middle to the highest tier in Maryland schools. Local assessments were deliberately aligned with standards as they were embedded in the state assessments.

■ Fort Logan Elementary School in Denver, Colorado, where scores rose significantly when teams of teachers analyzed weaknesses in performance relative to grade-level standards. Each team reviewed test data and developed strategies for helping students learn in identified areas of difficulty.

■ Lake Havasu City, Arizona, where teams of Title I teachers identified, defined, and focused instruction on common reading skills. Once teachers had a shared language about which skills to concentrate on, they improved strategies and systems to improve instructional quality and consistency. As a result, the number of students reading at or above grade level rose from 20 to 35 percent in just one year.

■ Glendale Union High School District near Phoenix, Arizona, where teams of teachers have increased student performance for almost every course offered. All district teachers—whether they teach algebra, U.S. history, biology, or senior English—are teaching to the same year-end assessments developed by subject-area teams. The same coordination is happening at Adlai Stevenson High School in Lincolnshire, Illinois, where teacher teams continue to set measurable achievement records on every kind of assessment.

■ Amphitheater High School in Tucson, Arizona, where teacher Bill Bendt routinely helps exceptional numbers of students pass advanced placement tests by carefully focusing instruction on the standards made explicit by the AP exam.

How did they get these results? Interestingly, not by focusing on standards contained in state or professional documents. Their efforts preceded those documents. Nonetheless, in each case, *teachers knew exactly what students needed to learn, what to teach to, where to improve, and what to work on with colleagues.* Clear, common learning standards—manageable in number—promote better results. They are essential to focus and to coherence.

If this is true, then educators face two important questions: (1) Do we already have sufficiently clear standards? and (2) Are state and professional standards documents truly helping us achieve the focus and the coherence that are vital to success? In too many cases, the answer to both questions is no.

Don't We Already Have Standards?

Curiously, standards in most districts are often similar. We have curriculums, scope, and sequence for each grade level, course, and subject area. But the perception of a common, coherent program of teaching and learning is a delusion. One of us once sat with a curriculum coordinator, poring through a dense curriculum notebook of the district's grade-by-grade "learner outcomes." The document was years in the making. Nonetheless, when the coordinator was asked what influence the curriculum was having on instruction, she was candid enough to reply "probably none." Consultant and author Heidi Hayes Jacobs likes to say that curriculum guides are "well-intended fictions." Her conclusion is that the current system actually encourages teachers to simply teach what they like to teach.

It is time to admit that at the ground level, where teachers teach and students learn, there is not coherence, but chaos. The chief problem is that there is simply too much to teach—arguably two to three times too much (Schmidt, McKnight, & Raizen, 1996)—and too many options for what can be taught (Rosenholtz, 1991). There are enormous differences in what teachers teach in the same subject at the same grade level in the same school. Even when common, highly structured textbooks are used as the basis for a curriculum, teachers make independent and idiosyncratic decisions regarding what should be emphasized, what should be added, and what should be deleted (see, for example, Doyle, 1992). Such practices create huge holes in the continuum of content to which students are exposed. *The Learning Gap,* researchers Stevenson and Stigler (1992, p. 140) observe that teachers are "daunted by the length of most textbooks." In a system that does little or nothing to help them coordinate priorities, they are forced to select or to omit different topics haphazardly. This only adds to the prevailing chaos.

Standards and School Improvement

The implications of this chaos go to the heart of school improvement. Researcher Susan Rosenholtz found that

> The hallmark of any successful organization is a shared sense among its members about what they are trying to accomplish. Agreed-upon goals and ways to attain them enhance the organization's capacity for *rational planning and action.* (1991, p. 13; our emphasis)

For this reason, she was dismayed to find that schools were unique among organizations in lacking common goals and that the goals of teaching were "multiple, shifting and frequently disputed" (p. 13).

This state of chaos was the rationale for the standards movement—and the most visible and influential manifestations are the state and professional standards documents. Yet these documents themselves have contributed to the very problems they were intended to solve.

The Perils of Standards-Based Education

"Less is more" we keep telling ourselves. Students learn more when we teach less—but teach it well (Dempster, 1993). Nowhere is this principle more obviously violated than in the standards documents. The official documents generated by 49 states and the professional subject-area organizations have had unintended consequences. Commentator Ronald Wolk has found some of them not only to be written in language that is "absurd" but also to contain such quantity that it would take a 10-hour teaching day to cover the material in them (1998).

Because it is easier to add and enlarge than to reduce and refine, we are caught in the snare of having honored (perhaps for political reasons) far too many suggestions for inclusion in the standards documents. We have often failed to place hard but practical limits on the number and the nature of the standards. The result? Bloated and poorly written standards that almost no one can realistically teach to or ever hope to adequately assess. We are making the same mistakes with these documents that we made with our district curriculums.

In the case of standards, quantity is not quality. The irony of the Third International Mathematics and Science Study (TIMSS) shouts at us: Although U.S. mathematics textbooks attempt to address 175 percent more topics than do German textbooks and 350 percent more topics than do Japanese textbooks, both German and Japanese students significantly outperform U.S. students in mathematics. Similarly, although U.S. science textbooks attempt to cover 930 percent more topics than do German textbooks and 433 percent more topics than do Japanese textbooks, both German and Japanese students significantly outperform U.S. students in science achievement as well (Schmidt, McKnight, & Raizen, 1996). Clearly, U.S. schools would benefit from decreasing the amount of content they try to cover. And teacher morale and self-efficacy improve when we confidently lay out a more manageable number of essential topics to be taught and assessed in greater depth.

Getting Standards Right

Too many of the state standards documents, informed as they are by the professional subject-area standards, have frustrated rather than helped

our attempt to provide common focus and clarity for teachers and students. The good news is this: Clear, intelligible standards are a pillar of higher achievement. *Aligned with appropriate assessments,* they can help us realize the dream of learning for all. They are the heart of the infrastructure for school improvement (Rosenholtz, 1991; Fullan & Stiegelbauer, 1991).

The Standards-Driven School

Consider a school where teachers know exactly what essential skills and knowledge students should learn that year and where they know that their colleagues are teaching to the same manageable standards. Because of this, their fellow teachers can collaborate with them on lessons and units.

This in turn leads to a living bank of proven, standards-referenced instructional materials—lessons, units, and assessments perfected through action research. Both new and veteran teachers can peruse these targeted materials, learning from and adding to the richness of the faculty's repertoire. Because of these rich resources, new and struggling teachers achieve confidence and competence much more rapidly, and experienced teachers have a sense of making a meaningful, ongoing contribution to their craft while being renewed by instructional ideas that are engaging for students. Proven methods, practices, and lessons aligned with established standards become the center of the professional dialogue. Results on local, state, and formative assessments get better and better. Such an alignment leads inevitably to better short- and long-term results on local and state assessments as well as on norm-referenced, alternative, and criterion-referenced assessments.

To create this infrastructure in schools, we can take a few concrete steps:

1. Start with the standards that are assessed. Be circumspect about standards that are not assessed. After thoroughly reviewing the state standards documents, we believe that many of them never will be thoroughly assessed. Many of the existing standards that educators are working manically to "cover" will disappear because of their own irrelevancy and imprecision. Expending organized effort on every standard is senseless because many of them will turn out to be ephemeral. Start by focusing teaching on the standards actually contained in current state norm-referenced or criterion-referenced assessments.

As state assessments develop, real priorities become clear. And we must learn all we can about how to teach to these priorities most effectively. Teachers in Colorado, now that they know the reading and writing standards through their experience with the state assessments, are responding in a positive and coordinated fashion. Many schools, like Bessemer Elementary in Pueblo, which has an 80 percent minority population, have realized dramatic gains. At Bessemer, from 1997 to 1998, the number of students performing at or above the standard in reading rose from 12 percent to 64 percent. In writing, they went from 2 percent to 48 percent. Weekly standards-based team meetings made the difference.

State and standardized assessments do not measure everything we deem important, but success on such tests in this age of accountability is vital. Strong standardized scores earn us the trust of our communities as we begin to demonstrate measurable progress on local criterion-referenced and alternative assessments. In districts where improvement on formal, public assessments is of the essence, we should assemble clear lists of the standards and proficiencies that the assessments will require of students. District offices and regional consortiums must take the initiative here: They must assemble representative teams of teachers to develop—and provide every teacher with—a precise, manageable list of the essential, assessed standards.

Every school year, the full faculty should conduct a review of assessment results. Teams of teachers should identify the most pronounced patterns of student weakness, then seek absolute clarity on the nature of these problems. Through staff development and regular, professional collaboration, teachers should focus on these areas, while monitoring progress regularly.

2. Beyond state assessments, add judiciously to the list of standards you will teach and assess. For Michael Fullan, "assessment is the coherence-maker" in school improvement (1998, personal communication). Because of the limitations of state and norm-referenced tests, we must develop local and district standards and assessments that take us beyond them. Districts should review the standards documents, but then exercise severe discipline in prioritizing on the basis of what students will most need if they are to become reflective thinkers, competent workers, and responsible citizens. For every grade or level, pilot your new standards and assessments while asking the question, Are the standards clear, relevant, and not so numerous that they sacrifice depth over breadth? Don't be afraid to do a rough accounting of time for teaching topics.

Adlai Stevenson High School has achieved world-class results in this way. Glendale Union High School District has done a masterful job of successfully concentrating on norm-referenced tests while implementing a coherent system of formative and end-of-course alternative assessments for high school courses. These assessments require students to do investigative science and to write analyses about social and historical issues—all according to clear standards and criteria. These common, teacher-made assessments embody and clarify precisely those thinking and reasoning standards that norm-referenced tests don't adequately assess. The result is an education that ensures a level of both breadth and substance that goes far beyond what is now required of the average high school graduate.

Perhaps the best time to develop such standards-based assessments is summer. Such work doesn't always require enormous amounts of time or resources. In Lake Havasu City, Arizona, educators developed common K–12 assessments in almost every subject area for about $25,000 over a two-year period. They took only four days to prioritize core science standards and generate common K–12 assessments.

3. Do not add more topics than can be taught and assessed reasonably and effectively. A key to developing science assessments in Lake Havasu City was following open discussions with fast, fair rank-ordering procedures that used weighted voting to quickly establish priority standards. Because we can expect educators to differ in philosophy and priority, every school employee could benefit from training in the use of these simple decision-making tools.

The tendency toward overload is strong in schools—and crippling to improvement efforts (Fullan & Hargreaves, 1996). A district we know has received high praise for showcase work by developing grade-by-grade benchmarks for the state standards. For 4th grade, educators developed 210 items to be taught in math, but 125 of these *were also to be taught in six to eight other grades*. In another district, in another state, there are only 17 items for 4th grade math, and they're written in language that is clear to parents and teachers.

At the local and state levels, we must demand that economy and clarity inform all standards and that they be meaningfully—not just rhetorically—aligned with assessments. Every teacher deserves a clear, manageable, grade-by-grade set of standards and learning benchmarks that make sense and allow a reasonable measure of autonomy. Anything less is frustrating, inhumane, and counterproductive.

Standards—when we get them right—will give us the results we want. But this will require hard-headed, disciplined effort. The lesson of TIMSS should considerably diminish the perceived risk of downsizing the curriculum. The very nature of organizations argues that we suc-ceed when all parties are rowing in the same direction. We will realize the promise of school reform when we establish standards and expectations for reaching them that are clear, not confusing; essential, not exhaustive. The result will be a new coherence and a shared focus that could be the most propitious step we can take toward educating all students well. ■

References

Dempster, F. N. (1993). Exposing our students to less should help them learn. *Phi Delta Kappan, 74*(6), 432–437.

Doyle, W. (1992). Curriculum and pedagogy. In P. W. Jackson (Ed.), *Handbook of research in curriculum* (pp. 486–516). New York: Macmillan.

Fullan, M., & Hargreaves, A. (1996). *What's worth fighting for in your school?* New York: Teachers College Press.

Fullan, M., & Stiegelbauer, S. (1991). *The new meaning of educational change.* New York: Teachers College Press.

Glaser, R., & Linn, R. (1993). Foreword. In L. Shepard (Ed.), *Setting performance standards for students achievement* (pp. xiii–xiv). Stanford, CA: National Academy of Education, Stanford University.

Rosenholtz, S. J. (1991). *Teacher's workplace: The social organization of schools.* New York: Teachers College Press.

Schmidt, W. H., McKnight, C. C., & Raizen, S. A. (1996). *Splintered vision: An investigation of U.S. science and mathematics education: Executive summary.* Lansing, MI: U.S. National Research Center for the Third International Mathematics and Science Study, Michigan State University.

Stevenson, H. W., & Stigler, J. W. (1992). *The learning gap: Why our schools are failing and what we can learn from Japanese and Chinese education.* New York: Summit.

Wolk, R. (1998). Doing it right. *Teacher Magazine, 10*(1), 6.

P O S T N O T E

Most Americans, if asked, would probably say that within any one school district there would be an agreed-upon common curriculum for each subject and grade level. Yet, as the authors point out, that belief is largely fiction. The strength of the standards-based movement in education is to forge common understandings for what should be taught and when. What we in the United States do is to create huge textbooks that try to cover every imaginable topic. In that way, no matter what a school district wants to teach, they can find the topic

Realizing the Promise of Standards-Based Education

in the textbook. The drawback to this approach is that textbooks may not cover the subjects in as much depth as teachers and students need.

As the authors also point out, the standards-based movement will not necessarily address the problem of trying to cover too many topics and may, in fact, exacerbate the problem. Quality over quantity is what we need.

DISCUSSION  QUESTIONS

1. What reasons can you think of for why American schools try to teach so many different topics within mathematics or science at any given grade level?

2. "Teachers will teach what students are tested on." Do you agree with this statement? Why or why not?

3. If the statement is true, what potential dangers might result?

Part Five
Instruction

What should we teach? is the fundamental question. But next in importance is: How do we teach it? Instructional questions range from the very nature of students as learners to how to organize a third-grade classroom.

In this section, we present a palette of new and old ideas about how to organize classrooms and schools to meet the needs of new students and a new society. A number of the most high-profile topics in education—such as cooperative learning, constructivism, and tracking—are presented. It is important to realize, however, as you read about an instructional methodology or set of procedures, that each represents a view of what the teaching-learning process is and what students are like. So, as you read these articles, we urge you to probe for their foundational ideas.

38 Engaging Students: What I Learned Along the Way

Anne Wescott Dodd

W hen I was a first-year teacher, I was concerned with survival. My attempts to control students led to many power struggles from which both the students and I emerged discouraged or defeated. These feelings were not conducive to teaching or learning.

I wish someone had told me then that knowing my students was as important as knowing my subject. I didn't realize until much later that to motivate and engage students, teachers must create a classroom environment in which every student comes to believe, "I count, I care, and I can."

The best advice I could give to beginning teachers now is the secret of the fox in Antoine de Saint-Exupéry's *The Little Prince* (1943): "What is essential is invisible to the eye." What teachers need most to know about students is hidden; unless they develop a trusting relationship with their students, teachers will not have access to the knowledge they need either to solve classroom problems or to motivate students.

At the time this article was written, Anne Wescott Dodd, a former secondary school teacher and principal, was a faculty member in the Education Department, Bates College, Lewiston, Maine. Dodd, Anne Wescott, "Engaging Students: What I Learned Along the Way." *Educational Leadership*, September 1995, pp. 65–67. Reprinted by permission from ASCD. All rights reserved.

I Wish I Had Known . . .

As a novice teacher, I didn't realize that a seemingly logical response to tardiness—detention—did not take into account students' reasons for being late, some of which were valid. If I had allowed students to explain why they were late before telling them to stay after school, I might have prevented hurt feelings and hostility. A 6th grader who hides from an 8th grade bully in the bathroom until the coast is clear shouldn't be treated the same as someone who chats too long with a friend in the hall.

I wish I had found out sooner that simply asking students to tell me their side of the story could make such a positive difference in their attitudes. When I tried to understand situations from their points of view, students were willing to consider them from my vantage point. These conversations opened the way for us to jointly resolve problems and did a great deal to build trust.

But, most of all, I wish someone had told me that understanding students' perspectives was the best way to foster engagement and learning. Like other novice teachers, I wasted a great deal of time searching for recipes to make learning more fun. Only much later did I find out that the most effective veteran teachers reflect on their classroom experience (Dodd 1994). Instead of thinking in terms of making learning *fun* (extrinsic motivation), they look for ways to make assignments and activities *engaging* (intrinsic motivation). Although they may express these ideas differently, effective teachers know that to become engaged, students must have some feelings of *ownership*—of the class or the task—and *personal power*—a belief that what they do will make a difference.

From the Student's Perspective

Because beginning teachers often focus on what they will do or require students to do, they often overlook some important principles about learning.

First, learning is personal and idiosyncratic. Thus, it helps to view students as individuals

(Marina, Hector, and Scott) rather than as groups (Period 1 Class, Sophomore English). Consider that even when there is only *one* right answer, there are *many* ways students can misunderstand. Thus, teachers need to find out how students individually make sense of any lesson or explanation.

Second, every student behavior—from the most outrageous classroom outburst to the more common failure to do homework—is a way of trying to communicate something the student cannot express any other way or doesn't consciously understand. Punishing the behavior without learning its possible cause does nothing to solve a problem and, in fact, may intensify it. Because the student may interpret detention or a zero in the gradebook as additional evidence that the teacher is uncaring, he or she may become less inclined to do future assignments.

Third, teachers should never assume, because too often they can be wrong. Low grades on tests do not necessarily mean that students haven't studied. Some students may have been confused when the material was covered in class. Incomplete homework isn't always a sign that students don't care. A student may be too busy helping care for younger siblings to finish assignments. The student who sleeps in class or responds angrily to a teacher's question may be exhausted, ill, or unable to cope with personal difficulties.

By inviting students to share their feelings and perceptions, teachers can establish positive relationships with them and thus minimize classroom problems. But even more important, they will discover how to modify their teaching methods and personalize assignments in ways that engage students in learning.

Getting Students to Open Up

There are many ways that teachers can get to know their students. Here are a few useful strategies.

■ *On the first day of class, give students a questionnaire to complete, or invite them to write you a letter about themselves.* The sooner you learn something about your students, the better equipped you will be to build personal relationships and address their concerns. By knowing which students consider themselves math phobics, poor writers, or reluctant readers, you can find ways to make sure they have a chance to feel good about a small success right away.

■ *Ask students who have not done the homework or who have come late to class to write a note explaining why.* Establish this requirement on the first day of class, but don't present it as a punishment. Students should see these notes as an opportunity to communicate privately with the teacher. As trust is established, students will feel freer about sharing personal concerns that affect their classroom performance. Even if you can do nothing to solve a problem a student has at home, you may be able to suggest better ways to deal with it.

■ *Ask students to write learning logs from time to time. Logs are especially useful at the end of a class in which new material has been introduced.* For example, "Briefly summarize what you learned today, and note any questions you have." Don't grade the logs; just read them quickly to note common problems to address in the next class, and list names of students who may need extra help. Taking the time to write a short comment or just draw a smiley face on each student's log before returning them also shows students that you care about them as people and want them to learn.

The same kind of assignment can be added to a homework paper or as the last question on a test: "What did you find confusing about this assignment?" or "How do you feel you did on this test? What would have helped you do even better?"

■ *Invite students to help you solve classroom problems, such as a lack of classroom participation or students' constantly interrupting one another.* Even if you wish to discuss the issue with the students, having them write their ideas down first will make the discussion more productive. Although students may not suggest any workable solutions to the problem, their comments can often lead to a strategy for solving the problem. Perhaps even more important, students will feel empowered.

Writing works because every student gets to share what he or she thinks, misunderstands, or needs to know. Teachers who depend on students to say aloud what they don't understand may be fooled into thinking that everything is okay when there are no questions. Many students, however, are reluctant to speak up in front of their peers for fear of looking foolish. Unfortunately, teachers don't have time for individual conversations with each student, but writing can be an invaluable substitute.

How to Personalize Assignments

All of the information teachers gather from students will be of little use if students do not have any opportunity to personalize their learning. While the idea of having students doing a variety of things at the same time may appear chaotic, there are some easy ways to try out this approach to see how it works.

■ Give students some choice of topics for research, books for reading, and planning methods for projects or papers (outlining, webbing, or focused free writing).

■ Let students prepare a lesson and teach their classmates (If teachers want students to be exposed to several aspects of the Civil War or three different novels, small groups of students learn about one aspect of the war or one of the novels in depth and the others in less detail. This approach is one way of solving the depth versus coverage dilemma all teachers wrestle with.)

■ Encourage students who understand a concept to help those who don't understand. This is a productive way of channeling students' desire to be social.

■ Allow students to choose how to demonstrate their understanding. (One student might draw the solution to a math problem or the plot in a novel; another might write about it; someone else might videotape a real-life connection for it.)

■ Give students permission occasionally to work on homework or routine assignments together. They can learn from one another, and a test will show what each has learned.

Reflection Is the Key

Trying out a practice offers fertile ground for reflection even if the trial fails. As teachers look for new ways to engage students in learning, they are likely to find that the search itself will re-energize their teaching.

Recipes are useful for beginners who haven't yet had time to analyze how and why students engage in learning, but reflection is the key to understanding why some recipes work better than others. That understanding depends on knowing more about students' perceptions. As teachers learn more about how students think and feel, they will be able to create classes where students have fun *because* they are engaged in learning in diverse, purposeful, and meaningful ways. ■

References

de Saint-Exupéry, A. (1943). *The Little Prince*. New York: Harcourt Brace.

Dodd, A. W. (1994). "Learning to Read the Classroom: The Stages Leading to Teacher Self-Actualization." *Northwords* 4: 13–26.

POST NOTE

This article is based on a fundamental principle of good teaching: engaging the student in his or her own learning. Along with the principle, the author offers several practical suggests and thus adds to our large literature on the subject of good teaching—a literature that has been evolving for centuries. But why, if the principle is so fundamental, do so few teachers follow it?

One possible explanation is that beginning teachers quite naturally lack confidence. They are on the defensive and, as a result, are "self-focused": "Will I survive?" "Will they accept me as a teacher, or are they seeing through this teacher-act I am performing?" "Will they like me?" "Can they tell how little I really know about what I'm doing?" The great majority of teachers pass out of this phase, but they survive by imposing their will, their lesson plans, their expectations (or some downsized version of their original expectations) on the class. And that habit of mind, focusing on *their* plans, takes over and becomes for them "teaching." To put it another way, "engaging" students involves risks, and most new teachers are not ready to take risks.

D I S C U S S I O N  U E S T I O N S

1. Can you recall teachers who engaged you in your own learning? How did they do it?

2. The article's author, Anne Wescott Dodd, offers four suggestions for "getting students to open up." What are they, and are there any suggestions you can add?

3. What are some of the potential problems and risks in this approach?

39

A Multiplicity of Intelligences

Howard Gardner

As a psychologist, I was surprised by the huge public interest in *The Bell Curve,* the 1994 book on human intelligence by the late Harvard University psychologist Richard J. Hernstein and policy analyst Charles Murray. Most of the ideas in the book were familiar not only to social scientists but also to the general public. Indeed, educational psychologist Arthur R. Jensen of the University of California at Berkeley as well as Hernstein had written popularly about the very same ideas in the late 1960s and the early 1970s. Perhaps, I reasoned, every quarter-century a new generation of Americans desires to be acquainted with "the psychologist's orthodoxy" about intelligence—namely, that there is a single, general intelligence, often called *g,* which is reflected by an individual's intelligence quotient, or IQ.

This concept stands in contrast to my own view developed over the past decades: that human intelligence encompasses a far wider, more universal set of competences. Currently I count eight intelligences, and there may be more. They include what are traditionally regarded as intelligences, such as linguistic and logical-mathematical abilities, but also some that are not

conventionally thought of in that way, such as musical and spatial capacities. These intelligences, which do not always reveal themselves in paper-and-pencil tests, can serve as a basis for more effective educational methods.

Defining Brainpower

The orthodox view of a single intelligence, widely, if wrongly, accepted today in the minds of the general population, originated from the energies and convictions of a few researchers, who by the second decade of this century had put forth its major precepts. In addition to its basic assumption, the orthodoxy also states that individuals are born with a certain intelligence or potential intelligence, that this intelligence is difficult to change and that psychologists can assess one's IQ using short-answer tests and, perhaps, other "purer" measures, such as the time it takes to react to a sequence of flashing lights or the presence of a particular pattern of brain waves.

Soon after this idea had been proposed—I like to call it "hedgehog orthodoxy"—more "foxlike" critics arose. From outside psychology, commentators such as American newspaper columnist Walter Lippmann challenged the criteria used to assess intelligence, contending that it was more complex and less fixed than the psychometricians had proposed.

From within psychology, scientists questioned the notion of a single, overarching intelligence. According to their analyses, intelligence is better thought of a set of several factors. In the 1930s Louis L. Thurstone of the University of Chicago said it makes more sense to think of seven, largely independent "vectors of the mind." In the 1960s Joy P. Guilford of the University of Southern California enunciated 120 factors, later amended to 150. Scottish investigator Godfrey Thomson of the University of Edinburgh spoke around the 1940s of a large number of loosely coupled faculties. And in our own day, Robert J. Sternberg of Yale University has proposed a triarchic theory of intellect. These arches comprise a component that deals with standard computational skill, *a*

Howard Gardner is a professor of education and codirector of Harvard's Project Zero—an umbrella project that encompasses some two dozen different studies related to cognition and creativity. Reprinted by permission from Dr. Howard Gardner.

component that is sensitive to contextual factors and a component that is involved with novelty.

Somewhat surprisingly, all these commentators—whether in favor of or opposed to the notion of single intelligence—share one conviction. They all believe that the nature of intelligence will be determined by testing and analyzing the data thus secured. Perhaps, reason orthodox defenders like Hernstein and Murray performance on a variety of tests will yield a strong general factor of intelligence. And indeed, there is evidence for such a "positive manifold," or high correlation, across tests. Perhaps, counter pluralists like Thurstone and Sternberg, the right set of tests will demonstrate that the mind consists of a number of relatively independent factors, with strength in one area falling to predict strength or weakness in other areas.

But where is it written that intelligence needs to be determined on the basis of tests? Were we incapable of making judgments about intellect before Sir Francis Galton and Alfred Binet cobbled together the first set of psychometric items a century ago? If the dozens of IQ tests in use around the world were suddenly to disappear, would we not longer be able to assess intellect?

Break from Orthodoxy

Nearly 20 years ago, posing these very questions, I embarked on quite a different path into the investigation of intellect. I had been conducting research primarily with two groups: children who were talented in one or more art form and adults who had suffered from strokes that compromised specific capacities while sparing others. Every day I saw individuals with scattered profiles of strengths and weaknesses, and I was impressed by the fact that a strength or a deficit could cohabit comfortably with distinctive profiles of abilities and disabilities across the variety of humankind.

On the basis of such data, I arrived at a firm intuition: human beings are better thought of as possessing a number of relatively independent faculties, rather than as having a certain amount

of intellectual horsepower, or IQ, that can be simply channeled in one or another direction. I decided to search for a better formulation of human intelligence. I defined an intelligence as "a psychobiological potential to solve problems or to fashion products that are valued in at least one cultural context." In my focus on fashioning products and cultural values, I departed from orthodox psychometric approaches, such as those adopted by Hernstein, Murray and their predecessors.

To proceed from an intuition to a definition of a set of human intelligences, I developed criteria that each of the candidate intelligences had to meet. [*See box on page 232.*] These criteria were drawn from several sources:

■ Psychology: The existence of a distinct developmental history for a capacity through which normal and gifted individuals pass as they grow to adulthood; the existence of correlations (or the lack of correlations) between certain capacities.

■ Case studies of learners: Observations of unusual humans, including prodigies, savants or those suffering from learning disabilities.

■ Anthropology: Records of how different abilities are developed, ignored or prized in different cultures.

■ Cultural studies: The existence of symbol systems that encode certain kinds of meanings—language, arithmetic and maps, for instance.

■ Biological sciences: Evidence that a capacity has a distinct evolutionary history and is represented in particular neural structures. For instance, various parts of the left hemisphere dominate when it comes to motor control of the body, calculation and linguistic ability; the right hemisphere houses spatial and musical capacities, including the discrimination of pitch.

The Eight Intelligences

Armed with the criteria, I considered many capacities, ranging from those based in the sense to those having to do with planning, humor and even sexuality. To the extent that a candidate's ability met all or most of the criteria handily, it

1. *Potential isolation by brain damage.* For example, linguistic abilities can be compromised or spared by strokes.
2. *The existence of prodigies, savants and other exceptional individuals.* Such individuals permit the intelligence to be observed in relative isolation.
3. *An identifiable core operation or set of operations.* Musical intelligence, for instance, consists of a person's sensitivity to melody, harmony, rhythm, timbre and musical structure.
4. *A distinctive developmental history within an individual, along with a definable nature of expert performance.* One examines the skills of, say, an expert athlete, salesperson or naturalist, as well as the steps to attaining such expertise.
5. *An evolutionary history and evolutionary plausibility.* One can examine forms of spatial intelligence in mammals or musical intelligence in birds.
6. *Support from tests in experimental psychology.* Researchers have devised tasks that specifically indicate which skills are related to one another and which are discrete.
7. *Support from psychometric findings.* Batteries of tests reveal which tasks reflect the same underlying factor and which do not.
8. *Susceptibility to encoding in a symbol system.* Codes such as language, arithmetic, maps and logical expression, among others, capture important components of respective intelligences.

gained plausibility as an intelligence. In 1983 I concluded that seven abilities met the criteria sufficiently well: linguistic, logical-mathematical, musical, spatial, bodily-kinesthetic (as exemplified by athletes, dancers and other physical performers), interpersonal (the ability to read other people's moods, motivations and other mental states), and intrapersonal (the ability to access one's own feelings and to draw on them to guide behavior). The last two can generally be considered together as the basis for emotional intelligence (although in my version, they focus more on cognition and understanding than on feelings). Most standards measures of intelligence primarily probe linguistic and logical intelligence; some survey spatial intelligence. The other four are almost entirely ignored. In 1995, invoking new data that fit the criteria, I added an eighth intelligence—that of the naturalist, which permits the recognition and categorization of natural objects. Examples are Charles Darwin, John James Audubon and Rachel Carson. I am currently considering the possibility of a ninth: existential intelligence, which captures the human proclivity to raise and ponder fundamen-

tal questions about existence, life, death, finitude. Religious and philosophical thinkers such as the Dalai Lama and Søren A. Kierkegaard exemplify this kind of ability. Whether existential intelligence gets to join the inner sanctum depends on whether convincing evidence accrues about the neural basis for it.

The theory of multiple intelligences (or MI theory, as it has come to be called) makes two strong claims. The first is that all humans possess all these intelligences: indeed, they can collectively be considered a definition of *Homo sapiens*, cognitively speaking. The second claim is that just as we all look different and have unique personalities and temperaments, we also have different profiles of intelligences. No two individuals, not even identical twins or clones, have exactly the same amalgam of profiles, with the same strengths and weaknesses. Even in the case of identical genetic heritage, individuals undergo different experiences and seek to distinguish their profiles from one another.

Within psychology, the theory of multiple intelligences has generated controversy. Many researchers are nervous about the movement away from standardized tests and the adoption of a set of criteria that are unfamiliar and less open to quantification. Many also balk at the use of the word "intelligence" to describe some of the abilities, preferring to define musical or bodily-kinesthetic intelligences as talents. Such a narrow definition, however, devalues those capacities, so that orchestra conductors and dancers are talented but not smart. In my view, it would be all right to call those abilities talents, so long as logical reasoning and linguistic facility are then also termed talents.

Some have questioned whether MI theory is empirical. This criticism, however, misses the mark. MI theory is based completely on empirical evidence. The number of intelligences, their delineation, their subcomponents are all subject to alteration in the light of new findings. Indeed, the existence of the naturalist intelligence could be asserted only after evidence had accrued that parts of the temporal lobe are dedicated to the naming and recognition of natural things, whereas others are attuned to human-made objects. (Good evidence for a neural foundation comes from clinical literature, which reported instances in which brain-damaged individuals lost the capacity to identify living things but could still name inanimate objects. Experimental findings by Antonio R. Damasio of the University of Iowa, Elizabeth Warrington of the Dementia Research Group at National Hospital in London and others have confirmed the phenomenon.)

Much of the evidence for the personal intelligences has come from research in the past decade on emotional intelligence and on the development in children of a "theory of mind"—the realization that human beings have intentions and act on the basis of these intentions. And the intriguing finding by Frances H. Rauscher of the University of Wisconsin–Oshkosh and her colleagues of the "Mozart effect"—that early musical experiences may enhance spatial capacities—raises the possibility that musical and spatial intelligences draw on common abilities.

It is also worth nothing that the movement toward multiple intelligences is quite consistent with trends in related sciences. Neuroscience recognizes the modular nature of the brain; evolutionary psychology is based on the notion that different capacities have evolved in specific environments for specific purposes; and artificial intelligence increasingly embraces expert systems rather than general problem-solving mechanisms. Within science, the believers in a single IQ or general intelligence are increasingly isolated, their positions more likely to be embraced by those, like Hernstein and Murray, who have an ideological ax to grind.

If some psychologists expressed skepticism about the theory of multiple intelligences, educators around the world have embraced it. MI theory not only comports with their intuitions that children are smart in different ways; it also holds out hope that more students can be reached more effectively if their favored ways of knowing are taken into account in curriculum, instruction and assessment. A virtual cottage industry has arisen to create MI schools, classrooms, curricula, texts, computer systems and the like. Most of this work is well intentioned, and some of it has proved quite effective in motivating students and in giving them a sense of involvement in intellectual life.

Various misconceptions, however, have arisen: for example, that every topic should be taught in seven or eight ways or that the purpose of school is to identify (and broadcast) students' intelligences, possibly by administering an octet of new standardized tests. I have begun to speak out against some of these less advisable beliefs and practices.

My conclusion is that MI theory is best thought of as a tool rather than as an educational goal. Educators need to determine, in conjunction with their communities, the goals that they are seeking. Once these goals have been articulated, then MI theory can provide powerful support. I believe schools should strive to develop individuals of a certain sort—civic-minded, sensitive to the arts, deeply rooted in the disciplines. And schools should probe pivotal topics with sufficient depth so that students end up with a comprehensive understanding of them. Curricular and assessment approaches founded on MI theory, such as Project Spectrum at the Eliot-Pearson Preschool at Tufts University, have demonstrated considerable promise in helping schools to achieve these goals.

The Future of MI

Experts have debated various topics in intelligence—including whether there is one or more—for nearly a century, and it would take a brave seer to predict that these debates will disappear. (In fact, if past cycles repeat themselves, a latter-day Hernstein and Murray will author their own *Bell Curve* around 2020.) As the person most closely associated with the theory of multiple intelligences, I record three wishes for this line of work.

The first is a broader but not infinitely expanded view of intelligence. It is high time that intelligence be widened to incorporate a range of human computational capacities, including those that deal with music, other persons and skill in deciphering the natural world. But it is important that intelligence not be conflated with other virtues, such as creativity, wisdom or morality.

I also contend that intelligence should not be so broadened that it crosses the line from description to prescription. I endorse the notion of emotional intelligence when it denotes the capacity to compute information about one's own or others' emotional life. When the term comes to encompass the kinds of persons we hope to develop, however, then we have crossed the line into a value system—and that should not be part of our conception of intelligence. Thus, when psychologist and *New York Times* reporter Daniel Goleman emphasizes in his recent best-seller, *Emotional Intelligence,* the importance of empathy as part of emotional intelligence, I go along with him. But he also urges that individuals care for one another. The possession of the capacity to feel another's suffering is not the same as the decision to come to her aid. Indeed, a sadistic individual might use her knowledge of another's psyche to inflict pain.

My second wish is that society shift away from standardized, short-answer proxy instruments to real-life demonstrations or virtual simulations. During a particular historical period, it was perhaps necessary to assess individuals by administering items that were themselves of little interest (for example, repeating numbers backward) but that were thought to correlate with skills or habits of importance. Nowadays, however, given the advent of computers and virtual technologies, it is possible to look directly at individuals' performances—to see how they can argue, debate, look at data, critique experiments, execute works of art, and so on. As much as possible, we should train students directly in these valued activities, and we should assess how they carry out valued performances under realistic conditions. The need for ersatz instruments, whose relation to real-world performance is often tenuous at best, should wane.

My third wish is that the multiple-intelligences idea be used for more effective pedagogy and assessment. I have little sympathy with educational efforts that seek simply to "train" the intelligences or to use them in trivial ways (such as singing the math times tables or playing Bach in the background while one is doing geometry). For me, the educational power of multiple intelligences is exhibited when these faculties are drawn on to help students master consequential disciplinary materials.

I explain how such an approach might work in my book, *A Well-Disciplined Mind.* I focus on three rich topics: the theory of evolution (as an example of scientific truth), the music of Mozart (as an example of artistic beauty), and the Holocaust (as an example of immorality in recent history). In each case, I show how the topic can be introduced to students through a variety of entry points drawing on several intelligences, how the subject can be made more familiar through the use of analogies and metaphors drawn from diverse domains, and how the core ideas of the topic can be captured not merely through a single symbolic language but rather through a number of complementary model languages or representations.

Pursuing this approach, the individual who understands evolutionary theory, for instance, can think of it in different ways: in terms of a

The examples of each intelligence are meant for illustrative purposes only and are not exclusive—one person can excel in several categories. Note also that entire cultures might encourage the development of one or another intelligence; for instance, the seafaring Puluwat of the Caroline Islands in the South Pacific cultivate spatial intelligence and excel at navigation, and the Manus children of New Guinea learn the canoeing and swimming skills that elude the vast majority of seafaring Western children.

1. *Linguistic* A mastery and love of language and words with a desire to explore them. Poets, writers, linguists: T. S. Eliot, Noam Chomsky, W. H. Auden

2. *Logical-Mathematical* Confronting and assessing objects and abstractions and discerning their relations and underlying principles. Mathematicians, scientists, philosophers: Stanislaw Ulam, Alfred North Whitehead, Henri Poincaré, Albert Einstein, Marie Curie

3. *Musical* A competence not only in composing and performing pieces with pitch, rhythm and timbre but also in listening and discerning. May be related to other intelligences, such as linguistic, spatial or bodily-kinesthetic. Composers, conductors, musicians, music critics: Ludwig van Beethoven, Leonard Bernstein, Midori, John Coltrane

4. *Spatial* An ability to perceive the visual world accurately, transform and modify perceptions and re-crete visual experiences even without physical stimuli. Architects, artists, sculptors, mapmakers, navigators, chess players: Michelangelo, Frank Lloyd Wright, Garry Kasparov, Louise Nevelson, Helen Frankenthaler

5. *Bodily-Kinesthetic* Controlling and orchestrating body motions and handling objects skillfully. Dancers, athletes, actors: Marcel Marceau, Martha Graham, Michael Jordan

6. and 7. *Personal Intelligences* Accurately determining moods, feelings and other mental states in oneself (intrapersonal and intelligence) and in others (interpersonal) and using the information as a guide for behavior. Psychiatrists, politicians, religious leaders, anthropologists: Sigmund Freud, Mahatma Gandhi, Eleanor Roosevelt

8. *Naturalist* Recognizing and categorizing natural objects. Biologists, naturalists: Rachel Carson, John James Audubon

9. *Existential* (possible intelligence) Capturing and pondering the fundamental questions of existence. More evidence, however, is needed to determine whether this is an intelligence. Spiritual leaders, philosophical thinkers: Jean-Paul Sartre, Søren A. Kierkegaard

historical narrative, a logical syllogism, a quantitative examination of the size and dispersion of populations in different niches, a diagram of species delineation, a dramatic sense of the struggle among individuals (or genes or populations), and so on. The individual who can think of evolution in only one way—using only one model language—actually has only a tenuous command of the principal concepts of the theory.

The issue of who owns intelligence has been an important one in our society for some time—and it promises to be a crucial and controversial one for the foreseeable future. For too long, the rest of society has been content to leave intelligence in the hands of psychometricians. Often these test makers have a narrow, overly scholastic view of intellect. They rely on a set of instruments that are destined to valorize certain capacities while ignoring those that do not lend themselves to ready formulation and testing. And those with a political agenda often skirt close to the dangerous territory of eugenics.

MI theory represents at once an effort to base the conception of intelligence on a much broader scientific basis, one that offers a set of tools to educators that will allow more individuals to master substantive materials in an effective way. Applied appropriately, the theory can also help each individual achieve his or her human potential at the workplace, in avocations and in the service of the wider world. ■

POST NOTE

Howard Gardner's theory of multiple intelligences refutes the widely accepted idea that there is a single, general intelligence. The eight intelligences—*linguistic, logical-mathematical, musical, spatial, bodily-kinesthetic, interpersonal, intrapersonal,* and *naturalist*—that he has identified appeal greatly to many educators, who see them as ways that schools can reach more students. In Gardner's theory, abilities in diverse areas would be valued as indicators of intelligence and would be considered worthy of further nurturance and development in school. If teachers provide multiple ways for students to be taught and assessed that recognize and value the kinds of differences that exist among students, then greater numbers of students will succeed and receive recognition. As a result, fewer students are likely to think of themselves as failures. The theory of multiple intelligences emphasizes the highly individualized ways in which people learn and recognizes that each of us has unique intellectual potential. Acknowledging and fostering individual abilities in a variety of areas is a way that teachers can help students. Currently, a number of schools across the country are applying the theory on a day-to-day basis in the classroom.

Teachers of gifted and talented students also see the theory of multiple intelligences as broadening conceptions of who is gifted or talented. The concept of giftedness can embrace dancers, athletes, musicians, artists, or naturalists, and programs can be established to help foster these talents. Gardner raises the issue of whether or not these abilities should be called intelligence or talent. He argues that to call linguistic or logical-mathematical ability intelligence, but spatial or musical ability talent, elevates certain types of ability and devalues others. Gardner's argument is not generally accepted, as society and most schools seem to value language and mathematical capabilities over other types of abilities.

DISCUSSION QUESTIONS

1. Do you believe that the eight different types of intelligences identified by Gardner are valued equally in our society? Why or why not do you think this is the case?

2. Can you think of any other kinds of intelligences that might exist?

3. Which of the eight intelligences are strengths of yours? How do you know this?

Students Need Challenge, Not Easy Success

Margaret M. Clifford

Hundreds of thousands of apathetic students abandon their schools each year to begin lives of unemployment, poverty, crime, and psychological distress. According to Hahn (1987), "Dropout rates ranging from 40 to 60 percent in Boston, Chicago, Los Angeles, Detroit, and other major cities point to a situation of crisis proportions." The term *dropout* may not be adequate to convey the disastrous consequences of the abandonment of school by children and adolescents; *educational suicide* may be a far more appropriate label.

School abandonment is not confined to a small percentage of minority students, or low ability children, or mentally lazy kids. It is a systemic failure affecting the most gifted and knowledgeable as well as the disadvantaged, and it is threatening the social, economic, intellectual, industrial, cultural, moral, and psychological well-being of our country. Equally disturbing are students who sever themselves from the flow of knowledge while they occupy desks, like mummies.

Student apathy, indifference, and underachievement are typical precursors of school abandonment. But what causes these symptoms? Is there a remedy? What will it take to stop the waste of our intellectual and creative resources?

To address these questions, we must acknowledge that educational suicide is primarily a motivational problem—not a physical, intellectual, financial, technological, cultural, or staffing problem. Thus, we must turn to motivational theories and research as a foundation for examining this problem and for identifying solutions.

Curiously enough, modern theoretical principles of motivation do not support certain widespread practices in education. I will discuss four such discrepancies and offer suggestions for resolving them.

Moderate Success Probability Is Essential to Motivation

The maxim, "Nothing succeeds like success," has driven educational practice for several decades. Absolute success for students has become the means *and* the end of education: It has been given higher priority than learning, and it has obstructed learning.

A major principle of current motivation theory is that tasks associated with a moderate probability of success (50 percent) provide maximum satisfaction (Atkinson 1964). Moderate probability of success is also an essential ingredient of intrinsic motivation (Lepper and Greene 1978, Csikszentmihalyi 1975, 1978). We attribute the success we experience on easy tasks to task ease; we attribute the success we experience on extremely difficult tasks to luck. Neither type of success does much to enhance self-image. It is only success at moderately difficult or truly challenging tasks that we explain in terms of personal effort, well-chosen strategies, and ability; and these explanations give rise to feelings of pride, competence, determination, satisfaction, persistence, and personal control. Even very young children show a preference for tasks that are just a bit beyond their ability (Danner and Lonky 1981).

Consistent with these motivational findings, learning theorists have repeatedly demonstrated

At the time this article was written, Margaret M. Clifford was professor of educational psychology, College of Education, University of Iowa, Iowa City.

that moderately difficult tasks are a prerequisite for maximizing intellectual development (Fischer 1980). But despite the fact that moderate challenge (implying considerable error-making) is essential for maximizing learning and optimizing motivation, many educators attempt to create error-proof learning environments. They set minimum criteria and standards in hopes of ensuring success for all students. They often reduce task difficulty, overlook errors, de-emphasize failed attempts, ignore faulty performances, display "perfect papers," minimize testing, and reward error-free performance.

It is time for educators to replace easy success with challenge. We must encourage students to reach beyond their intellectual grasp and allow them the privilege of learning from mistakes. There must be a tolerance for error-making in every classroom, and gradual success rather than continual success must become the yardstick by which learning is judged. Such transformations in educational practices will not guarantee the elimination of educational suicide, but they are sure to be one giant step in that direction.

External Constraints Erode Motivation and Performance

Intrinsic motivation and performance deteriorate when external constraints such as surveillance, evaluation by others, deadlines, threats, bribes, and rewards are accentuated. Yes, even rewards are a form of constraint! The reward giver is the General who dictates rules and issues orders; rewards are used to keep the troops in line.

Means-end contingencies, as exemplified in the statement, "If you complete your homework, you may watch TV" (with homework being the means and TV the end), are another form of external constraint. Such contingencies decrease interest in the first task (homework, the means) and increase interest in the second task (TV, the end) (Boggiano and Main 1986).

Externally imposed constraints, including material rewards, decrease task interest, reduce creativity, hinder performance, and encourage passivity on the part of students—even preschoolers (Lepper and Hodell 1989)! Imposed constraints also prompt individuals to use the "minimax strategy"—to exert the minimum amount of effort needed to obtain the maximum amount of reward (Kruglanski et al. 1977). Supportive of these findings are studies showing that autonomous behavior—that which is self-determined, freely chosen, and personally controlled—elicits high task interest, creativity, cognitive flexibility, positive emotion, and persistence (Deci and Ryan 1987).

Unfortunately, constraint and lack of student autonomy are trademarks of most schools. Federal and local governments, as well as teachers, legislate academic requirements; impose guidelines; create rewards systems; mandate behavioral contracts; serve warnings of expulsion; and use rules, threats, and punishments as routine problem-solving strategies. We can legislate school attendance and the conditions for obtaining a diploma, but we cannot legislate the development of intelligence, talent, creativity, and intrinsic motivation—resources this country desperately needs.

It is time for educators to replace coercive, constraint-laden techniques with autonomy-supportive techniques. We must redesign instructional and evaluation materials and procedures so that every assignment, quiz, text, project, and discussion activity not only allows for, but routinely *requires*, carefully calculated decision making on the part of students. Instead of minimum criteria, we must define multiple criteria (levels of minimum, marginal, average, good, superior, and excellent achievement), and we must free students to choose criteria that provide optimum challenge. Constraint gives a person the desire to escape; freedom gives a person the desire to explore, expand, and create.

Prompt, Specific Feedback Enhances Learning

A third psychological principle is that specific and prompt feedback enhances learning, performance, and motivation (Ilgen et al. 1979, Larson

1984). Informational feedback (that which reveals correct responses) increases learning (Ilgen and Moore 1987) and also promotes a feeling of increased competency (Sansone 1986). Feedback that can be used to improve future performance has powerful motivational value.

Sadly, however, the proportion of student assignments or activities that are promptly returned with informational feedback tends to be low. Students typically complete an assignment and then wait one, two, or three days (sometimes weeks) for its return. The feedback they do get often consists of a number or letter grade accompanied by ambiguous comments such as "Is this your best?" or "Keep up the good work." Precisely what is good or what needs improving is seldom communicated.

But, even if we could convince teachers of the value of giving students immediate, specific, informational feedback, our feedback problem would still be far from solved. How can one teacher provide 25 or more students immediate feedback on their tasks? Some educators argue that the solution to the feedback problem lies in having a tutor or teacher aide for every couple of students. Others argue that adequate student feedback will require an increased use of computer technology. However, there are less expensive alternatives. First, answer keys for students should be more plentiful. Resource books containing review and study activities should be available in every subject area, and each should be accompanied by a key that is available to students.

Second, quizzes and other instructional activities, especially those that supplement basic textbooks, should be prepared with "latent image" processing. With latent image paper and pens, a student who marks a response to an item can watch a hidden symbol emerge. The symbol signals either a correct or incorrect response, and in some instances a clue or explanation for the response is revealed. Trivia and puzzle books equipped with this latent image, immediate feedback process are currently being marketed at the price of comic books.

Of course, immediate informational feedback is more difficult to provide for composition work, long-term projects, and field assignments. But this does not justify the absence of immediate feedback on the learning activities and practice exercises that are aimed at teaching concepts, relationships, and basic skills. The mere availability of answer keys and latent image materials would probably elicit an amazing amount of self-regulated learning on the part of many students.

Moderate Risk Taking Is a Tonic for Achievement

A fourth motivational research finding is that moderate risk taking increases performance, persistence, perceived competence, self-knowledge, pride, and satisfaction (Deci and Porac 1978, Harter 1978, Trope 1979). Moderate risk taking implies a well-considered choice of an optimally challenging task, willingness to accept a moderate probability of success, and the anticipation of an outcome. It is this combination of events (which includes moderate success, self-regulated learning, and feedback) that captivates the attention, interest, and energy of card players, athletes, financial investors, lottery players, and even juvenile video arcade addicts.

Risk takers continually and freely face the probability of failing to attain the pleasure of succeeding under specified odds. From every risk-taking endeavor—whether it ends in failure or success—risk takers learn something about their skill and choice of strategy, and what they learn usually prompts them to seek another risk-taking opportunity. Risk taking—especially moderate risk taking—is a mind-engaging activity that simultaneously consumes and generates energy. It is a habit that feeds itself and thus requires an unlimited supply of risk-taking opportunities.

Moderate risk taking is likely to occur under the following conditions.

■ The success probability for each alternative is clear and unambiguous.

■ Imposed external constraints are minimized.

■ Variable payoff (the value of success increases as risk increases) in contrast to fixed payoff is available.

■ The benefits of risk taking can be anticipated.

My own recent research on academic risk taking with grade school, high school, and college students generally supports these conclusions. Students do, in fact, freely choose more difficult problems (a) when the number of points offered increases with the difficulty level of problems, (b) when the risk-taking task is presented within a game or practice situation (i.e., imposed constraint or threat is minimized), and (c) when additional opportunities for risk taking are anticipated (relatively high risk taking will occur on a practice exercise when students know they will be able to apply the information learned to an upcoming test). In the absence of these conditions we have seen students choose tasks that are as much as one-and-a-half years below their achievement level (Clifford 1988). Finally, students who take moderately high risks express high task interest even though they experience considerable error making.

In summary, risk-taking opportunities for students should be (a) plentiful, (b) readily available, (c) accompanied by explicit information about success probabilities, (d) accompanied by immediate feedback that communicates competency and error information, (e) associated with payoffs that vary with task difficulty, (f) relatively free from externally imposed evaluation, and (g) presented in relaxing and nonthreatening environments.

In today's educational world, however, there are few opportunities for students to engage in academic risk taking and no incentives to do so. Choices are seldom provided within tests or assignments, and rarely are variable payoffs made available. Once again, motivational theory, which identifies risk taking as a powerful source of knowledge, motivation, and skill development, conflicts with educational practice, which seeks to minimize academic risk at all costs.

We must restructure materials and procedures to encourage moderate academic risk taking on the part of students. I predict that if we fill our classrooms with optional academic risk-taking materials and opportunities so that all students have access to moderate risks, we will not only lower our educational suicide rate, but we will raise our level of academic achievement. If we give students the license to take risks and make errors, they will likely experience genuine success and the satisfaction that accompanies it.

Using Risk Can Ensure Success

Both theory and research evidence lead to the prediction that academic risk-taking activities are a powerful means of increasing the success of our educational efforts. But how do we get students to take risks on school-related activities? Students will choose risk over certainty when the consequences of the former are more satisfying and informative. Three basic conditions are needed to ensure such outcomes.

■ First, students must be allowed to freely select from materials and activities that vary in difficulty and probability of success.

■ Second, as task difficulty increases, so too must the payoffs for success.

■ Third, an environment tolerant of error making and supportive of error correction must be guaranteed.

The first two conditions can be met rather easily. For example, on a 10-point quiz, composed of six 1-point items and four 2-point items, students might be asked to select and work only 6 items. The highest possible score for such quizzes is 10 and can be obtained only by correctly answering the four 2-point items and any two 1-point items. Choice and variable payoff are easily built into quizzes and many instructional and evaluation activities.

The third condition, creating an environment tolerant of error making and supportive of error correction, is more difficult to ensure. But here are six specific suggestions.

First, teachers must make a clear distinction between formative evaluation activities (tasks that guide instruction during the learning process) and summative evaluation activities (tasks used to judge one's level of achievement and to determine one's grade at the completion of the learning activity). Practice exercises, quizzes, and skill-building activities aimed at acquiring and trengthening knowledge and skills exemplify formative evaluation. These activities promote learning and skill development. They should be scored in a manner that excludes ability judgments, emphasizes error detection and correction, and encourages a search for better learning strategies. Formative evaluation activities should generally provide immediate feedback and be scored by students. It is on these activities that moderate risk taking is to be encouraged and is likely to prove beneficial.

Major examinations (unit exams and comprehensive final exams) exemplify summative evaluation; these activities are used to determine course grades. Relatively low risk taking is to be expected on such tasks, and immediate feedback may or may not be desirable.

Second, formative evaluation activities should be far more plentiful than summative. If, in fact, learning rather than grading is the primary object of the school, the percentage of time spent on summative evaluation should be small in comparison to that spent on formative evaluation (perhaps about 1:4). There should be enough formative evaluation activities presented as risk-taking opportunities to satisfy the most enthusiastic and adventuresome learner. The more plentiful these activities are, the less anxiety-producing and aversive summative activities are likely to be.

Third, formative evaluation activities should be presented as optional; students should be enticed, not mandated, to complete these activities. Enticement might be achieved by (a) ensuring that these activities are course-relevant and varied (e.g., scrambled outlines, incomplete matrices and graphs, exercises that require error detection and correction, quizzes); (b) giving students the option of working together; (c) presenting risk-taking activities in the context of games to be played individually, with competitors, or with partners; (d) providing immediate, informational, nonthreatening feedback; and (e) defining success primarily in terms of improvement over previous performance or the amount of learning that occurs during the risk-taking activity.

Fourth, for every instructional and evaluation activity there should be at least a modest percentage of content (10 percent to 20 percent) that poses a challenge to even the best students completing the activity. Maximum development of a country's talent requires that *all* individuals (a) find challenge in tasks they attempt, (b) develop tolerance for error making, and (c) learn to adjust strategies when faced with failure. To deprive the most talented students of these opportunities is perhaps the greatest resource-development crime a country can commit.

Fifth, summative evaluation procedures should include "retake exams." Second chances will not only encourage risk taking but will provide good reasons for students to study their incorrect responses made on previous risk-taking tasks. Every error made on an initial exam and subsequently corrected on a second chance represents real learning.

Sixth, we must reinforce moderate academic risk taking instead of error-free performance or excessively high or low risk taking. Improvement scores, voluntary correction of errors, completion of optional risk-taking activities—these are behaviors that teachers should recognize and encourage.

Toward a New Definition of Success

We face the grim reality that our extraordinary efforts to produce "schools without failure" have not yielded the well-adjusted, enthusiastic, self-confident scholars we anticipated. Our efforts to mass-produce success for every individual in every educational situation have left us with cheap reproductions of success that do not even faintly represent the real thing. This overdose of synthetic success is a primary cause of the student apathy and school abandonment plaguing our country.

To turn the trend around, we must emphasize error tolerance, not error-free learning; reward error correction, not error avoidance; ensure challenge, not easy success. Eventual success on challenging tasks, tolerance for error making, and constructive responses to failure are motivational fare that school systems should be serving up to all students. I suggest that we engage the skills of researchers, textbook authors, publishers, and educators across the country to ensure the development and marketing of attractive and effective academic risk-taking materials and procedures. If we convince these experts of the need to employ their creative efforts toward this end, we will not only stem the tide of educational suicide, but we will enhance the quality of educational success. We will witness self-regulated student success and satisfaction that will ensure the intellectual, creative, and motivational well-being of our country. ■

References

Atkinson, J. W. (1964). *An Introduction to Motivation.* Princeton, N.J.: Van Nostrand.

Boggiano, A. K., and D. S. Main. (1986). "Enhancing Children's Interest in Activities Used as Rewards: The Bonus Effect." *Journal of Personality and Social Psychology* 51: 1116–1126.

Clifford, M. M. (1988). "Failure Tolerance and Academic Risk Taking in Ten- to Twelve-Year-Old Students." *British Journal of Educational Psychology* 58: 15–27.

Csikszentmihalyi, M. (1975). *Beyond Boredom and Anxiety.* San Francisco: Jossey-Bass.

Csikszentmihalyi, M. (1978). "Intrinsic Rewards and Emergent Motivation." In *The Hidden Costs of Reward,* edited by M. R. Lepper and D. Greene,. N.J.: Lawrence Erlbaum Associates.

Danner, F. W., and D. Lonky. (1981). "A Cognitive-Developmental Approach to the Effects of Rewards on Intrinsic Motivation." *Child Development* 52: 1043–1052.

Deci, E. L., and J. Porac. (1978). "Cognitive Evaluation Theory and the Study of Human Motivation." In *The Hidden Costs of Reward,* edited by M. R. Lepper and D. Greene. Hillsdale, N.J.: Lawrence Erlbaum Associates.

Deci, E. L., and R. M. Ryan. (1987). "The Support of Autonomy and the Control of Behavior." *Journal of Personality and Social Psychology* 53: 1024–1037.

Fischer, K. W. (1980). "Learning as the Development of Organized Behavior." *Journal of Structural Learning* 3: 253–267.

Hahn, A. (1987). "Reaching Out to America's Dropouts: What to Do?" *Phi Delta Kappan* 69: 256–263.

Harter, S. (1978). "Effective Motivation Reconsidered: Toward a Developmental Model." *Human Development* 1: 34–64.

Ilgen, D. R., and C. F. Moore. (1987). "Types and Choices of Performance Feedback." *Journal of Applied Psychology* 72: 401–406.

Ilgen, D. R., C. D. Fischer, and M. S. Taylor. (1979). "Consequences of Individual Feedback on Behavior in Organizations." *Journal of Applied Psychology* 64: 349–371.

Kruglanski, A., C. Stein, and A. Riter. (1977). "Contingencies of Exogenous Reward and Task Performance: On the 'Minimax' Strategy in Instrumental Behavior." *Journal of Applied Social Psychology* 2: 141–148.

Larson, J. R., Jr. (1984). "The Performance Feedback Process: A Preliminary Model." *Organizational Behavior and Human Performance* 33: 42–76.

Lepper, M. R., and D. Greene. (1978). *The Hidden Costs of Reward.* Hillsdale, N.J.: Lawrence Erlbaum Associates.

Lepper, M. R., and M. Hodell. (1989). "Intrinsic Motivation in the Classroom." In *Motivation in Education, Vol. 3,* edited by C. Ames and R. Ames. N.Y.: Academic Press.

Sansone, C. (1986). "A Question of Competence: The Effects of Competence and Task Feedback on Intrinsic Motivation." *Journal of Personality and Social Psychology* 51: 918–931.

Trope, Y. (1979). "Uncertainty Reducing Properties of Achievement Tasks." *Journal of Personality and Social Psychology* 37: 1505–1518.

P O S T   N O T E

In the 1980s, educators and their many critics recognized that our schools were failing many of our students and that our students were failing many of our schools. An avalanche of reports, books, television specials, and columns lambasted the schools' performance. In response, standards have been raised, graduation requirements increased, and more rigorous courses of study implemented.

However, as an old adage says, "You can lead a horse to water, but you can't make it drink." Vast numbers of students still continue to commit "educational suicide," and student apathy, indifference, and underachievement are widespread. Margaret Clifford's remedy first takes a realistic look at the mismatch between the student and the school and then suggests quite tangible modifications to match the student's motivational system with the goals of schooling.

DISCUSSION QUESTIONS

1. This article pinpoints student motivation as a major source of school problems. Do you agree with this assessment? Why or why not?

2. What are the most important remedies for our schools' ills offered by Clifford? In your review, will these remedies solve the problem?

3. What is the author's new definition of *success*? Do you agree with it? Why or why not?

Making the Grade: What Benefits Students?

Thomas R. Guskey

C harged with leading a committee that would revise his school's grading and reporting system Warren Middleton described his work this way:

> The Committee on Grading was called upon to study grading procedures. At first, the task of investigating the literature seemed to be a rather hopeless one. What a mass and a mess it all was! Could order be brought out of such chaos? Could points of agreement among American educators concerning the perplexing grading problem actually be discovered? It was with considerable misgiving and trepidation that the work was finally begun.

Few educators today would consider the difficulties encountered by Middleton and his colleagues to be particularly surprising. In fact, most probably would sympathize with his lament. What they might find surprising, however, is that this report from the Committee on Grading was published in 1933!

At the time this article was written, Thomas R. Guskey was professor of education policy studies and evaluation, College of Education, University of Kentucky. Guskey, Thomas R., "Making the Grade: What Benefits Students." *Educational Leadership,* October 1994, pp. 14–20. Reprinted by permission from ASCD. All rights reserved.

The issues of grading and reporting on student learning have perplexed educators for the better part of this century. Yet despite all the debate and the multitude of studies, coming up with prescriptions for best practice seems as challenging today as it was for Middleton and his colleagues more than 60 years ago.

Points of Agreement

Although the debate over grading and reporting continues, today we know better which practices benefit students and encourage learning. Given the multitude of studies—and their often incongruous results—researchers do appear to agree on the following points:

1. *Grading and reporting aren't essential to instruction.* Teachers don't need grades or reporting forms to teach well. Further, students don't need them to learn (Frisbie and Waltman 1992).

Teachers do need to check regularly on how students are doing, what they've learned, and what problems or difficulties they've experienced. But grading and reporting are different from checking; they involve judging the adequacy of students' performance at a specific time. Typically, teachers use checking to diagnose and prescribe and use grading to evaluate and describe (Bloom et al. 1981).

When teachers do both checking and grading, they become advocates as well as judges—roles that aren't necessarily compatible (Bishop 1992). Finding a meaningful compromise between these dual roles makes many teachers uncomfortable, especially those with a child-centered orientation (Barnes 1985).

2. *No one method of grading and reporting serves all purposes well.* Grading enables teachers to communicate the achievements of students to parents and others, provide incentives to learn, and provide information that students can use for self-evaluation. In addition, schools use grades to identify or group students for particular edu-

cational paths or programs and to evaluate a program's effectiveness (Feldmesser 1971, Frisbie and Waltman 1992). Unfortunately, many schools attempt to address all of these purposes with a single method and end up achieving none very well (Austin and McCann 1992).

Letter grades, for example, briefly describe learning progress and give some idea of its adequacy (Payne 1974). Their use, however, requires abstracting a great deal of information into a single symbol (Stiggins 1994). In addition, the cut-off between grade categories is always arbitrary and difficult to justify. If scores for a grade of B range from 80 to 89, students at both ends of that range receive the same grade, even though their scores differ by nine points. But the student with a score of 79—a one-point difference—receives a grade of C.

The more detailed methods also have their drawbacks. Narratives and checklists of learning outcomes offer specific information for documenting progress, but good narratives take time to prepare, and—not surprisingly—as teachers complete more narratives, their comments become increasingly standardized. From the parents' standpoint, checklists of learning outcomes often appear too complicated to understand. In addition, checklists seldom communicate the appropriateness of students' progress in relation to expectations for their level (Afflerbach and Sammons 1991).

Because one method won't adequately serve all purposes, schools must identify their primary purpose for grading and select or develop the most appropriate approach (Cangelosi 1990). This process often involves the difficult task of seeking consensus among several constituencies.

3. *Regardless of the method used, grading and reporting remain inherently subjective.* In fact, the more detailed the reporting method and the more analytic the process, the more likely subjectivity will influence results (Ornstein 1994). That's why, for example, holistic scoring procedures tend to have greater reliability than analytic procedures.

Subjectivity in this process, however, isn't always bad. Because teachers know their students, understand various dimensions of students' work, and have clear notions of the progress made, their subjective perceptions may yield very accurate descriptions of what students have learned (Brookhart 1993, O'Donnell and Woolfolk 1991).

When subjectivity translates into bias, however, negative consequences can result. Teachers' perceptions of students' behavior can significantly influence their judgments of scholastic performance (Hills 1991). Students with behavior problems often have no chance to receive a high grade because their infractions overshadow their performance. These effects are especially pronounced in judgments of boys (Bennett et al. 1993). Even the neatness of students' handwriting can significantly affect a teacher's judgment (Sweedler-Brown 1992).

Training programs can help teachers identify and reduce these negative effects and lead to greater consistency in judgments (Afflerbach and Sammons 1991). Unfortunately, few teachers receive adequate training in grading or reporting as part of their preservice experiences (Boothroyd and McMorris 1992). Also, few school districts provide adequate guidance to ensure consistency in teachers' grading or reporting practices (Austin and McCann 1992).

4. *Grades have some value as rewards, but no value as punishments.* Although educators would undoubtedly prefer that motivation to learn be entirely intrinsic, the existence of grades and other reporting methods are important factors in determining how much effort students put forth (Chastain 1990, Ebel 1979). Most students view high grades as positive recognition of their success, and some work hard to avoid the consequences of low grades (Feldmesser 1971).

At the same time, no studies support the use of low grades as punishments. Instead of prompting greater effort, low grades usually cause students to withdraw from learning. To protect their self-image, many students regard the low grade as irrelevant and meaningless. Other students may blame themselves for the low mark, but feel helpless to improve (Selby and Murphy 1992).

Sadly, some teachers consider grades or reporting forms their "weapon of last resort." In their view, students who don't comply with requests suffer the consequences of the greatest punishment a teacher can bestow: a failing grade. Such practices have no educational value and, in the long run, adversely affect students, teachers, and the relationship they share. Rather than attempting to punish students with a low mark, teachers can better motivate students by regarding their work as incomplete and requiring additional effort.

5. *Grading and reporting should always be done in reference to learning criteria, never on the curve.* Using the normal probability curve as a basis for assigning grades typically yields greater consistency in grade distributions from one teacher to the next. The practice, however, is detrimental to teaching and learning.

Grading on the curve pits students against one another in a competition for the few rewards (high grades) distributed by the teacher. Under these conditions, students readily see that helping others will threaten their own chances for success (Johnson et al. 1979, Johnson et al. 1980). Learning becomes a game of winners and losers—with the most students falling into the latter category (Johnson and Johnson 1989). In addition, modern research has shown that the seemingly direct relationship between aptitude or intelligence and school achievement depends upon instructional conditions, not a probability curve.

When the instructional quality is high and well matched to students' learning needs, the magnitude of this relationship diminishes drastically and approaches zero (Bloom 1976). Moreover, the fairness and equity of grading on the curve is a myth.

Learning Criteria

When grading and reporting relate to learning criteria, teachers have a clearer picture of what students have learned. Students and teachers alike generally prefer this approach because it seems fairer (Kovas 1993). The types of learning criteria usually used for grading and reporting fall into three categories:

- *Product criteria* are favored by advocates of performance-based approaches to teaching and learning. These educators believe grading and reporting should communicate a summative evaluation of student achievement (Cangelosi 1990). In other words, they focus on what students know and are able to do at that time. Teachers who use product criteria often base their grades or reports exclusively on final examination scores, overall assessments, or other culminating demonstrations of learning.

- *Process criteria* are emphasized by educators who believe product criteria don't provide a complete picture of student learning. From their perspective, grading and reporting should reflect not just the final results but also *how* students got there. Teachers who consider effort or work habits when reporting on student learning are using process criteria. So are teachers who take into consideration classroom quizzes, homework, class participation, or attendance.

- *Progress criteria*, often referred to as "improvement scoring" and "learning gain," consider how much students have gained from their learning experiences. Teachers who use progress criteria look at *how far* students have come rather than where they are. As a result, scoring criteria may become highly individualized.

Teachers who base their grading and reporting procedures on learning criteria typically use some combination of the three types (Frary et al. 1993; Nava and Loyd 1992; Stiggins et al. 1989). Most researchers and measurement specialists, on the other hand, recommend using product criteria exclusively. They point out that the more process and progress criteria come into play, the more subjective and biased grades become (Ornstein 1994). How can a teacher know, for example, how difficult a task was for students or how hard they worked to complete it? If these criteria are included at all, most experts recommend they be reported separately (Stiggins 1994).

Practical Guidelines

Despite years of research, there's no evidence to indicate that one grading or reporting method works best under all conditions, in all circumstances. But in developing practices that seek to be fair, equitable, and useful to students, parents, and teachers, educators can rely on two guidelines:

■ *Provide accurate and understandable descriptions of learning.* Regardless of the method or form used, grading and reporting should communicate effectively what students have learned, what they can do, and whether their learning status is in line with expectations for that level. More than an exercise in quantifying achievement, grading and reporting must be seen as a challenge in clear thinking and effective communication (Stiggins 1994).

■ *Use grading and reporting methods to enhance, not hinder, teaching and learning.* A clear, easily understood reporting form facilitates communication between teachers and parents. When both parties speak the same language, joint efforts to help students are likely to succeed. But developing such an equitable and understandable system will require the elimination of long-time practices such as averaging and assigning a zero to work that's late, missed, or neglected.

■ *Averaging* falls far short of providing an accurate description of what students have learned. For example, students often say, "I have to get a *B* on the final to pass this course." Such a comment illustrates the inappropriateness of averaging. If a final examination is truly comprehensive and students' scores accurately reflect what they've learned, why should a *B* level of performance translate to a *D* for the course grade?

Any single measure of learning can be unreliable. Consequently, most researchers recommend using several indicators in determining students' grades or marks—and most teachers concur (Natriello 1987). Nevertheless, the key question remains, "What information provides the most accurate depiction of students' learning at this time?" In nearly all cases, the answer is "the most current information." If students demonstrate that past assessment information doesn't accurately reflect their learning, new information must take its place. By continuing to rely on past assessment data, the grades can be misleading about a student's learning (Stiggins 1994).

Similarly, assigning a score of zero to work that is late, missed, or neglected doesn't accurately depict learning. Is the teacher certain the student has learned absolutely nothing, or is the zero assigned to punish students for not displaying appropriate responsibility (Canady and Hotchkiss 1989, Stiggins and Duke 1991)?

Further, a zero has a profound effect when combined with the practice of averaging. Students who receive a single zero have little chance of success because such an extreme score skews the average. That is why, for example, Olympic events such as gymnastics and ice skating eliminate the highest and lowest scores; otherwise, one judge could control the entire competition simply by giving extreme scores. An alternative is to use the median score rather than the average (Wright 1994) but use of the most current information remains the most defensible option.

Meeting the Challenge

The issues of grading and reporting on student learning continue to challenge educators today, just as they challenged Middleton and his colleagues in 1933. But today we know more than ever before about the complexities involved and how certain practices can influence teaching and learning.

What do educators need to develop grading and reporting practices that provide quality information about student learning? Nothing less than clear thinking, careful planning, excellent communication skills, and an overriding concern for the well-being of students. Combining these skills with our current knowledge on effective practice will surely result in more efficient and more effective reporting. ■

Although student assessment has been a part of teaching and learning for centuries, grading is a relatively recent phenomenon. The ancient Greeks used assessments as formative, not evaluative, tools. Students demonstrated, usually orally, what they had learned, giving teachers a clear indication of which topics required more work or instruction.

In the United States, grading and reporting were virtually unknown before 1850. Back then, most schools groups students of all ages and backgrounds together with one teacher. Few students went beyond the elementary education offered in these one-room schoolhouses. As the country grew—and as legislators passed compulsory attendance laws—the number and diversity of students increased. Schools began to group students in grades according to their age, and to try new ideas about curriculum and teaching methods. Here's a brief timeline of significant dates in the history of grading:

Late 1800s: Schools begin to issue progress evaluations. Teachers simply write down the skills that students have mastered; once students complete the requirements for one level, they can move to the next level.

Early 1900s: The number of public high schools in the United States increases dramatically. While elementary teachers continue using written descriptions to document student learning, high school teachers introduce percentages as a way to certify students' accomplishments in specific subject areas. Few educators question the gradual shift to percentage grading, which seems a natural by-product of the increased demands on high school teachers.

1912: Starch and Elliott publish a study that challenges percentage grades as reliable measures of student achievement. They base their findings on grades assigned to two papers written for a first-year English class in high school. Of the 142 teachers grading on a 0 to 100 scale, 15 percent give one paper a failing mark; 12 percent give the same paper a score of 90 or more. The other paper receives scores ranging from 50 to 97. Neatness, spelling, and punctuation influenced the scoring of many teachers, while others considered how well the paper communicated its message.

1913: Responding to critics—who argue that good writing is, by nature, a highly subjective judgment—Starch and Elliott repeat their study but use geometry papers. Even greater variations occur, with scores on one paper ranging from 28 to 95. Some teachers deducted points only for wrong answers, but others took neatness, form, and spelling into account.

1918: Teachers turn to grading scales with fewer and larger categories. One three-point scale, for example, uses the categories of Excellent, Average, and Poor. Another has five categories (Excellent, Good, Average, Poor, and Failing) with the corresponding letters of *A, B, C, D,* and *F* (Johnson 1918, Rugg 1918).

1930s: Grading on the curve becomes increasingly popular as educators seek to minimize the subjective nature of scoring. This method rank orders students according to some measure of their performance or proficiency. The top percentage receives an *A,* the next percentage receives a *B,* and so on (Corey 1930). Some advocates (Davis 1930) even specify the precise percentage of students to be assigned each grade, such as 6–22–44–22–6.

Grading on the curve seems fair and equitable, given research suggesting that students' scores on tests of innate intelligence approximate a normal probability curve (Middleton 1933).

As the debate over grading and reporting intensifies, a number of schools abolish formal grades altogether (Chapman and Ashbaugh 1925) and return to using verbal descriptions of student achievement. Others advocate pass-fail systems that distinguish only between acceptable and failing work (Good 1937). Still others advocate a "mastery approach": Once students have mastered a skill or content, they move to other areas of study (Heck 1938, Hill 1935).

1958: Ellis Page investigates how student learning is affected by grades and teachers' comments. In a now classic study,

74 secondary school teachers administer a test, and assign a numerical score and letter grade of *A, B, C, D,* or *F* to each student's paper. Next, teachers randomly divide the tests into three groups. Papers in the first group receive only the numerical score and letter grade. The second group, in addition to the score and grade, receive these standard comments: *A—Excellent! B—Good work. Keep at it. C—Perhaps try to do still better? D—Let's bring this up. F—Let's raise this grade!* For the third group, teachers mark the score and letter grade, and write individualized comments.

Page evaluates the effects of the comments by considering students' scores on the next test they take. Results show that students in the second group achieved significantly higher scores than those who received only a score and grade. The students who received individualized comments did even better. Page concludes that grades can have a beneficial effect on student learning, but only when accompanied by specific or individualized comments from the teacher.

Source: H. Kirschenbaum, S. B. Simon, and R. W. Napier, (1971), *Wad-ja-get? The Grading Game in American Education,* (New York: Hart).

References

Afflerbach, P., and R. B. Sammons. (1991). "Report Cards in Literacy Evaluation: Teachers' Training, Practices, and Values." Paper presented at the annual meeting of the National Reading Conference, Palm Springs, Calif.

Austin, S., and R. McCann. (1992). "'Here's Another Arbitrary Grade for Your Collection': A Statewide Study of Grading Policies." Paper presented at the annual meeting of the American Educational Research Association, San Francisco.

Barnes, S. (1985). "A Study of Classroom Pupil Evaluation: The Missing Link in Teacher Education." *Journal of Teacher Education* 36, 4: 46–49.

Bennett, R. E., R. L. Gottesman, D. A. Rock, and F. Cerullo. (1993). "Influence of Behavior Perceptions and Gender on Teachers' Judgments of Students' Academic Skill." *Journal of Educational Psychology,* 85: 347–356.

Bishop, J. H. (1992). "Why U.S. Students Need Incentives to Learn." *Educational Leadership* 49, 6: 15–18.

Bloom, B. S. (1976). *Human Characteristics and School Learning.* New York: McGraw-Hill.

Bloom, B. S., G. F. Madaus, and J. T. Hastings (1981). *Evaluation to Improve Learning.* New York: McGraw-Hill.

Boothroyd, R. A., and R. F. McMorris. (1992). "What Do Teachers Know About Testing and How Did They Find Out?" Paper presented at the annual meeting of the National Council on Measurements in Education, San Francisco.

Brookhart, S. M. (1993). "Teachers' Grading Practices: Meaning and Values." *Journal of Educational Measurement* 30, 2: 123–142.

Canady, R. L., and P. R. Hotchkiss. (1989). "It's a Good Score! Just a Bad Grade." *Phi Delta Kappan* 71: 68–71.

Cangelosi, J. S. (1990). "Grading and Reporting Student Achievement." In *Designing Tests for Evaluating Student Achievement,* pp. 196–213. New York: Longman.

Chapman, H. B., and E. J. Ashbaugh. (October 7, 1925). "Report Cards in American Cities." *Educational Research Bulletin* 4: 289–310.

Chastain, K. (1990). Characteristics of Graded and Ungraded Compositions." *Modern Language Journal,* 74, 1: 10–14.

Corey, S. M. (1930). "Use of the Normal Curve as a Basis for Assigning Grades in Small Classes." *School and Society* 31: 514–516.

Davis, J. D. W. (1930). "Effect of the 6–22–44–22–6 Normal Curve System on Failures and Grade Values." *Journal of Educational Psychology* 22: 636–640.

Ebel, R. L. (1979). *Essentials of Educational Measurement* (3rd ed.). Englewood Cliffs, N.J.: Prentice Hall.

Feldmesser, R. A. (1971). "The Positive Functions of Grades." Paper presented at the annual meeting of the American Educational Research Association, New York.

Frary, R. B., L. H. Cross, and L. J. Weber. (1993). "Testing and Grading Practices and Opinions of Secondary Teachers of Academic Subjects: Implications for Instruction in Measurement." *Educational Measurement: Issues and Practices* 12, 3: 23–30.

Frisbie, D. A., and K. K. Waltman. (1992). "Developing a Personal Grading Plan." *Educational Measurement: Issues and Practices* 11, 3: 35–42.

Good, W. (1937). "Should Grades Be Abolished?" *Education Digest* 2, 4: 7–9.

Heck, A. O. (1938). "Contributions of Research to Classification, Promotion, Marking and Certification." Reported in *The Science Movement in Education (Part II), Twenty-Seventh Yearbook of the National Society for the Study of Education.* Chicago: University of Chicago Press.

Hill, G. E. (1935). "The Report Card in Present Practice." *Education Methods* 15, 3: 115–131.

Hills, J. R. (1991). "Apathy Concerning Grading and Testing." *Phi Delta Kappan* 72, 2: 540–545.

Johnson, D. W., and R. T. Johnson. (1989). *Cooperation and Competition: Theory and Research.* Endina, Minn.: Interaction.

Johnson, D. W., L. Skon, and R. T. Johnson (1980). "Effects of Cooperative, Competitive, and Individualistic Conditions on Children's Problem-Solving Performance." *American Educational Research Journal* 17, 1: 83–93.

Johnson, R. H. (1918). "Educational Research and Statistics: The Coefficient Marking System" *School and Society* 7, 181: 714–716.

Johnson, R. T., D. W. Johnson, and M. Tauer. (1979). "The Effects of Cooperative, Competitive, and Individualistic Goal Structures on Students' Attitudes and Achievement." *Journal of Psychology* 102: 191–198.

Kovas, M. A. (1993). "Making Your Grading Motivating: Keys to Performance-Based Evaluation." *Quill and Scroll* 68, 1: 10–11.

Middleton, W. (1933). "Some General Trends in Grading Procedure." *Education* 54, 1: 5–10.

Natriello, G. (1987). "The Impact of Evaluation Processes On Students." *Educational Psychologists* 22: 155–175.

Nava, F. J. G., and B. H. Loyd. (1992). "An Investigation of Achievement and Nonachievement Criteria in Elementary and Secondary School Grading." Paper presented at the annual meeting of the American Educational Research Association, San Francisco.

O'Donnell, A., and A. E. Woolfolk. (1991). "Elementary and Secondary Teachers' Beliefs About Testing and Grading." Paper presented at the annual meeting of the American Psychological Association, San Francisco.

Ornstein, A. C. (1994). "Grading Practices and Policies: An Overview and Some Suggestions." *NASSP Bulletin* 78, 559: 55–64.

Page, E. B. (1958). "Teacher Comments and Student Performance: A Seventy-Four Classroom Experiment in School Motivation." *Journal of Educational Psychology* 49: 173–181.

Payne, D. A. (1974). *The Assessment of Learning.* Lexington, Mass.: Heath.

Rugg, H. O. (1918). "Teachers' Marks and the Reconstruction of the Marking System." *Elementary School Journal* 18, 9: 701–719.

Selby, D., and S. Murphy. (1992). "Graded or Degraded: Perceptions of Letter-Grading for Mainstreamed Learning-Disabled Students." *British Columbia Journal of Special Education* 16, 1: 92–104.

Starch, D., and E. C. Elliott. (1912). "Reliability of the Grading of High School Work in English." *School Review* 20: 442–457.

Starch, D., and E. C. Elliott. (1913). "Reliability of the Grading of High School Work in Mathematics." *School Review* 21: 254–259.

Stewart, L. G., and M. A. White. (1976). "Teacher Comments, Letter Grades, and Student Performance." *Journal of Educational Psychology* 68, 4: 488–500.

Stiggins, R. J. (1994). "Communicating with Report Card Grades." In *Student-Centered Classroom Assessment,* pp. 363–396. New York: Macmillan.

Stiggins, R. J., and D. L. Duke, (1991). "District Grading Policies and Their Potential Impact on At-risk Students." Paper presented at the annual meeting of the American Educational Research Association, Chicago.

Stiggins, R. J., D. A. Frisbie, and P. A. Griswold. (1989). "Inside High School Grading Practices: Building a Research Agenda." *Educational Measurement: Issues and Practice* 8, 2: 5–14.

Sweedler-Brown, C. O. (1992). "The Effect of Training on the Appearance Bias of Holistic Essay Graders." *Journal of Research and Development in Education* 26, 1: 24–29.

Wright, R. G. (1994). "Success for All: The Median Is the Key." *Phi Delta Kappan* 75, 9: 723–725.

POST NOTE

Grading students is one of the most troubling tasks that beginning teachers face. While working with students to help them learn and develop is a source of great pleasure for teachers, grading students provokes anxiety and avoidance. Unfortunately, grading is a part of almost all schooling and is not likely to go away anytime soon. Therefore, teachers need to learn how to grade in the fairest way possible.

To do this may require you to unlearn many aspects of grading that you have experienced as a student. For example, consider using the median instead of the mean when averaging a student's grades. Statistically, it is a more fair measure. In general, take time to learn effective and fair evaluation procedures.

DISCUSSION QUESTIONS

1. Did any of the author's recommendations surprise you? If so, which ones and why?

2. Can you think of any time when you thought you didn't get the grade you deserved? What were the circumstances? In what way do you think you were treated unfairly?

3. How would a zero score count differently in averaging scores if you used the median instead of the mean as the measure of central tendency?

Cooperative Learning and the Cooperative School

Robert E. Slavin

T he Age of Cooperation is approaching. From Alaska to California to Florida to New York, from Australia to Britain to Norway to Israel, teachers and administrators are discovering an untapped resource for accelerating students' achievement: the students themselves. There is now substantial evidence that students working together in small cooperative groups can master material presented by the teacher better than can students working on their own.

The idea that people working together toward a common goal can accomplish more than people working by themselves is a well-established principle of social psychology. What is new is that practical cooperative learning strategies for classroom use have been developed, researched, and found to be instructionally effective in elementary and secondary schools. Once thought of primarily as social methods directed at social goals, certain forms of cooperative learning are considerably more effective than traditional methods in increasing basic achievement outcomes, including performance on standardized tests of mathe-

Robert E. Slavin is Co-Director of the Center for Research on the Education of Students Placed at Risk, Johns Hopkins University, and chairman of the Success for All Foundation. Slavin, Robert E. (1987). "Cooperative Learning and the Cooperative School," *Educational Leadership*, 45, 3:7–13.

matics, reading, and language (Slavin 1983a, b; Slavin 1988).

Recently, a small but growing number of elementary and secondary schools have begun to apply cooperative principles at the school as well as the classroom level, involving teachers in cooperative planning, peer coaching, and team teaching, with these activities directed toward effective implementation of cooperative learning in the classroom. Many of these schools are working toward institutionalization of cooperative principles as the focus of school renewal.

This article reviews the research on cooperative learning methods and presents a vision of the next step in the progression of cooperative learning: the cooperative school.

What Is Cooperative Learning and Why Does It Work?

Cooperative learning refers to a set of instructional methods in which students work in small, mixed-ability learning groups. The groups usually have four members—one high achiever, two average achievers, and one low achiever. The students in each group are responsible not only for learning the material being taught in class, but also for helping their groupmates learn. Often, there is some sort of group goal. For example, in the Student Team Learning methods developed at Johns Hopkins University (Slavin 1986), students can earn attractive certificates if group averages exceed a pre-established criterion of excellence.

For example, the simplest form of Student Team Learning, called Student Teams-Achievement Division (STAD), consists of a regular cycle of activities. First, the teacher presents a lesson to the class. Then students, in their four-member mixed-ability teams, work to master the material. Students usually have worksheets or other materials; study strategies within the teams depend on the subject matter. In math, students might work problems and then compare answers, discussing and resolving any discrepancies. In spelling, students might drill one another on spelling lists. In social studies, students might work together to find information in the text relating to key concepts. Regardless of the subject matter, students are encouraged not just to give answers but to explain ideas or skills to one another.

At the end of the team study period, students take brief individual quizzes, on which they cannot help one another. Teachers sum the results of the quizzes to form team scores, using a system that assigns points based on how much individual students have improved over their own past records.

The changes in classroom organization required by STAD are not revolutionary. To review the process, the teacher presents the initial lesson as in traditional instruction. Students then work on worksheets or other practice activities; they happen to work in teams, but otherwise the idea of practice following instruction is hardly new. Finally, students take a brief, individual quiz.

Yet, even though changes in classroom organization are moderate, the effects of cooperative learning on students can be profound. Because one student's success in the traditional classroom makes it more difficult for others to succeed (by raising the curve or raising the teacher's expectations), working hard on academic tasks can cause a student to be labeled as a "nerd" or a "teacher's pet." For this reason, students often express norms to one another that discourage academic work. In contrast, when students are working together toward a common goal, academic work becomes an activity valued by peers. Just as hard work in sports is valued by peers because a team member's success brings credit to the team and the school, so academic work is valued by peers in cooperative learning classes because it helps the team to succeed.

In addition to motivating students to do their best, cooperative learning also motivates students to help one another learn. This is important for several reasons. First, students are often able to translate the teacher's language into "kid language" for one another. Students who fail to grasp fully a concept the teacher has presented can often profit from discussing the concept with peers who are wrestling with the same questions.

Second, students who explain to one another learn by doing so. Every teacher knows that we learn by teaching. When students have to organize their thoughts to explain ideas to teammates, they must engage in cognitive elaboration that greatly enhances their own understanding (see Dansereau 1985).

Third, students can provide individual attention and assistance to one another. Because they work one-on-one, students can do an excellent job of finding out whether their peers have the idea or need additional explanation. In a traditional classroom, students who don't understand what is going on can scrunch down in their seats and hope the teacher won't call on them. In a cooperative team, there is nowhere to hide; there *is* a helpful, nonthreatening environment in which to try out ideas and ask for assistance. A student who gives an answer in a whole-class lesson risks being laughed at if the answer is wrong; in a cooperative team, the fact that the team has a "we're all in this together" attitude means that, when they don't understand, students are likely to receive help rather than derision.

Under What Conditions Is Cooperative Learning Effective?

Cooperative learning is always fun; it almost always produces gains in social outcomes such as race relations; and it has never been found to reduce student achievement in comparison to traditional methods. However, a substantial body of research has established that two conditions must be fulfilled if cooperative learning is to enhance student achievement substantially. First, students must be working toward a group goal, such as earning certificates or some other recognition. Second, success at achieving this goal must depend on the individual learning of all group members (see Slavin 1983a, b; 1988).

Simply putting students into mixed-ability groups and encouraging them to work together are not enough to produce learning gains: students must have a reason to take one another's achievement seriously, to provide one another with the elaborated explanations that are critical to the achievement effects of cooperative learning (see Webb 1985). If students care about the success of the team, it becomes legitimate for them to ask one another for help and to provide help to each other. Without this team goal, students may feel ashamed to ask peers for help.

Yet team goals are not enough in themselves to enhance student achievement. For example, classroom studies in which students complete a common worksheet or project have not found achievement benefits for such methods. When the group task is to complete a single product, it may be most efficient to let the smartest or highest-achieving students do most of the work. Suggestions or questions from lower-achieving students may be ignored or pushed aside, as they may interfere with efficient completion of the group task. We can all recall being in lab groups in science class or in project groups in social studies in which one or two group members did all the work. To enhance the achievement of all students, then, group success must be based not on a single group product, but on the sum of individual learning performances of all group members.

The group's task in instructionally effective forms of cooperative learning is almost always to prepare group members to succeed on individual assessments. This focuses the group activity on explaining ideas, practicing skills, and assessing all group members to ensure that all will be successful on learning assessments.

When cooperative learning methods provide group goals based on the learning of all members, the effects on student achievement are remarkably consistent. Of 38 studies of at least four weeks' duration comparing cooperative methods of this type to traditional control methods, 33 found significantly greater achievement for the cooperatively taught classes, and 5 found no significant differences (Slavin 1988). In contrast, only 4 of 20 studies that evaluated forms of cooperative learning lacking group goals based on group members' learning found positive achievement effects, and 3 of these are studies by Shlomo Sharan and his colleagues in Israel that incorpo-

rated group goals and individual accountability in a different way (see Sharan et al. 1980, Sharan et al. 1984).

Successful studies of cooperative learning have taken place in urban, rural, and suburban schools in the U.S., Canada, Israel, West Germany, and Nigeria, at grade levels from 2 to 12, and in subjects as diverse as mathematics, language arts, writing, reading, social studies, and science. Positive effects have been found on such higher-order objectives as creative writing, reading comprehension, and math problem solving, as well as on such basic skills objectives as language mechanics, math computations, and spelling. In general, achievement effects have been equivalent for high, average, and low achievers, for boys and girls, and for students of various ethnic backgrounds. As noted earlier, positive effects of cooperative learning have also been found on such outcomes as race relations, acceptance of mainstreamed academically handicapped classmates, and student self-esteem and liking of class (see Slavin 1983a).

Comprehensive Cooperative Learning Methods

The cooperative learning methods developed in the 1970s—Student Teams-Achievement Divisions and Teams-Games-Tournaments (Slavin 1986); Jigsaw Teaching (Aronson et al. 1978); the Johnsons' methods (Johnson and Johnson 1986); and Group Investigation (Sharan et al. 1984)—all are generic forms of cooperative learning. They can be used at many grade levels and in many subjects. The broad applicability of these methods partly accounts for their popularity. A one- or two-day workshop given to a mixed group of elementary and secondary teachers of many subjects can get teachers off to a good start in most of the methods, which makes this an ideal focus of staff development.

However, because the early cooperative learning methods are generally applicable across grade levels and subjects, they tend not to be uniquely adapted to any particular subject or grade level.

254

Also, the methods developed earlier are mostly curriculum-free; they rarely replace traditional texts or teaching approaches. As a result, these methods are most often applied as supplements to traditional instruction and rarely bring about fundamental change in classroom practice.

Since 1980, research and development on cooperative learning conducted at Johns Hopkins University has begun to focus on comprehensive cooperative learning methods designed to replace traditional instruction *entirely* in particular subjects and at particular grade levels. Two major programs of this type have been developed and successfully researched: Team Accelerated Instruction (TAI) in mathematics for grades 3–6, and Cooperative Integrated Reading and Composition (CIRC) in reading, writing, and language arts for grades 3–5. The main elements of these programs are described below.

Team Accelerated Instruction (TAI) Team Accelerated Instruction shares with STAD and the other Student Team Learning methods the use of four-member mixed-ability learning teams and certificates for high-performing teams. But where STAD uses a single pace of instruction for the class, TAI combines cooperative learning with individualized instruction. TAI is designed to teach mathematics to students in grades 3–6 (or older students not ready for a full algebra course).

In TAI, students enter an individualized sequence according to a placement test and then proceed at their own rates. In general, team members work on different units. Teammates check each other's work against answer sheets and help one another with any problems. Final unit tests are taken without teammate help and are scored by student monitors. Each week, teachers total the number of units completed by all team members and give certificates or other rewards to teams that exceed a criterion score based on the number of final tests passed, with extra points for perfect papers and completed homework.

Because students are responsible for checking each other's work and managing the flow of materials, the teacher can spend most class time presenting lessons to small groups of students drawn from the various teams who are working at the same point in the mathematics sequence. For example, the teacher might call up a decimals group, present a lesson, and then send the students back to their teams to work on decimal problems. Then the teacher might call the fractions group, and so on.

In TAI, students encourage and help one another to succeed because they want their teams to succeed. Individual accountability is assured because the only score that counts is the final test score, and students take final tests without teammate help. Students have equal opportunities for success because all have been placed according to their level of prior knowledge; it is as easy (or difficult) for a low achiever to complete three subtraction units in a week as it is for a higher-achieving classmate to complete three long division units.

However, the individualization that is part of TAI makes it quite different from STAD. In mathematics, most concepts build on earlier ones. If the earlier concepts were not mastered, the later ones will be difficult or impossible to learn—a student who cannot subtract or multiply will fail to master long division, a student who does not understand fractional concepts will fail to understand what a decimal is, and so on. In TAI, students work at their own levels, so if they lack prerequisite skills they can build a strong foundation before going on. Also, if students can learn more rapidly, they need not wait for the rest of the class.

Individualized mathematics instruction has generally failed to increase student mathematics achievement in the past (see Horak 1981), probably because the teacher's time in earlier models was entirely taken up with checking work and managing materials, leaving little time for actually teaching students. In TAI, students handle the routine checking and management, so the teacher can spend most class time teaching. This difference, plus the motivation and help provided by students within their cooperative teams, probably accounts for the strong positive effects of TAI on student achievement.

Five of six studies found substantially greater learning of mathematics computations in TAI than in control classes, while one study found no differences (Slavin, Leavey, and Madden 1984; Slavin, Madden, and Leavey 1984; Slavin and Karweit 1985). Across all six studies, the TAI classes gained an average of twice as many grade equivalents on standardized measures of computation as traditionally taught control classes (Slavin in press a). For example, in one 18-week study in Wilmington, Delaware, the control group gained .6 grade equivalents in mathematics computations, while the TAI classes gained 1.7 grade equivalents (Slavin and Karweit 1985). These experimental-control differences were still substantial (though smaller) a year after the students were in TAI.

Cooperative Integrated Reading and Composition (CIRC) The newest of the Student Team Learning methods is a comprehensive program for teaching reading and writing in the upper elementary grades. In CIRC, teachers use basal readers and reading groups, much as in traditional reading programs. However, students are assigned to teams composed of pairs from two different reading groups. While the teacher is working with one reading group, students in the other groups are working in their pairs on a series of cognitively engaging activities, including reading to one another; making predictions about how narrative stories will come out; summarizing stories to one another; writing responses to stories; and practicing spelling, decoding, and vocabulary. Students also work in teams to master main idea and other comprehension skills. During language arts periods, a structured program based on a writing process model is used. Students plan and write drafts, revise and edit one another's work, and prepare for publication of team books. Lessons on writing skills such as description, organization, use of vivid modifiers, and on language mechanics skills are fully integrated into students' creative writing.

In most CIRC activities, students follow a sequence of teacher instruction, team practice, team pre-assessments, and a quiz. That is, students do not take the quiz until their teammates have determined they are ready. Certificates are given to teams based on the average performance of all team members on all reading and writing activities. Two studies of CIRC (Stevens et al. in press) found substantial positive effects from this method on standardized tests of reading comprehension, reading vocabulary, language expression, language mechanics, and spelling, in comparison to control groups. The CIRC classes gained 30 to 70 percent of a grade equivalent more than control classes on these measures in both studies. Significantly greater achievement on writing samples favoring the CIRC students was also found in both studies.

A New Possibility

The development and successful evaluation of the comprehensive TAI and CIRC models has created an exciting new possibility. With cooperative learning programs capable of being used all year in the 3 Rs, it is now possible to design an elementary school program based upon a radical principle: students, teachers, and administrators can work *cooperatively* to make the school a better place for working and learning.

There are many visions of what a cooperative elementary school might look like, but there is one model that my colleagues and I have begun to work toward in partnership with some innovative practitioners. Its major components are as follows.

1. *Cooperative learning in the classroom.* Clearly, a cooperative elementary school would have cooperative learning methods in use in most classrooms and in more than one subject. Students and teachers should feel that the idea that students can help one another learn is not just applied on occasion, but is a fundamental principle of classroom organization. Students should see one another as resources for learning, and there should be a schoolwide norm that every student's learning is everyone's responsibility, that every student's success is everyone's success.

2. *Integration of special education and remedial services with the regular program.* In the cooperative elementary school, mainstreaming should be an essential element of school and classroom

organization. Special education teachers may team-teach with regular teachers, integrating their students in teams with nonhandicapped students and contributing their expertise in adapting instruction to individual needs to the class as a whole. Similarly, Chapter I or other remedial services should be provided in the regular classroom. If we take seriously the idea that all students are responsible for one another, this goes as much for students with learning problems as for anyone else. Research on use of TAI and CIRC to facilitate mainstreaming and meet the needs of remedial readers has found positive effects on the achievement and social acceptance of these students (see Slavin 1984, Slavin et al. in press).

3. *Peer coaching.* In the cooperative elementary school, teachers should be responsible for helping one another to use cooperative learning methods successfully and to implement other improvements in instructional practice. Peer coaching (Joyce et al. 1983) is perfectly adapted to the philosophy of the cooperative school; teachers learn new methods together and are given release time to visit one another's classes to give assistance and exchange ideas as they begin using the new programs.

4. *Cooperative planning.* Cooperative activities among teachers should not be restricted to peer coaching. In addition, teachers should be given time to plan goals and strategies together, to prepare common libraries of instructional materials, and to make decisions about cooperative activities involving more than one class.

5. *Building-level steering committee.* In the cooperative elementary school, teachers and administrators should work together to determine the direction the school takes. A steering committee composed of the principal, classroom teacher representatives, representatives of other staff (e.g., special education, Chapter I, aides), and one or more parent representatives meets to discuss the progress the school is making toward its instructional goals and to recommend changes in school policies and practices to achieve these goals.

6. *Cooperation with parents and community members.* The cooperative school should invite the participation of parents and community members.

Development of a community sense that children's success in school is everyone's responsibility is an important goal of the cooperative school.

The Cooperative School Today

To my knowledge, there is not yet a school that is implementing all of the program elements listed here, but a few enterprising and committed schools are moving in this direction. In Bay Shore (New York) School District, teachers in two intermediate schools are using CIRC in reading, writing, and language arts, and STAD in math. In Alexandria, Virginia, Mt. Vernon Community School is working with the National Education Association's Mastery in Learning project to build a cooperative school plan. At Mt. Vernon, a building steering committee is planning and helping to implement a gradual phasing in of the TAI math program and CIRC reading, writing and language arts programs. Several schools throughout the U.S. that have successfully implemented TAI math are now planning to add CIRC for reading and writing instruction, and are looking toward full-scale implementation of a cooperative school plan. Most schools that have focused school renewal efforts on widespread use of cooperative learning are at the elementary level; but several middle junior high, and high schools have begun to work in this direction as well.

In a time of limited resources for education, we must learn to make the best use of what we have. Cooperative learning and the cooperative school provide one means of helping students, teachers, and administrators work together to make meaningful improvements in the learning of all students.

A Visit to a Cooperative School

It is Friday morning at "Cooper Elementary School." In Ms. Thompson's third-grade, the students are getting ready for reading. They are sitting in teams at small tables, four or five at each table. As the period begins, Ms. Thompson calls up the "Rockets." Pairs of students from several of the small groups move to a reading group area, while the remaining students continue working at their desks. In Ms. Thompson's class the students at their desks are working together on activities quite different from the usual workbooks. They are taking turns reading aloud to each other; working together to identify the characters, settings, problems, and problems solutions in stories; practicing vocabulary and spelling; and summarizing stories to one another. When Ms. Thompson finishes with the Rockets, they return to their groups and begin working together on the same types of activities. Ms. Thompson listens in on some of the students who are reading to each other and praises teams that are working well. Then she calls up the "Astros," who leave their teams to go to the reading group.

Meanwhile, in Mr. Fisher's fifth-grade, it is math period. Again, students are working in small teams, but in math, each team member is working on different materials depending on his or her performance level. In the teams students are checking one another's work against answer sheets, explaining problems to one another, and answering each other's questions. Mr. Fisher calls up the "Decimals" group for a lesson. Students working on decimals leave their teams and move to the group area for their lesson. When the lesson is over, the students return to their teams and continue working on decimals.

In Mr. Fisher's class there are five learning disabled students, who are distributed among the various teams. The special education resource teacher, Ms. Walters, is teaming with Mr. Fisher. While he is giving lessons, she is moving through the class helping students. At other times, Ms. Walters gives math lessons to groups of students who are having difficulties in math, including her five LD students, while Mr. Fisher works with students in their team areas.

In Mr. Green's fourth-grade class it is writing time. Mr. Green starts the period with a brief lesson on "*and* disease," the tendency to write long sentences connected by too many "*ands.*" Then the students work on compositions in teams.

They cooperatively plan what they will write and then do a draft. The students read their drafts to their teammates and receive feedback on what their teammates heard, what they liked, and what they wanted to hear more about. After revising their drafts, students hold editing conferences with teammates focusing on the mechanics of the composition.

While the students are writing, Mr. Green is moving from team to team, listening in on what they are saying to each other and conferencing with individual students to help them. Also in the class is Ms. Hill, another fourth-grade teacher. She and Mr. Green began using writing process methods at the same time and are coaching each other as they use them in their classes. At the end of the day the two teachers will meet to discuss what happened, and to plan the next steps jointly. On other days, a substitute will cover Mr. Green's class while he visits Ms. Hill's writing class.

All over Cooper Elementary School, students are working in cooperative teams, and teachers are working together cooperatively to help students learn. In the first grades, students are working in pairs taking turns reading to each other. In the sixth grades students are doing team science projects in which each team member is responsible for a part of the team's task. Second-graders are working in teams to master capitalization and punctuation rules.

At the end of the day, teachers award certificates to teams that did outstanding work that week. Those teams that met the highest standards of excellence receive "Superteam" certificates. Throughout the school the sounds of applause can be heard.

After the students have gone home, the school steering committee meets. Chaired by the principal, the committee includes representatives of teachers at several grade levels, plus two parent representatives. The committee discusses the progress they are making toward the goal of becoming a cooperative school. Among other things, the committee decides to hold a school fair to show what the school is doing, to display the students' terrific cooperative work in writing, science, and math; and to encourage parents to volunteer at the school and to support their children's success at home. ∎

References

Aronson, E., N. Blaney, C. Stephan, J. Sikes, and M. Snapp. *The Jigsaw Classroom.* Beverly Hills, Calif.: Sage, 1978.

Dansereau, D. F. "Learning Strategy Research." In *Thinking and Learning Skills: Relating Instruction to Basic Research, Vol. 1,* edited by J. Segal, S. Chipman, and R. Glaser. Hillsdale, N.J.: Erlbaum, 1985.

Horak, V. M. "A Meta-analysis of Research Findings on Individualized Instruction in Mathematics." *Journal of Educational Research* 74 (1981): 249–253.

Johnson, D. W., and R. T. Johnson. *Learning Together and Alone.* 2d ed. Englewood Cliffs, N.J.: Prentice-Hall, 1986.

Joyce, B. R., R. H. Hersh, and M. McKibbin. *The Structure of School Improvement.* New York: Longman, 1983.

Sharan, S., R. Hertz-Lazarowitz, and Z. Ackerman. "Academic Achievement of Elementary School Children in Small-Group vs. Whole Class Instruction." *Journal of Experimental Education* 48 (1980): 125–129.

Sharan, S., P. Kussell, R. Hertz-Lazarowitz, Y. Bejarano, S. Raviv, and Y. Sharan. *Cooperative Learning in the Classroom: Research in Desegregated Schools.* Hillsdale, N.J.: Erlbaum, 1984.

Slavin, R. E. *Cooperative Learning.* New York: Longman, 1983a.

Slavin, R. E. "When Does Cooperative Learning Increase Student Achievement?" *Psychological Bulletin* 94 (1983b): 429–445.

Slavin, R. E. "Team Assisted Individualization: Cooperative Learning and Individualized Instruction in the Mainstreamed Classroom." *Remedial and Special Education* 5, 6 (1984): 33–42.

Slavín, R. E. *Using Student Team Learning.* 3d ed. Baltimore, Md.: Center for Research on Elementary and Middle Schools, Johns Hopkins University, 1986.

Slavin, R. E. "Cooperative Learning: A Best-Evidence Synthesis." In *School and Classroom Organization,* edited by R. E. Slavin. Hillsdale, N.J.: Erlbaum, 1988.

Slavin, R. E. "Combining Cooperative Learning and Individualized Instruction." *Arithmetic Teacher.* In press a.

Slavin, R. E., and N. L. Karweit. "Effects of Whole-Class, Ability Grouped, and Individualized Instruction on Mathematics Achievement." *American Educational Research Journal* 22 (1985): 351–367.

Slavin, R. E., M. Leavey, and N. A. Madden. "Combining Cooperative Learning and Individualized Instruction: Effects on Student Mathematics Achievement, Attitudes, and Behaviors." *Elementary School Journal* 84 (1984): 409–422.

Slavin, R. E., N. A. Madden, and M. Leavey. "Effects of Team Assisted Individualization on the Mathematics Achievement of Academically Handicapped and Nonhandicapped Students." *Journal of Educational Psychology* 76 (1984): 813–819.

Slavin, R. E., R. J. Stevens, and N. A. Madden. "Accommodating Student Diversity in Reading and Writing Instruction: A Cooperative Learning Approach." *Remedial and Special Education.* In press.

Stevens, R. J., N. A. Madden, R. E. Slavin, and A. M. Farnish. "Cooperative Integrated Reading and Composition: Two Field Experiments." *Reading Research Quarterly.* In press.

Webb, N. "Student Interaction and Learning in Small Groups: A Research Summary." In *Learning to Cooperate, Cooperating to Learn,* edited by R. E. Slavin, S. Sharan, S. Kagan, R. Hertz-Lazarowitz, C. Webb, and R. Schmuck. New York: Plenum, 1985.

POST NOTE

In a country beginning to question the effects of unshackled individualism, cooperative learning strategies are a needed tonic. In addition to the moral values of tolerance and concern for others that are fostered through this methodology, it produces greater achievement, particularly in students who are typically low achievers. We suspect that these students, who are usually behind in class, find it much less threatening to take instruction from other students than from teachers.

School districts around the United States are conducting workshops for teachers to help them use these strategies in their teaching. Research evidence shows positive results on academic achievement, self-esteem, intergroup relations, and attitudes toward school. You would be well advised to develop your own skill in the use of cooperative learning strategies. Having these strategies in your instructional repertoire will certainly make you a more desirable candidate for a teaching position.

DISCUSSION QUESTIONS

1. Have you observed or participated in cooperative learning strategies? If so, how would you describe your experience?

2. From what you know of cooperative learning strategies, would you like to use them as described in Team Accelerated Instruction (TAI) and Cooperative Integrated Reading and Composition (CIRC)? Why or why not?

3. What drawbacks, if any, do you see in cooperative learning approaches? Explain your answer.

43 What's All the Noise About? Constructivism in the Classroom

Frank Betts

For years, we've been taught that maintaining control in the classroom is essential if students are to learn. This maxim translates to teacher control and quiet students. Suddenly (it seems) we're urged to give more control to students—and accept noisy classrooms and often unhappy parents. If you feel confused about all the fuss raised when people beat the drum for *constructivism* in the classroom, this article is for you.

The past 10–15 years have seen immense gains in knowledge and understanding about how people learn. In many cases, these new kinds of understanding have validated some past practice, for example, the work of Marilyn Adams (1990) in reading. For the most part, however, the new interpretations have shown us the weaknesses of the past and, to a great extent, present practice. These weaknesses in our educational foundations are convincingly discussed in detail in *Making Connections: Teaching and the Human Brain* (Caine and Caine 1991). The authors of this book show how we create, or construct, our own knowledge—and what conditions contribute to this construction.

At the time this article was written, Frank Betts was associate executive director, Association for Supervision and Curriculum Development, Alexandria, Virginia. Betts, Frank, "What's All the Noise About? Constructivism in the Classroom." *ASCD Curriculum/Technology Quarterly*, vol. 1, no. 1 (Fall 1991), pp. 1–4. Reprinted with permission from ASCD. All rights reserved.

What Is Constructivism?

Constructivism is both a set of assumptions (philosophical constructivism) and a set of behaviors consistent with them (pedagogical constructivism). Here is my working definition: Constructivism is a frame of reference, based on how children learn, for interpreting and organizing all classroom practice to enhance a child's ability to learn in any content area.

Some distributors of educational materials would have us believe that constructivism in the classroom is simply "hands-on science" or the use of manipulatives in mathematics. Although these approaches to science and math may both be consistent with the constructivist perspective on learning, they are only examples of behaviors that are necessary conditions of constructivism.

Following the interpretations of von Glaserfeld (1989) and others (Kamii 1982, Noelting 1978, Noddings 1990), the main canons of constructivism as it applies to classroom practice seem to be:

■ Knowledge is not passively received, but actively constructed by the learners on a base of prior knowledge, attitudes, and values. These are developed from and shaped by personal experience and the social and cultural environment. What students learn is heavily dependent on the understanding they bring to the task.

■ The function of cognition is adaptive; that is, learners need to create patterns, schema, strategies, and rules that increase their control over the environment. Learners identify and construct guidelines by experimenting, examining models, reflecting, and deciding on functional patterns that fulfill their personal needs. Most such guidelines are intuitive, not formal pronouncements.

According to Magoon (1977), three assumptions are critical to a constructivist:

1. Humans are "knowing beings." What they know has important consequences, especially as it affects behavior and their interpretation of actions. For example, according to Nuthall and Alton-Lee (1991), "Test items requiring knowledge of visual information require the child to experience a combination of both verbal descriptions and visual

information." To illustrate: Suppose you are studying Picasso's painting *Guernica*. You can read about the Spanish Civil War in a history book or a Hemingway novel, or you may read an art critic's description of the painting; but until you also see, study, and discuss the visual image of the painting within the context provided by the written material, you may not understand *Guernica* as both a political and aesthetic statement.

2. The locus of control is solely within the individual, although environmental factors or recognition of social norms may constrain action. "It is the child [not the teacher] who organizes, or reorganizes relevant memory content in an item-relevant manner. . . . Constructing a schema is a process of forming links or making connections between relevant already-known information" (Nuthall and Alton-Lee 1991, p. 47). The child makes meaning and organizes experience using basic models or schema, most often acquired informally from examples provided by adults and through observing the social consequences.

3. Humans develop knowledge by attending to "meanings of complex communications rather than surface elements" (Caine and Caine 1991), rapidly organizing the complexity they observe and taking on complex social roles or reconstructing them.

In a constructivist classroom, students must use higher order thinking skills to find meaning in the events they observe and experience. A constructivist approach is certain to fail in an educational environment that stresses having one right answer, does not encourage questioning and accepting a variety of interpretations, or depends solely on factual recall as evidence of learning. It has been my experience that many elementary school teachers avoid teaching science because "they don't know the right answer." In contrast, scientists are obsessed with the continuing search for answers.

Teachers using the constructivist approach change many of their prevalent instructional practices. For example, they reduce the amount of time spent in drill and practice activities and canned labs in favor of increased open-ended

questioning and Socratic dialogue with plenty of wait time. Heuristic learning (trial-and-error) through successive stages of experimentation, reflection, evaluation, and correction is their dominant mode of instruction. Constructivist teachers do not begin a lesson by offering correct model solutions or by correcting a student's work. They focus discussions on the reasoning that supports a variety of student-generated interpretations, including incorrect ones, as a part of the process of constructing knowledge. *The Polished Stones,* a videotape compiled by Harold Stevenson and Shin-Ying Lee (1989), demonstrates how this technique can be used effectively. Students are encouraged to discover how to add fractions by applying what they already know to construct guidelines for themselves as they consider why $\frac{1}{3} + \frac{1}{2}$ does not equal $\frac{2}{5}$.

Here are two examples that illustrate some implications of a constructivist interpretation of learning for the classroom.

Order of Operations

The order of operations in mathematics—exponentiation, multiplication or division, addition or subtraction—has for generations been taught as though it were an immutable fact rather than a social construction. The nonconstructivist approach requires it to be memorized, without questioning its origin. The constructivist interpretation recognizes it as a fact only because it is a rule of convenience agreed on by mathematicians as fitting within a particular schema. As such, it is one rule among a much larger set of socially constructed conventions that are kept in the "algebra" compartment of the box labeled "mathematics."

For example, what is the value of $16 - 2 \times 9 + 54 \div 3^3$? Your answer will depend entirely on the order of operations you apply to interpret this mathematical sentence. The socially constructed (correct) answer is zero only when the order of operations is exponentiation first, then division or multiplication, then addition or subtraction. If we reversed the order of operations and began with addition, the correct answer would be 32.66. The constructivist teacher would first ensure that the students had discovered this principle by examining the consequences of other orders and testing them in a variety of problem contexts before trying to convince the students that zero is the "right" answer.

Invented Spelling

Children acquire language through experimentation. "Wa-wa" becomes "water" though a process of experimentation and feedback. No one requires children to wait to speak until they can speak only in fully formed, accurate words and sentences. A word such as *water* is a social construction, one that varies from language to language—*agua, wasser,* and *mizu* work equally well when you're thirsty, if and only if the form used is supported by the local social construct for the substance scientists call H_2O.

Invented spelling is the child's attempt to express in symbols the group of sounds we call a word. The sentence "i c u cn red ths" mixes letter names and sounds. Invention of a symbol-sound relationship is an early and essential step on the way toward the social construction of the correctly spelled and phonetically similar word associated with a particular event or experience. Gregg shorthand is one form of invented spelling; the only thing about it that is more correct than a child's invented spelling is that it is a symbol-sound system we have collectively agreed to accept.

Though invented spelling is consistent with the assumptions of philosophical constructivism, its applications in actual classroom practice still lack a broad base of empirical support (Brown 1990). The little available research offers more hope than promise when it comes to *improving* children's spelling. What the research shows is that fluency, creativity, and quantity of children's writing increase when invented spelling is allowed, as a part of a comprehensive, developmentally appropriate language arts program.

The Role of Assessment

Q. How do you study?
A. I read, I take notes, I make outlines, and I memorize.

Q. Why do you do this?
A. For the test.

Q. What do you do after the test?
A. I forget it! (Caine and Caine 1991, pp. 13–15)

As the Caines point out, this could be a quote from any student in the United States for the past 50 years. Is this what we want from our students?

It should be evident from the assumptions of constructivism that "to teach well (from a constructivist perspective), we need to know what our students are thinking, how they produce the chain of little marks we see on their papers, and what they can do (or want to do) with the materials we present them" (Noddings 1990). This does not imply that we should be concerned only with what students want to learn. But teachers need to be prepared to help students clarify their own thinking and to build on their existing knowledge base from a student-centered perspective through activities perceived by the student as authentic—grounded in the student's experience, not an artificial implant. After 40 years, I still haven't figured out why it was important for me to read Thomas Hardy's *Return of the Native* in the 8th grade.

Constructivism requires the use of a greater variety of more sophisticated assessment tools and a greater degree of student autonomy to investigate the problem at hand through direct experience (Confrey 1990). Hence, portfolios, performances, and other observational measures become important assessment tools. An essential part of constructivist assessment requires developing protocols for valid, reliable interpretations of the data derived from these tools and correlating the results with other measures of student achievement, including standardized tests. The way we test students is a direct indication of what we value in learning.

Constructivist Classroom Practice in the '90s

As practice is more influenced by constructivist theory, classroom activity will exhibit some of the characteristics suggested by Lauren Resnick (1983), as well as by many other researchers and practitioners:

1. The classroom and school will become an environment in which the child can interact and be actively engaged in an experientially rich learning context—with things, with other children, and with adults.

2. The natural activities of children in interaction with their environment will be encouraged, both in and out of the classroom. "Play time" at recess, at lunch, or after school become learning opportunities. Paint a giant map of the United States on the playground and show young kids how to play Geography Tag—and you'll never have to teach state locations or capital cities again. Recreation is, after all, re-creation of the mind through intellectual exercise, as well as of the body through physical exercise.

3. Time in the classroom devoted to solitary drill and practice will be reduced.

4. Opportunities for invention and discovery will become a planned and valued element of instructional design. The kindergartner's pail of water is a high schooler's science lab; a rain puddle, the child's tidal pool.

5. The teacher's role will shift from *fact-giver to facilitator* who points out contradictions and lets the child work on resolving them. The teacher helps students increase their knowledge base by encouraging them to make "so what?" connections between facts, which are still important to learn. The teacher will become the "guide on the side" rather than the "sage on the stage."

6. Collaborative learning and teaching models will become key strategies, as will activities outside the classroom (constructivist homework). Cross-age learning will occur through mentoring and coaching.

7. Teachers will work more collaboratively in multidisciplinary and interdisciplinary teams to meet learner needs. As teachers give up the role of sole arbiter of knowledge, they are freed to explore issues and concepts more deeply and will feel the need to call on experts or expert systems to answer their own questions, as well as those of the students.

8. School will become more like the real world. Dependence on a single source of information, typically a textbook, will give way to using a variety of information sources, including original source material. This movement will accelerate as various emerging technologies become more readily available and less expensive—such as distance learning through satellite networks, mass storage media (like CD-ROM), and more user-friendly means to access information.

9. The boundaries of "classroom" will become more blurred; groupings based on age-grade distinctions will become less important as students become known for what they have learned rather than how old they are. Also, the amount of formal and informal learning, much of which will occur outside the classroom, for which the student is held accountable, will increase.

Changes will not come quickly, nor will they be easy, because they represent a radical departure from current practice in many cases. These changes require systemic involvement, beginning with a careful examination of constructivism's assumptions. Intellectual acceptance by an individual is insufficient to influence practice. A social commitment by the adult community is required—teachers, administrators, parents, everyone. Beyond intellectual acceptance, the community must make a commitment to action, which requires new behaviors and a reallocation of resources and efforts over an extended period of time. Constructivism is not simply an educational fad, doing the same old things in slightly different ways. It is a different, though not necessarily new, frame of reference or lens through which to view classroom practice and the world.

The constructivist teacher continually asks these questions:

■ In what way does this activity, question, or event contribute to a learner finding meaning—am I telling the student the answer or am I facilitating finding it?

■ Is the learning experience rooted in the child's understanding and experience or mine?

The child becomes the star performer in the spotlight at center stage. The teacher, out of the limelight, is ready in the wings to prompt and coach when needed. Or, to use another metaphor, education is like learning to cook: "None of us would argue that becoming skillful at measuring the ingredients for a recipe is all there is to cooking. Nor could we generate support for endless practice at beating egg whites. We recognize that a skillful cook not only knows the concepts and procedures that help to make a cake but has a sense of how these things fit together and need to be adjusted on a particular day with a particular batch of ingredients and a particular oven to produce an excellent cake" (Glatzer and Lappan 1990). ■

References

Adams, M. J. (1990). *Beginning to Read: Thinking and Learning About Print.* Cambridge, Mass.: Bradford Books/ MIT Press.

Brown, A. S. (1990). "A Review of Recent Research on Spelling." *Educational Psychology Review* 2, 4: 368–370, 379–382.

Caine, R. N., and G. Caine (1991). *Making Connections: Teaching and the Human Brain.* Alexandria, Va.: ASCD.

Kamii, C. (1982). *Constructivist Education: A Direction for the 21st Century.* (Paper with limited circulation). Chicago: Circle Children's Center.

Glatzer, D., and G. Lappan. (1990). "Enhancing the Maintenance of Skills." In *Algebra for Everyone,* edited by E. Edwards. Reston, Va.: National Council of Teachers of Mathematics.

Magoon, A. J. (1977). "Constructivist Approaches in Educational Research." *Review of Educational Research* 47, 4:651–693.

Noelting, G. (1978). *Constructivism as a Model for Cognitive Development and (Eventually) Learning: The Development of Proportional Reasoning in the Child and Adolescent.* Quebec, Canada: Ministry of Education.

Noddings, N. (1990). "Constructivism in Mathematics Education." *Journal for Research in Mathematics Education, Monograph No. 4, Constructivist Views of the Teaching and Learning of Mathematics,* edited by R. B. Davis, C. A. Maher, and N. Noddings. Reston, Va.: National Council of Teachers of Mathematics.

Nuthall, G., and A. Alton-Lee. (1991). "Making the Connection Between Teaching and Learning: Determining How Pupils Learn from the Information They Are Exposed to in the Classroom." Paper presented at the Annual Meeting of the American Educational Research Association, Chicago.

Resnick, L. (1983). "Toward a Cognitive Theory of Instruction." In *Learning and Motivation on the Classroom,* edited by S. G. Paris, G. M. Olson, and H. W. Stevenson. Hillside, N.J.: Lawrence Erlbaum.

Stevenson, H., and L. Shin-Ying. (1989). *The Polished Stone.* (Videotape). Reston, Va.: National Council of Teachers of Mathematics.

Von Glaserfeld, E. (1989). "Constructivism in Education." In *The Encyclopedia of Education—Research and Studies—Supplementary Volume One,* edited by T. Husen and T. N. Postelwaite. New York: Pergamon Press.

POST NOTE

Constructivism is an increasingly important idea in education. Research from cognitive scientists has taught us that when confronted with new learning, human beings "construct" new understandings of relationships and phenomena, rather than simply receiving others' understandings. Learners are always fitting new information into the schema they carry in their heads, or else they adjust or change the schema to fit the new information. As the author of this article states, knowledge is not passively received but actively constructed by learners on a base of prior knowledge, attitudes, and values.

The implications for teachers are enormous. Constructivism suggests that educators should invite students to explore the world's complexity, proposing situations for students to think about and observing how the students use their prior knowledge to confront the problems. When students make errors, teachers can analyze the errors to better understand just how the students are approaching the matter. Throughout the process, teachers must accept that there is no single "right" way to solve a problem.

DISCUSSION QUESTIONS

1. In what ways does constructivism challenge your ideas about how people learn?

2. How do you think constructivism will affect what goes on in classrooms? Describe a scenario in which a teacher, using constructivist principles, conducts a lesson. Choose any subject or grade level you wish.

3. How does constructivism dispute the notion of a fixed world that students need to understand?

Context Matters: Teaching in Japan and in the United States

*Nancy Sato and
Milbrey W. McLaughlin*

Even though such apparently straightforward terms as *teacher* and *student* can be translated easily into Japanese, these simple words convey significantly different meanings in the two cultures. Teachers in the U.S. and Japan hold different expectations, play different roles, and meet different responsibilities in the school workplace and in society. However, few comparative analyses of educational practices and outcomes acknowledge these different, culturally embedded conceptions of teachers and teaching. This article, which is based on a collaborative study between researchers at the University of Tokyo and at Standford University, examines the context surrounding teachers' professional lives with the goal of creating a more solid foundation

At the time this article was written, Nancy Sato was project director, Center for Research on the Context of Teaching, School of Education, Stanford University. Milbrey W. McLaughlin was professor of education and public policy and director of the federally supported Center for Research on the Context of Teaching at Stanford University. Sato, Nancy and Milbrey W. McLaughlin, "Context Matters: Teaching in Japan and in the United States," *Phi Delta Kappan,* January 1992. Copyright © 1992 by Phi Delta Kappa. Reprinted by permission of authors and publisher.

for mutual understanding and for comparative study between the U.S. and Japan.[1] . . .

We examine differences in teachers' roles and responsibilities in Japan and the United States in terms of four broad contexts for teachers and teaching: 1) social norms, values, and expectations; 2) norms of the teaching profession; 3) organizational environment of the school context; and 4) character of teacher/student relations.

Social Context

The broad social and cultural contexts of teachers and teaching in Japan and the United States differ in important ways, especially in terms of the goals society assigns to education, to educational governance, and to the place of learning in the broader culture.

Goals The goals for education and society's expectations for teachers are much broader in Japan than in the United States. America's educational purposes are framed primarily in terms of cognitive achievement and academic performance. For example, the Bush Administration's education plan, America 2000, adopts goals for students of "demonstrated competency in challenging subject matter" and reaching first place "in the world in science and mathematics achievement."[2]

In Japan, the "basic" goals for education encompass a greater range of competencies, including social, aesthetic, and interpersonal skills. As a Japanese science educator explained:

> One of the priorities in selecting [educational] objectives in Japan is to encourage the children to become aware of and respond in a positive manner to beauty and orderliness [in] their environment. One of the most important aspects of Japanese science education is to find ways to inculcate the ideals of beauty and orderliness in nature, love of nature, adjustments to nature, and not to conquer nature.[3]

Several aspects of Japanese educational philosophy support this more inclusive conception of the goals of education. First, skill in human relations is considered essential to the educated person, and Japanese teachers accordingly place high priority on developing students' interpersonal competencies and promoting a sense of social cohesion and collective responsibility among students. Many hours of teacher time, school time, and class time are spent in activities designed to develop peer socialization, peer supervision, and peer teaching/learning skills. The fact that Japanese students advance to each grade with age-level peers regardless of achievement reflects the priority Japanese society places on group identity and cohesion.

Second, the Japanese view academic knowledge as just one part of the more comprehensive goal of developing *ningen* (human beings). *Ningen*, a concept that transcends basic skills and academic achievement, assumes a holistic conception of the students' growth and learning. Japanese educators see a fundamental contrast between this Asian, phenomenological view of education and western concepts of learning that are rooted in scientism.[4] They believe that the broad educational goals set for children cannot be accomplished "if there is a separating and/or a differentiation of heart and body, and if knowledge is provided only through language."[5]

Thus "whole person" education is the ideal in Japan, and teachers' routine responsibilities pertain to aesthetic, physical, mental, moral, and social development. Student guidance, personal habits, motivation, interpersonal relations, and on- and off-campus behavior constitute important components of school activities and of the teachers' responsibility for developing *ningen*. Furthermore, experience with a wealth of non-academic learning activities, such as cultural ceremonies at each grade level, is considered essential to this process as well as to full comprehension of academic subject matter. Thus the longer Japanese school year (240 days compared with 180 days in the U.S.) supports the broader Japanese conception of goals for education and includes more time devoted to non-academic studies and activities (special events, ceremonies, and extracurricular activities) rather than simply more time in conventional academic instruction.

Governance Both Japanese and American teachers complain about what they consider excessive intrusion on their professional autonomy, but the realities of professional decision making are quite different in the two countries. Japanese schools operate in a centralized, nationally controlled school system; teachers throughout Japan must plan their instructional activities within the structure and guidelines prescribed by the Japanese Ministry of Education. . . .

Despite the central policy mandates and within an overall structure and curriculum dictated on a national level, Japanese teachers in fact have significant professional latitude to devise activities and create materials that meet the centrally defined instructional guidelines. In practice, Japanese teachers are actually less controlled in matters of instruction than are most of their American counterparts.

Although the U.S. system is more decentralized in terms of formal governance, many pressures work to restrict teachers' professional latitude. For one, district concerns about legal liability and insurance requirements limit such activities as field trips, sports, and science experiments, all of which Japanese teachers are free to initiate—often at the last minute. Textbooks, curriculum guides, and other "adopted" instructional materials in fact specify the details of the content of classrooms to a greater extent in the U.S. than in Japan.

Moreover, different roles for administrators have different effects on teachers' professional autonomy. Whereas many American administrators define their responsibilities in terms of close supervision and control of practice, most Japanese administrators frame their role in terms of maintaining good relations with the district, buffering teachers from outside influences, and managing the school environment in ways that enable teachers to act in accord with their best professional judgment. Japanese teachers respond to centrally determined objectives by choosing the materials, events, and opportunities appropriate to their students, their locale, and their school.[6] The highly centralized Japanese education system actually requires more planning, curriculum development, instructional decision making, and professional choices at the local level and engenders more diversity at the classroom level than does the apparently less controlled American system.

Social Status The pivotal position of schools in Japanese society and the esteem accorded teachers reflect the high value assigned education by the Japanese. Educating the nation's youth assumes top priority in Japan. One Japanese educator explains the different attitudes toward education in Japan and in the U.S. in terms of natural resources: "Japan has few natural resources, with little mineral and energy resources, and scarce agricultural lands. Many Japanese consider their people to be their most important resource."[7] This educator reasons that Americans assign lower priority to education because the country's many rich natural resources deflect attention from the importance of educating the nation's young.

Whether or not this analysis holds up, cultural factors do play an important role in the differing social importance assigned education in the two countries. Japan has a reading public with a high regard for intellectual and educational pursuits; the importance of literacy and book learning has been prominent since the 19th century. (One recent trend disturbing to adults, however, is that Japanese youths do not read newspapers or books as much as before.) In addition, learning—more generally conceived—constitutes an important aspect of life for all Japanese. Adults and children in Japan tend to have more hobbies (academic, artistic, and athletic) than Americans do, and formal lessons in a variety of activities—e.g., tennis, arts and crafts, languages, calligraphy—are common for people of all ages and from all walks of life.[8]

Given this broad social regard for and participation in learning, the responsibility for educating Japan's young people is shared by many segments of society. In contrast to the relative institutional isolation of schools in America, education in Japan takes place in an articulated and mutually reinforcing network, both inside and outside schools. This network includes business, the media, government, community organizations, and the family. It is assumed that a variety of educative agents and institutions contribute to the education of Japanese youth and adults.[9]

Compared with the U.S., there is a greater degree of mutual obligation and responsibility between teachers, parents, and students within Japanese schools and between schools and other institutions in society. The Japanese assume that everyone must share in the effort to educate the young. When problems occur, everyone is expected to accept responsibility, although schools and teachers bear the main responsibility for education. . . .

Professional Context

Norms established within the teaching profession combine with social expectations to further differentiate the roles and responsibilities of Japanese teachers from those of their American counterparts. Perhaps most striking are differences in the amount of time spent on professional growth and development.

Japanese teachers have a strong commitment to their profession and are dedicated to maximizing their own professional growth and that of their peers. Thus teachers in Japan systematically engage in a wide variety of activities aimed at expanding their professional expertise. Some participate in formal research groups; journal articles by teachers about their educational research outnumber by a third those of university educational researchers in Japan.[10] Other teachers form voluntary study groups in which members review and critically evaluate one another's curriculum activities and ideas. These groups meet outside of school time and take up such diverse topics as painting techniques, choir conducting, poetry, voice projection, teaching handsprings, and social studies concepts. Student work—drawings, cassette tapes of singing, and videotapes of classroom activity or of physical education—forms the basis for study group meetings. Some teachers participate in short training courses or institutes that deal with such topics as volleyball or computing.

In addition to these outside activities, Japanese teachers regularly hold professional development activities in the school with the dual goal of enhancing individual competence and fostering group identity. An observer comments: "Individual teachers are given the chance to demonstrate to the other teachers in the school the teaching techniques they are developing in order to emphasize the value of being recognized as an important part of the group, or school."[11] In short, Japanese teachers' involvement in professional growth activities is continuing and is a central aspect of their professional lives.

In contrast, American teachers report low levels of involvement in professional organizations and spend little of their personal time on activities related to their professional growth.[12] American teachers allocate their free time to family activities and social or religious groups, and they draw clear lines between their personal and their professional time. A teaching job in the U.S. carries no institutionalized expectation about professional development outside of school hours.

Professional norms and arrangements also require Japanese teachers to allocate more time to their jobs. Because schools run Monday through Saturday noon and fewer vacation days dot the calendar, Japanese teachers work many more days than do their American counterparts. Moreover, professional norms dictate that they work more than just the 240 scheduled school days. Various meetings, administrative tasks, and curriculum planning must be carried out during the two-week breaks at the New Year and between school years. Since teaching is considered a full-time occupation, teacher salaries reflect 12 months of work, and teachers are forbidden to do any other paid work, even on their own time. In contrast, approximately one-third of American teachers "moonlight" on other jobs, and most of those jobs are unrelated to education.[13]

The number of hours that Japanese teachers spend at school also greatly exceed the time put in by American teachers. Most Japanese teachers get to work early (between 7 and 7:30 a.m.) and stay late (until 5 or 6 p.m. and later) to prepare for the next day, to consult with one another, and to tend to other administrative tasks. Teachers' professional roles and socially defined responsibilities in Japan encompass a broad range of administrative, teaching, parental outreach, and counseling duties involving attention to the cognitive, social psychological, emotional, and physical well-being of their students—on and off campus. . . .

Just as teachers' duties are not limited to the classroom, students are accountable to their teachers for a wide range of personal and academic habits beyond school walls. For example, prior to each vacation period, students must submit to their teachers daily schedules, listing what they will do (watch TV, read) and when (wake-up times, bedtimes, study times, play times). Teachers read and approve or revise each schedule. Then parents, students, and teachers sign the document as a mutual pact. If any misbehavior happens outside of school, witnesses often report it to the school (rather than to the family). Teachers and principals are then responsible for contacting parents and handling the affair with them. In cases of stealing, teachers, principals, and parents must all apologize in person to the store owners. School rules regulate much of the students' personal lives: their appearance, their study and personal habits, and their behaviors. For Japanese students, the school is the primary organization in their lives.

School Context

Our surveys highlight many differences in the school context for Japanese and American teachers. U.S. teachers rate the support of principals and site administrators higher than do Japanese teachers. But Japanese teachers feel that they can depend on more help from fellow teachers. Japanese teachers also believe that they have more influence over school policy. Their lower ratings of support from principals and site administrators may reflect the fact that many responsibilities of school administration and program planning are delegated to teachers in Japan.

Interestingly, Japanese and American teachers' ratings of "collegiality" are quite similar. Yet what they mean by collegial relations and work arrangements differs substantially. Some of the differences can be explained by differing expectations of kinds, degrees, and frequency of collegial contact. And the high level of collaboration and collegiality among Japanese teachers surely derives in part from structural and cultural aspects of the school.

Interdependence The school context reflects and reinforces the professional context in Japan, especially in the degree of interdependence and networking required. Many areas of Japanese society mirror the expectations and demands placed on students, and the congruence between the adult world and the student world—particularly in terms of obligations, expectations, and work patterns—is invaluable to the successful daily operations of each classroom and of the school as a whole. Teachers' work arrangements often mirror those established for students. For example, one school-level integrating structure in Japanese schools is the whole-staff meeting. Every day begins with a whole-staff meeting; just as students meet in their classroom groups, so teachers meet to reaffirm purpose, to resolve problems, and to set goals. Teachers, like students, work together in cooperative groups, have interdependent work assignments, and have rotating duties that all must perform. Some of the duties assumed by teachers and students are even the same: teachers participate in school management and administration in the same way that students participate in classroom management and administration.

A complex subcommittee structure supports these activities and is outlined in each school's particular *komubunsho* (division of school duties). In addition, teachers are divided into grade-level and mixed-grade-level subcommittees to deal with such administrative areas as finance, health and nutrition, student guidance and activities, textbook selection, and schoolwide curriculum development and planning with representatives from each grade level.

In addition to teaching their homeroom classes, teachers share responsibilities for running student councils, club activities, and whole-grade and whole-school activities, events and ceremonies. These tasks are accepted as the duties of Japanese teachers. American teachers, by contrast, generally see such duties as "extra," and in many districts these activities are subjects for collective bargaining and are regulated by contracts. The result is that not all U.S. teachers involve themselves in extracurricular activities, and their opportunities to interact with colleagues and their sense of "professional responsibility" differ accordingly.

Physical Layout The physical arrangements of Japanese schools also shape the character and frequency of collegial interchange. Teachers' main work desks are in the faculty room, and their classroom desks are used just for teaching and student work, primarily during classroom time. The common working room for all teachers signals the existence of a cohesive work group, akin to a "family." Ongoing communication is facilitated by the open space in the working room, which allows for constant contact, interaction, and negotiations. In addition, this arrangement reflects the strong identification of the classroom as the students' "castle." The classroom is the realm of the students, not of the teachers.[14] High school teachers also have separate departmental rooms where faculty members from each department can gather. But high school teachers are criticized if they spend too much time sequestered from the rest of their colleagues.

By contrast, American teachers complain of the lack of common space where they can come together routinely, by grade level or department, to confer about students, practice, and problems. American teachers value the opportunities for such collegial interactions and assert that, without common space, the daily interactions that form the heart of substantive, positive collegial relations simply cannot occur. The physical layout of most American schools discourages rather than encourages regular teacher exchange, and the provision of the necessary common space seems low on planners' and administrators' lists of important organizational attributes.[15]

Contractual Arrangements The required rotation of teachers and administrators is another feature of Japanese schools that necessitates continuous communication. Districts throughout Japan differ, but in Tokyo administrators change schools every three or four years, and teachers change every six or seven years. Organizationally, this means that each year several veteran staff members leave and several new members arrive. The new members include a range of veteran teachers (those who have taught for many years) and of novice teachers. Incoming teachers—veterans and novices—are equally unfamiliar with the school's climate, relations, activities, and modes of operation. Thus, regardless of years of teaching experience, teachers come to depend on one another to learn about their new school.[16] With structural and normative interdependence, lively camaraderie and constant communication characterize the lives of students and teachers in Japan.

American schools and contexts for collegial exchange stand in stark contrast to those in Japan. The isolation of American teachers "behind the classroom door" and the "egg crate" compartmentalization of schools are commonplace in the U.S. Few American teachers have the physical space or the available time to work together in the way Japanese teachers do. And few school-level structures exist to stimulate collaboration or collective problem solving. Furthermore, professional norms of privacy constrain the open examination of practice and the collegial exchange that characterize Japanese schools. The strong collaborative relationships and the sense of belonging to a professional community that are the norm in Japan are the exception in the United States.

Classroom Context The classroom constitutes yet another culturally determined context for teaching and learning. Japanese teachers generally function more as facilitators and "knowledge guides" than as dispensers of information and facts.[17] Japanese teachers traditionally have subscribed to what Americans call "situated cognition" or "teaching for understanding." Accordingly, Japanese teachers view knowledge as something to be constructed by students rather than to be transmitted by the teacher. . . .

Consistent with this constructivist view of teaching and learning, much more authority for classroom management and control is delegated to students. Consequently, Japanese teachers spend much less time on direct discipline and classroom management issues than do American teachers. Instead, their time is spent guiding interpersonal relations and arranging the instructional patterns of mixed-ability grouping in the belief that peer supervision, peer teaching, and group learning can be more effective for all students.[18]

This conception of classroom processes and of the teacher's role is one strategy for dealing with diversity in Japanese classrooms. At the school level, diversity is also dealt with on an individual basis in terms of personality, academic interests, and accomplishments. For example, moving whole classes along together (regardless of achievement) may create a greater range of abilities within Japanese classrooms than is likely to occur in the U.S., where retention is common and skipping grades is not unheard of. However, Japanese teachers feel strongly that all students can learn from the diversity within the group.

Moreover, Japanese teachers assume that successful group work depends on substantial shared personal knowledge of individual students. Whereas American educators sometimes see "individualized instruction" or "whole-group instruction" as dichotomies, Japanese educators see them as complementary. Japanese teachers believe that the whole-group lesson, when done well, can benefit every child and teach important lessons about social interaction and problem solving, as well as about subject content.

With these different cultural norms and assumptions about classroom roles, "student disruption" in Japan is seen more as the students' mutual responsibility than as the sole responsibility of the teacher. Americans and Japanese also appear to have a different conception of what constitutes "disruption," at least at the elementary level. Most Americans visiting Japanese classrooms notice that noise levels are much higher than are typically permitted in American classrooms; these differences reflect different levels of tolerance as well as fundamental pedagogical differences: Japan's group processes, built around peer interaction, as opposed to America's teacher-led lessons or individual seatwork.

The idea of "personalization" is highly valued by teachers in both countries. But personalization conveys different meanings in the two cultures and carries different implications for the obligations and activities of teachers. In Japan, getting to know a student requires yearly visits to the student's home, active teacher involvement in vacation and leisure time planning, and, above all, universal participation of teachers and students in a variety of academic and nonacademic activities. The regularly scheduled extracurricular activities, school and classroom cleaning time, and numerous monitoring duties are central to student life and learning. Teachers see these activities as primary vehicles for getting to know the diverse strengths and weaknesses of the students and for increasing student motivation, engagement, and achievement.

Furthermore, participation in activities is every student's right, not a privilege to be manipulated for control or extended as a reward for achievement. No student is denied participation because of behavioral or academic problems, and—just as important—no student receives special attention or rewards because of excellent performance. Most significantly, in order to enhance group solidarity and individual recognition for all students, selection for various activities is by rotation (including all students), by chance (e.g., rock-scissors-paper game), or by student election rather than by teacher designation. These practices are seen as important ways to ensure fairness and avoid favoritism.[19]

Both Japanese and American teachers point to the value of interacting with students outside the homeroom as a way to obtain multiple views of their own and other students; such personal knowledge in turn contributes to the quality of relations that teachers and students build in classrooms. Yet only in Japan is this extra-classroom function an integral part of teachers' duties.

The structure of Japanese teachers' workdays accommodates this broader conception of role: Japanese teachers do not teach all day, as do American teachers. Japanese teachers spend many more hours at school each day than do American teachers, but they typically have fewer teaching hours. Only about 60% of their school time is spent in classroom activities; the remainder of the day is spent carrying out extracurricular responsibilities and fulfilling other duties to the school.[20]

Context Matters

Teachers' roles and responsibilities in Japan and in the U.S. are products of the cultures in which they are embedded. Both American and Japanese teachers distinguish clearly between their roles and those of students and their families. But because Japanese teachers are responsible for developing skills and knowledge "beyond the basics," their roles include—in addition to developing traditional academic competencies—overseeing the growth of youngsters' social skills, aesthetic sensitivity, and personal habits. This broader role for teachers and for schools reflects Japanese society's espoused goals for education and its conception of *ningen*.

Japanese teachers and American teachers also differ in the extent to which their professional and personal lives are clearly demarcated. Whereas American teachers protect their out-of-school time as "off duty" time to be used for friends, family, and social events and allocate little of this time to professional development activities, Japanese teachers routinely spend significant portions of their "free" time engaged in completing school obligations or in various types of professional growth activities. The high level of continuing professional development in Japan mirrors the high priority given learning of all forms by Japanese society. Teachers' engagement with professional activities beyond the "official" workday comports with this cultural norm.

Japanese teachers enjoy support for and take direction from an intricate social web of citizens, families and public and private agencies. In this context, such matters as student disruption, collegiality, parent involvement, professional development, public regard for education, and even educational goals carry meanings substantively different from those Americans associate with them. Comparisons of teachers and teaching—and of students and learning—across Japanese and American cultures must take account of these culturally embedded differences if the conclusions drawn from such comparisons are to be valid and the interpretations of survey responses clearly understood. ■

Notes

1. The collaborative study came about through the efforts of the Japan/United States Teacher Education Consortium (JUSTEC) a group of approximately 70 professors from schools of education that convenes annually to discuss issues in teacher education. Professors Tadahiko Inagaki and Yasuhiro Ito of the University of Tokyo developed the Japanese survey, administered both questionnaires, carried out analyses of the U.S. and Japanese survey data, and provided helpful comments on a draft of this article.

2. *America 2000: An Education Strategy* (Washington, D.C.: U.S. Department of Education, 1991), p. 19.

3. Shigekazu Takemura, "A Study of Knowledge Base for Science Teaching as Perceived by Elementary School Teachers in Japan and the United States," paper presented at the annual meeting of JUSTEC, Stanford University, July 1991, p. 8.

4. The distinction between these two philosophies of education occupied a prominent place in the discussions that took place at the July 1991 meeting of JUSTEC at Stanford University. In the view of Japanese professors of education, the two education systems reflect these root differences in many aspects of schooling and teacher training.

5. Takahisa Ichimura, "A Philosophical Approach to the 'Knowledge Base' in Teacher Education," paper presented at the annual meeting of JUSTEC, Stanford University, July 1991, p. 3.

6. See, for example, James W. Stigler and Harold W. Stevenson, "How Asian Teachers Polish Every Lesson to Perfection," *American Educator*, Spring 1991, pp. 12–47.

7. Takemura, p. 3.

8. Involvement in hobbies is true especially of housewives and those whose jobs do not require long hours. Japanese "salarymen" rarely have time for such pursuits, but they nonetheless see them as integral to family life.

9. One problematic feature of the Japanese education system is the existence of *juku* (private cram schools). Their function and their influence on schooling are serious issues in Japan, along with the strong pressures exerted by the system of college entrance examinations. Moreover, Japanese educators have noted a decline in participation in informal educational activities, especially those in the home.

10. Manabu Sato, "Issues in Japanese Teacher Education," in Howard Leavitt et al., eds., *International Handbook of Teacher Education* (San Francisco: Greenwood Press, forthcoming).

11. Takemura, p. 17.

12. Inagaki, Ito, and Sato, op. cit.

13. *1989 CRC Report to Field Sites* (Stanford, Calif.: Center for Research on the Context of Secondary School Teaching, Stanford University, November 1989).

14. In middle schools, the students stay in their homeroom throughout the day, and the teachers rotate in and out. In elementary schools, the classroom is occupied jointly by the students and their homeroom teacher, who is responsible for teaching all subjects. Typically, teachers stay with their students for at least two years.

15. CRC surveys found that measures of collegiality varied as much *within* schools as between them. When asked to explain these differences, teachers quickly pointed to the presence or absence of a common space, a place to gather as a department for coffee or for lunch. Most departments in our sample had no such spaces.

16. A commendable offshoot of this required rotation is that teachers develop friendships and professional contacts that span the boundaries of schools and districts and form an ever-widening network of professional contacts.

17. See, for example, Stigler and Stevenson, op cit.

18. For a discussion of teachers' roles in managing group processes in Japanese elementary schools, see Sato, op. cit.

19. As one teacher explained, those students who cause the worst behavior problems or who perform least well are the very ones who need additional opportunities to socialize, to build better relations with teachers and peers, and to take on responsibilities if they are to improve their performance and learning.

20. Stigler and Stevenson, p. 45.

POST NOTE

During the 1980s, as the Japanese economic system was booming, the American education system was under fire by critics. According to those critics, poor U.S. economic performance was the result of an inferior educational system; the Japanese system, on the other hand, produced the kind of workers required to support a high-technology economy. Accordingly, many studies of the Japanese educational system were conducted to determine what we might learn from the Japanese.

This particular study focused on teachers and their different roles in the United States and Japan. It concluded that the roles and expectations for teachers in the two countries differed considerably. The role of Japanese teachers is broader than that of American teachers; namely, Japanese teachers are expected to assist students in developing their "whole person," including aesthetic, physical, mental, moral, and social development. This means that Japanese teachers see their role as extending beyond the school and into the personal lives of their students; teachers enjoy a high level of support for this role from many elements of Japanese society. American teachers, however, make a much clearer distinction between their school role as teacher and their private role. American teachers also spend much less time on professional development activities than do Japanese teachers. The roles and responsibilities of Japanese and American teachers clearly differ.

Since this article first appeared, international comparisons of student achievement have continued. For example, in the Third International Mathematics and Science Study (TIMSS), the largest and most comprehensive international study of schools and students ever conducted, U.S. eighth graders scored slightly below average in mathematics and slightly above average in science. Early analyses of the data indicate that U.S. textbooks and teachers cover many more topics in less depth than those in high-scoring countries, and the content of U.S. mathematics classes is not as challenging. The report concludes that fundamental changes are needed in teacher knowledge, working conditions, curricula quality, student expectations, and textbook content.

DISCUSSION QUESTIONS

1. Which aspects of the Japanese system would you like to see implemented in the United States? Why?

2. In which country do you think teaching is more difficult? Why?

3. In what ways are the two societies different? How do those differences affect the countries' respective educational systems?

Part Six

Foundations

A s a career, education is a practical field like medicine or criminal justice. It is not a discipline or content area, such as anthropology, physics, or English literature. However, education draws on these various disciplines and fields of knowledge to guide teachers in their work.

The term *foundations* refers to the particular group of academic disciplines that the practice of education draws on quite heavily, including philosophy, history, psychology, and sociology. It is often said that a house is as good as the foundation upon which it rests. In our view, likewise, the most effective teaching is firmly grounded on these educational foundations.

Part Six

My Pedagogic Creed

John Dewey

Article I—What Education Is

I believe that

- all education proceeds by the participation of the individual in the social consciousness of the race. This process begins unconsciously almost at birth, and is continually shaping the individual's powers, saturating his consciousness, forming his habits, training his ideas, and arousing his feelings and emotions. Through this unconscious education the individual gradually comes to share in the intellectual and moral resources which humanity has succeeded in getting together. He becomes an inheritor of the funded capital of civilization. The most formal and technical education in the world cannot safely depart from this general process. It can only organize it or differentiate it in some particular direction.

- the only true education comes through the stimulation of the child's powers by the demands of the social situations in which he finds himself. Through these demands he is stimulated to act as a member of a unity, to emerge from his original narrowness of action and feeling, and to conceive of himself from the standpoint of the welfare of the group to which he belongs. Through the responses which others make to his own activities he comes to know what these mean in social terms. The value which they have is reflected back into them. For instance, through the response which is made to the child's instinctive babblings the child comes to know what those babblings mean; they are transformed into articulate language, and thus the child is introduced into the consolidated wealth of ideas and emotions which are now summed up in language.

- this educational process has two sides— one psychological and one sociological—and that neither can be subordinated to the other, or neglected, without evil results following. Of these two sides, the psychological is the basis. The child's own instincts and powers furnish the material and give the starting-point for all education. Save as the efforts of the educator connect with some activity which the child is carrying on of his own initiative independent of the educator, education becomes reduced to a pressure from without. It may, indeed, give certain external results, but cannot truly be called educative. Without insight into the psychological structure and activities of the individual the educative process will, therefore, be haphazard and arbitrary. If it chances to coincide with the child's activity it will get a leverage; if it does not, it will result in friction, or disintegration, or arrest of the child-nature.

- knowledge of social conditions, of the present state of civilization, is necessary in order properly to interpret the child's powers. The child has his own instincts and tendencies, but we do not know what these mean until we can translate them into their social equivalents. We must be able to carry them back into a social past and see them as the inheritance of previous race activities. We must also be able to project them into the future to see what their outcome and end will be. In the illustration just used, it is the ability to see in the child's babblings the promise and potency of a future social intercourse and conversation which enables one to deal in the proper way with that instinct.

- the psychological and social sides are organically related, and that education cannot be regarded as a compromise between the two, or a superimposition of one upon the other. We are told that the psychological definition of education is barren and formal—that it gives us only the

John Dewey was a philosopher and educator; he founded the progressive education movement. This article was published originally as a pamphlet by E. L. Kellogg and Co., 1897.

idea of a development of all the mental powers without giving us any idea of the use to which these powers are put. On the other hand, it is urged that the social definition of education, as getting adjusted to civilization, makes of it a forced and external process, and results in subordinating the freedom of the individual to a preconceived social and political status.

■ each of these objections is true when urged against one side isolated from the other. In order to know what a power really is we must know what its end, use, or function is, and this we cannot know save as we conceive of the individual as active in social relationships. But, on the other hand, the only possible adjustment which we can give to the child under existing conditions is that which arises through putting him in complete possession of all his powers. With the advent of democracy and modern industrial conditions, it is impossible to foretell definitely just what civilization will be twenty years from now. Hence it is impossible to prepare the child for any precise set of conditions. To prepare him for the future life means to give him command of himself; it means so to train him that he will have the full and ready use of all his capacities; that his eye and ear and hand may be tools ready to command, that his judgment may be capable of grasping the conditions under which it has to work, and the executive forces be trained to act economically and efficiently. It is impossible to reach this sort of adjustment save as constant regard is had to the individual's own powers, tastes, and interests—that is, as education is continually converted into psychological terms.

In sum, I believe that the individual who is to be educated is a social individual, and that society is an organic union of individuals. If we eliminate the social factor from the child we are left only with an abstraction; if we eliminate the individual factor from society, we are left only with an inert and lifeless mass. Education, therefore, must begin with a psychological insight into the child's capacities, interests, and habits. It must be controlled at every point by reference to these same considerations. These powers, interests, and habits must be continually interpreted—we must know what they mean. They must be translated into terms of their social equivalents—into terms of what they are capable of in the way of social service.

Article II—What the School Is

I believe that

■ the school is primarily a social institution. Education being a social process, the school is simply that form of community life in which all those agencies are concentrated that will be most effective in bringing the child to share in the inherited resources of the race, and to use his own powers for social ends.

■ education, therefore, is a process of living and not a preparation for future living.

■ the school must represent present life—life as real and vital to the child as that which he carries on in the home, in the neighborhood, or on the playground.

■ that education which does not occur through forms of life, forms that are worth living for their own sake, is always a poor substitute for the genuine reality, and tends to cramp and to deaden.

■ the school, as an institution, should simplify existing social life; should reduce it, as it were, to an embryonic form. Existing life is so complex that the child cannot be brought into contact with it without either confusion or distraction; he is either overwhelmed by the multiplicity of activities which are going on, so that he loses his own power of orderly reaction, or he is so stimulated by these various activities that his powers are prematurely called into play and he becomes either unduly specialized or else disintegrated.

■ as such simplified social life, the school life should grow gradually out of the home life; that it should take up and continue the activities with which the child is already familiar in the home.

■ it should exhibit these activities to the child, and reproduce them in such ways that the child will gradually learn the meaning of them, and be capable of playing his own part in relation to them.

- this is a psychological necessity, because it is the only way of securing continuity in the child's growth, the only way of giving a background of past experience to the new ideas given in school.

- it is also a social necessity because the home is the form of social life in which the child has been nurtured and in connection with which he has had his moral training. It is the business of the school to deepen and extend his sense of the values bound up in his home life.

- much of the present education fails because it neglects this fundamental principle of the school as a form of community life. It conceives the school as a place where certain information is to be given, where certain lessons are to be learned, or where certain habits are to be formed. The value of these is conceived as lying largely in the remote future; the child must do these things for the sake of something else he is to do; they are mere preparations. As a result they do not become a part of the life experience of the child and so are not truly educative.

- the moral education centers upon this conception of the school as a mode of social life, that the best and deepest moral training is precisely that which one gets through having to enter into proper relations with others in a unity of work and thought. The present educational systems, so far as they destroy or neglect this unity, render it difficult or impossible to get any genuine, regular moral training.

- the child should be stimulated and controlled in his work through the life of the community.

- under existing conditions far too much of the stimulus and control proceeds from the teacher, because of neglect of the idea of the school as a form of social life.

- the teacher's place and work in the school is to be interpreted from this same basis. The teacher is not in the school to impose certain ideas or to form certain habits in the child, but is there as a member of the community to select the influences which shall affect the child and to assist him in properly responding to these influences.

- the discipline of the school should proceed from the life of the school as a whole and not directly from the teacher.

- the teacher's business is simply to determine, on the basis of larger experience and riper wisdom, how the discipline of life shall come to the child.

- all questions of the grading of the child and his promotion should be determined by reference to the same standard. Examinations are of use only so far as they test the child's fitness for social life and reveal the place in which he can be of the most service and where he can receive the most help.

Article III—The Subject-Matter of Education

I believe that

- the social life of the child is the basis of concentration, or correlation, in all his training or growth. The social life gives the unconscious the unity and the background of all his efforts and of all his attainments.

- the subject-matter of the school curriculum should mark a gradual differentiation out of the primitive unconscious unity of social life.

- we violate the child's nature and render difficult the best ethical results by introducing the child too abruptly to a number of special studies, of reading, writing, geography, etc., out of relation to this social life.

- the true center of correlation on the school subjects is not science, nor literature, nor history, nor geography, but the child's own social activities.

- education cannot be unified in the study of science, or so-called nature study, because apart from human activity, nature itself is not a unity; nature in itself is a number of diverse objects in space and time, and to attempt to make it the center of work by itself is to introduce a principle of radiation rather than one of concentration.

- literature is the reflex expression and interpretation of social experience; that hence it must follow upon and not precede such experience. It, therefore, cannot be made the basis, although it may be made the summary of unification.

■ history is of educative value in so far as it presents phases of social life and growth. It must be controlled by reference to social life. When taken simply as history it is thrown into the distant past and becomes dead and inert. Taken as the record of man's social life and progress it becomes full of meaning. I believe, however, that it cannot be so taken excepting as the child is also introduced directly into social life.

■ the primary basis of education is in the child's powers at work along the same general constructive lines as those which have brought civilization into being.

■ the only way to make the child conscious of his social heritage is to enable him to perform those fundamental types of activity which make civilization what it is.

■ the so-called expressive or constructive activities are the center of correlation.

■ this gives the standard for the place of cooking, sewing, manual training, etc., in the school.

■ they are not special studies which are to be introduced over and above a lot of others in the way of relaxation or relief, or as additional accomplishments. I believe rather that they represent, as types, fundamental forms of social activity, and that it is possible and desirable that the child's introduction into the more formal subjects of the curriculum be through the medium of these activities.

■ the study of science is educational in so far as it brings out the materials and processes which make social life what it is.

■ one of the greatest difficulties in the present teaching of science is that the material is presented in purely objective form, or is treated as a new peculiar kind of experience which the child can add to that which he has already had. In reality, science is of value because it gives the ability to interpret and control the experience already had. It should be introduced, not as so much new subject-matter, but as showing the factors already involved in previous experience and

as furnishing tools by which that experience can be more easily and effectively regulated.

■ at present we lose much of the value of literature and language studies because of our elimination of the social element. Language is almost always treated in the books of pedagogy simply as the expression of thought. It is true that language is a logical instrument, but it is fundamentally and primarily a social instrument. Language is the device for communication; it is the tool through which one individual comes to share the ideas and feelings of others. When treated simply as a way of getting individual information, or as a means of showing off what one had learned, it loses its social motive and end.

■ there is, therefore, no succession of studies in the ideal school curriculum. If education is life, all life has, from the outset, a scientific aspect, an aspect of art and culture, and an aspect of communication. It cannot, therefore, be true that the proper studies for one grade are mere reading and writing, and that at a later grade, reading, or literature, or science, may be introduced. The progress is not in the succession of studies, but in the development of new attitudes towards, and new interests in, experience.

■ education must be conceived as a continuing reconstruction of experience; that the process and the goal of education are one and the same thing.

■ to set up any end outside of education, as furnishing its goal and standard, is to deprive the educational process of much of its meaning, and tends to make us rely upon false and external stimuli in dealing with the child.

Article IV—The Nature of Method

I believe that

■ the question of method is ultimately reducible to the question of the order of development of the child's powers and interests. The law for presenting and treating material is the law implicit within the child's own nature. Because this is so I believe the following statements are of supreme importance as determining the spirit in which education is carried on:

- the active side precedes the passive in the development of the child-nature; that expression comes before conscious impression; that the muscular development precedes the sensory; that movements come before conscious sensation; I believe that consciousness is essentially motor or impulsive; that conscious states tend to project themselves in action.

- the neglect of this principle is the cause of a large part of the waste of time and strength in school work. The child is thrown into a passive, receptive, or absorbing attitude. The conditions are such that he is not permitted to follow the law of nature; the result is friction and waste.

- ideas (intellectual and rational processes) also result from action and devolve for the sake of the better control of action. What we term reason is primarily the law of orderly and effective action. To attempt to develop the reasoning powers, the powers of judgment, without reference to the selection and arrangement of means in action, is the fundamental fallacy in our present methods of dealing with this matter. As a result we present the child with arbitrary symbols. Symbols are a necessity in mental development, but they have their place as tools for economizing effort; presented by themselves they are a mass of meaningless and arbitrary ideas imposed from without.

- the image is the great instrument of instruction. What a child gets out of any subject presented to him is simply the images which he himself forms with regard to it.

- if nine-tenths of the energy at present directed towards making the child learn certain things were spent in seeing to it that the child was forming proper images, the work of instruction would be indefinitely facilitated.

- much of the time and attention now given to the preparation and presentation of lessons might be more wisely and profitably expended in training the child's power of imagery and in seeing to it that he was continually forming definite, vivid, and growing images of the various subjects with which he comes in contact in his experience.

- interests are the signs and symptoms of growing power. I believe that they represent dawning capacities. Accordingly the constant and careful observation of interests is of the utmost importance for the educator.

- these interests are to be observed as showing the state development which the child has reached.

- they prophesy the stage upon which he is about to enter.

- Only through the continual and sympathetic observation of childhood's interests can the adult enter into the child's life and see what it is ready for, and upon what material it could work most readily and fruitfully.

- these interests are neither to be humored nor repressed. To repress interest is to substitute the adult for the child, and so to weaken intellectual curiosity and alertness, to suppress initiative, and to deaden interest. To humor the interests is to substitute the transient for the permanent. The interest is always the sign of some power below; the important thing is to discover this power. To humor the interest is to fail to penetrate below the surface, and its sure result is to substitute caprice and whim for genuine interest.

- the emotions are the reflex of actions.

- to endeavor to stimulate or arouse the emotions apart from their corresponding activities is to introduce an unhealthy and morbid state of mind.

- if we can only secure right habits of action and thought, with reference to the good, the true, and the beautiful, the emotions will for the most part take care of themselves.

- next to deadness and dullness, formalism and routine, our education is threatened with no greater evil than sentimentalism.

- this sentimentalism is the necessary result of the attempt to divorce feeling from action.

Article V—The School and Social Progress

I believe that

- education is the fundamental method of social progress and reform.

- all reforms which rest simply upon enactment of law, or the threatening of certain penalties, or upon changes in mechanical or outward arrangements, are transitory and futile.

- education is a regulation of the process of coming to share in the social consciousness; and that the adjustment of individual activity on the basis of this social consciousness is the only sure method of social reconstruction.

- this conception has due regard for both the individualistic and socialistic ideals. It is duly individual because it recognizes the formation of a certain character as the only genuine basis of right living. It is socialistic because it recognizes that this right character is not to be formed by merely individual precept, example, or exhortation, but rather by the influence of a certain form of institutional or community life upon the individual, and that the social organism through the school, as its organ, may determine ethical results.

- in the ideal school we have the reconciliation of the individualistic and the institutional ideals

- the community's duty to education is, therefore, its paramount moral duty. By law and punishment, by social agitation and discussion, society can regulate and form itself in a more or less haphazard and chance way. But through education society can formulate its own purposes, can organize its own means and resources, and thus shape itself with definiteness and economy in the direction in which it wishes to move.

- when society once recognizes the possibilities in this direction, and the obligations which these possibilities impose, it is impossible to conceive of the resources of time, attention, and money which will be put at the disposal of the educator.

- it is the business of every one interested in education to insist upon the school as the primary and most effective interest of social progress and reform in order that society may be awakened to realize what the school stands for, and aroused to the necessity of endowing the educator with sufficient equipment properly to perform his task.

- education thus conceived marks the most perfect and intimate union of science and art conceivable in human experience.

- the art of thus giving shape to human powers and adapting them to social service is the supreme art; one calling into its service the best of artists; that no insight, sympathy, tact, executive power, is too great for such service

- with the growth of psychological service, giving added insight into individual structure and laws of growth; and with growth of social science, adding to our knowledge of the right organization of individuals, all scientific resources can be utilized for the purpose of education.

- when science and art thus join hands the most commanding motive for human action will be reached, the most genuine springs of human conduct aroused, and the best service that human nature is capable of guaranteed.

- the teacher is engaged, not simply in the training of individuals, but in the formation of the proper social life.

- every teacher should realize the dignity of his calling; that he is a social servant set apart for the maintenance of proper social order and the securing of the right social growth.

- in this way the teacher always is the prophet of the true God and the usherer in of the true kingdom of God. ∎

POST **N** OTE

John Dewey, the father of progressivism, was the most influential educational thinker of the last 100 years. Many of the beliefs expressed in this article (originally published in 1897) have greatly affected educational practice in America. What we find most curious is how current some of these statements still are. On the other hand, many seem dated and clearly from another era. Those that appeal to altruism and idealism have a particularly old-fashioned ring to them. The question remains, however: Which is "out of sync"—the times or the appeals to idealism and altruism?

DISCUSSION QUESTIONS

1. How relevant do you believe Dewey's statements are today? Why?

2. Which of Dewey's beliefs do you personally agree or disagree with? Why?

3. How does Dewey's statement that "education . . . is a process of living and not a preparation for future living" compare with B. F. Skinner's position in his article "The Free and Happy Student" (see article 48)?

The Educated Person

46

Ernest L. Boyer

A s we anticipate a new century, I am drawn back to questions that have, for generations, perplexed educators and philosophers and parents. What *is* an educated person? What *should* schools be teaching to students?

In searching for answers to these questions, we must consider first not the curriculum, but the human condition. And we must reflect especially on two essential realities of life. First, each person is unique. In defining goals, it is crucial for educators to affirm the special characteristics of each student. We must create in schools a climate in which students are empowered, and we must find ways in the nation's classrooms to celebrate the potential of each child. But beyond the diversity of individuals, educators also must acknowledge a second reality: the deeply rooted characteristics that bind together the human community. We must show students that people around the world share a great many experiences. Attention to both these aspects of our existence is critical to any discussion of what all children should learn.

What, then, does it mean to be an educated person? It means developing one's own aptitudes and interests and discovering the diversity that makes us each unique. And it means becoming permanently empowered with language proficiency, general knowledge, social confidence, and moral awareness in order to be economically and civically successful. But becoming well educated also means discovering the connectedness of things. Educators must help students see relationships across the disciplines and learn that education is a communal act, one that affirms not only individualism, but community. And for these goals to be accomplished, we need a new curriculum framework that is both comprehensive and coherent, one that can encompass existing subjects and integrate fragmented content while relating the curriculum to the realities of life. This curriculum must address the uniqueness of students' histories and experiences, but it also must guide them to understand the many ways that humans are connected.

Some schools and teachers are aiming to fully educate students, but most of us have a very long way to go in reaching this goal. Today, almost all students in U.S. schools still complete Carnegie units in exchange for a diploma. The time has come to bury the old Carnegie unit; since the Foundation I now head created this unit of academic measure nearly a century ago, I feel authorized to declare it obsolete. Why? Because it has helped turn schooling into an exercise in trivial pursuit. Students get academic "credit," but they fail to gain a coherent view of what they study. Education is measured by seat time, not time for learning. While curious young children still ask why things are, many older children ask only, "Will this be on the test?" All students should be encouraged to ask "Why?" because "Why?" is the question that leads students to connections.

In abandoning the Carnegie unit, I do not endorse the immediate adoption of national assessment programs; indeed, I think we must postpone such programs until we are much clearer about what students should be learning. The goal, again, is not only to help students become well informed and prepared for lifelong learning, but also to help them put learning into the larger context of discovering the connectedness of things. Barbara McClintock, the 1983 winner of the Nobel

Prize for Physiology–Medicine, asserts: "Everything is one. There is no way to draw a line between things." Contrary to McClintock's vision, the average school or college catalog dramatizes the separate academic boxes.

Frank Press, president of the National Academy of Sciences, compares scientists to artists, evoking the magnificent double helix, which broke the genetic code. He said the double helix is not only rational, but beautiful. Similarly, when scientists and technicians watch the countdown to a space launch, they don't say, "Our formulas worked again." They respond, "Beautiful!" instinctively reaching for the aesthetic term to praise a technological achievement. When physicist Victor Weisskopf was asked, "What gives you hope in troubled times?" he replied, "Mozart and quantum mechanics." Most schools, however, separate science and art, discouraging students from seeing the connections between them.

How, then, can we help students see relationships and patterns and gain understanding beyond the separate academic subjects? How can we rethink the curriculum and use the disciplines to illuminate larger, more integrated ends?

Human Commonalities

In the 1981 book *A Quest for Common Learning*, I suggested that we might organize the curriculum not on the basis of disciplines or departments, but on the basis of "core commonalities." By core commonalities, I mean universal experiences that make us human, experiences shared by all cultures on the planet. During the past decade and a half, my thinking about this thematic structure has continued to evolve. I now envision eight commonalities that bind us to one another:

I. The Life Cycle. As life's most fundamental truth, we share, first, the experience that connects birth, growth, and death. This life cycle binds each of us to others, and I find it sad that so many students go through life without reflecting on the mystery of their own existence. Many complete twelve or sixteen years of formal schooling not considering the sacredness of their own bodies, not learning to sustain wellness, not pondering the imperative of death.

In reshaping the curriculum to help students see connections, I would position study of "The Life Cycle" at the core of common learning. Attention would go to nutrition, health, and all aspects of wellness. For a project, each student would undertake the care of some life form.

My wife is a certified nurse-midwife who delivers babies, including seven grandchildren of our own. Kay feels special pain when delivering the baby of a teenage girl because she knows that she is delivering one child into the arms of another, and that both have all too often lived for nine months on soda and potato chips. Some young mothers first learn about the birth process between the sharp pains of labor.

Too many young women and young men pass through our process of education without learning about their own bodies. Out of ignorance, they suffer poor nutrition, addiction, and violence. "Maintaining children's good health is a shared responsibility of parents, schools, and the community at large," according to former Secretary of Education William Bennett (1986, p. 37). He urges elementary schools "to provide children with the knowledge, habits, and attitudes that will equip them for a fit and healthy life."

Study of the Life Cycle would encourage students to reflect sensitively on the mystery of birth and growth and death, to learn about body functions and thus understand the role of choice in wellness, to carry some of their emotional and intellectual learning into their relations with others, and to observe, understand, and respect a variety of life forms.

II. Language. Each life on the planet turns to symbols to express feelings and ideas. After a first breath, we make sounds as a way of reaching out to others, connecting with them. We develop a variety of languages: the language of words (written and spoken), the language of symbols (mathematics, codes, sign systems), and the language of the arts (aesthetic expressions in language, music, paint, sculpture, dance, theater, craft, and so on). A quality education develops proficiency in the written and the spoken word, as well as a useful knowledge of mathematical symbol systems and an understanding that the arts provide countless ways to express ourselves.

Our sophisticated use of language sets human beings apart from all other forms of life. Through the created words and symbols and arts, we connect to one another. Consider the miracle of any moment. One person vibrates his or her vocal cords. Molecules shoot in the direction of listeners. They hit the tympanic membrane; signals go scurrying up the eighth cranial nerve. From that series of events, the listener feels a response deep in the cerebrum that approximates the images in the mind of the speaker. Because of its power and scope, language is the means by which all other subjects are pursued.

The responsible use of language demands both *accuracy* and *honesty*, so students studying "Language" must also learn to consider the ethics of communication. Students live in a world where obscenities abound. They live in a world where politicians use sixty-second sound bites to destroy integrity. They live in a world where clichés substitute for reason. To make their way in this world, students must learn to distinguish between deceit and authenticity in language.

Writers and mathematicians have left a long and distinguished legacy for students to learn from. Through words, each child can express something personal. Through symbols, each child can increase the capacity to calculate and reason. Through the arts, each child can express a thought or a feeling. People need to write with clarity, read with comprehension, speak effectively, listen with understanding, compute accurately, and understand the communicative capabilities of the arts. Education for the next century means helping students understand that language in all its forms is a powerful and sacred trust.

III. The Arts. All people on the planet respond to the aesthetic. Dance, music, painting, sculpture, and architecture are languages understood around the world. "Art represents a social necessity that no nation can neglect without endanger-ing its intellectual existence," said John Ruskin (Rand 1993). We all know how art can affect us. Salvador Dali's painting *The Persistence of Memory* communicates its meaning to anyone ever haunted by time passing. The gospel song "Amazing Grace" stirs people from both Appalachia and Manhattan. "We Shall Overcome," sung in slow and solemn cadence, invokes powerful feelings regardless of the race or economic status of singer or audience.

Archaeologists examine the artifacts of ancient civilization—pottery, cave paintings, and musical instruments—to determine the attainments and quality of a culture. As J. Carter Brown (1986) observes, "The texts of man's achievements are not written exclusively in words. They are written, as well, in architecture, paintings, sculpture, drawing, photography, and in urban, graphic, landscape, and industrial design."

Young children understand that the arts are language. Before they learn to speak, they respond intuitively to dance, music, and color. The arts also help children who are disabled. I once taught deaf children, who couldn't speak because they couldn't hear. But through painting, sculpture, and rhythm, they found new ways to communicate.

Every child has the urge and capacity to be expressive. It is tragic that for most children the universal language of the arts is suppressed, then destroyed, in the early years of learning, because traditional teaching does not favor self-expression and school boards consider art a frill. This is an ironic deprivation when the role of art in developing critical thinking is becoming more widely recognized.

Jacques d'Amboise, former principal dancer with the New York City Ballet, movie star, and founder of the National Dance Institute, offers his view on how art fits into education: "I would take the arts, science and sports, or play, and make all education involve all of them. It would be similar to what kindergarten does, only more sophisticated, right through life. All of the disciplines would be interrelated. You dance to a poem: poetry is meter, meter is time, time is science" (Ames and Peyser 1990).

For our most moving experiences, we turn to the arts to express feelings and ideas that words cannot convey. The arts are, as one poet has put it, "the language of the angels." To be truly educated means being sensitively responsive to the universal language of art.

IV. Time and Space While we are all nonuniform and often seem dramatically different from one another, all of us have the capacity to place ourselves in time and space. We explore our place through geography and astronomy. We explore our sense of time through history.

And yet, how often we squander this truly awesome capacity for exploration, neglecting even our personal roots. Looking back in my own life, my most important mentor was Grandpa Boyer, who lived to be one hundred. Sixty years before that, Grandpa moved his little family into the slums of Dayton, Ohio. He then spent the next forty years running a city mission, working for the poor, teaching me more by deed than by word that to be truly human, one must serve. For far too many children, the influence of such intergenerational models has diminished or totally disappeared.

Margaret Mead said that the health of any culture is sustained when three generations are vitally interacting with one another—a "vertical culture" in which the different age groups are connected. Yet in America today we've created a "horizontal culture," with each generation living alone. Infants are in nurseries, toddlers are in day care, older children are in schools organized by age. College students are isolated on campuses. Adults are in the workplace. And older citizens are in retirement villages, living and dying all alone.

For several years, my own parents chose to live in a retirement village where the average age was eighty. But this village had a day-care center, too, and all the three- and four-year-olds had adopted grandparents to meet with every day. The two generations quickly became friends. When I called my father, he didn't talk about his aches and pains, he talked about his little friend.

And when I visited, I saw that my father, like any proud grandparent, had the child's drawings taped to the wall. As I watched the two of them together, I was struck by the idea that there is something really special about a four-year-old seeing the difficulty and courage of growing old. And I was struck, too, by watching an eighty-year-old being informed and inspired by the energy and innocence of a child. Exposure to such an age difference surely increases the understanding of time and personal history.

The time has come to break up the age ghettos. It is time to build intergenerational institutions that bring together the old and young. I'm impressed by the "grandteacher" programs in the schools, for example. In the new core curriculum, with a strand called "Time and Space," students should discover their own roots and complete an oral history. But beyond their own extended family, all students should also become well informed about the influence of the culture that surrounds them and learn about the traditions of other cultures.

A truly educated person will see connections by placing his or her life in time and space. In the days ahead, students should study *Western* civilization to understand our past, but they should study *non-Western* cultures to understand our present and our future.

V. Groups and Institutions. All people on the planet belong to groups and institutions that shape their lives. Nearly 150 years ago, Ralph Waldo Emerson observed, "We do not make a world of our own, but rather fall into institutions already made and have to accommodate ourselves to them." Every society organizes itself and carries on its work through social interaction that varies from one culture to another.

Students must be asked to think about the groups of which they are members, how they are shaped by those groups, and how they help to shape them. Students need to learn about the social web of our existence, about family life, about how governments function, about the informal social structures that surround us. They also must discover how life in groups varies from one culture to another.

Civic responsibility also must be taught. The school itself can be the starting point for this education, serving as a "working model" of a healthy society in microcosm that bears witness to the ideals of community. Within the school, students should feel "enfranchised." Teachers, administrators, and staff should meet often to find their *own* relationship to the institution of the school. And students should study groups in their own community, finding out about local government.

One of my sons lives in a Mayan village in the jungle of Belize. When my wife and I visit Craig each year, I'm impressed that Mayans and Americans live and work in very similar ways. The jungle of Manhattan and the one of Belize are separated by a thousand miles and a thousand years, and yet the Mayans, just like us, have their family units. They have elected leaders, village councils, law enforcement officers, jails, schools, and places to worship. Life there is both different and very much the same. Students in the United States should be introduced to institutions in our own culture and in other cultures, so they might study, for example, both Santa Cruz, California, and Santa Cruz, Belize.

We all belong to many groups. Exploring their history and functions helps students understand the privileges and the responsibilities that belong to each of us.

VI. Work.
We all participate, for much of our lives, in the commonality of work. As Thoreau reminds us, we both "live" and "get a living." Regardless of differences, all people on the planet produce and consume. A quality education will help students understand and prepare for the world of work. Unfortunately, our own culture has become too preoccupied with *consuming*, too little with the tools for *producing*. Children may see their parents leave the house carrying briefcases or lunch pails in the morning and see them come home again in the evening, but do they know what parents actually do during the day?

Jerome Bruner (1971) asks: "Could it be that in our stratified and segmented society, our students simply do not know about local grocers and their styles, local doctors and their styles, local taxi drivers and theirs, local political activists and theirs? . . . I would urge that we find some way of connecting the diversity of the society to the phenomenon of school" (p. 7). A new, integrative curriculum for the schools needs to give attention to "Producing and Consuming," with each student studying simple economics, different money systems, vocational studies, career planning, how work varies from one culture to another, and with each completing a work project to gain a respect for craftsmanship.

Several years ago when Kay and I were in China, we were told about a student who had defaced the surface of his desk. As punishment, he spent three days in the factory where desks were made, helping the woodworkers, observing the effort involved. Not surprisingly, the student never defaced another desk.

When I was Chancellor of the State University of New York, I took my youngest son, then eight, to a cabin in the Berkshires for the weekend. My goal: to build a dock. All day, instead of playing, Stephen sat by the lake, watching me work. As we drove home, he looked pensive. After several miles, he said, "Daddy, I wish you'd grown up to be a carpenter—instead of you-know-what!"

VII. Natural World.
Though all people are different, we are all connected to the earth in many ways. David, my grandson in Belize, lives these connections as he chases birds, bathes in the river, and watches corn being picked, pounded into tortillas, and heated outdoors. But David's cousins in Boston and Princeton spend more time with appliances, asphalt roadways, and pre-cooked food. For them, discovering connectedness to nature does not come so naturally.

When I was United States Commissioner of Education, Joan Cooney, the brilliant creator of *Sesame Street*, told me that she and her colleagues at Children's Television Workshop wanted to start a new program on science and technology for junior high school kids. They wanted young people to learn a little more about their world and what they must understand as part of living. Funds were raised, and *3–2–1 Contact* went on the air. To prepare scripts, staff surveyed junior high school kids in New York City, asking questions such as "Where does water come from?"—which brought from some students the disturbing reply, "The faucet." They asked, "Where does light come from?" and heard, "The switch." And they asked, "Where does garbage go?" "Down the chute." These students' sense of connectedness stopped at the VCR or refrigerator door.

Canadian geneticist David Suzuki, host of *The Nature of Things*, says: "We ought to be greening the school yard, breaking up the asphalt and concrete. . . . We have to give children hand-held lenses, classroom aquariums and terrariums, lots of field trips, organic garden plots on the school grounds, butterfly gardens, trees. Then insects, squirrels—maybe even raccoons and rabbits—will show up, even in the city. We've got to reconnect those kids, and we've got to do it very early. . . . Our challenge is to reconnect children to their natural curiosity" (Baron Estes 1993).

With all our differences, each of us is inextricably connected to the natural world. During their days of formal learning, students should explore this commonality by studying the principles of science, by discovering the shaping power of technology, and, above all, by learning that survival on this planet means respecting and preserving the earth we share.

VIII. Search for Meaning. Regardless of heritage or tradition, each person searches for some larger purpose. We all seek to give special meaning to our lives. Reinhold Neibuhr said, "Man cannot be whole unless he be committed, he cannot find himself, unless he find a purpose beyond himself." We all need to examine values and beliefs, and develop convictions.

During my study of the American high school, I became convinced ours is less a school problem and more a youth problem. Far too many teenagers feel unwanted, unneeded, and unconnected. Without guidance and direction, they soon lose their sense of purpose—even their sense of wanting purpose.

Great teachers allow their lives to express their values. They are matchless guides as they give the gift of opening truths about themselves to their students. I often think of three or four teachers, out of the many I have worked with, who changed my life. What made them truly great? They were well informed. They could relate their knowledge to students. They created an active, not passive, climate for learning. More than that, they were authentic human beings who taught their subjects and were open enough to teach about themselves.

Service projects instill values. All students should complete a community service project, working in day-care centers and retirement villages or tutoring other students at school. The North Carolina School of Science and Math develops an ethos of responsible citizenship. To be admitted, a child must commit to sixty hours of community service per summer and three hours per week during the school year (Beach 1992, p. 56).

Martin Luther King, Jr., preached: "Everyone can be great because everyone can serve." I'm convinced the young people of this country want inspiration from this kind of larger vision, whether they come across it in a book or in person, or whether they find it inside themselves.

Values, Beliefs, and Connections

What, then, does it mean to be an educated person? It means respecting the miracle of life, being empowered in the use of language, and responding sensitively to the aesthetic. Being truly educated means putting learning in historical perspective, understanding groups and institutions, having reverence for the natural world, and affirming the dignity of work. And, above all, being an educated person means being guided by values and beliefs and connecting the lessons of the classroom to the realities of life. These are the core competencies that I believe replace the old Carnegie units.

And all of this can be accomplished as schools focus not on seat time, but on students involved in true communities of learning. I realize that remarkable changes must occur for this shift in goals to take place, but I hope deeply that in the century ahead students will be judged not by their performance on a single test but by the quality of their lives. It is my hope that students in the classrooms of tomorrow will be encouraged to create more than conform, and to cooperate more than compete. Each student deserves to see the world clearly and in its entirety and to be inspired by both the beauty and the challenges that surround us all.

Above all, I pray that Julie and David, my granddaughter in Princeton and my grandson in Belize, along with all other children on the planet, will grow to understand that they belong to the same human family, the family that connects us all.

Fifty years ago, Mark Van Doren wrote, "The connectedness of things is what the educator contemplates to the limit of his capacity." The student, he says, who can begin early in life to see things as connected has begun the life of learning. This, it seems to me, is what it means to be an educated person. ■

References

Ames, Katrine, and Marc Peyser. (Fall/Winter 1990). "Why Jane Can't Draw (or Sing, or Dance . . .)." *Newsweek* Special Edition: 40–49.

Baron Estes, Yvonne. (May 1993). "Environmental Education: Bringing Children and Nature Together." *Phi Delta Kappan* 74, 9: K2.

Beach, Waldo. (1992). *Ethical Education in American Public Schools*. Washington, D.C.: National Education Association.

Bennett, William J. (1986). *First Lessons*. Washington, D.C.: U.S. Department of Education.

Boyer, Ernest L. (1981). *A Quest for Common Learning: The Aims of General Education*. Washington, D.C.: Carnegie Foundation for the Advancement of Teaching.

Brown, J. Carter. (November/December 1983). "Excellence and the Problem of Visual Literacy." *Design for Arts in Education* 84, 3.

Bruner, Jerome. (November 1971). "Process of Education Reconsidered." An address presented before the 16th Annual Conference of the Association for Supervision and Curriculum Development.

Rand, Paul. (May 2, 1993). "Failure by Design," *The New York Times*, p. E19.

POST NOTE

There is no more important or fundamental question in education than "What is most worth knowing?" Schools have a mission, derived from the society at large, to prepare children to be fully developed people, to prepare them for the demands of adult life in an unknown future. As educators, our mission is to identify what our students need today and will need in the future. But the universe of knowledge, which once inched along at a snail's pace, is currently racing ahead like a sprinter. The child's future, which once we could say would be much like his or her parents' life, now is impossible to predict.

In this essay, the late Ernest Boyer, a great figure in twentieth-century education, lays out his answer to the question of what an educated person most needs to know. Though there is great merit in his educational vision, a question arises: How many of us as teachers have a clear sense of goals, guided by a similar vision of what a person really is and what a person ought to become?

1. What feature of Boyer's "educated person" do you believe currently receives the greatest attention in our schools today?

2. What feature of his vision do you believe receives the least attention today? Why?

3. Why do you think there is so little discussion of the question, "What is most worth knowing?"

47

The Basis of Education

Robert Maynard Hutchins

The obvious failures of the doctrines of adaptation, immediate needs, social reform, and of the doctrine that we need no doctrine at all may suggest to us that we require a better definition of education. Let us concede that every society must have some system that attempts to adapt the young to their social and political environment. If the society is bad, in the sense, for example, in which the Nazi state was bad, the system will aim at the same bad ends. To the extent that it makes men bad in order that they may be tractable subjects of a bad state, the system may help achieve the social ideals of the society. It may be what the society wants; it may even be what the society needs, if it is to perpetuate its form and accomplish its aims. In pragmatic terms, in terms of success in the society, it may be a "good" system.

But it seems to me clearer to say that, though it may be a system of training, or instruction, or adaptation, or meeting immediate needs, it is not a system of education. It seems clearer to say that the purpose of education is to improve men. Any system that tries to make them bad is not education, but something else. If, for example, democ-

Robert Maynard Hutchins (1899–1977) was a major figure in American education during the middle third of the twentieth century. A leading spokesperson for perennialist education, he was the long-time president of the University of Chicago. "The Basis of Education," from *The Conflict in Education in a Democratic Society* by Robert M. Hutchins. Copyright 1953 by Harper & Row, Publishers, Inc. Renewed © 1981 by Vesta S. Hutchins. Reprinted by permission of HarperCollins Publishers, Inc.

racy is the best form of society, a system that adapts the young to it will be an educational system. If despotism is a bad form of society, a system that adapts the young to it will not be an educational system, and the better it succeeds in adapting them the less educational it will be.

Every man has a function as a man. The function of a citizen or a subject may vary from society to society, and the system of training, or adaptation, or instruction, or meeting immediate needs may vary with it. But the function of a man as man is the same in every age and in every society, since it results from his nature as a man. The aim of an educational system is the same in every age and in every society where such a system can exist: it is to improve man as man.

If we are going to talk about improving men and societies, we have to believe that there is some difference between good and bad. This difference must not be, as the positivists think it is, merely conventional. We cannot tell this difference by any examination of the effectiveness of a given program as the pragmatists propose; the time required to estimate these effects is usually too long and the complexity of society is always too great for us to say that the consequences of a given program are altogether clear. We cannot discover the difference between good and bad by going to the laboratory, for men and societies are not laboratory animals. If we believe that there is not truth, there is no knowledge, and there are no values except those which are validated by laboratory experiment, we cannot talk about the improvement of men and societies, for we can have no standard of judging anything that takes place among men or in societies.

Society is to be improved, not by forcing a program of social reform down its throat, through the schools or otherwise, but by the improvement of the individuals who compose it. As Plato said, "Governments reflect human nature. States are not made out of stone or wood, but out of the characters of their citizens: these turn the scale and draw everything after them." The individual is the heart of society.

To talk about making men better we must have some idea of what men are, because if we have none, we can have no idea of what is good or bad for them. If men are brutes like other animals, then there is no reason why they should not be treated like brutes by anybody who can gain power over them. And there is no reason why they should not be trained as brutes are trained. A sound philosophy in general suggests that men are rational, moral, and spiritual beings and that the improvement of men means the fullest development of their rational, moral, and spiritual powers. All men have these powers, and all men should develop them to the fullest extent.

Man is by nature free, and he is by nature social. To use his freedom rightly he needs discipline. To live in society he needs the moral virtues. Good moral and intellectual habits are required for the fullest development of the nature of man.

To develop fully as a social, political animal man needs participation in his own government. A benevolent despotism will not do. You cannot expect the slave to show the virtues of the free man unless you first set him free. Only democracy, in which all men rule and are ruled in turn for the good life of the whole community, can be an absolutely good form of government.

The community rests on the social nature of men. It requires communication among its members. They do not have to agree with one another; but they must be able to understand one another. And their philosophy in general must supply them with a common purpose and a common concept of man and society adequate to hold the community together. Civilization is the deliberate pursuit of a common ideal. The good society is not just a society we happen to like or to be used to. It is a community of good men.

Education deals with the development of the intellectual powers of men. Their moral and spiritual powers are the sphere of the family and the church. All three agencies must work in harmony; for, though a man has three aspects, he is still one man. But the schools cannot take over the role of the family and the church without promoting the atrophy of those institutions and failing in the task that is proper to the schools.

We cannot talk about the intellectual powers of men, though we can talk about training them, or amusing them, or adapting them, and meeting their immediate needs, unless our philosophy in general tell us that there is knowledge and that there is a difference between true and false. We must believe, too, that there are other means of obtaining knowledge than scientific experimentation. If knowledge can be sought only in the laboratory, many fields in which we thought we had knowledge will offer us nothing but opinion or superstition, and we shall be forced to conclude that we cannot know anything about the most important aspects of man and society. If we are to set about developing the intellectual powers of men through having them acquire knowledge of the most important subjects, we have to begin with the proposition that experimentation and empirical data will be of only limited use to us, contrary to the convictions of many American social scientists, and that philosophy, history, literature, and art give us knowledge, and significant knowledge, on the most significant issues.

If the object of education is the improvement of men, and any system of education that is without values is a contradiction in terms. A system that seeks bad values is bad. A system that denies the existence of values denies the possibility of education. Relativism, scientism, skepticism, and anti-intellectualism, the four horsemen of the philosophical apocalypse, have produced that chaos in education which will end in the disintegration of the West.

The prime object of education is to know what is good for man. It is to know the goods in their order. There is a hierarchy of values. The task of education is to help us understand it, establish it, and live by it. This Aristotle had in mind when he said: "It is not the possessions but the desires of men that must be equalized, and this is impossible unless they have a sufficient education according to the nature of things."

Such an education is far removed from the triviality of that produced by the doctrines of adaptation, of immediate needs, of social reform, or of the doctrine of no doctrine at all. Such an education will not adapt the young to a bad environment, but it will encourage them to make it good. It will not overlook immediate needs, but it will place these needs in their proper relationship to more distant, less tangible, and more important goods. It will be the only effective means of reforming society.

This is the education appropriate to free men. It is liberal education. If all men are to be free, all men must have this education. It makes no difference how they are to earn their living or what their special interests or aptitudes may be. They can learn to make a living, and they can develop their special interests and aptitudes, after they have laid the foundation of free and responsible manhood through liberal education. It will not do to say that they are incapable of such education. This claim is made by those who are too indolent or unconvinced to make the effort to give such education to the masses.

Nor will it do to say that there is not enough time to give everybody a liberal education before he becomes a specialist. In America, at least, the waste and frivolity of the educational system are so great that it would be possible through getting rid of them to give every citizen a liberal education and make him a qualified specialist, too, in less time than is now consumed in turning out uneducated specialists.

A liberal education aims to develop the powers of understanding and judgment. It is impossible that too many people can be educated in this sense, because there cannot be too many people with understanding and judgment. We hear a great deal today about the dangers that will come upon us through the frustration of educated people who have got educated in the expectation that education will get them a better job, and who then fail to get it. But surely this depends on the representations that are made to the young about what education is. If we allow them to believe that education will get them better jobs and encourage them to get educated with this end in view, they are entitled to a sense of frustration if, when they have got the education, they do not get the jobs. But, if we say that they should

be educated in order to be men, and that everybody, whether he is a ditch-digger or a bank president, should have this education because he is a man, then the ditch-digger may still feel frustrated, but not because of his education.

Nor is it possible for a person to have too much liberal education, because it is impossible to have too much understanding and judgment. But it is possible to undertake too much in the name of liberal education in youth. The object of liberal education in youth is not to teach the young all they will ever need to know. It is to give them the habits, ideas, and techniques that they need to continue to educate themselves. Thus the object of formal institutional liberal education in youth is to prepare the young to educate themselves throughout their lives.

I would remind you of the impossibility of learning to understand and judge many of the most important things in youth. The judgment and understanding of practical affairs can amount to little in the absence of experience with practical affairs. Subjects that cannot be understood without experience should not be taught to those who are without experience. Or, if these subjects are taught to those who are without experience, it should be clear that these subjects can be taught only by way of introduction and that their value to the student depends on his continuing to study them as he acquires experience. The tragedy in America is that economics, ethics, politics, history, and literature are studied in youth, and seldom studied again. Therefore the graduates of American universities seldom understand them.

This pedagogical principle, that subjects requiring experience can be learned only by the experienced, leads to the conclusion that the most important branch of education is the education of adults. We sometimes seem to think of education as something like the mumps, measles, whooping-cough, or chicken-pox. If a person has had the education in childhood, he need not, in fact he cannot, have it again. But the pedagogical principle that the most important things can be learned only in mature life is supported by a sound philosophy in general. Men are rational animals. They achieve their terrestrial felicity by the use of reason. And this means that they have to use it for their entire lives. To say that they should learn only in childhood would mean that they were human only in childhood.

And it would mean that they were unfit to be citizens of a republic.[1] A republic, a true *res publica*, can maintain justice, peace, freedom, and order only by the exercise of intelligence. When we speak of the consent of the governed, we mean, since men are not angels who seek the truth intuitively and do not have to learn it, that every act of assent on the part of the governed is a product of learning. A republic is really a common educational life in process. So Montesquieu said that, whereas the principle of a monarchy was honor, and the principle of tyranny was fear, the principle of a republic was education.

Hence the ideal republic is the republic of learning. It is the utopia by which all actual political republics are measured. The goal toward which we started with the Athenians twenty-five centuries ago is an unlimited republic of learning and a world-wide political republic mutually supporting each other.

All men are capable of learning. Learning does not stop as long as a man lives, unless his learning power atrophies because he does not use it. Political freedom cannot endure unless it is accompanied by provision for the unlimited acquisition of knowledge. Truth is not long retained in human affairs without continual learning and relearning. Peace is unlikely unless there are continuous, unlimited opportunities for learning and unless men continuously avail themselves of them. The world of law and justice for which we yearn, the world-wide political republic, cannot be realized without the world-wide republic of learning. The civilization we seek will be achieved when all men are citizens of the world republic of law and justice and of the republic of learning al their lives long. ■

Note

1. I owe this discussion to the suggestions of Scott Buchanan.

P O S T N O T E

Much of the energy behind the current school reform movement grows out of concern that our young may be unable to meet the demands of the twenty-first century. Our global economic competitors, the argument goes, and possibly our military competitors as well, are more hard-working and disciplined than we are. Grown soft, we have created a soft educational system, at least by the standards of the nations with which we are in competition. Therefore, the public schools must do a better job of preparing our students, as future workers and citizens, to take over the reins of our economy and preserve the nation.

Robert Hutchins, one of the great educational thinkers and innovators of the twentieth century, took a different view. Education is for individual people first and foremost, Hutchins believed. Developing a person with the powers of understanding and judgment (as opposed to salable skills) is the true purpose of education. During his lifetime, Hutchins often reminded us that the state is designed to serve the ends of humans, not vice versa. Since Hutchins wrote this piece nearly half a century ago, the state has become bigger and bigger and more and more of a presence in our daily lives. In the face of this growth, educators need to wrestle continually with his question, "What is good for man?"

DISCUSSION QUESTIONS

1. How would you describe Hutchins's philosophy of education?

2. Do you agree with the idea that schools have become the state's training ground? Why or why not?

3. If Hutchins is correct, and "the prime object of education is to know what is good for man," how should this be reflected in the school curriculum?

48

The Free and Happy Student

B. F. Skinner

His name is Emile. He was born in the middle of the eighteenth century in the first flush of the modern concern for personal freedom. His father was Jean-Jacques Rousseau, but he has had many foster parents, among them Pestalozzi, Froebel, and Montessori, down to A. S. Neill and Ivan Illich. He is an ideal student. Full of goodwill toward his teachers and his peers, he needs no discipline. He studies because he is naturally curious. He learns things because they interest him.

Unfortunately, he is imaginary. He was quite explicitly so with Rousseau, who put his own children in an orphanage and preferred to say how he would teach his fictional hero; but the modern version of the free and happy student to be found in books by Paul Goodman, John Holt, Jonathan Kozol, or Charles Silberman is also imaginary. Occasionally a real example seems to turn up. There are teachers who would be successful in dealing with people anywhere—as statesmen, therapists, businessmen, or friends—and there are students who scarcely need to be taught, and together they sometimes seem to bring Emile to life. And unfortunately they do so just often enough to sustain the old dream. But Emile is a will-o'-the-wisp, who has led many

B. F. Skinner, a professor at Harvard University and the founder of *behaviorism*, died in 1990. "The Free and Happy Student" by B. F. Skinner. Reprinted with permission from *New York University Education Quarterly*, Vol. IV, No. 2 (Winter 1973), pp. 2–6. © New York University.

teachers into a conception of their role which could prove disastrous.

The student who has been taught *as if he were Emile* is, however, almost too painfully real. It has taken a long time for him to make his appearance. Children were first made free and happy in kindergarten, where there seemed to be no danger in freedom, and for a long time they were found nowhere else, because the rigid discipline of the grade schools blocked out progress. But eventually they broke through—moving from kindergarten into grade school, taking over grade after grade, moving into secondary school and on into college and, very recently, into graduate school. Step by step they have insisted upon their rights, justifying their demands with the slogans that philosophers of education have supplied. If sitting in rows restricts personal freedom, unscrew the seats. If order can be maintained only through coercion, let chaos reign. If one cannot be really free while worrying about examinations and grades, down with examinations and grades! The whole Establishment is now awash with free and happy students.

Dropping Out of School, Dropping Out of Life

If they are what Rousseau's Emile would really have been like, we must confess some disappointment. The Emile we know doesn't work very hard. "Curiosity" is evidently a moderate sort of thing. Hard work is frowned upon because it implies a "work ethic," which has something to do with discipline.

The Emile we know doesn't learn very much. His "interests" are evidently of limited scope. Subjects that do not appeal to him he calls irrelevant. (We should not be surprised at this, since Rousseau's Emile, like the boys in Summerhill, never got past the stage of knowledgeable craftsman.) He may defend himself by questioning the value of knowledge. Knowledge is always in flux, so why bother to acquire any particular stage of it? It will be enough to remain curious and interested.

In any case the life of feeling and emotion is to be preferred to the life of intellect; let us be governed by the heart rather than the head.

The Emile we know doesn't think very clearly. He has had little or no chance to learn to think logically or scientifically and is easily taken in by the mystical and the superstitious. Reason is irrelevant to feeling and emotion.

And, alas, the Emile we know doesn't seem particularly happy. He doesn't like his education any more than his predecessors liked theirs. Indeed, he seems to like it less. He is much more inclined to play truant (big cities have given up enforcing truancy laws), and he drops out as soon as he legally can, or a little sooner. If he goes to college, he probably takes a year off at some time in his four-year program. And after that his dissatisfaction takes the form of anti-intellectualism and a refusal to support education.

Are there offsetting advantages? Is the free and happy student less aggressive, kinder, more loving? Certainly not toward the schools and teachers that have set him free, as increasing vandalism and personal attacks on teachers seem to show. Nor is he particularly well disposed toward his peers. He seems perfectly at home in a world of unprecedented domestic violence.

Is he perhaps more creative? Traditional practices were said to suppress individuality; what kind of individuality has now emerged? Free and happy students are certainly different from the students of a generation ago, but they are not very different from each other. Their own culture is a severely regimented one, and their creative works—in art, music, and literature—are confined to primitive and elemental materials. They have very little to be creative with, for they have never taken the trouble to explore the fields in which they are now to be front-runners.

Is the free and happy student at least more effective as a citizen? Is he a better person? The evidence is not very reassuring. Having dropped out of school, he is likely to drop out of life too. It would be unfair to let the hippie culture represent young people today, but it does serve to clarify an extreme. The members of that culture do not ac-cept responsibility for their own lives; they sponge on the contributions of those who have not yet been made free and happy—who have gone to medical school and become doctors, or who have become the farmers who raise the food or the workers who produce the goods they consume.

These are no doubt overstatements. Things are not that bad, nor is education to be blamed for all the trouble. Nevertheless, there is a trend in a well-defined direction, and it is particularly clear in education. Our failure to create a truly free and happy student is symptomatic of a more general problem.

The Illusion of Freedom

What we may call the struggle for freedom in the Western world can be analyzed as a struggle to escape from or avoid punitive or coercive treatment. It is characteristic of the human species to act in such a way as to reduce or terminate irritating, painful, or dangerous stimuli, and the struggle for freedom has been directed toward those who would control others with stimuli of that sort. Education has had a long and shameful part in the history of that struggle. The Egyptians, Greeks, and Romans all whipped their students. Medieval sculpture showed the carpenter with his hammer and the schoolmaster with the tool of his trade too, and it was the cane or rod. We are not yet in the clear. Corporal punishment is still used in many schools and there are calls for its return where it has been abandoned.

A system in which students study primarily to avoid the consequences of not studying is neither humane nor very productive. Its byproducts include truancy, vandalism, and apathy. Any effort to eliminate punishment in education is certainly commendable. We ourselves act to escape from aversive control, and our students should escape from it too. They should study because they want to, because they like to, because they are interested in what they are doing. The mistake—a classical mistake in the literature of freedom—is to suppose that they will do so as soon as we stop punishing them. Students are not literally free when they have been freed from their teachers. They then simply come under the control of other conditions, and we must look at those conditions and their effects if we are to improve teaching.

Those who have attacked the "servility" of students, as Montessori called it, have often put their faith in the possibility that young people will learn what they need to know from the "world of things," which includes the world of people who are not teachers. Montessori saw possibly useful behavior being suppressed by schoolroom discipline. Could it not be salvaged? And could the environment of the schoolroom not be changed so that other useful behavior could occur? Could the teacher not simply guide the student's natural development? Or could he not accelerate it by teasing out behavior which would occur naturally but not so quickly if he did not help? In other words, could we not bring the real world into the classroom and turn the student over to the real world, as Ivan Illich has recommended? All these possibilities can be presented in an attractive light, but they neglect two vital points:

1. No one learns very much from the real world without help. The only evidence we have of what can be learned from a nonsocial world has been supplied by those wild boys said to have been raised without contact with other members of their own species. Much more can be learned without formal instruction in a social world but not without a good deal of teaching, even so. Formal education has made a tremendous difference in the extent of the skills and knowledge which can be acquired by a person in a single lifetime.

2. A much more important principle is that the real world teaches only what is relevant to the present; it makes no explicit preparation for the future. Those who would minimize teaching have contended that no preparation is needed, that the student will follow a natural line of development and move into the future in the normal course of events. We should be content, as Carl Rogers has put it, to trust

. . . the insatiable curiosity which drives the adolescent boy to absorb everything he can see or hear or read about gasoline engines in order to improve the efficiency and speed of his "hot rod." I am talking about the student who says, "I am discovering, drawing in from the outside, and making that which is drawn in a real part of me." I am talking about my learning in which the experience of the learner progresses along the line. "No, no, that's not what I want"; "Wait! This is closer to what I'm interested in, what I need." "Ah, here it is! Now I'm grasping and comprehending what I need and what I want to know!"[1]

Rogers is recommending a total commitment to the present moment, or at best to an immediate future.

Formal Education as Preparation for the Future

But it has always been the task of formal education to set up behavior which would prove useful or enjoyable *later* in the student's life. Punitive methods had at least the merit of providing current reasons for learning things that would be rewarding in the future. We object to the punitive reasons, but we should not forget their function in making the future important.

It is not enough to give the student advice—to explain that he will have a future, and that to enjoy himself and be more successful in it, he must acquire certain skills and knowledge now. Mere advice is ineffective because it is not supported by current rewards. The positive consequences that generate a useful behavior repertoire need not be any more explicitly relevant to the future than were the punitive consequences of the past. The student needs current reasons, positive or negative, but only the educational policy maker who supplies them need take the future into account. It follows that many instructional arrangements seem "contrived," but there is nothing wrong with that. It is the teachers' function to contrive conditions under which students learn. Their relevance to a future usefulness need not be obvious.

It is a difficult assignment. The conditions the teacher arranges must be powerful enough to compete with those under which the student tends to behave in distracting ways. In what has come to be called "contingency management in the classroom," tokens are sometimes used as rewards or reinforcers. They become reinforcing when they are exchanged for reinforcers that are already effective. There is no "natural" relation between what is learned and what is received. The token is simply a reinforcer that can be made clearly contingent upon behavior. To straighten out a wholly disrupted classroom, something as obvious as a token economy may be needed, but less conspicuous contingencies—as in a credit-point system, perhaps, or possibly in the long run merely expressions of approval on the part of teacher or peer—may take over.

The teacher can often make the change from punishment to positive reinforcement in a surprisingly simple way—by responding to the student's success rather than his failures. Teachers have too often supposed that their role is to point out what students are doing wrong, but pointing to what they are doing *right* will often make an enormous difference in the atmosphere of a classroom and in the efficiency of instruction. Programmed materials are helpful in bringing about these changes, because they increase the frequency with which the student enjoys the satisfaction of being right, and they supply a valuable intrinsic reward in providing a clear indication of progress. A good program makes a step in the direction of competence almost as conspicuous as a token.

Programmed instruction is perhaps most successful in attacking punitive methods by allowing the students to move at his own pace. The slow student is released from the punishment which inevitably follows when he is forced to move on to material for which he is not ready, and the fast student escapes the boredom of being forced to go too slow. These principles have recently been extended to college educa-tion, with dramatic results, in the Keller system of personalized instruction.[2]

The Responsibility of Setting Educational Policy

There is little doubt that a student can be given nonpunitive reasons for acquiring behavior that will become useful or otherwise reinforcing at some later date. He can be prepared for the future. But what *is* that future? Who is to say what the student should learn? Those who have sponsored the free and happy student have argued that it is the student himself who should say. His current interests should be the source of an effective educational policy. Certainly they will reflect his idiosyncrasies, and that is good, but how much can he know about the world in which he will eventually play a part? The things he is "naturally" curious about are of current and often temporary interest. How many things must he possess besides his "hot rod" to provide the insatiable curiosity relevant to, say, a course in physics?

It must be admitted that the teacher is not always in a better position. Again and again education has gone out of date as teachers have continued to teach subjects which were no longer relevant at any time in the student's life. Teachers often teach simply what they know. (Much of what is taught in private schools is determined by what the available teachers can teach.) Teachers tend to teach what they can teach easily. Their current interests, like those of students, may not be a reliable guide.

Nevertheless, in recognizing the mistakes that have been made in the past in specifying what students are to learn, we do not absolve ourselves from the responsibility of setting educational policy. We should say, we should be *willing* to say, what we believe students will need to know, taking the individual student into account wherever possible, but otherwise making our best prediction with respect to students in general. Value judgments of this sort are not as hard to make as is often argued. Suppose we undertake to prepare the student to produce his share of the goods he will consume and the services he will use, to get on well with his fellows, and to enjoy his life. In doing so are we imposing *our* values on someone else? No, we are merely choosing a set of specifications which, so far as we can tell, will at some time in the future prove valuable to the student and his culture. Who is any more likely to be right?

The natural, logical outcome of the struggle for personal freedom in education is that the teacher should improve his control of the student rather than abandon it. The free school is no school at all. Its philosophy signalizes the abdication of the teacher. The teacher who understands his assignment and is familiar with the behavioral processes needed to fulfill it can have students who not only feel free and happy while they are being taught but who will continue to feel free and happy when their formal education comes to an end. They will do so because they will be successful in their work (having acquired useful productive repertoires), because they will get on well with their fellows (having learned to understand themselves and others), because they will enjoy what they do (having acquired the necessary knowledge and skills), and because they will from time to time make an occasional

creative contribution toward an even more effective and enjoyable way of life. Possibly, the most important consequence is that the teacher will then feel free and happy too.

We must choose today between Cassandran and Utopian prognostications. Are we to work to avoid disaster or to achieve a better world? Again, it is a question of punishment or reward. Must we act because we are frightened, or are there positive reasons for changing our cultural practices? The issue goes far beyond education, but it is one with respect to which education has much to offer. To escape from or avoid disaster, people are likely to turn to the punitive measures of a police state. To work for a better world, they may turn instead to the positive methods of education. When it find its most effective methods, education will be almost uniquely relevant to the task of setting up and maintaining a better way of life. ■

Notes

1. Carl R. Rogers, *Freedom to Learn* (Columbus, Ohio: Merrill, 1969).

2. *P.S.I. Newsletter*, October 1972 (published by Department of Psychology, Georgetown University, J. G. Sherman, ed.).

P O S T N O T E

B. F. Skinner was one of America's most creative and controversial scientists. His psychological work is the foundation of an entire school of thought called *behaviorism*. In much of his scientific writing and in his famous utopian novel *Walden Two*, we can see his passionate concern for education.

Although we do not believe Skinner is directly responsible for it, his views have led to a new definition of *teacher* as "manager of the environment." In contrast to more conventional definitions, such as "fount of all knowledge and wisdom," and "creative spirit," the definition "manager of the environment" requires the teacher to be clear about his or her goals and then to take the important steps of arranging the classroom or other learning environment so that those goals are achieved. In this definition, teachers do not have to know everything or be able to do everything. Instead, they bring together the human and material resources to make learning a likely outcome.

DISCUSSION QUESTIONS

1. Do you agree or disagree with Skinner's position that we should prepare students for the future rather than the present? Why?

2. What major disagreement does Skinner have with the type of education Rousseau proposed for Emile?

3. Skinner urges teachers to respond to students' successes rather than their failures. How will doing this improve the classroom learning environment?

49 Personal Thoughts on Teaching and Learning

Carl Rogers

I wish to present some very brief remarks, in the hope that if they bring forth any reaction from you, I may get some new light on my own ideas.

I find it a very troubling thing to *think*, particularly when I think about my own experiences and try to extract from those experiences the meaning that seems genuinely inherent in them. At first such thinking is very satisfying, because it seems to discover sense and pattern in a whole host of discrete events. But then it very often becomes dismaying, because I realize how ridiculous these thoughts, which have much value to me, would seem to most people. My impression is that if I try to find the meaning of my own experience it leads me, nearly always, in directions regarded as absurd.

So in the next three or four minutes, I will try to digest some of the meanings which have come to me from my classroom experience and the experience I have had in individual and group therapy. They are in no way intended as conclu-

Carl Rogers, now deceased, was the most noted leader of the nondirective, client-centered theory of psychotherapy. He was president of the American Psychological Association and the American Academy of Psychotherapists. "Personal Thoughts on Teaching and Learning" by Carl Rogers, from *On Becoming a Person* (Boston: Houghton Mifflin, 1961), pp. 275–278. Copyright © 1961 by Houghton Mifflin Company. Used by permission of the publisher and Constable Publishers.

sions for someone else, or a guide to what others should do or be. They are the very tentative meanings, as of April 1952, which my experience has had for me, and some of the bothersome questions which their absurdity raises. I will put each idea or meaning in a separate lettered paragraph, not because they are in any particular logical order, but because each meaning is separately important to me.

a. I may as well start with this one in view of the purposes of this conference. *My experience has been that I cannot teach another person how to teach.* To attempt it is for me, in the long run, futile.

b. *It seems to me that anything that can be taught to another is relatively inconsequential, and has little or no significant influence on behavior.* That sounds so ridiculous I can't help but question it at the same time that I present it.

c. *I realize increasingly that I am only interested in learnings which significantly influence behavior.* Quite possibly this is simply a personal idiosyncrasy.

d. *I have come to feel that the only learning which significantly influences behavior is self-discovered, self-appropriated learning.*

e. *Such self-discovered learning, truth that has been personally appropriated and assimilated in experience, cannot be directly communicated to another.* As soon as an individual tries to communicate such experience directly, often with a quite natural enthusiasm, it becomes teaching, and its results are inconsequential. It was some relief recently to discover that Søren Kierkegaard, the Danish philosopher, had found this too, in his own experience, and stated it very clearly a century ago. It made it seem less absurd.

f. As a consequence of the above, *I realize that I have lost interest in being a teacher.*

g. When I try to teach, as I do sometimes, I am appalled by the results, which seem a little more than inconsequential, because sometimes the teaching appears to succeed. When this happens I find that the results are damaging. It seems to cause the individual to distrust his own experience, and to stifle significant learning. *Hence I have come to feel that the outcomes of teaching are either unimportant or hurtful.*

h. When I look back at the results of my past teaching, the real results seem the same—either damage was done, or nothing significant occurred. This is frankly troubling.

i. As a consequence, *I realize that I am only interested in being a learner, preferably learning things that matter, that have some significant influence on my own behavior.*

j. *I find it very rewarding to learn*, in groups, in relationship with one person as in therapy, or by myself.

k. *I find that one of the best, but most difficult ways for me to learn is to drop my own defensiveness, at least temporarily, and try to understand the way in which his experience seems and feels to the other person.*

l. *I find that another way of learning for me is to state my own uncertainties, to try to clarify my puzzlements, and thus get closer to the meaning that my experience actually seems to have.*

m. This whole train of experiencing, and the meanings that I have thus far discovered in it, seem to have launched me on a process which is both fascinating and at times a little frightening. *It seems to mean letting my experience carry me on, in a direction which appears to be forward, toward goals that I can but dimly define, as I try to understand at least the current meaning of that experience.* The sensation is that of floating with a complex stream of experience, with the fascinating possibility of trying to comprehend its ever changing complexity.

I am almost afraid I may seem to have gotten away from any discussion of learning, as well as teaching. Let me again introduce a practical note by saying that by themselves these interpretations of my own experience may sound queer and aberrant, but not particularly shocking. It is when I realize the *implications* that I shudder a bit at the distance I have come from the common-sense world that everyone knows is right. I can best illustrate that by saying that if the experiences of others had been the same as mine, and if they had discovered similar meanings in it, many consequences would be implied.

a. Such experience would imply that we would do away with teaching. People would get together if they wished to learn.

b. We would do away with examinations. They measure only the inconsequential type of learning.

c. The implication would be that we would do away with grades and credits for the same reason.

d. We would do away with degrees as a measure of competence partly for the same reason. Another reason is that a degree marks an end or a conclusion of something, and a learner is only interested in the continuing process of learning.

e. It would imply doing away with the exposition of conclusions, for we would realize that no one learns significantly from conclusions.

I think I had better stop there. I do not want to become too fantastic. I want to know primarily whether anything in my inward thinking as I have tried to describe it, speaks to anything in your experience of the classroom as you have lived it, and if so, what the meanings are that exist for you in *your* experience. ∎

P O S T N O T E

Rogers's personal philosophy of teaching and learning, so well expressed in this selection, is of course quite controversial. Give it a little test for yourself. Think of a couple of the most significant things you have learned as a human being. Now think of how you learned them. Did someone teach them to you, or did you discover them yourself through experience? Try it from a different approach and ask yourself what of significance you have ever been taught. Be specific. How do you feel about Rogers's statements now?

DISCUSSION QUESTIONS

1. Do you agree or disagree with Rogers's ideas on teaching and learning? Why?

2. Do Rogers's statements have any implications for you as a teacher? Explain your answer.

3. Compare the messages that Rogers presents with B. F. Skinner's in selection 48. How are they similar or different?

50

The Ethics of Teaching

Kenneth A. Strike

Mrs. Porter and Mr. Kennedy have divided their third-grade classes into reading groups. In her class, Mrs. Porter tends to spend the most time with students in the slowest reading group because they need the most help. Mr. Kennedy claims that such behavior is unethical. He maintains that each reading group should receive equal time.

Miss Andrews has had several thefts of lunch money in her class. She has been unable to catch the thief, although she is certain that some students in the class know who the culprit is. She decides to keep the entire class inside for recess, until someone tells her who stole the money. Is it unethical to punish the entire class for the acts of a few?

Ms. Phillips grades her fifth-grade students largely on the basis of effort. As a result, less-able students who try hard often get better grades than students who are abler but less industrious. Several parents have accused Ms. Phillips of unethical behavior, claiming that their children are not getting what they deserve. These parents also fear that teachers in the middle school won't understand Ms. Phillips' grading practices and will place their children in inappropriate tracks.

Kenneth A. Strike is professor of philosophy of education at Cornell University, Ithaca, N.Y. Strike, Kenneth A., "The Ethics of Teaching," *Phi Delta Kappan*, October 1988. Copyright © 1988 by Phi Delta Kappa. Reprinted by permission of author and publisher.

The Nature of Ethical Issues

The cases described above are typical of the ethical issues that teachers face. What makes these issues ethical?

First, ethical issues concern questions of right and wrong—our duties and obligations, our rights and responsibilities. Ethical discourse is characterized by a unique vocabulary that commonly includes such words as *ought* and *should*, *fair* and *unfair*.

Second, ethical questions cannot be settled by an appeal to facts alone. In each of the preceding cases, knowing the consequences of our actions is not sufficient for determining the right thing to do. Perhaps, because Mrs. Porter spends more time with the slow reading group, the reading scores in her class will be more evenly distributed than the scores in Mr. Kennedy's class. But even knowing this does not tell us if it is fair to spend a disproportionate amount of time with the slow readers. Likewise, if Miss Andrews punishes her entire class, she may catch the thief, but this does not tell us whether punishing the entire group was the right thing to do. In ethical reasoning, facts are relevant in deciding what to do. But by themselves they are not enough. We also require ethical principles by which to judge the facts.

Third, ethical questions should be distinguished from values. Our values concern what we like or what we believe to be good. If one enjoys Bach or likes skiing, that says something about one's values. Often there is nothing right or wrong about values, and our values are a matter of our free choice. For example, it would be difficult to argue that someone who preferred canoeing to skiing had done something wrong or had made a mistake. Even if we believe that Bach is better than rock, that is not a reason to make people who prefer rock listen to Bach. Generally, questions of values turn on our choices: what we like, what we deem worth liking. But there is nothing obligatory about values.

On the other hand, because ethics concern what we ought to do, our ethical obligations are often independent of what we want or choose. The fact that we want something that belongs to someone else does not entitle us to take it. Nor does a choice to steal make stealing right or even "right for us." Our ethical obligations continue to be obligations, regardless of what we want or choose.

Ethical Reasoning

The cases sketched above involve ethical dilemmas: situations in which it seems possible to give a reasonable argument for more than one course of action. We must think about our choices, and we must engage in moral reasoning. Teaching is full of such dilemmas. Thus teachers need to know something about ethical reasoning.

Ethical reasoning involves two stages: applying principles to cases and judging the adequacy or applicability of the principles. In the first stage, we are usually called upon to determine the relevant ethical principle or principles that apply to a case, to ascertain the relevant facts of the case, and to judge the facts by the principles.

Consider, for example, the case of Miss Andrews and the stolen lunch money. Some ethical principles concerning punishment seem to apply directly to the case. Generally, we believe that we should punish the guilty, not the innocent; that people should be presumed innocent until proven guilty; and that the punishment should fit the crime. If Miss Andrews punishes her entire class for the behavior of an unknown few, she will violate these common ethical principles about punishment.

Ethical principles are also involved in the other two cases. The first case involves principles of equity and fairness. We need to know what counts as fair or equal treatment for students of different abilities. The third case requires some principles of due process. We need to know what are fair procedures for assigning grades to students.

However, merely identifying applicable principles isn't enough. Since the cases described above involve ethical dilemmas, it should be possible to argue plausibly for more than one course of action.

For example, suppose Miss Andrews decides to punish the entire class. It could be argued that she had behaved unethically because she has punished innocent people. She might defend herself, however, by holding that she had reasons for violating ethical principles that we normally apply to punishment. She might argue that it was important to catch the thief or that it was even more important to impress on her entire class that stealing is wrong. She could not make these points by ignoring the matter. By keeping the entire class inside for recess, Miss Andrews could maintain, she was able to catch the thief and to teach her class a lesson about the importance of honesty. Even if she had to punish some innocent people, everyone was better off as a result. Can't she justify her action by the fact that everyone benefits?

Two General Principles

When we confront genuine ethical dilemmas such as this, we need some general ethical concepts in order to think our way through them. I suggest two: the principle of benefit maximization and the principle of equal respect for persons.

The principle of benefit maximization holds that we should take that course of actions which will maximize the benefit sought. More generally, it requires us to do that which will make everyone, on the average, as well off as possible. One of the traditional formulations of this principle is the social philosophy known as utilitarianism, which holds that our most general moral obligation is to act in a manner that produces the greatest happiness for the greatest number.

We might use the principle of benefit maximization to think about each of these cases. The principle requires that in each case we ask which of the possible courses of action makes people generally better off. Miss Andrews has appealed to the principle of benefit maximization in justifying her punishment of the entire class. Ms. Phillips might likewise appeal to it in justifying her grading system. Perhaps by using grades to reward effort rather than successful performance, the overall achievement of the class will be enhanced. Is that not what is important?

It is particularly interesting to see how the principle of benefit maximization might be applied to the question of apportioning teacher time between groups with different levels of ability. Assuming for the moment that we wish to maximize the overall achievement of the class, the principle of benefit maximization dictates that we allocate time in a manner that will produce the greatest overall learning.

Suppose, however, we discover that the way to produce the greatest overall learning in a given class is for a teacher to spend the most time with the *brightest* children. These are the children who provide the greatest return on our investment of time. Even though the least-able children learn less than they would with an equal division of time, the overall learning that takes place in the class is maximized when we concentrate on the ablest.

Here the principle of benefit maximization seems to lead to an undesirable result. Perhaps we should consider other principles as well.

The principle of equal respect requires that our actions respect the equal worth of moral agents. We must regard human beings as intrinsically worthwhile and treat them accordingly. The essence of this idea is perhaps best expressed in the Golden Rule. We have a duty to accord others the same kind of treatment that we expect them to accord us.

The principle of equal respect can be seen as involving three subsidiary ideas. First, it requires us to treat people as ends in themselves, rather than as means to further our own goals. We must respect their goals as well.

Second, when we are considering what it means to treat people as ends rather than as means, we must regard as central the fact that people are free and rational moral agents. This means that, above all, we must respect their freedom of choice. And we must respect the choices that people make even when we do not agree.

Third, no matter how people differ, they are of equal value as moral agents. This does not mean

that we must see people as equal in abilities or capacities. Nor does it mean that we cannot take relevant differences between people into account when deciding how to treat them. It is not, for example, a violation of equal respect to give one student a higher grade than another because that student works harder and does better.

That people are of equal value as moral agents does mean, however, that they are entitled to the same basic rights and that their interests are of equal value. Everyone, regardless of native ability, is entitled to equal opportunity. No one is entitled to act as though his or her happiness counted for more than the happiness of others. As persons, everyone has equal worth.

Notice three things about these two moral principles. First, both principles (in some form) are part of the moral concepts of almost everyone who is reading this article. These are the sorts of moral principles that everyone cites in making moral arguments. Even if my formulation is new, the ideas themselves should be familiar. They are part of our common ethical understandings.

Second, both principles seem necessary for moral reflection. Neither is sufficient by itself. For example, the principle of equal respect requires us to value the well-being of others as we value our own well-being. But to value the welfare of ourselves *and* others is to be concerned with maximizing benefits; we want all people to be as well-off as possible.

Conversely, the principle of benefit maximization seems to presuppose the principle of equal respect. Why, after all, must we value the welfare of others? Why not insist that only our own happiness counts or that our happiness is more important than the happiness of others? Answering these questions will quickly lead us to affirm that people are of equal worth and that, as a consequence, everyone's happiness is to be valued equally. Thus our two principles are intertwined.

Third, the principles may nevertheless conflict with one another. One difference between the principle of benefit maximization and the principle of equal respect is their regard for consequences. For the principle of benefit maximization, only consequences matter. The sole relevant factor in choosing between courses of action is which action has the best overall results. But consequences are not decisive in the principle of equal respect; our actions must respect the dignity and worth of the individuals involved, even if we choose a course of action that produces less benefit than some other possible action.

The crucial question that characterizes a conflict between the principle of benefit maximization and the principle of equal respect is this:

When is it permissible to violate a person's rights in order to produce a better outcome? For example, this seems the best way to describe the issue that arises when a teacher decides to punish an entire class for the acts of a few. Students' rights are violated when they are punished for something they haven't done, but the overall consequence of the teacher's action may be desirable. Is it morally permissible, then, to punish everyone?

We can think about the issue of fair allocation of teacher time in the same way. Spending more time with the brightest students may enhance the average learning of the class. But we have, in effect, traded the welfare of the least-able students for the welfare of the ablest. Is that not failing to respect the equal worth of the least-able students? Is that not treating them as though they were means, not ends?

The principle of equal respect suggests that we should give the least-able students at least an equal share of time, even if the average achievement of the class declines. Indeed, we might use the principle of equal respect to argue that we should allocate our time in a manner that produces more equal results—or a more equal share of the benefits of education.

I cannot take the discussion of these issues any further in this short space. But I do want to suggest some conclusions about ethics and teaching.

First, teaching is full of ethical issues. It is the responsibility of teachers, individually and collectively, to consider these issues and to have informed and intelligent opinions about them.

Second, despite the fact that ethical issues are sometimes thorny, they can be thought about. Ethical reflection can help us to understand what is at stake in our choices, to make more responsible choices, and sometimes to make the right choices.

Finally, to a surprising extent, many ethical dilemmas, including those that are common to teaching, can be illuminated by the principles of benefit maximization and equal respect for persons. Understanding these general ethical principles and their implications is crucial for thinking about ethical issues. ■

POST NOTE

Ethics seems to be making a comeback. We may not be behaving better, but we are talking about it more. Street crime and white-collar crime, drugs and violence, our inability to keep promises in our personal and professional lives— all these suggest a renewed need for ethics.

Kenneth Strike points out that teaching is full of ethical issues, and it is true that teachers make promises to perform certain duties and that they have real power over the lives of children. This article, however, speaks to only one end of the spectrum of ethical issues faced by the teacher: what we call "hard case" ethics, complex problems, often dilemmas. Certainly these are important, but there are also everyday teaching ethics—the issues that fill a teacher's day: Should I correct this stack of papers or watch *The Simpsons*? Should I "hear" that vulgar comment or stroll right by? Should I read this story again this year before I teach it tomorrow or spend some time with my colleagues in the teachers' lounge? Should I bend down and pick up yet another piece of paper in the hall or figure I've done my share for the day?

Like hard-case ethical issues, these questions, in essence, ask, What's the right thing to do? Our answers to these everyday questions often become our habits, good and bad. These, in turn, define much of our ethical behavior as teachers.

D I S C U S S I O N Q U E S T I O N S

1. What three factors or qualities make an issue an ethical one?

2. What two ethical principles are mentioned in the article? Give your own examples of classroom situations that reflect these principles.

3. Why is there a greater interest in the ethics of teaching today than thirty years ago?

The Teacher's Ten Commandments: School Law in the Classroom

Thomas R. McDaniel

I n recent years public school teachers have been made painfully aware that the law defines, limits, and prescribes many aspects of a teacher's daily life. Schools are no longer protected domains where teachers rule with impunity; ours is an age of litigation. Not only are parents and students ready to use the courts for all manner of grievances against school and teacher, the growing legislation itself regulates more and more of school life. In addition to an unprecedented number of laws at all levels of government, the mind-boggling array of complex case law principles (often vague and contradictory) adds to the confusion for the educator.

The Ten Commandments of School Law described below are designed to provide the concerned and bewildered teacher with some significant general guidelines in the classroom. While statutes and case law principles may vary from state to state or judicial circuit to judicial circuit, these school law principles have wide applicability in the United States today.

Thomas R. McDaniel is Provost of Converse College. "The Teacher's Ten Commandments: School Law in the Classroom" by Thomas R. McDaniel. Revised and updated from *Phi Delta Kappan,* June 1979. Reprinted by permission from Thomas R. McDaniel.

Commandment I: Though Shalt Not Worship in the Classroom

This may seem something of a parody of the Biblical First Commandment—and many teachers hold that indeed their religious freedom and that of the majority of students has been limited by the court cases prohibiting prayer and Bible reading—but the case law principles here have been designed to keep public schools *neutral* in religious matters. The First Amendment to the Constitution, made applicable by the Fourteenth Amendment to state government (and hence to public schools, which are agencies of state government), requires that there be no law "respecting the establishment of religion or prohibiting the free exercise thereof." As the Supreme Court declared in the *Everson* decision of 1947, "Neither [a state nor the federal government] can pass laws that aid one religion, aid all religions, or prefer one religion over another." Such rules, said the Court, would violate the separation of church and state principle of the First Amendment.

In 1971 the Supreme Court ruled in *Lemon v. Kurtzman* that separation of church and state required that government action or legislation in education must clear a three-pronged test. It must: 1) not have a religious purpose, 2) not have the primary effect of either enhancing on inhibiting religion, and 3) not create "excessive entanglement" between church and state. This Lemon Test has been attacked by Justice Anton Scalia and others in recent years but continues to be used (at least as a guideline) in court rulings. In a 1992 case, *Lee v. Wiseman,* the Supreme Court ruled that an invocation and benediction at commencement by a clergyman was unconstitutional—perhaps because the school principal chose the clergyman and gave him directions for the content of the prayer. In another 1992 case a circuit court of appeals upheld a policy that permitted high school seniors to choose student volunteers to deliver nonsectarian, nonproselytizing invocations at graduation ceremonies. Courts continue to wrestle with questions about "establishment" and "freedom" of religion. However, acts of worship in public schools usually violate the neutrality principle—especially when they appear to be planned and promoted by school officials.

On the other hand, public schools may offer courses in comparative religion, history of religion, or the Bible as literature, because these would be academic experiences rather than religious ones. "Released-time" programs during school hours for outside-of-school religious instruction have been held to be constitutional by the Supreme Court (*Zorach v. Clauson*, 1952). Other religious practices that have been struck down by the Supreme Court include a Kentucky statute requiring that the Ten Commandments be posted in every public school classroom, a Michigan high school's 30-year practice of displaying a 2-foot by 3-foot portrait of Jesus in the hallways, laws in Arkansas and Louisiana requiring that "scientific creationism" (based on Genesis) be taught in science classes to "balance" the teaching of evolution, the Gideons' distribution of Bibles in the public schools of Indiana. Other courts have questioned (or struck down) certain practices such as invocations at football games, nativity scenes and other religious displays, and laws requiring a "moment of silence" when the purpose is to promote prayer. Finding the line that separates church and state has not been easy. The "wall of separation" has often seemed more like a semi-permeable membrane.

In 1984, Congress passed the Equal Access Act. This statute made it unlawful for any public secondary school receiving federal funds to discriminate against any students who wanted to conduct a meeting on school premises during "non-instructional time" (before and after regular school hours) if other student groups (such as clubs) were allowed to use school facilities during these times. Religious groups that are voluntary and student initiated (not officially sponsored or led by school personnel) may, under the EAA, meet on school premises. Such meetings may not be conducted or controlled by others not associated with the school nor may they interfere with educational activities of the school. In a 1990 case (*Westside Community*

Schools v. Mergens) the Supreme Court upheld the constitutionality of the EAA and declared this federal statute did not violate the First Amendment or any of the three prongs of the Lemon Test. However, a 1993 case (*Sease v. School District of Philadelphia*) in Pennsylvania disallowed a gospel choir that advertised itself as sponsored by the school district, was directed by the school secretary, had another school employee attending all practices, and had non-school persons regularly attending meetings of the choir. There were several violations of the EAA in this case.

The application of the neutrality principle to education has resulted in some of the following guidelines for public schools:

1. Students may not be required to salute the flag nor to stand for the flag salute, if this conflicts with their religious beliefs.

2. Bible reading, even without comment, may not be practiced in a public school when the intent is to promote worship.

3. Prayer is an act of worship and as such cannot be a regular part of opening exercises or other aspects of the regular school day (including grace at lunch).

4. Worship services (e.g., prayer and Bible reading) are not constitutional even if voluntary rather than compulsory. Not consensus, not majority vote, nor excusing objectors from class or participation makes these practices legal.

5. Prayer and other acts of worship (benedictions, hymns, invocations, etc.) at school-related or school-sponsored events are increasingly under scrutiny by courts and may be disallowed when found to be initiated or controlled by school officials.

Commandment II: Thou Shalt Not Abuse Academic Freedom

Under First Amendment protection, teachers are given the necessary freedom and security to use the classroom as a forum for the examination and discussion of ideas. Freedom of expression is a prerequisite for education in a democracy—and the schools, among other responsibilities, are agents of democracy. Students are citizens too, and they are also entitled to freedom of speech. As Justice Abe Fortas, who delivered the Supreme Court's majority opinion in the famous *Tinker* decision (1969), put it:

> It can hardly be argued that either students or teachers shed their constitutional rights at the schoolhouse gate. . . . In our system state-operated schools may not be enclaves of totalitarianism . . . [and] students may not be regarded as closed-circuit recipients of only that which the state chooses to communicate.

Case law has developed over the years to define the parameters of free expression for both teachers and students:

1. Teachers may discuss controversial issues in the classroom if they are relevant to the curriculum, although good judgment is required. Issues that disrupt the educational process, are demonstrably inappropriate to the legitimate objectives of the curriculum, or are unreasonable for the age and maturity of the students may be prohibited by school officials. The routine use of profanity by teachers is not a protected First Amendment right (*Martin v. Parrish*, 1986, Fifth Circuit Court).

2. Teachers may discuss current events, political issues, and candidates so long as neutrality and balanced consideration prevail. When teachers become advocates and partisans, supporters of a single position rather than examiners of all positions, they run the risk of censure.

3. A teacher may use controversial literature containing "rough" language but must "take care not to transcend his legitimate professional purpose" (*Mailoux v. Kiley*, 1971, U.S. District Court, Massachusetts). Again, courts will attempt to determine curriculum relevance, disruption of the educational process, and appropriateness to the age and maturity of the students.

4. Teachers and students are increasingly (but not yet universally) guaranteed symbolic free speech, including hair length and beards, armbands, and buttons. Courts generally determine such issues in terms of the "substantial disruption" that occurs or is clearly threatened. Dress codes for students are generally allowable when they are intended to provide for health, safety, and "decency." When they exist merely to promote the "tastes" of the teacher or administration, they have usually been struck down by the courts.

5. Teachers have some control over school-sponsored publications and plays. In *Hazelwood School District v. Kuhlmeier* (1988) the Supreme Court held that "educators do not offend the First Amendment by exercising editorial control over the style and content of student speech in school-sponsored expressive activities so long as their actions are reasonably related to legitimate pedagogical concerns." This authority, however, does not extend to censorship of student expression. It does not appear to extend to a school board's banning and regulating textbooks and other "learning materials" (*Virgil v. School Board of Columbia County*, 1989, Eleventh Circuit).

6. Teachers do not have a constitutional right to use any teaching method they want. School district officials and boards may establish course content and teaching methods as matters of policy. Courts will support such policies but will examine the reasonableness of sanctions against teachers. For example, a California court ruled that firing a teacher for unwittingly permitting students to read obscene poetry was too severe (*De Groat v. Newark*, 1976) while a nine-month suspension of a West Virginia teacher showing cartoons of "Fritz the Cat" undressing was judged appropriate (*DeVito v. Board of Education*, 1984).

Teachers in short are free to deal with controversial issues (including politics and sex) and to use controversial methods and materials if these are educationally defensible, appropriate to the students, and not "materially and substantially" disruptive. But school boards also have authority to maintain curricular policies governing what (and even how) teachers should teach. Courts use a balancing test to determine when students' and teachers' rights to academic freedom must give way to the competing need of society to have reasonable school discipline.

Commandment III: Thou Shalt Not Engage in Private Activities That Impair Teaching Effectiveness

Of all the principles of school law, this commandment is probably the most difficult to delineate with precision. The private and professional areas of a teacher's life have been, for the most part, separated by recent court decisions. A mere 75 years ago teachers signed contracts with provisions prohibiting marriage, falling in love, leaving town without permission of the school board, smoking cigarettes, loitering in ice-cream stores, and wearing lipstick. But now a teacher's private life is considered his or her own business. Thus, for example, many court cases have established that teachers have the same citizenship rights outside the classroom that any other person has.

Teachers, however, have always been expected by society to abide by high standards of personal conduct. Whenever a teacher's private life undermines effective instruction in the class, there is a possibility that the courts will uphold his or her dismissal. To guard against this possibility, the teacher should consider some of the following principles:

1. Teachers may belong to any organization or association—but if they participate in illegal activities of that organization they may be dismissed from their job.

2. A teacher may write letters to newspapers criticizing school policies—unless it can be shown that such criticism impairs morale or working relationships. In the landmark *Pickering* decision (1968), the Supreme Court upheld a teacher who had written such a letter but pointed out that there was in this case "no question of maintaining either discipline by immediate supervisors or harmony among co-workers. . . ."

3. Teachers do not have a right to air private grievances or personnel judgments publicly. Free speech on public issues should not lead teachers to criticize superiors or other school employees in public settings. In a 1983 case, *Connick v. Myers*, the Supreme Court ruled against a discharged public employee, saying that he spoke out "not as a citizen upon matters of public concern but instead as an employee on matters of personal interest." A judge in Florida, applying *Connick* to a history teacher discharged for outspoken criticism of his administrators, ruled that the teacher's speech was "nothing more than a set of grievances with school administrators over internal school policies" (*Ferrara v. Mills*, 1984). Teachers should distinguish between *public* citizenship issues and *private* personnel issues before making controversial and critical public comments about their schools.

4. A teacher's private affairs do not normally disqualify him or her from teaching except to the extent that it can be shown that such affairs undermine teaching effectiveness. Teachers who are immoral in public, or who voluntarily (or through indiscretion) make known in public private acts of immorality, may indeed be dismissed. Courts are still debating the rights of homosexual teachers, with decisions falling on both sides of this issue.

5. Laws which say that teachers may be dismissed for "unprofessional conduct" or "moral turpitude" are interpreted narrowly, with the burden of proof on the employer to show that the particular circumstances in a case constitute "unfitness to teach." Dismissal must be based on fact, not mere rumor.

6. Whenever a teacher's private affairs include sexual involvement with students, it may be presumed that courts will declare that such conduct constitutes immorality indicating unfitness to teach.

Commandment IV: Thou Shalt Not Deny Students Due Process

The Fourteenth Amendment guarantees citizens "due process of law" whenever the loss of a right is at stake. Because education has come to be considered such a right (a "property" right), and because students are considered to be citizens, case law in recent years has defined certain procedures to be necessary in providing due process in particular situations:

1. A rule that is patently or demonstrably unfair or a punishment that is excessive may be found by a court to violate the "substantive" due process of a student (see, for example, the Supreme Court's 1969 *Tinker* decision). At the heart of due process is the concept of fair play, and teachers should examine the substance of their rules and the procedures for enforcing them to see if both are reasonable, nonarbitrary, and equitable.

2. The extent to which due process rights should be observed depends on the gravity of the offense and the severity of punishment that follows. The Supreme Court's *Goss v. Lopez* decision (1975) established minimal due process for suspensions of 10 days or less, including oral or written notice of charges and an opportunity for the student to present his or her side of the story.

3. When students are expelled from school, they should be given a statement of the specific charges and the grounds for expulsion, a formal hearing, names of witnesses, and a report of the facts to which each witness testifies (see the leading case, *Dixon v. Alabama State Board of Education*, 1961). Furthermore, it is probable that procedural due process for expelled students gives them the right to challenge the evidence, cross-examine witnesses, and be represented by counsel. (See, for example, the New York Supreme Court's 1967 *Goldwyn v. Allen* decision.) Finally, such students may appeal the decision to an impartial body for review.

4. Special education students have an added measure of due process protection. In 1990 Congress consolidated earlier special education federal statutes—including the 1975 Education of All Handicapped Children Act (Public Law 94-142) and section 504 of the Rehabilitation Act of 1973—into the Individuals with Disabilities Education Act (IDEA). These laws stipulate extensive due process rights for *all* children with disabilities (whether or not they have "the ability to benefit") to ensure a free, "appropriate" education. These provisions include prior written notice before any proposed change in a child's educational program; testing that is non-discriminatory in language, race, or culture; parental access to records; fair and impartial hearing by the State Education Agency or local district; and a student's right to remain in a current placement until due process proceedings are completed. These due process guarantees supersede district level policies relating to placement, suspension, or expulsion of students. As the Supreme Court ruled in *Honig v. Doe* (1988), the IDEA does not allow even for a "dangerous exception" to the "stay put" provision.

It is advisable for schools to develop written regulations governing procedures for such areas as suspension, expulsion, discipline, publications, and placement of the disabled. The teacher should be aware of these regulations and should provide his or her administration with specific, factual evidence whenever a student faces a serious disciplinary decision. The teacher is also advised to be guided by the spirit of due process—fairness and evenhanded justice—when dealing with less serious incidents in the classroom.

Commandment V: Thou Shalt Not Punish Behavior Through Academic Penalties

It is easy for teachers to lose sight of the distinction between punishing and rewarding academic performance, on the one hand, and disciplinary conduct on the other. Grades, for example, are frequently employed as motivation for both study behavior and paying-attention behavior. There is a great temptation for teachers to use one of the few weapons still in their arsenal (i.e., grades) as an instrument of justice for social infractions in the classroom. While it may indeed be the case that students who misbehave will not perform well academically because of their conduct, courts are requiring schools and teachers to keep those two domains separate.

In particular, teachers are advised to heed the following general applications of this principle:

1. Denial of a diploma to a student who has met all the academic requirements for it but who has broken a rule of discipline is not permitted.

Several cases (going back at least as far as the 1921 Iowa *Valentine* case) are on record to support this guideline. It is also probable that exclusion from a graduation ceremony as a punishment for behavior will not be allowed by the courts.

2. Grades should not be reduced to serve disciplinary purposes. In the *Wermuth* case (1965) in New Jersey, the ruling against such practice included this observation by the state's commissioner of education: "Whatever system of marks and grades a school may devise will have serious inherent limitations at best, and it must not be further handicapped by attempting to serve disciplinary purposes too." In a 1984 case in Pennsylvania (*Katzman v. Cumberland Valley School District*) the court struck down a policy requiring a reduction in grades by two percentage points for each day of suspension.

3. Lowering grades—or awarding zeros—for absences is a questionable legal practice. In the Kentucky case of *Dorsey v. Bale* (1975), a student had his grades reduced for unexcused absences, and under the school's regulation, was not allowed to make up the work; five points were deducted from his nine-weeks' grade for each unexcused absence. A state circuit court and the Kentucky Court of Appeals declared the regulation to be invalid. The courts are particularly likely to invalidate regulations that constitute "double jeopardy"—e.g., suspending students for disciplinary reasons and giving them zeros while suspended.

In general, teachers who base academic evaluation on academic performance have little to fear in this area. Courts do not presume to challenge a teacher's grades *per se* when the consideration rests only on the teacher's right or ability to make valid academic judgments.

Commandment VI: Thou Shalt Not Misuse Corporal Punishment

Corporal punishment is a controversial method of establishing discipline. The Supreme Court refused to disqualify the practice under a suit (*Ingraham v. Wright*, 1977) in which it was argued that corporal punishment was "cruel and unusual punishment" and thus a violation of the Constitution's Eighth Amendment. An increasing number of states—up from only two in 1979 to 27 in 1996—ban corporal punishment in public schools.

In those states not prohibiting corporal punishment, teachers may—as an extension of their *in loco parentis* authority—use "moderate" corporal punishment to establish discipline. There are, however, many potential legal dangers in the practice. *In loco parentis* is a limited, perhaps even a vanishing, concept, and teachers must be careful to avoid these misuses of corporal punishment if they want to stay out of the courtroom:

1. The punishment must never lead to permanent injury. No court will support as "reasonable" or "moderate" that physical punishment which permanently disables or disfigures a student. Many an assault and battery judgment has been handed down in such cases. Unfortunately for teachers, "accidents" that occur during corporal punishment and ignorance of a child's health problems (brittle bones, hemophilia, etc.) do not always excuse a teacher from liability.

2. The punishment must not be unreasonable in terms of the offense, nor may it be used to enforce an unreasonable rule. The court examines all the circumstances in a given case to determine what was or was not "reasonable" or "excessive." In 1980 the Fourth Circuit Court of Appeals ruled that "excessive" corporal punishment might well violate Fourteenth Amendment rights. In 1987 the Tenth Circuit Court of Appeal reached a similar conclusion.

3. The punishment must not be motivated by spite, malice, or revenge. Whenever teachers administer corporal punishment in a state of anger, they run a high risk of losing an assault and battery suit in court. Since corporal punishment is practiced as a method of correcting student behavior, any evidence that physical force resulted from a teachers' bad temper or quest for revenge is damning. On the other hand, in an explosive situation (e.g., a fight) teachers may protect themselves and use that force necessary to restrain a student from harming the teacher, others, or himself.

4. The punishment must not ignore such variables as the student's age, sex, size, and physical condition.

5. The punishment must not be administered with inappropriate instruments or to parts of the body where risk of injury is great. For example, a Texas case ruled that it is not reasonable for a teacher to use his fists in administering punishment. Another teacher lost a suit when he struck a child on the ear, breaking an eardrum. The judge noted, "Nature has provided a part of the anatomy for chastisement, and tradition holds that such chastisement should there be applied." It should be noted that creating mental anguish and emotional stress by demeaning, harassing, or humiliating a child may be construed as illegal punishment too.

6. Teachers must not only take care not to harm children by way of corporal punishment; they also have a responsibility to report suspected child abuse by parents or others. Congress passed the National Child Abuse Prevention and Treatment Act in 1974 and followed with stronger laws in 1988 and 1992. Child abuse is a state (not federal) crime with many variations in definition and reporting procedure. But *all* states require reporting if the neglect or abuse results in physical injury. Teachers need not be absolutely certain of abuse but must act "in good faith" if they have "reason to believe" a child is being subjected to abuse or neglect. Every state also provides legal protection from suit for such reporting. In most states, failure to report is a misdemeanor.

Courts must exercise a good deal of judgment in corporal punishment cases to determine what is "moderate," "excessive," "reasonable," "cruel," "unusual," "malicious," or "capricious." Suffice it to say that educators should exercise great care in the use of corporal punishment.

Commandment VII: Thou Shalt Not Neglect Students' Safety

One of the major responsibilities of teachers is to keep their students safe from unreasonable risk of harm or danger. The major cases involving teachers grow out of negligence charges relating to the teacher's failure to supervise properly in accordance with *in loco parentis* obligations (to act "in place of the parents"), contractual obligations, and professional responsibility. While the courts do not expect teachers to protect children from "unforeseeable accidents" and "acts of God," they do require teachers to act as a reasonably prudent teacher should in protecting students from possible harm or injury.

Negligence is a tort ("wrong") that exists only when the elements of *duty*, *violation*, *cause*, and *injury* are present. Teachers are generally responsible for using good judgment in determining what steps are necessary to provide for adequate supervision of the particular students in their charge, and the given circumstances dictate what is reasonably prudent in each case. A teacher who has a duty to his or her students but who fails to fulfill this duty because of carelessness, lack of discretion, or lack of diligence may violate this duty with a resultant injury to a student. In this instance the teacher may be held liable for negligence as the cause of the injury to the student.

Several guidelines can help teachers avoid this all-too-common and serious lawsuit:

1. Establish and enforce rules of safety in school activities. This is particularly important for the elementary teacher, since many injuries to elementary students occur on playgrounds, in hallways, and in classroom activity sessions. The prudent teacher anticipates such problems and establishes rules to protect students from such injuries. Generally, rules should be written, posted, and taught.

2. Be aware of school, district, and state rules and regulations as they pertain to student safety. One teacher was held negligent when a child was injured because the teacher did not know that there was a state law requiring safety glasses in a shop activity. It is also important that a teacher's own rules not conflict with regulations at higher levels. *Warn* students of any hazard in a room or in an instructional activity.

3. Enforce safety rules when violations are observed. In countless cases teachers have been found negligent when students repeatedly broke

important safety rules, eventually injuring themselves or others, or when a teacher should have foreseen danger but did not act as a "reasonably prudent" teacher would have in the same situation to correct the behavior. One teacher observing a mumblety-peg game at recess was held negligent for not stopping it before the knife bounced up and put out an eye of one of the players.

4. Provide a higher standard of supervision when students are younger, disabled, and/or in a potentially dangerous activity. Playgrounds, physical education classes, science labs, and shop classes require particular care and supervision. Instruction must be provided to insure safety in accordance with the children's maturity, competence, and skill.

5. Learn first aid, because teachers may be liable for negligence if they do not get or give prompt, appropriate medical assistance when necessary. While teachers should not give children medicine, even aspirin, they should, of course, allow any legitimate prescriptions to be taken as prescribed. There should be school policy governing such procedures.

6. Advise substitute teachers (and student teachers) about any unusual medical, psychological, handicapping, or behavioral problem in your class. If there are physical hazards in your class—bare light cords, sharp edges, loose boards, insecure window frames, etc.—warn everyone about these too. Be sure to report such hazards to your administration and janitorial staff—as a "prudent" teacher would do.

7. Be where you are assigned to be. If you have playground, hall, cafeteria, or bus duty, be there. An accident that occurs when you are someplace other than your assigned station may be blamed on your negligence, whereas if you had been there it would not be so charged. Your responsibility for safety is the same for extracurricular activities you are monitoring as it is for classes.

8. If you have to leave a classroom (particularly a rowdy one), stipulate the kind of conduct you expect and make appropriate arrangements—such as asking another teacher to check in. Even this may not be adequate precaution in terms of your duty to supervise if the students are known to be troublemakers, are quite immature, or are mentally retarded or emotionally disabled. You run a greater risk leaving a science class or a gym class than you do a social studies class.

9. Plan field trips with great care and provide for adequate supervision. Many teachers fail to realize that permission notes from home—no matter how much they disclaim teacher liability for injury—do not excuse a teacher from providing proper supervision. A parent cannot sign away this right of his or her child. Warn children of dangers on the trip and instruct them in rules of conduct and safety.

10. Do not send students on errands off school grounds, because they then become your agents. If they are injured or if they injure someone else, you may well be held liable. Again, the younger and less responsible the child, the greater the danger of a teacher negligence charge. To state the obvious, some children require more supervision than others.

Much of the advice is common sense, but the "reasonably prudent" teacher needs to be alert to the many requirements of "due care" and "proper supervision." The teacher who anticipates potentially dangerous conditions and actions and takes reasonable precautions—through rules, instruction, warnings, communications to superiors, and presence in assigned stations—will do a great deal in minimizing the chances of pupil injury and teacher negligence.

Commandment VIII: Thou Shalt Not Slander or Libel Your Students

This tort is much less common than negligence, but it is an area of school law that can be troublesome. One of the primary reasons for the Family Educational Rights and Privacy Act (1974) was that school records contains so much misinformation and hearsay and so many untrue (or, at least, questionable) statements about children's character, conduct, and morality that access to these records by students or their parents, in order to correct false information, seemed warranted. A teacher's right to write anything about a student under the protection of confidential files no longer exists. Defamation of character through written communication is "libel" while such defamation in oral communication is "slander." There are ample opportunities for teachers to commit both offenses.

Teachers are advised to be careful about what they say about students (let alone other teachers!) to employers, colleges, parents, and other personnel at the school. Adhere to the following guidelines:

1. Avoid vague, derogatory terms on permanent records and recommendations. Even if you do not intend to be derogatory, value judgments about a student's character, life-style, or home life may be found defamatory in court. In one case, a North Carolina teacher was found guilty of libel when she said on a permanent record card that a student was "ruined by tobacco and whiskey." Avoid characterizing students as "crazy," "immoral," or "delinquent."

2. Say or write only what you know to be true about a student. It is safer to be an objective describer of what you have observed than to draw possibly unwarranted and untrue conclusions and judgments. The truth of a statement is strong evidence that character has not been defamed, but in some cases where the intent has been to malign and destroy the person, truth is not an adequate defense.

3. Communicate judgments of character only to those who have a right to the information. Teachers have "qualified privileged communication," which means that so long as they communicate in good faith information that they believe to be true to a person who has reason to have this information, they are protected. However, the slandering of pupils in a teachers' lounge bull session is another thing altogether.

4 If a student confides a problem to you in confidence, keep that communication confidential. A student who is on drugs, let us say, may bring you to court for defamation of character and/or invasion of privacy if you spread such information about indiscriminately. On the other hand, if a student confides that he or she has participated in a felonious crime or gives you information that makes you aware of a "clear and present" danger, you are obligated to bring such information to the appropriate authorities. Find out the proper limits of communication and the authorized channels in your school and state.

5. As a related issue, be careful about "search and seizure" procedures too. Generally, school lockers are school property and may be searched by school officials if they have reasonable grounds to suspect that the locker has something dangerous or illegal in it. In its landmark 1985 decision in *New Jersey v. T.L.O.*, the Supreme Court rejected the notion that school officials had to have the police standard of "probable cause" before conducting a search; the court approved the lower standard of "reasonable suspicion." So long as both the grounds (i.e., reason) and scope are reasonable, school personnel can search student suspects. The growing concern in society about drugs and weapons in school has led courts to support school officials conducting searches for dangerous or illegal items. Strip searches, however, are often deemed to be too intrusive.

Teachers need to remember that students are citizens and as such enjoy at least a limited degree of the constitutional rights that adult citizens enjoy. Not only "due process," "equal protection," and "freedom of religion" but also protection from teacher torts such as "negligence" and "defamation of character" is provided to students through our system of law. These concepts apply to all students, including those in elementary grades.

Commandment IX: Thou Shalt Not Photocopy in Violation of Copyright Law

In January, 1978, the revised copyright law went into effect and with it strict limitations on what may be photocopied by teachers for their own or classroom use under the broad concept of "fair use." The "fair use" of copyrighted material means that the use should not impair the value of the owner's copyright by diminishing the demand for that work, thereby reducing potential income for the owner.

In general, educators are given greater latitude than most other users. "Spontaneous" copying is more permissible than "systematic" copying. Students have greater latitude than teachers in copying materials.

Teachers may:

1. Make a single copy for their own research or class preparation of a chapter from a book; an article from a periodical or newspaper; a short story, poem, or essay; a chart, graph, diagram, cartoon, or picture from a book, periodical, or newspaper.

2. Make multiple copies for classroom use only (but not to exceed one copy per student) of a complete poem, if it is fewer than 250 words and printed on not more than two pages; an excerpt from a longer poem, if it is fewer than 250 words; a complete article, story, or essay, if it is fewer than 2,500 word; an excerpt from a prose work, if it is fewer than 1,000 words or 10% of the work, whichever is less; one chart, graph, diagram, drawing, cartoon, or picture per book or periodical.

However, teachers may not:

1. Make multiple copies of work for classroom use if another teacher has already copied the work for use in another class in the same school.

2. Make copies of a short poem, article, story, or essay from the same author more than once in the same term.

3. Make multiple copies from the same collective work or periodical issue more than three times a term. (The limitation in Items 1–3 do not apply to current news periodicals or newspapers.)

4. Make a copy of works to take the place of anthologies.

5. Make copies of "consumable" materials such as workbooks, exercises, answer sheets to standardized tests, and the like.

More recent technologies have led to extended applications of the "fair use" doctrine:

1. The "fair use" doctrine does not apply to copyrighted computer software programs; however, teachers may load a copyrighted program onto a classroom terminal or make a "backup" copy for archival purposes. Teachers may not make copies of such programs for student use. In 1991 the Department of Justice and Department of Education called on schools to teach the ethical use of computers to counteract illegal copying of software.

2. Schools may videotape copyrighted television programs but may keep the tape no longer than 45 days without a license. Teachers may use the tapes for instruction during the first 10 consecutive days after taping but may repeat such use only once. Commercial videotapes may not be rented to be played for instruction (or entertainment) in classrooms.

3. Scanning copyrighted material into a computer and distributing it via the Internet is a violation of copyright law. The Internet should be viewed as a giant photocopying machine. Bills are now in Congress to restrict and punish those who misuse the Internet. We may expect to see other legal complications from this emerging technology: defamation, obscenity, threats of violence, disruption of the academic environment, and sexual harassment—to list but a few.

When teachers make brief, spontaneous, and limited copies of copyrighted materials other than consumables, they are likely to be operating within the bounds of fair use. Whenever multiple copies of copyrighted materials are made (within the guidelines above), each copy should include a notice of the copyright. Teachers should consult media specialists and others in their school about questions relating to "fair use"—whether for print, videotape, or computer materials.

Commandment X: Thou Shalt Not Be Ignorant of the Law

The axiom, "Ignorance of the law is no excuse," holds as true for teachers as anyone else. Indeed, courts are increasingly holding teachers to higher standards of competence and knowledge commensurate with their higher status as professionals. Since education is now considered a right—guaranteed to black and white, rich and poor, "normal" and disabled—the legal parameters have become ever more important to teachers in this litigious era.

How, then, can the teacher become aware of the law and its implications for the classroom? Consider the following possibilities:

1. Sign up for a course in school law. If the local college or university does not offer such a course, attempt to have one developed.

2. Ask your school system administration to focus on this topic in inservice programs.

3. Tap the resources of the local, state, and national professional organizations for pertinent speakers, programs, and materials.

4. Explore state department of education sources, since most states will have personnel and publications that deal with educational statutes and case law in your particular state.

5. Establish school (if not personal) subscriptions to professional journals. *Phi Delta Kappan*, *Journal of Law and Education*, and *Mental Disability Law Reporter* are only a few of the journals that regularly have columns and/or articles to keep the teacher aware of new developments in school law.

6. Make sure that your school or personal library includes such books as *Teachers and the Law* (Louis Fischer, et al., 4th edition, Longman, 1995); *The Law of Schools, Students, and Teachers* (Kern and David Alexander, 2nd edition, West, 1995); *Special Education Law* (Laura Rothstein, 2nd edition, Longman, 1995); and *Deskbook Encyclopedia of American School Law* (Data Research, Rosemount, Minnesota, 1996). Monthly newsletters can keep schools up-to-date in the school law area. Consider a subscription to *School Law Bulletin* (Quinlan Publishing Company, Boston) or *Legal Notes for Educators* (Data Research, Rosemount, Minnesota).

The better informed teachers are about their legal rights and responsibilities, the more likely they are to avoid the courtroom—and there are many ways to keep informed.

My Teacher's Ten Commandments are not exhaustive, nor are they etched in stone. School law, like all other law, is constantly evolving and changing so as to reflect the thinking of the times; and decisions by courts are made in the context of particular events and circumstances that are never exactly the same. But prudent professionals will be well served by these commandments if they internalize the spirit of the law as a guide to actions as teachers—in the classroom, the school, and the community. ∎

POST NOTE

The United States is an increasingly litigious society. Rather than settle disagreements and disputes face to face, we quickly turn over our problems to lawyers. In recent years, business owners and managers, doctors, and even lawyers have been held liable for various consequences of their work. Such situations were almost unknown to their colleagues twenty or thirty years ago.

Although relatively few teachers have been prosecuted successfully in the courts, the number of cases has dramatically increased. Therefore, it is important for teachers—both in training and in service—to be aware of areas of legal vulnerability. McDaniel, himself a former teacher, has presented an outstanding summary of the law as it affects teachers.

1. Before reading this article, were you aware that school law governed teachers' behavior as much as it does? In which of the areas described by McDaniel do you, personally, feel most vulnerable? Why?

2. What steps can you take to protect yourself as a teacher from legal liability?

3. Which of these "commandments" has the most negative impact on the effectiveness of the average teacher? Why?

You Ask, "Why Have School Costs Increased So Greatly During the Last 20 Years?"

Otis K. LoVette

I t has become increasingly popular to throw stones at the public education system in this country. Everyone would like to place the blame for many of society's ills and students' shortcomings at the doorsteps of our schoolhouses. Along with this blame goes a negative attitude toward helping schools improve, especially if that involves dedicating more public funds to what many believe are inefficient efforts. Schools are constantly criticized because costs have increased dramatically during the past 20 years. Is this criticism warranted? Have schools been inefficient in their use of public funds, or are there reasons beyond the control of schools that have caused costs to rise dramatically?

As an educator for the past 32 years, 20 of which were spent in some type of administrative position, I would like to offer a different perspective on the escalation of school costs. During my tenure as both a teacher and an administrator, I witnessed a proliferation of state and federal mandates to schools. Court decisions were ren-

dered that seemed to be totally out of touch with the financial realities of schools and society. Many other changes over which educators and school boards had little or no control were also imposed from outside the school.

In an effort to provide some insight into the ultimate impact on schools and educators of these outside demands, I have compiled a descriptive listing of some of them. I hope that this information will be useful to school leaders and others in the education community to help explain why costs have risen and why increased funding may be necessary just to maintain required programs at an "adequate" level. The public needs to be properly informed as to why school costs have increased so greatly. It is obvious that many of the new reforms and restructuring efforts being proposed in most parts of the U.S. will be even more costly.

Court Decisions

Busing. Many school districts throughout the country are still involved in extensive busing programs aimed at the integration of schools. Most of these programs have been court-ordered and have been very costly to districts, taking resources away from other programs.

Provisions for private schools. Even though the courts have tried to prevent "excessive entanglement" between private schools and the government, many public funds and benefits have been diverted to these schools as a result of court rulings. Private schools now receive funding for transportation, textbooks, and many other services dictated by federal programs and supported by our courts.

Education of children of illegal aliens. Our courts require that we educate the children of illegal aliens. We must also provide these children with related services, such as special education, breakfast, lunch, and numerous types of remediation. Some states feel the impact more severely than others, but the drain on public school coffers has been tremendous.

Otis K. LoVette is an associate professor of educational leadership, Northeast Louisiana University. LoVette, Otis K., "You Ask, 'Why Have School Costs Increased So Greatly During the Last 20 Years?'" *Phi Delta Kappan*, October 1995. Copyright © 1995 by Phi Delta Kappa. Reprinted by permission of Phi Delta Kappa and the author.

Bilingual education and English as a second language. Children who enter our schools from other countries must be provided with instruction in their native language when they arrive and while they are learning English. This has been very expensive for many districts.

Use of school facilities. Many schools have stopped renting school facilities to outside groups because the courts have held that if you rent to one group you must rent to all (open forum). This has not been good for the public relations efforts of schools and has cost them much-needed revenues. The cost of insurance associated with the rental of facilities has also increased greatly because of the large sums granted by courts in injury cases.

Removal of hazards. Of course we must have school environments that are safe for our students, but the cost of securing them has been great. Schools have spent billions of dollars on programs to remove, encapsulate, and monitor asbestos. Schools have also been responsible for replacing drinking fountains that contained lead, removing certain hazardous chemicals from labs, and eliminating radon gas from facilities. These efforts all required dollars that would otherwise have been available for other school needs.

Litigation. Schools have been forced to spend large amounts of money on suits brought against them for student injuries and for alleged violations of students' personal freedoms. Playground accidents, athletic accidents, regulations regarding hair length or dress, requirements for participation in graduation, suspensions and expulsions, searches and seizures, incidents of student harassment, and the use of corporal punishment have all been causes for litigation. The courts have often sided with students. Such court action gives rise to additional litigation, and schools are forced to defend themselves in court over many cases that are frivolous or designed to get a large monetary settlement from the school or its insurer.

It should also be noted that school insurance costs have skyrocketed at least partly because insurers will often settle a dispute by making a large payment to the "injured" party rather than incur the exorbitant costs associated with litigation. Schools have no control over this action, and the result is that more students and their parents are encouraged to bring suit against the school or district because they know that there is a good chance that the insurer will be willing to settle out of court.

Federal Legislation and Regulations

Title IX. Title IX is part of the Education Amendments of 1972. It requires that schools provide equal opportunities for female students, especially in the area of school activities. If schools do not comply, their federal funds, which includes school lunch subsidies, can be withheld. As a result of this law, many new athletic programs for women were created, at considerable expense to schools. The law also forced schools to make major pay adjustments in the salaries of women coaches.

Age Discrimination in Employment Act of 1978. This act stipulates that teachers and others cannot be forced to retire, as long as they are able to carry out the responsibilities of their positions. Thus schools have been forced to keep older employees, who are far more costly than newer employees. Some would also say that newer employees are generally more effective in their positions than those over age 65.

Legislation for special students. The biggest financial impact on public education has come from legislation that deals with the rights of students with disabilities. These laws, which require schools to provide services for students from ages 3 through 21, have resulted in major expenditures of school funds. The programs all have rigid enforcement standards and agencies that monitor school compliance.

Schools must provide such services as speech therapy, physical therapy, occupational therapy, adaptive programs of all types, and special classes for students with many different kinds of disabilities and learning problems. Schools must also make available an extended school year (summer school) for students who might regress more than normal students during the summer. Many students require expensive medical and custodial care, the costs of which must be borne by the schools. Classes for special students are often small, and the costs of equipment and accommodations are large, when compared with those for "regular" classrooms.

Schools have also been required to make major renovations or additions to accommodate special students. Such items as elevators, ramps, special toilet facilities, drinking fountains, desks, showers, and modified buses have been added at major cost to schools. Legislation has recently been approved that identifies additional categories of students—those with Attention Deficit Disorder and Attention Deficit Hyperactivity Disorder, to mention two—who must receive special services in schools. It is estimated that nearly 20% of our school population is now eligible for expensive special programs.

Students with AIDS and other communicable diseases. Our courts have determined that students with AIDS must not be discriminated against in our schools. In fact, they are to remain anonymous to most persons in the school setting, including teachers. As a result, most schools are now providing teachers and others with rubber gloves to be worn when they must give assistance to students who are bleeding or when they must come into contact with other bodily fluids or waste from these students. Continuing expenditures are also necessary to provide training and education for those who might have contact with infected students. Finally, sophisticated and costly procedures must be used for disposing of materials that may have been contaminated by these students.

State Legislation and Regulations

New bus safety standards. Many states have adopted new safety standards for school buses. Legislation concerning such things as seat belts,

lighting, and the number of students to be transported on each bus has increased transportation costs. Schools have also had to absorb greatly increased costs associated with the purchase, maintenance, and operation of school buses. In addition, many schools have had to install expensive video equipment on buses as a deterrent to unruly students.

Mandates for reducing class size. Many states have passed legislation that identifies the maximum class size allowable at various grade levels. Consequent reductions in class size have been very costly for schools.

Required kindergarten. Most states now require that kindergarten be offered for students. The addition of another grade has meant that schools have had to acquire additional space, teaching staff, and equipment.

Collective bargaining laws. Many states have passed laws that allow or require collective bargaining with teachers and other school groups. Some states have also sanctioned the use of strikes by education groups. Such laws have severely limited school boards in their decision making about the expenditure of scarce resources.

Required testing programs. In efforts to hold schools accountable, state legislatures have mandated a variety of testing programs for local schools, and a national testing program is being actively promoted. Such programs are added on to the testing that schools are already doing and therefore require additional funds.

New safety standards. Legislatures have upgraded regulations pertaining to school safety and convenience. New standards for fire protection; handicapped accessibility; number of toilets and lavatories; and wiring, plumbing, and other mechanical systems all mean increased school costs. Educators have also realized that more must be spent on construction to make schools "vandal proof." New safety standards for football equipment (especially helmets), science laboratories, industrial programs, and playground equipment have also driven up costs.

Increased accountability requirements. In addition to increasing testing requirements, many states are imposing more rigid standards for student accounting, inventory control, financial accounting, and adherence to state regulations. To demonstrate compliance with these standards, school staff members must put in additional time maintaining records and completing other paperwork. To facilitate the submission of statistical data, schools have also been required to purchase computer equipment that interfaces with equipment at the state level. The amount of record keeping that must be carried out for federal programs has also increased. Directors of food service programs have been particularly burdened by the new requirements.

Imposed programs and curricular offerings. During the past 20 years states have asked schools to make numerous additions to their curricula and programs. Sex education; AIDS education; consumer education; family life education; drug education; classes in boating and hunting safety; foreign language, economics, and law courses—all have been required, often without additional or appropriate funding. The national goal (which has been adopted by many states) of being number one in the world in science and mathematics by the year 2000 has meant that schools have also found it necessary to increase their offerings in those areas.

Societal Expectations and Demands

Weapon detection systems. Because guns and other weapons are being brought to school, there is public pressure for schools to invest in security personnel and costly detection systems.

School security systems. School have found it necessary to protect the taxpayers' investments in buildings and facilities by installing security systems. Schools spend millions of dollars each year as a result of vandalism to facilities and equipment. Some systems even have staff members who are hired solely to remove graffiti and to repair other damage from vandalism.

Paid police patrols. Schools have become easy targets for drug dealers and others conducting illegal activities. Police are hired to eliminate these undesirable activities, but they are also hired to control student conduct in the halls and on school grounds.

Alternative settings. Many students today will not conform to the normal routines of our schools and do not seem to be able to benefit from the usual curriculum. Society has vigorously opposed the expulsion of these students, who are unmotivated and often disruptive or even dangerous. Thus schools have found it necessary to provide different opportunities and settings for these students. Such provisions are expensive and often require additional facilities, equipment, and staff.

School health clinics and other health services. Health clinics have been established in many schools to provide information and services that relate to communicable diseases, birth control, and so on. The number of school nurses also continues to rise as regulations and the fear of liability limit what teachers and administrators can do for students, even in emergency situations.

Pursuing truants. Attendance has become a major problem in many of the nation's schools, which find it necessary to hire employees to pursue those who are chronically absent. This is an important issue, because school funding is often tied to student attendance.

Air conditioning. Schools of 20 and 30 years ago were seldom air-conditioned. Today, most of our schools are air-conditioned, at considerable expense. It is reasonable to expect that schools be cooled, as are many of our prisons, but the costs for acquisition, energy usage, and maintenance have been high.

Increased use of technology. Schools have essentially been forced to computerize and have had to bear the major expense of doing so. As a means of improving the efficiency of various management functions, computers were sorely needed, and the expense was probably justified. Computers have also proliferated in classrooms, libraries, and laboratories, and the costs for acquisition, software, maintenance, and replacement have been tremendous. Schools have been expected to adopt this and other new technologies in order to produce graduates who are technologically literate.

Greatly increased costs for purchasing. It is hard to believe the prices of today's textbooks, workbooks, and library books. Schools often find themselves waiting many years beyond the planned adoption dates for new texts and materials because funds are not available. In addition, schools must pay for the purchase, maintenance, and operation of computers, televisions, video equipment, and copiers—expenditures that were minimal or nonexistent 20 years ago.

Before- and after-school care. Schools have become heavily involved in extended-day programs designed to assist families in which the sole parent or both parents must work outside the home. These programs are usually designed to be self-supporting, but overhead costs are often not taken into account. More schools are also providing preschool programs.

In addition to the costs associated with all the changes just discussed, school personnel have been forced to dedicate extra time to complying with ever-growing reporting, monitoring, and administrative requirements. Schools are often criticized for having too many administrators. But a closer look would reveal that many of the administrative positions that have come into being during the past 20 years were created to oversee the new mandated programs. It should also be noted that student conduct in many schools has deteriorated, and administrators have been added to perform various disciplinary functions.

While this article was not intended to be exhaustive, I hope that my listing of the pressures and demands that schools face will provide insight into some of the reasons for increased school costs. I recognize that many of the changes mentioned have been desirable or even necessary, but schools have been required to carry the resulting financial burdens.

We in the U.S. have never paid a high price for education (witness teacher salaries), and we won't in the future—at least not until we can understand why school costs have risen so rapidly during the last 20 years. Educators at all levels must carry this information to the public. ■

POST NOTE

A recent international study found that, compared with other nations, the United States spends a lot on public and private education. In average expenditure per pupil in elementary and secondary grades, the United States ranked second to Switzerland among the 22 countries studied. This average, however, masks huge differences among our states, with New Jersey spending over $10,000 per pupil and Utah about $3,700. The other states fall between these two extremes.

For expenses other than teacher pay, the international study also found that the United States spends more than any of the other countries for which data were collected, except the Czech Republic. The author of this article tells us that much of what we are currently spending on education is hardly going for student learning, but represents new missions for the school, missions that, in other times, were carried out by the home and the community.

DISCUSSION QUESTIONS

1. In your opinion, how important or vital are the various programs on which the United States spends its educational dollars?

2. Which of these programs could be curtailed or eliminated to save money or to pay teachers more?

3. Many critics of the public schools say that just "throwing more money at the schools" won't improve education. What would be your response to this charge?

53

The Return of Character Education

Thomas Lickona

To educate a person in mind and not in morals is to educate a menace to society.

—Theodore Roosevelt

Increasing numbers of people across the ideological spectrum believe that our society is in deep moral trouble. The disheartening signs are everywhere: the breakdown of the family; the deterioration of civility in everyday life; rampant greed at a time when one in five children is poor; an omnipresent sexual culture that fills our television and movie screens with sleaze, beckoning the young toward sexual activity at ever earlier ages; the enormous betrayal of children through sexual abuse; and the 1992 report of the National Research Council that says the United States is now *the* most violent of all industrialized nations.

As we become more aware of this societal crisis, the feeling grows that schools cannot be ethical bystanders. As a result, character education is making a comeback in American schools.

Thomas Lickona is a developmental psychologist at the State University of New York at Cortland and one of the leading experts in character education. Lickona, Thomas, "The Return of Character Education." *Educational Leadership,* November 1993, pp. 6–11. Reprinted by permission from ASCD. All rights reserved.

Early Character Education

Character education is as old as education itself. Down through history, education has had two great goals: to help people become smart and to help them become good.

Acting on that belief, schools in the earliest days of our republic tackled character education head on—through discipline, the teacher's example, and the daily school curriculum. The Bible was the public school's sourcebook for both moral and religious instruction. When struggles eventually arose over whose Bible to use and which doctrines to teach, William McGuffey stepped onto the stage in 1836 to offer his McGuffey Readers, ultimately to sell more than 100 million copies.

McGuffey retained many favorite Biblical stories but added poems, exhortations, and heroic tales. While children practiced their reading or arithmetic, they also learned lessons about honesty, love of neighbor, kindness to animals, hard work, thriftiness, patriotism, and courage.

Why Character Education Declined

In the 20th century, the consensus supporting character education began to crumble under the blows of several powerful forces.

Darwinism introduced a new metaphor— evolution—that led people to see all things, including morality, as being in flux.

The philosophy of logical positivism, arriving at American universities from Europe, asserted a radical distinction between *facts* (which could be scientifically proven) and *values* (which positivism held were mere expressions of feeling, not objective truth). As a result of positivism, morality was relativized and privatized—made to seem a matter of personal "value judgment," not a subject for public debate and transmission through the schools.

In the 1960s, a worldwide rise in personalism celebrated the worth, autonomy, and subjectivity of the person, emphasizing individual rights and freedom over responsibility. Personalism rightly protested societal oppression and injustice, but it also delegitimized moral authority, eroded belief in objective moral norms, turned people inward toward self-fulfillment, weakened social commitments (for example, to marriage and parenting), and fueled the socially destabilizing sexual revolution.

Finally, the rapidly intensifying pluralism of American society (Whose values should we teach?) and the increasing secularization of the public arena (Won't moral education violate the separation of church and state?) became two more barriers to achieving the moral consensus indispensable for character education in the public schools. Public schools retreated from their once central role as moral and character educators.

The 1970s saw a return of values education, but in new forms: values clarification and Kohlberg's moral dilemma discussions. In different ways, both expressed the individualist spirit of the age. Values clarification said, don't impose values; help students choose their values freely. Kohlberg said, develop students' powers of moral reasoning so they can judge which values are better than others.

Each approach made contributions, but each had problems. Values clarification, though rich in methodology, failed to distinguish between personal preferences (truly a matter of free choice) and moral values (a matter of obligation). Kohlberg focused on moral reasoning, which is necessary but not sufficient for good character, and underestimated the school's role as a moral socializer.

The New Character Education

In the 1990s we are seeing the beginnings of a new character education movement, one which restores "good character" to its historical place as the central desirable outcome of the school's moral enterprise. No one knows yet how broad or deep this movement is; we have no studies to tell us what percentage of schools are making

what kind of effort. But something significant is afoot.

In July 1992, the Josephson Institute of Ethics called together more than 30 educational leaders representing state school boards, teachers' unions, universities, ethics centers, youth organizations, and religious groups. This diverse assemblage drafted the Aspen Declaration on Character Education, setting forth eight principles of character education.[1]

The Character Education Partnership was launched in March 1993, as a national coalition committed to putting character development at the top of the nation's educational agenda. Members include representatives from business, labor, government, youth, parents, faith communities, and the media.

The last two years have seen the publication of a spate of books—such as *Moral, Character, and Civic Education in the Elementary School*, *Why Johnny Can't Tell Right from Wrong*, and *Reclaiming Our Schools: A Handbook on Teaching Character, Academics, and Discipline*—that make the case for character education and describe promising programs around the country. A new periodical, the *Journal of Character Education*, is devoted entirely to covering the field.[2]

Why Character Education Now?

Why this groundswell of interest in character education? There are at least three causes:

1. *The decline of the family.* The family, traditionally a child's primary moral teacher, is for vast numbers of children today failing to perform that role, thus creating a moral vacuum. In her recent book *When the Bough Breaks: The Cost of Neglecting Our Children*, economist Sylvia Hewlett documents that American children, rich and poor, suffer a level of neglect unique among developed nations (1991). Overall, child well-being has declined despite a decrease in the number of children per family, an increase in the educational

level of parents, and historically high levels of public spending in education.

In "Dan Quayle Was Right" (April 1993) Barbara Dafoe Whitehead synthesizes the social science research on the decline of the two biological-parent family in America:

> If current trends continue, less than half of children born today will live continuously with their own mother and father throughout childhood. . . . An increasing number of children will experience family break-up two or even three times during childhood.

Children of marriages that end in divorce and children of single mothers are more likely to be poor, have emotional and behavioral problems, fail to achieve academically, get pregnant, abuse drugs and alcohol, get in trouble with the law, and be sexually and physically abused. Children in stepfamilies are generally worse off (more likely to be sexually abused, for example) than children in single-parent homes.

No one has felt the impact of family disruption more than schools. Whitehead writes:

> Across the nation, principals report a dramatic rise in the aggressive, acting-out behavior characteristic of children, especially boys, who are living in single-parent families. Moreover, teachers find that many children are so upset and preoccupied by the explosive drama of their own family lives that they are unable to concentrate on such mundane matters as multiplication tables.

Family disintegration, then, drives the character education movement in two ways: schools have to teach the values kids aren't learning at home; and schools, in order to conduct teaching and learning, must become caring moral communities that help children from unhappy homes focus on their work, control their anger, feel cared about, and become responsible students.

2. *Troubling trends in youth character.* A second impetus for renewed character education is the sense that young people in general, not just those from fractured families, have been adversely affected by poor parenting (in intact as well as broken families); the wrong kind of adult role models; the sex, violence, and materialism portrayed in the mass media; and the pressures of the peer group. Evidence that this hostile moral environment is taking a toll on youth character can be found in 10 troubling trends: rising youth violence; increasing dishonesty (lying, cheating, and stealing); growing disrespect for authority; peer cruelty; a resurgence of bigotry on school campuses, from preschool through higher education; a decline in the work ethic; sexual precocity; a growing self-centeredness and declining civil responsibility; an increase in self-destructive behavior; and ethical illiteracy.

The statistics supporting these trends are overwhelming.[3] For example, the U.S. homicide rate for 15- to 24-year-old males is 7 times higher than Canada's and 40 times higher than Japan's. The U.S. has one of the highest teenage pregnancy rates, the highest teen abortion rate, and the highest level of drug use among young people in the developed world. Youth suicide has tripled in the past 25 years, and a survey of more than 2,000 Rhode Island students, grades six through nine, found that two out of three boys and one of two girls thought it "acceptable for a man to force sex on a woman" if they had been dating for six months or more (Kikuchi 1988).

3. *A recovery of shared, objectively important ethical values.* Moral decline in society has gotten bad enough to jolt us out of the privatism and relativism dominant in recent decades. We are recovering the wisdom that we do share a basic morality, essential for our survival; that adults must promote this morality by teaching the young, directly and indirectly, such values as respect, responsibility, trustworthiness, fairness, caring, and civil virtue; and that these values are not merely subjective preferences but that they have objective worth and a claim on our collective conscience.

Such values affirm our human dignity, promote the good of the individual and the common good, and protect our human rights. They meet the classic ethical tests of reversibility (Would you want to be treated this way?) and universalizability (Would you want all persons to act this way in a similar situation?). They define our responsibilities in a democracy, and they are recognized by all civilized people and taught by all enlightened creeds. *Not* to teach children these core ethical values is grave moral failure.

What Character Education Must Do

In the face of a deteriorating social fabric, what must character education do to develop good character in the young?

First, it must have an adequate theory of what good character is, one which gives schools a clear idea of their goals. Character must be broadly conceived to encompass cognitive, affective, and behavioral aspects of morality. Good character consists of knowing the good, desiring the good, and doing the good. Schools must help children *understand* the core values, *adopt* or commit to them, and then *act upon* them in their own lives.

The cognitive side of character includes at least six specific moral qualities: awareness of the moral dimensions of the situation at hand, knowing moral values and what they require of us in concrete cases, perspective-taking, moral reasoning, thoughtful decision making, and moral self-knowledge. All these powers of rational moral thought are required for full moral maturity and citizenship in a democratic society.

People can be very smart about matters of right and wrong, however, and still choose the wrong. Moral education that is merely intellectual misses the crucial emotional side of character, which serves as the bridge between judgment and action. The emotional side includes at least the following qualities: conscience (the felt obligation to do what one judges to be right), self-respect, empathy, loving the good, self-control, and humility (a willingness to both recognize and correct our moral failings.).

At times, we know what we should do, feel strongly that we should do it, yet still fail to translate moral judgment and feeling into effective moral behavior. Moral action, the third part of character, draws upon three additional moral qualities: competence (skills such as listening, communicating, and cooperating), will (which mobilizes our judgment and energy), and moral habit (a reliable inner disposition to respond to situations in a morally good way).

Developing Character

Once we have a comprehensive concept of character, we need a comprehensive approach to developing it. This approach tells schools to look at themselves through a moral lens and consider how virtually everything that goes on there affects the values and character of students. Then, plan how to use all phases of classroom and school life as deliberate tools of character development.

If schools wish to maximize their moral clout, make a lasting difference in students' character, and engage and develop all three parts of character (knowing, feeling, and behavior), they need a comprehensive, holistic approach. Having a comprehensive approach includes asking, Do present school practices support, neglect, or contradict the school's professed values and character education aims?

In classroom practice, a comprehensive approach to character education calls upon the individual teacher to:

■ *Act as caregiver, model, and mentor*, treating students with love and respect, setting a good example, supporting positive social behavior, and correcting hurtful actions through one-on-one guidance and whole-class discussions;

■ *Create a moral community*, helping students know one another as persons, respect and care about one another, and feel valued membership in, and responsibility to, the group;

■ *Practice moral discipline*, using the creation and enforcement of rules as opportunities to foster moral reasoning, voluntary compliance with rules, and respect for others;

■ *Create a democratic classroom environment*, involving students in decision making and the responsibility for making the classroom a good place to be and learn;

- *Teach values through the curriculum,* using the ethically rich content of academic subjects (such as literature, history, and science), as well as outstanding programs (such as *Facing History and Ourselves*[4] and *The Heartwood Ethics Curriculum for Children*[5]), as vehicles for teaching values and examining moral questions;

- *Use cooperative learning* to develop students' appreciation of others, perspective taking, and ability to work with others toward common goals;

- *Develop the "conscience of craft"* by fostering students' appreciation of learning, capacity for hard work, commitment to excellence, and sense of work as affecting the lives of others;

- *Encourage moral reflection* through reading, research, essay writing, journal keeping, discussion, and debate;

- *Teach conflict resolution,* so that students acquire the essential moral skills of solving conflicts fairly and without force.

Besides making full use of the moral life of classrooms, a comprehensive approach calls upon the school *as a whole* to:

- *Foster caring beyond the classroom,* using positive role models to inspire altruistic behavior and providing opportunities at every grade level to perform school and community service;

- *Create a positive moral culture in the school,* developing a schoolwide ethos (through the leadership of the principal, discipline, a schoolwide sense of community, meaningful student government, a moral community among adults, and making time for moral concerns) that supports and amplifies the values taught in the classrooms;

- *Recruit parents and the community as partners in character education,* letting parents know that the school considers them their child's first and most important moral teacher, giving parents specific ways they can reinforce the values the school is trying to teach, and seeking the help of the community, churches, businesses, local government, and the media in promoting the core ethical values.

The Challenges Ahead

Whether character education will take hold in American schools remains to be seen. Among the factors that will determine the movement's long-range success are:

- *Support for schools.* Can schools recruit the help they need from the other key formative institutions that shape the values of the young—including families, faith communities, and the media? Will public policy act to strengthen and support families, and will parents make the stability of their families and the needs of their children their highest priority?

- *The role of religion.* Both liberal and conservative groups are asking, How can students be sensitively engaged in considering the role of religion in the origins and moral development of our nation? How can students be encouraged to use their intellectual and moral resources, including their faith traditions, when confronting social issues (for example, what is my obligation to the poor?) and making personal moral decisions (for example, should I have sex before marriage?)?

- *Moral leadership.* Many schools lack a positive, cohesive moral culture. Especially at the building level, it is absolutely essential to have moral leadership that sets, models, and consistently enforces high standards of respect and responsibility. Without a positive schoolwide ethos, teachers will feel demoralized in their individual efforts to teach good values.

- *Teacher education.* Character education is far more complex than teaching math or reading; it requires personal growth as well as skills development. Yet teachers typically receive almost no preservice or inservice training in the moral aspects of their craft. Many teachers do not feel comfortable or competent in the values domain. How will teacher education colleges and school staff development programs meet this need?

"Character is destiny," wrote the ancient Greek philosopher Heraclitus. As we confront the causes of our deepest societal problems, whether in our intimate relationships or public institutions, questions of character loom large. As we close out a turbulent century and ready our schools for the next, educating for character is a moral imperative if we care about the future of our society and our children. ■

Notes

1. For a copy of the Aspen Declaration and the issue of *Ethics* magazine reporting on the conference, write the Josephson Institute of Ethics, 310 Washington Blvd., Suite 104, Marina del Rey, CA 90292.

2. For information write Mark Kann, Editor, *The Journal of Character Education*, Jefferson Center for Character Education, 202 S. Lake Ave., Suite 240, Pasadena, CA 91101.

3. For documentation of these youth trends, see T. Lickona, (1991), *Educating for Character: How Our Schools Can Teach Respect and Responsibility* (New York: Bantam Books).

4. *Facing History and Ourselves* is an 8-week Holocaust curriculum for 8th graders. Write Facing History and Ourselves National Foundation, 25 Kennard Rd., Brookline, MA 02146.

5. *The Heartwood Ethics Curriculum for Children* uses multicultural children's literature to teach universal values. Write The Heartwood Institute, 12300 Perry Highway, Wexford, PA 15090.

References

Benninga, J. S., ed. (1991). *Moral, Character, and Civic Education in the Elementary School.* New York: Teachers College Press.

Hewlett, S. (1991). *When the Bough Breaks: The Cost of Neglecting Our Children.* New York: Basic Books.

Kikuchi, J. (Fall 1988). "Rhode Island Develops Successful Intervention Program for Adolescents." *National Coalition Against Sexual Assault Newsletter.*

National Research Council. (1992). *Understanding and Preventing Violence.* Washington D.C.: National Research Council.

Whitehead, B. D. (April 1993). "Dan Quayle Was Right." *The Atlantic* 271: 47–84.

Wynne, E. A., and K. Ryan. (1992). *Reclaiming Our Schools: A Handbook on Teaching Character, Academics, and Discipline.* New York: Merrill.

P O S T   N O T E

Education for good character is one of our schools' latest fads—and also one of their oldest missions. This article by the nation's leading proponent of character education lays out the case for our schools' involvement in teaching core moral values and helping children acquire good habits, such as respect and responsibility.

But despite the call for character education from our parents, pulpits, and politicians, schools and teachers are often unsure what to do. Because character education has been absent from the great majority of our schools for fully three decades, few educators know how to translate their good intentions into practice. Many schools are having one or two inservice days, buying boxes of character-oriented banners to put up on their walls, and purchasing "Character Counts!" coffee cups for the teachers' lounge.

Developing in our young the strong moral habits that constitute good character needs to be a central priority for a school community. What Lickona calls a "comprehensive approach" will take time, energy, and deep commitment to achieve. But, curiously, schools that take on this mission wholeheartedly find that many of their other goals—academic, athletic, and social—are achieved in the process.

DISCUSSION QUESTIONS

1. What is your personal experience with character education in the schools?

2. Do you agree with the thrust of this article, that schools have a major role in the fostering of good character?

3. From your perspective, what are the hard questions that schools must grapple with if they are to engage in character education responsibly?

Part Seven

Educational Reform

Since the publication of *A Nation at Risk* in 1983 (a report of President Reagan's National Commission on Excellence in Education), American schools have been in what is referred to as an "era of school reform." Both educators and private citizens are worried about our schools' ability to supply an adequately educated workforce. New jobs in the information age require a worker to solve problems, often as a member of a team, write and speak proficiently, and carry out higher levels of mathematical computations. Dismal research reports on the academic achievement of American students, particularly when compared with students from other countries, have sent a clear message: Something must be done.

The primary response has been at the state level, where governors and legislatures across the country have passed laws requiring higher standards for students and teachers alike. Ways of more effectively and efficiently organizing schools have surfaced—some borrowed from industry, some from schools in other nations. This section offers an overview of some of the most important developments in reforming education.

What Matters Most: A Competent Teacher for Every Child

Linda Darling-Hammond

We propose an audacious goal . . . by the year 2006, America will provide all students with what should be their educational birthright: access to competent, caring, and qualified teachers.[1]

With these words, the National Commission on Teaching and America's Future summarized its challenge to the American public. After two years of intense study and discussion, the commission—a 26-member bipartisan blue-ribbon panel supported by the Rockefeller Foundation and the Carnegie Corporation of New York—concluded that the reform of elementary and secondary education depends first and foremost on restructuring its foundation, the teaching profession. The restructuring, the commission made clear, must go in two directions: toward increasing teachers' knowledge to meet the demands they face and toward redesigning schools to support high-quality teaching and learning.

The commission found a profession that has suffered from decades of neglect. By the standards of other professions and other countries, U.S. teacher education has historically been thin, uneven, and poorly financed. Teacher recruitment is distressingly ad hoc, and teacher salaries lag significantly behind those of other professions. This produces chronic shortages of qualified teachers in fields like mathematics and science and the continual hiring of large numbers of "teachers" who are unprepared for their jobs.

Furthermore, in contrast to other countries that invest most of their education dollars in well-prepared and well-supported teachers, half of the education dollars in the United States are spent on personnel and activities outside the classroom. A lack of standards for students and teachers, coupled with schools that are organized for 19th-century learning, leaves educators without an adequate foundation for constructing good teaching. Under these conditions, excellence is hard to achieve.

The commission is clear about what needs to change. No more hiring unqualified teachers on the sly. No more nods and winks at teacher education programs that fail to prepare teachers properly. No more tolerance for incompetence in the classroom. Children are compelled to attend school. Every state guarantees them equal protection under the law, and most promise them a sound education. In the face of these obligations, students have a right to competent, caring teachers who work in schools organized for success.

The commission is also clear about what needs to be done. Like the Flexner report that led to the transformation of the medical profession in 1910, this report, *What Matters Most: Teaching for America's Future*, examines successful practices within and outside the United States to describe what works. The commission concludes that children can reap the benefits of current knowledge about teaching and learning only if schools and schools of education are dramatically redesigned.

The report offers a blueprint for recruiting, preparing, supporting, and rewarding excellent educators in all of America's schools. The plan is aimed at ensuring that all schools have teachers with the knowledge and skills they need to enable all children to learn. If a caring, qualified

Linda Darling-Hammond is a professor of education at Stanford University. Darling-Hammond, Linda, "What Matters Most: A Competent Teacher for Every Child," *Phi Delta Kappan*, November 1996. Copyright © 1996 by Linda Darling-Hammond. Reprinted by permission of the author.

teacher for every child is the most important ingredient in education reform, then it should no longer be the factor most frequently overlooked.

At the same time, such teachers must have available to them schools and school systems that are well designed to achieve their key academic mission: they must be focused on clear, high standards for students; organized to provide a coherent, high-quality curriculum across the grades; and designed to support teachers' collective work and learning.

We note that this challenge is accompanied by an equally great opportunity: over the next decade we will recruit and hire more than two million teachers for America's schools. More than half of the teachers who will be teaching 10 years from now will be hired during the next decade. If we can focus our energies on providing this generation of teachers with the kinds of knowledge and skills they need to help students succeed, we will have made an enormous contribution to America's future.

The Nature of the Problem

The education challenge facing the U.S. is not that its schools are not as good as they once were. It is that schools must help the vast majority of young people reach levels of skill and competence that were once thought to be within the reach of only a few.

After more than a decade of school reform, America is still a very long way from achieving its educational goals. Instead of all children coming to school ready to learn, more are living in poverty and without health care than a decade ago.[2] Graduation rates and student achievement in most subjects have remained flat or have increased only slightly.[3] Fewer than 10% of high school students can read, write, compute, and manage scientific material at the high levels required for today's "knowledge work" jobs.[4]

This distance between our stated goals and current realities is not due to lack of effort. Many initiatives have been launched in local communities with positive effects. Nonetheless, we have reached an impasse in spreading these promising efforts to the system as a whole. It is now clear that most schools and teachers cannot produce the kind of learning demanded by the new reforms—not because they do not want to, but because they do not know how, and the systems they work in do not support their efforts to do so.

The Challenge for Teaching

A more complex, knowledge-based, and multicultural society creates new expectations for teaching. To help diverse learners master more challenging content, teachers must go far beyond dispensing information, giving a test, and giving a grade. They must themselves know their subject areas deeply, and they must understand how students think, if they are to create experiences that actually work to produce learning.

Developing the kind of teaching that is needed will require much greater clarity about what students need to learn in order to succeed in the world that awaits them and what teachers need to know and do in order to help students learn it. Standards that reflect these imperatives for student learning and for teaching are largely absent in our nation today. States are just now beginning to establish standards for student learning.

Standards for teaching are equally haphazard. Although most parents might assume that teachers, like other professionals, are educated in similar ways so that they acquire common knowledge before they are admitted to practice, this is not the case. Unlike doctors, lawyers, accountants, or architects, all teachers do not have the same training. Some teachers have very high levels of skills—particularly in states that require a bachelor's degree in the discipline to be taught—along with coursework in teaching, learning, curriculum, and child development; extensive practice teaching; and a master's degree in education. Others learn little about their subject matter or about teaching, learning, and child development—particularly in states that have low requirements for licensing.

And while states have recently begun to require some form of testing for a teaching license, most licensing exams are little more than multiple-choice tests of basic skills and general knowledge, widely criticized by educators and experts as woefully inadequate to measure teaching skill.[5] Furthermore, in many states the cutoff scores are so low that there is no effective standard for entry.

These difficulties are barely known to the public. The schools' most closely held secret amounts to a great national shame: roughly one-quarter of newly hired American teachers lack the qualifications for their jobs. More than 12% of new hires enter the classroom without any formal training at all, and another 14% arrive without fully meeting state standards.

Although no state will permit a person to write wills, practice medicine, fix plumbing, or style hair without completing training and passing an examination, more than 40 states allow districts to hire teachers who have not met basic requirements. States pay more attention to the qualifications of the veterinarians treating America's pets than to those of the people educating the nation's youngsters. Consider the following facts:

- In recent years, more than 50,000 people who lack the training required for their jobs have entered teaching annually on emergency or substandard licenses.[6]

- Nearly one-fourth (23%) of all secondary teachers do not have even a minor in their main teaching field. This is true for more than 30% of mathematics teachers.[7]

- Among teachers who teach a second subject, 36% are unlicensed in that field, and 50% lack a minor in it.[8]

- Fifty-six percent of high school students taking physical science are taught by out-of-field teacher, as are 27% of those taking mathematics and 21% of those taking English.[9] The proportions are much greater in high-poverty schools and lower-track classes.

- In schools with the highest minority enrollments, students have less than a 50% chance of getting a science or mathematics teacher who holds a license and a degree in the field in which he or she teaches.[10]

In the nation's poorest schools, where hiring is most lax and teacher turnover is constant, the results are disastrous. Thousands of children are taught throughout their school careers by a parade of teachers without preparation in the fields in which they teach, inexperienced beginners with little training and no mentoring, and short-term substitutes trying to cope with constant staff disruptions.[11] It is more surprising that some of these children manage to learn than that so many fail to do so.

Current Barriers

Unequal resources and inadequate investments in teacher recruitment are major problems. Other industrialized countries fund their schools equally and make sure there are qualified teachers for all of them by underwriting teacher preparation and salaries. However, teachers in the U.S. must go into substantial debt to become prepared for a field that in most states pays less than any other occupation requiring a college degree.

This situation is not necessary or inevitable. The hiring of unprepared teachers was almost eliminated during the 1970s with scholarships and loans for college students preparing to teach, Urban Teacher Corps initiatives, and master of arts in teaching (MAT) programs, coupled with wage increases. However, the cancellation of most of these recruitment incentives in the 1980s led to renewed shortages when student enrollments started to climb once again, especially in cities. Between 1987 and 1991, the proportion of well-qualified new teachers—those entering teaching with a college major or minor and a license in their fields—actually declined from about 74% to 67%.[12]

There is no real system for recruiting, preparing, and developing America's teachers. Major problems include:

Inadequate teacher education. Because accreditation is not required of teacher education programs, their quality varies widely, with excellent programs standing alongside shoddy ones that are allowed to operate even when they do an utterly inadequate job. Too many American universities still treat their schools of education as "cash cows" whose excess revenues are spent on the training of doctors, lawyers, accountants, and almost any students other than prospective teachers themselves.

Slipshod recruitment. Although the share of academically able young people entering teaching has been increasing, there are still too few in some parts of the country and in critical subjects like mathematics and science. Federal incentives that once existed to induce talented people into high-need fields and locations have largely been eliminated.

Haphazard hiring and induction. School districts often lose the best candidates because of inefficient and cumbersome hiring practices, barriers to teacher mobility, and inattention to teacher qualifications. Those who do get hired are typically given the most difficult assignments and left to sink or swim, without the kind of help provided by internships and residencies in other professions. Isolated behind classroom doors with little feedback or help, as many as 30% leave in the first few years, while others learn merely to cope rather than to teach well.

Lack of professional development and rewards for knowledge and skill. In addition to the lack of support for beginning teachers, most school districts invest little in ongoing professional development for experienced teachers and spend much of these limited resources on unproductive "hit-and-run" workshops. Furthermore, most U.S. teachers have only three to five hours each week for planning. This leaves them with almost no regular time to consult together or to learn abut new teaching strategies, unlike their peers in many European and Asian countries who spend between 15 and 20 hours per week working jointly on refining lessons and learning about new methods.

The teaching career does not encourage teachers to develop or use growing expertise. Evaluation and tenure decisions often lack a tan-gible connection to a clear vision of high-quality teaching, important skills are rarely rewarded, and—when budgets must be cut—professional development is often the first item sacrificed. Historically, the only route to advancement in teaching has been to leave the classroom for administration.

In contrast, many European and Asian countries hire a greater number of better-paid teachers, provide them with more extensive preparation, give them time to work together, and structure schools so that teachers can focus on teaching and can come to know their students well. Teachers share decision making and take on a range of professional responsibilities without leaving teaching. This is possible because these other countries invest their resources in many more classroom teachers—typically constituting 60% to 80% of staff, as compared to only 43% in the United States—and many fewer nonteaching employees.[13]

Schools structured for failure. Today's schools are organized in ways that support neither student learning nor teacher learning well. Teachers are isolated from one another so that they cannot share knowledge or take responsibility for overall student learning. Technologies that could enable alternative uses of personnel and time are not yet readily available in schools, and few staff members are prepared to use them. Moreover, too many people and resources are allocated to jobs and activities outside of classrooms, on the sidelines rather than at the front lines of teaching and learning.

High-performance businesses are abandoning the organizational assumptions that led to this way of managing work. They are flattening hierarchies, creating teams, and training employees to take on wider responsibilities using technologies that allow them to perform their work more efficiently. Schools that have restructured their work in these ways have been able to provide more time for teachers to work together and more time for students to work closely with teachers around more clearly defined standards for learning.[14]

Goals for the Nation

To address these problems, the commission challenges the nation to embrace a set of goals that will put us on the path to serious, long-term improvements in teaching and learning for America. The commission has six goals for the year 2006.

- All children will be taught by teachers who have the knowledge, skills, and commitment to teach children well.
- All teacher education programs will meet professional standards, or they will be closed.
- All teachers will have access to high-quality professional development, and they will have regularly scheduled time for collegial work and planning.
- Both teachers and principals will be hired and retained based on their ability to meet professional standards of practice.
- Teachers' salaries will be based on their knowledge and skills.
- High-quality teaching will be the central investment of schools. Most education dollars will be spent on classroom teaching.

The Commission's Recommendations

The commission's proposals provide a vision and a blueprint for the development of a 21st-century teaching profession that can make good on the nation's educational goals. The recommendations are systemic in scope—not a recipe for more short-lived pilot and demonstration projects. They describe a new infrastructure for professional learning and an accountability system that ensures attention to standards for educators as well as for students at every level: national, state, district, school, and classroom.

The commission urges a complete overhaul in the systems of teacher preparation and professional development to ensure that they reflect current knowledge and practice. This redesign should create a continuum of teacher learning based on compatible standards that operate from recruitment and preservice education through licensing, hiring, and induction into the profession, to advanced certification and ongoing professional development.

The commission also proposes a comprehensive set of changes in school organization and management. And finally, it recommends a set of measures for ensuring that only those who are competent to teach or to lead schools are allowed to enter or to continue in the profession—a starting point for creating professional accountability. The specific recommendations are enumerated below.

1. Get serious about standards for both students and teachers. "The Commission recommends that we renew the national promise to bring every American child up to world-class standards in core academic areas and to develop and enforce rigorous standards for teacher preparation, initial licensing, and continuing development."

With respect to student standards, the commission believes that every state should work on incorporating challenging standards for learning—such as those developed by professional bodies like the National Council of Teachers of Mathematics—into curriculum frameworks and new assessments of student performance. Implementation must go beyond the tautology that "all children can learn" to examine what they should learn and how much they need to know.

Standards should be accompanied by benchmarks of performance—from "acceptable" to "highly accomplished"—so that students and teachers know how to direct their efforts toward greater excellence.

Clearly, if students are to achieve high standards, we can expect no less from teachers and other educators. Our highest priority must be to reach agreement on what teachers should know and be able to do in order to help students succeed. Unaddressed for decades, this task has recently been completed by three professional bodies: the National Council for Accreditation of Teacher Education (NCATE), the Interstate New Teacher Assessment and Support Consortium (INTASC), and the National Board for

Professional Teaching Standards (the National Board). Their combined efforts to set standards for teacher education, beginning teacher licensing, and advanced certification outline a continuum of teacher development throughout the career and offer the most powerful tools we have for reaching and rejuvenating the soul of the profession.

These standards and the assessments that grow out of them identify what it takes to be an effective teacher: subject-matter expertise coupled with an understanding of how children learn and develop; skill in using a range of teaching strategies and technologies; sensitivity and effectiveness in working with students from diverse backgrounds; the ability to work well with parents and other teachers; and assessment expertise capable of discerning how well children are doing, what they are learning, and what needs to be done next to move them along.

The standards reflect a teaching role in which the teacher is an instructional leader who orchestrates learning experiences in response to curriculum goals and student needs and who coaches students to high levels of independent performance. To advance standards, the commission recommends that states:

- establish their own professional standards boards;
- insist on professional accreditation for all schools of education;
- close inadequate schools of education;
- license teachers based on demonstrated performance, including tests of subject-matter knowledge, teaching knowledge, and teaching skill; and
- use National Board standards as the benchmark for accomplished teaching.

2. Reinvent teacher preparation and professional development.
"The Commission recommends that colleges and schools work with states to redesign teacher education so that the two million teachers to be hired in the next decade are adequately prepared and so that all teachers have access to high-quality learning opportunities."

For this to occur, states, school districts, and education schools should:

- organize teacher education and professional development around standards for students and teachers;
- institute extended, graduate-level teacher preparation programs that provide yearlong internships in a professional development school;
- create and fund mentoring programs for beginning teachers, along with evaluation of teaching skills;
- create stable, high-quality sources of professional development—and then allocate 1% of state and local spending to support them, along with additional matching funds to school districts;
- organize new sources of professional development, such as teacher academies, school/university partnerships, and learning networks that transcend school boundaries; and
- make professional development an ongoing part of teachers' daily work.

If teachers are to be ready to help their students meet the new standards that are now being set for them, teacher preparation and professional development programs must consciously examine the expectations embodied in new curriculum frameworks and assessments and understand what they imply for teaching and for learning to teach. Then they must develop effective strategies for preparing teachers to teach in these much more demanding ways.

Over the past decade, many schools of education have changed their programs to incorporate new knowledge. More than 300 have developed extended programs that add a fifth (and occasionally a sixth) year to undergraduate training. These programs allow beginning teachers to complete a degree in their subject area as well as to acquire a firmer ground in teaching skills. They allow coursework to be connected to extended practice teaching in schools—ideally, in professional development schools that, like teaching hospitals in medicine, have a special mission to support research and training. Recent studies show that graduates of extended programs are rated as better-prepared and more effective teachers and are far more likely to enter and remain in teaching than are their peers from traditional four-year programs.[15]

New teachers should have support from an expert mentor during the first year of teaching. Research shows that such support improves both teacher effectiveness and retention.[16] In the system we propose, teachers will have completed initial tests of subject-matter and basic teaching knowledge before entry and will be ready to undertake the second stage—a performance assessment of teaching skills—during this first year.

Throughout their careers, teachers should have ongoing opportunities to update their skills. In addition to time for joint planning and problem solving with in-school colleagues, teachers should have access to networks, school/university partnerships, and academies where they can connect with other educators to study subject-matter teaching, new pedagogies, and school change. The benefit of these opportunities is that they offer sustained work on problems of practice that are directly connected to teachers' work and student learning.

3. Overhaul teacher recruitment and put qualified teachers in every classroom.
"The Commission recommends that states and school districts pursue aggressive policies to put qualified teachers in every classroom by providing financial incentives to correct shortages, streamlining hiring procedures, and reducing barriers to teacher mobility."

Although each year the U.S. produces more new teachers than it needs, shortages of qualified candidates in particular fields (e.g., mathematics and science) and particular locations (primarily inner city and rural) are chronic.

In large districts, logistics can overwhelm everything else. It is sometimes the case that central offices cannot find out about classroom vacancies, principals are left in the dark about applicants, and candidates cannot get any information at all.

Finally, it should be stressed that large pools of potential mid-career teacher entrants—former employees of downsizing corporations, military and government retirees, and teacher aides

already in the schools—are for the most part untapped.

To remedy these situations, the commission suggests the following actions:

- increase the ability of financially disadvantaged districts to pay for qualified teachers and insist that school districts hire only qualified teachers;
- redesign and streamline hiring at the district level—principally by creating a central "electronic hiring hall" for all qualified candidates and establishing cooperative relationships with universities to encourage early hiring of teachers;
- eliminate barriers to teacher mobility by promoting reciprocal interstate licensing and by working across states to develop portable pensions;
- provide incentives (including scholarships and premium pay) to recruit teachers for high-need subjects and locations; and
- develop high-quality pathways to teaching for recent graduates, mid-career changers, paraprofessionals already in the classroom, and military and government retirees.

4. Encourage and reward knowledge and skill.
"The Commission recommends that school districts, states, and professional associations cooperate to make teaching a true profession, with a career continuum that places teaching at the top and rewards teachers for their knowledge and skills."

Schools have few ways of encouraging outstanding teaching, supporting teachers who take on the most challenging work, or rewarding increases in knowledge and skill. Newcomers who enter teaching without adequate preparation are paid at the same levels as those who enter with highly developed skills. Novices take on exactly the same kind of work as 30-year veterans, with little differentiation based on expertise. Mediocre teachers receive the same rewards as outstanding ones. And unlicensed "teachers" are placed on the same salary schedule as licensed teachers in high-demand fields such as mathematics and science or as teachers licensed in two or more subjects.

One testament to the inability of the existing system to understand what it is doing is that it rewards experience with easier work instead of encouraging senior teachers to deal with difficult learning problems and tough learning situations. As teachers gain experience, they can look forward to teaching in more affluent schools, working with easier schedules, dealing with "better" classes, or moving out of the classroom into administration. Teachers are rarely rewarded for applying their expertise to the most challenging learning problems or major needs of the system.

To address these issues, the commission recommends that state and local education agencies:

■ develop a career continuum linked to assessments and compensation systems that reward knowledge and skill (e.g., the ability to teach expertly in two or more subjects, as demonstrated by additional licenses, or the ability to pass examinations of teaching skill, such as those offered by INTASC and the National Board);

■ remove incompetent teachers through peer review programs that provide necessary assistance and due process; and

■ set goals and enact incentives for National Board certification in every district, with the aim of certifying 105,000 teachers during the next 10 years.

If teaching is organized as are other professions that have set consistent licensing requirements, standards of practice, and assessment methods, then advancement can be tied to professional growth and development. A career continuum that places teaching at the top and supports growing expertise should 1) recognize accomplishment, 2) anticipate that teachers will continue to teach while taking on other roles that allow them to share their knowledge, and 3) promote continued skill development related to clear standards.

Some districts, such as Cincinnati and Rochester, New York, have already begun to develop career pathways that tie evaluations to salary increments at key stages as teachers move from their *initial license* to *resident teacher* (under the supervision of a mentor) to the designation of *professional teacher*. The major decision to grant *tenure* is made after rigorous evaluation of performance (including both administrator and peer review) in the first several years of teaching. Advanced certification from the National Board for Professional Teaching Standards may qualify teachers for another salary step and/or for the position of lead teacher—a role that is awarded to those who have demonstrated high levels of competence and want to serve as mentors or consulting teachers.

One other feature of a new compensation system is key. The central importance of teaching to the mission of schools should be acknowledged by having the highest-paid professional in a school system be an experienced, National Board–certified teacher. As in other professions, roles should become less distinct. The jobs of teacher, consultant, supervisor, principal, curriculum developer, researcher, mentor, and professor should be hyphenated roles, allowing many ways for individuals to use their talents and expertise without abandoning the core work of the profession.

5. Create schools that are organized for student and teacher success.
"The Commission recommends that schools be restructured to become genuine learning organizations for both students and teachers: organizations that respect learning, honor teaching, and teach for understanding."

Many experts have observed that the demands of serious teaching and learning bear little relationship to the organization of the typical American school. Nothing more clearly reveals this problem than how we allocate the principal resources of school—time, money, and people. Far too many people sit in offices on the sidelines of the school's core work, managing routines rather than improving learning. Our schools are bureaucratic inheritances from the 19th century, not the kinds of learning organizations required of the 21st century.

Across the United States, the ration of school staff to students is 1 to 9 (with "staff" including district employees, school administrators, teachers, instructional aides, guidance counselors, librarians, and support staff). However, actual class size averages about 24 and reaches 35 or more in some cities. Teaching loads for high school teachers generally exceed 100 students per day. Yet many schools have proved that it is possible to restructure adults' use of time so that more teachers and administrators actually work in the classroom, face-to-face with students on a daily basis, thus reducing class sizes while creating more time for teacher collaboration. They do this by creating teams of teachers who share students; engaging almost all adults in the school in these teaching teams, where they can share expertise directly with one another; and reducing pullouts and nonteaching jobs.

Schools must be greed from the tyrannies of time and tradition to permit more powerful student and teacher learning. To accomplish this the commission recommends that state and local boards work to:

- flatten hierarchies and reallocate resources to invest more in teachers and technology and less in nonteaching personnel;

- provide venture capital in the form of challenge grants that will promote learning linked to school improvement and will reward effective team efforts; and

- select, prepare, and retain principals who understand teaching and learning and who can lead high-performing schools.

If students have an inalienable right to be taught by a qualified teacher, teachers have a right to be supervised by a highly qualified principal. The job began as that of a "principal teacher," and this conception is ever more relevant as the focus of the school recenters on academic achievement for students. Principals should teach at least part of the time (as do most European, Asian, and private school directors), and they should be well prepared as instructional leaders, with a solid understanding of teaching and learning.

Next Steps

Developing recommendations is easy. Implementing them is hard work. The first step is to recognize that these ideas must be pursued together—as an entire tapestry that is tightly interwoven.

The second step is to build on the substantial work of education reform undertaken in the last decade. All across the country, successful programs for recruiting, educating, and mentoring new teachers have sprung up. Professional networks and teacher academies have been launched, many teacher preparation programs have been redesigned, higher standards for licensing teachers and accrediting education schools have been developed, and, of course, the National Board for Professional Teaching Standards is now fully established and beginning to define and reward accomplished teaching.

While much of what the commission proposes can and should be accomplished by reallocating resources that are currently used unproductively, there will be new costs. The estimated additional annual costs of the commission's key recommendations are as follows: scholarships for teaching recruits, $500 million; teacher education reforms, $875 million; mentoring supports and new licensing assessments, $750 million; and state funds for professional development, $2.75 billion. The total is just under $5 billion annually—less than 1% of the amount spent on the federal savings-and-loan bailout. This is not too much, we believe, to bail out our schools and to secure our future.

A Call to Action

Setting the commission's agenda in motion and carrying it to completion will demand the best of us all. The commission calls on governors and legislators to create state professional boards to govern teacher licensing standards and to issue annual report cards on the status of teaching. It asks state legislators and governors to set aside at least 1% of funds for standards-based teacher training. It urges Congress to put money behind the professional development programs it has already approved but never funded.

Moreover, the commission asks the profession to take seriously its responsibilities to children and the American future. Among other measures, the commission insists that state educators close the loopholes that permit administrators to put unqualified "teachers" in the classroom. It calls on university officials to take up the hard work of improving the preparation and skills of new and practicing teachers. It asks administrators and teachers to take on the difficult task of guaranteeing teaching competence in the classroom. And it asks local school boards and superintendents to play their vital role by streamlining hiring procedures, upgrading quality, and putting more staff and resources into the front lines of teaching.

If all of these things are accomplished, the teaching profession of the 21st century will look much different from the one we have today. Indeed, someone entering the profession might expect to advance along a continuum that unfolds much like this:

For as long as she could remember, Elena had wanted to teach. As a peer tutor in middle school, she loved the feeling she got whenever her partner learned something new. In high school, she served as a teacher's aide for her community service project. She linked up with other students through an Internet group started by Future Educators of America.

When she arrived at college she knew she wanted to prepare to teach, so she began taking courses in developmental and cognitive psychology early in her sophomore year. She chose mathematics as a major and applied in her junior year for the university's five-year course of study leading to a master of arts in teaching. After a round of interviews and a review of her record thus far, Elena was admitted into the highly selective teacher education program.

The theories Elena studied in her courses came to life before her eyes as she conducted a case study of John, a 7-year-old whom she tutored in a nearby school. She was struck by John's amazing ability to build things, in contrast with his struggles to learn to read. She carried these puzzles back to her seminar and on into her other courses as she tried to understand learning.

Over time, she examined other cases, some of them available on a multimedia computer system that allowed her to see videotapes of children, samples of their work, and documentation from their teachers about their learning strategies, problems, and progress. From these data, Elena and her classmates developed a concrete sense of different learning approaches. She began to think about how she could use John's strengths to create productive pathways into other areas of learning.

Elena's teachers modeled the kinds of strategies she herself would be using as a teacher. Instead of lecturing from texts, they enabled students to develop and apply knowledge in the context of real teaching situations. These frequently occurred in the professional development school (PDS) where Elena was engaged in a yearlong internship, guided by a faculty of university- and school-based teacher educators.

In the PDS, Elena was placed with a team of student teachers who worked with a team of expert veteran teachers. Her team included teachers of art, language arts, and science, as well as mathematics. They discussed learning within and across these domains in many of their assignments and constructed interdisciplinary curricula together.

Most of the school- and university-based teacher educators who made up the PDS faculty had been certified as accomplished practitioners by the National Board for Professional Teaching Standards, having completed a portfolio of evidence about their teaching along with a set of rigorous performance assessments. The faculty members created courses, internship experiences, and seminars that allowed them to integrate theory and practice, pose fundamental dilemmas of teaching, and address specific aspects of learning to teach.

Elena's classroom work included observing and documenting the learning and behavior of specific children, evaluating lessons that illustrated important concepts and strategies, tutoring and working with small groups, sitting in on family conferences, engaging in school and team planning meetings, visiting homes and community agencies to learn about their resources, planning field trips and curriculum segments, teaching lessons and short units, and ultimately taking major responsibility for the class for a month at the end of the year. This work was supplemented by readings and discussions grounded in case studies of teaching.

A team of PDS teachers videotaped all their classes over the course of the year to serve as the basis for discussions of teaching decisions and outcomes. These teachers' lesson plans, student work, audiotaped planning journals, and reflections on lessons were also available in a multimedia database. This allowed student teachers to look at practice from many angles, examine how classroom situations arose from things that had happened in the past, see how various strategies turned out, and understand a teacher's thinking about students, subjects, and curriculum goals as he or she made decisions. Because the PDS was also wired for video and computer communication with the school of education, master teachers could hold conversations with student teachers by teleconference or e-mail when on-site visits were impossible.

When Elena finished her rich, exhausting internship year, she was ready to try her hand at what she knew would be a demanding first year of teaching. She submitted her portfolio for review by the state professional standards board and sat for the examination of subject-matter and teaching knowledge that was required for an initial teaching license. She was both exhilarated and anxious when she received a job offer, but she felt she was ready to try her hand at teaching.

Elena spent that summer eagerly developing curriculum ideas for her new class. She had the benefit of advice from the district mentor teacher already assigned to work with her in her first year of teaching, and she had access to an on-line database of teaching materials developed by teachers across the country and organized around the curriculum standards of the National Council of Teachers of Mathematics, of which she had become a member.

Elena's mentor teacher worked with her and several other new middle school mathematics and science teachers throughout the year, meeting with them individually and in groups to examine their teaching and provide support. The mentors and their first-year colleagues also met in groups once a month at the PDS to discuss specific problems of practice.

Elena met weekly with the other math and science teachers in the school to discuss curriculum plans and share demonstration lessons. This extended lunch meeting occurred while her students were in a Project Adventure/physical education course that taught them teamwork and cooperation skills. She also met with the four other members of her teaching team for three hours each week while their students were at community-service placements. The team used this time to discuss cross-disciplinary teaching plans and the progress of the 80 students they shared.

In addition to these built-in opportunities for daily learning, Elena and her colleagues benefited from the study groups they had developed at their school and the professional development offerings at the local university and the Teachers Academy.

At the Teachers Academy, school- and university-based faculty members taught extended courses in areas ranging from advances in learning theory to all kinds of teaching methods, from elementary science to advanced calculus. These courses usually featured case studies and teaching demonstrations as well as follow-up work in teachers' own classroom. The academy provided the technologies needed for multimedia conferencing, which allowed teachers to "meet" with one another across their schools and to see one another's classroom work. They could also connect to courses and study groups at the university, including a popular master's degree program that helped teachers prepare for National Board certification.

With the strength of a preparation that had helped her put theory and practice together and with the support of so many colleagues, Elena felt confident that she could succeed at her life's goal: becoming—and, as she now understood, *always* becoming—a teacher. ∎

Notes

1. *What Matters Most: Teaching for America's Future* (New York: National Commission on Teaching and America's Future, 1996). Copies of this report can be obtained from the National Commission on Teaching and America's Future, P.O. Box 5239, Woodbridge, VA 22194-5239. Prices, including postage and handling, are $18 for the full report, $5 for the summary report, and $20 for both reports. Orders must be prepaid.

2. *Income, Poverty, and Valuation of Non-Cash Benefits: 1993* (Washington, D.C.: U.S. Bureau of the Census, Current Population Reports, Series P-60, No. 188, 1995), Table D-5, p. D-17. See also *Current Population Survey: March 1988/March 1995* (Washington, D.C.: U.S. Bureau of the Census, 1995).

3. *National Education Goals Report: Executive Summary* (Washington, D.C.: National Education Goals Panel, 1995).

4. National Center for Education Statistics, *Report in Brief: National Assessment of Educational Progress (NAEP) 1992 Trends in Academic Progress* (Washington, D.C.: U.S. Department of Education, 1994).

5. For reviews of teacher licensing tests, see Linda Darling-Hammond, "Teaching Knowledge: How Do We Test It?," *American Educator*, Fall 1986, pp. 18–21, 46; Lee Shulman, "Knowledge and Teaching: Foundations of the New Reform," *Harvard Educational Review*, January 1987, pp. 1–22; C. J. MacMillan and Shirley Pendlebury, "The Florida Performance Measurement System: A Consideration," *Teachers College Record*, Fall 1985, pp. 67–78; Walter Haney, George Madaus, and Amelia Kreitzer, "Charms Talismanic: Testing Teachers for the Improvement of American Education," in Ernest Z. Rothkopf, ed., *Review of Research in Education, Vol. 14* (Washington, D.C.: American Educational Research Association, 1987), pp. 169–238; and Edward H. Haertel, "New Forms of Teacher Assessment," in Gerald Grant, ed., *Review of Research in Education, Vol. 17* (Washington D.C.: American Educational Research Association, 1991), pp. 3–29.

6. C. Emily Feistritzer and David T. Chester, *Alternative Teacher Certification: A State-by-State Analysis* (Washington, D.C.: National Center for Education Information, 1996).

7. Marilyn M. McMillen, Sharon A. Bobbitt, and Hilda F. Lynch, "Teacher Training, Certification, and Assignment in Public Schools: 1990–91," paper presented at the annual meeting of the American Educational Research Association, New Orleans, April 1994.

8. National Center for Education Statistics, *The Condition of Education 1995* (Washington, D.C.: U.S. Department of Education, 1995), p. x.

9. Richard M. Ingersoll, *Schools and Staffing Survey: Teacher Supply, Teacher Qualifications, and Teacher Turnover, 1990–1991* (Washington, D.C.: National Center for Education Statistics, 1995), p. 28.

10. Jeannie Oakes, *Multiplying Inequalities: The Effects of Race, Social Class, and Tracking on Opportunities to Learn Mathematics and Science* (Santa Monica, Calif.: RAND Corporation, 1990).

11. *Who Will Teach Our Children?* (Sacramento: California Commission on Teaching, 1985); and Linda Darling-Hammond, "Inequality and Access to Knowledge," in James Banks, ed., *Handbook of Research on Multicultural Education* (New York: Macmillan, 1995), pp. 465–83.

12. Mary Rollefson, *Teacher Supply in the United States: Sources of Newly Hired Teachers in Public and Private Schools* (Washington, D.C.: National Center for Education Statistics, 1993).

13. *Education Indicators at a Glance* (Paris: Organisation for Economic Cooperation and Development, 1995).

14. Linda Darling-Hammond, "Beyond Bureaucracy: Restructuring Schools for High Performance," in Susan Fuhrman and Jennifer O'Day, eds., *Rewards and Reform* (San Francisco: Jossey-Bass, 1996), pp. 144–94; Linda Darling-Hammond, Jacqueline Ancess, and Beverly Falk, *Authentic Assessment in Action: Studies of Schools and Students at Work* (New York: Teachers College Press, 1995); Fred Newman and Gary Wehlage, *Successful School Restructuring: A Report to the Public and Educators by the Center on Organization and Restructuring of Schools* (Madison: Board of Regents of the University of Wisconsin System, 1995); and Ann Lieberman, ed., *The Work of Restructuring Schools: Building from the Ground Up* (New York: Teachers College Press, 1995).

15. For data on effectiveness and retention, see Michael Andrew, "The Differences Between Graduates of Four-Year and Five-Year Teacher Preparation Programs," *Journal of Teacher Education*, vol. 41, 1990, pp. 45–51; Thomas Baker, "A Survey of Four-Year and Five-Year Program Graduates and Their Principals," *Southeastern Regional Association of Teacher Educators (SRATE) Journal*, Summer 1993, pp. 28–33; Michael Andrew and Richard L. Schwab, "Has Reform in Teacher Education Influenced Teacher Performance? An Outcome Assessment of Graduates of Eleven Teacher Education Programs," *Action in Teacher Education*, Fall 1995, pp. 43–53; Jon J. Denton and William H. Peters, "Program Assessment Report: Curriculum Evaluation of a Nontraditional Program for Certifying Teachers," unpublished report, Texas A & M University, College Station, 1988; and Hyun-Seok Shin, "Estimating Future Teacher Supply: An Application of Survival Analysis," paper presented at the annual meeting of the American Educational Research Association, New Orleans, April 1994.

16. Leslie Huling-Austin, ed., *Assisting the Beginning Teacher* (Reston, Va.: Association of Teacher Educators, 1989); Mark A. Smylie, "Redesigning Teachers' Work: Connections to the Classroom," in Linda Darling-Hammond, ed., *Review of Research in Education, Vol. 20* (Washington, D.C.: American Educational Research Association, 1994); and Linda Darling-Hammond, ed., *Professional Development Schools: Schools for Developing a Profession* (New York: Teachers College Press, 1994).

The education of teachers has been a long-standing concern both inside and outside the profession. As Linda Darling-Hammond points out, many school reform efforts have been stymied because the teaching force was ill-equipped to put the reforms into effect. Two issues in particular have threatened efforts to reform teacher education. One is an on-the-cheap approach to the preparation of teachers. As a society, we spend few social resources on training teachers. While the preparation of most other professions has evolved out of the undergraduate years into concentrated graduate study and practical experience, most teachers still must skimp on their basic liberal education. Until we are ready to support the education of teachers at a much higher level, we will be sending teachers into schools with too much to learn on the job.

The second issue is related to the first: the underestimation of what it takes to be a teacher. If teaching is simply a matter of standing in front of students and transferring information, then perhaps our limited teacher education programs are adequate. However, if we want our teachers to help children engage in their own discoveries and become self-starting inquirers, we need a larger vision of the teacher to guide teacher education. The report described by Darling-Hammond offers such a vision.

D I S C U S S I O N Q U E S T I O N S

1. What are some of the developments leading to the call for reform of teacher education?

2. According to Darling-Hammond, what workplace factors are currently affecting the education of teachers?

3. In your own view, what aspect of teacher education is most in need of reform? Why?

From Aptitude to Effort: A New Foundation for Our Schools

Lauren B. Resnick

Two challenges face American education today: We must raise overall achievement levels, and we must make opportunities for achievement more equitable. The importance of both derives from the same basic condition—our changing economy. Never before has the pool of developed skill and capability mattered more in our prospects for general economic health. And never before have skill and knowledge mattered as much in the economic prospects for individuals. There is no longer a welcoming place in low-skill, high-wage jobs for people who have not cultivated talents appropriate to an information economy. The country, indeed each state and region, must press for a higher overall level of such cultivated talents. Otherwise, we can expect a continuation of the pattern of falling personal incomes and declining public services that has characterized the past twenty years.

Lauren B. Resnick is director of the Learning Research and Development Center and professor of psychology at the University of Pittsburgh. "From Aptitude to Effort: A New Foundation for Our Schools" reprinted by permission of *Daedalus*, Journal of the American Academy of Arts and Sciences, from the issue entitled, "American Education: Still Separate, Still Unequal," Fall 1995, Vol. 124, No. 4, and from Lauren B. Resnick.

The only way to achieve this higher level of skill and ability in the population at large is to make sure that all students, not just a privileged and select few, learn skills that our society requires. Equity and excellence, classically viewed as competing goals, must now be created as a single aspiration.

To do this will require a profound transformation of our most basic assumptions about the conditions that enable people to learn. What we learn is a function both of our talents—our aptitude for particular kinds of learning—and of how hard we try—our effort. But what is the relationship between aptitude and effort? Are they independent of each other, and, if so, which is more important? Do strengths in one compensate for weaknesses in the other? Or does one help to create the other?

Facing Up to Our Aptitude-Oriented Education System

Historically, American education has wavered between the first and second of these possibilities, the independent and the compensatory. But it has never seriously considered the third possibility—that effort that can create ability. Early in this century, we built an educational system around the assumption that aptitude is paramount in learning and that it is largely hereditary. The system was oriented toward selection, distinguishing the naturally able from the less able and providing students with programs thought suitable to their talents. In other periods, most notably during the Great Society reforms, we worked on a compensatory principle, arguing that special effort, by an individual or an institution, could make up for low aptitude. The third possibility—that effort actually creates ability, that people can become smart by working hard at the right kinds of learning tasks—has never been taken seriously in America or indeed in any European society, although it is the guiding assumption of education institutions in societies with a Confucian tradition.

Although the compensatory assumption is more recent in the history of American education, many of our tools and standard practices are inherited from the earlier period in which aptitude reigned supreme. As a result, our schools largely function as if we believed that native ability is the primary determinant in learning, that the "bell curve" of intelligence is a natural phenomenon that must necessarily be reproduced in all learning, that effort counts for little. Consider the following examples: (1) IQ tests or their surrogates determine who will have access to the enriched programs for the "gifted and talented." This curriculum is denied to students who are judged less capable. (2) Our so-called achievement tests are normed to compare students with one another rather than with a standard of excellence, making it difficult to see the results of learning, and, in the process, actively discouraging effort: Students stay at about the same relative percentile rank, even if they have learned a lot, so why should they try hard? (3) We group students, sometimes within classrooms, and provide de facto different curricula to different groups. As a result, some students never get the chance to study a high-demand, high-expectation curriculum. (4) College entrance is heavily dependent on tests that have little to do with the curriculum studied and that are designed—like IQ tests—to spread students out on a scale rather than to define what one is supposed to work at learning. (5) Remedial instruction is offered in "pullout" classes, so that students who need extra instruction miss some of the regular learning opportunities. (6) We expect teachers to grade on a curve. If every student gets an A or a B, we assume that standards are too low. We seldom consider the possibility that the students may have worked hard and succeeded in learning what was taught.

These are commonplace, everyday, taken-for-granted features of the American educational landscape. They are institutionalized expressions of a belief in the importance of aptitude. These practices are far more powerful than what we might say about effort and aptitude. Their routine, largely unquestioned use continues to create evidence that confirms aptitude-based thinking.

Students do not try to break through the barrier of low expectations because they, like their teachers and parents, accept the judgment that aptitude matters most and that they do not have the right kinds of aptitude. Not surprisingly, their performance remains low. Children who have not been taught a demanding, challenging, thinking curriculum do not do well on tests of reasoning or problem solving, confirming our original suspicions that they did not have the talent for that kind of thinking. The system is a self-sustaining one in which hidden assumptions are continually reinforced by the inevitable results of practices that are based on those assumptions.

Organizing for Effort

It is not necessary to continue this way. Aptitude is not the only possible basis for organizing schools. Educational institutions could be built around the alternative assumption that effort actually creates ability. Our education system could be designed primarily to foster effort. What would such a system look like? How might it work? There are five essential features of an effort-oriented education system: (1) clear expectations for achievement, well understood by everyone, (2) fair and credible evaluations of achievement, (3) celebration and payoff for success, (4) as much time as is necessary to meet learning expectations, and (5) expert instruction. Let us consider each of these features and what the implications may be.

1. *Clear expectations.* Achievement standards—publicly announced and meant for everyone—are the essential foundation of an equitable, effort-oriented education system. If students are to work hard, they need to know what they are aiming for. They need not only to try hard, but also to point their efforts in a particular direction. To direct their efforts, students need to know what they are trying to learn, what the criteria of "good" performance are. Artists building a portfolio of work engage in a continuous process of self-evaluation—aided, when they are fortunate, by friendly but critical teachers and peers. If clear

standards of achievement existed, elementary and secondary students could work that way, too, building portfolios of work that they continually evaluate, eventually submitting their best work for external "jurying" to see whether it meets the standards they have been working toward.

An equitable standards system must not just make the goals clear but must also set the same expectations for all students. In the absence of publicly defined standards, our inherited assumptions about aptitude lead us to hold out lower expectations for some children than for others. We will go on doing this as long as official standards of achievement do not exist. The best remedy, the equitable solution, is to set clear, public standards that establish very high minimum expectations for everyone, providing a solid foundation for effort by students and teachers alike.

2. *Fair and credible evaluations.* If I am to put out serious effort, I need to know that I will be evaluated fairly, and that those evaluations will be honored and respected. But there is more to fairness than the simple absence of bias in tests and examinations: Fair evaluations are also transparent. Students know their content in advance; they can systematically and effectively study for such an evaluation. In America today, students rarely have the experience of studying hard to pass an examination that they know counts in the world and for which they have been systematically prepared by teachers who themselves understand what is to be examined.

Local tests and exams, usually made up by teachers and administered at the end of teaching units or marking periods, may appear to contradict my claim. Students can study for those, and they are clearly related to the taught curriculum. But, especially for students from poor schools, those tests do not really "count." They are not credible to the world at large. It is understood that an A or B in an inner-city school does not equal the same grade in an upscale suburban or private school.

A credible evaluation system, one that will evoke sustained effort by students and teachers throughout the system, must evaluate students from all kinds of schools against the same criteria.

It must include some externally set exams graded by people other than the students' own teachers, along with an external quality control of grades based on classwork (as in an audited portfolio grading system, for example). Neither of these is a new idea. Some version of external exams and audited class work is used in virtually every country except ours as the basis for diplomas, university entrance, and employment. Joined with the other elements of an effort-oriented system, this kind of evaluation system constitutes a strategy for optimizing both equity and excellence in our schools.

3. *Celebration and the payoff for success.* Hard work and real achievement deserve celebration. And celebration encourages future effort. An education system that actively tries to promote effort will make sure that its schools organize visible, important events highlighting the work students are doing and pointing clearly to achievements that meet the publicly established standards of quality. There are many options for organizing celebrations. School-community nights can become occasions for displaying work, organizing exhibitions, and putting on performance. Local newspapers and radio and television stations can be recruited to publish exemplary student work or otherwise mark achievements. Community organizations can be asked to participate. It is critical that these celebrations include people who matter to the students, and that what is celebrated is work that meets or is clearly en route to meeting the established standards.

For older students, celebration alone may no longer be enough to sustain effort. Adolescents are increasingly concerned with finding their way into adult roles. They will want to see connections between what they are accomplishing in school and the kinds of opportunities that will become available to them when they leave school. This is why many today advocate some kind of high school credential that is based on specific achievements and that is honored for entrance into both college and work. Celebration coupled with payoff will keep the effort flowing; achievement will rise accordingly.

4. *Time and results—inverting the relationship.* Schools today provide roughly equal instructional time to all students: a certain number of hours per day, days per year, and years of schooling. As much instruction and learning as can be fitted into that time is offered. Then, at the end of the prescribed period of study, some kind of evaluation takes place. The spread of results confirms the assumptions about aptitude of American schooling.

What if, instead of holding time fixed and allowing results to vary, we did the opposite: set an absolute standard of expectation and allowed time (and the other resources that go with it) to vary? That arrangement would recognize that some students need more time and support than others but would not change expectations according to an initial starting point. Everyone would be held to the same high minimum. Effort could really pay because all students would know that they would have the learning opportunities they need to meet the standards.

Allowing time to vary does not have to mean having young people remain indefinitely in school, repeating the same programs at which they failed the year before. We already know that this kind of additional time produces very little. Instead, schools and associated institutions would need to offer extra learning opportunities early on. For example, pullout instruction could be replaced with enriched, standards-oriented after-school, weekend, and summer programs. Churches, settlement houses, Scouts, 4-H clubs, and other youth service organizations could be asked to join with the schools in providing such programs. A results-oriented system of this kind would bring to all American children the benefits that some now receive in programs organized by their parents and paid for privately.

5. *The right to expert instruction.* I have been arguing that we ought to create the right to as much instruction as each child needs. That is what the time-results inversion is about. But an equitable system requires more than that. It requires expert instruction for all children. We are far from providing that. With notable exceptions, the best teachers, and, therefore, the best instruction, gravitate to the schools that teach children with the fewest educational problems. Children who start out with the greatest need for expert instruction are the ones least likely to get it.

That will not do. An effort-oriented system that sets high expectations for all will create a demand—indeed, a right—to expert instruction. To fulfill that demand, it will be necessary to create enhanced instructional expertise up and down the teaching force, so that there is enough expert instruction to go around. This means that new forms of professional development, for teachers now in the force as well as for those preparing to enter the field, are an essential ingredient of the standards and effort revolution.

From Effort to Ability

My proposal is, in some respects, a radical one. The effort-oriented education that I am calling for—a system in which everyone in the schools knows what they are working toward, in which they can see clearly how they are doing, and in which effort is recognized in ways that people value—is based on assumptions about the nature of human ability that are very different from those that predominate today. But in other respects, my proposal is a practical and feasible one. It calls for a return in institutional practice to values that most Americans subscribe to: effort, fair play, the chance to keep trying. Most of the elements of the proposal—standards, exams, celebrations of achievement, extended time for those who want to meet a higher standard, expert instruction, and professional development—already exist somewhere in our educational practice. These elements need to be brought together in a few major demonstrations that show the possibilities of effort-oriented practices. Just as aptitude-oriented practices have created evidence that confirms our assumptions about aptitude, so a few effort-oriented demonstrations can begin to create evidence of the power of effort to create ability. As evidence accumulates, beliefs will begin to change, and we can, perhaps, look forward to education in America that is equitable in the deepest sense of the word because it creates ability everywhere. ■

POST NOTE

Lauren Resnick posits an interesting hypothesis, that is, that effort can create ability. For virtually all of U.S. history, schools have served as sorting mechanisms that distinguish the talented and privileged from those less fortunate. Some students were seen as being "naturally smart" in certain subjects. Resnick argues that if all students are accorded clear expectations, fair and credible evaluations, payoffs for success, enough time as needed to learn, and access to expert instruction, then they can learn at high levels.

It is interesting that in western cultures aptitude has reigned supreme, while in some eastern cultures student effort is seen as the determining factor in schools success. Everyone is considered gifted and talented in various ways.

DISCUSSION QUESTIONS

1. Do you agree or disagree with Resnick's propositions? Why or why not?

2. What needs to change for Resnick's ideas to be implemented?

3. Do you think Resnick's ideas are likely to be implemented? Why or why not?

New Hope for High Schools: Lessons from Reform-Minded Educators

Theodore R. Sizer

The leap from traditional school practice to commonsense reform is for most Americans a heroic one. Contrast familiar life outside school with that commonly found inside school. Few parents want to spend, or can even rationally contemplate spending, a full day all alone penned up in one room with 27 12-year-olds, day after day. . . . Nonetheless, most parents assume that a middle-school teacher can cope well every day of the week with five groups of 27 12-year-olds drawn from every sort of community, following a regimen over which that teacher has almost no control.

Most college English department faculty members would mightily object—and do strenuously object—if those of them who teach writing classes are forced to carry more than 60 students at once, in four classes of 15 students each. Nonetheless, most school boards assume that high school English instructors can teach 120 to 180 students, in groups of 20 to 40, to write clearly and well.

Theodore Sizer is professor emeritus, Brown University, and the founder of the Coalition of Essential Schools. This selection is from his book *Horace's Hope*. Copyright © 1996 by Theodore R. Sizer. Reprinted by permission of Houghton Mifflin Company. All rights reserved. This abridged excerpt was published in *The American School Board Journal*.

Few businesses hire people on the basis of test scores alone, or even principally so. Most businesses hire people on the basis of evidence about their previous work, its substance, and how faithfully and imaginatively they dealt with that substance. Yet most policy makers assume that for serious purposes of judgment, one can pinpoint the present effectiveness and future chances of a child, or even an entire school, on the basis of some congeries of numerical data.

Few successful businesses change the content of each employee's work every hour and regularly and insistently interrupt the workers' efforts with announcements on a public address system. Nonetheless, a seven- or eight-period day and an incessant blare of administrative matters over PA systems characterize most high schools.

Few serious enterprises let all their employees take long vacations at the same time every year. Few such enterprises assume that all work can be reduced to a predictable schedule, which implies that every worker will produce at the same speed. Few serious businesses believe that those who are immediately swifter are always better. Nonetheless, most high schools accept these practices without challenge.

And more. The typical routines of high school . . . often defy elementary logic and the experience of the typical citizen. Yet, curiously, they seem exceedingly difficult to change.

I believe that there are at least four reasons for this extraordinary gap between common sense and common school practice.

First, high schools in America serve more symbolic than substantive purposes. The routines of adolescence carry great weight—taking the expected courses, coping with Mom and Dad over a report card festooned with challenging letter or numerical grades, meeting girls or boys, dating (made possible by the rituals of the high school hallways), attending homecoming, the prom, and above all graduation, that choreographed rite of passage expected of every American around the age of 18. One messes with these very familiar icons of practice at one's peril. . . .

Second, the high school mechanism is highly complex and interconnected. The curriculum, for example, is divided into familiar subjects. To teach a particular subject in a public school, one has to be formally certified in that academic area by the state. One gains certification by attending a college where specified courses leading to that credential are given. The college is divided into departments that correspond with the certification needs of those at the high school. College faculty get their tenure by providing the expected courses and writing their books in the expected areas. The collective bargaining agreements reflect these subject categories. State and federal assessments and regulations depend on them. . . . Seemingly everything important within and outside a high school affects everything else. To change anything means changing everything. The prospect is daunting, usually paralyzing.

Third, and not surprisingly, school routines tend to be remarkably similar in high schools across the country, even those in the private sector, where one might expect significantly different approaches. There are few examples, especially state-endorsed examples, of a school organized in ways and on assumptions that diverge sharply from the conventional. Thus we have a chicken-and-egg problem; there is no critical mass of different schools across the country to bear witness to a better kind of schooling, and this makes the argument in their favor a difficult one, based on promises rather than evidence.

Finally, the people who make many crucial decisions about educational policy and practice—those at the top—do not have to live with those decisions. After giving the order to charge, they do not have to lead the troops—that is, to serve directly in the schools. Accordingly, there is little incentive for many of them to study the realities. . . . They can require and recommend and finance with little immediate accountability. If kids do not improve, someone else is always there to blame. . . .

Change comes hard, even when the need for the change is blatantly obvious. The system carries on, even when the carrying on is irrational. In Essential schools, [schools affiliated with the Coalition of Essential Schools, a group of second-ary schools trying to reform themselves on the basis of principles developed by Sizer], as well as in schools in kindred projects, there is usually a battle over even the most obviously needed reforms. Realistically, we must expect that a majority of the schools attempting significant change will flounder, smothered by the forces of mindless tradition, fear, and obstruction, which, because of the complexity of high school work, are so easy to rally. As a result, we have learned to be very straight with the schools and with the authorities directing them about the rigors and costs of serious change. . . .

Human-scale places are critical. "I cannot teach well a student whom I do not know." How many students at once can one high school teacher know well? At the start, the Coalition, somewhat arbitrarily, asserted that no teacher should have responsibility for more than 80 students. Even though the leap to this number from the more usual 100 to 180 students is heroic, the record of demonstrably successful Essential schools shows that this number is still too large.

However, we have learned that there is much more to the whole matter of scale. It is not only that each teacher must have a sensible load of students. It is that the school itself has to be of human scale—a place where everyone can know everyone else. Of course, smallness is just the beginning, but it is a necessary precondition.

More than one teacher must know each child (and her family) well, and there must be time for those teachers, and, as necessary, her parents, to discuss that child. It is fine for me to know Jessica, a ninth-grader; but my knowledge of her is necessarily limited to her participation in my classes and our personal relationship. She may well be known quite differently by another teacher, who is a different person and who teachers her a different subject. Together that teacher and I and her parents can construct a fuller, fairer portrait of Jessica than any of us can alone.

Such sharing of knowledge about kids requires trusting colleagueship among teachers. If we are hired merely on the basis of our certification areas ("secondary school U.S. and European history teacher") and seniority in the school system (First hired, last fired"), we join a school as independent operators, are given our classrooms, and consult and collaborate only when the spirit moves us. But when we are chosen to work in a school on the basis of a commitment to the philosophy of that school and because our arrival will strengthen the corps of staff members already there, the relationship of each of us to the others is always crucial, particularly so if the school is taking on tough reforms.

How many colleagues can work effectively together? No more, or hunch is, than can attend a crowded potluck supper. So much of importance in schools depends upon trust, and trust arises from familiarity and from time spent together getting divisive issues out on the table and addressing them. A team of 25 or 30 teachers, a number large enough for variety and small enough for trust, might be ideal. This implies, given average secondary school pupil-teacher ratios, a school of 325 to 420 pupils, itself a human-scale number. Adolescent anonymity is unlikely in such a place.

How, some protest, does one create such small units when school buildings are very large? The answer is to divide the students into small, fully autonomous units, each in effect its own school within a large "educational apartment building."

What does it take to work together effectively? A mix of inspired leadership, candor, and restraint. Schools are difficult places, filled with issues over which reasonable people will disagree. A process to work the inevitable kinks out is necessary, as is the time for that process to proceed.

A kid has just been caught with a pinch of marijuana; he is a first-time offender. Should we suspend him? "We need to set an example." Or do we just slap his wrist hard? "He's really scared—he needs support now."

Those English prize essays; which is best and why? Who gets the prize? Should there be a prize? What signals, good and bad, do prizes send?

An unmarried teacher is pregnant. As she comes to term, should she continue to teach? "She models the very behavior that we must not condone." "She's a stellar teacher; the kids love her."

"Her private life is her own business." "Each case deserves to be decided on its merits." . . .

The very existence of such confrontations, of course, makes teaching an endlessly stimulating occupation. These are real issues that affect real people every day, and they are issues as influential in people's lives as they are controversial. They can be dealt with well only in schools small enough to allow for trusting relationships among the staff and with the students.

Human scale is only the beginning. The culture of the place is also critical. Essential schools with high morale reflect the dignity deserved by teachers as well as students. The little things symbolize it well. Teachers are given not only the time to struggle with the substance and standards of the students' daily work but also the civilities of access to telephones and trust in their use. A copying machine is available for all, not just the administrative staff. There are no time clocks or check-ins. Teachers are expected to consult with one another, and easy relationships among colleagues—formal or informal, as the individuals like—are the norm. These matters are the important minutiae of school keeping, the little things that send institutional signals.

Work in an Essential school (as in most others) is hard. The pressure is bearable if the work is respected, not only in word but in the way the adult community functions. Essential schools that have worked out their relationships clearly serve their students better than those in which the adults go their own ways civilly or are full of tension and disrespect. . . .

The evidence in favor of human-scale environments and a teacher-student ratio of one to 80 or fewer comes largely from negative findings. Some schools, however devoted to redesign, have not been able to reduce teacher loads dramatically. They thereby remain wracked with faculty dissension, which paralyzes all reform beyond generalized rhetoric. Big schools remain the prisoners of procedures rather than relationships to get through a day, and many of their students thus remain aloof and difficult to engage. The poor performance of such students reflects this.

The limited but growing number of small Essential schools (or small autonomous units within a larger institution) that have been able to build coherent relationships demonstrably outperform their large and bureaucratically ensnared brethren. . . .

Clusters of schools proceed more effectively than schools alone. The Coalition in its early years was a group of individual schools, each making its own way in its own setting. As the numbers of schools grew, for administrative convenience we organized regional centers to provide the kind of support usually delivered from the Coalition's central office at Brown University. We have since realized that clustering has important substantive virtues.

The schools play off against one another, comparing work, consulting on new directions, promoting honest talk by faculty members across schools, serving each other as sustained "critical friends." A cluster of schools can help others in their midst get started, both through the small staffs they hire and by lending veteran teachers as consultants.

The schools protect one another politically. In one extraordinary instance, a new district superintendent threatened to fire a principal because she had raised substantial moneys on her own for her school's library, which made it far richer than comparable libraries in nearby schools. The superintendent found this inequitable; no school should have a much bigger library than others. The principal had to cease this fund-raising, he ordered. Principals at the other schools in the cluster and the cluster's staff had contacts with the local newspaper, and the story quickly reached page one. The superintendent backed off. Entrepreneurial energy was applauded, and the poverty of school library budgets was exposed.

In some places, such as New York City, clusters in fact operate in some respects as formal school districts. They collectively prepare standards and expectations for exhibitions, and they make the work of their students public. They monitor and support one another. When it is efficient, they make collective purchases. They have negotiated with the state for collective waivers of regulations. They are professional and governmental units in all but name. They profoundly redefine what is meant by the top and the bottom.

The relationship between the top and the bottom of the educational hierarchy must be fundamentally rethought. Our experience with the governance of schools has led to four principal conclusions. First, stability of leadership within the system is crucial. Schools endlessly affected by changes—new superintendents, each with a new plan; new governors, also with "new initiatives"; new legislative leadership—are pulled in frustratingly different directions. We have seen school principals and teachers figuring out practically, and often cynically, how to fend off the worst of any new order, knowing that this year's innovation may well not be operative next year. . . .

Second, the way the policy community and the bureaucracy view schooling is crucial. If the metaphor of the bloodless assembly line persists, little change happens. Dealing with children in the aggregate ("all the eighth-graders in this state," "all children from families below the poverty line") and perceiving each child as an individual ("just like each of my own very different children") lead policy in very different directions. The latter, obviously—as it reflects reality—is preferable.

Policy makers, of course, have to view the large scene, but they do not have to reduce the scene to crude generalities. Accepting both the diversities implicit in schooling—the differences among children, neighborhoods, and professionals—and the need to attend carefully to the wishes, commitments, and proper rights of parents make system policy and practice complex, and thus a nuisance. We have found that when the subtleties are honored and when there has been bipartisan commitment to a reform direction, the results are promising.

In 1988, the Coalition of Essential Schools formally allied with the Education Commission of the States (an association of state governments for collective study of educational policy and practice) in a project dubbed Re:Learning to pursue what we called a strategy of reform "from the schoolhouse to the statehouse." The assumption here was that the governmental "top" and the school-level "bottom" would work as close allies, with the demands and particular needs of the bottom—the individual schools—profoundly shaping the top's specific policies.

Over the past years some 15 states have been involved, directly or indirectly, in this project, which has led to efforts to bring together the teaching and policy communities for greater understanding of each other's roles (gatherings rarely held in previous times), state assignment of staff to support Essential schools and kindred reforming schools, state funds to support the reform, and waivers of regulations to give the schools room to redesign their work. In several states this activity has led to reform legislation—specific support to risk-taking schools. Most important, Re:Learning has given legitimacy to the work of those schools trying to break with unwise practices. The informed blessing of the top has provided substantial support for the bottom , as the rapid growth of Essential schools after 1988 evidences.

Third, leaders at both the top and the bottom have to understand that managing a school is rather like sailing a boat. There is a chart, there is a planned course, and there are plotted shoals and sandbars, but those on board have to adjust all the time to changing winds and attitudes, even redrawing the course to the destination from time to time. There are goals for a school and a framework of expectations for how those goals may be reached, but the means, and even the framework itself, are subject to constant ad-justment on the basis of what is going on with the children, the staff, and the community. The hand of government has to be a light one, and a trusting one. Directing the sailboat from an office ashore is as imprudent as directing the activities of an individual school from a school system's central headquarters.

Finally, respect and sustained, genuine communication between top and bottom are essential. Where there are differences, they should be addressed. Too often they are swept under a rug while the state or district tries to ram its views home and the locals sit on their hands, griping.

Of course, the conventional wisdom implies that higher government has the right to overrule lower government. The fact that these "levels" of government arise more from the realities of scale (towns are smaller than states) and from political arrangements than from citizens' rights obscures the fact that the compulsory nature of public education put an enormous responsibility for restraint on governmental leaders. Some give that responsibility too little respect, with predictable resentment and opposition at the bottom.

The shape and obligations of all the pieces of the public school system as we know it are under fresh scrutiny. State and city leaders' willingness to contemplate radical changes in that system is strikingly more prevalent today than when the Coalition's work started. The system is under criticism unprecedented in this century. We hope that the new forms it takes adhere carefully to the convictions represented by Re:Learning's slogan, "*from* the schoolhouse to the statehouse." ∎

POST NOTE

For many years Theodore Sizer has been one of the foremost advocates and leaders in reforming public high schools. His trilogy of books, *Horace's Compromise*, *Horace's School*, and *Horace's Hope*, focuses on an imaginary high school English teacher named Horace Smith and his trials and tribulations as he tries to become a better teacher. Together, these three books present an agenda for high school reform based on the principles of the Coalition of Essential Schools, a network of over 1,000 high schools that Sizer led until 1997. The excerpt included here, from the third book in the trilogy, *Horace's Hope*, touches on four of the thirteen lessons Sizer has learned from his work with the Coalition of Essential Schools (www.essentialschools.org).

DISCUSSION UESTIONS

1. What are the four lessons of reform that Sizer identifies in this selection?

2. What is it about high schools, as opposed to elementary schools, that makes them so intractable to reform efforts?

3. On the basis of your own experiences, what reforms would you like to see implemented in high schools?

57

The Who, What, and Why of Site-Based Management

Jane L. David

S
ite-based management may be the most significant reform of the decade—a potential force for empowering educators and communities. Yet no two people agree on what it is, how to do it, or even why to do it.

Kentucky requires virtually every school to have a site-based council with three teachers, two parents, and the principal, and endows councils with considerable fiscal and policy authority. Maryland and Texas require schools to have school-based decision-making teams, but in contrast to Kentucky, do not specify their composition or legally transfer authority from the district to the school.

In Chicago, state law places significant authority in the hands of local school councils and defines their makeup: six parents, two community representatives, two teachers, and the principal. In Cincinnati, reorganization and downsizing of the central office has shifted considerable responsibility, but no additional legal authority, to school principals.

Colorado governor Roy Romer initiated site-based management in Denver as part of stalled contract negotiations between the school district

Jane L. David is director of the Bay Area Research Group, Palo Alto, California. David, Jane, "The Who, What, and Why of Site-Based Management." *Educational Leadership*, December 1995/January 1996, pp. 4–9. Reprinted by permission from ASCD. All rights reserved.

and the teachers' association and required a business representative on each council. In Memphis, site-based management never got beyond a small pilot phase. In Dade County, Florida, the pilot was expanded but in a much weaker form.

These are only a few examples. According to Ogawa and White (1994), one-third of all school districts had some version of site-based management between 1986 and 1990. Since 1990 at least five states have jumped on the bandwagon. And during the same time, more than 20 states have passed legislation to create charter schools— individual schools that are de facto site-based managed, even though they do not carry that title. All this activity excludes individual schools that have instituted reforms but have not been delegated authority by their district or state, although some of these may be excellent models of democratic decision making (see, for example, Apple and Beane 1995, Wohlstetter and Smyer 1994).

What Is It?

So what is site-based management? It has almost as many variants as there are places claiming to be "site-based." And they differ on every important dimension—who initiates it, who is involved, what they control, and whether they are accountable to an outside authority. Site-based management may be instituted by state law or by administrative action, by a district, or by a school. It may be linked to an accountability system with consequences tied to student performance, or it may not be.

Most variants of site-based management involve some sort of representative decision-making council at the school, which may share authority with the principal or be merely advisory. Some councils have the power to hire principals, some hire and fire, some do neither. Some can hire other personnel when there are vacancies. Some councils specify that the principal be the chair, others specify that the principal not be the chair.

The composition of site councils also varies tremendously. In addition to teachers, parents, and the principal, they may include classified staff, community members, students, and business representatives. Educators may outnumber non-educators, or vice versa. States or districts may list constituencies who must be represented, or simply leave it to individual schools. Chicago and Kentucky are exceptions in specifying exact membership of the site council—who and how many of each type of constituent.

Why Do It?

Reasons for initiating site-based management run the gamut, yet virtually all are cloaked in the language of increasing student achievement. To some, site-based management is a governance reform designed to shift the balance of authority among schools, districts, and the state. This tends to be the rationale behind state efforts rather than district reforms, and it is often part of a larger reform agenda that claims to trade school autonomy for accountability to the state.

To others, site-based management is a political reform initiated to broaden the decision-making base, either within the school, the larger community, or both. But democratization of decision making as an end in itself leaves open the question of who should be involved in which decisions.

Site-based management may also be an administrative reform to make management more efficient by decentralizing and deregulating it. Here, too, management efficiency presumably serves the ultimate goal of organization—student learning. Yet another premise of site-based management as educational reform is that the way to enhance student learning is to let education professionals make the important professional decisions.

Further complicating the landscape, there are often underlying motives. Stated purposes may obscure far less lofty aims, such as weakening entrenched and distrusted local school boards, creating the illusion of reform without investing additional resources, putting a positive spin on central office downsizing by calling it decentralization, or simply trying to shift the blame for failure to the school itself.

Linking Decentralization and Achievement

Although site-based management appears in many guises, at its core is the idea of participatory decision making at the school site. And despite all the variations in rationale, its main stated objective is to enhance student achievement. Participatory decision making and school improvement are presumed to be related, but that's not always the case.

Consider what happens when any group is formed by bringing together people who have never worked as a group, who may have no experience in collaborative decision making, and who may in fact have a history of being adversaries (parents and teachers, for example). To make matters worse, some members may be subject to evaluation by other members (teachers by the principal, most obviously). Why would such a group be expected to improve student learning?

Indeed, groups like these that do function well tend to spend most of their time on issues of discipline, facilities, and extracurricular activities. They limit themselves to these issues for good reason—these are the issues that people are passionate about and have some idea how to tackle. Moreover, these are concerns that parents and teachers share (David 1994).

Curriculum and instruction are much more difficult to deal with, for educators and non-educators alike. And these issues are even more difficult to tackle when states or districts mandate new assessments that require teaching methods that are unfamiliar to many parents and teachers. When there are serious consequences for unsatisfactory student performance—especially teacher or principal dismissal—but a lack of knowledge about how to improve student performance, trust and constructive dialogue are further undermined.

Who Decides What?

For site-based decisions to be sound, attention must be paid to who decides what. Sound decisions are made by those who are informed about and care about the issues and who know the context in which the decision will be carried out. Otherwise, there is no guarantee that these decisions will be any better than those made by policy-makers many steps removed. In fact, school-based decisions could be made by only one person, and that person could be uninformed and insensitive to the context.

Participatory management does not mean that everyone decides everything. Some decisions are best left to the professionals in the school, some to parents, and others to students. Some decisions are appropriately made by representatives of several constituencies, others by a formal schoolwide body. Nor does site-based management mean that all decisions are appropriately made at the school level. Schools belong to larger systems—districts and states—that must provide a strong center if decentralization is to create something other than anarchy (Murphy 1989).

Schools are unlikely to improve unless community members—and particularly parents—participate meaningfully. And in secondary schools, students should be involved as well. Schools are also unlikely to improve unless teachers—the main implementers—shape the direction of change. In general, those who have the strongest personal stake in and the most immediate connection to the school are the ones who should tackle the issues. The challenge is to maximize the likelihood that decisions will be appropriately participatory, informed, and sensitive to the context.

Internal Elements

Site councils that truly flourish in the school community tend to have a number of characteristics in common, most notably the following.

- *A well-thought-out committee structure.* In a well-structured system of council committees, there is a good matchup between the types of decisions to be made and the most appropriate people to debate and resolve those issues. Some committees may be standing, others ad hoc. Some may be composed of teachers, and so

defined by naturally existing groups like teams, departments, and grade levels. Some may consist only of parents; other may be representative of all constituencies. Whether the relationship between the committees and the site council is formal (approval) or informal (advisory), the committee structure with overlapping memberships provides a communication network that is critical to an effective council.

- *Enabling leadership.* Strong councils are usually led, though not always chaired, by strong principals (and sometimes teachers) who exercise leadership by mobilizing others. They encourage all parties to participate. And they model inquiry and reflection. Such leaders create schoolwide ownership of the improvement agenda so that principal turnover or a change in council membership does not bring efforts to a halt.

- *Focus on student learning.* Not all issues have a direct influence on student learning, but strong councils consciously connect non-instructional decisions with conditions that maximize learning opportunities. For example, a decision to invest in classroom telephones to facilitate communication between teachers and parents will also affect students. By linking all issues to teaching and learning, council members don't lose sight of the ultimate goal.

- *Focus on adult learning.* There are two points here. First, council members need new skills, assistance, and practice in asking hard questions and gathering evidence about what is and is not working. Second, councils need to appreciate that their constituencies—parents and educators—require access to new knowledge and skills, both to be active decision makers and to change their teaching and learning practices and beliefs.

- *Schoolwide perspective.* Functioning councils focus on the collective interests of the parties, devoting their energy to school goals and direction, coordination and communication, and allocation of resources and equity. They do not get caught up in details of management or curriculum, and they do not get waylaid by individual agendas. Naturally most parents will be thinking about their own children's needs, and most teachers will be thinking about their own classrooms, and so they might be defensive. Moreover, everyone may lack confidence in a new process that carries considerable responsibility.

External Elements

Not many schools are able to create on their own the conditions I have described, particularly when strong enabling leadership is absent. To learn how to do it, most schools require support from their district or state agencies, including the following:

■ *Long-term commitment.* Councils cannot evolve into effective decision-making bodies at the school site if the pendulum swings from one extreme to the other every two or three years. Site-based management cannot be the reform *du jour* that changes authority and flexibility when the superintendent changes. Sustained commitment is essential. The process is hard work and takes time.

■ *Curricular guidance.* Schools need a substantive framework within which to make appropriate choices. Whether that guidance is best communicated in the form of learning goals and standards, curriculum or content guides, or assessments is an open question—as is the way in which choices about such guidance are made. The goal of site-based management is not to let a thousand flowers bloom nor to force every school to reinvent itself from scratch.

In addition, everyone from classroom teachers to other members of committees who diagnose problems must have opportunities to learn new ways of operating, including mediating techniques. School councils must reflect the existing culture. For most schools, if real improvement is to occur, individual beliefs and, ultimately, the school culture will need to change.

■ *Opportunities for learning and assistance.* Districts can provide resources for the kinds of learning opportunities that adults in schools need to change classroom practices and to function effectively as council and committee members. School councils will necessarily reflect the existing culture. Most councils, but especially those with local conflicts and limited experience in collaborative problem solving, will need assistance and access to facilitation and mediation. For most schools, if site-based management is to lead to improvement, individual beliefs and, ultimately, the culture of the school will need to change.

■ *Access to information.* Schools must have easy access to the information needed to make decisions, including everything from budget to performance data. A decentralized system can function well only when each unit knows how it is doing. Although schools can gather certain data from students, teachers, and the community, they cannot be expected to have the data collection and analysis capability that a larger organization can support. Moreover, because the system has its own needs for information, the flow must go in both directions.

Open Questions

Making fundamental changes in systems as complex as state and local school systems raises a number of questions for which there are no pat answers. The solutions simply have to be worked out by those involved. Among these difficult issues are questions of equity, adult learning, decision making, and changing conceptions of teaching and community. In particular:

■ What policies and supports will ensure that site-based management does not exacerbate resource differences among schools? Schools in poorer neighborhoods tend to have fewer resources and less educated populations. They are at risk of being further disadvantaged under a decentralized system.

■ How can site-based management create a sense of community in schools that draw from a large geographic area, as do most secondary schools; and in schools in districts with desegregation plans, choice, open enrollment, or magnet schools? Parents and staff at such schools may not have access to transportation or time to participate in school decision making.

■ New ideas for teacher professional development are emerging, but where are the opportunities for principals, central office staff, and parents to learn new roles and ways to assist site councils?

■ How should teachers' jobs be redefined to allow time for collaborative decision making and ongoing professional development? Both teachers and the public believe that teachers should devote their time to students, and teachers are finding classroom demands take increasing time and energy.

■ How can site-based management be structured to balance school autonomy and flexibility with certain centralized operations that require consistency, coordination, and legal constraints? For example, collective bargaining, transportation, and government regulations may all affect class size, schedules, services, and how facilities are used.

■ What is the best public education analogue to private sector work teams, and where do parents and community members fit in? That is, decentralized private organizations delegate authority to work teams that don't involve the public. But in schools, neither site councils nor groups of teachers are really teams that carry out the work of the organization (teachers typically work in isolation).

■ Should schools have mandates that require them to involve parents and the community in decisions? What is the likelihood that without such mandates, parents and community members would continue to have little voice in some local schools?

Risks and Benefits

In theory, the benefits of site-based management overwhelm the costs: the goals of education reform are unlikely to be met in any other way. As public support for public education in general, and reform in particular, dwindles, community members' engagement in their local schools offers the most promise for rebuilding support.

Without a school and community culture that supports ongoing learning, student achievement is unlikely to improve. The challenge is to open avenues for informed conversation and for be-coming informed. Ultimate accountability rests on the ability of individuals to influence what is not working (Wiggins 1993). That is certainly far preferable to a state takeover or school closure.

Although the ultimate goal of participatory site-based management is to improve schools in order to improve student performance, the intermediate goals are desired ends in themselves. Involving teachers in decisions about their work must be valued in its own right, as must giving parents and other community members more involvement in their schools.

One risk is that the public will judge site-based management prematurely on the ultimate goals, derailing sound practices whose success is not yet reflected in test scores. When there is more than one desired end and the means to those ends are not clear, it is difficult to assess progress along the way. Therefore, it is critically important to devise new ways of measuring progress for such an undertaking (Bryk et al. 1994).

Another risk, however, is that participants will not judge site-based management in terms of any of its goals—intermediate or ultimate—but simply allow the process to absorb time and energy to no good purpose. Unfortunately, in practice, the potential of site-based management is rarely realized. It can even have deleterious effects, exhausting limited energy and good will in futile exercises. Only with visible progress and results will folks willingly put in the hard work.

The key is to identify and exploit ways to ensure that decisions will be appropriately participatory, informed, and context-sensitive, thereby increasing the likelihood that they will lead to better school practices and stronger instruction. Ultimately, it will be the people who carry out site-based management who determine what it is—and can become. Their success or failure will also help others decide whether it is worthwhile in terms of the human costs it exacts.

Finally, the goal of transforming schools into communities where everyone has a voice goes beyond issues of school reform to the heart of our democratic society. The creation of models of collaboration and participatory decision making for students to witness and become involved in—not only in classrooms but also in their community—ultimately benefits not just the school community but our entire society. ■

References

Apple, M. W., and J. A. Beane, eds. (1995). *Democratic Schools*. Alexandria, Va.: Association for Supervision and Curriculum Development

Bryk, A. S., et al. (1994). "The State of Chicago School Reform." *Phi Delta Kappan* 76: 74–78.

David, J. L. (1994). *School-Based Decision Making: Linking Decisions to Learning*. Lexington, Ken.: The Prichard Committee for Academic Excellence.

Murphy, J. T. (1989). "The Paradox of Decentralizing Schools Lessons from Business, Government, and the Catholic Church." *Phi Delta Kappan* 70: 808–812.

Ogawa, R. T., and P. A. White. (1994). "School-Based Management An Overview." In *School-Based Management Organizing for High Performance*, edited by S. A. Mohrman, P. Wohlstetter, and Associates. San Francisco: Jossey-Bass.

Wiggins, G. P. (1993). *Assessing Student Performance Exploring the Purpose and Limits of Testing*. San Francisco: Jossey-Bass.

Wohlstetter, P., and R. Smyer. (1994). "Models of High-Performance Schools." In *School-Based Management Organizing for High Performance*, edited by S. A. Mohrman, P. Wohlstetter, and Associates. San Francisco: Jossey-Bass.

POST NOTE

Like many other educational reforms, site-based management came to education via the business community. During the 1980s and 1990s, many businesses moved away from large, bureaucratic, and centralized decision making to give more decision-making responsibility to the workers on the front line. Workers were empowered to detect and solve problems, without having to "kick the matter upstairs." Businesses found that by decentralizing the decision making, they improved both the quality and the swiftness of the decisions, and employees took more pride in their work.

Since businesses were having such success, why wouldn't the same ideas work to reinvigorate the American educational system and create more of a sense of professionalism among America's teachers? In education, however, site-based management (also known as school-based management and site-based decision making) is having mixed success. Although it is still early in the reform movement, the ultimate impact of site-based management on education remains to be seen.

DISCUSSION QUESTIONS

1. What differences do you see between the business and education arenas in the implementation of shared decision making?

2. Are any of the schools with which you are familiar engaged in site-based management? If so, what have been their successes and failures?

3. Would you like to be a teacher in a school that employs site-based management? Why or why not?

58

The Power of Innovative Scheduling

Robert Lynn Canady and Michael D. Rettig

Scheduling is a valuable but untapped resource for school improvement. Through our work in schools across the country, we have seen again and again how a well-crafted schedule can

- result in more effective use of time, space, and resources (human as well as material);
- improve instructional climate;
- help solve problems related to the delivery of instruction; and
- assist in establishing desired programs and instructional practices.

We believe that Deming was right when he said that it is more often the structure of an organization than the inadequacies of the people who work within it that causes problems (Bonstingl 1992). The examples we'll discuss only hint at the power of scheduling to improve schools. But, first, let's review some problems that scheduling can help alleviate.

Robert Lynn Canady is a professor emeritus at the Curry School of Education, University of Virginia; and Michael D. Rettig is an associate professor at the School of Education, College of Education and Psychology, James Madison University. Canady, Robert Lynn and Michael D. Rettig, "The Power of Innovative Scheduling." *Educational Leadership*, November 1995, pp. 4–10. Reprinted by permission from ASCD. All rights reserved.

Three Issues All Schools Face

Although scheduling varies from elementary school through high school, three areas of concern span all levels.

1. Providing Quality Time Fragmented instructional time is an issue at all levels. In elementary school, a variety of practices contribute to this problem. For example, haphazardly scheduled pullout programs (for ESL or special education, for example) disrupt classroom instruction; and because the schedules of specialists (for music and art, for example) are created for periods of varying length, core teachers must plan instruction around the remaining chopped-up time. In addition, when special programs classes meet just once a week for a short period, students receive piecemeal instruction.

At the middle and high school levels, fragmentation occurs in a different way. Students traveling through a six-, seven-, or eight-period day encounter the same number of pieces of unconnected curriculum each day, with little opportunity for in-depth study. In middle schools, this problem may have been exacerbated by exploratory programs, which in many schools have evolved from risk-free explorations to full academic courses with tests, grades, and homework.

Recently we worked with a district where students spent four periods daily in English, mathematics, social studies, and science, and two periods in six-week exploratory "wheels." In other words, students saw 4 core teachers and 12 exploratory teachers during the year. Is having so many teachers per day and per year consistent with what we know about middle school students?

2. Creating a School Climate The daily schedule can have a great effect on a school's climate. At the elementary level, discipline problems can result from the way small-group reading and math instruction is scheduled. Many teachers continue to divide their classes into reading, language arts, and math groups, which meet separately with the teacher while other students complete worksheets or work in learning centers. All too often, teachers must interrupt small-group instruction to address discipline problems that arise in the back of the room.

In middle and high schools, traditional schedules create at least four situations that may contribute to the number of discipline problems.

■ Many disciplinary referrals result from scheduled transitions, when large numbers of students spill into hallways, lunchrooms, and commons areas, or congregate in locker rooms and bathrooms. If students are not sent to the office directly, the problems often carry over into the classroom, where teachers must deal with them before beginning instruction.

■ The assembly-line, traditional period schedule contributes to the depersonalizing nature of high schools. When teachers are responsible for 100–180 students daily, and students must answer to six, seven, or eight teachers a day, it is nearly impossible to develop close relationships, which may help reduce discipline problems.

■ Short instructional periods may also contribute to a negative classroom climate. When students who misbehave do not respond to a quick correction, many teachers send them to the office. With only 40- to 55-minute class periods, these teachers view any time taken away from classwork as unacceptable.

■ The middle school schedule, in particular, often makes teaming efforts difficult. Students in seven-period schools often are enrolled in three non-core classes, while the four-teacher teams—one teacher each from English, math, science, and social studies—are assigned five classes daily. Thus, during many periods of the day, 20 percent of the students are "off core." As a result, teams must remain in a period schedule, and the team structure, which usually facilitates disciplinary control, is weakened.

3. Providing Varying Learning Time   Perhaps the most critical (and unresolved) time allocation issue that schools face is the indisputable fact that some students need more time to learn than others. In secondary schools, reliance on the Carnegie unit has made all students "Prisoners of Time" (National Education Commission on Time and Learning

1994). High schools, and to a lesser extent, middle schools, experience this problem, especially in late January. After receiving their first-semester grades, some students conclude that they will not pass the subject regardless of their performance during the second semester. Believing they have nothing to gain by doing the work, some of these students act out and skip classes. In a way, we *have* created a system to handle students who need more time to learn: we give them *F*s and make them repeat the course during summer school or the next academic year!

On the other end of the spectrum, possibilities for acceleration in U.S. schools are still very limited. Most districts, however, offer one celebrated occasion for advancement. At the end of 7th grade in middle and junior high schools, teachers must decide whether or not a student should enroll in algebra during the 8th grade. This inflexible system forces instructors to make premature decisions about a student's potential in mathematics. If the school schedule were not as rigid, perhaps educators could make the decision to accelerate students at more appropriate times.

In elementary school, our usual reaction to the need for different amounts of time for learning is to provide individual assignments to those who learn quickly, and to regroup, slow down, and provide pullout programs for those who need more time. The problems with these accommodations are that 1) sometimes the activities provided for those who learn quickly are thrown together haphazardly (Renzulli 1986), and 2) students placed in the lower groups fall farther behind. In addition, students in pullout programs often are stigmatized by their participation in them.

Scheduling as a Solution

Redesigning the school schedule can help address each of these three issues. We begin with the elementary school.

Elementary School Scheduling   A number of elementary schools across the country have adopted parallel block scheduling to reduce instructional

Figure 1 A Parallel Block Elementary School Schedule for Four Base Teachers and an Extension Center

TEACHERS	50 MINS.	50 MINS.	50 MINS.	50 MINS.
Teacher A	Language Arts and Social Studies (Reading-Writing Groups 1 and 2)		Reading-Writing Group 1	Reading-Writing Group 2
Teacher B	Language Arts and Social Studies (Reading-Writing Groups 3 and 4)		Reading-Writing Group 3	Reading-Writing Group 4
Teacher C	Reading-Writing Group 5	Reading-Writing Group 6	Language Arts and Social Studies (Reading-Writing Groups 5 and 6)	
Teacher D	Reading-Writing Group 7	Reading-Writing Group 8	Language Arts and Social Studies (Reading-Writing Groups 7 and 8)	
Extension Center	Reading-Writing Groups 6 and 8	Reading-Writing Groups 5 and 7	Reading-Writing Groups 2 and 4	Reading-Writing Groups 1 and 3

Note: Depending on the size of the school, this plan can work with four 5th grade teachers, two 4th and two 5th grade teachers, or four teachers of four different grade levels.

fragmentation, improve discipline, and provide regularly scheduled, yet flexible, opportunities for extended learning and enrichment (Canady 1988, 1990; Canady and Reina 1993). Figure 1 illustrates part of such a schedule, designed for four base teachers and an extension center.

Teachers A and B work with their homeroom classes for an uninterrupted 100 minutes to begin the time block shown. They can use this time for language arts and social studies or perhaps for a whole class reading lesson. Teachers A and B may team together for this block if desired.

During the next 50 minutes, Teacher A works with Reading-Writing Group 1; Teacher B instructs Group 3. Teaching about half of the class, the base teacher conducts a reading group, or a writers' workshop, or perhaps conferences with individual students. Discipline is improved because independent groups are no longer in the back of the room. The extension teacher picks up Reading-Writing Group 2 from Teacher A and

Group 4 from Teacher B and escorts these students to the extension center.

At the end of this 50-minute period, the extension center teacher returns Reading-Writing Groups 2 and 4 to their classrooms and picks up Groups 1 and 3 for their extension time. The rest of the school day is devoted to math, science, music, the arts, and physical education. Sleepy Hollow Elementary School in Fairfax County, Virginia, has operated a similar schedule for the past four years.

In the extension center, students who need more time to learn receive assistance through reteaching and reinforcement, and they have opportunities for practice. Any pullouts for special services—special education, English as a second language, gifted and talented, or Chapter 1—are provided during extension center time. Students who have mastered basic concepts work on enrichment activities.

The extension center position can be staffed in different ways. Increasing homeroom size frees up regular teaching staff. An alternative is to staff the center with Chapter 1, English-as-a-second-language, gifted and talented, or special education teachers. Still other options are to use the computer lab or a foreign language program as the extension center or to rotate library/media, guidance, and reading enrichment professionals for a specific period of time (three weeks, for example).

Other Tips for Elementary Schools

- Schedule all specialists for equal periods of instruction on a rotating schedule during the same time block each day. Consider four- or six-day cycles, rather than the unwieldy and unfair Monday through Friday schedule.

- Rotate shared itinerant specialists who travel to different schools on a nine-week or semester basis, rather than two days a week here and two days a week there.

- Schedule recess time contiguous to another class change such as for lunch or specials' classes to reduce time lost to movement.

- Avoid short periods of time such as 15-minutes between lunch and specials. These often are wasted.

Middle School Scheduling Models

We'll look at three models at the middle school level.

The four-block schedule. One schedule being used with increasing frequency across the country greatly reduces fragmented instruction. In the four-block schedule, students spend one block of the day (about 90 minutes) in language arts, a second block in mathematics, and a third block in either social studies/science. The block of social studies/science is rotated every other day, every other unit, by semester, or on some other basis. Students spend the fourth block of the day in physical education, music, and/or exploratory courses, which meet for 90 minutes every other day. They attend only three academic courses daily.

Language arts and mathematics teachers teach three groups every day for the entire year; social studies and science teachers work with three groups per day, but with six groups for the year; and physical education, exploratory, and elective teachers work with only three groups per day. With this scheduling plan, both teachers and students experience less stress and fragmentation.

The four-block middle school schedule significantly reduces the daily number of class changes, thereby reducing discipline problems. Examples of schools operating this schedule during the 1994–95 year include: Newberry Middle School in Newberry, South Carolina; Goochland Middle School in Goochland, Virginia; and Wilbur Wright Middle School in Dayton, Ohio. Districts that operate the 4×4 semester block high school may find this plan a logical transition for middle schools.

The 75–75–30 plan. (Canady and Rettig 1993). W. Marshall Sellman School in the Madeira School District in Cincinnati, Ohio, implemented this unique 180-day school calendar for the 1994–95 school year. According to teachers, students, and parents, the program was a great success.

Under the Sellman plan, the school follows a fairly typical middle school team block schedule for the first 150 days. Courses end after two 75-day terms, and students begin their final six weeks of school enrolled in specialized courses, created and designed by teachers. Such specialized courses provide 1) additional learning time for students who have yet to master grade-level objectives, and 2) academically enriching activities for all students. Course titles at Sellman School include Principles of Mathematics, Team-Accelerated Instruction, Water Science, Inventioneering, Mock Trial, and Fun with Poetry.

The concept-progress model. This approach is another attempt to address students' differing needs for learning time (Canady and Rettig 1992, Canady 1989). Several elementary and middle schools across the country are using it to provide mathematics instruction to heterogeneous groups. Figure 2 illustrates one version of this plan.

Math teachers A, B, and C present the basic concepts of a mathematical topic to their entire classes two days of every six-day cycle. Math Teacher A's Concept Math Group meets on Days

Figure 2 A Concept/Progress Middle School Model for a Six-Day Cycle with 50- to 60-Minute Periods per Day

TEACHERS	1 MONDAY	2 TUESDAY	3 WEDNESDAY	4 THURSDAY	5 FRIDAY	6 MONDAY
Math A	Concept Math Groups 1 and 4	Concept Math Groups 1 and 4	Progress Math Group 1	Progress Math Group 1	Progress Math Group 4	Progress Math Group 4
Math B	Progress Math Group 2	Progress Math Group 2	Concept Math Groups 2 and 5	Concept Math Groups 2 and 5	Progress Math Group 5	Progress Math Group 5
Math C	Progress Math Group 3	Progress Math Group 3	Progress Math Group 6	Progress Math Group 6	Concept Math Groups 3 and 6	Concept Math Groups 3 and 6
Computer Lab	Groups 5 and 6	Groups 5 and 6	Groups 3 and 4	Groups 3 and 4	Groups 1 and 2	Groups 1 and 2

1 and 2 of the six-day cycle. During concept math time, the teacher focuses on grade-level instruction, ideally using cooperative learning, providing direct instruction, and, when needed, illustrating with manipulatives. The teacher does not test and grade students in concept groups.

After working with their whole groups, Teachers A, B, and C divide students into two Progress Math Groups—temporary, flexible, homogenous groupings of students, based on their understanding of the basic ideas taught in the Concept Math Group. Math Teacher A instructs Progress Math Group 1 on Days 3 and 4, and Group 4 on Days 5 and 6. (Note that Progress Math Groups 1 and 4 equal Teacher A's Concept Math Group.) Teachers monitor and adjust instruction during this time, providing enrichment and additional assistance as needed; however, Progress Math Groups remain on the same topic. For example, if teachers have planned to work on long division for 18 days, Progress Math Group 2 might focus on dividing two digits into three digits, while Progress Math Group 5 might be dividing three digits into four. Note, however, that

all groups work in long division for the number of days determined by the pacing guide that teachers developed at the beginning of the school year. Students are graded based on their progress within the topic.

In the computer lab, similar adjustments are made in the selection of software for each group. The concept-progress model is just one way of designing the school schedule to serve students with varying instructional needs by providing

- whole-group instruction without the pressure of testing and grading;
- small groups so that teachers can monitor and adjust instruction without having to teach one group while policing another group; and
- both extended learning and enrichment time on an individual student basis.

Other Middle School Scheduling Tips

- Many middle schools can benefit from operating on some of the more popular high school block scheduling models, such as the Day 1/Day 2 schedule. Students have fewer classes daily, and fewer class changes are necessary.

■ Consider adding a nontraditional core teacher to the interdisciplinary team. At Glasgow Middle School in Fairfax County, Virginia, a foreign language teacher is now on each 8th grade interdisciplinary team. At other schools, related arts teachers are on teams on a rotating basis. For example, an art teacher might be the fifth person on a team for nine weeks of art, followed by nine weeks of computer technology, nine weeks of teen living, and nine weeks of drama. Being part of the team increases the likelihood that the content of these exploratory subjects will be integrated with the core.

■ Another way of reorganizing the 180-day calendar, which is similar to the 75–75–30 Plan, is the 35–(5)–35–(15)–35–(5)–35–(15) Plan. Each semester students attend regular classes for 35 days and have 5 days for reteaching and/or enrichment. Then they continue regular classes for 35 days and end the semester with 15 days for extended learning time or enrichment/electives (see Canady and Rettig 1995, Chapter 5).

High School Scheduling Models

During the past 10 years, high schools across the country have begun to implement block schedules to address curriculum fragmentation. Many schools operate alternate-day schedules, the 4 × 4 semester plan, and many variations (for a detailed treatment of these plans see Canady and Rettig 1995). Each plan can also have a positive effect on school discipline. Here are two examples.

A trimester plan with daily periods for extended learning. In the fall of 1994, Parry McCluer High School in Buena Vista, Virginia, used a trimester schedule with extended classes for enhanced learning (Canady and Rettig 1995, Chapter 4). In such a plan, students enroll in two classes per trimester; each class meets for two hours in the morning and reconvenes for an additional 45 minutes of extended learning time each afternoon. Nearly all students require this additional time for learning; however, a few have been permitted to contract out of the extended learning time for advanced study with another faculty member. An equally small number of students

require more time than can be allocated each trimester to complete course objectives. If these students need more time, they may be granted an "Incomplete," which they can make up during extended learning time of the next trimester.

A schedule that provides algebra for all students. In one school district—where 40 percent of the students enrolled in first-year algebra failed the course, and where approximately one-third of the students who passed the course the previous year failed the state proficiency examination—we designed the following schedule to provide varying learning time for students in Algebra I.

As shown in Figure 3 (on the following page), four sections of Algebra I are scheduled in the same period or block, and the curriculum is divided into four distinct segments. During Quarter 1, all students begin together as heterogeneous groups with teachers A, B, C, and D. After completing Quarter 1, students who need more learning time are regrouped into a separate section, which repeats Part 1 with Teacher D during Quarter 2. Teachers A, B, and C continue Part 2 of the course with students who, at the time, are performing successfully. At the end of each quarter, teachers determine whether a regrouping is necessary. When a group must repeat one of the four parts of the course, we recommend using a different teaching approach—for example, having that teacher reteach the group using a software package in the computer lab or having one of the other four teachers reteach that part of the course.

Figure 3 shows some students finishing the course in four quarters, and some in five, six, seven, or even eight quarters. Variable learning time is provided for students, and no student is forced to sit through a repeat of the entire class. The same idea shown in Figure 3 can be designed for English, particularly for grade 9 students, by basing the parts of the course on an identified sequence of writing and reading skills.

Other High School Scheduling Tips

■ Schools may periodically alter the regular schedule so that each class meets for a full day on a rotating basis. For example, in a six-period

Figure 3 A Middle School Schedule That Provides Varying Learning Times for Students Taking Algebra I

QUARTERS	1	2	3	4	5	6	7	8
TEACHER A	Part 1	Part 2	Part 3	Part 4	Students take new course. Teacher offers new course.			
TEACHER B	Part 1	Part 2	Part 3	Part 4	Part 4	Computer Lab	½-credit electives available	
TEACHER C	Part 1	Part 2	Part 2	Part 3	Part 3	Part 4		
TEACHER D	Part 1	Part 1	Part 2	Part 2	Part 3	Part 3	Part 4	Part 4

Note: The Algebra I curriculum is divided into four parts. Quarters indicate the time it would normally take to complete ¼ of the course. In a single period or A/B schedule, this would be nine weeks. In a 4 × 4 semester plan, this would be four and a half weeks. (For more information about these scheduling plans, see Canady and Rettig 1995.)

school (on a six-day cycle), teachers would meet with each of their five classes for a full day and then have a full day off for planning or professional development.

- Some schools have scheduled one long lunch period rather than two or three short periods. During this extended time the library, gym, computer lab, and outdoor recreational areas are opened for student use. Teachers schedule office hours for extra help; club meetings and other activities also may be held. Several serving sites are necessary to accommodate students purchasing lunch.

Harnessing the Power of Scheduling

We've looked at ways that some elementary, middle, and high schools have redesigned their schedules to reduce curriculum fragmentation, discipline problems, and student failure. We need to move beyond individual school models of scheduling, however, and toward districtwide plans. Ultimately, we envision students progressing from school to school in a seamless design. Such a plan may even enable 5th and 8th grade

teachers, for example, on an every-other-year basis, to continue with their students during their first year in middle or high school.

Only in the last decade have educators begun to capitalize on the potential of scheduling to improve schools. With open minds and equal doses of creativity and technical expertise, school administrators, teachers, parents, and students can harness this power. ■

References

Bonstingl, J. J. (1992). *Schools of Quality: An Introduction to Total Quality Management in Education*. Alexandria, Va.: Association for Supervision and Curriculum Development.

Canady, R. L. (October 1988). "A Cure for Fragmented School Schedules in Elementary Schools." *Educational Leadership* 46: 65–67.

Canady, R. L. (March 1989). "Design Scheduling Structures to Increase Student Learning." *Focus in Change* 1, 2: 1–2, 7–8.

Canady, R. L. (January 1990). "Parallel Block Scheduling: A Better Way to Organize a School." *Principal* 69, 3: 34–36.

Canady, R. L., and J. M. Reina. (January 1993). "Parallel Block Scheduling: An Alternative Structure." *Principal* 72, 3: 26–29.

Canady, R. L., and M. D. Rettig. (Summer 1992). "Restructuring Middle Level Schedules to Promote Equal Access." *Schools in the Middle*: 20–26.

Canady, R. L., and M. D. Rettig. (December 1993). "Unlocking the Lockstep High School Schedule." *Kappan*: 310–314.

Canady, R. L., and M. D. Rettig. (1995). *Block Scheduling: A Catalyst for Change in High Schools*. Princeton, N. J.: Eye on Education.

National Education Commission on Time and Learning. (1994). *Prisoners of Time: Report of the National Education Commission on Time and Learning*. Washington, D.C.: U.S. Government Printing Office.

Renzulli, J. S., ed. (1986). *Systems and Models for Developing Programs for the Gifted and Talented*. Mansfield Center, Conn.: Creative Learning Press.

POST NOTE

A 1994 national report, *Prisoners of Time*, called time "the missing element in the school-reform debate." Advising schools to be less rigid in how they used time, the report recommended the use of block scheduling and an extended school year.

Block scheduling can be the catalyst for numerous school improvements. While the research on block scheduling so far is relatively scarce, it is a hot topic in school reform. Anecdotal evidence indicates that students like the new type of schedule if teachers hold the students' interest through various learning activities. But if teachers rely primarily on lectures, which are longer under block scheduling, students complain. The key seems to be to work with teachers to change their teaching models so that they can make better use of the additional time they have each day the class meets.

DISCUSSION QUESTIONS

1. Have you ever experienced block scheduling as a student or an observer? If so, what were your impressions?

2. What evidence would you want to have to evaluate the effectiveness of block scheduling?

3. From a teacher's perspective, what are the strengths and weaknesses of block scheduling?

59
The Educational Consequences of Choice

Paul T. Hill

Many members of the education establishment claim that universal public school choice would be of little value to low-income and minority students who now attend the worst schools. They say that the best schools would take advantage of a larger pool of applicants to become even more selective than they are now and that schools that did admit disadvantaged children would not work very hard to meet their needs.

However, there is ample evidence that choice strongly benefits all children, including the disadvantaged. Choice promotes the candid and demanding relationships among teachers, parents, and students that are essential to effective schooling. It can make the difference between schools that are apathetic providers of routine academic courses and schools that are true communities that develop students as whole people.

Much of the evidence for these conclusions comes from my study of a privately funded voucher program, the Student-Sponsor Partnership Program in New York City. Under that program, individual sponsors pay tuition for low-income minority students—many of whom have failed in public schools and are not Catholic—to

Paul T. Hill is a research professor of public affairs, Daniel J. Evans School of Public Affairs, University of Washington, Seattle. Hill, Paul T., "The Educational Consequences of Choice," *Phi Delta Kappan*, June 1996. Copyright © by Phi Delta Kappa. Reprinted by permission of author and publisher.

attend New York City Catholic high schools. The program selects students from the bottom of the New York City public school population. They and their parents have only to accept the opportunity offered. My study compared the educational experiences and achievement of these private voucher students with the experiences of similar students in public high schools in New York City.[1] Other evidence is drawn from Robert Crain's study of nonselective magnet schools in New York City and my subsequent studies of site-based management and foundation-funded public high school reform efforts.[2]

How Choice Affects Schools

Starting with Milton Friedman, the advocates of choice have argued that competition is a powerful force for school quality. The attitudes and behavior of teachers and administrators in schools of choice show how competition affects schooling. Schools of choice need to attract students in order to survive. Though some can rely on a reputation for exclusivity or superior quality, not all schools can credibly claim to be the best. But every school *can* offer something that gives it an identity—a specific curriculum, social climate, or extracurricular program—that attracts the interest of parents and students. Once a school has established an identity, it must deliver on its promises well enough to keep current students from transferring out, to create "brand loyalty" among families with several children, and to attract enough new families to fill the entering class each year.

The need for product differentiation encourages a number of behaviors that advocates of "effective schools" have tried to promote in public school staffs. School staffs have a strong incentive to articulate a mission for the school and to ensure that all elements of the school contribute to its attainment. This mission must also be easy to explain to parents. That means that it must be focused on what children will experience in school and what they will be able to do when they leave—not on subtleties of educational technique that may matter only to professionals.

Once a school of choice has established an identity, the staff has a strong incentive to avoid major disruptions in the program. The demands of sheer economic survival also make teachers concerned about the performance of the school as a whole. If a school is forced to close because too few students want to attend it, all teachers have to find new jobs, no matter how well they have been teaching their own classes. Teachers therefore have strong incentives to keep their own work in line with the school's mission, to help one another, to identify weaknesses, and to ensure that variations in teacher performance do not harm the school's ultimate product and reputation.

All these behaviors are evident in public magnet schools, which must continually justify their existence in the face of pressures for uniformity, and in the financially struggling non-elite religious schools such as those attended by the Partnership students. Staff members in such schools are eligible to work in regular public schools for equal or greater pay, but they stay in schools of choice either out of commitment to the kind of education being offered in them or because they prefer the working conditions. They therefore value their jobs, which they know would go away if their schools were forced to close.

Staff members know that the continuation of their jobs depends on their own performance and that of their co-workers. Thus they are quick to seek advice from other teachers if a particular class is not going well and to alert their colleagues or the school management if another teacher is not pulling his or her weight. They are also very reluctant to give up on a student, knowing that too many stories of failure can wreck a school's reputation. Even when the student population changes because of worsening economic conditions or demographic shifts, teachers and administrators in schools of choice have the strongest possible incentive to maintain the level of students performance.

In contrast, staff members in a compulsory attendance public school need not fear for their jobs if their school fails to perform. As long as there are students in the neighborhood, they will be assigned to attend the school. Even if (as can happen in New York) the state intervenes to close the school, the teachers and administrators will be assigned to a similar school in the local system. The school's reputation may be a source of pride, but people's livelihoods do not depend on it. Though most teachers want to do a good job, they are not driven by economic necessity to question their own performance or to confront others who are not producing. Students who fail do not constitute a particular threat to the school. Staff members, knowing that serious self-assessment can lead to painful adult confrontations, have strong incentives to assign blame for declining student performance or rising dropout rates to factors over which the school has no control.

A small number of schools of choice may have so many applicants that they can reject a student who shows the first sign of becoming an academic or behavior problem. But in a competitive situation, such as that faced by the New York City Catholic and nonselective magnet schools, schools of choice have no such luxury. Such schools must be, in Robert Slavin's term, relentless in improving their own performance and in helping students achieve. Contrary to the claims of the antichoice education establishment, schools of choice cannot survive by hand-picking the easiest students to educate. They must, instead, work to influence the attitudes and motivations, as well as the academic performance, of their students.

Staff members in schools of choice must treat all students as if they are educable, not frozen in either their academic abilities or their attitudes. This difference between schools of choice and compulsory attendance public schools is epitomized in a sign displayed in a private school classroom: "Attitude is a choice."

How Choice Affects Parents

Most of the literature promoting choice stresses the importance of making parents consumers, courted and feared by school staffs. As the preceding section shows, the possibility that parents will withdraw their children from a school of choice is a powerful motivator for teachers and principals. That same possibility also means that parents can intervene effectively if schools mistreat or neglect their children.

But the connections between parents and schools of choice are more complex than this raw economic relationship. For all but the most opinionated and aggressive parents, the choice of a school is more akin to the choice of a family doctor or pastor than to the choice of a car dealer or grocery store. The parent's status as a consumer is important, but it is only the foundation of a much richer set of trust relationships between parent and child and child and school.

As James Coleman has pointed out, parents who choose a school for their child give the school a grant of parental authority. Parents who could have chosen any number of schools have selected this one. For whatever reason—religious conviction, educational taste, confidence in the school staff, or personal convenience—the parents want the child to attend a particular school. Though the parents might change their minds if things go especially badly, the child knows that a change of school can upset and inconvenience the parents. Most children, not wanting to risk an upheaval at home, have a strong incentive to succeed in the school their parents have chosen for them.

As the experience of Partnership students demonstrates, this grant of parental authority greatly increases the school's leverage over its students. As one student put it, "My mother says that I am lucky to be going to this school, and I had better not mess up." Another reported, "My uncle said [the public school the student previously attended] was no good, but if I couldn't do good here, there is something wrong with me." A student who skips school, does not study, or displays a sullen attitude is risking a confrontation with a parent. Though a few children will endure such a confrontation, the vast majority will not. School staff members are therefore able to use the parent's grant of authority to make demands on the student, as did one principal in the Partnership program who told a student, "Your mother didn't send you here to hang out in the rest room. She sent you here to learn."

Chosen schools also have leverage in dealing with parents. The threat of rejection that motivates teachers and principals cuts both ways: the school can likewise decide not to continue educating a student. Once they have chosen a school and adjusted their transportation plans and schedules accordingly, parents do not like to make changes. Unless the school has failed to keep its part of the bargain, parents are also reluctant to see their children's education disrupted. Schools can, consequently, make demands on parents—to monitor homework, ensure student attendance, and see to it that the student comes to school fed, rested, and ready to learn.

Schools in the Partnership program unhesitatingly made such demands on parents. They understood that parents lacked the time and money to make donations, raise funds, or attend frequent meetings. But the schools were direct and demanding about what parents had to do if their children were to succeed in school. Partnership schools found foster homes for students whose families were disrupted by death, unemployment, illness, or imprisonment. But they expected the family to support the educational process whenever it was physically possible.

Much of a school's influence is based on the parents' trust in the school's competence and concern for its students. Schools of choice, like family doctors, are influential because they are trusted. Patients follow their doctors' advice primarily because they believe it will make them healthier and only secondarily because they fear that the doctor will refuse to see them again if they do not take the medicine prescribed. The same is true with families. Because parents have chosen a school and because the school has an incentive to be as helpful as possible, a relationship of trust is created. Families that deal with the same school over a long time, especially those that have sent several children there, develop particularly strong bonds of sentiment and loyalty toward the school.

Any relationship of trust can be misused, and some schools of choice may retain parents' confidence longer than their performance merits. But in most cases major benefits accrue to all parties.

The Partnership schools felt confident in exhorting parents to become important forces in their children's lives and to reinforce the school's opposition to the harmful elements of students' peer culture. One Partnership school principal required that parents attend only one meeting each year, before classes started in September, so that she could urge parents to hold their children to traditional family standards, no matter how much children appeared to reject them.

These conditions are not impossible to achieve in compulsory attendance public schools, but there they require a great deal of personal effort, whereas they are intrinsic to choice schools. An attendance-zoned school, to which children are assigned because they are of mandatory school age and live in the neighborhood, has no definite grant of parental authority. As a result, teachers in regular public schools all over the country complain, "We can't teach these kids if their families don't care."

Choice affects the relationships between schools and parents even if a chosen school falls short of a parent's ideal. As long as the parent thinks the chosen school is better than any available alternative, the parent has reason to feel commitment to it. Schools need not be highly distinctive to get the benefit of a parent's choice. Even though educators may think low-cost parochial schools are all quite similar, the parents who choose among them usually think the differences are important. The longer a family stays with a school, the more importance history and personal relationships assume.

Compulsory attendance schools can build personal loyalties, and a parent whose children attend such a school can come to believe that it is just the right one. In such cases, the school probably gains an important grant of parental authority. But choice may play an important part even then. Higher-income parents, who always have the capacity to remove their children from compulsory attendance schools, are the ones most likely to develop close relationships with teachers and administrators. Lower-income parents, who have little choice about where their children attend school, seldom develop strong feelings of

confidence and loyalty. Parent advisory councils and other mechanisms for parent involvement in school governance affect only the few parents who participate.

As experience with the Partnership program shows, however, choice gives low-income parents the same sense of commitment and loyalty that higher-income parents enjoy. The schools' religious identity obviously builds some trust. But the fact that the parents have been able to accept or reject the scholarship creates a sense of mutual commitment between parent and school.

How Choice Affects Students

Many of the effects of choice on students are implicit in the foregoing discussion. Students in schools of choice benefit from the teachers' and principals' need to create a defined image and reputation. Students also benefit from their parents' commitment to the school and from the school's consequent ability to make demands on their parents and themselves.

Beyond these advantages, students derive two other benefits from being in schools of choice. First, they gain from being in a situation in which they must make commitments and take them seriously. Second, they gain from observing adults working in a common enterprise in which performance matters and both success and failure have real consequences.

Student commitment. Students may prefer not to attend any school at all, but if they have a preference for the school they attend over other alternative schools, they are susceptible to influence by the chosen school. This is true even if the school preference is based on nonacademic factors, such as location, sports teams, or presence of friends. It is especially important if students have knowingly chosen a school that offers a particular academic emphasis or makes special demands on effort and performance. When students make such a commitment, they implicitly affirm that the chosen school is more attractive than the alternatives. Though they may prefer not to do everything the school requires, they know that acting on those impulses could result in their being forced to leave the chosen school and go to another one that is less attractive to them.

Students in the Partnership schools frankly admitted that they had made a tradeoff in accepting scholarships to attend private schools. All knew that leaving public school would separate them from friends of the neighborhood and would subject them to firm demands about attendance and academic effort. They accepted the scholarships for many reasons—because the private schools were safer, because they hoped (along with virtually all high school students) to attend college someday, or because they liked the schools' traditions and sports teams. But they all understood what the schools would demand of them because the school admissions counselors and the Partnership program itself made sure that they knew.

Once they accepted the school's demands, they had given the schools leverage: teachers and administrators could assign homework, take attendance, grade performance, and administer consequences, just as they had said they would. Armed with this power, the Partnership schools exercised their authority confidently—not in a harsh or morally superior way, but matter-of-factly, as the simple consequence of a well-understood bargain.

Less than 10% of the students who were offered scholarships rejected them, and less than 5% of the students admitted to private schools left, either voluntarily or at the schools' initiative. The vast majority of students understood the bargain they had made, and they accepted, albeit grudgingly, the schools' rigorous execution of it. When students failed to complete assigned work or broke school rules, teachers consistently said, "You made an agreement when you came here—now live up to it." For the vast majority of students, the need to abide by their prior commitments both influenced their behavior and changed their attitudes. In surveys and interviews, virtually all students said that their effort, attendance, and attitudes about schooling had all changed since they joined the Partnership program.

Emulation of adult working relationships. During the fieldwork for my study in subsequent work in urban high schools, I saw students encounter a hidden curriculum, taught not didactically but by example. The example is provided by teachers and administrators, the only people whom students routinely see at work. It can send a powerful message to students about whether or not the work of adults is informed by clear goals and requires or rewards collaborative effort, initiative, reciprocity, or risk-taking.

As Carl Glickman and others confirm, teachers in compulsory attendance schools often feel that they have little control over the conditions of their own work and think that they and their colleagues are neither rewarded for diligence nor punished for negligence. For adults in such situations, the apparently rational response is to do exactly what their formal job descriptions require and not take responsibility for the overall product of the organization in which they work. Albert Shanker's quote from an urban teacher, "I taught them but they didn't learn it," sums up the phenomenon. Many teachers and administrators in compulsory attendance schools think differently, but they are not rewarded by the organization or, in many cases, appreciated by their co-workers. For students, who seldom observe any adults other than teachers at work, the message can be powerful: large organizations that employ adults do not have clear goals and do not require or support effective work.

The hidden curriculum in schools of choice is different. The adults in such schools are not necessarily more virtuous than teachers and administrators elsewhere, but because they are linked in a common enterprise they have incentives to work together and to hold one another accountable. The version of adult life and responsibility modeled in such schools is very different from that evident in schools that lack a clear mission and in which staff members do not have to perform in order to keep their jobs. The message to students is that adults depend on and influence one another and that they care about whether they and others are contributing to the success of a broader enterprise.

Students get the message. One student interviewed at a compulsory attendance school stated bluntly what other students had said less directly: "Nobody here does any more than you have to do. I'm not going to be a chump." Students in Partnership schools, on the contrary, saw how hard faculty members worked to make the school succeed. As one Partnership student who had recently transferred from public school told me, "In public school the teachers say, 'I get paid whether you learn this or not.' Here they say, 'You are going to learn this if it takes all day. I don't care how long it takes: I live upstairs.'"

It does not take a private or religious school to teach these lessons. Many of the nonselective magnet schools in Crain's and my studies provide similar examples of earnest adult collaboration. There are, furthermore, many teachers and administrators in compulsory attendance schools who offer sterling personal examples. But these individuals are forced to overcome the context in which they work, whereas teachers and administrators in schools of choice are reinforced by everything about their working environment.

Conclusion

Several current educational reform movements—going under such names as decentralization, charters, and school contracting—all hope to create the conditions under which public schools can develop these attributes. Doing so will re-

quire profound change in the missions and operations of public schools. It surely requires choice—choice of schools by teachers, students, and parents; choice by schools concerning how long to stick with a student who will not fulfill the school's work requirements; and choice by public officials regarding whether to continue supporting a failing school or to close and recommission it with a new staff and management.

As educational environments, schools of choice are profoundly different from compulsory attendance schools. Even when their academic offerings are not much different from those of compulsory attendance schools, schools of choice become places in which parents and teachers are collaborators, bargains among adults and between adults and children are made and kept, effort is rewarded, and actions have consistent consequences. Such environments motivate student effort in the short run. In the long run, they socialize students into the values and attitudes required in real life. ∎

Notes

1. Paul T. Hill, *High Schools with Character* (Santa Monica, Calif.: RAND Corporation, 1990).

2. Robert Crain et al., *The Effectiveness of New York City's Career Magnets* (Berkeley, Calif.: National Center for Research on Vocational Education, 1992); and Paul T. Hill and Josephine J. Bonan, *Decentralization and Accountability in Public Education* (Santa Monica, Calif.: RAND Corporation, 1991).

P O S T N O T E

Although the nation continues to debate the merits of a school choice system, many important ideas raised by school choice studies deserve to be brought into our public schools immediately. One of these ideas is what Paul Hill calls the "grant of parental authority" that parents confer on teachers in noncompulsory schools. Once teachers were given such authority in all schools, public and private, but today the teacher's position has been weakened. Without a sense of authority coming from the children's parents and from the front office, teachers often feel vulnerable and uncertain.

Contrary to some popular belief, possessing authority does not mean being arbitrary, insensitive to others' needs, or authoritarian. Nor does it mean dumping information on children through "frontal" teaching. Being an authoritative yet open presence in the lives of students is quite different from being controlling and authoritarian.

DISCUSSION QUESTIONS

1. Hill argues that choice positively affects three entities. What are they, and for which of the three do you believe he makes the strongest case?

2. Taking these three entities, can you come up with arguments *against* choice for each of them?

3. Considering all the factors discussed in this article, as well as your own knowledge of educational choice, what do you think is the strongest argument for or against choice?

60

School Choice: Panacea or Pandora's Box?

*Kevin B. Smith and
Kenneth J. Meier*

Taken at face value, school choice is a pretty simple idea. Take the control of education away from school boards and state legislatures and replace it with the freedom of the market. Schools will supply the educational "product," and parents and students will act as "customers," choosing the school that best fits their educational desires and needs.

Because tax dollars follow students, schools will have to attract students in order to survive, and they will be allowed the freedom to respond to the demands and needs of their customers in creative ways. Schools that offer the best education will prosper; those that do not will close. The end result will be innovative approaches to education and an overall improvement of the nation's schools, with no more bothersome mandates from state legislatures and no more stifling layers of bureaucracy. At least, that is the theory. But will it work?

Yes, say John Chubb and Terry Moe, two of the most persuasive backers of school choice. The

Kevin B. Smith is an associate professor in the Department of Political Science at the University of Nebraska, Lincoln. Kenneth J. Meier is a professor in the Department of Political Science at Texas A&M University.
Smith, Kevin B. and Kenneth J. Meier, "School Choice: Panacea or Pandora's Box?" *Phi Delta Kappan*, December 1995. Copyright © 1995 by Phi Delta Kappa. Reprinted by permission of authors and publisher.

market will respond to individual and localized needs in ways that the current public education monopoly cannot. From their perspective, whatever the education ill, "choice *is* a panacea."[1]

No, say such committed debunkers as Gerald Bracey. In his Fourth Bracey Report on the condition of education, he argues that interest in school choice is on the wane, and for good reason: the evidence says that choice does not live up to its claims.[2] Opponents of choice argue that, instead of promoting performance, a market-driven system of education will promote everything from racial and religious segregation to quickie diploma mills and souped-up day-care centers.

Other observers say that choice falls somewhere between a panacea and a Pandora's box. In a thoughtful analysis, Jeffrey Henig, a political scientist, argues that backers have underestimated the potential for harm in school choice—particularly with regard to segregation and to religion—but that choice may work in limited circumstances.[3]

Social science research has managed to muddy the waters of the debate with a string of contradictory reports. John Witte's reports on the choice experiment in Milwaukee, a closely watched program that pays for low-income children to attend private schools, suggest no evidence of improvement over the existing system.[4] Meanwhile, the choice reforms in New York City's East Harlem are touted as miraculously effective.[5] And the choice reforms in Richmond, California, are blamed for driving the local school system into bankruptcy for no apparent gain in performance.[6]

Adding to the confusion generated by these conflicting results is the delicate question of ideology. As Ernest Boyer has written, "There is intensity, even a zealousness, in the debate on school choice that smothers thoughtful discourse. Political concerns seem more and more to outweigh educational objectives."[7] Indeed, the "correct" answer on choice all too often depends on the ideological prism through which it is viewed. Supporters and detractors can extrapolate the scant empirical evidence to fit their own agendas.

Does choice work? The current answer is yes. And no. And maybe.

There's Choice—And Then There's Choice

The failure of social science to provide an empirical resolution to this largely ideological debate stems from a number of factors. One is the lack of any real agreement on what school choice is. As Henig has pointed out, choice works well as a metaphor, but it is not a concrete policy option.[8] While many people are attracted to the abstract idea of "choice," this general agreement disappears in a welter of specifics. Should choice involve private and religious schools? Should it involve single-sex schools? Single-race schools? A number of students we interviewed saw school choice not as an option *between* institutions, but as an opportunity to pick an individualized curriculum *within* an institution. Does this also constitute school choice? In three months of interviews we found a lot of people who favored school choice, but few who seemed to be talking about the same thing.[9]

If school choice is viewed as a minimally regulated, market-based system of education, then no such entity currently exists. While states and localities continue to experiment with options such as open enrollment, these represent only small steps toward the concept envisioned by backers of choice such as Chubb and Moe. Even these small steps confuse the issue, because they often seem to be going in different directions—each having varying degrees of restriction and regulation.[10]

Thus two considerable problems immediately confront any researcher seeking to answer definitively whether school choice will work. First, there is no agreement on what should be analyzed. What policy or experiment actually represents a real test of school choice? With no clear answer, picking what to analyze becomes a partisan decision. Even critics agree that East Harlem has had its successes. Advocates say, unsurprisingly, that this experience represents a true test of choice; detractors say that other programs that did not have the political backing of U.S. Presidents would be better social laboratories. Still others argue that programs that do not include private schools are not a real test of choice at all.

The second problem is the flip side of the first. There are no comprehensive systems of school choice to test. The only way to resolve the issue of whether applying economic principles to education will work is to try them on a broad scale, and no one has been able to do this. Judging from the steady rejection of choice programs in statewide ballots, it does not appear to be politically feasible.

So a real system of choice—whatever it may be—does not exist in any universal or comprehensive form and is unlikely to exist for the foreseeable future. And it can be argued that examining anything less would not be a fair and representative test of choice. Thus the results of any particular study can be embraced or dismissed by those on either side of the debate. Small wonder that evidence supports virtually every opinion on school choice. Our goal here is to use existing data to attempt to resolve this problem, to put school choice to the empirical acid test, and to arrive at a definitive answer regarding its possibilities.

The Institutional Theory

The core of the argument in favor of school choice presents one possible way of getting around the problem of what to test. We can look not only at how an education market *would* work, but at how the existing education system *does* work. Then we can see if reality supports the theory.

This approach is best articulated by Chubb and Moe, who put forward a cogent and comprehensive explanation of education, the so-called institutional model. This theory argues that "school organization does indeed have a significant impact on how much students learn."[11] Why is America's education system failing? Because, Chubb and Moe answer, it is designed to fail.[12] The system is set up to respond not to parents' and students' demands for quality education, but rather to the demands of state legislatures, school boards, and a large, professionalized education bureaucracy. Chubb and Moe's solution is to free schools from the demands of the latter and to make their survival dependent on meeting the demands of the former. As Chubb and Moe sum it up, "If Americans want effective schools, it appears they must first create new institutions. . . ."[13]

To illustrate the fundamental premise of their theory, Chubb and Moe contrast the organizational structure of public and private schools. The key institutional differences are that, in the private sector, "society does not control [the schools] directly through democratic politics, and society does control them—indirectly— through the marketplace."[14] The decisions on what to teach, how to teach, and who will teach are made at the school level. These decisions are based on a need for institutional survival: if a private school fails to attract students, it closes. Thus these decisions respond to the educational demands of parents and students. Private schools are better at educating, Chubb and Moe argue, because their organizational structure focuses on meeting the demands of the market.

Contrast this with the organizational structure of public schools. While private schools have customers, public schools have constituents, and "parents and students are but a small part of this constituency."[15] Public schools are agencies of society, controlled by democratic institutions. These institutions—school boards and state legislatures—respond to a wide variety of constituents' demands generated by the democratic process. While parents and students can participate in the process, "they have no right to win. In the end, they have to take what society gives them."[16]

The function of democratic control is to impose "higher-order values" on the schools—that is, to carry out the wishes of those in political power. Those who hold the keys to this power use a thick layer of bureaucracy to ensure that their goals are met. Unlike private schools, public schools are not autonomous. They must rigidly conform to the rules and regulations passed by democratic institutions and enforced by a bureaucracy. The whats, hows, and whos of teaching are decided far from the individual school. Moreover, the wishes of parents and students often seem irrelevant to this process. Public schools are not controlled by parents and students "and are literally not supposed to provide them with the kind of education they want."[17]

Essentially, the institutional theory holds that, to improve education, public schools should be organized more like private schools. That is, public schools should be controlled by the market and not by bureaucracy.

Although the institutional theory put forward by Chubb and Moe has come under a rising barrage of criticism, it remains the intellectual foundation of the school choice argument, and its basic tenets are widely accepted. For example, virtually all choice advocates agree that public schools are failing and that the institutional structure of public education is a root cause of this problem.

Here is the basis for at least one comprehensive empirical test: How does the existing public school system—not some abstract, vaguely defined market system—actually function? The relationships that the institutional theory of choice argues govern public and private school performance and enrollments are straightforward empirical propositions. We have a theory, we have a system in existence, and we have some data. In short, we have a means to reach a definitive answer on at least one fundamental proposition of school choice. If the relationships argued by choice theory to be important are found, then school choice theory will be supported, and we can consider choice a viable option. If they are not, then the theory is false to the reality of today's education system. If this is the case, a primary intellectual support of the choice option collapses, and ideology alone is left to shore up the damage. The tasks before us now are to draw hypotheses from the theory and to gather data to test them. This is what we offer here.

Hypothesis 1. The education system is failing. School choice is predicated on the assumption that the existing education system is failing. However, this assumption is not supported by available data. The most commonly offered "proof" of educational decline is the decline in scores on the SAT I (formerly the Scholastic Aptitude Test).[18] This contention has been thoroughly discredited as evidence that schools are performing less well,[19] and, indeed, the developers of the test have never claimed that SAT scores can be used to measure school performance.

The major reason that SAT I scores have fallen over the decades is the changing demographic makeup of the test-takers. Beginning in the late 1960s, those who took the SAT I became less white, less well off, and less likely to have graduated in the top 20% of their high school classes. Raw scores on the SAT I have fallen since the 1970s, but scores for all ethnic subgroups (save only for whites) have risen. The Sandia National Laboratories weighted the 1990 scores to reflect the demographics of the 1975 pool of test-takers and found that scores actually increased 30 points over that 15-year span.[20] In short, the most commonly used yardstick of educational performance—whatever its inherent shortcomings—contradicts a basic assumption of choice theory.

Some of the other data quoted by choice advocates are much more firmly rooted in empirical fact. These primarily deal with such issues as teen violence and pregnancy. While these figures may be accurate enough, there seems to be a failure of causal logic here. Even granting arguments that classrooms have become too permissive, the culpability of schools for such problems seems limited. Schools must deal with such problems, but they do not cause them. When we asked students in the Milwaukee area about these problems, they uniformly put the causes beyond the confines of the school yard, placing them squarely on parents and the students themselves.[21]

Hypothesis 2. Parents are dissatisfied with public schools. Parental dissatisfaction is also a fundamental assumption of choice theory, and it is particularly critical because it represents the ignored demand for a better educational product—the fuel that will ultimately drive the engine of the education market. Yet, once again, the assumption is not wholly justified by the available data. This has been known for some time. In 1984 John Goodlad reported the results of a survey of 8,624 parents in which only 10% gave their schools a grade of D or lower. "Overall," Goodlad concluded, "the data do not convey the deep parental concern that supposedly has prevailed widely."[22] Similarly, the Phi Delta Kappa/Gallup Poll reported annually in this magazine belies the notion of a rising tide of public dissatisfaction with education. Roughly half of those surveyed give their public schools a grade of A or B (and the percentage ranges even higher for parents grading their children's schools). Only about 5% assign the schools an F.

Other studies indicate that growth in private school enrollments is not necessarily driven by dissatisfaction with the quality of public schools. For example, a sudden spurt of private school enrollments in the Omaha, Nebraska, area recently prompted officials of the Millard School District to commission a survey of those parents who switched. About one-third mentioned academic rigor as "a" (not "the") reason for opting to go private. Three-quarters mentioned religion.[23]

On closer examination the assumptions of school failure and public dissatisfaction do not seem justified. Failure and dissatisfaction are ideological points, not facts. There is ample evidence to support the arguments that education is not failing and that it is providing service that most of its users consider satisfactory.

Hypothesis 3. Poor public school performance increases private school enrollment. Many choice advocates bolster their arguments by using private schools as an example of how market forces can improve the quality of education. Private schools are institutions geared to their customers, the advocates of choice argue. They know what their customers want—high-quality education—and they are free to meet those demands. This argument is given empirical backing by comparisons of achievement test scores at public and private schools, and the test scores at private schools tend to be higher. Such findings have prompted fierce debate. While backers of choice say that the higher scores are evidence of the superior quality of a private school education, opponents of private school choice argue that the higher scores are the result of selection bias—that private schools "skim" the best students from the public education system.

Theoretically, private schools do not have to attempt to provide a high-quality education to survive. The most common type of private schools in America are Catholic schools. While Catholic schools have a well-deserved reputation for high academic standards, this is not the only value that they offer to their "customers." They offer a religion-based curriculum that is unavailable in public schools. Thus it does not seem unreasonable to argue that the demand for religious instruction plays an important role in the success of private schools.

One of the other arguments put forward for the success of private schools is more disturbing—the demand for racial segregation. This argument has strong historical roots. In the era of desegregation, Southern parents who wanted the right to send their children to racially segregated schools were among the strongest backers of school choice. While de jure segregation is illegal, minority students today are twice as likely, as a percentage of total enrollment, to attend public rather than private schools.[24]

What is being argued here is not only the heart of choice theory, but also a testable question: What drives private school enrollments? If choice theorists are correct, then as the quality of the public schools drops, enrollment in private schools should increase. This assumes, of course, that parents have the necessary financial resources to move their children to private schools. With regression analysis—a statistical approach that allows us to judge the impact of one variable independent of the effects of other variables—we can control for financial resources and look at the independent impact of public school quality.

This is exactly what we did. We attempted to predict enrollment shifts in Florida's private schools for the latter half of the 1980s. And we were quite successful. We built a model that explained 98% of the variance in these enrollment shifts. The results of our analysis contradict the expectations of choice theory.

Public school quality—as measured by achievement test scores—had no impact on changes in private school enrollment. We looked at both short- and long-term trends in public school test scores and found nothing to indicate that, as scores fell, parents with the necessary financial resources shifted their children to private schools.

However, one consistent and positive predictor of private school enrollment was the percentage of a school district's population that is Catholic. The more Catholic the district, the greater the likelihood of increases in private school enrollment. While this finding does not offer much comfort to choice theorists—who tend to downplay the demand for religious instruction—it makes sense to those who run the Catholic schools. John Norris, superintendent of the Milwaukee Catholic Schools, told us that Catholic schools emphasize values and curricula with religious content precisely because these features are attractive to many parents.

Minority enrollment in public schools was also a significant predictor of private school enrollments. As the number of black students increased in the public system, private school enrollments grew. This offers some empirical backing for those who argue that racial segregation will play a role in an education market. Choice advocates consistently deny charges that a market-regulated education system would be divisive. But these results raise serious questions about the effects of a market-based education system. And they are supported by more anecdotal evidence that we collected. As we conducted field interviews in the Milwaukee area, we asked students whether race would play any role in their choice if they were allowed to pick their schools. A disturbing number said yes.

Taken together, these results deal a blow to choice theory. There is no evidence that poorly performing public schools are driving up enrollments in private schools. However, religion and a desire for racial segregation do seem to play a role in these shifts in enrollment. The theory does not fit with the evidence we have.

Choice supporters can deal with the uncomfortable matters of religion and race by recognizing that they will play an important role in any education marketplace and by advocating tight government regulation of them. Even Chubb and Moe find themselves forced into this position, saying that schools should be able to set their own admissions procedures, "subject only to nondiscrimination requirements."[25] Of course, enforcing nondiscrimination requirements would be a complex and difficult job, and it would require a centralized agency with considerable monitoring and enforcement powers. This agency would almost certainly have to be placed under the control of a democratic institution. In this fashion, choice theory not only has to modify its explanation of the success of private schools, but it also has to accept a good deal of assistance from the very institutional structure it seeks to eliminate.

Because we have data for several years, we took our analysis one step further on this question. In order to get a better understanding of the public school/private school relationship, we turned our research question on its head. Instead of looking at whether public school performance drives private school enrollment, we looked at what impact private school enrollment has on public school performance. We used statistical techniques to determine whether private school enrollments affected student performance or whether student performance led to greater private enrollments. As we noted above, we found that public school performance did not affect private enrollments. But in this part of the analysis, we found that, as private school enrollments rise, public school performance drops.

Combined with our earlier research, this offers strong evidence that private schools "skim" the best students from the available enrollment pool. In other words, private school performance is likely to be a function more of enrolling the most educable students than of superior instruction or organizational structure.

Based on these and our earlier findings, we conclude that choice theory does not accurately account for the relationship between the success of private schools and public school performance. Although an attractive argument, school choice theory failed every empirical test that we administered. While the debate on an as yet nonexistent choice system continues, we believe that we have supplied a reasonably definitive answer to a question with enormous implications for this debate: Does choice theory accurately describe the structures of the existing education system? No. Most definitely not.

We do not contend that we have proved the inadequacy of the cure offered by school choice enthusiasts. But we have brought into serious question the validity of their diagnosis of education's ills and the logic mustered in support of their proposed cure. While it is theoretically possible to derive a cure from an inaccurate diagnosis that lacks a logical connection between problem and remedy, we believe it is highly unlikely. Choice is more Pandora's box than panacea. ■

Notes

1. John E. Chubb and Terry Moe, *Politics, Markets, and America's Schools* (Washington, D.C.; Brookings Institution, 1990), p. 217.

2. Gerald W. Bracey, "The Fourth Bracey Report on the Condition of Public Education," *Phi Delta Kappan*, October 1994, pp. 123–24.

3. Jeffrey R. Henig, *Rethinking School Choice: Limits of the Market Metaphor* (Princeton, N.J.: Princeton University Press, 1994).

4. John F. Witte et al., *Second-Year Report: Milwaukee Parental Choice Program* (Madison: Department of Political Science and Robert M. La Follette Institute of Public Affairs, University of Wisconsin, 1992).

5. Seymour Fliegel and James MacGuire, *Miracle in East Harlem* (New York: Random House, 1993).

6. Barbara Chriss, Greta Nash, and David Stern, "The Rise and Fall of Choice in Richmond, California," *Economics and Education Review*, vol. 11, 1992, pp. 395–406.

7. Ernest L. Boyer, *School Choice* (Princeton, N.J.: Carnegie Foundation for the Advancement of Teaching, 1992), pp. xv–xvi.

8. Henig, pp. 174–95.

9. Kevin B. Smith and Kenneth J. Meier, *The Case Against School Choice: Politics, Markets, and Fools* (New York: M. E. Sharpe, 1995), pp. 132–40.

10. Thomas Timar and David L. Kirp, "State Efforts to Reform Schools: Treading Between a Regulatory Swamp and an English Garden," *Educational Evaluation and Policy Analysis*, vol. 10, 1988, pp. 75–88.

11. Chubb and Moe, p. 16.

12. Ibid., pp. 1–2.

13. Ibid., p. 21.

14. Ibid., p. 27.

15. Ibid., p. 31.

16. Ibid., p. 32.

17. Ibid.

18. Henig, p. 27.

19. Bracey, pp. 116–18.

20. C. C. Carson, R. M. Huelskamp, and T. D. Woodall, "Perspectives on Education in America," *Journal of Educational Research*, May/June 1993, pp. 267–270.

21. Smith and Meier, pp. 1–13.

22. John I. Goodlad, *A Place Called School: Prospects for the Future* (New York: McGraw-Hill, 1984), p. 36.

23. Deborah Shanahan, "Religion Cited in School Choices," *Omaha World-Herald*, 21 July 1994, p. 20.

24. John F. Witte, "Private School Versus Public School Achievement: Are There Findings That Should Affect the Educational Choice Debate?," *Economics of Education Review*, vol. 11, 1992, pp. 371–94.

25. Chubb and Moe, p. 221.

P O S T N O T E

This impressive article poses some thoughtful objections to the arguments of school-choice advocates. Yet it seems to ignore one important fact: a large and growing number of Americans want school choice. These adults know they have choice in almost every aspect of their lives except how they educate their children. Many also feel that it is fundamentally unfair that wealthy Americans have educational choice, but those of lesser means do not.

We are convinced that the school-choice issue will be with us for some time. We fear, however, that the debate will become a highly charged political argument featuring overblown rhetoric with racial and class-struggle overtones. What we urge are several large-scale experiments, comparing the current system with the various choice and voucher plans. Instead of hanging on to what we have (and thereby angering many of our citizens) or taking a huge leap to a choice plan, let's be educators. Let's try some different approaches, examine the results carefully, and then decide what is best for our students.

D I S C U S S I O N Q U E S T I O N S

1. What is Chubb and Moe's institutional model, and how does it apply to American education?

2. Are you satisfied with Smith and Meier's conclusions about whether our schools are failing and whether parents are dissatisfied with the schools?

3. Where do you stand on the issue of school choice? Why?

Part Eight

Educational Technology

For much of the past decade, schools have emphasized the acquisition of technology hardware as a major objective. By 1998, it was estimated that there was one instructional computer for every six students in our public schools. Educators have now reached the point where their goal should not be just to acquire technology. Instead, they should ask how technologies should be used to help students reach the higher standards being developed by states and to prepare students for the world they will enter when they leave school.

Although most educators, policy makers, and business leaders believe that technology has the potential to alter dramatically how teachers teach and students learn, there are some who remain skeptical that technology will have a significant effect on education. These skeptics cite as evidence the "hype" that accompanied previous technologies, such as television, that failed to deliver on their promises.

It is clear that if computer and other related technologies are to transform educational practice, much time and effort must go into working with teachers, who need to understand what technology can do and to develop the skills necessary to deliver on the promise. If this teacher development does not occur, then the latest educational technology, like some earlier ones, will prove to be a bust.

The Mad Dash to Compute

Jane M. Healy

"I feel as if we're being swept down this enormous river—we don't know where we're going or why, but we're caught in the current. I think we should stop and take a look before it's too late."

This comment about the use of technology in schools was voiced plaintively by an assistant superintendent from Long Island, N.Y. It was typical of many I collected recently in a three-year investigation of our heavily hyped technological revolution.

Having started this saga as a wide-eyed advocate for educational computing, I now must admit that the school official was right. New technologies hold enormous potential for education, but before any more money is wasted, we must pause and ask some pointed questions that have been bypassed in today's climate of competitive technophilia ("My district's hard drives are bigger than yours!").

Educators, who are seen as one of the ripest growth markets in hardware, software and Internet sales, have been carefully targeted by an industry that understandably wants to convince us that its products will solve all our problems. (Did you ever previously see multiple double-page

Jane Healy is an educational psychologist and author of *Endangered Minds*, *Your Child's Growing Mind* and *Failure to Connect: How Computers Affect Our Children's Minds for Better and Worse*. Reprinted with permission from the April 1999 issue of *The School Administrator* magazine.

ads in *Education Week* for any educational product? Have you been offered "free" equipment—that eventually demands as much upkeep and fiscal lifeblood as the man-eating plant in "Little Shop of Horrors"?). The advertising's thrust to both educators and parents is that you should invest in as much technology as early as possible or students will be left hopelessly behind. The parents, failing to appreciate the nonsense inherent in this assumption, in turn put additional pressure on schools to "get with the program."

As educators, we should have the wit to evaluate these pressures, resist public opinion and shun manipulative marketing. It also becomes our obligation to interpret to the public what we know is really good for kids. Yet three major issues are being largely overlooked as we rush to capture the trend. I will call them (1) trade-offs, (2) developmental questions and (3) winners in the long run?

The Trade-Offs

During my recent research, which involved visits to dozens of elementary and secondary schools across the United States, I was invited to observe the flagship elementary school of a district that prides itself on the scope of its technology budget. Yet I had difficulty finding students using computers. Many expensive machines were sitting idle (and becoming increasingly obsolete) in classrooms where teachers have not learned to incorporate them into daily lessons. ("When they break, I just don't get them repaired," one 1st-grade teacher confided.)

Finally, in the computer lab, I found 32 5th-grade students lined up at two rows of machines and confronted the following scenario: The technology coordinator—technologically adept but with virtually no background in either teaching or curriculum development—explains that this group comes four times a week to practice reading and math skills. Many students are below grade level in basic skills.

I randomly select a position behind Raoul, who was using a math software program. The director, now occupied in fixing a computer that eager young fingers have crashed, hastily reminds the students to enter the program at the correct level for their ability, but I begin to suspect something is amiss when Raoul effortlessly solves a few simple addition problems and then happily accepts his reward—a series of smash-and-blast games in which he manages to demolish a sizeable number of aliens before he is electronically corralled into another series of computations. Groaning slightly, he quickly solves these problems and segues expertly into the next space battle.

By the time I move on, Raoul has spent many more minutes zapping aliens than he has in doing math. My teacher's soul cringes at the thought of important learning time squandered. I also wonder if what we are really teaching Raoul is that he should choose easy problems so he can play longer or that the only reason to use his brain even slightly is to be granted—by an automaton over which he has no personal control—some mindless fun as a reward. I wonder who selected this software or if any overall plan dictates the implementation of this expensive gadgetry.

Moreover, this computer lab, like so many others, has been morphed from a music room. In this school system, cutbacks in arts, physical education and even textbooks are used to beef up technology budgets.

The trade-offs inherent in this all-too-typical situation should be troubling to all of us:

- *Haste and pressure for electronic glitz.* These should not replace a carefully designed plan based on sound educational practice. Grafting technology onto schools without good curriculum or excellent teaching guarantees failure. First things first.

- *Money on hardware, software and networks instead of essential teacher education.* Informed estimates suggest it takes five years of ongoing in-service training before teachers can fully integrate computer uses into lesson plans. They must also have solid technical support so that instructional time is not spent repairing machines.

- *Technology coordinators without adequate preparation in education.* Rather, the key instructional decisions should be made by teachers who are adept

in linking computer use to significant aspects of curriculum. "The 3rd-graders made T-shirts in computer lab today," one techie boasted during one of my school visits. "Why?" I asked. "Well, we can—and besides, the kids just loved it." If this sort of justification prevails in your schools, don't be surprised if your test scores start to drop!

- *Cuts in vital areas used to finance technology purchases.* Computers, which have as yet demonstrated questionable effects on student learning, must not be bought at the expense of proven staples of mental development, such as art, music, drama, debate, physical education, text literacy, manipulatives and hands-on learning aids. One teacher in a Western state told me her district "could be IBM for all the technology we have," yet she was refused money to purchase a set of paperback literature books for her classroom. Why? "The money had all been spent on the machines," she sighed.

- *Pie-in-the-sky assumptions.* Don't be mislead by claims that computers, instead of proven interventions, will remediate basic skills. Many of today's youngsters need solid, hands-on remediation in reading and math delivered by teachers trained in established programs such as Reading Recovery. Don't forget that those "proven studies" about the impact of electronic learning systems and their cost effectiveness were financed by people with products to sell.

- *Installing computers instead of reducing class size.* To my surprise, I found that good technology use is actually more teacher intensive than traditional instruction and works best with smaller classes! Research also is beginning to show the skill/drill software that manages learning for large groups actually may limit students' achievement once the novelty wears off. We need good, objective long-range data before committing money and growing minds to such programs.

- *Funding electronic glitz instead of quality early childhood programs.* Again, we must weigh a large expense of unproven value against proven upstream prevention of academic and social problems. Ironically, estimated costs for connecting all classrooms to the Internet also could provide every child with an adequate preschool program.

■ *Time wasted vs. productive learning.* Without good planning and supervision, youngsters tend to use even the best educational programs for mindless fun rather than meaningful learning. Moreover, if you do not have a district policy on selecting software, implement one today. Poorly selected "edutainment" and drill-and-practice programs actually can depress academic gains, whereas well-implemented simulations and conceptually driven programs may improve learning—if a good teacher is in charge.

Engaged Learning

Consider a different scenario that I observed at a middle school in a suburban school district. A small group of 12-year-olds eagerly surround a computer terminal but don't complain about the slightly fuzzy image. They are too busy following the action on the screen where a disheveled-looking young man in bicycling clothes stands in a jungle talking earnestly with someone in a bush jacket who appears to be a scientist.

One of the students giggles, pokes another and attempts a whispered comment, but he is rapidly silenced. "Shush, Damon. Don't be such a jerk. We can't hear!" hisses his neighbor.

What has inspired such serious academic purpose among these kids? They and their teacher are involved in directing (along with others around the globe) a three-month bicycle expedition, manned by a team of cyclists and scientists, through the jungles of Central America in search of lost Mayan civilizations. At the moment, they are debating the possibility of sending the team through a difficult, untravelled jungle track to a special site. How fast can they ride? How far? What obstacles will they encounter? What are the odds of success? What plans must be made?

Like others in a new breed of simulations, this activity uses on-line and satellite phone communications to establish real-time links between students around the world and the adventurers. Because students' votes actually determine the course of the journey, they must problem-solve right along with the scientists. To acquire the necessary knowledge, the class also has plunged into a variety of real-life, hands-on learning: history, archaeology, visual arts, math (e.g., Mayans calculated in base 20), science of flora and fauna, Mayan poetry, building a miniature rain forest, reading the daily journals of the adventurers, researching, developing theories and debating about why the civilization collapsed.

This example is only one of many powerful supplements to a well-planned curriculum. New technologies can be used wisely—or they can be a costly impediment to educational quality. As you debate the trade-offs of your technology choices, you might keep these questions in mind:

1. What can this particular technology do that cannot be accomplished by other less expensive or more proven methods?

2. What will we gain—and what will we lose?

3. How can we sell wise educational decisions to a public foolishly buying the message that computers are a magic bullet for education?

Developmental Questions

A question too rarely considered is what effect extended computer use will have on children's developing bodies and brains. Moreover, it is imperative to ask at what age this technology should really be introduced. My observations have convinced me that normally developing children under age seven are better off without today's computers and software. Technology funds should be first allocated to middle and high schools where computer-assisted learning is much more effective and age-appropriate.

■ *Physical effects:* Too little is known about technology's physical effects on digitized youngsters, but troubling evidence of problems resulting from computer use include: vision (e.g., near-sightedness), postural and orthopedic complaints (e.g., neck and back problems; carpal tunnel syndrome), the controversial effects of electromagnetic radiation emitted from the backs and sides of machines and even the rare possibility of seizures triggered by some types of visual displays. Administrators should be on top of this.

Nonetheless, I found a woeful disregard in schools of even the basic safety rules mandated for the adult workplace. Clear guidelines exist, and before you consign all your 3rd-graders to laptops you would be wise to check the suggestions out.

■ *Brain effects:* In terms of what happens to children's cognitive, social and emotional development as a function of computer use, even less is known. The brain is significantly influenced by whatever media we choose for education, and poor choices now may well result in poor thinkers in the next generation.

In my book, *Failure to Connect,* I trace the course of brain development with technology use in mind, and one thing is clear. Computers can either help or hurt the process. For younger children, too much electronic stimulation can become addictive, replacing important experiences during critical periods of development: physical exploration, imaginative play, language, socialization and quiet time for developing attention and inner motivation. For children of any age, improper software choices can disrupt language development, attention, social skills and motivation to use the mind in effortful ways. (The next time you see a classroom of students motivated by computer use, be sure to question whether they are motivated to think and learn—or simply to play with the machines.)

By mid-elementary school, students can start to capitalize on the multimedia and abstract-symbolic capabilities of computers—if an effective teacher is present to guide the learning. For middle and high school students, new technologies can make difficult concepts (e.g., ratio, velocity) more accessible and provide new windows into visual reasoning, creativity and the challenges of research. Yet the first step must still be the filtering process: What is worthwhile in support of the curriculum, and what is merely flashy? Districts that take this job seriously and gear computer use to students' developmental needs are beginning to show real benefits from technology use.

Winners in the Long Run

"Kids need computers to prepare them for the future."

Like so many advertising slogans, this one bears closer examination. First, learning to use a computer today is a poor guarantee of a student's future, since workplace equipment will have changed dramatically for all but our oldest students. Moreover, because so much current use is harming rather than helping students' brain power and learning habits, the computer "have-nots" today actually may end up as the "haves" when future success is parcelled out.

But even more important is the question of what skills will really prepare today's students for the future. Surely the next decades will be ones of rapid change where old answers don't always work, where employers demand communication and human relations skills as well as the ability to think incisively and imagine creative solutions to unforeseen problems. Many of today's computer applications offer poor preparation for such abilities.

One skill of critical importance in a technological future is symbolic analysis, with reading and writing the common entry point. Yet while cyberspace may be filled with words, "a growing portion of the American population will not be able to use, understand or benefit from those words," contend Daniel Burstein and David Kline in their book, *Road Warriors.* "Some of these people may be digitally literate, in that they feel at home with joysticks and remote controls and are perfectly capable of absorbing the sights and sounds of multimedia entertainment. But if you are not functionally literate, your chances of getting a significant piece of the cyberspace pie are slim, even if you have access to it."

Our future workers also will need other abstract-symbolic skills. As the creation of wealth moves farther and farther away from raw materials and hands-on labor, successful workers will need to synthesize information, judge abstract numbers and acquire multiple-symbol systems in foreign languages, math or the arts; they will also need a familiarity with new digital languages and images. As software improves, computers will doubtless help with such preparation, but the key will continue to lie in the quality of the teachers who plan, mediate and interpret a thoughtful curriculum.

The future also will favor those who have learned how to learn, who can respond flexibly and creatively to challenges and master new skills. At the moment, the computer is a shallow and pedantic companion for such a journey. We should think long and carefully about whether our purpose is to be trendy or to prepare students to be intelligent, reasoning human beings whose skills extend far beyond droid-like button clicking.

If we ourselves cannot think critically about the hard sell vs. the real business of schooling, we can hardly expect our students to do so. ■

P O S T N O T E

Jane Healy raises a number of valuable points concerning education's embrace of technology. Two points seem particularly significant: teacher education and trade-offs. Citing research that indicates teachers need five years of in-service training before they can successfully integrate technology into the curriculum, Healy deplores the vast expenditure on hardware and software without concomitant spending on teacher training. The second important point revolves around the question of how else the money might be spent. What are schools not doing in order to buy technology? These are good issues worth thinking about.

D I S C U S S I O N Q U E S T I O N S

1. What arguments would you state to counter Healy's concerns?

2. In your opinion, is the technology emphasis in schools here to stay or just a fad? Why do you think so?

3. Do you think there is an appropriate age at which to introduce children to computers? How would you address Healy's concern about the potential physical effects of using technology at too young an age?

62

Making a Living, Making a Life: Technology Reconsidered

Neil Postman

I should like to begin by presenting a short poem that I found in a book by Lawrence Cuban that illustrates the history of the relationship between technology and schools. The poem, written by a teacher in the early 1920s, is not very good, but it is instructive and provides a good beginning for this reconsideration of the topic.

> *Mr. Edison says*
> *That the radio will supplant the teacher.*
> *Already one may learn languages by means of*
>   *Victrola records.*
> *The moving picture will visualize*
> *What the radio fails to get across.*
> *Teachers will be relegated to the backwoods*
> *With fire-horses*
> *And long-haired women.*
> *Or perhaps shown in museums.*
> *Education will become a matter*
> *Of pressing a button.*
> *Perhaps I can get a position at the switchboard.*

Neil Postman is chairperson, Department of Culture and Communications, School of Education, New York University, New York, New York.

I think this poem is worth taking seriously because it describes a few things that are often forgotten. It reminds us, for example, that two things always occur when a new kind of technology is developed. First, the technology is always oversold and frequently envisioned as a panacea; second, businessmen are always interested in exploiting the technology for economic gain. I do not hold that against them; it's what businessmen do. But educators do not always have to accommodate them, and, as the poem's sarcasm suggests, teachers are permitted to be skeptical about technology's powers. They are, perhaps, *obliged* to be skeptical.

Another thing the poem tells us is that television, the computer, and their associated technologies do not, by any means, pose an unprecedented challenge to traditional educational practices, including the role of the teacher. Such challenges have presented themselves before. I am not old enough to remember when educators believed that the radio and Victrola would forever change the nature of the classroom. However, I do remember when they thought 16-millimeter film would do so. Then closed-circuit television. Then 8-millimeter film. Then structured, teacher-proof textbooks. Now, of course, the computer, and, if we are to believe Chris Whittle, television again.

In this context, I can't help recalling H. L. Mencken's comment on the educator's quest for panaceas. He said, ". . . there is no sure-cure so idiotic that some superintendent of schools will not swallow it. The aim seems to be to reduce the whole teaching process to a sort of automatic reaction, to discover some master formula . . . [to] take the place of competence and resourcefulness in the teacher." Mencken wrote that in 1918, but the quest for sure cures continues today. There are as many true believers as ever—people who think that our newest technological advances will, at long last, change the structure and even the very purpose of schooling.

At least one of these true believers comes from Arkansas. Late last year, in an address to educators, President Clinton focused his remarks on the great technological changes now taking place. In a remarkable statement, he said, "In the nineteenth century, at most, young Americans needed a high school education to make their way. . . . It was good enough if they could read well and understand basic numbers. In the twenty-first century, our people will have to keep learning all their lives." I call this statement "remarkable" only as a sign of respect. To put it gently, in the nineteenth century, it was also desirable for people to continue learning all their lives; they *had* to because they experienced vast and continuous technological change. I would even say that far more technological change occurred during the nineteenth century than is likely to occur during the twenty-first, despite flamboyant prophecies to the contrary. The nineteenth century gave us telegraphy, photography, the rotary press, the telephone, the typewriter, the phonograph, the transatlantic cable, the electric light, radio waves, movies, the locomotive, the suspension bridge, the steamboat, the X ray, the factory, the revolver, the computer, and the stethoscope, not to mention canned food, the penny press, the modern magazine, the advertising agency, the modern bureaucracy, and even the safety pin. Let us suppose that the president might be willing to concede that the technological challenges of the nineteenth century were as traumatic as any faced by people today.

This does not mean that schools ought not to be doing things that the schools of the nineteenth and twentieth centuries did not do. If, for example, the president wants our schools to concentrate as never before on producing young men and women who, as resourceful, adaptable, questioning, and open-minded students, are not paralyzed by technological change, I would expect him to make an impassioned plea for the humanities, not, as he did, for technical-vocational training. Though educators may not be the smartest people around, we do know that it is mainly through the study of history, philosophy, literature, science, and the arts that people's minds are opened to change and to new possibilities. I might note in passing that just about all the people who invented our new technologies were educated with a heavy concentration in humanistic studies. And, just in case anyone be-

lieves that no self-respecting school can carry on without high-tech equipment, it should also be noted that those who invented our high-tech world were themselves educated exclusively with pen, paper, and books. How did they get so smart, I wonder?

I should make it clear that I have no serious complaint against schools buying computers or spending lavishly on state-of-the-art video. If school systems wish to purchase these rather than pay their teachers more or hire more teachers, and if teachers do not object, I am not inclined to speak against this practice.

I would, however, speak out if such investments distracted educators from providing our youth with a serious form of technology education. By technology education I do not mean instruction in using computers to process information, which strikes me as a rather trivial thing to do for two reasons. First, approximately 35 million people have already learned how to use computers without the benefit of school instruction. If schools do nothing, most of the population will know how to use computers in the next 10 years, just as most of the population learned how to drive cars without school instruction. Second, what we needed to know about cars—which is what we now need to know about computers, television, and other important technologies—is not how to use them, but rather how *they* use us. In the case of cars, what we needed to think about in the early twentieth century was not how to drive them, but what they would do to our air, our landscape, our social relations, our family life, and our cities. I'm afraid we didn't take the combustion engine as seriously as we should have. Similarly, suppose that in 1946 we had started to address significant questions about television. What effects would it have upon our political institutions, our psychic habits, our children, our religious conceptions, our families, our economy? Wouldn't we be better positioned today to control television's massive assault on American culture?

I think we should make technology itself an object of inquiry, not an object of celebration. The idea is that our youth should be more interested in asking questions *about* the computer than in getting answers from it. As for television, using it as an aid to learning is seductive but quite beside the point. The average American youngster clocks 5,000 hours in front of a television set before entering the first grade, 19,000 hours by high school's end, and will have seen approximately 700,000 television commercials by age 20. Television, in other words, is the primary vehicle for communicating social values to our young, not to mention its enormous role in shaping their psychic habits and political biases.

What is the schools' response to this? Did someone actually say, "I have a good idea. Let's spend some money to bring television into the classroom to help the students learn"? You can be assured that television is helping them learn many things without the school's complicity; for example, to value immediate gratification; to believe that consumership is the highest aim in life; to be estranged from the written word; to be impatient with reasoned discourse; to believe that what is not instantly accessible is not worthwhile; to be inured to, if not fascinated by, violence. Yes, television *can* be used to enliven lessons in the classroom. It is not, however, necessary, and in my opinion is not the sort of thing educators need to spend their time thinking about, not when there *are* things worth thinking about. Here are some examples.

Since 1960, our population has increased 41 percent. During that same period, violent crimes have increased 560 percent; illegitimate births have increased 400 percent; divorces have quadrupled; the percentage of children living in single-parent homes has tripled; the teenage suicide rate has increased by more than 200 percent; and, I'm told, a considerable drop in the average SAT scores of high school students has occurred. When teachers were asked in 1940 to identify the most serious problems in schools, they listed talking out of turn, chewing gum, making noise, running in the halls, cutting in line, dress code infractions, and littering. When asked the same question in 1990, they listed drug use, alcohol abuse, pregnancy, suicide, rape, robbery, and assault.

I do not say that schools can fix most of these problems. Some of them were brought on by

the technological fury of the past two centuries. Others result from factors so complex that their origins are difficult to trace. But if schools cannot fix these problems, they can at least *respond* to them. They can acknowledge that these problems exist and embark on a journey to discover what our students need most in a culture stumbling into the twenty-first century. That is to say, we all know that schools cannot remake America, but they can make Americans who have the power and will to undertake the task.

What kind of journey would that be? Not, I fear, a journey into the world of technological wonders. A far more useful journey would take us on an exploration of the human heart, which is more mysterious and more unknown than any other terrain. For it seems to me that we are not suffering in America from a lack of information, and our children in particular are not suffering from technological deprivation. They live in a culture that has 260,000 billboards; 17,000 newspapers; 12,000 periodicals; 27,000 video outlets for renting tapes; 400 million television sets; and well over 500 million radios, not including those in automobiles. There are 40,000 new book titles published every year, and every day in America 41 million photographs are taken. And, just for the record (and thanks to the computer), over 60 billion pieces of advertising junk mail come into our mailboxes every year. Everything from telegraphy and photography in the nineteenth century to the silicon chip in the twentieth has amplified the din of information. From millions of sources all over the globe, through every possible channel and medium—light waves, air waves, ticker tapes, computer banks, telephone wires, television cables, satellites, and printing presses—information pours in. Behind it, in every imaginable form of storage—on paper, on video and audio tape, on disks, film, and silicon chips—is an even greater volume of information waiting to be retrieved. Information has become a form of garbage. It comes indiscriminately, directed at no one in particular, disconnected from usefulness. We are swamped by information, have no control over it, and don't know what to do with it. And we don't know what to do with it because a corresponding loss of meaning, a growing skepticism toward legitimate authority, and a confusing absence of clear moral direction have occurred. We are suffering, if I may put it metaphorically, from a broken heart: a separation of ourselves from any inspiring, life-enhancing narratives or transcendent stories that give meaning to the past, explain the present, and provide guidance for the future.

If there is a single problem that plagues American education at the moment, it is that our children no longer believe, as they once did, in some of the powerful and exhilarating narratives that were the underpinning of American culture. To get an idea of one of these narratives, I suggest we turn away from Bill Gates and pay some attention to Thomas Jefferson, who was among those who wrote the story of our origins. It is a story in which America is brought forth out of revolution, not merely as an experiment in governance, but as part of God's own plan, the story of America as a moral light unto the world. That story provided people with a purpose for learning. As Jefferson saw it, the purpose of school was not to enhance students' economic productivity or to aid them in becoming better consumers. Its purpose was to provide students with the tools with which to protect their liberty and to know when their liberty was threatened. Does anyone take this seriously today?

Does anyone take seriously another great American narrative, the one that was summarized so elegantly in a poem written by Emma Lazarus and that is lodged at the base of the Statue of Liberty? It includes the words, "Give me your tired, your poor, your huddled masses yearning to breathe free." This is the story of America as a nation of many nations, and it provided the schools with a specific imperative: to help make Americans out of the teeming masses; to help the lost and lonely find freedom, peace, and sustenance. Who believes this today? Or the great story—sometimes referred to as the Protestant Ethic—that tells of how self-restraint, discipline, and hard work form the pathway to a fulfilled life. There are still other narratives by which life in America was given form, ideals,

and energy, and which gave the whole enterprise of education a profound purpose.

My point is that the great problem of American education is of a social, moral, and spiritual nature, and has nothing to do with dazzling new technologies. In fact, it has nothing to do with teacher accountability, national standards of assessment, class size, or school financing. These are matters with which we must deal, but they are essentially engineering problems, which, in the end, can be solved by technicians. Far more formidable is the problem of how to mend a broken heart; that is, the problem of finding narratives in which students can believe and that will provide them with transcendent reasons for learning. Without such reasons, schools have no point. They become houses of detention rather than attention no matter how much technology you stuff into them.

I take it as a matter of course that the reason educators are so enthusiastic about technology is that it helps us to evade the central problem we know we must face but that is so difficult we hardly know how to begin. Here's how serious the problem is: It is not enough to say we will teach critical thinking. The question is, about what do we want students to think critically, and for what purpose?

It is not enough to say we want students to be adaptable to change. The question is, to what changes ought they adapt, and what changes ought they resist?

It is not enough to say we want to teach them to be good citizens. The question is, by whose authority do we judge good citizenship?

It is not enough to say we will build our students' self-esteem. The question is, what will they esteem other than self?

It is not even enough to say we will teach them to read. The Germans taught their young to read to become Nazis. The Russians taught their young to read to become communists. Do we have something better in mind? Or have we lost our minds altogether?

I began this sermon by presenting to you an instructive, "bad" poem. I should like to move toward a close by presenting to you an instructive, "good" poem. It was written by Vachel Lindsay of Springfield, Illinois. Lindsay died in 1931, but he knew, even then, what we would need to give to our children. This is the poem.

Let not young souls be smothered out before
They do quaint deeds and fully flaunt their pride.
It is the world's one crime its babes grow dull
Its poor are ox-like, limp and leaden-eyed.

Not that they starve, but starve so dreamlessly
Not that they sow, but that they seldom reap
Not that they serve, but have no gods to serve.
Not that they die, but that they die like sheep.

In closing, I should like to call your attention to the line that says our children have "no gods to serve," because that speaks to the heart of the matter. The gods of consumership, and economic utility—and, especially, the god of technology—may say something to our young about how to make a living. They are silent on the question of how to make a life. Perhaps someday soon, educators will get together to address that question. Who knows? Maybe the College Board will sponsor such a meeting. ■

POST NOTE

Technology has always been an important topic in education. However, the rapid invasion of the personal computer, CD-ROMs, and the Internet have caught many veteran teachers off guard. The acquisition of new classroom hardware and software represents an invasion from above; the interests and skills of today's students, many of whom are used to computer games and have access to the Internet at home, represent an invasion from below. In response, teachers are scrambling to become literate in the new technology and to integrate it into their instruction.

Neil Postman, a long-time student of human communication and education, offers some wise counsel in this article written for the *College Board Review*. He warns us to keep our heads, not to be carried away with our new toys, not to think ours is the first era to undergo a dramatic technological change. More positively, he calls on us to help students find the "transcendent reasons for learning."

DISCUSSION QUESTIONS

1. What are Postman's major points about technology and schools?

2. What do you think he meant to convey by quoting the line that our children have "no gods to serve"?

3. Rather than getting rid of new technology, what is Postman suggesting we do?

63

School Reform in the Information Age

Howard D. Mehlinger

. . . Technology has always been an important part of schooling in America, but until recently the technology employed was rather simple and changed slowly. No one reading this article can remember when there were no textbooks, but the kind of textbooks we have today are largely products of the 20th century. Nor did teachers always have their primary tools—the blackboard and chalk. Slate blackboards did not appear in urban schools until the 1830s.

When I was a young boy, one of the rituals at the start of the school year was a trip to the local department store to purchase school supplies: a "Big Chief" tablet, pencils, rubber erasers, pens with removable points (they became dull quickly), and a bottle of ink. Sometimes a pencil box would be added so that I could keep track of my personal supplies. Parents and students today go through similar shopping rituals each year. The technology has changed somewhat (ball-point pens have replaced ink and straight pens, pencil boxes have given way to backpacks), but it is essentially the same.

There have been many attempts to change the technology of schooling. They have each appeared with great fanfare and expressions of optimism by advocates. In the 1920s, radio was

Howard Mehlinger is director of the Center for Excellence in Education and a professor of education and history at Indiana University, Bloomington. Mehlinger, Howard H., "School Reform in the Information Age," *Phi Delta Kappan,* February 1996. Copyright © 1996 by Phi Delta Kappa. Reprinted by permission of author and publisher.

expected to have a major impact on schools; in the 1930s, it was to be film; in the 1950s, television; and in the 1960s, teaching machines. The one piece of new technology from those bygone years that truly found a place was the overhead projector. Introduced in the 1940s by the military, it gradually found its way into the schools. The overhead projector is easy to use and relatively inexpensive, it permits the teacher to prepare notes in advance of class and to project then onto the screen for all to see, and it can be used without darkening the room or turning one's back to the students. In many ways it is the perfect technology for supporting the kind of instruction that takes place in most classrooms today.

More advanced technology has hit the schools at about the same time as have ideas for school restructuring and findings from the cognitive sciences. According to Karen Sheingold, "The successful transformation of student learning and accomplishment in the next decade requires effectively bringing together three agendas—an emerging consensus about learning and teaching, well-integrated uses of technology, and restructuring. Each agenda alone presents possibilities for educational redesign of a very powerful sort. Yet none has realized or is likely to realize its potential in the absence of the other two."[1] I agree.

Skeptics will argue that we are merely going through another cycle of reform. School reforms come almost every decade; the schools absorb as many of the new ideas as they want and reject the rest. The result is that schools change very little where it truly counts—in the classroom. But the synergy of school restructuring, new forms of learning and teaching, and new technology will make the difference this time.

The forces driving the Information Age seem irresistible. It is impossible both to participate fully in the culture and yet resist its defining features. Thus, if the schools are an "immovable object" (and I don't believe they are), they are beginning to meet the "irresistible force"—Information Age technology.

The analogy I carry in my head is that of a volcano erupting in Hawaii, spewing forth ash and lava. We have all seen pictures of such eruptions and what follows. The lava slowly oozes its way down the mountain toward the sea. No device or structure raised by human beings can block it. It either consumes all obstacles in fire or rolls over them. Finally, the lava reaches the sea—nature's immovable object. Throughout the process there is a lot of noise, smoke, and steam that can distract one's attention from the fundamental process that is taking place: the transformation of the landscape. In the most dramatic cases, entirely new islands appear. A volcanic eruption changes the environment in unpredictable ways; it is also irresistible.

Information Age technology is like that volcano. It is changing the landscape of American culture in ways we either take for granted or scarcely notice. There are holdouts. Many of us see no need for placing telephones in our cars or buying mobile telephones. Some believe that television is a corrupting influence and refuse to have a set in their homes. I know such people; I am largely sympathetic to their views. But most people who think television can be corrosive buy one anyway and try to control its use.

I cannot predict how schools will accommodate themselves to the force of computers and other electronic technologies. Some schools will move more quickly than others; some teachers will not change at all. The process may be slow enough that many teachers will be able to retire before they are forced to change. Some will quit teaching, and it is likely that some will remain anachronisms in a greatly altered school environment—antiques of a sort, surrounded by modernity but refusing even to use the telephones in their classrooms.

But schools will change! I don't know whether teachers will use the new technologies in the ways constructivists anticipate; other reformers have urged teachers to adopt similar progressive ideas in the past with mostly negative results. Perhaps technology will support constructivist approaches and make learner-centered instruction a practice as well as a theory this time. I don't know whether schools will have site-based management or some other kind of organizational structure. Other theories of learning and school organization will certainly appear. The exact shape of future schools is unclear, but of this I am certain: schools will be unable to resist the new technology. The new technology will be used in schools because it appeals to students and may enhance learning and because the schools can offer no reasonable defense for rejecting it.

The use of the new technologies will have a profound effect on schools. The very relationship between students and teachers will be challenged because the technologies enable learners to gain control of their own learning. In the past, schools have been places where people in authority decided what would be taught (and possibly learned), at what age, and in what sequence. They also decided what would *not* be taught—what would not be approved knowledge. The new technologies provide students access to information that was once under the control of teachers.

Years ago, as a high school teacher, I received a note from a colleague who was teaching a course in American history for the first time. He had given students reading assignments from one set of books while he turned to other books as sources for his lectures. The note said, "The game is up. The students know where I am getting my information." That is happening everywhere today, and the game is truly up. No teacher can compete with the power and the capability of the new technology as a presenter of information. If teachers and schools try to sustain that role, they will be whipped. On the other hand, no teachers will be replaced by a machine unless they attempt to do only what the machine can do better.

It may be that the technology will be used most extensively first by privately financed schools, such as Sylvan Learning Systems, Kaplan Educational Centers, or the schools of the Edison Project. Privately financed schools that successfully demonstrate the value of technology may provide the incentive to persuade public institutions of the instructional value of technology. Perhaps public schools that employ the new technologies successfully in restructured environments will begin as magnet schools or even charter schools; if they succeed, then the use of technology may spread to the remainder of the schools in a district. Possibly the technological challenge to public education will come from home schooling, when parents discover that through technology they not only retain the current advantages of home schooling but also gain access to the academic resources of the public schools and of the world.

The genie is out of the bottle. It is no longer necessary to learn about the American War of Independence by sitting in Mrs. Smith's classroom and hearing her version of it. There are more powerful and efficient ways to learn about the Revolutionary War, and they are all potentially under the control of the learner. Either schools will come to terms with this fact, or schools will be ignored.

It has never been easy for schools to change, and it is not going to be easy now. The current reform effort has been compared to changing a tire on a car that is continuing to speed down the highway. The job is actually much harder than that, because it is not repair but transformation that is required. It is more akin to changing a car into an airplane while continuing to drive the car. We are asking schools to become something different, without a clear picture of what the new institution should look like, even as we continue to satisfy the public that the old purposes of schooling are being served as well as or better than in the past.

Availability and Use of Technology in Schools Today

No one knows for certain what kind of technology exists in schools, how it is used, how much it is used, whether what exists is actually available to teachers, and whether what exists is broken, worn-out, or still in unopened boxes.[2] It is hard enough to maintain an up-to-date inventory within a given school district without trying to do the same for the nation. Various individuals and organizations have conducted surveys on technology use, and these provide some clues as to the situation generally.

Computers. We know that the number of computers in schools has grown enormously since 1983. At that time it was estimated that there were fewer than 50,000 computers in the nation's schools; by 1994 the estimate was revised to 5.5 million. In 1981 only about 18% of schools had one or more computers for instructional use; by 1994 this figure had risen to 98%. There is hardly a school in America today without at least one computer.

These figures tell us very little about student access to computers, however. In 1985 the median number of computers in K–6 elementary schools that used computers was three; that number rose to about 18 in 1989. In high schools for the same two years the numbers were 16 and 39, respectively. By 1994 the ratio of students to computers across all grades was 14 to 1. Thus, while there has been rapid growth in the number of computers in each school, the opportunity for a typical student to have access to a computer is still limited. For example, as late as 1989 a student might have had access to a computer for one hour per week— about 4% of instructional time.

A second issue concerns the location of computers and how they are used. The most common pattern in schools is to cluster 20 or so machines in a single laboratory and then to schedule classes for time in the lab once a week. A decade ago computers were used mainly to teach programming, to teach about computers (computer literacy), and to run drill-and-practice exercises. More recently, computers have been used for enrichment, as work tools, and—less frequently— for purposes of computer literacy. However, computers in elementary schools continue to be used heavily to teach basic skills, and this pattern is growing in high schools. Federal funds for at-risk children have been a major source of school funding for computers, so it is hardly surprising that schools rely on them primarily for teaching basic skills and for remedial instruction. The use of computers to support instruction in the academic areas or to allow students independent exploration is sharply limited. Indeed, many American students have more access to a computer at home than at school.

Most computers are purchased as stand-alone machines. It is possible to connect computers, either through a local area network (LAN) or through a wide area network (WAN). The advantage of networks is that people can work together and share information. Computer networks are common in business and higher education; the use of networks in schools, though it is growing, is still small. Moreover, school LANs are used mainly to support integrated learning systems (ILSs) within a school. Thus far, relatively little has been done to foster communication among classrooms. Schools with modems have access to commercial network services, such as Prodigy, CompuServe, Apple Link, or America Online. And a rapidly increasing number of schools are beginning to use the Internet, a service originally created by the U.S. Department of Defense to connect researchers at labs and universities and that now connects many kinds of groups worldwide. The Clinton Administration wishes to build a national electronic infrastructure that would increase opportunities for schools to be connected to outside resources.

Video. Video use in schools seems to be growing and taking different forms. Instructional television, in which a program is broadcast to schools at scheduled times during the day from a state-operated or district-run studio, continues to exist, but it is not as significant as in the past. Many of these broadcasts were developed nationally through a consortium led by the Agency for Instructional Technology. The programs were designed to fit the school curriculum as determined by the state departments of education that were the most prominent consortium members.

As a result of federal financing through the Star Schools program, many schools are able to use courses delivered nationwide by satellite and originating from a single source at a predetermined time. These programs typically feature courses that are difficult for small schools to offer on their own, e.g., courses in German or Japanese or advanced courses in mathematics and the sciences. Rural schools in particular have taken advantage of these offerings; about one-third of all rural schools have the capability of receiving satellite broadcasts.

Commercial sources also provide programming to schools. In 1994 Whittle Communications, Inc., reportedly offered its programs to more than 12,000 schools and reached eight million students. The principal program offering was a 10-minute news show called Channel One. The program and all the equipment provided to the schools were paid for by the two minutes of commercial advertising that accompanied each show. CNN offers a rival news program called *CNN Newsroom*. This 15-minute news show is broadcast early in the morning over the regular CNN cable channel. Schools are permitted to tape the program and use it as they please.

The Corporation for Public Broadcasting is developing new programming for schools, and the Learning Channel and the Discovery Channel both provide programs that offer useful information for schools.

As a result of this proliferation of educational programming, the VCR has become a nearly ubiquitous piece of school technology. Virtually every school in the United States has at least one, and many teachers routinely collect tapes to use with their classes. Because it is more flexible and user friendly, the videotape has taken the place of film for instruction.

CD-ROM and videodiscs offer other ways for schools to employ video. The use of these media, while still limited, is growing rapidly. According to Quality Education Data, Inc., 26% of all school districts had videodisc technology in 1994, as compared to 18% in 1992–93.

Results. It would be wonderful if we could point to specific data that would demonstrate conclusively that the use of one technology or approach produced better results than the use of some other technology or approach. Alas, the problem is not so simple.

First, the existence of a particular technology does not prescribe the way in which it will be used. Yet how a technology is actually used is critically important. One English teacher might use computers mainly for drill on grammar and spelling, while another English teacher might allow students to use the computers for word processing.

Much of the evaluation research on media use is based on a specific intervention and focuses on short-term results. It seeks to determine, for example, whether the students receiving computer-assisted instruction (CAI) perform better on short-answer examinations than do those in a control group. In studies of this kind, the experimental group nearly always wins, but seldom does the investigator study the two groups a year or two later to find out if the gain has survived. Studies of short-term results, though interesting, are of marginal value to policy makers.[3]

What we need are studies of an altogether different order. When students and teachers are immersed in technology *over time*, will we detect changes in how students learn and how teachers teach? While it may be important to see some gain on a particular test, those who are trying to reform schools have larger goals in mind. Before we spend billions of dollars to equip every student with a computer at home and one at school and before we spend millions to equip teachers and to provide them with the necessary training, we need to know whether such a colossal investment of public funds makes sense. We cannot be certain, but the study reported below should encourage us.

A Suggestive Experiment

In 1986 Apple Computer, Inc., launched a project called Apple Classrooms of Tomorrow (ACOT).[4] The project began with seven classrooms representing what was intended to be a cross section of K–12 schools. Each participating student and teacher received two computers: one for home and one for school. The goal of the project was to see how the routine use of computers would affect how students learn and how teachers teach.

One issue the project hoped to confront was the possibility of any negative effects from prolonged exposure to computers. Some critics have worried that students who use computers extensively will become "brain dead" or less social from looking at the computer screen all day. At the end of two years, the investigators learned that some of their worst fears had been groundless.

■ Teachers were not hopeless illiterates where technology was concerned; they could use computers to accomplish their work.

■ Children did not become social isolates. ACOT classes showed more evidence of spontaneous cooperative learning than did traditional classes.

■ Children did not become bored by the technology over time. Instead, their desire to use it for their own purposes increased with use.

■ Even very young children had no problem becoming adept users of the keyboard. With very little training, second- and third-graders were soon typing 25 to 30 words per minute with 95% accuracy—more than twice as fast as children of that age can usually write.

■ Software was not a major problem. Teachers found programs—including productivity tools—to use in their classes.

Standardized test scores showed that students were performing as well as they might have been expected to do without the computers; some were doing better. The studies showed that ACOT students wrote better and were able to complete units of study more rapidly than their peers in non-ACOT classrooms. In one case, students finished the year's study of mathematics by the beginning of April. In short, academic productivity did not suffer and in some cases even improved.

What I find most interesting, however, is that classroom observers noticed changes in the behavior of teachers and students. Students were taking more responsibility for their own learning, and teachers were working more as mentors and less as presenters of information.

By the end of the fourth year, ACOT classrooms had changed; teachers were teaching differently, though they did not all teach alike. Each teacher seemed to have adjusted his or her own style to the computer-rich environment, but all the teachers were aware of the changes that had occurred in their own professional outlooks.

The students had also changed, especially the ACOT students at West High School, a school serving urban, blue-collar families in Columbus, Ohio. Twenty-one freshmen were selected at random from the student body to participate in a study of ACOT. They stayed with the program until their graduation four years later. All 21 graduated, whereas the student body as a whole had a 30% dropout rate. Nineteen of the ACOT students (90%) went on to college, while only 15% of non-ACOT students sought higher education. Seven of the ACOT students were offered full college scholarships, and several businesses offered to hire those who did not intend to go on to college. ACOT students had half the absentee rate, and they had accumulated more than their share of academic honors. But perhaps the most important finding was the difference exhibited by these students in how they did their work. The ACOT students routinely and without prompting employed inquiry, collaboration, and technological and problem-solving skills of the kind promoted by the school reform movement.

This is only one study, of course, and it would be unwise to place too much weight on its findings. But those who believe that technology is the key to school reform and to more powerful learning by students can take hope from this investigation.

They may also find encouragement in the results of a 1994 study commissioned by the Software Publishers Association and conducted by an independent technology consulting firm, Interactive Educational Systems Design, Inc.[5] The study reviewed research on educational technology that had been conducted from 1990 through 1994. The report was based on 133 research reviews and reports on original research projects. Some of the conclusions of that study follow.

- Educational technology has a significant positive impact on achievement in all subject areas, across all levels of school, and in regular classrooms as well as those for special-needs students.

- Educational technology has positive effects on student attitudes.

- The degree of effectiveness is influenced by the student population, the instructional design, the teacher's role, how students are grouped, and the levels of student access to technology.

- Technology makes instruction more student-centered, encourages cooperative learning, and stimulates increased teacher/student interaction.

- Positive changes in the learning environment evolve over time and do not occur quickly.

While this study was commissioned by an organization that had a stake in the results, the conclusions seem consistent with other research findings, especially with those of the ACOT study.

The Future of Technology in the Schools

Thus far I have focused on the technology available to schools today. What about the future? We are only at the threshold of the Information Age. Tools we now treat as technical marvels will seem primitive in five years. Commodore Pets, IBM PC jrs., and the first Apple machines are throwaway items today. We can predict with certainty that technology will become faster, cheaper, more powerful, and easier to use. We can also predict that new devices that we can scarcely imagine today will be on the market before the end of this decade. Schools that expect to invest in a single computer system and then forget about technology purchases for several years will be surprised and disappointed. Schools must make decisions regarding additions and/or upgrades to their technology every year, in line with their own strategic plans.

Without going into detail regarding specific pieces of hardware, I can say with confidence that schools should expect more *integration, interaction,* and *intelligence* from future technology. In their early days in school, computers and video were regarded as separate entities, and it was assumed they would stay that way. In fact, we can expect a continuing *integration* of these technologies. Voice, data, and images will be brought together into one package. One current example of this process is desktop video. In a single, relatively inexpensive unit, one has telephone (voice), computer (data storage and manipulation), and video (sending and receiving moving images) capabilities. Those who use the machine can talk to people at a distance, exchange documents, work collaboratively, and even see their collaborators on screen.

Technology will also become more *interactive*. In the field of distance learning, rather than rely strictly on one-way video and two-way audio communication, teachers and students will see one another simultaneously, thereby making distance learning more like fact-to-face classroom interaction. Computer-based instruction will also be designed to respond to learners' interests and abilities, giving them greater control over what they need to learn and the pace at which they learn it. And computer searches, which can now be bewildering to the casual user, will become easier and more responsive to what a user needs. Greater interactivity will make instructional programs even more powerful than they are today.

Finally, technology will have greater *intelligence*. This intelligence will be displayed in several ways. First, the technology will have more features and greater capacity. Second, it will have the capability to learn from the user, so that it can customize its services to fit the user's learning style and interests. Future technology will provide not only databases but knowledge bases. And the technology will be able to stay abreast of that information most valued by the user and to alert him or her to its availability.

Integration, interaction, and intelligence. These are three features we can expect of technology in the future. And they will change the way technology is employed in schools.

Technology Revolution in Schools

What is this revolution? It is the transformation of schooling through the use of technology, and it is occurring in classrooms all over the country.

The seeds of the revolution are being planted everywhere, though seldom dramatically. Occasionally, there is an announcement that District A has received a major grant that will lead to the installation of Brand X equipment in all its schools. But these are the exceptions.

What is occurring nearly every week is that one school board has approved the purchase of 10 or 20 computers for use in a school to improve writing skills; another board has approved the high school's use of Channel One; still another has set aside funds so that a high school or middle school can subscribe to online, commercial information services, and so on. This revolution is not characterized by a major assault leading to the rapid sweeping away of every custom and practice of the past. This is a slow but steady revolution. Each decision by a school board, each act of support by a principal, and each initiative by a teacher is changing the nature of schooling.

This revolution is not like any other school reform movement that I have observed, and I have been in the profession for more than 40 years. First, it is a grassroots movement. Actions by state and federal governments and by business and industry have helped fuel the revolution, but they did not provide the spark. Teachers and local school administrators are leading this revolution, and they are not leading it in order to save American business or to prove a new theory of learning. They are buying, installing, and using technology simply because they believe that students will be less bored and will learn more through the use of the technology than without it. In short, they are using technology to make schools better.

This revolution is eclectic and largely devoid of ideology; therefore, what schools do with the technology varies widely. Much technology is used for remediation, especially in the elementary grades; it provides drill-and-practice exercises that are boring for teachers to teach. School officials hope that computers used in this way will hold pupils' attention longer and save wear and tear on teachers. This approach to learning may irritate the constructivists and many others, but as long as society emphasizes mastering basic skills we need not be surprised if some schools use technology to meet these goals and to help students pass required tests.

Other schools are using the technology primarily to provide students with productivity tools, such as word processing and spreadsheets, to inspire students to make their work more professional in quality and appearance. In other places, such technology as compressed, interactive video is used to share an instructor across one or more school sites. Technology has its foot in the door of classrooms all across America, and the schools will never be the same.

Some people will be annoyed to learn that there is a revolution under way and that they have not been informed of it or invited to participate. While they may know that millions of dollars have been invested in computers and other technology during the past decade and a half, they have assumed that most teachers have been resisting the technology. They may also believe that these investments have accomplished little because there has been no evidence of sharp improvements in scores on the SAT I or on national achievement tests.

In response to the first point, I agree that many teachers do not yet employ instructional technology and probably will not do so for some time. As in every revolutionary movement, those teachers in the vanguard are the dedicated ones with a special interest in the cause; the rest must be persuaded that the revolution is in their own interests. In the case of technology, we don't make it easy to convince them. Few schools currently provide computers for each teacher, so the computers they do have must be shared. Teachers are provided little training in how to use the new technology, and seldom is there adequate technical support when something breaks down. In such a situation, it makes sense to some teachers to continue doing what they have always done rather than to spend time learning to use technology with all the attendant frustrations.

With regard to the second point, we have considerable evidence that the appropriate use of technology *does* contribute to student learning.

These small-scale experimental results, however, are often overlooked when national results are reported. On a national scale, despite major investments to date, we have only begun to provide schools what they need. Except in a few cases, students have access to a computer for only a short time each week and then often for the purpose of working on preselected exercises. Imagine the outcry if students had access to a textbook only one day a week or if they had to share a pencil with 15 other students. Imagine a business, say, an insurance company, that had only one computer for each 15 workers and made them take turns entering their data. When access to computers has been sufficient, the results have been positive for student learning.

We cannot blame teachers or students if technology has failed to transform all schools. There has not been enough time or enough money for the purchase of equipment, for training, or for support. Transforming schooling through technology will work; we have evidence that it does. But it will take time, and it will be expensive.

There are also people who do not want the technology revolution to succeed. Some are offended that this reform is truly a grassroots effort. While the technology revolution is certainly abetted by business and government, unlike most education reforms it has not been a top-down effort. This is not a reform hatched in universities or think tanks and handed on to schools to implement. Indeed, universities and most think tanks are largely unconnected to this reform. Obviously, specific professors and researchers are deeply involved, but institutional responses have been erratic: sometimes positive, occasionally negative, usually absent.

Other people want to improve schools, but they want to do it on the cheap. They hope that more regulation, stiffer accountability measures, and stirring speeches, alternating with scolding lectures when results do not improve, will do the job. They are wrong, and they are cheapskates.

A few, mainly in universities, are offended by the thought of linking technology to learning. For ideological reasons they wish to keep technology out of schools because it might "de-skill" teachers. Technology might place schools in the service of business and industry; it might exacerbate equity problems. These issues are fundamentally important to some college professors, but few teachers are listening. What may be most threatening to university professors is that they have spent their lives becoming experts in narrow areas, and now technology threatens to make their hard-won knowledge available to everyone. Much is made of the threat that the computer poses to K–12 teachers because the computer challenges their role as keepers and presenters of knowledge. If that threat disturbs some K–12 teachers, it is all the more frightening to many college professors.

What Are the Chances for Success?

The likelihood of success for the educational technology revolution cannot be judged in the same way as chances for the success of other educational innovations. First, the movement is driven by teachers rather than by outside experts. Second, teachers are not required to use the technology in prescribed ways; they use it as they choose or reject it if they wish. Third, their students are eager to use technology, and parents want their children to have access to technology in school. Fourth, once teachers have overcome their initial concern about feeling stupid while they learn to use a new tool, they find themselves using the technology in various instructional situations. They are pleased to have learned a new skill, and they gradually change the way they teach. Because of these factors, I cannot imagine that this reform will fail for the same reasons as previous reforms.

The progress of technology in the schools will surely proceed more slowly than its proponents would prefer. The reasons are mainly lack of time and lack of money. While Americans talk expansively about creating "break the mold" schools, by and large they want cheap reforms. They hope that by reorganizing the administration of schools (leading to "site-based management") or

by allowing parents to choose schools for their children, school reform will be successful. They are wrong. These cheap solutions will have little impact. In contrast, enormous amounts of money will have to be spent on rewiring and equipping schools, and still more money must be devoted to staff training. It is not yet clear that Americans want new kinds of schools badly enough to pay for them.

Lack of money will slow the revolution—making it seem more like evolution—but it won't stop it. If you believe that schools are a part of the American culture, that the American culture is increasingly influenced by Information Age technology, and that teachers participate in the American culture as much as other Americans, then you cannot also believe that teachers will use the technology outside of school but fail to employ it in their classrooms. Technology will be used extensively in schools. That much is inevitable. ■

Notes

1. Karen Sheingold, "Restructuring for Learning with Technology: The Potential for Synergy," in Karen Sheingold and Marc Tucker, eds., *Restructuring for Learning with Technology* (New York: Center for Technology in Education and National Center on Education and the Economy, 1990), p. 9.

2. Establishing precise figures regarding the availability and use of technology in schools is a reckless enterprise. Even when data are gathered carefully and systematically, the numbers are quickly out-of-date. Readers should judge my figures as "best estimates." In arriving at these estimates, I drew heavily on data compiled by Barbara Means et al., *Using Technology to Support Education Reform* (Washington, D.C.: U.S. Department of Education, 1993), and on data assembled for me by Media Management Services, Inc., which drew upon several databases available to the firm.

3. "Integrated Learning Systems: What Does the Research Say?," *Computing Teacher*, February 1995, pp. 7–10.

4. My description of the ACOT project was based on an article by David Dwyer, "Apple Classrooms of Tomorrow: What We've Learned," *Educational Leadership.* April 1994, pp. 4–10.

5. *Report on the Effectiveness of Technology in Schools, 1990–1994* (Washington, D.C.: Software Publishers Association, 1994).

Louis Gerstner, Jr., chairman of IBM, made the following statement at the 1995 National Governors Association meeting: "We need to recognize that our public schools are low-tech institutions in a high-tech society. The same changes that have brought cataclysmic change to every facet of business can improve the way we teach students and teachers." Obviously, Gerstner is not an impartial observer because IBM has strong economic interests in getting schools to use more technology. But is he right? Does technology—in particular, the Information Age technology described by Mehlinger in this article—have the potential to transform how teaching and learning occur?

Pointing to past revolutionary technologies, such as television, that were predicted to change how schools function, skeptics note that their impact was marginal at best. The skeptics conclude that when all the fuss is over, computers and other current technologies will have had limited effects on education. We believe differently, however. No other technology has had the power that computers have to put students in control of their own learning. As students learn to use computers, videodisks, multimedia materials, electronic networks, and satellite transmissions to access information, they gain control of their education and thus of their future.

DISCUSSION QUESTIONS

1. What strategies could be employed at the local, state, and national levels to speed up the infusion of technology into our schools?

2. What technology skills do you possess that you think will be useful as a teacher? What skills do you think you need to develop?

3. What concerns, if any, do you have regarding this tremendous momentum to incorporate technology in our schools?

Technology and Equity Issues

Michael N. Milone, Jr., and Judy Salpeter

A mong the issues that face educators in the next decade, perhaps none is more important than providing all students with comparable educational opportunities, particularly with respect to technology. To understand how important schooling—and indirectly, exposure to technology—is to a student's future, one need look no further than the U.S. Department of Labor's 1992 publication, *What Work Requires of Schools: A SCANS Report for America 2000.* In the report, the authors assert that "More than half of our young people leave school without the knowledge or foundation required to find and hold a good job." The report was not addressing technology specifically, but given the rapid infiltration of technology into all careers, the inference one can draw is that today's young people are not being prepared as well as they should be to succeed in tomorrow's highly technical careers. . . .

It is in the best interest of both today's young people and the nation as a whole that *all* students have an opportunity to master the elements of technology they will need to have a productive future. Further, it is also clear that technology should be one of the principal tools by which students learn to manage the ever-

Michael N. Milone, Jr., is a freelance author, consultant, and software developer. Judy Salpeter is editor-in-chief of *Technology & Learning.* "Technology and Equity Issues," by Michael N. Milone, Jr., and Judy Salpeter from *Technology & Learning,* January 1996, pp. 38–47. Copyright © 1996 Miller Freeman, Inc. Used by permission.

increasing base of knowledge they will need to achieve success. After all, today's students are tomorrow's mechanics and doctors, teachers and political leaders. Given this indisputable need, the issue then centers on access and quality: Do all students have equitable access to technology, and is the quality of their access comparable?

From Home to School

If we begin with a look at the home scene, it becomes clear that there is a serious gap between higher-income students, many of whom have access to personal computers, and children from families that lack the resources to purchase such hardware.

The Link Resources Home Media Consumer Survey found that, in 1995, almost 42 percent of households with children had a personal computer. As computer prices drop, middle-income homes are gaining greater access. For example, a new study from Dataquest indicates that 52 percent of the people planning to buy a home computer during the next year have household incomes of $40,000 or less. Nevertheless, this leaves a sizable group of children whose families still cannot afford a home computer.

How can schools deal with this inequity? As *T&L* columnist Daniel Kinnaman pointed out in his April 1994 "Leadership Role" column, some educators might be tempted to respond by forbidding students to use home computers to complete assignments. After all, he quotes one teacher as saying, "Not every student has a computer at home, so it's unfair for those that have computers to use them." Kinnaman's response: "That's not equity. That's foolishness. Not every child has two parents at home either. Should we tell those who do that they can get help from only one parent?"

Taking away access from one group is clearly not the solution. But the inequality of home access does place a greater burden on schools to provide technology resources to students (and families) with the greatest need for them. How are we doing with this difficult task?

The School Numbers

A look at the condition of education in general might lead us to worry. The funding differences between rich and poor schools are both statistically significant and educationally meaningful. The National Center for Educational Statistics' Indicator of the Month for September, 1995, points out that the wealthiest districts in terms of household income have access to about 36 percent more revenue per student. Similarly, school districts with less than five percent of children living in poverty have about 27 percent more revenue than those with many children (more than 25 percent) living in poverty.

To some degree the same sort of pattern holds true for technology. In a recent conference paper entitled "Equality and Technology," Jeanne Hayes, President of Denver-Colorado-based Quality Education Data, reported socioeconomic and ethnic differences in access to new technology. A closer look at the QED numbers, however, reveals that the inequities are smaller than one might fear. For example, schools with the lowest percentage of Title I students (ten percent or fewer) had a student-to-computer ratio of approximately 12:1, while schools with the highest number of Title I students (26 percent or more) had a ratio closer to 14:1. Analyzing by ethnicity yielded almost identical results—schools with "low multicultural" populations (more than 80 percent white) averaged 12 students per computer, while those with "high multicultural" ratings (50 percent or more non-white students) had a 14:1 ratio. In both cases, that's a difference of about 15 percent—significant but smaller than in other areas of education, and less than half the discrepancy found by Henry Jay Becker a decade ago. (In his 1983 report, *School Uses of Microcomputers: Reports from a National Survey*, Becker showed ratios of 155:1 for students in high socioeconomic-status (SES) schools, 215:1 in low SES, predominantly minority schools—a 33 percent average difference.)

A 1992 study conducted by the Instructional Association for the Evaluation of Educational Achievement (IEA), and edited by Ron Anderson, found a disturbing 25 percent discrepancy in computer ratios when comparing low and high multicultural settings at the middle school level, but on 11 percent in elementary schools and no difference at all in high schools. Even better news is the fact that in responding to interview questions, ethnic minority students were slightly more likely than white students to report using computers at school. The authors of the report conclude, as we do, that the increased access is probably related to the success of targeted programs such as Title I (formerly Chapter I).

Our conclusions concerning computer access: We still have a long way to go, but we do seem to have made considerable progress over the past decade.

Inequitable Uses?

Perhaps an even greater concern than *access* is the question of *how* computers are being used by different students. In recent years, many writers have contended that poor, minority, and inner-city students are given fewer opportunities for higher-level applications and thus are not reaping the full benefits of technology. In many cases, this contention has been based on research conducted by Henry Jay Becker back in the 1980s.

In both the 1983 and 1985 national surveys conducted at Johns Hopkins University, Becker looked at the two most common types of computer use at the time—programming and drill-and-practice—and found that students in the lower SES schools were approximately three times as likely to be using drill-and-practice software as those in the higher SES schools, while students at the higher socioeconomic level were three times as likely to be learning to program the computer. As Rosemary E. Sutton summarized in "Equity and Computers in the Schools: A Decade of Research," published in the *Review of Educational Research* in 1991:

> This means that the low-SES children, who are disproportionately African American and Hispanic, were gaining most of their experience with a computer when it was in control, asking

questions, expecting a response, and informing the student when he or she was correct. In contrast, the high-SES students, who are disproportionately White, were gaining considerable experience when they were in control, giving the computer a series of instructions, and observing the consequences of these instructions.

If such a discrepancy in types of use continues to be true, that is indeed a serious concern. One of the few recent reports that addresses the topic of how computers are used by different groups of students is the 1992 IEA study mentioned above. According to the IEA numbers, differences do persist, although they are far less dramatic than they were in the past. For example, while students from high-SES families were pretty close to the national average in time spent using computers for skill-building, they were 13 or 14 percent more likely than average to use computers for higher-order activities and 26 percent more likely to experience what the study called "diverse" use (a mix of skill-building and higher-order thinking).

Another relevant study, also from 1992, is Henry Jay Becker's paper "How Our Best Computer-Using Teachers Differ from Other Teachers." He focused on "exemplary computer-using teachers" (those who, based on their responses on a questionnaire, appeared to "provide intellectually exciting educational experiences" to students rather than using the computers as "substitutes for paper-and-pencil worksheets and for 'enrichment' to reward the completion of other work"). His conclusion was that "exemplary computer-using teachers are as likely to be found in low-income districts and low socio-economic-status schools as they are in other schools."

Our own anecdotal evidence confirms the observation that—with leadership from creative computer-using teachers and school administrators—much is going *right* for at-risk students. In attending conferences, reviewing article submissions to this magazine, and judging our annual Teacher of the Year contest, we have found an overwhelming number of success stories coming from schools in low-income areas. Of our eight

national Teacher of the Year winners this year, for example, four worked with at-risk students of one kind or another, including minority and rural or urban-poor.

This is not to suggest that the technology education offered to poor and minority students is consistently as good as it should be. It is clear that we have a long way to go before *all* students receive a quality education on a predictable basis. Nonetheless, for once, the news on the education front appears to be better than many people believe.

Making Equity a Reality

Here are just a few examples of schools that have overcome economic obstacles to provide their students with a quality education in which technology plays an important role. These and many other success stories demonstrate that technological inequity need not be a fact of life for this generation of young people.

■ **At the Perry Middle School in Miramar, Florida,** a multicultural school that falls at the low end of family incomes in Broward County, high-risk students participate in a "school within a school," the A.C.E. Academy. School/business partnerships are key to the A.C.E. program. The students broadcast the school morning news with help from one of their business partners, Telecommunications International, and regularly visit the training and repair departments of another partner, CompUSA, to learn about technology applications in the real world. In addition to serving as cross-age and peer tutors within the school, A.C.E. students even offer introductory computer classes to new employees at partner businesses.

Judy Shasek, resource teacher at the school, tells about one student who at age 15 was still in eighth grade because he'd been at home (in one of the poorest, roughest Broward County neighborhoods) caring for his mother, who was disabled with cancer. Shasek describes how the A.C.E. program inspired him to move on to high school, participate successfully in the academic program (during the day and at night and summer school), become A.C.E. Academy's first graduate, and head for community college on a basketball scholarship. She has all sorts of helpful tips for others, but perhaps her best explanation for A.C.E.'s success is that, "Everyone else told these kids, 'You can't,' but A.C.E. said, 'You can'—and they believed it and proved us right."

■ **Chinle Elementary School, located on the huge, rural Navajo reservation in Chinle, Arizona,** is a true technology success story. Tribal leaders made a commitment to integrating technology into the curriculum and instituted a "saturation" program that equipped the school with a 30-station lab and five-station mini-labs in each classroom. The 700 students in the school now have access to 200 computers, which they use for everything from mastering the basic curriculum to compiling research-based writing portfolios.

Fifth-grade teacher Camala Natay feels the writing portfolio activities have motivated her students more than any other activity and have improved their achievement significantly, as measured by scores on the Iowa Test of Basic Skills. Since the Chinle students rarely have computers at home (many of them come from traditional homes where electricity is unavailable), another important venture is the school's "lab night," during which students and their parents work together at the computer. Natay and her colleagues hope the school's technology saturation approach will help the students break the cycle of poverty, which runs about 49 percent among Native peoples in Arizona.

■ **Clear View Elementary School, located just a few miles north of the Mexican border in Chula Vista, CA,** has been featured in a number of publications in recent years. The highly multicultural, low-income school made a serious commitment to technology and went, in just one year, from being barely computer literate to defining the term "cutting edge." Introduced to technology in kindergarten and first grade, students are experts at logging onto the Internet, creating multimedia projects, and using integrated application software by the time they reach grade six.

They've also had the chance to explore the interface between computers and ham radios, edit videos, use laptop computers, and gain experience with many other aspects of technology.

Clear View's principal, Ginger Hovenic, explains, "We have an attitude here that our students can excel if given the proper motivation and opportunity. That's what our teachers do, and that's how we view technology."

■ **The Nixon Elementary School in El Paso, TX,** uses technology in concert with peer tutoring and other interventions in its Dual Language Program to teach Spanish to English-speakers and English to Spanish-speakers. A border school with high numbers of poor, non-English-speaking students, it has made headlines with its creative technology solutions, earning a Texas Successful Schools Award and recognition by *Redbook* magazine as the best school in Texas and one of the best in the nation.

■ **At Rowland High School, situated in a low-wealth district about 25 miles east of Los Angeles,** some of Hollywood's future stars are now in training. Started by *Technology & Learning*'s 1991 national Teacher of the Year, Dave Master, Rowland's film-making program is one of the best in the nation. Almost every piece of equipment in the school was donated, a result of successful partnerships with community, businesses, and industry groups. In the early days, Master solicited additional needed equipment by bringing student products to the community to show what they could accomplish with donated technology resources.

Students in the program, which is open to anyone in the school, have won almost a thousand awards, and typically go on to successful (and lucrative) careers in the film industry or related fields.

■ **The C. Melvin Sharpe Health School in Washington, DC,** serves mentally and physically disabled students from throughout the city. With a limited budget but boundless enthusiasm and dedication—and some generous help from business partners AT&T and the Internal Revenue Service—the school's staff has put together one of the best adaptive technology centers in the country.

It is not unusual for Ramona Medane, the technology coordinator, and her colleagues to work well into the evening doing whatever is necessary to make technology accessible to their students. According to Medane, "Most of the technology we have here was donated or obtained through grants the teachers have written. We have a lab and computers in every classroom, all of which have been adapted to the needs of various students. We hold a computer fair at the school yearly and work with satellite schools throughout the city. I think people hear too much of the bad news about education in the cities. If anyone thinks our students are getting short-changed, they should come and visit us."

The Keys to Success

Ask the teachers and administrators at the schools described above how their programs were made possible and you're likely to hear a multi-faceted response like this one from A.C.E. Academy's Judy Shasek: "We do everything you can imagine, including writing grants—constantly—for additional public and private support, seeking out community partners, promoting parent and community involvement, pairing up with community-based social service providers, and changing our school culture. We stiffened up our rules, upgraded our curriculum, and raised our expectations for all students. If there is something we aren't doing, we aren't aware of it. And as soon as we find out what it is, we'll try it."

Here's a closer look at some of the successful approaches used by educators we interviewed for this article.

■ **After-hours open labs.** It's helpful to have computers available before and after school and in the evenings, for families that don't have them at home. Chinle's Camala Natay says of her school's lab night, "It is one of the most important things we do at our school. Most of the time, the students are teaching their parents. This gives the children a chance to build their confidence and gets their parents more interested in what's going on at school."

■ **Loaners.** Another response to inequities in home access is to allow students to borrow computers for specified periods of time. Although the risk of equipment being lost or stolen is a real one, the schools that are involved in this type of program generally report very few problems— and a highly positive response on the part of parents and students. The Indiana Buddy System Project, a partnership among the state education department, the Indiana Corporation for Science and Technology, the Lilly Foundation, Apple, and IBM, is a great example of what can be accomplished with outside funding. This statewide effort so far has provided 2,000 students with technology in their homes. Many individual schools have initiated similar take-home programs for their own students. . . .

■ **Teacher training.** In a survey recently completed by Cable in the Classroom, lack of knowledge was cited as one of the most significant barriers to widespread implementation of technology in classrooms. There is no question that an ongoing staff development program is necessary not only to maintain teachers' technology skills but also to develop awareness and ensure that poor, minority, female, and disabled students are receiving a fair deal.

■ **Seeking additional funding.** Since technology is expensive, schools that have developed successful equity programs have generally obtained additional funding from state and federal grants or private foundations. Many programs are targeted at communities with the greatest economic need. Even when equity is not a stated goal, granting organizations are likely to look favorably on a well-conceived proposal that also happens to serve a population with limited economic means. . . .

■ **Local partnerships.** Partnerships between schools and local businesses are central to many equity success stories. Sometimes these partnerships are initiated by the company. For example, AT&T has set up Community Involvement

Councils (CICs) in many cities where it has 1,000 or more employees. Each CIC oversees philanthropic efforts focused on the specific needs of that community—including its schools. In other communities, partnerships are initiated by parents or school personnel approaching businesses (in the immediate or neighboring communities) with ideas about mutually beneficial educational programs. The local Chamber of Commerce can often put you in touch with organizations that are willing to provide schools with financial assistance or volunteer hours.

■ **Using telecommunications to connect.** Giving students a chance to "chat" or exchange electronic mail with their peers and adult experts from other schools, states, or countries allows them to build a sense of community that transcends economics and other factors that sometimes separate young people within a school.

■ **Mentors and role models.** Nothing gives students a better understanding of what technology can do for them than showing them potential careers and allowing them to learn from individuals who are using computers in their daily work. Some schools set up annual career days that focus on technology-related fields and include everything from word processing in an office to programming or working as a computer chip fabrication technician. Others recruit community members to serve as ongoing mentors to students. It's important to find role models who are both male and female and represent a broad range of ethnic groups—including those groups most common in your student population.

■ **Rethinking your expectations.** Far too often, well-meaning educators make decisions about technology use that impact negatively on the success of the lower-achieving or less-advantaged students in the school. When an innovative new program or approach—portfolio assessment, for example, or a project involving multimedia authoring—is being piloted in your school, do you find yourself automatically starting off with the "honors" students and others who have traditionally done well in school? If so, it's time to rethink your approach. All the equity success stories we know of involve a "Can do" attitude on the part of teachers and students alike.

■ **Nurturing internal leadership.** A key success factor present in virtually every successful educational technology program is an individual or small group of people who are leading the way. The notion of the "champion" and the "skunk works," a highly motivated group of people dedicated to solving a common problem, was highlighted in Thomas Peters and Robert Waterman's classic text, *In Search of Excellence*. Although the book focused on America's most successful companies, the lessons it contains are just as valuable in education. It is essential for us to nurture and encourage those teachers and administrators who have the vision, energy, and enthusiasm to help all children reach lofty goals.

Maintaining the Momentum

Although we've seen real progress in the movement toward equitable technology access and use, the battle is far from won. If all students are to be given an opportunity to become productive adults who are both self-fulfilled and capable of contributing to the common good, then the entire school experience must be restructured to maintain equity and promote students' respect for themselves and one another.

The goal of equity is to empower all students to make the most of their lives. Unfortunately, past efforts toward this goal have often exacerbated the problems they were intended to solve. We who are involved in technology-based education have a unique opportunity to expect a great deal from students while being able to provide them with the tools they will need to meet these high expectations. Our field is still young and vibrant, and we are not saddled with the baggage of the past that has hampered others within and outside education. It is an opportunity that does not present itself often, and we should certainly do our best to take advantage of it so that all of our students can achieve the fullness of their potential. ■

In addressing the questions of educational fairness in this article, our focus has been on socioeconomic differences—traditionally those resulting in the most dramatic inequities. However, this is not to say that poor and minority students are the only young people who have suffered from below-average access to computers over the years. Many of the 1980 studies also pointed to inequitable access by girls and students with disabilities.

Although a more in-depth analysis will need to wait for another article, here's a quick look at the issues and resources available to help in these areas.

Girls and Technology

Female students are in a unique circumstance since they enjoy virtually equal institutional access to computers when compared with their male peers, but appear to have very different attitudes about computers. Suzanne Lavon Burgo, who completed an interpretive analysis of more than a hundred studies on gender, computers, and education as her doctoral dissertation at the University of Virginia in 1993, found that female students are less likely to be exposed to out-of-school computer activities, less likely to participate in optional computer activities in school, and less likely to major in computer science at the university level.

Despite these attitudinal differences, the female and male students had comparable performance on post-instructional measures. Burgo also found that experience with computers had a greater effect on students' attitudes than did gender differences—supporting the idea that we like what we can do well. This finding suggests that looking for ways to encourage additional technology use by girls at crucial periods in their education can have a long-term positive impact on their attitudes.

One of the best ways to locate resources to help address issues of gender and equity is to visit the Women in Technology World Wide Web site (http://gseweb.harvard.edu/~tie/studentgroups/wit/wit2.html), established by the Harvard Graduate School of Education. It contains a wealth of information about various organizations' efforts to promote female students' interest and achievement in technology-related fields, including the Society of Women Engineers, the Ada Project, the International Network of Women in Technology, and Women and Computer Science.

Technology Help for Students with Special Needs

Students with disabilities are arguably the kids who can benefit most from educational technology, and yet their access has not always been what it should be. Although special education programs were some of the first to obtain technology for use with students, equipment budgets have often lagged, causing those programs to continue to function with extremely outdated equipment. Although little hard data exist to define the current status of technology access for disabled students, signs indicate that the situation is improving because of legislation, changing attitudes, and the advances that have been made in technology itself. Nevertheless, we believe we have a long way to go before all students with special needs have adequate access to the types of adaptive devices and other technologies that can make a major difference in their lives.

Fortunately, there are numerous organizations and clearinghouses to help educators, students, and parents looking for technology for special needs. Here are two of the best places to start:

The National Database of Assistive Technology Information (ABLEDATA) offers extensive listings of commercially and non-commercially available assistive technology. You can reach ABLEDATA at 8401 Colesville Road, Suite 200, Silver Spring, MD 20910-3319; (800) 227-0216; BBS line (301) 589-3563 (you need to set your modem to 2400, 8-1-N).

Alliance for Technology Access is a national network of community-based service providers with 44 resource centers across the country. To learn the location of a center near your district or to order their comprehensive 1994 book, *Computer Resources for People with Disabilities*, call (800) 455-7970; or write to Alliance for Technology Access, 2175 E. Francisco Blvd., Suite L, San Rafael, CA 94901; or send e-mail to atafta@aol.com.

POST NOTE

As the authors of this article note, there is good news and bad news regarding equitable access and use of technology for low-income students. The bad news is that a discrepancy still exists between high- and low-income students, both in access to technology and in use of the technology for intellectually exciting experiences rather than drill-and-practice exercises. The good news is that the gap has closed dramatically and is likely to continue to narrow in the future.

More important than the equipment gap is the issue of how the technology is used. Teachers' expectations for students will play a key role. If teachers expect *all* students, regardless of socioeconomic status, gender, race, or ethnicity, to use technology to promote higher-level thinking and problem solving, then the equity gap can and will be eliminated.

DISCUSSION QUESTIONS

1. Which of the school examples cited in this article appealed to you? Why?

2. What uses of technology have you observed in schools? Did these uses focus primarily on drill-and-practice exercises or on more creative thinking?

3. What observations have you made regarding equitable access to technology for females and students with disabilities?

Technology Changes Intelligence: Societal Implications and Soaring IQs

Robert J. Sternberg

W ith all the moaning and groaning we constantly hear about the way schools educate our children, we often lose sight of an important and startling fact: intelligence, as measured by so-called intelligence quotients, or IQs, has been increasing over the past 30 years, and the increases are large—about 20 points of IQ per generation for tests of fluid intelligence such as the Raven Progressive Matrices, which require thinking with relatively abstract and novel kinds of problems.

This effect, first pointed out by James Flynn and sometimes called the "Flynn effect" in his honor, has been found in every country where it has been possible to compare IQs across successive generations. We know it's there. But what's behind it?

No one knows for sure, but I think we can make an educated guess, and a good guess is that a major factor behind the massive IQ gains is an important force that has penetrated all but the most remote regions of the globe—technology.

Robert Sternberg, IBM Professor of Psychology and Education at Yale University, is the author of several books, including the new *Successful Intelligence: How Practical and Creative Intelligence Determines Success in Life*. Reprinted by permission from *TECHNOS: Quarterly for Education and Technology*, Vol. 6, No. 2, Summer 1997.

Technology changes society profoundly, but in ways to which we become so accustomed that we hardly notice them. First radio and now television have brought to children concepts and points of view to which they would not have been exposed at the turn of the century. These days we continue to get weak programming, but we also get more and more coverage of a kind that was not formerly available, such as all-day news channels, the Discovery Channel, and the History Channel.

My goal here is to discuss the effects technology may have on human intelligence, not just with levels of intelligence but also what intelligence is. I will discuss some stunningly positive effects but some distressing negative effects as well.

The Blessings of Technology

Let's start with the positive effects, as illustrated by examples that highlight two of the kinds of academic skills we care most about in our kids: mathematical and writing skills.

1. Computational Devices When I went to elementary and secondary school in the 1950s and 1960s, we did all our mathematical computations by hand, and only as high school seniors did we begin to use the now almost forgotten slide rule to help us in these computations. To succeed in mathematics a student had to be skilled in computation because no matter how strong he or she was in conceptual and problem-solving skills, a wrong computation could easily lead to wrong answers in problem solving, as on homework, a quiz, or a test.

Most schools are quite different today. My children were using calculators in elementary school; and as high school students, they regularly use powerful programmable calculators that not only compute but also plot mathematical functions. They can use these calculators for homework, for teacher-made tests, and even for high-stakes testing such as the SAT.

In several important senses, our children's informed use of calculators has increased their intelligence. First, the calculators have removed virtually all of the computational errors they once would have been likely to have made in their work. Just in terms of the answers they can produce, therefore, what was once a common source of error has been removed. Second, the use of calculators changes the way they think about mathematics—and for the better. In the past, they would have had to devote substantial mental resources to the adequate implementation of computational formulas. Much of the time they would have spent doing mathematics would therefore have been spent in fairly mindless computations. Today those computations—done by calculator—take only a fraction of a second. The mental resources they once would have placed into computation can now be spent more productively on important mathematical operations—figuring out what the problem is, visualizing how to represent the problem, formulating a strategy for solving the problem, and programming or performing the operations that will enable the calculator to compute answers. Third, the very act of using the calculator forces them to learning programming skills, which are important for developing computer-based skills as well as for developing the kind of logical thinking one needs to succeed in disciplines including but not limited to mathematics.

The availability of calculators has also changed what intelligence is. Since the beginning of the twentieth century, intelligence has been defined in terms of individual differences that are meaningful for school performance. Indeed, Alfred Binet and Theodore Simon, in creating the first intelligence tests, were asked to develop an instrument that would distinguish children who were truly deficient in academic potential from children who were merely behavior problems.

To the extent that we have greatly decreased the importance of computational skills as a meaningful source of individual differences in school performance, the nature of mathematical ability for school has changed. Conceptual and problem-solving abilities, focal both to mathematics and to intelligence, have now become more important to success in school mathematics. In other words, we have made school mathematics more like real

mathematics and more like the kind of activity we want students to do to develop their intellectual abilities. Moreover, as children learn to use more powerful computational devices, such as full-fledged computers, in their mathematical work, their opportunities to develop their intellectual skills will only increase.

2. Word Processing The changes we have produced both in levels and in the nature of abilities apply not only in the mathematical domain but in other domains as well. Consider the case of word processing in the domain of writing.

Not so long ago, when someone wanted to write a poem, a short story, an essay, or whatever, the options were to use a pen or to use a pencil. Then typewriters came along, offering people the opportunity to increase greatly the efficiency with which words could be processed. When I learned touch-typing, a whole new world opened up to me. I could produce documents much more efficiently and quickly, and, perhaps even more important. I no longer needed to worry about what effect my awful penmanship would have on my teachers' evaluations of my work. Penmanship has become a less important ability not because it is any less a source of individual differences, but because its importance to how students are evaluated in the school setting has decreased.

Typewriters were an improvement, but correcting errors with a typewriter eraser was a slow operation. Recognizing this, my ninth-grade typing teacher subtracted 10 words per minute for every error we made in our timed tests: and I made a lot of errors! Two technological developments came along—eraser paper and liquid eraser fluid—and the correcting of errors became more rapid, less painful, and less disruptive of the flow of thoughts during writing.

As typewriters improved, so did the efficacy with which students could write. Manual typewriters were gradually replaced by electric typewriters, and then electronic typewriters became available. But a much bigger shift occurred when typewriters gave way to word-processing programs on computers. Where are those Royal,

Remington, and Smith-Corona typewriters today? Many of them can be found only in antique shops.

With computers, typing mistakes can be corrected with the push of a button. Whole passages can be deleted, transformed, or moved from one place in a document to another in a fraction of the time it once took. My own productivity has increased many times over as a result of my being able to use a computer-based word-processing program to do my writing, including the writing of this article.

With word processors, students and other people can devote more time to thinking about the quality of their writing and less to the low-level mechanics of getting the writing done. If they make a typing error, they can correct it in seconds, thereby holding onto their train of thought. If they decide that a sentence doesn't work, deleting it can be done in seconds rather than in the minutes it once took to make the erasures on a document. If they wish to move one or more paragraphs to improve the flow of their writing, they can do in seconds what once might easily have taken several hours to rewrite or retype a document. Word processors enable writers to concentrate on composition, on logic, and on being creative rather than on the low-level mechanics of producing a finished-looking document.

Notice that, once again, technology has both increased the intelligence of students and transformed it. Their products are, or at least should be, better. Individual differences in analytical and creative writing skills have become more important as individual differences in penmanship, typing speed, and erasure speed have become less important to teachers' evaluations of students' products.

Technology can enable people better to develop their intelligence—no question about it. And the two cases I've given are only a small sample of those that might be mentioned. Computer games can help develop children's rapid thinking as well as spatial and perceptual-motor skills. New software also enables students to learn about science and scientific research in ways that were never possible before. What a blessing!

The Challenges of Technology

But technology can also be a curse. Almost anything that can be used to good purposes can be twisted to bad ones, and technology is no exception. Two more cases illustrate the challenges we face in implementing the technology we have available.

3. Television Children, not to mention adults, spend enormous—some would say monstrous—amounts of time watching television. What return are they getting for the time they are spending?

Along with a fair amount of good television, there is a much larger amount of trash. It's easy to blame the networks, but we need to remember that they produce programming in response to what their surveys show people watch. People say they want one thing but often respond to another, as many chain restaurants found when they introduced healthful, low-fat food, only to find that the demand to have such products available was in no way matched by the demand to consume them.

Typical noneducational television can help children acquire some concepts and some vocabulary, but only to the relatively low level allowed on most shows. Not only are many shows relatively mindless, but so is the kind of information processing required to understand them. Anyone who has ever appeared on shows quickly learns that even responses to interviews on supposedly educational programs need to be kept short, simple, and direct. Banal questions encourage banal answers. For the most part, television does not encourage the development of active, mindful, and critical thinking.

The problem is not inherent in the medium, as anyone who has watched educational shows can confirm. It is in the use of the medium. This use is dictated, in turn, by demand, which determines the dollars sponsors are willing to pay to advertise their products on the shows. If we want change, we need to be willing to pay for it, which means financial support for educational programming. But it also requires parents who insist that if their children are going to watch television, at least a fair share of it needs to be educational programming.

4. Weapons We do not often associate weapons with education, but in the final days of the twentieth century we have little choice. Every year seems to bring both greater technological sophistication and, unfortunately, easier availability of weapons to schoolchildren. The problem is one we cannot afford to duck, because it has many effects on children's thinking and lives, some of them not so easily observable to middle-class adults.

First, children who are spending their time worrying about violence in school and on the way to school are not thinking about lessons. The psychologist Abraham Maslow was among the first to point out that human motivation tends to be hierarchically structured, so that we need to worry about safety and survival needs before we can worry about needs for cognitive growth. Children worried about self-protection cannot be expected to engage fully in the educational program of the school.

Second, research shows that children who watch aggressive and violent models end up behaving in kind. The models we provide on TV shows do not speak well for the values we wish to foster in our children.

Third, kids are killing kids with weapons. More and more children are dying at each others' hands. The waste to our pool of human resources is enormous, both in terms of the children who die and in terms of the children who, having killed, inevitably find their lives permanently altered for the worse. It this what we want for our children?

Fourth, in many nations of the world, sophisticated but cheap weapons like land mines are leaving a generation of permanently maimed children who are and will be severely challenged in their ability to adapt to the world in which they must live. The time other children are able to spend learning school subjects is time these children have to spend, day after day, week after

week, and year after year, learning to cope with their injuries.

Summing Up

Technology can be and, from all the evidence available, has been a highly constructive force in the development of intelligence in our children. It has made it possible for them to experience events and even virtual words that were never available to their parents when they were children. Technology is helping to raise levels of intelligence and even reshaping what intelligence is. Increasingly, the intelligence one needs for coping with the environment will involve complex, higher-order thinking skills rather than routine, lower-order skills. At the same time, technology is creating challenges that we have been much less than effective in solving, challenges such as those challenges posed by television and weapons in the school environment.

As technology increases the importance of higher-order thinking skills and decreases the importance of lower-order and more routinized ones, there is a risk of greater and greater socioeconomic polarization of our society. Those with good conceptual and technological skills will increasingly be able to advance to more meaningful and higher-paying jobs, whereas those without these skills will increasingly be relegated to lower-level jobs. Jobs that once were in the middle will start to creep upward or downward, or even disappear.

An effective secretary today, for example, must have the conceptual and technological skills to use sophisticated word-processing machinery effectively; the job has gone up scale. But to operate most cash registers, one needs only to be able to scan a bar code—no longer does one need to add, subtract, multiply, and divide; the job has gone downscale. And more and more middle-level jobs, such as those of telephone operator and bank teller, are dying out as technology does what was formerly done by humans. The middle is disappearing in the job market and in our socioeconomic stratification as well.

Sociologists speak of "Matthew effects," an expression coined by sociologist Robert Merton from the Biblical Book of Matthew based on the notion that to those who have much, more will come, and to those who have little, even less will come. Technology can create Matthew effects as it increasingly separates the skilled from the unskilled among both students and workers.

As a society, we need to be prepared for the changes to come. Most important, we need to educate all our students so that they do not get left out in the technological cold. We need to develop not only their technological skills but their conceptual ones as well. Those who have doubts only have to go through supermarket checkout lines, and watch the look of utter puzzlement that crosses the faces of some checkers when a product lacks the proper bar code.

Technology can bring a wonderful future to our children. But we have to shape it and teach children how to use it effectively and constructively. We need to remember that technology will not be a substitute for intelligence. It will change levels of intelligence and even what intelligences is. As educators, we need to ensure that the changes are for the better and not for the worse. ■

POST NOTE

Sternberg makes the case that IQs have been rising with each generation and that technology is a major factor in these rises. Unless you are a psychologist or a psychology major, you may not have been aware of the "Flynn" effect. While the effect is interesting, what's more interesting is the way that technology changes the kind of thinking we expect of students in schools. Technology encourages higher-order thinking (applications, analyses, syntheses, and evaluation) because students are freed from the routines that often consume great amounts of time. Instead of expecting students to spend most of their time actually doing computations in mathematics, students are now asked to conceptualize problems, and to figure out various ways to solve the problems. Nor are the influences of technology limited to mathematics. Social studies teachers can now make great use of digitized primary sources; science teachers can use probes that measure speed and temperature changes and feed that information directly into computers for analysis along multiple dimensions. It's a new world.

DISCUSSION QUESTIONS

1. Do you think Sternberg makes a persuasive argument for technology being a major factor in the generational rise is IQ scores? Why or why not?

2. In addition to technology, what other factors can you suggest as reasons why IQ tests have risen?

3. On balance, do you believe technology's influence on schooling and education are positive or negative? Why?

Educating the Net Generation

Don Tapscott

Every time I enter a discussion about efforts to get computers into schools, someone insists that computers aren't the answer. "It won't help to just throw computers at the wall, hoping something will stick. I've seen lots of computers sitting unused in classrooms."

Agreed. Computers alone won't do the trick. They are a necessary but insufficient condition for moving our schools to new heights of effectiveness. We've still got to lean how best to use this technology. And I have become convinced that the most potent force for change is the students themselves.

Why look to the kids? Because they are different from any generation before them. They are the first to grow up surrounded by digital media. Computers are everywhere—in the home, school, factory, and office—as are digital technologies—cameras, video games, and CD-ROMs. Today's kids are so bathed in bits that they think technology is part of the natural landscape. To them, digital technology is no more intimidating than a VCR or a toaster. And these new media are increasingly connected by the Internet, that ex-

Don Tapscott is President of New Paradigm Learning Corporation and Chairman of Alliance for Converging Technologies, 133 King St. E., Ste. 300, Toronto, ON M5C 1G6, Canada (Web site: http://nplc.com; e-mail: nplc@nplc.com). Copyright © 1999 Don Tapscott. "Educating the Net Generation" by Don Tapscott, originally appeared in *Educational Leadership*, February 1999, pp. 7–11. Reprinted by permission from Don Tapscott.

panding web of networks that is attracting one million new users a month.

The Net Generation

The Net affects us all—the way we create wealth, the nature of commerce and marketing, the delivery system for entertainment, the role and dynamics of learning, and the nature of government. It should not surprise us that those first to grow up with this new medium are defined by their relationship to it. I call them the Net Generation—the N-Geners.

According to Teenage Research Unlimited (1997), teens feel that being online is as "in" as dating and partying! And this exploding popularity is occurring while the Net is still in its infancy and, as such, is painfully slow; primitive; limited in capabilities; lacking complete security, reliability, and ubiquity; and subject to both hyperbole and ridicule. Nevertheless, children love it and keep coming back after each frustrating experience. They know its potential.

What do students do on the Net? They manage their personal finances; organize protest movements; check facts; discuss zits; check the scores of their favorite team and chat online with its superstars; organize groups to save the rain forest; cast votes; learn more about the illness of their little sister; go to a virtual birthday party; or get video clips from a soon-to-be-released movie.

Chat groups and computer conferences are populated by young people hungry for expression and self-discovery. Younger kids love to meet people and talk about anything. As they mature, their communications center on topics and themes. For all ages, "E-mail me" has become the parting expression of a generation.

Digital Anxiety

For many adults, all this digital activity is a source of high anxiety. Are kids really benefitting from the digital media? Can technology truly improve the process of learning, or is it dumbing down and misguiding educational efforts? What about Net addiction? Is it useful for children to spend time in online chat rooms, and what are they doing there? Are some becoming glued to the screen? What about cyberdating and cybersex? Aren't video games leading to a violent generation? Is technology stressing kids out—as it seems to be doing to adults? Has the Net become a virtual world—drawing children away from parent authority and responsible adult influence—where untold new problems and dangers lie? What is the real risk of online predators, and can children be effectively protected? How can we shield kids from sleaze and porn? As these children come of age, will they lack the social skills for effective participation in the work force?

These questions are just a sampling of the widespread concern raised not just by cynics, moralists, and technophobes, but also by reasonable and well-meaning educators, parents, and members of the community.

Everybody, relax. The kids are all right. They are learning, developing, and thriving in the digital world. They need better tools, better access, better services—*more* freedom to explore, not less. Rather than convey hostility and mistrust, we need to change *our* way of thinking and behaving. This means all of us—parents, educators, lawmakers, and business leaders alike.

Digital kids are learning precisely the social skills required for effective interaction in the digital economy. They are learning about peer relationships, teamwork, critical thinking, fun, friendships across geographies, self-expression, and self-confidence.

Conventional wisdom says that because children are multitasking—jumping from one computer-based activity to another—their attention span is reduced. Research does not support this view. Ironically, the same people who charge that today's kids are becoming "glued to the screen" also say that kids' attention spans are declining.

At root is the fear that children will not be able to focus and therefore will not learn. This concern is consistent with the view that the primary challenge of learning is to absorb specific information. However, many argue—and I agree—that the content of a particular lesson is less important than learning how to learn. As John Dewey wrote,

> Perhaps the greatest of all pedagogical fallacies is the notion that a person learns only the particular thing he is studying at the time. Collateral learning . . . may be and often is more important than the spelling lesson or lesson in geography or history that is learned. (1963, p. 48)

The Challenge of Schooling

The new technologies have helped create a culture for learning (Papert, 1996) in which the learner enjoys enhanced interactivity and connections with others. Rather than listen to a professor regurgitate facts and theories, students discuss ideas and learn from one another, with the teacher acting as a participant in the learning. Students construct narratives that make sense out of their own experiences.

Initial research strongly supports the benefits of this kind of learning. For example, in 1996, 33 students in a social studies course at California State University in Northridge were randomly divided into two groups, one taught in a traditional classroom and the other taught virtually on the Web. The teaching model wasn't fundamentally changed—both groups received the same texts, lectures, and exams. Despite this, the Web-based class scored, on average, 20 percent higher than the traditional class. The Web class had more contact with one another and were more interested in the class work. The students also felt that they understood the material better and had greater flexibility to determine how they learned (Schutte, n.d.).

The ultimate interactive learning environment is the Internet itself. Increasingly, this technology includes the vast repository of human knowledge, the tools to manage this knowledge, access to people, and a growing galaxy of services ranging from sandbox environments for pre-schoolers to virtual laboratories for medical students studying neural psychiatry. Today's baby will tomorrow learn about Michelangelo by walking through the Sistine Chapel, watching Michelangelo paint, and perhaps stopping for a conversation. Students will stroll on the moon. Petroleum engineers will penetrate the earth with the drill bit. Doctors will navigate the cardiovascular system. Researchers will browse through a library. Auto designers will sit in the back seat of the car they are designing to see how it feels and to examine the external view.

Eight Shifts of Interactive Learning

The digital media is causing educators and students alike to shift to new ways of thinking about teaching and learning.

1. From linear to hypermedia learning. Traditional approaches to learning are linear and date back to using books as a learning tool. Stories, novels, and other narratives are generally linear. Most textbooks are written to be tackled from the beginning to the end. TV shows and instructional videos are also designed to be watched from beginning to end.

But N-Gen access to information is more interactive and nonsequential. Notice how a child channel surfs when watching television. I've found that my kids go back and forth among various TV shows and video games when they're in the family room. No doubt that as TV becomes a Net appliance, children will increasingly depend on this nonlinear way of processing information.

2. From instruction to construction and discovery. Seymour Papert says,

> The scandal of education is that every time you teach something, you deprive a child of the pleasure and benefit of discovery. (de Pommereau, 1996, p. 68)

With new technologies, we will experience a shift away from traditional types of pedagogy to the creation of learning partnership and learning cultures. This is not to say that teachers should not plan activities or design curriculums. They might, however, design the curriculum in partnership with learners or even help learners design the curriculum themselves.

This constructivist approach to teaching and learning means that rather than assimilate knowledge that is broadcast by an instructor, the learner constructs knowledge anew. Constructivists argue that people learn best by *doing* rather than simply by *listening*. The evidence supporting constructivism is persuasive, but that shouldn't be too surprising. When youngsters are enthusiastic about a fact or a concept that they themselves discovered, they will better retain the information and use it in creative, meaningful ways.

3. From teacher-centered to learner-centered education. The new media focus the learning experience on the individual rather than on the transmitter. Clearly, learner-centered education improves the child's motivation to learn.

The shift from teacher-centered to learner-centered education does not suggest that the teacher is suddenly playing a less important role. A teacher is equally crucial and valuable in the learner-centered context, for he or she creates and structures what happens in the classroom.

Learner-centered education begins with an evaluation of abilities, learning styles, social contexts, and other important factors that affect the student. Evaluation software programs can tailor the learning experience for each individual child. Learner-centered education is also more active, with students discussing, debating, researching, and collaborating on projects with one another and with the teacher.

4. From absorbing material to learning how to navigate and how to learn. This means learning how to synthesize, not just analyze. N-Geners can assess and analyze facts—a formidable change in a data galaxy of easily accessible information sources. But more important, they can synthesize. They are engaged in information sources and people on the Net, and then they construct higher-level structures and mental images.

5. From school to lifelong learning. For young baby boomers looking forward to the world of work, life often felt divided—between the period when you *learned* and the period when you *did*. You went to school and maybe to university and learned a trade or profession. For the rest of your life, your challenge was simply to keep up with developments in your field. But things have changed. Today, many boomers reinvent their knowledge base constantly. Learning has become a continuous, lifelong process. The N-Gen is entering a world of lifelong learning from day one, and unlike the schools of the boomers, today's educational system can anticipate how to prepare students for lifelong learning.

6. From one-size-fits-all to customized learning. The digital media enables students to be treated as individuals—to have highly customized learning experiences based on their backgrounds, individual talents, age levels, cognitive styles, and interpersonal preferences.

As Papert puts it,

> What I see as the real contribution of digital media to education is a flexibility that could allow every individual to find personal paths to learning. This will make it possible for the dream of every progressive educator to come true: In the learning environment of the future, every learner will be "special." (1996, p. 16)

In fact, Papert believes in a "community of learning" shared by students and teachers:

> Socialization is not best done by segregating children into classrooms with kids of the same age. The computer is a medium in which what you make lends itself to be modified and shared. When kids get together on a project, there is abundant discussion; they show it to other kids, other kids want to see it, kids learn to share knowledge with other people—much more than in the classroom. (1997, p. 11)

7. From learning as torture to learning as fun. Maybe torture is an exaggeration, but for many kids, class is not exactly the highlight of their day. Some educators have decried the fact that a generation schooled on *Sesame Street* expects to be entertained at school—and to enjoy the learning experience. They argue that learning and entertainment should be clearly separated.

Why shouldn't learning be entertaining? In *Merriam-Webster's Collegiate Dictionary*, the third definition of the verb *to entertain* is "to keep, hold, or maintain in the mind" and "to receive and take into consideration." In other words, entertainment has always been a profound part of the learning process, and teachers throughout history have been asked to convince their students to entertain ideas. From this perspective, the best teachers were the entertainers. Using the new media, the learner also becomes the entertainer and, in doing so, enjoys, is motivated toward, and feels responsible for learning.

8. From the teacher as transmitter to the teacher as facilitator. Learning is becoming a social activity, facilitated by a new generation of educators.

The topic is saltwater fish. The 6th grade teacher divides the class into teams, asking each team to prepare a presentation on a fish of its choice. Students have access to the Web and are allowed to use any resources. They must cover the topics of history, breathing, propulsion, reproduction, diet, predators, and "cool facts." They must also address questions to others in their team or to others in the class, not to the teacher.

Two weeks later, Melissa's group is first. The students have created a shark project home page with hot links for each topic. As the students talk, they project their presentation onto a screen at the front of the class. They have video clips of different types of sharks and also a clip from Jacques Cousteau discussing the shark as an endangered species. They then use the Web to go live to Aquarius, an underwater site located off the Florida Keys. The class can ask questions of the Aquarius staff, although most inquiries are directed to the project team. One such discussion focuses on which is greater: the dangers posed by sharks to humans or the dangers posed by humans to sharks.

The class decides to hold an online forum on this topic and invites kids from classes in other countries to participate. The team asks students to browse through its project at any time, from any location, because the forum will be up for the rest of the school year. In fact, the team decides to maintain the site by adding new links and fresh information throughout the year. The assignment becomes a living project. Learners from around the world find the shark home page helpful and build links to it.

In this example, the teachers acts as consultant to the teams, facilitates the learning process, and participates as a technical consultant on the new media. The teacher doesn't have to compete with Jacques Cousteau's expertise on underwater life; her teaching is supported by his expertise.

Turning to the Net Generation

Needless to say, a whole generation of teachers needs to learn new tools, new approaches, and new skills. This will be a challenge, not just because of resistance to change by some teachers, but also because of the current atmosphere of financial cutbacks, low teacher morale, increased workloads, and reduced retraining budgets.

But as we make this inevitable transition, we may best turn to the generation raised on and immersed in new technologies. Give students the tools, and they will be the single most important source of guidance on how to make their schools relevant and effective places to learn. ■

References

de Pommereau, I. (1997, April 21). Computers give children the key to learning. *Christian Science Monitor*, p. 68.

Dewey, J. (1963). *Experience and education.* London: Collier Books.

Papert, S. (1996). *The connected family: Bridging the digital generation gap.* Marietta, GA: Longstreet Press.

Schutte, J. G. (n.d.) *Virtual teaching in higher education* [On-line]. Available: http://www.csun.edu/sociology/virtexp.htm

Teenage Research Unlimited, Inc. (1996, January). Press release. Northbrook, IL; Author.

Teenage Research Unlimited, Inc. (1997, Spring). Teenage marketing and lifestyle update. Northbrook, IL: Author.

POST NOTE

The author identifies eight shifts in the ways teachers and students will think about teaching and learning as a result of the growth of digital media. The author acknowledges that as these new digital technologies are implemented in classrooms, the role of the teacher will change from being an information dispenser to being more of a coach. Some teachers will be comfortable with this coaching role; others will cling to the more traditional role of information dispenser. Clearly, if this shift in roles is to occur, teacher education programs must address the ways in which teachers can make effective use of technologies.

It is also important for university faculty members, in both education and the arts and sciences, to model the uses of new technologies. It won't work for them to say, "Do as I say, not as I do." Teachers learn best by seeing and using contemporary technologies in their college and university courses, as well as in the classrooms in which their practicum experiences occur.

D I S C U S S I O N Q U E S T I O N S

1. Do you disagree with any of the eight shifts in ways of teaching and learning? Which ones, and why?

2. Which of the new technologies seem particularly well suited for the subject matter that you plan on teaching? Are some technologies less suited to your subject than others?

3. What obstacles stand in the way of these eight shifts in teaching and learning from occurring?

Part Nine
Diversity

The United States is a nation of great diversity: races, cultures, religions, languages, and lifestyles. Although these forms of diversity are part of what makes the United States strong, they nevertheless create challenges. The major challenge is how to recognize and respect these forms of diversity while still maintaining a common culture to which each subgroup can feel welcomed and valued. Early in the twentieth century, American schools tried to create a "melting pot," where group differences were boiled away so that just "Americans" survived. Today, the notion of cultural pluralism has replaced the assimilationist perspective, with the metaphor of a "mosaic" or "salad" replacing that of the melting pot.

The readings in this section of the book address diversity issues such as multicultural education, bilingual education, gender issues, and inclusion of children with disabilities. Many of these topics are controversial, with both strong proponents and opponents of the various positions articulated in the articles. As you read the selections, try to sort out your own positions on the issues.

Multiculturalism: E Pluribus Plures

Diane Ravitch

Q uestions of race, ethnicity, and religion have been a perennial source of conflict in American education. The schools have often attracted the zealous attention of those who wish to influence the future, as well as those who wish to change the way we view the past. In our history, the schools have been not only an institution in which to teach young people skills and knowledge, but an arena where interest groups fight to preserve their values, or to revise the judgments of history, or to bring about fundamental social change.

Given the diversity of American society, it has been impossible to insulate the schools from pressures that result from differences and tensions among groups. When people differ about basic values, sooner or later those disagreements turn up in battles about how schools are organized or what the schools should teach. Sometimes these battles remove a terrible injustice, like racial segregation. Sometimes however, interest groups politicize the curriculum and attempt to impose their views on teachers, school officials, and textbook publishers. When groups cross the line into extremism, advancing their own agendas without regard to reason or to others, they threaten public education itself, making it difficult to

Diane Ravitch is a research professor at New York University and nonresident senior scholar at the Brookings Institute. Diane Ravitch, "Multiculturalism: E Pluribus Plures," *The Key Reporter*, Vol. 56, No. 1, Autumn 1990, pp. 1–4. Reprinted with permission.

teach any issues honest and making the entire curriculum vulnerable to political campaigns.

For many years, the public schools attempted to neutralize controversies over race, religion, and ethnicity by ignoring them. The textbooks minimized problems among groups and taught a sanitized version of history. Race, religion, and ethnicity were presented as minor elements in the American saga; slavery was treated as an episode, immigration as a sidebar, and women were largely absent. The textbooks concentrated on presidents, wars, national politics, and issues of state. An occasional "great black" or "great woman" received mention, but the main narrative paid little attention to minority groups and women.

With the ethnic revival of the 1960s, this approach to the teaching of history came under fire, because the history of national leaders—virtually all of whom were white, Anglo-Saxon, and male—ignored the place in American history of those who were none of the above. The traditional history of elites had been complemented by an assimilationist view of American society, which presumed that everyone in the American melting pot would eventually lose or abandon those ethnic characteristics that distinguished each from mainstream Americans. The ethnic revival demonstrated that many groups did not want to be assimilated or melted. Ethnic studies programs popped up on campuses to teach not only that "black is beautiful," but also that every other variety of ethnicity is "beautiful" as well; everyone who had "roots" began to look for them so that they, too, could recover that ancestral part of themselves that had not been homogenized.

As ethnicity became an accepted subject for study in the late 1960s, textbooks were assailed for their failure to portray blacks accurately; within a few years, the textbooks in wide use were carefully screened to eliminate bias against minority groups and women. At the same time, new scholarship about the history of women, blacks, and various ethnic minorities found its way into the textbooks. Today's history textbooks routinely incorporate the experiences of women, blacks, American Indians, and various immigrant groups.

As a result of the political and social changes of recent decades, cultural pluralism is now generally recognized as an organizing principle of this society. In contrast to the idea of the melting pot, which promised to erase ethnic and group differences, children now learn that variety is the spice of life. They learn that America has provided a haven for many different groups and has allowed them to maintain their cultural heritage or to assimilate, or—as is often the case—to do both; the choice is theirs, not the state's. They learn that cultural pluralism is one of the norms of a free society; that differences among groups are a national resource rather than a problem to be solved. Indeed, the unique feature of the United Stats is that its common culture has been formed by the interaction of its subsidiary cultures. It is a culture that has been influenced over time by immigrants, American Indians, Africans (slave and free) and by their descendants. American music, art, literature, language, food, clothing, sports, holidays, and customs all show the effects of the commingling of diverse cultures in one nation. Paradoxical though it may seem, the United States has a common culture that is multicultural.

This understanding of the pluralistic nature of American culture has taken a long time to forge. It is based on sound scholarship and has led to major revisions in what children are taught and what they read in school. The new history is—indeed, must be—a warts-and-all history; it demands an unflinching examination of racism and discrimination in our history. Making these changes is difficult, raises tempers, and ignites controversies but gives a more interesting and accurate account of American history. Accomplishing these changes is valuable, because there is also a useful lesson for the rest of the world in America's relatively successful experience as a pluralist society. Throughout human history, the clash of different cultures, races, ethnic groups, and religions has often been the cause of bitter hatred, civil conflict, and international war. The ethnic tensions that now are tearing apart Lebanon, Sri Lanka, Kashmir, and various republics of the Soviet Union remind us of the costs of unfettered group rivalry. Thus, it is a matter of more than domestic importance that we closely examine and try to understand that part of our national history in which different groups competed, fought, suffered, but ultimately learned to live together in relative peace and even achieved a sense of common nationhood.

Particularism

Alas, these painstaking efforts to expand the understanding of American culture into a richer and more varied tapestry have taken a new turn, and not for the better. Almost any idea, carried to its extreme, can be made pernicious, and this is what is happening now to multiculturalism. Today, pluralistic multiculturalism must contend with a new, particularistic multiculturalism. The pluralists seek a richer common culture; the particularists insist that no common culture is possible or desirable.

The new particularism is entering the curriculum in a number of school systems across the country. Advocates of particularism propose an ethnocentric curriculum to raise the self-esteem and academic achievement of children from racial and ethnic minority backgrounds. Without any evidence, they claim that children from minority backgrounds will do well in school *only* if they are immersed in a positive, prideful version of their ancestral culture. If children are of, for example, Fredonian ancestry, they must hear that Fredonians were important in mathematics, science, history, and literature. If they learn about great Fredonians and if their studies use Fredonian examples and Fredonian concepts, they will do well in school. If they do not, they will have low self-esteem and will do badly.

The particularistic version of multiculturalism is unabashedly filiopietistic and deterministic. It teaches children that their identity is determined by their "cultural genes"—that something in their blood or their racial memory or their cultural DNA defines who they are and what they may achieve; that the culture in which they live is not their own culture, even though they were born here; that American culture is "Eurocentric," and therefore hostile to anyone whose ancestors are not European. Perhaps the most invidious implication of particularism is that racial and ethnic minorities are not and should not try to be part of American culture; it implies that American culture belongs only to those who are white and European; it implies that those who are neither white nor European are alienated from American culture by virtue of their race or ethnicity; it implies that the only culture they do belong to or can ever belong to is the culture of their ancestors, even if their families have lived in this country for generations.

The pluralist approach to multiculturalism promotes a broader interpretation of the common American culture and seeks due recognition for the ways that the nation's many racial, ethnic, and cultural groups have transformed the national culture. The pluralists say, in effect, "American culture belongs to us, all of us; the United States is us, and we remake it in every generation." But particularists have no interest in extending or revising American culture; indeed, they deny that a common culture exists. Particularists reject any accommodation among groups, any interactions that blur the distinct lines between them. The brand of history that they espouse is one in which everyone is a descendant of victims or oppressors. By taking this approach, they fan and re-create ancient hatreds in each new generation.

Particularism has its intellectual roots in the ideology of ethnic separatism and in the black nationalist movement. In the particularist analysis, the nation has five cultures: African American, Asian American, European American, Latino/Hispanic, and American Indian. The huge cultural, historical, religious, and linguistic differences within these categories are ignored, as is the considerable intermarriage among these groups, as are the linkages (like gender, class, sexual orientation, and religion) that cut across these five groups. No serious scholar would claim that all Europeans and white Americans are part of the same culture, or that all Asians are part of the same culture, or that all people of Latin American descent are of the same culture, or that all people of African descent are of the same culture. Any categorization this broad is essentially meaningless and useless.

Particularism is a bad idea whose time has come. It is also a fashion spreading like wildfire through the education system, actively promoted by organizations and individuals with a political and professional interest in strengthening ethnic power bases in the university, in the education profession, and in society itself. One can scarcely pick up an educational journal without learning about a school district that is converting to an ethnocentric curriculum in an attempt to give "self-esteem" to children from racial minorities. A state-funded project in a Sacramento high school is teaching young black males to think like Africans and to develop the "African Mind Model Technique," in order to free themselves of the racism of American culture. A popular black rap singer, KRS-One, complained in an op-ed article in the *New York Times* that the schools should be teaching blacks about their cultural heritage, instead of trying to make everyone Americans. "It's like trying to teach a dog to be a cat," he wrote. KRS-One railed about having to learn about Thomas Jefferson and the Civil War, which had nothing to do (he said) with black history.

Ethnomathematics

Pluralism can easily be transformed into particularism, as may be seen in the potential uses in the classroom of the Mayan contribution to mathematics. The Mayan example was popularized in a movie called *Stand and Deliver*, about a charismatic Bolivian-born mathematics teacher in Los Angeles who inspired his students (who are Hispanic) to learn calculus. He told them that their ancestors invented the concept of zero; but that wasn't all he did. He used imagination to put across mathematic concepts. He required students to do homework and to go to school on Saturdays and during the Christmas holidays, so that they might pass the advanced placement mathematics examination. The teacher's reference to the Mayans' mathematical genius was a valid instructional device: It was an attention-getter and would have interested even students who were not Hispanic. But the Mayan example would have had little effect without the teacher's insistence that the class study hard for a difficult examination.

Ethnic educators have seized on the Mayan contribution to mathematics as the key to simultaneously boosting the ethnic ride of Hispanic children and attacking Eurocentrism. One proposal claims that Mexican-American children will be attracted to science and mathematics if they study Mayan mathematics, the Mayan calendar, and Mayan astronomy. Children in primary grades are to be taught that the Mayans were first to discover the zero and that Europeans learned it long afterward from the Arabs, who had learned it in India. This will help students see that Europeans were latecomers in the discovery of great ideas. Botany is to be learned by study of the agricultural techniques of the Aztecs, a subject of somewhat limited relevance to children in urban areas. Furthermore, "ethnobotanical" classifications of plants are to be substituted for the Eurocentric Linnaean system. At first glance, it may seem curious that Hispanic children are deemed to have no cultural affinity with Spain; but to acknowledge the cultural tie would confuse the ideological assault on Eurocentrism.

This proposal suggests some questions: Is there any evidence that the teaching of "culturally relevant" science and mathematics will draw Mexican-American children to the study of these subjects? Will Mexican-American children lose interest or self-esteem if they discover that their ancestors were Aztecs or Spaniards, rather than Mayans? Are children who learn in this way prepared to study the science and mathematics that are taught in American colleges and universities and that are needed for advanced study in these fields? Are they even prepared to study the science and mathematics taught in *Mexican* universities? If the class is half Mexican-American and

half something else, will only the Mexican-American children study in a Mayan and Aztec mode or will all the children? But shouldn't all children study what is culturally relevant for them? How will we train teachers who have command of so many different systems of mathematics and science?

The interesting proposal to teach ethnomathematics comes at a time when American mathematics educators are trying to overhaul present practices, because of the poor performance of American children on national and international assessments. Mathematics educators are attempting to change the teaching of their subject so that children can see its uses in everyday life. There would seem to be an incipient conflict between those who want to introduce real-life applications of mathematics and those who want to teach the mathematical systems used by ancient cultures. I suspect that most mathematics teachers would enjoy doing a bit of both, if there were time or student interest. But any widespread movement to replace modern mathematics with ancient ethnic mathematics runs the risk of disaster in a field that is struggling to update existing curricula. If, as seems likely, ancient mathematics is taught mainly to minority children, the gap between them and middle-class white children is apt to grow. It is worth noting that children in Korea, who score highest in mathematics on international assessments, do not study ancient Korean mathematics.

Particularism is akin to cultural Lysenkoism, for it takes as its premise the spurious notion that cultural traits are inherited. It implies a dubious, dangerous form of cultural predestination. Children are taught that if their ancestors could do it, so could they. But what happens if a child is from a cultural group that made no significant contribution to science or mathematics? Must children find a culturally appropriate field in which to strive? How does a teacher find the right cultural buttons for children of mixed heritage? And how in the world will teachers use this technique when the children in their classes are drawn from many different cultures, as is usually the case? By the time that every culture gets its due, there may be no time left to teach the subject itself. This explosion of filiopietism (which, we should remember, comes from adults, not from students) is reminiscent of the period some years ago when the Russians claimed that they had invented everything first; as we now know, this nationalistic braggadocio did little for their self-esteem and nothing for their economic development. We might reflect, too, on how little social prestige has been accorded in this country to immigrants from Greece and Italy, even though the achievements of their ancestors were at the heart of the classical curriculum.

In school districts where most children are black and Hispanic, there has been a growing tendency to embrace particularism rather than pluralism. Many of the children in these districts perform poorly in academic classes and leave school without graduating. They would fare better in school if they had well-educated and well-paid teachers, small classes, good materials, encouragement at home and school, summer academic programs, protection from the drugs and crime that ravage their neighborhoods, and higher expectations of satisfying careers upon graduation. These are expensive and time-consuming remedies that must also engage the large society beyond the school. The lure of particularism is that it offers a less complicated anodyne, one in which the children's academic deficiencies may be addressed—or set aside—by inflating their racial pride. The danger of this remedy is that it will detract attention from the real needs of schools and the real interests of children, while simultaneously arousing distorted race pride in children of all races, increasing racial antagonism and producing fresh recruits for white and black racist groups.

The Effects of Particularism

The rising tide of particularism encourages the politicization of all curricula in the schools. If education bureaucrats bend to the political and ideological winds, as is their wont, we can anticipate a generation of struggle over the content of the curriculum in mathematics, science, litera-

ture, and history. Demands for "culturally relevant" studies, for ethnostudies of all kinds, will open the classroom to unending battles over whose version is taught, who gets credit for what, and which ethno-interpretation is appropriate.

The spread of particularism throws into question the very idea of American public education. Public schools exist to teach children the general skills and knowledge that they need to succeed in American society, and the specific skills and knowledge that they need in order to function as American citizens. They receive public support because they have a public function. Historically, the public schools were known as "common schools" because they were schools for all, even if the children of all the people did not attend them. Over the years, the courts have found that it was unconstitutional to teach religion in the common schools, or to separate children on the basis of their race in the common schools. In their curriculum, their hiring practices, and their general philosophy, the public schools must not discriminate against or give preference to any racial or ethnic group. Yet they are permitted to accommodate cultural diversity by, for example, serving food that is culturally appropriate or providing library collections that emphasize the interests of the local community. They should not, however, be expected to teach children to view the world through an ethnocentric perspective that rejects or ignores the common culture.

For generations, those groups that wanted to inculcate their religion or their ethnic heritage have instituted private schools—after school, on weekends, or on a full-time basis. There, children learn with others of the same group—Greeks, Poles, Germans, Japanese, Chinese, Jews, Lutherans, Catholics, and so on—and are taught by people from the same group. Valuable as this exclusive experience has been for those who choose it, this has not been the role of public education. One of the primary purposes of public education has been to create a national community, a definition of citizenship and culture that is both expansive and *inclusive*.

The multicultural controversy may do wonders for the study of history, which has been neglected for years in American schools. At this time, only half of our high school graduates ever study any world history. Any serious attempt to broaden students' knowledge of Africa, Europe, Asia, and Latin America will require at least two, and possibly three, years of world history (a requirement thus far only in California). American history, too, will need more time than the one-year high-school survey course. Those of us who have insisted for years on the importance of history in the curriculum may not be ready to assent to its redemptive power, but hope that our new allies will ultimately join a constructive dialogue that strengthens the place of history in the schools.

Some Solutions

As cultural controversies arise, educators must adhere to the principle of "E Pluribus Unum." That is, they must maintain a balance between the demands of the one—the nation of which we are common citizens—and the many—the varied histories of the American people. It is not necessary to denigrate either the one or the many. Pluralism is a positive value, but it is also important that we preserve a sense of an American community—a society and a culture to which we all belong. If there is no overall community with an agreed-upon vision of liberty and justice; if all we have is a collection of racial and ethnic cultures, lacking any common bonds, then we have no means to mobilize public opinion on behalf of people who are not members of our particular group. We have, for example, no reason to support public education. If there is no larger community, then each group will want to teach its own children in its own way, and public education ceases to exist.

History should not be confused with filiopietism. History gives no grounds for race pride. No race has a monopoly on virtue. If anything, a study of history should inspire humility, rather than pride. People of every racial group have committed terrible crimes, often against others of the same group. Whether one looks at the history of Europe or Africa or Latin America or Asia,

every continent offers examples of inhumanity. Slavery has existed in civilizations around the world for centuries. Examples of genocide can be found around the world, throughout history, from ancient times right through to our own day. Governments and cultures, sometimes by edict, sometimes simply following tradition, have practiced not only slavery, but human sacrifice, infanticide, cliterodectomy, and mass murder. If we teach children this, they might recognize how absurd both racial hatred and racial chauvinism are.

What must be preserved in the study of history is the spirit of inquiry, the readiness to open new questions and to pursue new understandings. History, at its best, is a search for truth. The best way to portray this search is through debate and controversy, rather than through imposition of fixed beliefs and immutable facts. Perhaps the most dangerous aspect of school history is its tendency to become Official History, a sanctified version of the Truth taught by the state to captive audiences and embedded in beautiful mass-market textbooks as holy writ. When Official History is written by committees responding to political pressures, rather than by scholars synthesizing the best available research, the errors of the past are replaced by the politically fashionable errors of the present. It may be difficult to teach children that history is both important and uncertain, and that even the best historians never have all the pieces of the jigsaw puzzle, but it is necessary to do so. If state education departments permit the revision of their history courses and textbooks to become an exercise in power politics, the entire process of state-level curriculum-making becomes suspect, as does public education itself.

The question of self-esteem is extraordinarily complex, and it goes well beyond the content of the curriculum. Most of what we call self-esteem is formed in the home and in a variety of life experiences, not only in school. Nonetheless, it has been important for blacks—and for other racial groups—to learn about the history of slavery and of the civil rights movement; it has been important for blacks to know that their ancestors actively resisted enslavement and actively pursued equality; and it has been important for blacks and others to learn about black men and women who fought courageously against racism and who provide models of courage, persistence, and intellect. These are instances where the content of the curriculum reflects sound scholarship, and at the same time probably lessens racial prejudice and provides inspiration for those who are descendants of slaves. But knowing about the travails and triumphs of one's forebears does not necessarily translate into either self-esteem or personal accomplishment. For most children, self-esteem—the self-confidence that grows out of having reached a goal—comes not from hearing about the monuments of their ancestors but as a consequence of what they are able to do and accomplish through their own efforts.

As I reflected on these issues, I recalled reading an interview a few years ago with a talented black runner. She said that her model is Mikhail Baryshnikov. She admires him because he is a magnificent athlete. He is not black; he is not female; he is not American-born; he is not even a runner. But he inspires her because of the way he trained and used his body. When I read this, I thought how narrow-minded it is to believe that people can be inspired *only* by those who are exactly like them in race and ethnicity. ■

POST NOTE

The term *multiculturalism* means different things to different people. For some, it represents an attempt to replace the traditional, time-tested legacy of Western civilization with the literature and history of people from other cultures and of women—groups whose achievements are often judged to have less perennial value. For others, multiculturalism is an attempt to recognize the contributions of the many different cultures represented in our pluralistic society. For still others, it represents an ethnocentric approach designed to raise academic achievement and self-esteem for children of particular racial or ethnic backgrounds.

Diane Ravitch argues strongly for cultural pluralism and the recognition that, paradoxical as it may seem, the United States has a common culture that is multicultural. She believes that the particularistic, ethnocentric version of multiculturalism damages the fabric of American culture and divides society. A culturally pluralistic approach to curriculum, she believes, will help reduce racial, ethnic, socioeconomic, and gender divisions in the United States, whereas an ethnocentric approach is likely to exacerbate differences.

DISCUSSION QUESTIONS

1. To what degree has your education been multicultural? In what ways?

2. What do you see as the greatest threats of multiculturalism? The greatest benefits? Explain your answers.

3. Ravitch ends her essay with the recollection of a Black female runner who thought of Mikhail Baryshnikov as her hero. Do you have a hero or heroine from a culture other than your own? If so, describe that individual, and explain why he or she is important to you.

68

Multicultural Education in the New Century

James A. Banks

An important goal of multicultural education is to educate citizens who can participate successfully in the workforce and take action in the civic community to help the nation actualize its democratic ideals. These ideals, such as justice, equality and freedom, are set forth in the Declaration of Independence, the U.S. Constitution and the Bill of Rights.

Democratic societies, such as the United States, are works in progress that require citizens who are committed to democratic ideals, who are keenly aware of the gap between a nation's ideals and realities and who are able and willing to take thoughtful action that will help make democratic ideals a reality.

Distortion by Critics

Although some critics have misrepresented multicultural education and argued it is divisive and will Balkanize the nation, the aim of multicultural education is to unify our nation and to help put in place its ideal of *e pluribus unum*—"out of many, one."

James Banks is professor and director of the Center for Multicultural Education, University of Washington. He is author of *Educating Citizens in a Multicultural Society*. Reprinted with permission from the May 1999 issue of *The School Administrator* magazine.

The claim by conservative social commentators that multicultural education will divide the nation assumes that it is now united. However, our nation is deeply divided along racial, ethnic and social-class lines. Multicultural education is trying to help unify a deeply divided nation, not to divide one that is united.

Multicultural theorists assume that we cannot unite the nation around its democratic ideals by forcing people from different racial, ethnic and cultural groups to leave their cultures and languages at the schoolhouse door. An important principle of a democratic society is that citizens will voluntarily participate in the commonwealth and that their participation will enrich the nation-state.

When citizens participate in society and bring their cultural strengths to the national civic culture, both they and the nation are enriched. Renato Rosaldo, the Stanford anthropologist, calls this kind of civic participation *cultural citizenship*.

We can create an inclusive, democratic and civic national community only when we change the center to make it more inclusive and reflective of the diversity that enriches our nation. This will require that we bring people and groups that are now on the margins of society into the center.

Schools should be model communities that mirror the kind of democratic society we envision. In democratic schools the curriculum reflects the cultures of the diverse groups within society, the languages and dialects that students speak are respected and valued, cooperation rather than competition is fostered among students and students from diverse racial, ethnic and social-class groups are given equal status in the school.

Major Challenges

Several societal trends present challenges for educating effective citizens in the new century. These trends include the growing ethnic, racial, cultural and language diversity in the United States, caused in part by the largest influx of immigrants to the nation since the beginning of the 20th century.

Unlike in the past, most immigrants are coming from nations in Asia and Latin America. Only a small percentage of the immigrants are coming from European nations. U.S. Census projections indicate that people of color will make up 47.5 percent of the nation's population by 2050. Students of color will make up about 48 percent of the nation's school-age youth by 2020. In 1995, they made up 35 percent of the nation's public school students.

The increasing percentage of school-age youth who speak a first language other than English and the widening gap between the rich and poor also present challenges to educating effective citizens in the new century. In 1990, 14 percent of school-age youth spoke a first language other than English. One in every five was living below the official government poverty line.

Addressing Diversity

The challenge to school leaders is to find ways to ensure that the rich contributions that diverse groups can make to our nation and the public schools becomes a reality. The cultural and language groups within our nation have values, perspectives and languages that can help the nation solve some of its intractable problems and humanize the lives of all of its citizens. During World War II the lives of many American soldiers were saved because the Navajo language was used in a secret code that perplexed military leaders in Japan. The code contributed to the victory of the Allies in the South Pacific and also was used in the Korean and Vietnam wars.

In order for multicultural education to be implemented in ways that will help actualize effective citizenship education, improve race relations and increase the academic achievement of students from diverse groups, the field must be viewed broadly and attention must be paid to the research that has accumulated during the last two decades. This research, briefly summarized below, is reviewed extensively in the *Handbook of Research on Multicultural Education.*

Too often multicultural education is conceptualized narrowly to mean adding content about diverse groups to the curriculum or expanding the canon taught in schools. It also should help students to develop more democratic racial and ethnic attitudes and to understand the cultural assumptions that underlie knowledge claims.

Another important dimension of multicultural education is equity pedagogy, in which teachers modify their teaching in ways that will facilitate the academic achievement of students from diverse racial, cultural, language and social-class groups.

What Research Says

Educational leaders should become familiar with the research evidence about the effects of multicultural education and not be distracted by the critics of multicultural education who disregard or distort this significant body of research.

Research indicates that students come to school with many stereotypes, misconceptions and negative attitudes toward outside racial and ethnic groups. Research also indicates that the use of multicultural textbooks, other teaching materials and cooperative teaching strategies can help students to develop more positive racial attitudes and perceptions.

This research also indicates that these kinds of materials and teaching strategies can result in students choosing more friends from outside racial, ethnic and cultural groups.

Research indicates that teachers can increase the classroom participation and academic achievement of students from different ethnic groups by modifying their instruction so that it draws upon their cultural strengths. In Susan Philips' study, *The Invisible Culture: Communication in Classroom and Community on the Warm Spring Indian Reservation,* American Indian students participated more actively in class discussions when teachers used group-oriented participation structures that were consistent with their community cultures.

Researchers Kathryn Au and Roland G. Tharp, working in the Kamehameha Early Education Program in Honolulu, Hawaii, found that both student participation and standardized achievement test scores increased when they incorporated teaching strategies consistent with the cultures of Native Hawaiian students and used the children's experiences in reading instruction.

Studies summarized by Linda Darling-Hammond, a Stanford University professor and executive director of the National Center for Restructuring Education and Teaching, indicate that the academic achievement of students of color and low-income students increases when they have high-quality teachers who are experts in their content specialization, pedagogy and child development. She points to a significant study by Robert Dreeben, the University of Chicago sociologist. He found that when African American students receive high-quality instruction their reading achievement was as high as that of white students. The quality of instruction, not the race of the students, was the significant variable.

The Future

School leaders should recognize that the goals of multicultural education are highly consistent with those of the nation's schools: to develop thoughtful citizens who can function effectively in the world of work and in the civic community. Ways must be found for schools to recognize and respect the cultures and languages of students from diverse groups while at the same time working to develop an overarching national culture to which all groups will have allegiance.

This can best be done by bringing groups that are on the margins of society into the center, educating students who have the knowledge, skills and values needed to rethink and change the center so that it is more inclusive and incorporating the research and theory in multicultural education into school reform.

Rethinking and re-imaging our nation in ways that will make it more just and equitable will enrich us all because the fates of all groups are tightly interconnected. Martin Luther King Jr. said, "We will live together as brothers and sisters or die separate and apart as strangers." ∎

POST NOTE

Multicultural education is a controversial issue, partly because there is no generally accepted definition. Some people see multicultural education as being divisive, creating separate pockets of different cultures, rather than helping to create a common culture. Others see multicultural education as valuing cultural pluralism, and recognizing that cultural diversity is a valuable resource that should be preserved and extended. James Banks rejects both assimilation and separatism as ultimate goals. He recognizes that each subculture exists as part of an interrelated whole. Multicultural education reaches beyond awareness and understanding of cultural differences to recognize the right of these different cultures to exist and to value that existence.

In addition to valuing cultural diversity, multicultural education is also based on the concept of *social justice,* which seeks to do away with social and economic inequalities for those in our society who have been denied these benefits of a democratic society. African Americans, Native Americans, Asian Americans, Hispanic Americans, women, disabled individuals, people with limited English proficiency, persons with low incomes, members of particular religious groups, and gays are among those groups that have at one time or another been denied social justice. Educators who support multicultural education see establishing social justice for all groups of people who have experienced discrimination as a moral and ethical responsibility. Extending the concept of multicultural education to include a broader population has also contributed to its controversy.

DISCUSSION QUESTIONS

1. In your own words, what does multicultural education mean?

2. In your opinion, should cultural pluralism be a goal of our society and its schools? Why or why not?

3. What examples of multicultural education can you describe from your own education?

69

Multicultural Illiteracy

Sandra Stotsky

The meaning of the word "diversity" has been badly abused in recent decades. American educators have long honored diversity in the only educationally meaningful sense of the word—individual difference.

For generations teachers were trained to look at students as individuals. Each student was supposedly endowed with a different combination of talents, abilities, interests and opinions. There is no question that this way of understanding diversity created strong positive educational outcomes and could continue to do so. Intellectual or social conformity has never been an American trait.

But in an Orwellian transformation of the meaning of the word, diversity has come to mean looking at a student as a representative of a particular demographic category. It now conveys the erroneous notion that, for example, all girls think and learn in one way, all boys in another or that all black students think and learn in one way, all Asians in another, all white students in yet another. To see students as members of a particular racial category or "culture" (to use current educational jargon), rather than as unique individuals, makes all the difference in the world.

Few positive outcomes are possible in an educational system that slots all students into spurious racial categories and then attaches fictitious ways

Sandra Stotsky is Deputy Commissioner for Academic Affairs and Planning for the Massachusetts Department of Education and a research associate with the Philosophy of Education Research Center at the Harvard University Graduate School of Education. She is the author of *Losing Our Language: How Multicultural Classroom Instruction Is Undermining Our Children's Ability to Read, Write, and Reason*. Reprinted with permission from the May 1999 issue of *The School Administrator* magazine.

of thinking, learning and knowing to each. The result is not the elimination of stereotypes but the freezing of them.

Classified by Category

We always have had different races and ethnic groups in our schools, although not in the same numbers or kinds in all schools. I grew up in a small Massachusetts town in which the children or grandchildren of early 20th century immigrants were as numerous as the children of those whose families had lived in the town for several hundred years.

As children, we all knew each others' backgrounds. We knew who spoke Italian, Armenian, Greek, Portuguese, Lithuanian, Polish or French Canadian in their home. We knew which families attended the local Catholic church, one of the many Protestant churches in town or the synagogue in a neighboring city. But not one of my teachers, in my presence, ever denigrated our ethnic, linguistic or religious backgrounds. Indeed, what they emphasized was something all our parents wanted them to stress. All of us, we were told repeatedly, were American citizens. And we were individual American citizens, not Lithuanian Americans, Irish Americans and so on, even though our parents may have belonged to the local Lithuanian, Polish or Italian social club or read an Armenian or Polish newspaper. We were not classified into racial or ethnic categories for any purpose.

Yes, there was prejudice in America. Why should this country be different from the others? But we all knew from our families there was even more prejudice elsewhere in the world, especially in those countries from which our families had come. Furthermore, the prejudice here was not just in those families who had been here for generations, it was also in the newcomers.

Every group had its own prejudices toward outsiders, as we all learned through experience, and it didn't bother us much. It was just another one of life's many hurdles to surmount. What was more important was that we all lived under the same set of laws as American citizens. These were ideals, to be sure, not always realities, but they were official ideals with teeth behind them, and we learned that they could be appealed to or drawn on, as women found in the early part of the century in gaining the right to vote, or as court decisions and civil rights legislation showed us in the 1950s and 1960s.

Fortunately for us, our teachers didn't subject us to endless lessons on tolerance and on how to be respectful of each other's "culture." They simply modeled tolerance for us and dealt, briefly, with problematic incidents whenever they arose in school. We were thus able to spend most of our school time on academic matters. Our main responsibility was to go to school every day, to be respectful of our teachers and to do our homework.

It's true we didn't see our home cultures in what we read in school, but we identified with each other as American citizens, something we and our parents were proud to be, despite our country's flaws. We probably would have welcomed attempts at a realistic curriculum that included more information or literature on the many immigrant groups in this country, as well as on the African Americans and Native Americans, but only if it did not end up making it more difficult for us to learn how to read and write English or giving us a warped or dishonest view of our own country and the larger world within which we live.

Negative Connotations

It is highly ironic that multiculturalism has evolved as an educational philosophy from its original and positive meaning of inclusion to mean something very negative, especially for us. This was one of the major findings of my research on the contents of all the grade 4 and grade 6 readers in six leading basal reading series, published between 1993 and 1995, as reported in *Losing Our Language*.

Rather than broadening students' horizons about the ethnic diversity of this country, today's

version of multiculturalism has led to the suppression of the stories of most immigrant groups to this country. Overall, the selections in these readers convey the picture of an almost monolithic white world, with none of the real ethnic diversity that can be seen in just the listing of restaurants in a telephone directory for any city in this country. Almost all of the various European ethnic groups I grew up with have been excluded. Instead of the real America, we find a highly shrunken mainstream culture in most series, surrounded by Native Americans, Asian Americans, African Americans and Hispanics, none of whom seem to interact much with each other.

Nor do today's readers give children an informed understanding of the real world within which they live. Nowhere do children read about the first airplane flight, the first transatlantic flight, the first exploration of space, the discovery of penicillin or the polio vaccine or how such inventions as the light bulb, radio, telegraph, steamboat, telephone, sewing machine, phonograph or radar came about. Apparently, accounts of these significant discoveries or inventions have been banished from students' common knowledge because most portray the accomplishments of white males.

But without the stories about the pioneers in science and technology (a few of whom were females, like Marie Curie), both boys and girls are unlikely to acquire a historically accurate timeframe for sequencing the major discoveries that have shaped their life today. The greater loss is that of an educational role model. The current substitutes for these stories in the readers—stories about people who have overcome racism or sexism or physical disabilities—are unlikely to give children insights into the power of intellectual curiosity in sustaining perseverance or the role of intellectual gratification in rewarding this perseverance.

Wayward Literacy

The most visible problem I found in the readers is at the level of language itself. The kinds of selections now featured in the readers make it almost impossible for children to develop a rich, literate vocabulary in English over the grades. In some series, children must learn a dazzling array of proper nouns, words for the mundane features of daily life, words for ethnic foods in countries around the world and other non-English words, most of which contribute little if anything to the development of their competence in the English language.

For example, consider this paragraph near the end of a story in a grade 4 reader: "In the wee hours of the morning, the family made a circle around Grandma Ida, Beth and Chris. Grandma Ida gave the *tamshi la tutaonana:* 'In this new year let us continue to practice *umoja, kujichagulia, ujima, ujamaa, nia, kuumba* and *imani.* Let us strive to do something that will last as long as the earth turns and water flows.'"

Or consider this sentence in another grade 4 reader: "The whole family sat under wide trees and ate arroz con gandules, pernil, viandas and tostones, ensalada de chayotes y tomates and pasteles."

Or these sentences in a grade 6 reader: "On the *engawa* after dinner, Mr. Ono said to Mitsuo, 'Take Lincoln to the dojo. You are not too tired, are you, Lincoln-kun?'"

Not only are children in this country unlikely to see any of these Swahili, Spanish or Japanese words in any of their textbooks in science, mathematics or history, they are unlikely to see them in any other piece of literature as well. They have wasted their intellectual energy not only learning their meaning but also learning how to pronounce them. It is not clear why these academically useless words, some of which are italicized, some not, are judged to be of importance by contemporary teacher educators.

These educators also seem to think that children should spend a considerable amount of class time engaged in conversations with each other about each other's ethnic cultures and daily lives—in the name of building self-esteem and group identity. But using precious class time for frequent conversations about intellectually barren topics that draw on intellectually limited vocabularies deprives the very students who most need it of opportunities to practice using the lexical building blocks necessary for conceptual growth and analytical thinking.

The present version of multiculturalism may well be largely responsible, through its effects on classroom materials and instruction, for the growing gap between the scores of minority students and other students on the National Assessment of Educational Progress examinations in reading. We need public discussions of the goals that should dominate reading instruction. Do we want teachers absorbed with the development of their children's egos, intent on shaping their feelings about themselves and others in specific ways? Or do we want teachers to concentrate on developing their children's minds, helping them acquire the knowledge, vocabulary and analytical skills that enable them to think for themselves and to choose the kind of personal identity they find most meaningful? ■

POST NOTE

Raw perception of people and things can quickly overpower us and submerge us in a sea of confusion. The human mind fights back by organizing perceptions into categories and putting labels on those categories: boys, girls, friends, enemies, tall people, short people, conservatives, liberals. However, as soon as we have labeled someone, distortions and mischief tend to set in. Tim with his enormous array of talents is labeled "the ADD [attention deficient disorder] kid." Teresa with all her budding potentialities is "that Hispanic girl." Although we can't live without categories and a method of labeling, we must be constantly vigilant of their limitations and their dangers. Sandra Stotsky's essay points out how, in her lifetime, a system of labeling has changed. She raises serious questions about the education consequences of this change.

D I S C U S S I O N Q U E S T I O N S

1. State three major points from this essay.

2. What is the difference between the meaning of "diversity" in today's schools and the schools of Stotsky's youth?

3. How do you believe the reality of multiculturalism should be dealt with in our schools?

The Culture/Learning Style Connection: Educating for Diversity

Pat Guild

Cultures do have distinctive learning style patterns, but the great variation among individuals within groups means that educators must use diverse teaching strategies with all students.

Our ability to give every child a chance to succeed in school depends upon a full understanding of culture and learning styles. After all, effective educational decisions and practices must emanate from an understanding of the ways that individuals learn. Consequently, knowing each student, especially his or her culture, is essential preparation for facilitating, structuring, and validating successful learning for all students.

This imperative leads to three critical questions. Do students of the same culture have common learning style patterns and characteristics? If they do, how would we know it? And most important, what are the implications for educators?

These questions are both important and controversial. They are important because we need all the information we can get to help every learner succeed in school and because our understanding of the learning process is the basis for decisions about curriculum and instruction. They

Pat Guild is owner of Pat Guild Associates. From Guild, Pat, "The Culture/Learning Style Connection." *Educational Leadership*, May 1994. Reprinted by permission from ASCD and the author. All rights reserved.

are important because success for the diverse populations that schools serve calls for continual reexamination of educators' assumptions, expectations, and biases. And they are important because, ultimately, every educational decision is evaluated according to its impact on individual students' learning.

One reason that the linkage between culture and learning styles is controversial is that generalizations about a group of people have often led to naive inferences about individuals within that group. Although people connected by culture do exhibit a characteristic pattern of style preferences, it is a serious error to conclude that all members of the group have the same style traits as the group taken as a whole.

A second source of controversy is the understandable sensitivity surrounding attempts to explain the persistent achievement differences between minority and nonminority students—it is all too easy to confuse descriptions of differences with explanations for deficits. Finally, the relationship between culture and learning styles is controversial because it brings us face to face with philosophical issues that involve deeply held beliefs. Debaters in the uniformity versus diversity dispute, for instance, differ over whether instructional equality is synonymous with educational equity. Another debate concerns the ultimate purpose of schooling. Is it "cultural pluralism" or the "melting pot"?

A highly public example of how sensitive these issues are occurred in 1987 when the state of New York published a booklet to help decrease the student dropout rate. A small section of the booklet described the learning styles typical of minority students and identified certain patterns associated with African-American students.

These descriptions became the subject of intense scrutiny and animated debate. Eventually, the descriptions were deleted from the booklet. Nonetheless, in the New York State Regent's Report, a review panel reiterated that:

> learning style and behavioral tendency do exist, and students from particular socialization and cultural experiences often possess approaches

to knowledge that are highly functional in the indigenous home environment and can be capitalized upon to facilitate performance in academic settings (Claxton 1990).

How We Know That Culture and Ways of Learning Are Linked

There is very little disagreement that a relationship does exist between the culture in which children live (or from which they are descended) and their preferred ways of learning. This relationship, further, is directly related to academic, social, and emotional success in school.

These conclusions are not as simple or definite as they seem, however. Though many syntheses and surveys have discussed the interdynamics of different cultures and ways of learning, each comes from a very distinctive approach, focusing either on a specific learning style model or a particular cultural group. No work, to my knowledge, claims to be comprehensive on the topic of culture and learning styles.

In general, researchers have reported three kinds of information about culture and learning styles.

The first is the set of observation-based descriptions of cultural groups of learners. For the most part, people who are familiar with each group have written these descriptions to sensitize people outside the culture to the experiences of children inside the culture. They have often contrasted minority students' learning patterns with European-American students' ways of learning and the school practices designed for such students.

Researchers have identified typical learning patterns among African Americans (Hale-Benson 1986, Shade 1989, Hilliard 1989), Mexican Americans (Ramirez 1989, Vasquez 1991, Berry 1979, Cox and Ramirez 1981), and Native Americans (Bert and Bert 1992, More 1990, Shade 1989).

The reports conclude that Mexican Americans regard family and personal relationships as important and are comfortable with cognitive generalities and patterns (Cox and Ramirez 1981,

Vasquez 1991). Such traits explain why Mexican-American students often seek a personal relationship with a teacher and are more comfortable with broad concepts than component facts and specifics.

Research about the African-American culture shows that students often value oral experiences, physical activity, and loyalty in interpersonal relationships (Shade 1989, Hilliard 1989). These traits call for classroom activities that include approaches like discussion, active projects, and collaborative work.

Descriptions indicate that Native-American people generally value and develop acute visual discrimination and skills in the use of imagery, perceive globally, and have reflective thinking patterns (Shade 1989, More 1990, Bert and Bert 1992). Thus, schooling should establish a context for new information, provide quiet times for thinking, and emphasize visual stimuli.

In contrast, the observers describe mainstream white Americans as valuing independence, analytic thinking, objectivity, and accuracy. These values translate into learning experiences that focus on competition, information, tests and grades, and linear logic. These patterns are prevalent in most American schools.

A second way that we know about the links between culture and learning styles is data-based descriptions of specific groups. In this class of inquiry, researchers administer learning style/cognitive style instruments to produce a profile of a cultural group, compare this group with another previously studied one (usually white Americans), or validate a particular instrument for cross-cultural use.

The various formal assessment instruments that purport to measure learning styles detect differences in two general ways. In the category of instruments that looks for style preferences, respondents usually self-report their favored approaches to learning. The best known instrument of this kind is probably the Myers-Briggs Type Indicator. It infers learning style patterns from basic perceptual and judging traits.

Another type of assessment instrument tests style strengths, that is, the ability to do tasks with a certain approach. The Swassing-Barbe Modality Index, for example, asks test takers to repeat patterns given auditorily, visually, and tactilely. Another example is the well-known series of assessments that distinguishes between field-dependence and independence. In this series, the test taker tries to find a simple figure embedded in a more complex one. The results show differences in cognitive strengths, such as global, holistic learning in contrast to analytic, part-to-whole approaches.

Formal assessment data should be interpreted (though often, it is not) in the light of the kind of assessment used. An important fact about self-report instruments, for instance, is that they are language- and culture-specific. In other words, when test takers respond to specific words, they interpret the words through their cultural experiences.

Further, different assessments may yield conflicting results. For instance, someone might self-report a preference for learning something in a certain way and yet test out in a different way on a task involving strengths. It is equally possible for descriptions based on observations to conflict with self-reported preferences.

These inconsistencies do not invalidate the usefulness of each of the ways of assessing learning styles. They do point out, however, that understanding learning patterns is a complex task and that the scope of the diagnostic tool used imposes limits on generalizations that can be drawn on the basis of it. Further, the characteristics of the assessment instruments used often account for the seemingly contradictory information reported about groups of learners.

The third way we know about the relationship of learning and culture is through direct discussion. Shade (1989), for instance, comments that:

> . . . perceptual development differs within various ethnocultural groups. It is therefore an erroneous assumption in the teaching-learning process to assume children "see" the same event, idea, or object in the same way.

Cognitive styles research, Ramirez (1989) believes, could help accommodate children who see

things differently. The research findings, he notes, provide "a framework to look at and be responsive to diversity within and between cultures."

Bennett (1986) warns that ignoring the effects of culture and learning styles would depress learning among nonmainstream students:

> If classroom expectations are limited by our own cultural orientations, we impede successful learners guided by another cultural orientation. If we only teach according to the ways we ourselves learn best, we are also likely to thwart successful learners who may share our cultural background but whose learning styles deviate from our own.

Accepted Conclusions about Culture and Learning Styles

Those who study culture and those who study learning styles generally agree on at least five points.

1. Educators concur that students of any particular age will differ in their ways of learning. (Guild and Garger 1985). Both empirical research and experiences validate these learning style differences, which in their cognitive, affective, and behavioral dimensions, help us to understand and talk about individual learning processes.

2. Most researchers believe that learning styles are a function of both nature and nurture. Myers (1990) asserts that:

> Type development starts at a very early age. The hypothesis is that type is inborn, an innate predisposition like right- or left-handedness, but the successful development of type can be greatly helped or hindered by environment.

Some researchers downplay the innate aspects of learning style, preferring to focus on the impact of environment. Many place great importance on the early socialization that occurs within the family, immediate culture, and wider culture.

3. Most researchers also believe that learning styles are neutral (Guild and Garger 1985). Every learning style approach can be used successfully, but can also become a stumbling block if applied inappropriately or overused.

This concept in the learning styles literature says a great deal about the effects of different learning approaches with different school tasks. Without question, for example, an active, kinesthetic learner has a more difficult time in school because of the limited opportunities to use that approach, especially for the development of basic skills. Nonetheless, the kinesthetic approach is a successful way to learn, and many adults, including teachers and administrators, use this approach quite effectively. Howard Gardner's (1983, 1991) identification of various intelligences has helped people appreciate the strengths of various approaches to learning.

4. In both observational and data-based research on cultures, one consistent finding is that, within a group, the variations among individuals are as great as their commonalities. Therefore, no one should automatically attribute a particular learning style to all individuals within a group (Griggs and Dunn 1989).

This subtle point is often verbally acknowledged, but ignored in practice. Cox and Ramirez (1981) explain the result:

> Recognition and identification of . . . average differences have had both positive and negative effects in education. The positive effect has been the development of an awareness of the types of learning that our public schools tend to foster. . . . The negative effect . . . is that the great diversity within a culture is ignored and a construct that should be used as a tool for individualization becomes yet another label for categorizing and evaluating.

5. Finally, many authors acknowledge the cultural conflict between some students and the typical learning experiences in schools. When a child is socialized in ways that are inconsistent with school expectations and patterns, the child needs to make a difficult daily adjustment to the culture of the school and his or her teachers. Hale-Benson (1986) points out the added burden this adjustment places on black youngsters:

> Black children have to be prepared to imitate the "hip," "cool" behavior of the culture in

which they live and at the same time take on those behaviors that are necessary to be upwardly mobile.

Debates about Applying Theory on Culture and Learning Styles

The published literature recommends caution in applying knowledge about culture and learning styles to the classroom. This prudence seems advisable because, despite the accepted ideas, at least five differences of opinion persist.

1. People differ, for instance, on whether educators should acquire more explicit knowledge about particular cultural values and expectations. Proponents say that such knowledge would enable educators to be more sensitive and effective with students of particular cultures. Certain states even mandate such information as part of their goals for multiculturalism.

Other authors argue, however, that describing cultures has resulted in more stereotyping and may well lead to a differentiated, segregated approach to curriculum. For example, Cox and Ramirez (1981) note that "the concept of cognitive or learning styles of minority and other students is one easily oversimplified, misunderstood, or misinterpreted." The authors go on to say that misuse of the concept has led to stereotyping and labeling rather than the identification of educationally meaningful differences among individuals.

2. Authors also debate the proper response to the fact that the culture-learning styles relationship affects student achievement. Evidence suggests that students with particular learning style traits (field-dependent, sensing, extraversion) are underachievers in school, irrespective of their cultural group. Students with such dominant learning style patterns have limited opportunities to use their style strengths in the classroom.

Even more disheartening is the practice of remediating problems so that the learner conforms to school expectations, rather than structuring school tasks in ways that respond to students' strengths. With the current emphasis on the inclusion of all learners in classrooms, it seems essential to change that practice.

Another achievement problem is the serious inequity that results when certain cultures value behaviors that are undervalued in school. Will increased attention to culture and learning styles eradicate this problem?

Hilliard (1989) thinks not:

I remain unconvinced that the explanation for the low performance of culturally different "minority group" students will be found by pursuing questions of behavioral style. . . . Children, no matter what their style, are failing primarily because of systemic inequities in the delivery of whatever pedagogical approach the teachers claim to master—not because students cannot learn from teachers whose styles do not match their own.

Bennett (1986) agrees that accommodating learning styles won't solve all problems:

We must be careful . . . not to view learning styles as the panacea that will eliminate failure in the schools. To address learning styles is often a necessary, but never sufficient, condition of teaching.

3. Another unresolved issue is how teachers working from their own cultures and teaching styles can successfully reach diverse populations. Bennett (1986) sums up the problem this way:

To the extent that teachers teach as they have been taught to learn, and to the extent that culture shapes learning style, students who share a teacher's ethnic background will be favored in class.

Some argue, though, that teachers properly play a special role in representing their own culture. Hale-Benson (1986), for example, says:

It is incumbent upon black professionals to identify the intelligences found especially in black children and to support the pursuit of their strengths.

Yes, that seems sensible. But we have all learned successfully from teachers who were neither like us in learning style or in culture. Often, these were masterful, caring teachers. Sometimes our own motivation helped us learn in spite of a teacher. Clearly, neither culture nor style is destiny. Just as clearly, though, teachers of all cultures and styles will have to work conscientiously to provide equitable opportunities for all students.

4. How cultural identity and self-esteem are related remains an open question, too. Many large city school systems are wrestling with the appropriateness of ethnically identified schools, such as an African-American academy. Bilingual programs continue to debate the value of instruction in the students' first language.

I would add to this discussion a remark of Carl Jung's: "If a plant is to unfold its specific nature to the full, it must first be able to grow in the soil in which it is planted" (Barger and Kirby 1993). This comment has led me to argue against the approach to learning so prevalent in our schools (especially in special education programs), which emphasizes the identification and remediation of deficiencies.

An acceptance of learning styles demands an approach that develops skills through strengths. Should the same not be said of cultural identity?

5. Perhaps the most weighty of the application issues has to do with ways to counteract our tendency toward instructional pendulum swings. This oscillation has become so predictable in schooling in our country. Today it's phonics. Tomorrow whole language. The day after that, phonics again. We are always seeking one right way to teach, and when we accumulate evidence that a strategy is effective with some students, we try to apply it to every student in every school.

A deep understanding of culture and learning styles makes this behavior seem naive. If instructional decisions were based on an understanding of each individual's culture and ways of learning, we would never assume that uniform practices would be effective for all. We would recognize that the only way to meet diverse learning needs would be to intentionally apply diverse strategies. As Bennett (1986) says, equitable opportunities for success demand "unequal teaching methods that respond to relevant differences among students."

Ideas about culture and learning styles can be of great help to teachers as they pursue such intentional instructional diversity. A teacher who truly understands culture and learning styles and who believes that all students can learn, one way or another, can offer opportunities for success to all students.

Not Easy, but Crucial

While the culture/learning styles relationship is deceptively simple and the issues surrounding it are complex, it is a crucially important idea to contemplate. We should not be reluctant to do so for fear of repeating past mistakes. With a better understanding of these missteps, we can avoid them in the future. As Hilliard (1989) assures us:

Educators need not avoid addressing the question of style for fear they may be guilty of stereotyping students. Empirical observations are not the same as stereotyping, but the observations must be empirical and must be interpreted properly for each student.

As we try to accommodate students' cultural and learning differences, it is most important to deeply value each person's individuality. If we believe that people do learn—and have the right to learn—in a variety of ways, then we will see learning styles as a comprehensive approach guiding all educational decisions and practices. The ideas will not become ends in themselves, which would merely support the uniformity found in most schools.

Using information about culture and learning styles in sensitive and positive ways will help educators value and promote diversity in all aspects of the school. This task will not be easy, but then teaching is not a profession for the faint of heart. It requires courage and a willingness to grapple with real questions about people and their learning. Many students stand to benefit from that effort. ■

References

Barger, N. J., and L. K. Kirby. (Fall 1993). "The Interaction of Cultural Values and Type Development: INTP Women Across Cultures." *Bulletin of Psychological Type* 16: 14–16.

Bennett, C. (1986). *Comprehensive Multicultural Education, Theory and Practice.* Boston: Allyn and Bacon.

Berry, J. W. (1979). "Culture and Cognitive Style." In *Perspectives on Cross-Cultural Psychology,* edited by A. Marsella, R. Tharp, and T. Ciborowski. San Francisco: Academic Press.

Bert, C. R. G., and M. Bert. (1992). *The Native American: An Exceptionality in Education and Counseling.* (ERIC Document Reproduction Service No. ED 351 168).

Claxton, C. S. (Fall 1990). "Learning Styles, Minority Students, and Effective Education." *Journal of Developmental Education* 14: 6–8, 35.

Cox, B., and M. Ramierez III. (1981). "Cognitive Styles: Implications for Multiethnic Education." In *Education in the '80s,* edited by J. Banks, Washington, D.C.: National Education Association.

Gardner, H. (1983). *Frames of Mind.* New York: Basic Books.

Gardner, H. (1991). *The Unschooled Mind: How Children Think and How Schools Should Teach.* New York: Basic Books.

Griggs, S. A., and R. Dunn. (1989). "The Learning Styles of Multicultural Groups and Counseling Implications." *Journal of Multicultural Counseling and Development* 17: 146–155.

Guild, P., and S. Garger. (1985). *Marching to Different Drummers.* Alexandria, Va.: Association for Supervision and Curriculum Development.

Hale-Benson, J. E. (1986). *Black Children: Their Roots, Culture, and Learning Styles,* Rev. ed. Baltimore: Johns Hopkins University Press.

Hilliard, A. G., III. (January 1989). "Teachers and Cultural Styles in a Pluralistic Society." *NEA Today:* 65–69.

More, A. J. (1990). "Learning Styles of Native Americans and Asians." Paper presented at the Annual Meeting of the American Psychological Association, Boston. (ERIC Document Reproduction Service No. ED 330 535)

Myers, I. B. (1990). *Gifts Differing,* 2nd ed. Palo Alto, Calif.: Consulting Psychologists Press.

Ramirez, M., III. (1989). "Pluralistic Education: A Bicognitive-Multicultural Model." *The Clearinghouse Bulletin 3:* 4–5.

Shade, B. J. (October 1989). "The Influence of Perceptual Development in Cognitive Style: Cross Ethnic Comparisons." *Early Child Development and Care 51:* 137–155.

Vasquez, J. A. (1991). "Cognitive Style and Academic Achievement." In *Cultural Diversity and the Schools: Consensus and Controversy,* edited by J. Lynch, C. Modgil, and S. Modgil. London: Falconer Press.

The author correctly points out that one's cultural background does affect preferred ways of learning. Guild also warns about the dangers of assuming that all people from a particular cultural background exhibit these preferred ways of learning. So what's a teacher to do? Should the teacher try to understand how different cultures emphasize traits that might influence what classroom activities are employed, and plan those activities accordingly? Or would such planning be guilty of stereotyping members of a particular culture? And what about teachers who have a number of different cultures represented by the students in their classes? How can all these cultural preferences be incorporated in the classroom?

The answer to these questions, according to the author, is for teachers to deliberately employ diverse instructional strategies, rather than rely on a few strategies that reflect the teacher's own personal learning preferences. Certainly, knowing about students' culture and learning styles can only help teachers to diversify their practices so all of their students find ways of learning that fit their own individual preferences and strengths.

DISCUSSION **Q**UESTIONS

1. Have you ever taken any of the learning styles inventories, such as the Myers-Briggs Type Indicator or the Swassing-Barbe Modality Index? If so, what did you learn about how you prefer to learn?

2. What are some ways that you can learn about preferred learning patterns among different cultural groups, for example, African Americans or Mexican Americans?

3. After reading this article, what questions or issues concern you?

Where We Stand on the Rush to Inclusion

Albert Shanker

United States education is in trouble and there are a lot of reasons for it. One of them is the tendency of American education to be moved—massively moved—by fads and ideologies. We can think back to the 1950s when I started teaching and something swept the country called the New Math. The overwhelming majority of teachers said it doesn't work; the kids don't get it; we don't get it. But it took 25 to 30 years before there was recognition of its weaknesses and a movement away from it. And New Math is not the only example of this phenomenon.

If we think of a field like medicine, we see that in the medical and pharmaceutical worlds, there are all sorts of cautions taken before new medicine is placed on the market. When something is discovered and you read about it in the newspapers, you know that you can't go out the next day and buy it at the drugstore because it has to be thoroughly tested before it becomes available. You know that there will be many additional experiments before this new remedy is marketed. When it finally becomes available, there are always all sorts of warnings attached.

Unfortunately, in education we tend to operate in such a way that one or two or a handful of people or advocacy groups grab on to some new idea, present it as a panacea, and "sell" it to an ed-

The late Albert Shanker was president of the American Federation of Teachers. From Albert Shanker, "Where We Stand on the Rush to Inclusion," *Vital Speeches of the Day,* vol. 60, no. 10 (March 1, 1994). Copyright © 1994 by Albert Shanker. Reprinted by permission.

ucational community that is hungry for answers. And once a fad is adopted, it takes a long, long period of time after the damage is done to undo it.

Now we have a rush towards something called inclusion. We don't know what the long-term effects are. We have had mainstreaming for more than 15 years, but in mainstreaming disabled students' progress was always being monitored by special education teachers. Inclusion was tried in only a few small places and immediately was viewed as the panacea, the only moral answer, the only way to educate students with disabilities. In addition, some people now claim that anybody who's against inclusion is immoral, a new segregationist, or antieducation. That kind of rhetoric is quite effective in shutting off discussion. There may be a lot of people who are intimidated or afraid to say anything, even though they don't like what's happening.

The inclusion that is being advocated is the placement of all students with disabilities into general education classrooms *without regard to the nature or severity of the students' disabilities, without regard to their ability to behave and function appropriately in a regular classroom, without regard to the educational benefits they derive, and without regard to the impact that that inclusion has on the other students in the class.* In other words, it's basically a view that this is the right thing to do, and it's the right thing under all circumstances. And there is a tremendous push on the part of some U.S. government officials, state boards of education, and a number of advocacy groups to implement that brand of inclusion.

Before we go any further with our discussion of inclusion, it's important to start with what schools are about. Schools have three functions: the development of knowledge and skills, the development of adults who are economically viable, and the development of social and interpersonal relations. Looked at another way, there are intellectual benefits, there are economic benefits, and there are political and social benefits in terms of developing the ability to function within a democracy. The argument on the part of the full inclusionists rests on the social benefits of education. Some have even stated that they don't care if other children don't learn to read and write, if they have learned to "get along."

Any new policy in American education that will affect what students learn and their interpersonal and social development should not be implemented hastily and certainly should not be implemented before there is full discussion and scrutiny of the issues. New programs should not be implemented without some periods of experimentation where we have an opportunity to see and judge the effects of actual implementation.

Large numbers of books are written about well-intentioned programs, things that the government tried to do in the '50s and '60s and '70s that didn't work out quite the way they were supposed to. I think many of these programs were worthwhile, even if they had some unintended consequences. But the fact is that we now know that we often get something that's quite different from what was envisioned in the first place. And, therefore, it's important to engage in some trial, some experimentation, before deciding that everybody has to do it in this particular way.

There is no doubt that every child, regardless of abilities, disabilities, problems, or status, has a right to a free public education. But that does not mean that any particular child has a right to a particular placement in a particular class or a particular school.

I believe that large numbers of students who are now separated in special education could undoubtedly be included and integrated in regular classrooms. I believe that it would be profitable for many students with disabilities and for the rest of the class if many disabled students not now being educated in regular classrooms were placed there. Therefore, I agree with those who say that we probably have too many youngsters separated out and many who could be integrated. Many of our members who are very concerned about this movement toward inclusion feel that way, too.

The AFT's [American Federation of Teachers'] position is not a movement to label and to separate and to create two systems. It is a position that says that we cannot make blanket decisions about every student. We cannot say that all students should be in regular classrooms whatever their disability, whatever their ability to function in a classroom and profit from it, and whatever the impact on the other youngsters.

We offer an alternative to the full inclusionists' point of view, and that alternative is that placement ought to depend on those very things. It ought to depend on the nature of the disability. It ought to depend on the ability of that child to function within a regular classroom. It ought to depend upon the impact of such a placement on that child and on all the other children.

In other words, we are staying away from ideology, away from the notion that the same thing fits all kids, that all kids have to be treated the same even though they're different. We need to treat youngsters in terms of what's best for them and not according to some ideological theory.

In each case, we need to ask what is the impact of a particular placement on the child who has a disability, and we also have to ask what is the impact on all the others in the class. We are especially concerned with children who are very emotionally disturbed and with children who are medically fragile and need medical attention throughout the day. Very little good is done by including children in a regular class if the entire academic mission of that class, the entire focus, becomes "How do we adjust to this child?" When the teacher and the paraprofessional and everybody else in the class focus on how to handle one particular child, what is the effect on the rest of the class?

If parents see that their kids are not getting out of school what they're supposed to be getting, that the entire class is focused on adjusting to one very disruptive child or on a child whose many medical needs must be met by the teacher, those parents are going to start pressing for vouchers. They're going to start pressing for the privatization of education, and instead of a public school system which includes many children of many different races, religions, nationalities, we're going to end up with highly separated and segregated schools. So that in the name of inclusion, we may end up getting the most separated and segregated school system that we can possibly have in this country. That is one of the central dangers of this movement.

One argument for inclusion is a civil rights argument. But this is based on a faulty analogy. Once upon a time, we used to segregate black youngsters and send them to separate schools. The Supreme Court of the United States ruled that even if you tried to provide equal facilities in those schools, separate can never be equal. The view in the full inclusion movement is that once you separate kids out, you label them, and there is a stigma attached to the label. Therefore, the argument goes, a judgement that was true for black youngsters during the period of segregation is also true for youngsters today who suffer from some disability. Therefore, it follows, we must end all separation.

The problem with the analogy is that it's not very accurate. Black youngsters were being kept out for one reason, because they were black, because of the color of their skin. There is the same range of learning abilities among black youngsters as among white youngsters, and the black students were kept out for a reason that was totally irrelevant and totally racist. It was race and not their ability to function within normal classrooms that kept them out. But if a youngster is kept out of the classroom because that youngster needs instruction in Braille or if a youngster is kept out of a classroom because his or her medical problems are not likely to be attended to in a regular classroom, we have something that's very different.

In one case, youngsters were separated out for a reason that was totally irrelevant to their education. As a matter of fact, it was destructive of their education. In another case, youngsters are being separated out because of special needs and special problems that they have. Two very, very different motivations and two very, very different attitudes.

We are saying that some children need separate classrooms not to harm them or because anyone desires that the youngsters be separated, but to meet their different and special educational needs. If a youngster is constantly violent and constantly noisy and disruptive, so the class can't function when that youngster is there, we need to separate that youngster out so that he or she can learn and so that the rest of the class can function.

I see no basis for the civil rights analogy. Black youngsters then were so eager to learn that, when the civil rights movement reached its height, they were willing to risk a great deal walking through lines of hostile people protected by troops, they were so eager to learn. This is very different from a youngster who is yelling and screaming and fighting and throwing things. The analogy just does not stand.

I would very strongly suggest that the way we should behave as educators and the way we should behave as individuals would be very much the way a caring and intelligent parent would act. What was very interesting about my appearance on a number of radio shows on this issue was that a number of parents who called in and talked about the fact that they had four or five children and they were very, very different. And parents who had an extremely disturbed youngster who was violent would not insist that that youngster be at all the other activities with all the other children. One youngster might be taking piano lessons; another might be athletically inclined; a third might be doing something else. Many of these parents were very concerned that one of the youngsters would disturb and disrupt and destroy the work of the other youngsters. It seems to me that the same kind of judgment that an intelligent parent would exercise ought to be exercised by all of us as a society.

Not very long ago, a film came out called "Educating Peter." I saw it last year at the AFT QuEST Conference . . . where we had a session on this issue. It is a very moving film, which was really put together to be an argument in favor of inclusion. What the film did not tell you was that inclusion there was really done right. That is, the teacher involved was given time off and given special training. There were additional personnel assigned to the class. All of the supports that are frequently missing were there.

But as I watched that film, I saw that Peter was very unpredictable and very disruptive, and on occasion violent. At the end of the film, he was less disruptive and able to relate to the teacher and the other youngsters a little bit more. The other youngsters had learned to accept him and live with him, and my heart went out. It is a tearjerker and you see that something very good was accomplished there because the kids were a little closer together. My emotional reactions were the same as everybody else who watched the film.

But I had another reaction, too. I wondered whether the youngsters in that class had spent a whole year in adjusting to how to live with Peter and whether they did any reading, whether they did any writing, whether they did any mathematics, whether they did any history, whether they did any geography. And it seems to me that it's a terrible shame that we don't ask that question. Is the only function of the schools to get kids to learn to live with each other? Would we be satisfied if that's what we did and if all the youngsters came out not knowing any of the things that they're supposed to learn academically? Will any of them, disabled or non-disabled, be able to function as adults?

We now have legislation, Goals 2000, that President Clinton is supporting and the governors are supporting. We have a National Educational Goals Panel. We have an attempt to lift the nation very quickly from a low level of performance to a high level of performance. There's great doubt as to whether we can do it, because it will be very difficult. We need coordination of three levels of government. We need substantial retraining of teachers. We need different attitudes on the part of students towards their work.

Do we really believe that we can simultaneously accomplish that mission and at the same time do something that no other country in the world has ever done? Do we really believe that we can take youngsters with very, very severe disabilities and, at the same time we're trying to get world-class education, include youngsters who need extensive medical attention and youngsters who are extremely disturbed and deal with all of their problems?

The advocates hope that by mixing all children, children with disabilities will gain the respect of children who are not disabled. I think the underlying motive is undeniably excellent— we're all going to be living together as adults; we're going to be working together as adults; and therefore, if we can live with each other as much as possible as youngsters in school, that will be the beginning of learning to live and work with each other as grownups. But if extremely disturbed, violent youngsters are put in the regular classrooms, do we really think that the other youngsters are going to learn respect—or are they going to learn contempt? Are they going to develop hostility? This rush to inclusion has created a situation where placements of students with disabilities are being made incorrectly in many cases. Because this is so, we may develop exactly the opposite values that we say that we want to develop.

One of the reasons for the push to inclusion is that taking youngsters with special needs out of small classrooms, not giving them special teachers, psychologists, social workers, therapists and other professionals, and including them with everybody else saves money. And during a period of time like this when school budgets are under attack, many of these youngsters are likely to lose their special help when they are placed in regular classrooms. Part of the thrust of the inclusion movement is saving money.

Some school districts see that special education is more expensive and reason that if they could push all disabled youngsters into regular education, they can squeeze some of the money out of their special education budgets and have special education go away. In theory, youngsters with special problems who are integrated into a regular class are supposed to have special services follow them. But given the financial situation of our states and school districts, and given the fact that the federal government has never met its commitment to fund its share of education for the disabled, does anybody really believe that the large amount of money that's necessary to provide these services in individual classrooms is going to be made available?

What we are doing here is very difficult to do. There are other organizations out there. There are people in those organizations who have thought

Where We Stand on the Rush to Inclusion

the same thoughts and felt the same things and had the same experiences and had letters and telephone calls from teachers and from parents and from administrators and from different constituents. Many have made public statements about their concerns. But it didn't seem that anyone who is pushing this movement would listen. In this climate, the AFT could not sit back and remain silent. We have joined them.

I want to conclude by saying that I think that we can turn this around. There are many, many advocacy groups in the special education field who are unhappy and uneasy with this policy. In the radio shows that I was on, there were parents whose youngsters were included who said they agreed with us because they weren't sure that their kids would be able to adjust, and they wanted the option of being able to move their kids back if it didn't work out. They liked the idea that they could try this out and if it worked, of course, they wanted it that way. But they didn't want it that way as a matter of policy. And they didn't want it that way as a matter of ideology.

I have a copy of a letter that appeared in the Eugene, Oregon, newspaper called *The Register-Guard*. It's a short letter, but it's one that really shows that somebody out there understands the issues and the politics of it very clearly. The headline is "Challenge and Inclusion." The letter says,

"Albert Shanker, President of the American Federation of Teachers, spoke the unspeakable when he suggested that not all special needs children should be fully mainstreamed or included in the regular classroom. The inclusion movement is both politically correct, namely satisfying the liberals, and cost-effective, namely satisfying the conservatives. By challenging it, Shanker has guaranteed himself attacks from both camps.

"I applaud his willingness to accept such attacks. I hope his comments will remind us that placement of special needs students should be based not on political correctness or economic expediency, but on a careful consideration of the physical, emotional, educational and social welfare of all the students involved. I have taught special needs students in special programs for 28 years. My goal and the goal of every special needs teacher I have known has always been to help students develop those skills, behaviors, and attitudes that would allow them to return to and succeed in the regular classroom, or upon leaving school, to succeed on the job and in their personal lives.

"Every special needs teacher I've ever known is dedicated to each student's placement in the least restrictive appropriate educational setting. However, in this era of cutbacks, special needs programs are being dismantled and special needs students are being included in regular classes. Classes . . . are increasing in size by five to ten students and . . . teacher's aides are being eliminated as further cost-saving measures. Certainly the inclusion movement is politically correct and certainly it's cost-effective. But please don't try to tell me it's good for the kids."

That's our view. ∎

POST NOTE

In this article Albert Shanker, who served for over two decades as president of the American Federation of Teachers, the second largest teacher organization in the United States, articulates the concerns that many AFT members have expressed about the inclusion movement in education. Many regular education teachers are angry about the full-inclusion movement because they see it as yet another educational idea that has been forced upon them.

As school budgets have become ever tighter, many teachers have come to believe that school boards and administrators are saving money on special education simply by placing students with disabilities in regular classrooms without providing adequate support for teachers. Further, since severely disabled students often require extra attention, Shanker's article raises concerns about whether the majority of students in classrooms are getting the best education. The issue is complicated and is likely to continue to provoke controversy.

DISCUSSION QUESTIONS

1. Which, if any, of Shanker's points seem most valid to you?

2. Is full inclusion a good idea? What limitations, if any, do you see in its implementation?

3. What retort to Shanker's arguments could you make?

What Do I Do Now?
A Teacher's Guide to
Including Students
with Disabilities

Michael F. Giangreco

A s students with disabilities are increasingly being placed in general education classrooms, teachers are asking many legitimate questions about what to do about their instruction and how to do it. For the past seven years, I've consulted with teachers, administrators, support personnel, and families who are grappling with these concerns. I've also joined with colleagues in conducting 12 research studies at some of these schools. The following suggestions are concrete actions to consider as you pursue success for both students with disabilities and their classmates.

1. Get a Little Help from Your Friends

No one expects teachers to know all the specialized information about every disability, or to do everything that may be necessary for a student with disabilities.

At the time this article was written, Michael F. Giangreco was research assistant professor, College of Education and Social Services, University of Vermont. Michael F. Giangreco, "What Do I Do Now? A Teacher's Guide to Including Students with Disabilities," from *Educational Leadership*, February 1996, Vol. 53, No. 5, pp. 56–59. Copyright © Michael F. Giangreco. Reprinted by permission.

Thus, in schools where students with disabilities are successful in general education classes, teams usually collaborate on individualized educational programs. Team members often include the student and his or her parents, general educators, special educators, para-educators, and support staff, such as speech and language pathologists, and physical therapists. And don't forget: each classroom includes some 20–30 students who are creative and energetic sources of ideas, inspiration, and assistance.

Although teamwork is crucial, look out for some common problems. When groups become unnecessarily large and schedule too many meetings without clear purposes or outcomes, communication and decision making get complicated and may overwhelm families. Further, a group is not necessarily a team, particularly if each specialist has his or her own goals. The real team shares a single set of goals that team members pursue in a coordinated way.

2. Welcome the Student in Your Classroom

Welcoming the student with disabilities may seem like a simple thing to do, and it is. But you'd be surprised how often it doesn't happen. It can be devastating for such a student (or any student) to feel as if he or she must earn the right to belong by meeting an arbitrary standard that invariably differs from school to school.

Remember, too, that your students look to you as their primary adult model during the school day. What do you want to model for them about similarities and differences, change, diversity, individuality, and caring?

So when children with disabilities come to your classroom, talk with them, walk with them, encourage them, joke with them, and teach them. By your actions, show all your students that the child with disabilities is an important member of your class and, by extension, of society.

3. Be the Teacher of All the Students

When a student with disabilities is placed in a general education class, a common practice is for the teacher to function primarily as a host rather than a teacher. Many busy teachers actually embrace this notion because it means someone else is responsible for that student. Many teachers, in fact, think of these students as the responsibility of the special education teacher or para-educator.

Merely hosting a student with disabilities, however, doesn't work very well (Giangreco et al. 1992). Inevitably, these other professionals will work with the student, and the "host" will end up knowing very little about the student's educational program or progress. This perpetuates a lack of responsibility for the student's education and often places important curricular and instructional decisions in the hands of hardworking, but possibly underqualified, paraprofessionals.

Be flexible, but don't allow yourself to be relegated to the role of an outsider in your own classroom. Remember that teachers who successfully teach students without disabilities have the skills to successfully teach students with disabilities (Giangreco et al. 1995).

4. Make Sure Everyone Belongs to the Classroom Community

How, where, when, and with whom students spend their time is a major determinant of their affiliations and status in the classroom (Stainback and Stainback 1996). Too often, students with disabilities are placed with mainstream students, but take part in different activities and have different schedules from their peers. These practices inhibit learning with and from classmates, and may contribute to social isolation.

To ensure that students with disabilities are part of what's happening in class, seat them with their classmates, and at the same kind of desk, not on the fringe of the class.

Make sure, too, that the student participates in the same activities as the rest of the class, even though his or her goals may be different. If the class is writing a journal, the student with a disability should be creating a journal, even if it's in a nonwritten form. If you assign students homework, assign it to this student at an appropriate level. In like manner, if the class does a science experiment, so should this student. Although individualization and supports may be necessary, the student's daily schedule should allow ample opportunities to learn, socialize, and work with classmates.

5. Clarify Shared Expectations with Team Members

One of the most common sources of anxiety for classroom teachers is not understanding what other team members expect them to teach. "Do I teach this student most of or all of what I'm teaching the other students?" Sometimes the answer will be yes, sometimes no. In either case, team members must agree on what the student should learn and who will teach it.

To do this, the team should identify a few of the student's learning priorities, as well as a larger set of learning outcomes as part of a broad educational program. Doing so will clarify which parts of the general curriculum the student will be expected to pursue and may include learning outcomes that are not typically part of the general program.

Many students with disabilities also need supports to participate in class. These supports should be distinguished from learning outcomes. If the supports are inadvertently identified as learning outcomes, the educational program may be unnecessarily passive.

Finally, on a one- or two-page program-at-a-glance, summarize the educational program, including, for example, priority learning outcomes, additional learning outcomes, and necessary supports (Giangreco et al. 1993). This concise list will help the team plan and schedule, serve as a reminder of the student's individual needs, and help you communicate those needs to teachers in special areas, such as art, music, and physical education. By clarifying what the team expects the student to learn, you set the stage for a productive school year.

6. Adapt Activities to the Student's Needs

When the educational needs of a student with disabilities differ from those of the majority of the class, teachers often question the appropriateness of the placement. It's fair to ask, for example, why an 11-year-old functioning at a 2nd grade level is placed in a 6th grade class.

The answer is that such a student can still have a successful educational experience. In fact, many schools are purposely developing multigrade classrooms, where teachers accommodate students with a wide range of abilities.

When a student's needs differ from other members of the class, it is important to have options for including that student in activities with classmates. In some cases, the student requires instructional accommodations to achieve learning outcomes within the same curriculum area as his or her classmates, but at a different level.

The student might need to learn, for example, different vocabulary words, math problems, or science concepts. Or the student may be pursuing learning outcomes from different curriculum areas. For example, during a science activity, the student could be learning communication, literacy, or socialization skills, while the rest of the class focuses on science.

7. Provide Active and Participatory Learning Experiences

I've heard teachers of students with disabilities say, "He wouldn't get much out of being in that class because the teacher does a lot of lecturing, and uses worksheets and paper-and-pencil tests." My first reaction is, "You're right, that situation doesn't seem to match the student's needs." But then I wonder, Is this educational approach also a mismatch for students without disability labels?

Considering the diversity of learning styles, educators are increasingly questioning whether passive, didactic approaches meet their students' needs. Activity-based learning, on the other hand, is well suited to a wide range of students. The presence of a student with disabilities may simply highlight the need to use more active and participatory approaches, such as individual or cooperative projects and use of art media, drama, experiments, field study, computers, research, educational games, multimedia projects, or choral responding (Thousand et al. 1994). Interesting, motivating activities carry an added bonus—they encourage positive social behaviors, and can diminish behavior problems.

8. Adapt Classroom Arrangements, Materials, and Strategies

Alternate teaching methods or other adaptations may be necessary. For example, if a group lecture isn't working, try cooperative groups, computer-assisted instruction, or peer tutoring. Or make your instruction more precise and deliberate.

Adaptations may be as basic as considering a different way for a student to respond if he or she has difficulty speaking or writing, or rearranging the chairs for more proximity to peers or access to competent modeling.

You may also have to adapt materials. A student with visual impairments may need tactile or auditory cues. A student with physical disabilities may require materials that are larger or easier to manipulate. And a student who is easily bored or distracted may do better with materials that are in line with his or her interests.

Rely on the whole team and the class to assist with adaptation ideas.

9. Make Sure Support Services Help

Having many support service personnel involved with students can be a help or a hindrance. Ideally, the support staff will be competent and collaborative, making sure that what they do prevents disruptions and negative effects on students' social relationships and educational programs. They will get to know the students and classroom routines, and also understand the teacher's ideas and concerns.

Teachers can become better advocates for their students and themselves by becoming informed consumers of support services. Learn to ask good questions. Be assertive if you are being asked to do something that doesn't make sense to you. Be as explicit as you can be about what type of support you need. Sometimes you may need particular information, materials, or someone to demonstrate a technique. Other times, you may need someone with whom to exchange ideas or just validate that you are headed in the right direction.

won't predict the impact of your teaching on the student's post-school life. Unfortunately, far too many graduates with disabilities are plagued by unemployment, health problems, loneliness, or isolation—despite their glowing school progress reports.

We need to continually evaluate whether students are applying their achievements to real life, by looking at the effects on their physical and emotional health, personal growth, and positive social relationships; and at their ability to communicate, advocate for themselves, make informed choices, contribute to the community, and increasingly access places and activities that are personally meaningful. The aim is to ensure that our teaching will make a real difference in our students' lives. ■

10. Evaluate Your Teaching

We commonly judge our teaching by our students' achievements. Although you may evaluate students with disabilities in some of the same ways as you do other students (for example, through written tests, reports, or projects), some students will need alternative assessment, such as portfolios adapted to their needs.

Often it is erroneously assumed that if students get good grades, that will translate into future educational, professional, and personal success. This is a dangerous assumption for any student, but particularly for those with disabilities. Although traditional tests and evaluations may provide certain types of information, they

References

Giangreco, M., D. Baumgart, and M.B. Doyle. (1995). "How Inclusion Can Facilitate Teaching and Learning." *Intervention in School land Clinic* 30, 5: 273–278.

Giangreco, M., C.J. Cloninger, and V. Iverson. (1993). *Choosing Options and Accommodations for Children: A Guide to Planning Inclusive Education.* Baltimore: Brookes.

Giangreco, M., R. Dennis, C. Cloninger, S. Edelman, and R Schattman. (1992). "I've Counted Jon': Transformational Experiences of Teachers Educating Students with Disabilities." *Exceptional Children* 59: 359–372.

Stainback, W., and S. Stainback. (1996). *Inclusion: A Guide for Educators.* Baltimore: Brookes.

Thousand, J., R. Villa, and A. Nevin. (1994). *Creativity and Collaborative Learning: A Practical Guide to Empowering Students and Teachers.* Baltimore: Brookes.

POST NOTE

The previous article on inclusion dealt mainly with policy issues. This article addresses what teachers can do to help ensure success for disabled students in their classrooms. Working successfully with disabled students is one of the most challenging tasks facing beginning teachers.

Almost 5 million students, about 11 percent of the total public school population, receive federal aid for their disabilities, so it is likely that you will have students with disabilities in your classroom. It is important that you approach instruction for these children as you do for other students: expect diversity, expect a range of abilities, and look for the particular strengths and learning profiles of each student. Work with the special education teachers in your school to coordinate instruction and services for your students with disabilities.

D I S C U S S I O N  U E S T I O N S

1. Which of the ten recommendations in the article did you find most helpful, and why?

2. The author asserts that "far too many graduates with disabilities are plagued by unemployment" despite their good performance in school. Why do you suppose this is true?

3. What concerns, if any, do you have about teaching children with disabilities? What can you do to address these concerns?

School Reform and Student Diversity

Catherine Minicucci,
Paul Berman,
Barry McLaughlin,
Beverly McLeod,
Beryl Nelson, and
Kate Woodworth

About one in seven of the nation's 5- to 17-year-olds speaks a home language other than English, and the number of such young people is growing.[1] During the 1980s the number of students considered to be limited English proficient (LEP) grew 2½ times faster than the general school enrollment.[2] LEP students are concentrated in large urban areas in a few states—California, New York, Texas, Florida, Illinois, and New Jersey—and in the rural areas of the Southwest.[3]

Nearly all language-minority students are also poor, and many are members of racial or ethnic minority groups as well. Most LEP children live in communities beset by poverty and violence and

At the time this article was written, Catherine Minicucci was head of Minicucci Associates, Sacramento, California; Paul Berman was president of BW Associates, Berkeley, California; Barry McLaughlin was director of the National Center for Research on Cultural Diversity and Second Language Learning, University of California, Santa Cruz; Beverly McLeod was a research affiliate at the National Center; Beryl Nelson was senior researcher at BW Associates; and Kate Woodworth was a researcher at BW Associates. Minicucci, Catherine, Paul Berman, Barry McLaughlin, Beverly McLeod, Beryl Nelson, and Kate Woodworth, "School Reform and Student Diversity," *Phi Delta Kappan*, September 1995. Copyright © 1995 by Phi Delta Kappa. Reprinted by permission of authors and publisher.

offering limited economic opportunity. LEP children attending public schools frequently do not have access to adequate nutrition, housing, or health and dental care. The misconnections between the school and the community, coupled with the lack of economic opportunity, create an atmosphere of alienation between the home and the school. For their part, schools cannot predict the numbers, literacy levels, or previous school experience of incoming immigrant students.

It should not be surprising, then, that children who come from cultural- and linguistic-minority backgrounds often founder in American schools. By the time they enter high school, many still lack a solid grounding in reading, writing, mathematics, and science. Moreover, most secondary schools do not offer an academic program in science, math, or social studies that is geared toward LEP students.[4] While dropout rates are not tallied for LEP students per se, it is clear that LEP students in some ethnic groups are dropping out of school at a high rate. The dropout rate for Hispanic immigrants is estimated to be 43%.[5] As young adults, many LEP students are inadequately prepared for higher education or high wage/high skill employment.

Recent reports have called for making the needs of LEP students more central to the national school reform effort. At a time when America seeks to reform its schools so that all students meet high standards, the challenge of educating language-minority students assumes even greater importance. But many schools undergoing restructuring fail to include LEP students in their attempts to revitalize their curriculum and instruction.[6]

There are schools that have made significant breakthroughs in educating LEP students, however.[7] In our study of student diversity, we examined eight such exemplary school reform efforts for language-minority students in grades 4 through 8 in language arts, science, or mathematics.[8] We identified theory-based and practice-proven strategies that effectively teach language arts, mathematics, and science to students from linguistically and culturally diverse backgrounds.[9]

Solutions Found in Exemplary Schools

The case studies of eight exemplary schools demonstrate that, while they are becoming literate in English, LEP students can learn the same curriculum in language arts, science, and math as native English speakers. The success of these schools challenges the assumption that students must learn English first, before they learn grade-level science or math. The elements that come together in these schools are 1) a schoolwide vision of excellence that incorporates LEP students and embraces the students' language and culture, 2) the creation of a community of learners engaged in active discovery, and 3) well-designed and carefully executed programs to develop LEP students' skills in English and in their native languages.

While the vision of each exemplary school we studied was unique, they all held high expectations for the learning and personal development of LEP students. The exemplary sites developed a meaningful curriculum that made connections across disciplines, built real-life applications into the curriculum, related the curriculum to student experiences, and emphasized depth of understanding rather than breadth of knowledge. Schools relied on thematic learning that connected science, math, social science, and language arts and validated students' cultural and linguistic backgrounds. Working in teams, teachers developed, assessed, and refined thematic units over a period of years.

The exemplary schools used innovative approaches to help LEP students become independent learners who could take responsibility for their own learning. Teachers understood that they were not the sole sources of information and wisdom, and they acted as facilitators for student learning. The students were the center of classroom activity; they collaborated with their peers and teachers in the processes of inquiry and active discovery. Students understood what was expected of them and viewed each other as resources for learning.

Cooperative learning was used extensively in all eight of the exemplary schools. Cooperative learning strategies are particularly effective with LEP students because they provide opportunities for students to produce language in a setting that is less threatening than speaking before the entire class. Cooperative learning groups promote the development of language related to a subject area, which serves the dual purpose of developing language skills and enhancing understanding of core content.

All the schools were "parent friendly" and welcomed parents in innovative ways. The schools were also "family friendly," and some took unusual steps to bring health care, dental care, counseling, and social services onto their campuses to serve the families of students. The schools embraced the cultural and linguistic backgrounds of students by employing bilingual staff members, by communicating with parents in their native language when necessary, by honoring the multicultural quality of the student population, and by ensuring a safe school environment. The value placed on students' culture pervaded the classroom curriculum, whether taught in the student's native language or in sheltered English.

In order to build consensus through broad-based decision making, the exemplary schools developed new governance structures involving teachers, parents, and community members. The teachers in the exemplary schools were treated as professionals, encouraged to learn from one another, and given the time to develop programs. The schools used the findings of educational research to hone their approaches, and they sought assistance from external partners in curriculum development and professional development. In schools with exemplary science programs, external partners played a very important role in adapting innovative science curriculum materials for LEP students.

The exemplary schools created smaller school organizations, such as "families" or "houses," that strengthened the connections among students and teachers alike. Smaller school units set the stage for cross-disciplinary instruction and enhanced teachers' sense of commitment by allowing them to focus on a smaller group of students. One exemplary school kept students together with the same teacher for five years. This continuity offers distinct advantages to students who are learning English. Gaps in student learning between grades taught by different teachers were avoided. Parent involvement was enhanced. LEP students in such long-term "continuum" classes became skilled at cooperative learning, were highly responsible for their own learning tasks, and built a remarkable level of academic self-confidence.

The exemplary schools used time in inventive ways. For the most part, teachers controlled their own daily schedules, and they zealously protected students' time to learn. Several exemplary schools extended the school day and year. This added student learning time and freed time for teacher collaboration and professional development. LEP students making the transition to English instruction need additional time to learn, and the schools meet that need through Saturday programs, summer programs, and after-school tutorials.

Exemplary schools paid special attention to the main goal, which is helping students achieve English literacy. The schools used qualified faculty members fluent in the native language of students and trained in second-language learning. Teachers had the flexibility to tailor transitional paths to meet each child's needs. The schools had more than one program path for students to move to English literacy. In these schools native language literacy was universally regarded as a critical foundation for successful attainment of English literacy. The exemplary schools made special academic support (through homework clubs or after-school tutorials) available to LEP students when they were mainstreamed into all-English classes.[10]

The stories of two of these schools will illustrate the dynamic quality of the interplay of school reform, high-quality language development programs, and challenging curriculum for LEP students.

Inter-American School

Inter-American School is a public school enrolling 650 Chicago students from prekindergarten to eighth grade. It was founded in 1975 by a small group of parents and teachers as a bilingual preschool under the auspices of the Chicago Public Schools. The parents and teachers envisioned a multicultural school in which children would be respected as individuals and their languages and cultures would be respected as well.

Today, the school is a citywide magnet school whose students are 70% Hispanic, 13% African American, and 17% white. The developmental bilingual program at the school has the goal of bilingualism and biliteracy for all students including native speakers of English. At all grade levels, English-dominant and Spanish-dominant students are assigned to classrooms in roughly equal proportions. In prekindergarten, all core subjects are taught in Spanish to all students. Spanish-dominant students take English as a second language, and English-dominant students take Spanish as a second language. An 80/20 ratio of Spanish to English instruction remains through third grade; then English instruction is gradually increased to 50/50 by eighth grade. Students enrolled in fifth and sixth grades at Inter-American School are fully bilingual and biliterate in Spanish and English.

Much of the school's curriculum is integrated across the disciplines and built around themes that reflect the history, culture, and traditions of students. The school emphasizes the study of the Americas and Africa, especially how African history and culture have influenced the Americas. Teachers at each grade level work together to develop their curriculum around themes. For example, fourth-grade teachers use a thematic unit on Mayan civilization to integrate content across the curriculum. In social studies, students study the geographic spread of Mayan civilization, Mayan religion, and Mayan cultural traditions. In science, students study Mayan architecture and agriculture. In language arts, they read and write stories about the Mayans. A volunteer parent taught an art lesson in which students painted Mayan gods. The unit began with a visit to the Field Museum to see an exhibit on Mayan culture, architecture, and religion.

Throughout the year teachers work together intensively in groups that span two grade levels.

The teachers at prekindergarten and kindergarten, grades 1 and 2, and so on, plan together, exchange students across grade levels and classrooms, and work together on thematic units.

Like other Chicago schools, Inter-American School has a local school council that sets school policies, hires and evaluates the principal, interviews prospective teachers, and controls the school budget. the professional personnel advisory committee, made up entirely of faculty members, sets priorities and takes responsibility for the instructional program.

Hanshaw Middle School

Hanshaw Middle School serves 860 sixth- through eighth-graders from a predominantly low-income Latino community in Modesto, California. It opened in the fall of 1991. The Hanshaw student body is roughly 56% Hispanic, 26% white, 11% Asian, and 5% African American. After interviewing 500 families in their homes, the principal and faculty agreed on four principles for the foundation of Hanshaw's program: high expectations for all students, support for the Latino and Chicano experience, a meaning-centered curriculum, and a conscious effort to impart life skills as part of the curriculum. The principal recruited teachers from industry—for example, a former museum director teaches science, and a former wildlife biologist teaches science. Life skills such as patience, flexibility, integrity, initiative, and effort are taught at the start of each school year. Students are rewarded throughout the year for demonstrating life skills.

Hanshaw is organized into five houses, each named for a campus of the California State University system. Each house is made up of from six to nine teachers, led by a team leader. Teams of two teachers (one for the math/science core and one for the language arts/social studies core) teach groups of 30 to 35 students. All students take two 90-minute core classes, one for math/science and one for language arts/social studies. Each year students visit the college campus their house is named after, meet college students from various ethnic backgrounds, hear lectures, and receive a T-shirt and a "diploma." Students identify strongly with the college campus, which provides them with an alternative to gang affiliation. Teachers within each house make decisions about the school's budget.

The curriculum design decisions that Hanshaw teachers make are based on a simple principle: every lesson or skill must be relevant to the students' lives. Teachers strive to help students know the "why" of an answer or of multiple answers or to help them understand multiple ways of getting to an answer. Teachers build on students' own experiences in thematic instruction. Themes unify instruction across science, math, language arts, and social studies, incorporating topics from the California curriculum frameworks.

Hanshaw offers several programs for LEP students: instruction in Spanish in core curricular areas, sheltered instruction for advanced Spanish-speaking LEP students and students who speak other primary languages, and mainstream English instruction for clusters of LEP students who speak the same first language. When LEP students are considered ready to move to full English instruction, they are clustered together in mainstream classes. Many of the teachers of mainstream classes have special training and credentials in second-language acquisition.

Hanshaw teachers use a constructivist approach to teaching math. A mainstream eighth-grade algebra class we observed included 15 LEP students. The math teacher is a former carpenter who had training in second-language acquisition. The spatial math lesson she was conducting challenged students to modify the profile of a building and to graph that profile. Students working in cooperative groups used Lego blocks to re-create the profile in three dimensions. The teacher's role was to set up the challenge and to facilitate the work of cooperative student groups in solving the problem. When students finished the assignment, she asked them to solve it another way. LEP students speaking the same language worked together in both English and their native language in their cooperative groups.

Hanshaw's program is supported by a vigorous relationship with an external partner, Susan Kovalik and Associates from the state of Washington; that partner works with Hanshaw faculty members in intensive summer and weekend retreats. A Kovalik coach assists the school on a monthly basis, designing curriculum, providing instructional coaching, and helping the faculty identify problems and solutions. The school uses both state and federal funds to purchase assistance from Kovalik. Hanshaw also has a comprehensive health and social services center on campus that is staffed by social workers and counselors who are bilingual in Spanish and English.

These two schools provide concrete examples of the broader solutions listed above. Both schools have a schoolwide vision that incorporates high standards for LEP students. Both schools take a number of concrete steps to validate and honor the languages and cultures of their students. Both schools teach challenging academic content to LEP students in their native languages. Both schools use the thematic approach to deliver a meaning-centered curriculum that relates to students' life experiences. And teachers at both schools take responsibility for making decisions about the uses of resources and time.

Exemplary schools, such as Inter-American and Hanshaw, illustrate the way such concepts of school reform as smaller school organizations, protected time for learning, thematic instruction, and teacher collaboration can be harnessed to meet the needs of LEP students. They demonstrate that high-quality LEP programs, which include the development of native language literacy, are certainly compatible with learning science and math through active discovery. The dynamic interplay of greater school autonomy, protected time to learn for smaller groups of students with a small group of teachers, intensive professional development, and development of

LEP students' literacy in English and in their native languages holds the promise for success in educating growing numbers of LEP students. ■

Notes

1. General Accounting Office, "Limited English Proficiency: A Growing and Costly Educational Challenge Facing Many School Districts," Report to the Chairman, Committee on Labor and Human Resources, U.S. Senate, Washington, D.C., January 1994; and Diane August and Kenji Hakuta, *Federal Educational Programs for Limited-English-Proficient Students: A Blueprint for the Second Generation* (Stanford, Calif.: Stanford Working Group, 1993).

2. Cynthia A. Chavez, "'State of the Play' in Educational Research on Latino/Hispanic Youth," unpublished manuscript, Rockefeller Foundation, New York, N.Y., May 1991. The phrase "limited English proficient" is used to refer to students whose home language is other than English and who have been determined, using tests of oral English fluency, to require special instruction in order to acquire sufficient English skills to participate in all English instruction.

3. *Numbers and Needs: Ethnic and Linguistic Minorities in the United States*, newsletter published by Dorothy Waggoner, Washington, D.C., May 1992; and Lorraine M. McDonnell and Paul T. Hill, *Newcomers in American Schools: Meeting the Education Needs of Immigrant Youth* (Santa Monica, Calif.: RAND Corporation, 1993).

4. Catherine Minicucci and Laurie Olsen, *Programs for Secondary Limited English Proficient Students: A California Study*, Focus #5 (Washington, D.C.: National Clearinghouse for Bilingual Education, 1992).

5. *School Success for Limited English Proficient Students: The Challenge and State Response* (Washington, D.C.: Resource Center on Educational Equity, Council of Chief State School Officers, 1990).

6. Laurie Olsen et al., *The Unfinished Journey: Restructuring Schools in a Diverse Society* (San Francisco: California Tomorrow, 1994).

7. See Paul Berman et al., *Meeting the Challenge of Language Diversity*, 5 vols. (Berkeley, Calif.: BW Associates, February 1992).

8. The eight exemplary schools selected after an extensive nationwide search are: Del Norte Heights Elementary School, Ysleta Independent School District (El Paso); Hollibrook Elementary School, Spring Branch Independent School District (Houston); Linda Vista Elementary School, San Diego Unified School District; Inter-American School, Chicago Public Schools; Graham and Parks Alternative School, Cambridge (Mass.) School District; Evelyn

Hanshaw Middle School, Modesto (Calif.) City Schools; Horace Mann Middle School, San Francisco Unified School District; and Charles Wiggs Middle School, El Paso Independent School District.

9. *School Reform and Student Diversity*, 3 vols. (Santa Cruz: National Center for Research on Cultural Diversity and Second Language Learning, University of California, in collaboration with BW Associates, September 1995).

10. We conducted focus groups with LEP students who had made the transition to all-English instruction. The students told us that they relied on their bilingual teachers, their older siblings, and their English-speaking peers in learning English and that they benefited from the after-school tutorial opportunities, summer programs, and extracurricular opportunities.

POST NOTE

The recent wave of immigration to the United States has had tremendous consequences for our schools. One estimate puts the number of students with limited English proficiency (LEP) at around 3 million, and the numbers are increasing much more rapidly than the overall student enrollment. As these students enter school, most will need to make sense of a new language, a new culture, and possibly new ways of behaving.

The authors of this article studied eight schools with exemplary approaches to working with LEP students. They discovered that the approaches that work for these students are also the approaches that many reformers urge all schools to follow: high expectations for all learners, cross-disciplinary curricula, depth rather than breadth, thematic units, cooperative learning, parental involvement, site-based management, smaller school organizations, and innovative use of time. In other words, what works for "regular" students also works for students with limited English proficiency.

DISCUSSION QUESTIONS

1. Have you ever traveled or lived in a country where you couldn't speak the language? If so, how did you feel? How did you cope?

2. Were there any aspects of the programs at the Inter-American and Hanshaw schools that particularly appealed to you? Why?

3. Would you like to work with LEP students? Why or why not? If so, what can you do to prepare yourself for success?

74

The Changing Face of Bilingual Education

Russell Gersten

The past year or so has brought a virtual avalanche of dramatic events in the field of bilingual education, portending a significant shift in how English language learners are taught in the United States.

In April 1998, Secretary of Education Richard Riley announced a major shift in policy, calling for a goal of English language proficiency in three years for virtually all English language learners. Riley asserted that "new immigrants have passion to learn English, and they want the best for their children" (p. 2). A survey of 420 randomly selected members of the Association of Texas Educators (both inside and outside the field of bilingual education) found that the majority agreed with the secretary. They believed that children spend too much time in native language instruction (Tanamachi, 1998). Traub (1999) also argues that Latino students spend far too much time in native language instruction, concluding that, in its current form, "bilingual education seems to be hurting" Latino students the most—"the one group it was initially designed to help" (p. 33).

This view stands in stark contrast to the position of several noted scholars in the field, who feel that English language learners should be taught all academic subjects in their native language for no fewer than five, and preferably seven, years (for example, Cummins, 1994). These scholars believe that extensive academic instruction in the native language is necessary for students to benefit from mainstream classrooms.

Recent events indicate that some large school districts (for example, New York and Denver) and some states (for example, California) are seriously rethinking how they educate English language learners. Invariably, the initiatives call for students to enter English language academic instruction at a much earlier age, and they propose a significant reduction in academic instruction in native languages. An article in the *New York Times* reports that "in response to years of criticism of the city's bilingual education programs . . . New York City plans to dramatically increase the amount of time devoted to English language development" (Archibold, 1998). The article concludes with a summary of major lawsuits. Lawsuits or threatened litigation in Sacramento, Denver, and Albuquerque convey the emotional tenor of the debate.

Increasingly, parents and teachers (most notably Jaime Escalante and Gloria Tuchman) have begun to question the small amount of time devoted to English language development in many bilingual education programs in the primary grades. Advocacy groups have consistently raised such issues as parental choice in the amount of English language instruction each child receives, how early a child is introduced to substantive English language instruction, and when a child should exit classrooms that use a great deal of native language instruction.

It seems reasonable to expect that after so much attention, controversy, and discussion, research would provide answers to questions such as these:

- At what age is it best to introduce academic instruction in English to young students?
- To what extent—if any—does native language instruction benefit students' cognitive and academic growth?
- Which are the best instructional methods for developing English language proficiency?

Russell Gersten is Professor at the University of Oregon and Senior Researcher at the Eugene Research Institute. Gersten, Russell, "The Changing Face of Bilingual Education." *Educational Leadership*, April 1999, pp. 41–45. Reprinted by permission from ASCD. All rights reserved.

Unfortunately, research findings have stubbornly failed to provide answers to the first two questions. Ironically, we have more research-based information on the third—and least emotional—of these guiding research questions.

Searching for Answers

An unbiased review of research addressing the first question indicates that we do not have adequate information to determine the optimal time for a child to be taught academic content in English.[1] This is not to say that researchers have not passionately debated the issue or that they have not developed and disseminated a vast array of complex theories. This issue has been debated extensively and serves as the basis of some of the aforementioned lawsuits.

The cornerstone of most contemporary models of bilingual education is that content knowledge and skills learned in a student's primary language will transfer to English once the student has experienced between five and seven years of native language instruction. Yet absolutely no empirical research supports this proposition. Methodological problems so severe that the question cannot be adequately answered plague the research on the subject (August & Hakuta, 1997). These problems appear to be most severe in some of the larger studies intended to "answer" major policy questions.

The recent report released by the National Academy of Sciences, *Improving Schooling for Language Minority Children* (August & Hakuta, 1997), offers a laundry list of complaints concerning these studies:

> The major national-level program evaluations suffer from design limitations, lack of documentation of study objectives, poorly articulated goals, lack of fit between goals and research designs and excessive use of elaborate statistical designs to overcome shortcomings. (P. 138)

In addition, the report concludes that "it is difficult to synthesize the program evaluations of bilingual education because of the extreme politicization of the process" (p. 138). The report makes clear that the prevalence of writings by "advocates who are convinced of the absolute correctness of their positions" (p. 138) presents serious barriers to attempts to improve the quality of instruction for English language learners.

Trying to unravel the issues behind these conflicts and debates can be frustrating. Even the National Academy of Sciences report is of little immediate help. It is as filled with contradictions as most other writing in the field. For example, the authors savagely critique the research on effective schooling and classroom processes, yet report the findings from these seriously flawed studies as if they represented solid facts. Similarly, the authors indicate that there is no empirical support for the effectiveness of native language instruction in the early grades, yet still advocate its use. However, the report also demonstrates an awareness of the contradictory nature of the database by noting:

> It is clear that many children first learn to read in a second language without serious negative consequences. These include children who successfully go through early-immersion, two-way, and English as a second language (ESL)-based programs in North America. (P. 23)

Michael Kirst of Stanford University (Schnaiberg, 1998) recently provided some valuable insight into the problems within the bilingual education knowledge base. In discussing California, he noted:

> From its inception . . . in the 1970s, bilingual education has been oriented toward inputs, process and compliance. . . . The assumption was if you have this input, the outputs would take care of themselves. So . . . [we monitor] . . . whether you mounted the program, *and not its results*. (P. 16, emphasis added)

Although Kirst was discussing California, similar problems have been noted in states such as Texas and Massachusetts. This concern with compliance as opposed to learning outcomes helps explain why the bilingual education knowledge base is so inadequate—which in turn contributes to many of the current problems in the field.

Increasingly, researchers argue that we need to focus on aspects of instruction that lead to improved learning outcomes as opposed to political labels that at best crudely describe complex instructional interventions. Several years ago, my colleagues and I received support from the U.S. Department of Education to begin to articulate these components. Our charge was to synthesize the knowledge base on effective classroom practices that simultaneously promote English language development and academic learning. We intentionally eschewed the ongoing political debates. Our goal was to delineate specific techniques that teachers could use to simultaneously promote learning and English language development.

English Language Development

Although questions about optimal age remain unanswered, at some point all English language learners begin academic instruction in English. The initial transition is often called "content area ESOL," "structured immersion," or "sheltered content instruction." The common feature is teachers' use of English designed for students who are not proficient in the language. In sheltered instruction, teachers modulate their use of English so that it is comprehensible to the student and base their degree of support on their knowledge of that student. In some cases, teachers use native language to help a child complete a task, to clarify a point, or to respond to a question.

Almost invariably, sheltered content instruction is coupled with instruction geared toward building the student's knowledge of the English language. In years past, this component has been referred to as ESL or ESOL. Increasingly, educators are using "English language development" (ELD). Historically, teachers focused on the formal structure of language (for example, grammar and mechanics). Critics routinely attacked this approach, however, because it failed to capitalize on the communication function of language, did not generate student interest, and resulted in very limited generalization.

The 1980s brought more "natural" conversational approaches to teaching English. These also attracted criticism, primarily because they did not necessarily help students learn the highly abstract, often decontextualized language of academic discourse. A movement began about 10 years ago to merge English language learning with content acquisition. The rationale is that students can learn English while learning academic content and that this type of learning will build academic language (Cummins, 1994)—that is, the abstract language of scientific, mathematical, or literary discourse. However, too often teachers merely "hope that language occurs [during lessons]. There is a risk during content instruction of neglecting language development" (Gersten & Baker, in press).

The erratic quality of ELD instruction is at the root of the growing dissatisfaction with current practice. Inadequate attention has been devoted to curriculum development, *pragmatic teacher training and professional development*, and applied research. In a recent professional work group that I conducted in California for the U.S. Department of Education (Gersten & Baker, in press), an educator from the district bilingual education office articulated the problem: "It's important for teachers to be clear about objectives and goals . . . yet an explicit statement of goals does not exist [in district or state curricular materials]."

I would argue, however, that we have made definite progress in understanding what instructional goals are feasible for this group of students and what *specific classroom practices are likely to help meet these goals*. In our two-year research synthesis project (Gersten & Baker, in press), we concluded that the beginning of an empirical knowledge base on effective instructional practices for English language learners exists. It is important to emphasize, however, that this knowledge base is emerging and should be the topic of controlled, high-quality classroom research.

Principles for Merging ELD with Content Area Learning

ELD programs must include the development of oral and written proficiency, the development of basic conversational English and academic language, and the systematic proactive teaching of conventions and grammar (Saunders, O'Brien, Lennon, & McLean, 1998; Fashola, Drum, Mayer, & Kang, 1996). As they undertake these tasks, teachers should keep in mind the following instructional principles derived from the limited research in this area:[2]

- Avoid oversimplifying with contrived, intellectually insulting material when teaching academic content in English. Subjects such as science and math can be excellent venues for merging English language development because all students are learning a new technical vocabulary and there is great potential to use concrete objects (Chamot, 1998).

- Use visuals to reinforce verbal content when teaching in English (Saunders et al., 1998; Reyes & Bos, 1998).

- Use both oral and written modalities frequently (Saunders et al., 1998).

- Employ strategic use of synonyms. Word choice and sentence structure need to be consistent and concise during second language learning. Pay attention to use of metaphors and similes and other highly culture-specific phrases and expressions (Gersten & Jiménez, 1994).

- Focus on approximately five to eight core vocabulary words in each lesson. Some strategies include (1) carefully selecting words (evocative words that stimulate instruction, key words for understanding a story), (2) linking words or concepts to words known in the native language, (3) showing new words in print, and (4) using visuals (for example, concept maps) to depict concepts or word meanings (Saunders et al., 1998).

- Use native language during ELD strategically. At times, it might be helpful to use both native language and English during instruction; however, be aware of the risk of overreliance on simultaneous translations.

- During the early phases of language learning, modulate and be sensitive when providing feedback and correcting language usage; however, during later stages, identify errors and provide specific feedback to students (Reyes, 1992).

To date, much has evolved from grassroots experimentation and attempts by researchers to describe practices that appear to engage students and enhance their learning. Nonetheless, it is becoming increasingly clear that a set of practices exists that teachers can use to persistently but sensitively, encourage students to learn content while expressing their ideas in a new language. This information may be particularly helpful as the shift toward greater emphasis on instruction in English takes effect. ■

Notes

1. An unpublished meta-analysis by Jay Greene (1998) has been occasionally cited as support for native language instruction. However, when we examined his data, we found that his results show no benefits of native language instruction for Latino students in the elementary grades. We also noted numerous methodological problems in his meta-analysis (Baker, Gersten, & Otterstedt, 1999). Thus we conclude that there is no empirical evidence of benefits to extensive native language instruction.

2. For a more complete description see Gersten, Baker, and Marks (1998). The practices are embedded in programs such as Instructional Conversations (Echevarria & Graves, 1998), Bilingual CIRC (Calderon, Hertz-Lazarowitz, & Slavin, 1998), Cognitive Academic Language Learning Approach (Chamot, 1998), collaborative strategic reading (Klingerner, Vaughn, & Schumm, 1998), Peer-Mediated Instruction (Arreaga-Mayer, 1998), and the Effective Strategies for Studying Literature model used successfully in Los Angeles schools by Saunders and colleagues (1998).

References

Archibold, R. C. (1998, June 21). Crew plans an overhaul of bilingual education. *New York Times*, p. 27.

Arreaga-Mayer, C. (1998). Language sensitive peer mediated instruction for culturally and linguistically diverse learners in the intermediate elementary grades. In R. R. Gersten & R. Jiménez (eds.), *Promoting learning for culturally and linguistically diverse students: Classroom applications from contemporary research* (pp. 73–90). Belmont, CA: Wadsworth.

August, D., & Hakuta, K. (Eds.). (1997). *Improving schooling for language-minority children*. Washington, DC: National Academy Press.

Calderon, M., Hertz-Lazarowitz, R., & Slavin, R. (1998). Effects of bilingual cooperative integrated reading and composition on students making the transition from Spanish to English reading. *Elementary School Journal, 99*(2), 153–165.

Chamot, A. U. (1998). Effective instruction for high school English language learners. In R. Gersten & R. Jiménez (Eds.), *Promoting learning for culturally and linguistically diverse students: Classroom applications from contemporary research* (pp. 187–209). Belmont, CA: Wadsworth.

Cummins, J. (1994). Primary language instruction and the education of language minority students. In *Schools and language minority students: A theoretical framework* (2nd ed.). Los Angeles: California State University, National Evaluation, Dissemination and Assessment Center.

Echevarria, J., & Graves, A. (1998). *Sheltered content instruction: Teaching English-language learners with diverse abilities*. Des Moines, IA: Allyn & Bacon.

Fashola, O. S., Drum, P. A. Mayer, R. E., & Kang, S. (1996). A cognitive theory of orthographic transitions: Predictable errors in how Spanish-speaking children spell English words. *American Educational Research Journal, 33*, 825–844.

Gersten, R., & Baker, S. (in press). The professional knowledge base on instructional interventions that support cognitive growth for language minority students. In R. Gersten, E. Schiller, S. Vaughn, & J. Schumm (Eds.), *Research synthesis in special education*. Mahwah, NJ: Erlbaum.

Gersten, R., Baker, S., & Marks, S. U. (1998). *Productive instructional practices for English-language learners: Guiding principles and examples from research-based practice*. Reston, VA: Council for Exceptional Children.

Gersten, R., Baker, S., & Otterstedt, J. (1999). Further analysis of "A meta-analysis of the effectiveness of bilingual education," by J. P. Greene (1989). Technical Report No. 99-01. Eugene, OR: Eugene Research Institute.

Gersten, R., & Jiménez, R. (1994). A delicate balance: Enhancing literacy instruction for students of English as a second language. *The Reading Teacher, 47*(6), 438–449.

Greene, J. P. (1998). *A meta-analysis of the effectiveness of bilingual education*. Unpublished technical report. Austin, TX: University of Texas & the Thomas Rivera Policy Institute.

Klingner, J. K., Vaughn, S., & Schumm, J. S. (1998). Collaborative strategic reading during social studies in heterogeneous fourth-grade classrooms. *Elementary School Journal, 99*(1), 3–22.

Reyes, M. (1992). Challenging venerable assumptions: Literacy instruction for linguistically different students. *Harvard Educational Review, 62*(4), 427–446.

Reyes, E., & Bos, C. (1998). Interactive semantic mapping and charting: Enhancing content area learning for language minority students. In R. Gersten & R. Jiménez (Eds.), *Promoting learning for culturally and linguistically diverse students: Classroom applications from contemporary research* (pp. 133–152). Belmont, CA: Wadsworth.

Riley, R. W. (1998, April 27) *Helping all children learn English*. Washington, DC: U.S. Department of Education, Office of Public Affairs.

Saunders, W., O'Brien, G., Lennon, D., & McLean, J. (1998). Making the transition to English literacy successful: Effective strategies for studying literature with transition students. In R. Gersten & R. Jiménez (Eds.), *Effective strategies for teaching language minority students: Classroom applications from contemporary research* (pp. 99–132). Belmont, CA: Wadsworth.

Schnaiberg, L. (1998, April 29). What price English? *Education Week*, pp. 1, 16.

Tanamachi, C. (1998, July 18). Educators poll: Set bilingual time limit. *Austin American Statesman*, p. B1.

Truab, J. (1999, January 31). The bilingual barrier. *The New York Times Magazine*, pp. 32–35.

Author's note: This article was supported, in part, by the United States Department of Education, Office of Special Education Programs, grant number H023E50013. Mark Harniss and Scott Baker contributed to the writing of this article.

POST NOTE

One of the most politicized issues in education concerns bilingual education. Advocates argue strongly for the need to conduct extensive academic instruction for limited English proficient (LEP) students in their native language. Opponents believe LEP students are ill-served by prolonging instruction in the native language and not focusing on learning English sooner. In 1998, California voters passed Proposition 227, which called for LEP students to be taught in a special English-immersion program in which nearly all instruction is in English, in most cases for no more than a year, before moving into mainstream English classrooms. Proposition 227 basically ended transitional and maintenance models of bilingual education in California, except when sufficient numbers of parents specifically request that their children continue in them. Other states are considering following California's lead. The movement is definitely headed toward less instruction in the LEP student's native language, and earlier instruction in English.

DISCUSSION UESTIONS

1. What reasons can you offer for why the discussion of bilingual education is so heated?

2. Have you studied a foreign language? If so, how long did it take you to master its basic elements so you could understand when the language was being spoken?

3. In the case of California, do you think LEP students can learn sufficient English in one year to begin receiving instruction in mathematics, social studies, and science in English?

Shortchanging Girls and Boys

Susan McGee Bailey

R ecently gender equity in education has become a hot, or at least a "reasonably warm," topic in education. Higher education institutions across the country are under renewed pressure to provide equal athletic opportunities for female students. The U.S. Supreme Court is considering cases involving the admission of women to all-male, state-supported military institutions. And the continued under-representation of women in tenured faculty positions is prompting many donors to withhold contributions to Harvard University's fundraising campaign.

But it is at the elementary and secondary school levels that the shortchanging of girls has been most extensively documented (Wellesley College Center for Research on Women 1992, AAUW 1995, Orenstein 1994, Sadker and Sadker 1994, Thorne 1993, Stein et al. 1993). Twenty-four years after the passage of Title IX—which prohibits discrimination on the basis of sex in any educational programs receiving federal funds—girls and boys are still not on equal footing in our nation's classrooms. Reviews of curricular materials, data on achievement and persistence in science, and research on teacher-to-student and student-to-student interaction patterns all point to school experiences that create significant bar-

Susan McGee Bailey is director of the Wellesley Center for Research on Women at Wellesley College, Wellesley, MA. Susan McGee Bailey, "Shortchanging Girls and Boys," *Educational Leadership,* May 1996, pp. 75–79. Reprinted by permission of the author.

riers to girls' education. These factors have fostered widespread discussion and action among parents, educators, and policymakers.

Barriers to Gender Equitable Education

As the principal author of the 1992 study, *How Schools Shortchange Girls,* I have followed the discussion with considerable interest and mounting concern. The central problem posed in the opening pages of this report continues to be ignored in our discussions of public K–12 education

> [There are] critical aspects of social development that our culture has traditionally assigned to women that are equally important for men. Schools must help girls *and* boys acquire both the relational and the competitive skills needed for full participation in the workforce, family, and community (Wellesley College Center for Research on Women 1992, p. 2).

Too much of the discussion and too many of the proposed remedies rely on simplistic formulations that obscure, rather than address, the complex realities confronting our society.

First among these are the assumptions that 1) gender equity is something "for girls only" and 2) if the situation improves for girls, boys will inevitably lose. These constructions are dangerously narrow and limit boys as well as girls. Gender equity is about enriching classrooms, widening opportunities, and expanding choices for all students.

The notion that helping girls means hurting boys amounts to a defense of a status quo that we all know is serving too few of our students well. Surely it is as important for boys to learn about the contributions of women to our nation as it is for girls to study this information. Surely adolescent pregnancy and parenting are issues for young men as well as young women. And surely boys as well as girls benefit from instructional techniques that encourage cooperation in learning.

A second set of assumptions concern the single-sex versus coed dichotomy. During discussions of gender equity, rarely does anyone stop to consider that coeducation, as the term is generally used, implies more than merely attending the same institution. It is usually assumed to mean a balanced experience as compared to an exclusive, one-sided, single-sex, all-female or all-male one. Thus the term itself undercuts our ability to achieve genuine coeducation by implying that it already exists.

We would do better to describe U.S. public elementary and secondary education as mixed-sex education rather than as coeducation. Girls and boys are mixed together in our schools, but they are not receiving the same quality or quantity of education—nor are they genuinely learning from and about each other. Our task is to find ways to provide the gender equitable education the term coeducation promises, but does not yet deliver.

Lessons from All-Girl Schools

It may indeed be easier in an all-girl setting both to value skills, career fields, and avocations generally considered feminine *and* to encourage girls in nontraditional pursuits. Pressures on students from peers, from popular culture, and even from many adults around them all define gender stereotypic behavior as normal, expected, and successful. Particularly for young adolescents, the clarity of these stereotypes can be reassuring; questioning them can be uncomfortable and risky. In a world where being labeled a "girl" is the classic insult for boys, single-sex environments for girls can provide a refuge from putdowns and stereotypes.

But these environments may also send messages that can perpetuate rather than eliminate negative gender stereotyping. Removing girls from classes in order to provide better learning opportunities for them can imply that girls and boys are so different that they must be taught in radically different ways. When all-girl classes are set up specifically in science or math, an underlying, if unintended, message can be that girls are less capable in these subjects. Separating boys from girls in order to better control boys' behavior can indicate that boys are "too wild" to control.

Rather than assuming that we must isolate girls in order to protect them from boys' boisterous, competitive behavior—or that boys will be unduly feminized in settings where girls are valued and comfortable—we must look carefully at why some students and teachers prefer single-sex settings for girls. We must understand the positive aspects of these classrooms in order to begin the difficult task of bringing these positive factors into mixed-sex classes.

In U.S. public schools, this is not only a matter of good sense, but it is a matter of law. Title IX permits single-sex instruction only in very specific situations.[1] In doing so, we will be moving toward genuinely coeducational environments where the achievements, perspectives, and experiences of both girls and boys, women and men, are equally recognized and rewarded whether or not they fall into traditional categories.

How to Eliminate Barriers

As long as the measures and models of success presented to students follow traditional gender stereotypes and remain grounded in a hierarchy that says paid work is always and absolutely more important and rewarding than unpaid work, that the higher the pay the more valuable the work *and* the worker who does it, we will be unfairly limiting the development of, and the opportunities available to, all our students. Gender equitable education is about eliminating the barriers and stereotypes that limit the options of *both* sexes. To move in this direction, we need to take three major steps.

1. *We must acknowledge the gendered nature of schooling.* Schools are a part of society. Educators cannot single-handedly change the value structure we ourselves embody, but we can acknowledge and begin to question the ways in which gender influences our schooling. *How Schools Shortchange Girls* points out that the emotions and the power dynamics of sex, race, and social class are all present, but evaded, aspects of our classrooms. We can begin to change this by fostering classroom discussions that explicitly

include these issues and that value expressions of feelings as well as recitations of facts.

2. *We must take a careful look at our own practices.* Years ago as a first-year teacher, I was proud of my sensitivity to the needs of my 6th graders. I carefully provided opportunities for boys to take part in class discussions and lead group projects in order to channel their energies in positive ways. I was equally careful to ensure that two very shy, soft-spoken girls never had to be embarrassed by giving book reports in front of the class.

Only much later did I realize that rather than helping the boys learn cooperative skills, I may merely have reinforced their sense that boys act while girls observe, and that I may have protected the girls from exactly the experiences they needed in order to overcome their initial uncertainties. Further, in protecting the girls, I also deprived the boys of opportunities to learn that both girls and boys can take the risks and garner the rewards of speaking up in class and speaking out on issues.

One technique that teachers can use to gain a picture of their classes is to develop class projects in which students serve as data collectors. Students are keen observers of the world around them. Having them keep a record of who is taking part in class can serve as a springboard for important discussions. These discussions can raise everyone's awareness of classroom dynamics, dynamics sometimes so ingrained that they have become invisible.

3. *We must learn from all-girl environments about teaching techniques and curricular perspectives that have particular appeal to girls and determine how to use these approaches successfully in mixed-sex classes.* In talking with teachers working in all-girl environments, I hear three frequent suggestions: 1) place less emphasis on competition and speed and more emphasis on working together to ensure that everyone completes and understands the problem or project; 2) place more emphasis on curricular materials that feature girls and women; and 3) increase the focus on practical, real-life applications of mathematics and the sciences.

Three Practical Suggestions

Teachers can apply these three suggestions in mixed-sex settings. The first is the most difficult. What appears to happen naturally in all-girl settings—for example, girls' working together in an environment where they feel empowered to set the pace—must be deliberately fostered in settings where a different style has been the norm. Girls and their teachers speak of all-girl classes as places where fewer students shout out answers and interrupt one another. Teachers indicate that they deliberately work to ensure that all girls take some active part in class activities. If teachers can directly address these factors in an all-girl setting, surely we can begin to address them in mixed-sex settings.

Further, teachers must experiment with instructions and with reward systems that will encourage students to value a thorough understanding of a task as well as a quick answer, and of group success as well as individual performance. In doing so, we will be encouraging strengths many girls have developed and helping boys acquire skills that they need.

The second suggestion is also not without difficulties when transported to mixed-sex settings. As television producers have discovered, girls may watch programs with male characters, but programs featuring girls are less likely to attract or hold boys' interests. But schools are places where students come to learn. Boys *and* girls need to learn to appreciate and value the accomplishments of women and women's groups who have succeeded in traditionally male fields: Shirley Chisholm, Indira Gandhi, Sally Ride, the Women's Campaign Fund, as well as those whose success has been in traditionally female areas of employment and avocation: Jane Addams, Mary McLeod Bethune, the Visiting Nurses Association.

In *Natural Allies, Women's Associations in American History,* Anne Firor Scott notes that "by the 1930s the landscape was covered with libraries, schools, colleges, kindergartens, museums, health clinics, houses of refuge, school lunch programs, parks, playgrounds, all of which owed their existence to one or several women's societies" (1991,

p. 3). Our students—male and female—need to learn more of this work if they are to grow into adults who can carry on activities vital to our survival as a viable, humane society.

The third factor is perhaps the least problematic. Although girls may be most enthusiastic about pursuing science when they see it as relevant to daily life, boys will surely not be less interested when presented with more relevance! For teachers to develop new lesson plans and materials in the sciences, however, will require increased support from school administrators and school boards for professional development, new materials and equipment, and perhaps a reorganization of class time.

Operation Smart, an after-school informal science program for girls developed by Girls, Inc., is just one example of new relevant science programs. A unit on water pollution, for example, offers middle school and junior high school girls an opportunity to study the effects of pollution in their own communities and to gain an understanding of the value of scientific knowledge and procedures in improving living conditions (Palmer 1994).

Mixed-sex classes can easily adapt such projects, and many have. Last year my nieces, both middle school students in mixed-sex classes in Mystic, Connecticut, eagerly showed me their science projects. Sarah's, done with her close friend Caitlin, contained several different pieces of cloth, each of which had been put through a series of trials: burned, washed, stretched, and frozen. "We thought the synthetic pieces of cloth would be stronger, but they weren't! Now we know natural material is very tough."

Aidan, a year older, collected samples of river water at points varying in distance from the mouth of the Mystic River where it joins the salt water of Fisher's Island Sound. Expecting that the water would be less salty the farther away it was from the Sound, she was surprised to find that her graph was not a straight line: a very salty sample appeared at a point quite far upriver. Trying to figure out what might account for this became the most interesting aspect of the project. For both Sarah and Aidan, science is about their own questions, not out of a book or in a laboratory and it is certainly not a boys-only activity!

Moving Beyond Stereotypes

As we move into a new century, we must leave behind our boys-only and girls-only assumptions and stereotypes. On any given measure of achievement or skill, we can find greater similarity between the average score of girls as a group and the average score of boys as a group than we can find when comparing among individual girls or among individual boys. We must no longer allow stereotypic assumptions to guide our expectations or obscure the reality that empathy, cooperation, and competition are all important skills—and are important for all our students. ■

Note

1. Under Title IX, portions of elementary and secondary school classes dealing with human sexuality and instruction in sports that involve bodily contact may, but do not have to be, separated by sex. (Title IX Rules and Regulations of the Educational Amendments of 1972, section 86.34)

References

Orenstein, P. (1994). *SchoolGirls: Young Women, Self-Esteem, and the Confidence Gap.* New York: Doubleday.
Palmer, L. (1994). *The World of Water: Environmental Science for Teens.* New York: Girls Incorporated.
Sadker, D., and M. Sadker, (1994). *Failing at Fairness: How America's Schools Cheat Girls.* New York: C. Scribner's Sons.
Scott, A. F. (1991). *Natural Allies: Women's Associations in American History.* Urbana, Ill.: University of Illinois Press.
Stein, N., N. Marshall, and L. Tropp. (1993). *Secrets in Public: Sexual Harassment in Our Schools.* Wellesley, Mass.: The Wellesley College Center for Research on Women.
Thorne, B. (1993). *Gender Play: Girls and Boys in School.* New Brunswick, N.J.: Rutgers University Press.
Wellesley College Center for Research on Women. (1992). *The AAUW Report: How Schools Shortchange Girls.* Washington, D.C.: American Association of University Women Educational Foundation; reprint ed., (1995), New York: Marlowe and Company.

This article raises a number of hotly debated issues. Many educators agree with Bailey's contention that certain practical steps can and should be taken to increase gender equity in our schools. Other scholars, though, have sharply criticized the body of research on which these arguments rest, debating both the methodologies and the conclusions. Indeed, some studies claim that boys, who have much higher dropout rates and significantly poorer achievement scores than girls, are the ones being shortchanged by our schools.

Bailey's reference to findings from single-sex schools that can be applied to mixed-sex schools raises yet another issue. Research on single-sex schools by Anthony Bryk and his colleagues demonstrates rather conclusively that girls flourish academically in a girls-only setting. Why, then, is there not more interest in expanding single-sex education, particularly during the tumultuous preadolescent and adolescent years? From a historical perspective, coeducation or mixed-sex education is an innovation. If we are unhappy with the performance of girls and/or boys in our mixed-sex system, shouldn't we consider abandoning this innovation?

DISCUSSION QUESTIONS

1. What suggestions from single-sex schools does Bailey want to apply to mixed-sex schools?

2. What are your views on the value of single-sex education in middle schools and high schools?

3. Which group, girls or boys, do you believe is shortchanged the most in schools today?

Glossary

Note: Boldfaced terms that appear within definitions can be found elsewhere in the glossary.

Academic learning time Time spent by students performing academic tasks with a high success rate.

Acceptable use policy (AUP) A statement of rules governing student use of school computers, especially regarding access to the Internet.

Accountability movement Reform movement in the 1970s embracing the idea that schools and educators should be required to demonstrate what they are accomplishing and should be held responsible for student achievement and learning.

American Federation of Teachers (AFT) The nation's second-largest teacher's association or union. Founded in 1916, it is affiliated with the AFL-CIO, the nation's largest union.

Apple Classroom of Tomorrow (ACOT) A classroom model of the effective implementation of computer technology created by Apple Computers; characterized by cooperative and engaged learning and teacher facilitation rather than teacher direction.

At risk A term used to describe conditions, for example, poverty, poor health, or learning disabilities, that put children in danger of not succeeding in school.

Attendance-zoned school School to which children are assigned because they are of mandatory school age and live within the school's designated neighborhood boundaries.

Back-to-basics movement A theme in education reform during the late 1970s and early 1980s that called for more emphasis on traditional subject matter such as reading, writing, arithmetic, and history. It also included the teaching of basic morality and called for more orderly and disciplined student behavior.

Benefit maximization An ethical principle suggesting that individuals should choose the course of action that will make people generally better off.

Bilingual education A variety of approaches to educating students who speak a primary language other than English.

Block grants Federal aid to states or localities that comes with only minimal federal restrictions on how the funds should be spent (as opposed to *categorical* aid, which restricts federal funds to specified uses or categories of use).

Block scheduling An approach to class scheduling in which students take fewer classes each school day, but spend more time in each class.

Brown v. Board of Education of Topeka U.S. Supreme Court ruling in 1954 holding that segregated schools are inherently unequal.

Buckley Amendment An act passed by Congress in 1974, the real name of which is the Family Educational Rights and Privacy Act. It stipulates that students have the right to see the files kept on them by colleges and universities, and that parents should be allowed to see school files kept on their children.

Busing The controversial practice of transporting children to different schools in an attempt to achieve racial desegregation.

CD-ROM An acronym for Compact Disc—Read-Only Memory, a type of computer disk that stores several hundreds megabytes of data and is currently used for many kinds of multimedia software.

Carnegie Forum (on Education and the Economy) A program of the Carnegie Corporation of New York that was created to draw attention to the link between economic growth and the skills and abilities of the people who contribute to that growth, as well as to help develop education policies to meet economic challenges. In 1986 the Forum's Task

Force on Teaching as a Profession issued *A Nation Prepared: Teachers for the 21st Century*, a report that called for establishing a national board for professional teaching standards.

Carnegie unit A measure of clock time used to award high school credits toward graduation.

Certification Recognition by a profession that one of its practitioners has met certain standards. Often used as a synonym for *licensure*, which is governmental approval to perform certain work, such as teaching.

"Channel One" A controversial commercial program that delivers ten minutes of high-quality news programming directly to public school classrooms free of cost in exchange for two minutes of advertising.

Chapter 1 *See* **Title 1**.

Character The sum of an individual's enduring habits, which largely determines how one responds to life's challenges and events.

Charter school School in which the educators, often joined by members of the local community, have made a special contract, or charter, with the school district. Usually the charter allows the school a great deal of independence in its operation.

CIRC (Cooperative Integrated Reading and Composition) A cooperative learning method used for teaching reading and writing in upper elementary grades, in which students are assigned to teams composed of pairs from two different reading groups.

Citizenship education A curriculum that includes teaching the basic characteristics and responsibilities of good citizenship, including neighborliness, politeness, helpfulness, and respect.

Civil Rights Act of 1964 Established that discrimination on the basis of race, color, or national origin is illegal in any program or activity receiving federal funding.

Classical humanism Renaissance philosophy centered on human values and exalting humans' free will and their superiority to the rest of nature.

Coalition of Essential Schools An organization of high schools, established by Theodore Sizer, committed to reforming high schools on the basis of nine basic principles, including an intellectual focus, covering less content but making certain students master it, and emphasizing students as workers.

Collective bargaining A procedure for reaching agreements and resolving conflicts between employers and employees; in education, it covers the teacher's contract and work conditions.

Common curriculum A curriculum in which there is agreement about what students ought to know and be able to do and, often, about the age or grade at which they should be able to accomplish these goals.

Comprehensive high school The predominant form of secondary education in the United States in the twentieth century. It provides both a preparation for college and a vocational education for students not going to college.

Compulsory education The practice of requiring school attendance by law.

Computer literacy Basic knowledge of and skills in the use of computer technology; considered an essential element of contemporary education.

Conant Report A study of the American comprehensive high school written by James B. Conant, a former president of Harvard University.

Conservation, concept of Demonstrated through Jean Piaget's famous demonstration of pouring water from a narrow container into a wider one and then posing the question to children of various ages, "Is this more water, less water, or the same amount of water?" Used to show the importance of providing children with **developmentally appropriate** learning experiences.

Constructivism A theory, based on research from cognitive psychology, that people learn by constructing their own knowledge through an active learning process, rather than by simply absorbing knowledge directly from another source.

Cooperative learning An educational strategy, composed of a set of instructional methods, in which students work in small, mixed-ability groups to master the material and to ensure that all group members reach the learning goals.

Core knowledge curriculum A curriculum based on a strong, specific elementary core of studies as a prerequisite for excellence and fairness in education; intended to be the basis for about 50 percent of a school's curriculum. The Core Knowledge Foundation is directed by E. D. Hirsch, Jr., of the University of Virginia.

Council for Exceptional Children A national organization of individuals concerned about the education of children with disabilities or gifts. The organization promotes research, public policies, and programs that champion the rights of exceptional individuals.

Creative thinking skills The set of skills involving creative processes as means of analysis and decision making.

Criterion-referenced testing Assessment in which an individual's performance is evaluated against a set of preestablished objectives or standards (for comparison, *see* **norm-referenced testing**).

Critical thinking A general instructional approach intended to help students evaluate the worth of ideas, opinions, or evidence before making a decision or judgment.

Cultural literacy Being aware of the central ideas, stories, scientific knowledge, events, and personalities of a culture; a concept that led to the **core knowledge curriculum.**

Cultural milieu The characteristics of a particular culture, particularly the characteristics that determine one's value or success. For instance, the self-made person is valued in a highly competitive culture such as that of the United States. The cultural milieu is strongly promulgated by the mass media.

Cultural pluralism An approach to the diversity of individuals that calls for understanding and appreciation of differences.

Curriculum All the organized and intended experiences of the student for which the school accepts responsibility.

Curriculum integration Integration of the subject matter from two or more disciplines, such as English and history, often using themes such as inventions, discoverers, or health as overlays to the study of the different subjects.

Decentralization The practice of diffusing the authority and decision making of a central individual or agency and allocating these responsibilities and privileges among others. As a restructuring approach in education, decentralization is intended to achieve more responsive and flexible management and decision making; **site-based decision making** is an example.

Desegregation The practice of eliminating **segregation;** that is, bringing together students of different racial, ethnic, and socioeconomic levels.

Developmentally appropriate The term used to describe learning tasks appropriate to the child's level of intellectual development.

Dewey, John American philosopher, educator, and author (1859–1952) who taught that learning by doing should form the basis of educational practice.

Didactic instruction A lecture approach to teaching that emphasizes compliant behavior on the part of the student while the teacher dispenses information.

Didactic philosophy The view that teachers should be masters of particular subject areas and that their role is to transmit their knowledge to students. Under this philosophy, teaching methods include lectures and recitations. Students are expected to memorize facts and concepts and practice skills until mastery has been achieved. (For comparison, *see* **constructivism.**)

Directive teaching Instructional method in which the teacher leads the students through the learning process rather than allowing learning to be student-led.

Early childhood education Programs that concentrate on educating young children (usually up to age eight). Early childhood education has become an important priority in helping children from disadvantaged backgrounds achieve educational parity with other children.

Edison Project Experiment in entrepreneurial education begun in 1992 that seeks to establish partnerships with the public schools to create schools with a common curriculum and greater use of technology, among other characteristics. Now called the Edison Schools.

Educable mentally retarded (EMR) A classification of individuals who are mentally retarded but capable of learning basic skills and information.

Educational Testing Service (ETS) A nonprofit organization, located in Princeton, New Jersey, that develops educational tests like the Scholastic Aptitude Test (SAT).

Emotional intelligence A recent notion advanced by Daniel Goleman, referring to an individual's capacity to compute information about one's own or others' emotional life.

English as a second language (ESL) Method of teaching English to non-English speakers.

Epistemic knowledge Representational or symbolic knowledge; the understanding that explicit concepts and domains connect or correspond. Such knowledge is demonstrated by the use of manipulatives such as blocks in teaching mathematics.

Equal Access Act of 1984 Statute making it unlawful for any public secondary school receiving federal funds to discriminate against any students who want to conduct a meeting on school premises during "non-instructional time" (before and after regular school hours) if other student groups (such as clubs) are allowed to use school facilities during these times.

Equal educational opportunity The legal principle that all children should have equal chances to develop their abilities and aptitudes to the fullest extent regardless of family background, social class, or individual differences.

Equal respect for persons An ethical principle suggesting that our actions acknowledge the equal worth of humans (i.e., the Golden Rule).

Eurocentrism Term used to describe the heavy focus in school curricula on European history and contributions to Western civilization and the effective exclusion from instruction of the history and advances of other peoples.

"Evaded" curriculum A term coined to describe issues central to students' lives that are addressed briefly, if at all, in most schools; examples include teenage pregnancy and sexually transmitted disease.

Excellence movement Education reform movement of the mid-1980s, in which greater academic rigor and higher standards were required of both students and teachers.

Extended school year Provision of education programs beyond the minimum number of school days mandated by law. Often referred to as "summer school."

Fair use doctrine A legal principle defining specific, limited ways in which copyrighted material can be used without permission from the author.

Family Educational Rights and Privacy Act (1974) *See* **Buckley Amendment.**

Filtering software Utilities that may be installed on computers or workstations connected to the Internet to block access to sexually explicit, violent, or otherwise objectionable material.

Formal curriculum Subjects taught in school and the instructional approaches used to transmit this knowledge.

Formative evaluation Evaluation used as a means of identifying a particular point of difficulty and prescribing areas in need of further work or development. Applied in developmental or implementation stages.

Fourteenth Amendment Requires that there be no law "respecting the establishment of religion or prohibiting the free exercise thereof." Relevant case law has been applied to keep public schools neutral in matters of religion.

Frontal teaching Traditional teaching method, now much criticized, in which the teacher's primary instructional method is lecturing in front of the classroom.

Full-service schools Schools where the educational, health, psychological, and social requirements of students and their families are addressed by coordinating the services of professionals from these various disciplines at the school site.

Globalization The recent move toward heightened connection among nations and people around the world, fed by technology, free markets, and the free flow of information.

Goals 2000 *See* **National Education Goals.**

Group investigation Form of cooperative learning in which students work in small groups using cooperative inquiry, group discussion, and projects.

Groupware Allows users in a computer network to jointly author, share, and disseminate electronic documents.

Guided Reflection Protocol Method developed to aid teachers, alone or with colleagues, to think about their teaching practice.

Head Start A federally funded compensatory education program, in existence since the mid-1960s, that provides additional educational services to young children suffering the effects of poverty.

Heuristic learning Educational method in which the student is encouraged to learn independently through extensive and reflective trial-and-error investigation.

Hidden curriculum *See* **Informal curriculum.**

Higher-order thinking skills Skills involving critical analysis of a problem or situation; the ability to apply one's whole range of knowledge and cognitive skills to problem evaluation and decision making. To do so involves moving beyond such skills as memorization and demonstration to application and conceptual understanding.

Holistic scoring Grading a student's work as a whole, considering achievement in all relevant skill areas; the opposite of *analytic scoring*, which involves grading work according to specific, quantifiable achievement criteria.

Hypermedia A framework for creating interconnected, weblike assemblages of content in a computer application or network. Hypermedia can be thought of as interlinked **multimedia** that the user can explore in a nonlinear manner, following embedded links from one piece of content (text, graphics, video, sound) to another.

Inclusion The commitment to educate each child, to the maximum extent appropriate, in the regular school and classroom, rather than moving children with disabilities to separate classes or institutions.

Individualized education program/plan (IEP) A management tool required for every student covered by the provisions of the **Individuals with Disabilities Education Act.** It must indicate a student's current level of performance, short- and long-term instructional objectives, services to be provided, and criteria and schedules for evaluation of progress.

Individuals with Disabilities Education Act (IDEA) Federal law passed in 1990, extending and expanding the provisions of the Education for All Handicapped Children Act of 1975.

Informal curriculum The teaching and learning that occur in school but are not part of the formal, or explicit, curriculum; also called the *hidden curriculum.*

In loco parentis The responsibility of the teacher to function "in the place of the parent" when a student is in school.

Inservice training Training provided by a school or school district to improve the skills and competencies of its professional staff, particularly teachers.

Integrated learning system (ILS) Computerized, individualized academic tutorials, often supported through a **local area network** within a school.

Intelligence According to classical theory, a single and general human capacity to think and solve problems.

Internet A worldwide computer network that can be accessed by individuals to communicate with others and to retrieve various kinds of information stored electronically in many locations throughout the world.

Interstate New Teacher Assessment and Support Consortium (INTASC) A project sponsored by the Council of Chief State School Officers that is identifying standards for what beginning teachers should know and be able to do.

Intrinsic motivation Motivation that comes from the satisfaction of doing something, in contrast to *extrinsic motivation,* which comes from the reward received for doing something.

Invented spelling Child's attempt to express in symbols (letters) the group of sounds that make up a word.

Iowa Test of Basic Skills A series of standardized achievement tests that measure learning in reading, mathematics, language, and word study skills in grades K–9.

IQ Intelligence quotient, a measure of an individual's general intelligence.

Jigsaw teaching Form of cooperative learning in which each student on a team becomes "expert" on one topic by working with members from other teams assigned the same topic. On return to the home team, each expert teaches the group, and all students are assessed on all aspects of the topic.

Kohlberg's moral dilemma discussions Values education methodology involving presentation of moral dilemmas as catalysts for student discussions and the development of moral reasoning.

Learning criteria Specific statements of what students should know and be able to do after having completed a learning experience.

Learning disability (LD) A disability classification referring to a disorder in basic psychological processing that affects the individual's ability to listen, think, speak, read, write, spell, or do mathematical calculations. A learning disability is not primarily the result of visual, hearing, or motor disabilities; of mental retardation; of emotional disturbance; or of environmental, cultural, or economic disadvantage.

Learning style Characteristic way a student learns, including such factors as the way an individual processes information, preference for competition or cooperation, and preferred environmental conditions such as lighting or noise level.

Lemon test A set of three requirements, established by the Supreme Court ruling in the case *Lemon v. Kurtzman,* that limits government action or legislation with respect to religion in the schools. Government action must not 1) have a religious purpose, 2) have the primary effect of either enhancing or inhibiting religion, and 3) create "excessive entanglement" between church and state.

Licensure Governmental approval to perform certain work, such as teaching.

Limited English Proficient (LEP) Term for students whose native language is not English and who have difficulty understanding and using English.

Linear thinking The process of thinking through a concept or idea from start to finish by using step-by-step reasoning to reach a logical conclusion.

Local area network (LAN) A method of connecting computers within a relatively small area to allow people to work together and share information. Especially useful for fostering communication among classrooms within a school.

Magnet schools Alternative schools that provide instruction in specified areas such as the fine arts, for specific groups such as the gifted and talented, or using specific teaching styles such as open classrooms. In many cases, magnet schools are established as a method of promoting voluntary desegregation in schools.

Mainstreaming The practice of placing special education students in general education classes for at least part of the school day, while also providing additional services, programs, or classes as needed.

Matthew effect An expression based on the Book of Matthew in the Bible that refers to the notion that to those who have much, more will come, and to those who have little, even less will come.

McGuffey Readers A six-volume series of textbooks, written by William Holmes McGuffey, that sold over 100 million copies during the nineteenth century. The books contained poetry, moral teachings, and writings of statesmen and religious leaders, as well as grammar teaching.

Merit pay The system of paying teachers according to the quality of their performance, usually by means of a bonus given for meeting specific goals.

Metaknowledge "Knowing what you know"; awareness of what knowledge one possesses.

Mixed-ability (or heterogeneous) grouping A placement approach in which students of different abilities are grouped together. Rooted in the belief that peer supervision, peer teaching, and group learning are effective means of educating all students, this approach is the opposite of **tracking** or ability grouping.

Multicultural education An approach to education intended to recognize cultural diversity and foster the cultural enrichment of all children and youth.

Multiculturalism A concept or situation in which individuals understand, respect, and participate in aspects (such as sports, food, customs, music, and language) of many different cultures.

Multimedia The combination of various media, such as text, graphics, video, music, voice narration, and manipulative objects; today, the term is often applied to computerized applications that incorporate two or more media.

Multiple intelligence (MI) theory A theory of human intelligence advanced by Howard Gardner, which suggests that humans have the psychobiological potential to solve problems or to fashion products that are valued in at least one cultural context. Gardner's research indicates at least eight separate faculties.

National Child Abuse Prevention and Treatment Act of 1974 Federal law that defines child abuse and neglect as "the physical or mental injury, sexual abuse or exploitation, negligent treatment, or maltreatment of a child under the age of eighteen, or the age specified by the child protection law of the state in question, by a person who is responsible for the child's welfare."

National Commission on Teaching and America's Future Blue-ribbon panel that in 1996 released the report *What Matters Most: Teaching for America's Future*. The report emphasized the importance of high-quality teaching and recommended the National Board certification of 105,000 teachers by the year 2006.

National Council for Accreditation of Teacher Education (NCATE) Nationally recognized organization awarding voluntary **accreditation** to college-level teacher education programs. Approximately 500 colleges and universities in the United States are accredited through NCATE.

National Education Association (NEA) The nation's largest teachers' association, founded in 1857 and having a membership of over 2.2 million educators.

National Education Goals Goals for U.S. education, established by the president and the fifty state governors and intended to be reached by the year 2000.

National Education Summit of 1996 Meeting of the nation's governors and business leaders called to address the need to create high standards for both teacher and student achievement. It was spurred by concern about American students' ability to compete effectively in a modern global work force.

A Nation at Risk: The Imperative for Educational Reform A highly influential 1983 national commission report calling for extensive education reform, including more academic course requirements, more stringent college entrance requirements, upgraded and updated textbooks, and longer school days and years.

New England Primer An illustrated book of religious texts and other readings that was the most famous basic school text for the period between 1690 and 1790.

New math A mathematics curriculum popular in the 1960s that focused on teaching students to understand the structure of the discipline of mathematics rather than on teaching computation techniques.

Norming The process of establishing norms for standardized tests, based on reviews of norm groups and their scores. Most tests are renormed approximately every seven years; the trend has been to raise norms on subsequent evaluations, so that increasingly higher performance has been required to reach the 50th percentile (or normal performance).

Norm-referenced testing Assessment in which an individual's performance is evaluated against what is typical of others in his or her peer group (i.e., *norms*) (for comparison, *see* **criterion-referenced testing**).

OERI The Office of Educational Research and Improvement, a division of the U.S. Department of Education.

Outcomes-based education (OBE) A highly controversial curriculum reform movement that emphasizes the specification of learning outcomes instead of topics to be covered, along with assessment measures to determine if students have achieved the outcomes.

Paideia From the Greek *pais,* meaning "the upbringing of a child"; used as the equivalent of the Latin *humanitas* (from which came "the humanities"), signifying the general learning that should be the possession of all human beings.

Particularism A narrow ethnocentrism in which individuals acknowledge the importance and value of only their own culture.

Pedagogy The art or profession of teaching.

Peer coaching A method by which teachers help one another learn new teaching strategies and material. It often involves release time to allow teachers to visit one another's classes as they start to use new programs, such as cooperative learning.

Performance-based tests Tests that require students to actually perform, as by writing or drawing, to demonstrate the skill being measured.

Phonics An instructional strategy used to teach letter-sound relationships to beginning readers by having them sound out words.

Platform for Internet Content Selection (PICS) technology Technology that allows Internet content providers and third-party rating bureaus to embed rating labels, such as those provided by the **Recreational Software Advisory Council rating system,** into the programming code of Internet-accessible documents. Users with PICS-compatible software can then block access to undesirable sites from their own workstation.

Politically correct (PC) A term coined to describe thinking that is politically popular. Taken to extreme, such thinking is so euphemistic and generalized as to be opinionless.

Portfolio assessment A means of assessment based on a collection of a person's work. For students, portfolios may contain a great range of work, from paper and pen work to sculpture.

Positivism A philosophy asserting a radical distinction between facts, which can be scientifically proven, and values, which positivism holds are mere expressions of feelings, not objective truth. Positivism provides the philosophical underpinnings for moral **relativism.**

Pragmatism Belief that one tests truth by its practical consequences. Therefore, truth is relative.

Presage characteristics Characteristics of teachers resulting from formative experiences, training, and individual properties such as intelligence and personality.

Problem-solving skills Skills involving the application of knowledge and information to solving a given problem, for example, definition, analysis, comparison/contrast, and sequencing; synonymous with **higher-order thinking skills.**

Process criteria Learning criteria used for grading and reporting in which teachers take into account effort, work habits, classroom quizzes, homework, class participation, or attendance. (For comparison, *see* **product criteria** and **progress criteria.**)

Product criteria Learning criteria used for grading and reporting in which teachers base their grades or reports exclusively on final examination scores, overall assessments, or other culminating demonstrations of learning. (For comparison, *see* **process criteria** and **progress criteria.**)

Professionalization of teaching The movement toward establishing or recognizing teaching as a profession, not merely an application of skills toward a particular task. This movement supports such practices as **site-based decision making** and other efforts that give teachers more authority and control over educating students.

Progress criteria Highly individualized learning criteria used for grading and reporting in which teachers look at how far students have come rather than where they are. (For comparison, *see* **process criteria** and **product criteria.**)

Progressive school A school that focuses on students' personal and social development.

Pull-out groups Groups of students who periodically leave the regular classroom for special education services. For instance, students with hearing impairments may attend regular sessions of instruction in sign language.

Real-time interactive programming Two-way, delay-free transmission of audio and visual images through computers or television sets allowing the delivery of high-quality, interactive instructional programming.

Reciprocal teaching An instructional procedure designed to teach students cognitive strategies that might lead to improved reading comprehension.

Examples include summarization, question generation, clarification, and prediction, supported through dialogue between teacher and students and the attempt to gain meaning from the text.

Recreational Software Advisory Council rating system (RSACi) A rating system for the Internet through which content providers assign ratings to their own sites according to a five-level, four-category arrangement. Parents, educators, and students can use these standards to make informed choices regarding access to sites with objectionable violence, sex, or language content.

Reflection An inner process in which the individual thinks back on events, attempting to see them in a more objective matter with a view toward improvement.

Regression analysis A statistical approach that allows judgment regarding the impact of one variable independent of the effects of other variables.

Relativism The theory that all truth is relative to the individual and to the time or place in which he or she acts.

Saxon Math Program A traditional skills-based approach for teaching mathematics developed by John Saxon; it emphasizes repetition of mathematical operations.

School choice Allowing parents to select alternative educational programs for their children, either within a given school or among different schools.

Scientific creationism A theory of world creation, based on the Book of Genesis, that some Christians have proposed as a counterbalance to the teaching of evolution in science classes.

SCORE Acronym for the essential goals in Strong, Silver, and Robinson's model of student engagement: *Success, Curiosity, Originality,* and *Relationships,* resulting in *Energy* to complete tasks and work productively.

Secularism An educational approach that ignores religious and spiritual perspectives in favor of a scientific and totally human perspective, excluding, too, the role of religious motivation in historical events [e.g., the movement to free slaves in nineteenth-century America].

Segregation The act of separating people according to such characteristics as race, ethnicity, or **socioeconomic status.** In education, the fact that most students attend schools in the areas in which they live means that student populations will be homogeneous and thus segregated; **desegregation** is achieved when student populations are mixed.

Self-actualization The status of having achieved one's potential through one's own efforts. Providing opportunities for self-actualization greatly promotes self-esteem.

Self-fulfilling prophecy Students' behavior that comes about as a result of teachers' expectations that the students will behave in a certain way. Teachers expect students to behave in a certain way, they communicate those expectations by both overt and subtle means, and students respond by behaving in the way expected.

Sexism Discriminatory attitudes and actions against a particular gender group, especially women.

Sexual harassment Acts directed against an individual of the opposite sex that are intended to humiliate, intimidate, or oppress. Sexual harassment includes making comments of a sexual nature, propositioning, touching, making unwelcome sexual advances, or making one's successful employment or education contingent upon accepting or tolerating such harassment.

Site- or school-based decision making A school reform effort to decentralize, allowing decisions to be made and budgets to be established at the school-building level, where most of the changes need to occur. Usually teachers become involved in the decision-making process. Also known as *site-based management* or *school-based management.*

Socialization The general process of social learning whereby the child learns the many things he or she must know to become an acceptable member of society.

Socioeconomic status The status one occupies on the basis of social and economic factors such as income level, educational level, occupation, area of residence, family background, and the like.

Socratic instruction A method of teaching in which the teacher asks questions and leads the student through responses and discussion to an understanding of the information being taught.

Split-brain theory Theory suggesting that certain intellectual capacities and functions are controlled by the left hemisphere of the brain and others by the right hemisphere.

Sputnik 1 The Soviet rocket launched into space in 1957 that threatened American security and thus stimulated educational reform.

STAD (Student Teams-Achievement Division) A cooperative learning method, developed by Robert Slavin, consisting of a cycle of work starting with the teacher presenting lessons to the class and ending with the students taking a quiz.

Standard   Exemplary performance that serves as a benchmark.

Standards movement   Efforts at the local, state, and federal level to make clear exactly what students need to know and be able to do and, therefore, what schools need to teach. Implicit in the standards movement is an attempt to increase the academic achievement of students.

Star Schools   Federally financed program providing nationwide video education courses (in such areas as advanced math, science, and foreign languages) using satellite broadcasts. Especially helpful for small schools that are typically unable to offer such classes on their own.

Summative evaluation   Evaluation used to assess the adequacy or outcome of a program after the program has been fully developed and implemented.

Teacher competencies   The characteristics that make a teacher qualified to do the job, including various areas of subject-matter expertise and a wide range of personality variables. Some school reform proposals urge that teachers undergo periodic assessment of their competencies to maintain licensure or earn incentives.

Teacher empowerment   The process of giving teachers (or of teachers taking) greater control over their professional lives and how they deliver their educational services.

Teaching for understanding   An educational approach in which the goal is to enable students to explain information in their own words and use it effectively in school and nonschool settings. This approach fosters the development of **critical thinking** or **problem-solving skills** through the direct application of knowledge and information.

Teaching portfolio   Collection of such items as research papers, pupil evaluations, teaching units, and videocassettes of lessons to reflect the quality of a teacher's teaching. Portfolios can be used to illustrate to employers the teacher's expertise or to obtain national board certification.

Team Accelerated Instruction (TAI)   A cooperative learning method using mixed-ability student groups but combining this approach with individualized instruction and students checking one another's work.

Teams-Games-Tournament   Form of cooperative learning in which students compete in academic tournaments for team points and recognition. Most appropriately used for teaching well-defined objectives with single right answers.

TIMSS   The Third International Mathematics and Science Study, which is the largest and most extensive international study of academic achievement in mathematics and science ever undertaken.

Tinker v. Des Moines Independent Community School District   The 1969 decision in which the Supreme Court held that the schools cannot prohibit students' expression of opinions when the expression does not materially and substantially interfere with the requirements of appropriate discipline in the schools; to do so would violate the First Amendment of the Constitution.

Title 1 (Chapter 1)   Part of the 1965 Elementary and Secondary Education Act that delivers federal funds to local school districts and schools for the education of students from low-income families. It also supplements the educational services provided to low-achieving students in those districts.

Title IX   A provision of the 1972 federal Education Amendment Act that prohibits discrimination on the basis of sex for any educational program or activity receiving federal financial assistance.

Tracking   The homogeneous grouping of students for learning tasks on the basis of some measure(s) of their abilities.

Traditional school   A school that seeks to transmit to its students the best knowledge, skills, and values in society.

Values clarification   A values education methodology advocating the presentation of values to students free from imposed value judgments. Students should then be allowed freedom to choose their own values.

Virtual reality   Technology providing users opportunities to actively explore three-dimensional environments that mimic real life. In current applications, users must wear special goggles connected to an input device such as a data glove.

Voucher plan   A type of **school choice** plan that gives parents a receipt or written statement that they can exchange for the schooling they feel is most desirable for their child. The school, in turn, can cash in its received vouchers for the money to pay teachers and buy resources.

White flight   A response to public school racial integration efforts in which white citizens move out of the central city into the suburbs so their children can attend neighborhood schools with a lower percentage of minority students.

Index

Article Review Form

Feel free to photocopy this page and use it to help you review each article you read in this edition of *Kaleidoscope*.

Name: _____ Date: _____ Article no.: _____

In your own words, briefly state the main idea of the article:

_____

_____

_____

_____

With what points or arguments made by the author(s) do you agree or disagree?
Agree:

_____

_____

_____

Disagree:

_____

_____

_____

What did you learn from the article that you think is (1) important, (2) interesting, and (3) unclear?

(1) _____

(2) _____

(3) _____

List any new terms or concepts you found in the article, and briefly define them.

_____

_____

_____

_____

Student Response Form

We'd like to make this book as useful as we can for readers, and your views are vital to our task. What did you think about the selection of articles in this ninth edition of *Kaleidoscope?* Your comments on the form below will help us revise the book for the next edition. You can use a scale of 1 to 5 to "grade" the articles you've read:

> 5—Excellent   4—Good   3—Average   2—Below average   1—Poor

Please mail the completed form to College Marketing, Houghton Mifflin Company, 222 Berkeley Street, Boston, MA 02116-3764.

Grade Author/Title

____ 1. Csikszentmihalyi & McCormack, *The Influence of Teachers*

____ 2. Crowley, *Letter from a Teacher*

____ 3. Michie, *Room to Learn*

____ 4. Metzger, *Calling in the Cosmos*

____ 5. Hole & McEntee, *Reflection Is at the Heart of Practice*

____ 6. Fried, *The Heart of the Matter*

____ 7. Ducharme, *The Great Teacher Question: Beyond Competencies*

____ 8. Jesness, *Why Johnny Can't Fail*

____ 9. Haberman, *Selecting "Star" Teachers for Children and Youth in Urban Poverty*

____ 10. Wolf, *Developing an Effective Teaching Portfolio*

____ 11. Barr, *Who Is This Child?*

____ 12. Eitzen, *Problem Students: The Sociocultural Roots*

____ 13. Shakeshaft, Mandel, Johnson, Sawyer, Hergenrother, & Barber, *Boys Call Me Cow*

____ 14. Wasicsko & Ross, *How to Create Discipline Problems*

____ 15. Cates, Markell, & Bettenhausen, *At Risk for Abuse: A Teacher's Guide for Recognizing and Reporting Child Neglect and Abuse*

____ 16. Strong, Silver, & Robinson, *What Do Students Want (and What Really Motivates Them)?*

____ 17. O'Neil, *On Emotional Intelligence: A Conversation with Daniel Goleman*

Grade Author/Title

____ 18. Wolfe & Brandt, *What Do We Know from Brain Research?*

____ 19. Edelman, *Leaving No Child Behind*

____ 20. Berliner, *Mythology and the American System of Education*

____ 21. Cuban, *A Tale of Two Schools*

____ 22. Meier, *The Big Benefits of Smallness*

____ 23. Finders & Lewis, *Why Some Parents Don't Come to School*

____ 24. Comer, *Parent Participation: Fad or Function?*

____ 25. Lines, *Home Schooling Comes of Age*

____ 26. Nathan, *Early Lessons of the Charter School Movement*

____ 27. Molnar, *Charter Schools: The Smiling Face of Disinvestment*

____ 28. Peddiwell, *The Saber-Tooth Curriculum*

____ 29. Adler, *The Paideia Proposal: Rediscovering the Essence of Education*

____ 30. Hirsch, *The Core Knowledge Curriculum— What's Behind Its Success?*

____ 31. Glasser, *The Quality School Curriculum*

____ 32. Beane, *Curriculum Integration and the Disciplines of Knowledge*

____ 33. Nord, *The Relevance of Religion to the Curriculum*

____ 34. Noddings, *Teaching Themes of Care*

____ 35. Ryan, *Mining the Values in the Curriculum*

____ 36. Eisner, *Standards for American Schools: Help or Hindrance?*

Grade	Author/Title
_____	37. Schmoker & Marzano, *Realizing the Promise of Standards-Based Education*
_____	38. Dodd, *Engaging Students: What I Learned Along the Way*
_____	39. Gardner, *A Multiplicity of Intelligences*
_____	40. Clifford, *Students Need Challenge, Not Easy Success*
_____	41. Guskey, *Making the Grade: What Benefits Students?*
_____	42. Slavin, *Cooperative Learning and the Cooperative School*
_____	43. Betts, *What's All the Noise About? Constructivism in the Classroom*
_____	44. Sato & McLaughlin, *Context Matters: Teaching in Japan and in the United States*
_____	45. Dewey, *My Pedagogic Creed*
_____	46. Boyer, *The Educated Person*
_____	47. Hutchins, *The Basis of Education*
_____	48. Skinner, *The Free and Happy Student*
_____	49. Rogers, *Personal Thoughts on Teaching and Learning*
_____	50. Strike, *The Ethics of Teaching*
_____	51. McDaniel, *The Teacher's Ten Commandments: School Law in the Classroom*
_____	52. LoVette, *You Ask, "Why Have School Costs Increased So Greatly During the Last 20 Years?"*
_____	53. Lickona, *The Return of Character Education*
_____	54. Darling-Hammond, *What Matters Most: A Competent Teacher for Every Child*
_____	55. Resnick, *From Aptitude to Effort: A New Foundation for Our Schools*
_____	56. Sizer, *New Hope for High Schools: Lessons from Reform-Minded Educators*

Grade	Author/Title
_____	57. David, *The Who, What, and Why of Site-Based Management*
_____	58. Canady & Rettig, *The Power of Innovative Scheduling*
_____	59. Hill, *The Educational Consequences of Choice*
_____	60. Smith & Meier, *School Choice: Panacea or Pandora's Box?*
_____	61. Healy, *The Mad Dash to Compute*
_____	62. Postman, *Making a Living, Making a Life: Technology Reconsidered*
_____	63. Mehlinger, *School Reform in the Information Age*
_____	64. Milone & Salpeter, *Technology and Equity Issues*
_____	65. Sternberg, *Technology Changes Intelligence: Societal Implications and Soaring IQs*
_____	66. Tapscott, *Educating the Net Generation*
_____	67. Ravitch, *Multiculturalism: E Pluribus Plures*
_____	68. Banks, *Multicultural Education in the New Century*
_____	69. Stotsky, *Multicultural Illiteracy*
_____	70. Guild, *The Culture/Learning Style Connection: Educating for Diversity*
_____	71. Shanker, *Where We Stand on the Rush to Inclusion*
_____	72. Giangreco, *What Do I Do Now? A Teacher's Guide to Including Students with Disabilities*
_____	73. Minicucci, Berman, McLaughlin, McLeod, Nelson, & Woodworth, *School Reform and Student Diversity*
_____	74. Gersten, *The Changing Face of Bilingual Education*
_____	75. Bailey, *Shortchanging Girls and Boys*

Title of course in which you used this book: _____

Name of your school: _____

Your name (optional): _____

Suggestions for next edition (topics, types of articles, specific selections—any ideas you'd like to share with us):

_____

_____

_____

_____

_____

Topic	Author	Abbreviated Title	Kaleido-scope (pages)	Those Who Can, Teach (chapters)	Foundations of Education (chapters)
Philosophy of education	Adler	The Paideia Proposal	166–171	8, 10	12, 14
	Boyer	The Educated Person	285–292	8, 10	12, 14
	Dewey	My Pedagogic Creed	278–284	3, 8, 10	4, 12
	Hutchins	The Basis of Education	293–297	8, 10	4, 12, 14
	Rogers	Personal Thoughts on Teaching and Learning	304–306	6, 10	12, 14
	Skinner	The Free and Happy Student	298–303	10	12
Reforming education	Eisner	Standards for American Schools	211–218	8, 13	2, 16
	Resnick	From Aptitude to Effort	351–355	8, 13	16
	Schmoker & Marzano	Realizing the Promise of Standards-Based Education	219–224	8, 13	2, 16
Religion and education	Nord	The Relevance of Religion to the Curriculum	194–198	8, 12, 13	3, 5, 8
Scheduling	Canady & Rettig	The Power of Innovative Scheduling	368–375	3, 8	16
Schools	Berliner	Mythology and the American System of Education	106–115	3, 13	10, 16
	Cuban	A Tale of Two Schools	116–120	3, 13	10, 16
	Meier	The Big Benefits of Smallness	121–125	13	6, 16
Site-based management	David	The Who, What, and Why of Site-Based Management	362–367	9, 13	2, 6
Standards movement	Eisner	Standards for American Schools	211–218	8, 13	2, 16
	Schmoker & Marzano	Realizing the Promise of Standards-Based Education	219–224	8, 13	2, 16
Student motivation and engagement	Clifford	Students Need Challenge	237–243	6, 13	9, 14, 16
	Csikszentmihalyí & McCormack	The Influence of Teachers	2–8	1, 6, 13	9, 14, 16
	Dodd	Engaging Students	226–229	6, 13	9, 14, 16
	Gardner	A Multiplicity of Intelligences	230–236	4, 6, 13	9, 16
	Strong, Silver, & Robinson	What Do Students Really Want?	85–90	6, 13	9, 16
Student needs	Barr	Who Is This Child?	58–59	4, 5	9, 10, 11
	Edelman	Leaving No Child Behind	102–104	4, 5	9, 10, 11
	Eitzen	Problem Students	60–66	4, 5	9, 10, 11